An Alaska Antho

Interpreting the Past

An Alaska Anthology

Interpreting the Past

Edited by

Stephen W. Haycox

and

Mary Childers Mangusso

University of Washington Press

Seattle and London

Printed in the United States of America

Library of Congress Cataloging-in-Publication Data

An Alaska anthology : interpreting the past / edited by Stephen W. Haycox and Mary Childers Mangusso.
p. cm.
ISBN 0-295-97495-8
1. Alaska—History. I. Haycox, Stephen W. II. Mangusso, Mary Childers.
F904.5.A42 1996 96-10463
979.8—dc20 CIP

The paper used in this publication meets the minimum requirements of American National Standard for Information Sciences—Permanence of Paper for Printed Library Materials, ANSI Z39.48-1984. ♾

Contents

Preface

This anthology is a revised and expanded version of a volume edited by Professors Stephen Haycox and Mary Mangusso that first appeared in 1989. Five successive printings of that collection have demonstrated the continuing need for a selection of articles that complements the narrative histories of Alaska used in undergraduate courses and available to general readers. But an explosion of fresh scholarship has occurred since the original collection. The Alaska Historical Society's journal, *Alaska History,* has printed numerous important articles by established and new historians, and *Pacific Northwest Quarterly* has continued its strong commitment to scholarship of the region. In addition, new monographs have appeared, along with a number of significant essays in other collections and journals, and several useful doctoral dissertations. Symposia on the history of Russian America have also stimulated work in that field. Frequent users of the first collection have made known their wishes for a revision that would gather together some of this new work. We are grateful for their comments and confidence; this new selection is a response to their requests.

Like the original, this collection is intended to provide a deeper, more focused interpretation of significant events and developments in Alaska history than the general histories or the casual literature. In addition to the work on political, social, and economic history, the editors have added material on environmental history and have expanded the section on Russian America. Ten of the pieces from the original have been retained for this edition, to which have been added fifteen new selections. We hope that together they will be as useful as the original.

Acknowledgments

This anthology is a tribute to all those who pursue a scholarly interest in Alaska history. We have tried to explain its purpose and context in the Introduction. The editors wish to express here their appreciation to all those who helped to make the work possible and without whose generous assistance it could not have been completed. Most particularly, we thank Professors Morgan Sherwood, Richard Pierce, Lydia Black, Ted C. Hinkley, and Barbara Smith, whose support was essential. We also want to thank all those authors who graciously agreed to permit their work to be reprinted here, and the publishers and editors who gave their permission, especially John Findlay of *Pacific Northwest Quarterly*, Robert Craig of *Pacifica* (a publication now regrettably defunct), Dave Nicandri of the Washington State Historical Society, and Jim Ducker of *Alaska History*. We owe Jan Ingram, formerly of Alaska Pacific University Press, much thanks, and special appreciation to Julidta Tarver of the University of Washington Press, without whose generous confidence and legendary patience no revision would have been possible. Also special thanks to Carol Zabilski of *Pacific Northwest Quarterly*, for her fine editorial eye.

Introduction

History is at once a scientific attempt to reconstruct the events of the past and an individual human attempt to understand their meaning. Historians, professional and amateur, constantly pursue both enterprises, sometimes simultaneously, sometimes separately. But the second aspect of writing history, interpretation, is not often as well understood as the first. The image comes readily to mind of a researcher assembling old diaries, letters, reports, and memos and poring over their details so as to present an orderly progression of the sequence of events. But it is not well appreciated that the interpretation of such data, once assembled and ordered, is an act of individual judgment. It is often assumed either that the facts will tell their own meaning, and thus do not need interpretation, or else that the way they have been understood traditionally is the only way they can be understood.

History differs from science in that every writer, indeed every reader, understands the facts differently. Partly this is so because every act of reconstructing the past represents a different selection of the facts themselves. There are too many facts to be included in any one reconstruction of the past; some have to be left out. Which ones should be included and which not? The reader's first impulse is to answer that only the important ones should be included. But who is to be the judge of which are the most important ones? No two readers, or historians, will agree on which are the most important facts, and should be included, and which are the ones which should be left out.

In their reading of the very same letters and memoranda of officials in Russia and the United States in the early 19th century, for example, Howard Kushner (who is not included in this volume) and Nikolai Bolkhovitinov (who is included) came to different conclusions about which were the most important facts and what they meant. Kushner concluded that relations between the two countries were characterized by antagonism and conflict, while Bolkhovitinov thought their nature was friendly and cooperative. The fact that Kushner is American and Bolkhovitinov Russian explains little about their disagreement. Rather, each proceeded from different assumptions about the meaning of the facts: Kushner assumed that disagreement over policy necessarily meant conflict, Bolkhovitinov, that the outcome demonstrates that neither party allowed conflict to destroy the mutual pursuit of objectives useful to both countries. It is not necessary that one historian be right and the other wrong. Instead, together they contribute to understanding by giving the subject a broader context than either of their works gives separately.

Every student of history, casual or professional, will come to an individual conclusion about what the significance of a particular historical episode really is. And as in any intellectual enterprise, reasonable people will disagree. The credibility of any particular writer must be determined by the character of that writer's intellectual judgment and common sense, and how he or she has handled the factual evidence, i.e., whether the facts are accurate, and how they have been weighted in reaching conclusions and forming judgments. In this regard, history resembles any intellectual judgment or analysis in the present; it differs only in that its subject is mankind's past activity, and the analysts have the benefit of the passage of time.

Not all readers of history are aware of these subtleties. Some are impatient with differing interpretations and particularly with new interpretations which challenge widely held, time-honored versions of the past. Reflection, though, suggests that truth is not easily obtained in any intellectual endeavor and that it is not the product of popularity contests.

Alaska history has been the beneficiary of much interpretation over the past several decades. As more scholars and students have joined those already practicing the historian's craft, subjects long neglected have been studied in greater detail, and interpretations thought beyond change have been exposed to new, sometimes dramatically different light. The purchase of Alaska, for example, commonly assumed to have been unpopular in the United States, was in fact heartily endorsed by most major newspaper editors, as well as by the two-thirds of the U.S. Senate necessary to pass the purchase treaty. The Alaska Highway, usually presented as a military supply road made necessary by war, actually was built for very different reasons and accepted only grudgingly by the U.S. Army. There are many other examples of familiar nostrums which have been challenged by closer, more recent study.

Most, though by no means all, of the work of reinterpretation has taken place in the professional historical journals which publish articles on Alaska history. Most of the essays in this collection appeared originally in such journals, including, in addition to the two already noted, *Pacific Historical Review, Western Historical Quarterly, Journal of the West, Pacific Historian, Arctic Anthropology,* and *Canadian Historical Review.*

The selections in this volume were chosen principally for their contribution to a more complete understanding of Alaska history, to provide greater depth than is available in the more widely used narrative histories, and to present, in the judgment of the editors, the best interpretations of those pivotal events and significant themes in the Alaskan past to which writers have given their attention. The articles complement the region's history as presented in such texts as Ernest Gruening's *State of Alaska,* William R. Hunt's *Alaska: A Bicentennial History,* and the second edition of Claus-M. Naske's popular *Alaska: A History of the 49th State.*

This collection includes anthropology and oral history as well as traditional documentary history. The new discipline of ethnohistory, a combination of the methods of anthropology and history, is represented by Lydia Black's work on Aleut culture. Six of the articles deal directly with Alaska Natives and Native conditions. Other articles also deal with Native affairs, though less directly. In addition to political history, the pieces treat economic development, social conditions, environmental history, and myth and ideology. Limited space has prevented the treatment of many themes and topics and the inclusion of many articles which the editors would like to have reprinted.

The theme of the Alaskan past most central to this collection is Alaska's relationship to broader contexts—geographical, political, environmental, economic, social, and ideological. It has been common in much Alaskan historical writing to present the state's history either as if what happened here were independent of events, forces, and ideas elsewhere or, if not, should have been. Such a view is encouraged by the notion that Alaska is unique, exceptional, and universally so. Certainly Alaska is unique in some ways. The largest state in the union, it is vast in size and diverse in resources. In many parts of the state, population is sparse, and the number of persons per total acres of land is much lower than elsewhere in the U.S. Not only does Alaska have a significant Native population, but it has as well the only non-Indian aboriginal Native people in the United States, the Eskimos and Aleuts. Alaska is one of only two states not contiguous with the continental United States and was the first noncontiguous U.S. territorial acquisition.

But writers who have described Alaska have usually focused on the assumption that the people and the culture of Alaska are unique as well. Many have taken it as axiomatic that Alaskans are more independent, more self-reliant, and more individualistic than people in the rest of the U.S. and that they are less patient with the constraints which circumscribe thought and action in other parts of the country. People come to Alaska, it has been written, to live more freely and to be more fully themselves than is possible in the more settled, more heavily bureaucratic continental states. By extension, it has often been assumed that there is an Alaskan culture which is unique and which inspires a characteristically Alaskan self-reliance.

When this thesis of uniqueness has been applied to Alaska history, it has produced an interpretation particularly celebratory of individual heroes, such as sourdoughs, for example, and of individualistic enterprises, such as placer mining and fur trapping. At the same time, it has been critical of federal bureaucracy and the federal government's role in Alaska's development.

Like any interpretation, the thesis of Alaskan uniqueness is a way of understanding the facts, and like other interpretations, it explains some of them better than others. Today, with nearly universal access to air travel and instant worldwide communication, people move into and out of Alaska with an ease not possible in earlier times and are as much a part of American culture as any other American residents with access to television, telephones, public schools, and supermarkets. Essentially, non-Native Alaskans are virtually indistinguishable from people in the rest of the country in their experiences and attitudes.

Moreover, when historically considered, the thesis of Alaskan uniqueness contradicts Alaska's high degree of dependence on Outside investment and on the federal government for Alaskans' livelihood and development. Private investment in the Pacific salmon industry, in the industrial mining of gold and copper and, more recently, in oil has been a basic ingredient of the Alaskan economy. So have such public projects as construction of the Alaska Railroad, the Richardson Highway, and the numerous military facilities. Moreover, Alaska, like the rest of the western states, felt the transforming effect of World War II on its economic and social history. Its postwar development was categorically different from that of the prewar period, being characterized by even greater federal investment and involvement.

Some of the interpretations in this collection complement the notion of Alaskan uniqueness, while others challenge it. But all set Alaska history into broader contexts and show the relationships between Alaska and the Outside, between Alaskan experiences, ideas, and circumstances and those of the rest of the U.S. and the world. Many recent writers have found that those relationships were much more complex than once supposed, and also that Alaskan dependence was much greater than has sometimes been understood.

The editors of this anthology will regard their work as successful if readers take from it a deeper understanding of the true circumstances of the Alaskan past, a deeper understanding than that provided in the general treatments and casual representations which characterize popular literature. These have their necessary place. But this volume has been prepared to aid those who wish to go beyond popular history, to learn what the corps of dedicated researchers has found to be the meaning behind the facts and how that meaning has changed as more is learned. The meaning of Alaska history will continue to change, as still more is learned through additional documentation, study, and reflection and as the needs and circumstances of the present stimulate yet newer ways of understanding the past. As that work continues, this anthology will become outdated and will need to be replaced with yet another. We look forward to that day, for such is the true nature of history.

Alaska History

An Outline

Alaska has long been inhabited. Its preliterate history extends back at least 10,000 years, and some scholars believe that humans migrated from Asia to the Americas across the Bering Sea Land Bridge 27,000 or 28,000 years ago. Whenever they came, these travelers included the ancestors of today's Haida and Tlingit of southeastern Alaska and of the Athabascan people of the Interior. Eskimos and Aleuts, however, may have come later by boat, either across Bering Strait or via the Aleutians. In any case, they have been in western and northern Alaska and in the Aleutians for at least 8,000 years. Historians depend upon archaeologists and anthropologists for information about the precontact lives of these Native Alaskans.

Alaska history in the traditional sense (that is, as dependent upon written documentation or eyewitness accounts) began only in 1741. Despite its comparative brevity, Alaska history is complex. For example, it encompasses a series of international rivalries, the collision of several cultures, and economic difficulties characteristic of any resource-rich but remote area.

In a political sense, Alaska history may be divided into five eras: (1) the Russian period, 1741–1867; (2) the early American era, 1867–97; (3) the gold rush years, 1897 to about 1912; (4) the territorial period, 1912–59; and (5) the period since statehood, 1959 to the present. Some of these eras, such as the Russian period, may easily be subdivided. And naturally none is completely separate and distinct from that which preceded or followed it. But, for purposes of convenience, always remembering that this scheme of categorization is political and therefore somewhat artificial, such periodization may help the reader gain an understanding of both general trends and the significance of specific events.

The Russian Period, 1741–1867

In 1741 Vitus Bering led the first successful Russian expedition to Alaska. Although his crew landed on Kayak Island southeast of Cordova and charted part of the southcentral coast, the human toll was high; almost half of Bering's men perished. Those who survived, however, returned to Siberia in 1742 with many valuable furs, including fox, seal, and sea otter pelts.

The knowledge that pelts of high quality could be obtained readily in the islands east of Kamchatka led increasing numbers of *promyshlenniki* (fur hunters-traders) to the Commander Islands and the Aleutians. Whenever the *promyshlenniki* could not obtain pelts easily themselves, they forced the Aleuts to hunt for them. Within 20 years, the *promyshlenniki* reached Kodiak Island; within 40, the Russian fur merchant Gregory Shelikhov had established a permanent settlement there.

Furs attracted others as well. Spain, interpreting Russian fur trading on the mainland of Alaska as a threat to its claim to all of the west coast of North America, dispatched a number of expeditions into Alaskan waters between 1774 and the early 1795. Great Britain sent Captain James Cook into the area in 1778; George Vancouver followed in 1791–94. The private commercial British and American fur trade on the coast had begun in 1785. The Russian government, meanwhile, tried without success first to tax the Aleuts, then to protect them from the worst excesses perpetrated by the *promyshlenniki*.

Free-booting Russian exploitation of Alaska ended in 1799 with creation of the Russian-American Company, a privately owned, government-chartered monopoly modeled on Western European trading companies. Aleksandr Baranov, formerly resident manager of the Golikov-Shelikhov Company, became the Chief Manager of the Company and Governor of Russian America. Baranov expanded the Company's operations. He established a post at Sitka which, despite the open hostility of local Tlingits, became the Company's Alaskan headquarters. Because of continual difficulty in procuring supplies, Baranov built a post in northern California (Fort Ross) and twice attempted to set up trading posts in Hawaii. He also traded freely with British and American ship captains, upon whom he became increasingly dependent.

Russia's Imperial Navy objected to Baranov's dealings with foreigners and criticized his treatment of Natives, whom Baranov expected to work whenever and wherever required. He loaned Natives to foreign captains to poach otter on the California coast, and he also dispatched them to Fort Ross and Hawaii. The Navy's opposition led to Baranov's removal in 1818, and Russian America subsequently fell under naval control.

Under the Company's second and third charters, issued in 1821 and 1844 respectively, the colony's governor and his top assistants were to be naval officers, although the Company remained nominally under the control of its stockholders, who continued to vote themselves handsome dividends. When he granted the second charter in 1821, Czar Alexander I also attempted to eliminate foreign trading in Alaska. He extended Russian America's boundary southward from 55° to 51°, and he decreed that no foreign ships were to be permitted within 100 miles of the coast. These directives brought immediate protests from Britain and the United States and also caused considerable hardship in Russian America by cutting off the colony's major sources of supply. Treaties between Russia and the United States (1824) and Russia and Great Britain (1825) reopened trade. The Anglo-Russian treaty of 1825 also delineated the Canadian–Russian American boundary. Russian America's supply problems remained unresolved until 1839, when Company officials negotiated an agreement by which the Hudson's Bay Company leased what is now the mainland of southeastern Alaska in return for providing specified supplies annually to the Russians.

Under the second and third charters a distinctively Russian American culture began to emerge in the Aleutians, southcentral, and southeastern Alaska. Partly this resulted from the work of Russian Orthodox priests, especially Father Ioann Veniaminov, later Bishop Innocent. Veniaminov arrived at Unalaska in the 1820s, learned the Fox Aleut dialect, helped to devise a Fox alphabet, and through example converted many Natives to Christianity. Veniaminov soon moved to Sitka, where he established a seminary to train Native Alaskan priests. Despite his efforts, few of the local Tlingits converted to Russian Orthodoxy. The Russians, in fact, never subdued the Tlingits at all. But, among other Native employees of the Company Veniaminov's influence was great.

Russian authorities took steps to improve the lives of Native workers as well as to Christianize them. Under the second charter, the "half-village rule" went into effect: only half of the men in any village could be conscripted for labor by the Company at once, and the village headman had the right to determine who would go and who would stay. The Russians also tried several times to immunize people against smallpox. Their efforts proved partly successful during the continent-wide epidemic of the late 1830s.

As the fur supply became depleted, the Russian-American Company tried to diversify. Distance, transportation costs, and lack of skilled labor operated to the Company's disadvantage, however. Of potentially valuable exports, only ice proved profitable, but by 1860 the ice trade produced only about 2 percent of the Company's revenues. Declining Company income necessitated increased subsidies from the Russian government, already beset with domestic financial difficulties. In addition, Russian officials in Alaska had watched the California gold rush of 1849 with alarm. California's population had increased from about 8,000 in 1848 to roughly 100,000 in 1850. Since the total number of Russians in Alaska probably never exceeded 800, obviously a stampede of that magnitude would have rendered Alaska ungovernable. And the Crimean War (1853–56) had further demonstrated Alaska's vulnerability; only the fact that Great Britain honored a mutual neutrality agreement negotiated by the Hudson's Bay and Russian American companies had saved Russian America from possible British attack and conquest. Russia's acquisition of the left bank of the Amur River from China in the 1850s brought Russia a new region far more accessible and potentially much more profitable than Alaska. For those reasons and others Czar Alexander II approved Alaska's sale to the United States in 1867 for $7.2 million.

The United States, traditionally expansionist, proved eager to buy Alaska, partly due to a desire to keep it out of British hands. But knowledge about Alaska's potential resources also contributed to Americans' willingness to purchase the area. Yankee whalers had exploited Alaskan waters for years, obtaining quantities of whale and walrus oil, baleen, and ivory. Scientists from the Smithsonian Institution had accompanied the Alaskan branch of the unsuccessful Western Union Telegraph Expedition (1865–66), and their glowing reports about potential wealth confirmed others' accounts. The formal transfer of Alaska from Russian to American hands occurred in October 1867, some months prior to appropriation of the necessary purchase funds by the Congress. The speed with which the transfer was completed indicates the desire of both governments to consummate the deal quickly.

The Early American Era, 1867–1897

Following American acquisition of Alaska, the United States Congress designated it a "customs and military district" and extended U.S. mining law to Alaska. In 1873, Congress categorized Alaska as "Indian territory" in order to prohibit the sale of distilled alcohol to Natives. No other governmental arrangements were made. No way existed to obtain title to land other than a mining claim. No civil government could be established legally. The United States Army was placed in control, but without formal declaration of martial law. The Army "governed" Alaska until 1877, when troops were withdrawn to suppress the Nez Perce rebellion in Washington and Idaho. For two years the highest federal official in Alaska was the Customs Collector at Sitka. In 1879, following trouble between Tlingits and non-Natives at Sitka, U.S. authorities dispatched the Navy to govern Alaska, again without declaration of martial law. Naval personnel at least possessed the advantage of mobility, although they had little more success at governance than had army officers.

A number of land speculators and other optimists had moved to Alaska in 1867, confidently expecting the area to boom immediately under American rule. Alaska, however, did not develop quickly, a fact related to its geographic location, its size, and to the state of technology in the 1860s. New residents, like frontiersmen throughout the American West, blamed the federal government for Alaska's problems. The government, they noted, had not provided adequate mail service, did not allow Alaska to be represented in Congress, had not passed a homestead law, and did not give Alaska the right to self-government.

With hindsight it is apparent that Alaska in the late 1860s and early 1870s lacked any economic base. Given the prevailing laissez-faire philosophy, the federal government could have done little to correct this condition. But slowly, without federal assistance, a Western-based economy began to develop. Commercial salmon processing began in the late 1870s and grew rapidly. A major gold strike at Juneau in 1880 brought attention and outside investors to the area, and the Juneau-Douglas mines soon became the largest employers in Alaska.

Economics aside, the need for civil government became increasingly apparent. Alaska especially needed a judicial system. In both Sitka and Angoon, Tlingits with claims for compensation clearly legal under Western law were denied redress by military authorities. In Angoon, the naval commander went so far as to punish the Tlingits, who had requested compensation for the death of a villager in a job-related accident, by shelling the village.

The Juneau gold strike; the census of 1880, which, although incomplete, found more than 33,000 people residing in Alaska (but only 435 non-Natives); the restiveness of the several hundred non-Natives drawn north by Alaska's apparent promise; pressure exerted in Washington,

D.C., by the Presbyterian leader Sheldon Jackson; and the obvious need for a fair and effective judicial system finally induced Congress to establish a rudimentary form of civil government in Alaska with the Organic Act of 1884, soon after the Juneau rush. The act provided for a Governor, a federal district judge, and various other court officials, including a General Agent of Education, each of whom would be appointed by the President and confirmed by the Senate. The laws of Oregon were to apply insofar as they did not conflict with federal law. The act reserved the Natives' rights to their land, pending final disposition of land claims by Congress. Dr. Sheldon Jackson was appointed the education agent, serving from 1885 until 1906. He was to oversee the schooling of Alaska's children "without regard to race," which meant there would be separate schools for white and for Native children.

Native Alaskans faced rapid social change during this period. Perhaps the greatest outside influence was that of missionaries. Sheldon Jackson encouraged Protestant missionaries to go north; at his suggestion, Protestants divided Alaska into exclusive districts to avoid competition and insure an Alaska-wide missionary effort. Roman Catholic missionaries soon followed their Protestant counterparts. Most missionaries combined the cultural assumptions of middle-class Americans with a belief in saving souls. Thus, missionary activity in the early American era stressed education as well as Christianization, the goals being to avoid mistakes made earlier in the contiguous United States and to prepare Alaska's Natives for assimilation into America's mainstream. The missionaries exercised mixed influences, of course. They suppressed Native languages and cultural traditions. They also operated orphanages, supervised a reindeer-herding program instituted in northwestern Alaska by Jackson, brought literacy, and spread the Gospel. Perhaps they cushioned the worst of the cultural collisions. Certainly they helped many Natives prepare for the changes that the turn-of-the-century gold rushes brought.

The Gold Rush, 1897–1912

Alaska's gold rush era began, of course, with the Klondike strike in Canada's Yukon Territory. This strike affected Alaska in two ways. First, major routes to the goldfields crossed Alaska, resulting in a demand for goods and services by stampeders on their way north. By the time the stampeders of 1898 reached Dawson City, the best ground had already been staked. Many simply returned home, but others drifted into Alaska to seek gold.

Knowledge of the Klondike also stimulated prospecting by Alaskan residents. Consequently, major strikes occurred in Nome in 1898 and near Fairbanks in 1902. Each of these triggered a rush, as did several dozen other strikes throughout Alaska.

The gold rushes spurred other economic activity. The Alaska Syndicate, a consortium formed by J. P. Morgan, the Guggenheim brothers, and others, bought the Kennicott copper mine, built the Copper River and Northwestern Railroad, and operated gold mines, canneries, and a steamship line. Southcentral Alaska particularly benefited from the Syndicate's investments.

During the gold rush era, Alaska's population more than doubled in 10 years. For the first time, a substantial non-Native population existed north of the Yukon River. Native Alaskans not previously affected by outside contact now experienced its effects. Miners brought influenza, measles, and smallpox. They depleted game in areas near goldfields. They disregarded traditional Native land use patterns. At the same time, jobs, education, and medical care became more widely available. Again, prolonged contact between cultures brought mixed results.

In political terms, the gold rushes brought the beginnings of self-government and increased federal attention. The government hurried to formalize settlement of a boundary dispute with Canada which stemmed from ambiguities in the 1825 Anglo-Russian treaty. Congress provided new civil and criminal codes expressly for Alaska and expanded the judicial system, permitted towns of more than 300 people to incorporate and set up municipal services, granted non-Natives the right to homestead and Natives the right to acquire land allotments. Finally, in 1906 Congress authorized Alaskans to elect a nonvoting delegate to the United States House of Representatives, legislation similar to that adopted earlier for the other western territories.

Despite these changes, many Alaskans remained dissatisfied. Natives worried about losing their land. At the same time, they sought the benefits of education and Western technology. Non-Natives became more frustrated than ever with federal control of Alaska's resources. Theodore Roosevelt's creation of the Tongass and Chugach National Forests and his withdrawal of Alaska's coal lands from public entry provoked spirited protests and sparked a debate about the proper federal role in Alaska, a debate which continues today.

The Territorial Period, 1912–1959

Alaska formally became a territory when Congress passed the Organic Act of 1912 establishing a legislature. The powers of the legislature were severely limited. For example, acts passed by the legislature could be vetoed by the Governor (subject to override) or disallowed by the United States Congress, as had been the case in the other western territories. The Alaska legislature could pass no land laws. Neither the territory nor its incorporated municipalities could incur bonded indebtedness without Congressional enactment. The Alaskan legislature operated under two unique restrictions: it could neither establish a territorial judicial system nor regulate fish, game, and fur-bearing animals. These restrictions resulted from pressure exerted by the salmon packers, who feared that a larger government would necessitate increased revenues, leading to higher taxes. The packers also benefited throughout this period from relatively lax federal fisheries regulation and thus preferred federal to territorial control.

In areas where the legislature could act, members generally favored Progressive measures. For instance, the first act passed by the first session of the first legislature gave women the right to vote.

Despite the promise of the gold rush years and federal funding of the Alaska Railroad in 1914, World War I brought depression to Alaska. Men left the territory to join the service, and many failed to return. Nature played a part, too; the Treadwell gold mines on Douglas Island closed following collapse and flooding in April 1917. And after the war the prices of copper and salmon, Alaska's major products, fell sharply. Alaska's economy remained depressed throughout the 1920s in spite of efforts to promote tourism and encourage agriculture, the completion of the Alaska Railroad, and the introduction of air travel, a means by which to solve the territory's remaining transportation problems. Policy makers in Washington, D.C., could only contrast Alaska with the booming contiguous United States and conclude that something must be wrong with Alaska. Once again, expectations had been foiled by impersonal factors, particularly a geographic location which rendered much large-scale industrial and virtually any agricultural development economically unfeasible.

The interwar years marked the entry into politics of the Tlingit and Haida, the first Native Alaskans to participate actively in the Western-imposed political process. The Tlingit lawyer William L. Paul, Sr., led the way, becoming in 1925 the first Native Alaskan to serve in the territorial legislature. Paul also played a role in insuring that Alaska Natives could establish village councils and qualify for the grants and loans provided by the Indian Reorganization Act of 1934. Concern about land lost with the creation of Tongass National Forest led to a request for, and passage of, the Tlingit-Haida Jurisdictional Act of 1935, which permitted the Tlingit and Haida people to sue the United States government in the Court of Claims for compensation.

Other Alaskans continued to fret about federal-territorial relations, particularly the control which the federal government exercised over Alaska's land and resources. Federal fisheries policy remained a major issue as the size of the annual salmon pack began to decline beginning in 1937. The federal Bureau of Fisheries blamed the decline on Japanese fishing in Alaskan waters. Alaskans more correctly blamed it on overfishing as a result of ineffective regulation by the federal government.

Although Alaskans criticized some federal policies, residents also benefited from major federal expenditures during the 1930s. The Civilian Conservation Corps, a New Deal relief program, employed both Natives and non-Natives in a variety of projects. The Public Works Administration furnished grants and loans to municipalities for proposals as diverse as a new schoolhouse in Skagway, a federal building in Fairbanks, a bridge crossing Gastineau Channel to connect Douglas with Juneau, and a city hall in Anchorage. As the 1930s wore on, the Works Progress Administration began to finance defense-related projects, such as emergency landing strips. And the New Deal administration raised the price of gold from $20.77 to $35.00 per ounce, providing some stimulus to the gold-mining industry. Social Security payments also helped to bring needed funds to the territory. And in one of its more experimental undertakings, the government brought 200 low income families from the upper Midwest to open new settlement in the Matanuska Valley, hoping to stimulate population growth and agricultural self-sufficiency in Alaska while at the same time inspiring Americans with a model of determined self-betterment. The Matanuska Colony failed to meet these ambitious goals, although some colony families continue to farm in the Valley today. Then the remilitarization of Alaska began in 1939, leading to construction of military installations at Fairbanks, Anchorage, Kodiak, Ketchikan, and Unalaska.

World War II changed Alaska even more drastically than had the gold rushes. People flooded into the territory: soldiers, contractors, construction workers, support personnel. The Japanese Navy came, too, bombing Dutch Harbor near Unalaska in early June 1942 and occupying Kiska and Attu, the outermost Aleutian Islands, a few days later. A counteroffensive followed, driving the Japanese from Alaska by mid-1943. Eventually some of the airfields and harbors built for defense purposes would serve the burgeoning civilian population, as would the Alaska Highway, which for the first time provided an overland link to the "lower 48."

To all Alaskans the war brought confusion and inconvenience: travel restrictions, censorship of mail, shortages of specific commodities. To a few, it brought suffering. The Japanese interned the Aleuts captured on Attu in Hokkaido. More than 40 percent died there. The United States government evacuated all other Aleuts from Unalaska west through the Pribilofs. Taken to southeastern Alaska, housed in deplorable and unsanitary conditions, many returned home to find their houses demolished, their personal belongings vandalized, and their communities surrounded by unsightly, often dangerous, military debris. In addition, as in the western states, Alaska's Japanese-American citizens were held in internment camps in the American West for the duration of the war.

For other Alaskans, World War II meant promise for the future. Alaska's Governor Ernest Gruening and its Delegate to Congress Anthony J. (Tony) Dimond believed that the attention drawn to Alaska by the war might insure statehood for the territory in the foreseeable future. Both worked to prepare. Gruening presented a tax reform proposal which the territorial legislature initially rejected but finally passed in 1949, insuring that Alaska could support a state government financially. And Dimond sponsored legislation enlarging the legislature and apportioning its lower house according to population, thereby giving statehood advocates in the more populous districts a greater voice in legislation. In 1947 Gruening had worked with Congress, over the protests of Alaska's Tlingit and Haida Indians and in disregard of the environmental impact, to open the Tongass National Forest to timber lease sales and eventually to construct two pulp mills.

Defense spending had become increasingly important to Alaska's economy, and it continued to grow during the Cold War of the early 1950s. Alaska's population grew as well. Many who had come to Alaska during the war remained. Others who had been in the territory in military service returned. More professionals came—teachers, doctors, lawyers—all necessary to provide the infrastructure required by a developing community. These people came from areas which possessed all the rights and privileges of United States citizens. They expected the government to provide many services, and they did not begrudge paying the taxes necessary to support such services. These newcomers, along with a cadre of reform-minded longtime residents, formed the core of the statehood movement.

Alaska played a significant role in the Cold War. Construction of strategic bomber runways, the Distant Early Warning radar network and the White Alice communications system which accompanied it, together with substantial expansion of the various federal agencies operating in the territory kept the level of government spending in the territory near wartime levels, especially during the Korean War, 1950–53. Several federal agencies had special interest in Alaska. The Atomic Energy Commission, thinking Alaska remote and virtually unpeopled, sought to demonstrate the peaceful use of nuclear weapons by blasting out an artificial harbor at Cape Thompson on the Arctic Coast. Researchers forced abandonment of the project by demonstrating the deleterious effects radioactive fallout would have on Eskimo subsistence resources. The Army Corps of Engineers proposed construction of a massive dam on the Yukon River in Rampart Canyon to produce electric power which could be marketed in central Canada and the U.S., but that project, too, was abandoned when analysts raised concerns over the planned forced resettlement of Athabascan villagers and devastation to millions of acres of migratory waterfowl habitat. The AEC did undertake an underground nuclear weapons testing program on Amchitka Island, but the series was discontinued when environmental safeguards were found wanting. In each of these efforts the government learned that Alaska was no more empty or unaffected than sparsely settled areas of the continental states. If it ever had been, Alaska was no longer a frontier in the 1950s, a fact that proponents of statehood understood clearly.

Advocates of statehood faced a long battle. Serious questions persisted about Alaska's ability to support a state government financially. Opponents of statehood included the salmon packers; some Republicans in the U.S. Congress, who opposed admission of then-Democratic Alaska solely on partisan grounds; and many southern Democrats in Congress who feared (correctly) that two more senators from a state with a sizable minority population would equal two more votes for civil rights bills. A formula for conveyance of federal land to state ownership had to be worked out. Active opposition combined with indifference to delay statehood long enough to frustrate many initial supporters. But when proponents found a way to finance state government, they cleared the major hurdle to broad public approval. The federal government agreed to turn over to the new state 90 percent of royalty revenue collected from the sale of exploration and development leases on federal land within state boundaries.

During the winter of 1955–56 the Alaska Constitutional Convention met on the University of Alaska campus at Fairbanks. There, statehood advocates sought to demonstrate Alaskans' political maturity by adopting a model state constitution. No one knew whether or not that constitution would actually go into effect. The convention, however, galvanized the statehood movement. Then, in 1956 Alaskan voters adopted the Tennessee Plan, so named for the first territory to use the device to speed the attainment of statehood. Under this plan, Alaskans selected an unofficial Congressional delegation, one U.S. Representative and two Senators. Members of the delegation (Ernest Gruening, William Egan, and Ralph Rivers) joined Alaska's delegate to Congress (E. L. [Bob] Bartlett) in lobbying for statehood in Washington, D.C., and otherwise publicizing the cause.

Alaska became a state in 1959. The constitution drawn up three years earlier went into effect and remains, according to political scientists, one of the best in the nation.

Alaska since Statehood

Statehood did not solve all of Alaska's problems, of course. The most immediate problems faced by the state proved to be financial ones. In 1959 the state had only $18.5 million in unrestricted revenues, much of that derived from personal and corporate income taxes. The state had anticipated revenue from sales of land, but conveyance to the state of the 103.5 million acres to which Alaska was entitled under terms of the statehood act proceeded very slowly. Essentially, the state depended upon periodic oil and gas lease sales for the revenue which enabled it to keep operating. The Prudhoe Bay oil strike, the Prudhoe Bay lease sale of 1968, and eventual completion of the pipeline in 1977 changed that. For the first time the state had more than adequate revenue, and Alaskans benefited from increased expenditures for education, from establishment of a state telecommunication network, and, in rural areas, from the improved health care that telecommunications made possible. Oil has replaced salmon and government as the mainstay of the economy, and at present the economy remains tied to a resource controlled by outside investors and world prices. In 1976 Alaskans, by constitutional amendment, created a permanent investment fund for about 10 percent of the earnings from taxation on petroleum production. About half of the earnings of the Permanent Fund, which had grown to about $15 billion by 1995, are distributed annually to all state residents and about half are reinvested to "inflation-proof" the fund. The legislature governs the use of the fund, but the distribution program mitigates against its use as general revenue. But the permanent fund has not provided economic self-sufficiency for Alaska; nor was it intended to. Geographic imperatives continue to determine the economic and, to a large extent, the political context of Alaska's existence.

Finances were not the only challenge to the new state. The statehood act contained within it a basic contradiction which would become clear only as national priorities shifted. In section 4 of the act, Alaskans renounced claims to Native land within the state. But in 1958, those lands had not yet been identified. In section 6 of the act, Congress provided that the state should select for state ownership 30 percent of the economically viable land in Alaska, 103 million acres. Many Alaskans considered the land provision to be a solemn promise which could not be altered without their consent, perhaps an unrealistic interpretation of constitutional history but one felt keenly in a state where many enthusiastically embraced an image of fierce self-reliance and closely guarded personal freedom.

When the state began to propose its selections, Natives responded with competing claims of aboriginal title to many selected areas; from their combined protests arose a new statewide organization, the Alaska Federation of Natives. The Alaska Native Claims Settlement Act in 1971, written with the full involvement of the AFN, sought to protect the Native land base by conveying title to 12 percent (44 million acres) of Alaska's land to Natives and paying a billion dollars in compensation for relinquishment of title to the remainder ($962.5 million), federal legislation which was hastened by the need to clear title to a corridor for the Trans-Alaska Pipeline to move North Slope oil. In 1980 Congress passed the Alaska National Interest Lands Conservation Act which withdrew 100 million acres of Alaska in conservation reserves (federal parks, forests, fish and wildlife reserves, and wilderness areas), adding these to more than 50 million acres already in various federal reserves. Both the Native and conservation withdrawals reflected major changes in national opinion in the 1960s regarding minority rights to land and the claim of future generations. But the withdrawals were interpreted by many Alaskans as a violation of the statehood "compact." Environmentalists, development-minded Alaskans, and rural subsistence resource users remain pitted against each other, and often against the federal government, over land use and management practices. Solutions to many of today's problems will require care, thought, and time.

Until recently the themes of exceptionality and economic development have dominated Alaska history. Newer scholarship has emphasized the role of Natives and the significance of environment. The articles in this collection demonstrate the complex relationship between these various lines of interpretation and thereby provide texture to a history which often has been presented as one-dimensional. Undoubtedly future scholars will pursue yet others avenues of understanding which will deepen our grasp of the meaning of the Alaskan past and its relation to broader contexts.

An Alaska Anthology

Interpreting the Past

Finding America

RAYMOND H. FISHER

The late Raymond Fisher, Professor Emeritus at the University of California at Los Angeles, made several significant contributions to the history of Russian America. His area of specialty was Russian investigation of the geography of the North Pacific and its adjacent lands.

The Russians reached the Pacific in 1647, but not until nearly 100 years later did Vitus Bering and Alexi Chirikov discover North America in the latitudes of today's Alaska. Stories from Natives on the Chukotsk Peninsula, directly across Bering Strait from Alaska, told of a "great land," or mainland, a land which was not an island, to the east. Later stories about a land to the north related by Spanish sailors following the Japan Current across the North Pacific as they returned from the Philippines to Mexico suggested to geographers that there must be a subcontinent where the Bering Sea is known to be today. They called the supposed (but nonexistent) land mass variously Gamaland, Company Land, or on some maps, simply "unnamed land." Russian explorers spent considerable time looking for Gamaland.

Professor Fisher first sought to unravel ambiguities in Peter the Great's instructions to Bering for the First Kamchatka Expedition. Those instructions are not entirely clear, and Fisher concluded that many historians in the 19th and 20th centuries misinterpreted them. Peter did not assume, as a number of historians supposed, that there was a land connection between Asia and America. Instead, he sent Bering in 1725 to look for Gamaland. It not being there, Bering did not find it. In fact, on that expedition he decided not even to look for it.

On the Second Kamchatka Expedition, however, Bering did look for Gamaland. Again he did not find it, and after many weeks and thousands of miles at sea, he decided instead to concentrate his efforts on finding where the North American continent lay in the northern latitudes. This led him to the discovery of Alaska in 1741.

This article appeared originally in Barbara Sweetland Smith and Redmond Barnett, eds., *Russian America: The Forgotten Frontier* (Tacoma: Washington State Historical Society, 1990), 3–19; it is reprinted here by permission.

Fisher also examined the matter of the voyage of Semen Dezhnev, a Russian cossack who led an expedition of seven ships along the northeastern Siberian coast in 1648. For many generations historians both in Russia and North America doubted the reality of Dezhnev's voyage, a view endorsed by Frank Golder, the chief American historian of Russian Pacific exploration writing in the first part of the 20th century. Fisher was able to demonstrate conclusively from the documentary record that the voyage indeed took place, and he interpreted its role in the saga of Russian maritime exploration.

Finally, Fisher studied and came to accept the reality of yet another disputed voyage, that of Mikhail Gvozdev in 1732 from the mouth of the Anadyr' River, across Bering Strait to the North American mainland in the vicinity of Cape Prince of Wales. Not all historians have accepted this last conclusion of Fisher's, but all acknowledge his work in developing a better understanding of Russian Pacific exploration and the Russians' enormous contribution to geographic knowledge.

The article reprinted here was written for a scholarly symposium on the history of Russian America held in Anchorage in 1990 in conjunction with the opening of the major museum exhibit "Russian America: The Forgotten Frontier." Many of the symposium papers, including this one, were published in 1990 in the book by the same name. The remaining papers were published in the journal Pacifica *(November 1990). Two of the papers from* Pacifica *are reprinted in this anthology.*

Finding America—that was the intention behind the two voyages of Vitus Bering, often referred to as the First and Second Kamchatka expeditions. The first voyage in the summer of 1728, carried Bering, captain in the Russian Imperial Navy, through the strait later named after him, but he did not find America. The second voyage, of two vessels commanded by Bering and his cocaptain Alexeii Chirikov in the summer of 1741, resulted in the sighting of the coast of southeastern Alaska, portions of its southern coast, and some of the Aleutian Islands. Chirikov and his crew made it back to Kamchatka that same summer. Bering and his crew were forced to winter on Bering Island, where he and half of his crew perished from scurvy. The survivors returned to Kamchatka the next summer. With one minor exception, these voyages mark the beginning of the Russian discovery of America. America had been found, but not explored.[1]

The search for America was initiated by Peter the Great. Just when he became interested in finding America is not known. Several individuals in the course of his reign urged him to arrange a search for a northeast passage to the Pacific, but to look for America was another matter. There is evidence from the report of a conversation he had in Amsterdam in 1697 with Nicolaas Witsen, a Dutch visitor to and student of Russia, that the latter thought there existed a close connection between Kamchatka and America in the form of a large island or American peninsula called Juan de Gama Land. Until Bering's second voyage it would seem that the Russians underestimated the distance between America and Kamchatka in the middle latitudes. By 1719 Peter was sufficiently interested to direct Ivar Evreinov and Fedor Luzhin to describe the local areas around Kamchatka and ascertain whether America was joined with Asia, making a search in the south and north, east and west. They reached Kamchatka by sea from the west, and visited the east coast in the winter of 1720–21, and the northern Kurile Islands to the south in the summer of 1721. The land to the north was already known to the Russians. They found no connection with America, and Evreinov reported this to Peter in 1722 in Kazan, where he was pausing on his way to the campaign against Persia. A further hint that Peter had been thinking of a search for America is seen in a conversation reported by Fedor Soimonov, naval officer, cartographer, and future governor of eastern Siberia. In an exchange with Peter in 1722 during the Persian campaign, Soimonov pointed out the advantages enjoyed by the Russians in searching for the Japanese and Philippine archipelagoes and the areas from Kamchatka to America itself along the west coast of the island of California compared to the western European maritime countries. Peter replied: "Listen, I know all this, but not now, in the future."[2]

The future came rather soon. In January 1725, just before his death, Peter drafted the instructions for Bering's first voyage. Although for more than two hundred years it has been believed that Peter sent Bering into the North Pacific to determine whether Asia and America were joined at their northeastern and northwestern extremities, one searches Peter's instructions in vain for any reference to that question as the reason for the voyage. To be sure, he ordered Bering to sail "along the land which goes to the north and according to expectations (because its end is not known) that land appears to be part of America." But then, in paragraph three, he goes on to order Bering to search for the place where this land is joined with America, to seek a European settlement or vessel, find out what the coast is called, explore and map it, and return to Kamchatka. The most likely identification of "the land which goes to the north" is the unnamed land to the east of Kamchatka depicted on a map of Kamchatka in Johann B. Homann's *Grosser Atlas,* published in 1725 in Nuremberg, a map printed in 1722 from one prepared in Russia and sent to Homann for publication. The eastern part of the land was not known because it was cut off by the right border of the map. It is believed that Bering carried a copy of this map with him on his voyage. This northward-going land reflected the belief in the existence of the mythical Juan de Gama Land between Asia and America. If I am right in my reading of Peter's instructions, what he had in mind was that Bering should sail east along the southern coast of this land until he reached America and there look for a European settlement, which not only would serve to ascertain the northern limit of European settlement on the west coast of America, but also would reinforce any future claim Russia might make to unclaimed land there. It is significant that Bering's vessel, the *St. Gabriel,* was built and equipped only for coastal sailing, not for open-sea navigation.

Why Peter was interested in America is not known with any certainty. No statement by him has turned up telling his reasons for sending Bering to America. Any answer has to be conjectural. But it is quite plausible that he wanted to find a new Siberia rich in fur-bearing animals to replenish a treasury hard hit by his reforms, the long Great Northern War with Sweden, and a decline in fur revenue from Siberia. Perhaps, too, he had in mind America's wealth in precious metals. Furs, gold, and silver clearly motivated the planners of Bering's second voyage, men who had been associated with Peter.

But somewhere en route across Siberia to Kamchatka, Bering came to the conclusion that there was no such "Unnamed Land" as shown on the map. That meant for him and his two lieutenants, Chirikov and Martin Spanberg, that the land going north was the coast north of Kamchatka, and if it was joined to America, it would have to be in the north that Bering would look for a land connection, one that if followed far enough would take him in an arching curve to America and a European settlement—a roundabout route certainly, but how else interpret Peter's instructions in the absence of Juan de Gama Land? This belief in and search for a land connection emerges clearly, though not explicitly, from a careful reading of statements by Chirikov and Bering in the last few days of the outbound voyage.

Having followed the coast from the lower Kamchatka River northward and northeastward to the face of the Chukotskii Peninsula, on August 13 (nautical dating), 1728, at 65°30′ north latitude, the voyagers found themselves out of sight of land as they approached and passed through the strait.[3] Heavy fog concealed the land on both sides. Chukchi Natives previously interviewed by the Russians had reported that the coast would turn west farther up the line. This led Bering to consult with his two lieutenants about what should be done next: continue on or turn around and go back to Kamchatka. Chirikov's advice is revealing. In a written statement he remarks that the land they had been following they thought to be joined with America. That being so, he argued that by virtue of Peter's instructions they had to proceed along that land to a European settlement—that is, to return to the coast and follow it, unless, he wrote, further advance was blocked by ice or *"unless the coast led away to the Kolyma River"* (emphasis added). If it turned north, by the twenty-fifth of the month they should look for a winter haven, preferably on the land reported to lie east of the Chukotskii Peninsula. In other words, disbelief in a land connection with America had not yet set in; and he rejected sailing westward to the Kolyma. Bering chose to continue north, possibly on the theory that, by following the chord of the arc formed by the land connection, he would find America.

The climax of the voyage occurred during the next three days. It has long been believed that during those three days Bering continued sailing north until he reached 67°18′ north latitude in the Chukchi Sea. Concluding that the land no longer went north, he decided to turn around and head back to Kamchatka. But a recent study by the Soviet scholar Arkadii Sopotsko reveals a different picture. In 1973 he uncovered in the naval archives the official logbook of the *St. Gabriel,* long thought to have been lost. From its navigational data he has traced the course of the voyage in detail, day by day, often hour by hour. According to his reconstruction of the voyage, Bering reached 67°18′ north latitude at midnight August 14, and until four o'clock August 16 he followed a back-and-forth course east and west that took him as far north as 67°24′ north latitude and east to longitude 167°50′ west.[4] Here, fearful of being trapped in a hostile environment by adverse winds, he turned around and sailed back to Kamchatka on a more-or-less straight course, passing through the strait near Cape Dezhnev, the easternmost tip of Asia. Cape Prince of Wales on the American side was not seen because it was shrouded in fog. Sopotsko believes that this back-and-forth sailing constituted an effort by Bering to find America. He finds his explanation in two earlier episodes, when Bering followed a back-and-forth course that enabled him to find Cape Chukotsk, at the southeast corner of the Chukotskii Peninsula, and St. Lawrence Island to the south, where taking a straight course had failed.

But his third use of this technique failed to produce the desired result, since at 68° north latitude the coast of America is one hundred miles to the east, for the Seward Peninsula recedes markedly to the northeast from Cape Prince of Wales. Subsequently, after returning to St. Petersburg on March 1, 1730, Bering explained why he turned back in the "Short Account" of his expedition, which he presented to the empress Anna the following month:

> On August 15 [civil time] we arrived at 67°18′ N. lat. I judged that according to everything that had been seen and to the instructions given by his Imperial Majesty, there had been fulfillment because the land no longer extended to the north and no land of any kind approached the Chukotsk or eastern corner, and I turned back.[5]

He said nothing about sailing west. He also expressed his concern over the safety of his vessel and crew because of the lateness of the navigation season (August 15 was August 26 by the Western calendar). He had sailed along the land that went north, seeking its juncture with America, but now it was evident that there was no such juncture. He had done as much as time permitted, and in that sense he had carried out Peter's order, though obviously he had not fulfilled that part of the assignment contained in the third paragraph of Peter's instructions, to reach a European settlement in America. This latter failure may explain the entry in the logbook for August 16, repeated in the journal of Petr Chaplin, a junior officer, which seems to contradict Bering's claim of fulfillment of his instructions. It reads: "At 3:00 p.m. the *gospodin* [captain] declared that contrary to the *ukaz* [Peter's instructions] in [its] execution he must return, and turning the boat around, ordered keeping to the SW."[6] The instructions in the second paragraph of Peter's order he had carried out; those in the third paragraph he had not.

Bering returned to the lower Kamchatka River, and thereafter his efforts to find America were directed to the east, as Peter originally had in mind. Noting signs that he took to indicate land east of Kamchatka, in June 1729 Bering made a short excursion to the east. He sailed some one hundred thirty miles before, frustrated by fog, he turned around and sailed southwest around Kamchatka to Okhotsk and traveled thence across Siberia to St. Petersburg. After his arrival he presented to the Admiralty College a proposal for a second voyage to find America. Still believing that America lay not too far east of Kamchatka, he thought that it would "be possible to search for this route *directly* [emphasis added] if a vessel [were to be] built of a size, for example, of 40 or 50 lasts [80 or 100 tons]."[7]

I must confess that until recently I have missed the significance of Bering's use of the word "directly," as have all the previous investigators of his voyages. If one assumes that Peter sent Bering to the Pacific to determine the union or separation of Asia and America, as scholars until recently have, then his proposal for a second voyage that would go east appears irrelevant. But if Peter sent Bering to find the route to America, the word "directly" becomes relevant, for it tells us that Bering recognized that by sailing east he might well achieve that objective as he had not been able to do by sailing the roundabout route to the north of the first voyage. There would be no coastal sailing to America this time, but open-sea navigation, for which a bigger vessel would be needed.

At the outset of Bering's 1728 voyage he appears to have believed in a land connection between Asia and America. However, the purpose of the voyage was not to demonstrate that connection, but to find America in light of that belief. Nevertheless, demonstrating the actuality or absence of that land connection came to be generally understood as the purpose of the voyage, and, ironically, it was Bering's conversations with Gerhard F. Müller of the Academy of Sciences that gave rise to that understanding, a thesis I plan to develop elsewhere at a future date. Meanwhile, the fact remains that the disconnection between Asia and America had been demonstrated eighty years before. In 1648 a merchant's agent, Fedor Alekseev Popov, organized at Srednekolymsk a party of ninety members, mostly *promyshlenniki* (fur hunters), with several cossack interlopers, to search for the Anadyr' River, reported to be rich in sables and have a considerable Native population. At the last hour, one Semen Dezhnev, a cossack in government employ, was assigned to represent the state's interests (i.e., collect tribute in furs). In June 1648 the party departed from the Kolyma River in seven boats called *koches* and headed east along the Siberian coast. Four of the boats and their occupants were lost before reaching the end of the Chukotskii Peninsula. A fifth was wrecked on the peninsula and its occupants taken by Alekseev into his boat. The two remaining boats rounded the peninsula only to be thrown ashore south of the Anadyr' River in a storm. Alekseev and his companions were later killed by Natives. Dezhnev and his twenty-four companions survived the wreck, but half of them subsequently disappeared in a snowstorm. Dezhnev and the survivors reached the Anadyr' overland and moved upstream to the forest line, where they founded the Anadyrsk outpost and imposed tribute on the Natives. Seven years later he sent in two reports to the commandant at Iakutsk in which he mentioned the voyage and described "the great rocky cape" on the Chukotskii Peninsula, around which he had sailed. He survived to tell about the voyage; Alekseev did not, so the voyage has come down in history under Dezhnev's name. A hazy knowledge of the voyage, of the fact of such a voyage, without dates or names of the participants, seems to have filtered through northern Siberia and northern Russia, but there is no evidence that either Peter I or Bering knew about it. Nevertheless, eighty years before Bering's voyage, Semen Dezhnev, an illiterate cossack, and his party of Russian fur hunters demonstrated the separation of Asia and America by sailing around the northeastern corner of Siberia. They were the first Europeans to do so.

Two years after Bering's first voyage and nine years before his second, another expedition, sailing in his vessel, did find a bit of America, Cape Prince of Wales, the westernmost tip of the American mainland. This voyage, though authorized by the Governing Senate and with some personnel assigned by the Admiralty College in St. Petersburg, was largely the outgrowth of Siberian initiative. An Iakutsk cossack, Afanasii Shestakov, went to St. Petersburg in 1724, where he proposed an ambitious expedition including a move against the recalcitrant Chukchi and Koriaks in northeastern Siberia and an investigation of the "Big Land" reported by the Chukchi to lie across the water from the Chukotskii Peninsula. In 1727 he was given command of fifteen hundred men to be recruited in Siberia and assembled in Iakutsk, then the main administrative center of northeastern Siberia. However, once in Siberia he had to share command with Dmitrii Pavlutskii, captain of dragoons, selected by the governor of Siberia in Tobol'sk and assigned four hundred of the fifteen hundred men. Pavlutskii's task was to subdue the Chukchi in their homeland, the Chukotskii Peninsula. In July 1729 Shestakov arrived in Okhotsk, where he made his base, taking over the supplies and vessels, including the *St. Gabriel,* that Bering had left there. His first move was against the Chukchi, who had invaded Koriak territory north of Kamchatka. In a fight with them in March 1730 he was killed and his force destroyed.

This left Pavlutskii in command of what remained of the expedition. He proceeded to order the navigator Iakov Gens, assistant navigator Ivan Fedorov, and geodesist (or surveyor) Mikhail Gvozdev, then in Okhotsk and Tauisk—all appointees of the Admiralty College—to take the *St. Gabriel* to the Anadyr' River, whence they were to sail east and investigate the "Big Land" and any islands en route. Pavlutskii relieved Gens of command because of the latter's blindness and an ulcerated leg, and placed Gvozdev in charge. Fedorov, also suffering from a badly ulcerated leg, tried to beg off but was forcefully carried aboard the *St. Gabriel.* Leaving the Anadyr' on July 23, 1732, the expedition, which consisted of the two top commanders, Gvozdev and Fedorov, a junior officer, four sailors, thirty-two service men (to collect tribute?), and an interpreter, reached Big Diomede Island on August 17, where the Russians landed, and Little Diomede Island on the twentieth. They found no forests on either island, and the Natives refused to pay tribute. On the twenty-first the Russians sighted the "Big Land" at Cape Prince of Wales. Seeing no habitations ashore, they moved southward to where habitations were seen, but were prevented from landing by shallow water and adverse winds. Continuing southward, they discovered King Island, but could not land, again because of contrary winds. Lateness of the navigation season (September 8 by the Western calendar), low food supply, and a leaking vessel prompted return to Kamchatka, where they arrived on September 27.

This voyage was an extension of the pattern of conquest of Siberia: the search for and subjugation of Natives, who could be made to pay tribute in furs, in the course of which geographical information was obtained. This was why Gvozdev was added to the expedition by the Admiralty College. Provision for a geodesist was not a part of Shestakov's original proposal. Even so, there was a lack of direction and control of the Shestakov-Pavlutskii expedition from St. Petersburg, which was also a part of the pattern. Admittedly, the Governing Senate authorized the expedition, and the Admiralty College provided personnel and instruments for an accurate survey of far eastern Siberia, but thereafter they seem to have lost contact with the development of the expedition as it took form in Siberia. There the two leaders quarreled, and each acted increasingly as a law unto himself. The authorities in Tobol'sk and Iakutsk failed to maintain a firm control over the two men. There was little communication between the two leaders or between them and Tobol'sk, and less between Tobol'sk and St. Petersburg. It was Shestakov, and after Shestakov's death, Pavlutskii, who gave the search for the Bering Strait islands and the "Big Land" a high priority. And after taking over full command, it was Pavlutskii who replaced Gens with Gvozdev without consulting higher authority. It is striking that the Admiralty College, which oversaw naval operations, did not learn of Gvozdev's and Fedorov's voyage and discoveries until 1738, presumably from one of the sailors who had been sent to St. Petersburg on criminal charges.

This tenuous relation between center and field, as well as between the officers in the field, is noticeable in the reporting of the voyage and its findings. Upon returning to Kamchatka, Gvozdev wrote a detailed report of the voyage and sent it to Pavlutskii along with the official logbook, incomplete because Fedorov, a sick man, had not always made the entries required of the navigator. Both logbook and report disappeared after reaching Iakutsk, Pavlutskii not being there. No map of the voyage was made since Fedorov, in the last stages of his illness, rejected Gvozdev's request to add the missing entries in the logbook, essential to the drafting of a map. Thereafter, Fedorov's death in June 1733 and Gvozdev's assignment to other activities unrelated to the voyage removed the two principals on the voyage from further involvement in it. Nearly a decade passed before the voyage again received attention, this time from the local officials at Okhotsk. First to show interest was Anton Devier, the new commandant at Okhotsk. In 1713, Spanberg, who had taken over command of the Second Kamchatka Expedition after Bering's death, visited Okhotsk. There Gvozdev had petitioned for promotion to naval rank (he was a geodesist). As a condition for approval, Spanberg required him to write a detailed account of the 1732 voyage and submit the logbook and map of the voyage. The logbook he had long since sent to Iakutsk, and the map had never been made. At this juncture there appeared—how is unknown—an unsuspected primary document, the personal journal kept on the journey by Fedorov for his own information, a journal with more entries than he had made in the official logbook. In September 1743 Spanberg turned the journal over to Gvozdev and ordered him, with the assistance of two subpilots, to prepare a map of coastal Siberia from the Kamchatka River to the Chukotskii Peninsula. This they did. The map showed part of the route of the voyage, from the Diomede Islands to Cape Prince of Wales (Cape Gvozdev to the Russians) and along its southern coast. Neither map, journal, nor logbook identified the "Big Land" as America, though others later made the connection. The new information led Spanberg to promise the Okhotsk authorities that he would send another expedition to the strait, but this was before he learned that the Second Kamchatka Expedition had been officially terminated.

Thus did the Russians discover and record a tiny bit of northwestern America. Even so, it is not clear that the discoverers understood the significance of their discovery, that the "Big Land" was America. But perhaps more to the point, it was a discovery without important consequences such as followed the discovery of northwestern America by Bering and Chirikov in 1741. There was no follow-up; there were no attempts to subjugate the Natives, probably because the areas seen promised no profit for the sovereign. Only a bit of geographical knowledge, little disseminated, had been obtained. Bering no doubt knew of the discovery while preparing for his second expedition; but the effect of this knowledge on the planning of that expedition appears to have been negligible. The planning of the voyage to America focused on the area south of the Aleutian Islands.

Bering's proposal to the Admiralty College for a second voyage to find America also contained proposals for voyages to Japan and along the Siberian Arctic coast from the Ob' to the Lena River. In 1732 the Governing Senate acted on these proposals and expanded them into the most extensive program of exploration undertaken by a European state up to that time, if not beyond. Placed under the supreme command of Bering, it became known as the Second Kamchatka Expedition and later by other names. Our interest, however, is confined to the component expedition sent to find America, which was the last of the Second Kamchatka Expedition to be mounted. It will be referred to as the American expedition.

Bering was named the supreme expeditionary commander of the two vessels that made up the American expedition. He captained the *St. Peter,* and Chirikov, the *St. Paul.* The purpose of the expedition has long been thought to have been scientific, but though its leaders did record much information of scientific interest, it was not planned or organized as a scientific enterprise with a contingent of scientists aboard, as was Captain James Cook's first voyage into the South Pacific in 1768–71—the first truly scientific maritime expedition. To be sure, Georg Wilhelm Steller, the German naturalist and member of the Imperial Academy of Sciences, accompanied Bering on the *St. Peter* but was employed as a mineralogist and assayer, not as a scientist. Louis Delisle de la Croyère, an astronomer and also a member of the Academy of Sciences, accompanied Chirikov on the *St. Paul.* He was to assist in choosing the route to America and in making celestial observations. Given to drink, he was increasingly ignored by Chirikov. Rather, the purpose of the expedition was political and economic—that is, to lay the foundation for an empire in that part of North America not yet claimed by other European powers—and for the exploitation of its natural resources: fur-bearing animals and precious metals. This purpose was clearly expressed by two of the expedition's major proponents. In October 1732 Vice Admiral Nikolai Golovin, vice president of the Admiralty College, proposed sending two frigates and a transport to Kamchatka to assist Bering in his preparations for the American expedition. Russian naval presence in the North Pacific, Golovin wrote, would enable the Russians "to go everywhere without danger and to look for lands and islands . . . passages, harbors, straits, and the like." Further, he wrote:

> In exploring America there may be the following great gains for the state: very rich mines, of both gold and silver, are there which are still unknown, [and it is known] what profits the Spanish, English, and Portuguese kingdoms receive and how important commerce and navigation to the regions are for these kingdoms now.[8]

Sometime in 1733 or 1734 Ivan Kirilov, senior secretary of the Governing Senate and a prime mover in organizing the Second Kamchatka Expedition, presented a memorandum to the empress Anna regarding the expedition. He stated that the American expedition was to search for new lands and islands not yet conquered, to bring them under Russian dominion, and to search for minerals and precious metals. He explained the thinking behind the enterprise as follows:

> The benefit to be expected is that from the eastern side Russia will extend its possessions as far as California and Mexico, although it will not receive immediately the rich metals the Spanish have there. However, without preparing for war we can in time acquire them through kindness. . . . [T]he local people are greatly embittered against the Spanish and for that reason have to escape to unknown places farther away (and it appears that there are no other places except closer to us). Here on our side it is firmly established not to embitter such people. . . .[9]

However unrealistic this analysis, it does express the ambitions in America of the Russian leadership. Late in December 1732 instructions were issued by the Governing Senate to the Admiralty College regarding the Second Kamchatka Expedition, including the American component. They reflect the Russian technique in the conquest of Siberia. Bering was to investigate a "Big Land" reported to be situated opposite the Chukotskii Peninsula and to have many fur-bearing animals and forests.[10] The Natives in the land discovered were to be invited to pay tribute and to give hostages. Gifts were to be given to the Native chiefs to induce submission. The members of the expedition were to look for islands en route to America and for landing places, harbors, and forests. They were to go ashore and undertake a search for mineral ores and metals, samples being provided to help in identifying them. A mineralogist was to accompany the expedition to assist in the search.

For the most part, the expedition failed to accomplish its official tasks. The two vessels left Petropavlosk (Avacha Bay) in Kamchatka on June 4, 1741. After searching in vain as far south as 46° north latitude (that of Astoria, Oregon) for Juan de Gama Land, the alleged land en route to America, the two vessels became separated in a storm on June 20 and thereafter went their individual ways. Chirikov made his American landfall at the southern end of the present-day Alaska Panhandle on July 15 (July 26 by the Western calendar), and Bering made his the next day at the northern end. Two weeks later Chirikov lost both of his shore boats and fifteen men in a disappearance that to this day remains unsolved. Unable to go ashore to investigate and obtain fresh water, he had no choice but to start back to Kamchatka. Bering found himself in strange waters late in the navigation season—precious time had been spent looking for Juan de Gama Land—and, fearful of being locked in by adverse winds, he turned back.

On their return trips both captains sighted sections of the Alaska mainland and some of the Aleutian Islands. Chirikov made it back to Kamchatka. Bering did not. On November 6 his vessel was thrown into a lagoon on Bering Island, where he and half of his crew died of scurvy over the winter. The rest survived to rebuild the vessel in smaller form and reached Petropavlovsk in August 1742. Thus ended the American expedition. It had found northwestern America, and stretches of its coast and islands had been sighted and placed on a map. But beyond that, few of the objectives set forth in the instructions to Bering had been achieved. Only two visits ashore were made, to replenish the water supply of the *St. Peter.* No Natives were brought under submission, no tribute collected, no hostages taken. On top of that, Chirikov had lost his two shore boats and fifteen members of his crew, making it impossible for him to carry out the instructions. The state's efforts to extend Russian dominion into North America had failed.

Yet, the expedition had its successes, unplanned and unintended. They were the work mainly of one man, the physician and naturalist Steller. Though his official role was only that of mineralogist, he made it clear from the beginning that he would "make various observations on the voyage concerning the natural history, peoples, conditions of the land, etc." "Ever in a hurry, circling half the globe, and never in a position to prepare his manuscripts for publication, Steller had too much to do in too little time. He explored, collected, described, speculated, and moved on to do more of the same. Others after him gained reputation from the use of his information. . . ." So writes O. W. Frost in his excellent introduction to a new translation of the journal Steller kept on the voyage.[11] Given a few hours on Kayak Island, against Bering's initial resistance, and permitted ashore during the water stop at the Shumagin Islands, Steller gathered and recorded an amazing amount of information and specimens. The eight-month sojourn on Bering Island provided much more time and opportunity to examine the environment. His interests embraced medicine, botany, zoology, and ethnology. He discovered a cure for scurvy made of local herbs and roots, and applied it to Bering's crew. He described the Arctic fox, the sea otter, the now-extinct sea cow, and their behavior, as well as other animals. His knowledge and conduct were probably the main reason why as many as did survived the severe winter on barren Bering Island. It is clear that such scientific character as the American expedition acquired was due to the extracurricular activity of this remarkable man.

America, or more precisely northwestern America, had been found by Russians from the west, not by Spanish or English from the south or east. But Bering and Chirikov had seen only a small part of northwestern America—some stretches of coast, some offshore islands, several of the Aleutian Islands, and Bering Island. The distance from America to Siberia was now known, as were the latitudes at which it would be found; but the sightings left some questions unanswered, particularly the question of whether the land seen was continental or insular, or a combination of both. Two maps made later on the basis of the data gathered on the two voyages depicted the land bordering the Gulf of Alaska on the north as a large sausage-shaped peninsula extending far to the southwest, its northern side running northeast to north to the cape seen by Gvozdev in 1732. One map, not published until the mid-twentieth century, was made in 1746 in the Naval Academy under the supervision of Chirikov. The other was made in the Academy of Sciences under the direction of Gerhard Müller, author of the first published account of Bering's voyages, and published in 1758. Only where the coast had been seen was a solid line used; where it had not been seen and was speculative, a broken line appeared. It does show some of the islands. Thus, the task remained to find the rest of coastal and insular America.

Following the return of the survivors of Bering's wrecked ship, in 1743 began the rush of fur traders to the Eastern (Aleutian) Islands. This task was carried out by private individuals, entrepreneurs who invested their own capital, built their own boats, and hired their own crews with only modest aid from local government officials. Their objective, however, was finding not America, but two sea mammals, the sea otter (or sea beaver, as the Russians called it) and the fur seal. The survivors of Bering's crew, upon returning to Kamchatka after the winter on Bering Island, brought with them some nine hundred pelts of the sea otter, fur seal, and blue Arctic fox, killed for food and body covering. The Russians were not unfamiliar with the sea otter, having caught it in the waters off Kamchatka; but they were ignorant of its habitat. It is a playful animal with luxuriant fur, more luxuriant and more valuable even than that of the Siberian sable, which had drawn the Russians across Siberia to the Pacific. The fur seal pelt was not particularly luxuriant, but it commanded a good price. The best market for these pelts was Kiakhta, on the Siberian-Mongolian border south of Lake Baikal, visited by Chinese merchants.

The news about the whereabouts of the sea otter set off a fur rush to the east that resulted in finding more of northwestern America. The move was financed by merchants and traders from European Russia and Siberia. The manpower was furnished by *promyshlenniki*—fur hunters and trappers—petty entrepreneurs, peasants, and Kamchadals in Siberia. In locally constructed vessels, some eighty voyages were made between 1743 and 1790. The voyages were carried out by independent companies, typically organized on the basis of a single voyage. Merchants or traders, even *promyshlenniki* or state servitors with some capital to invest, individually or as a group, would organize a so-called company. Shares in the company would be assigned to investors, skipper, and crew, usually *promyshlenniki*. A boat would be built by them and equipment and supplies laid in. After a cargo of furs had been acquired and the boat returned to Kamchatka, assuming that disaster at sea or at the hands of Natives had not occurred, a ten percent tax was paid to the state, and the proceeds from the venture were distributed according to the shares assigned at the outset. The company then went out of existence. Investors were free to organize other such companies concurrently or subsequently, and did.

The boats used for these voyages have traditionally been described as crudely built, lasting scarcely one trip, and their crews as landlubbers unskilled in navigation, with a high casualty rate at sea. Though this was true often enough to provide a basis for this characterization, it is an overdrawn picture. Lydia Black points out that several boats, *shitiki,* constructed without nails in the absence or scarcity of metal, their planks and joints lashed together with thongs, are known to have made five or six trips. The average was three. Many *promyshlenniki* were landlubbers to begin with; others were experienced navigators of the Siberian rivers. Those who survived the perils of the sea became proficient mariners. Many spent a lifetime sailing the Aleutian waters, learning the currents, winds, and vagaries of the weather. They could sail these waters better than many navy men who came later in imperial ships and felt only contempt for these men, who were rough and hardy and not gentlemen. The naval officers' prejudiced appraisal has prevailed. Nonetheless, official naval expeditions had several of these experienced fur hunters aboard their vessels when they sailed from Kamchatka to the American coast.

The fur rush got underway in 1743 with the voyage of Emel'ian Basov to Bering Island. For the next thirteen years the Russians went no farther east than the Near Islands, the group closest to Kamchatka. Then, between 1756 and 1780 some forty-eight voyages were made, in the course of which the rest of the Aleutian chain was found, as well as the southwesternmost part of Alaska and the Alaska Peninsula. The order of discovery was not a progressive eastward succession; it had a hit-or-miss character.

Many skippers on these fur-gathering voyages made maps, often crude ones in the absence or scarcity of navigation instruments; or they provided information used by local authorities to have maps made. But not all skippers provided cartographic data. Some, to protect their hunting grounds, withheld information or deliberately distorted their maps. Enough reasonably accurate information was assembled, however, so that more and more of America became known. This information, on the other hand, was confined to official circles and not disseminated abroad.

The heavy hunting among the islands nearer Kamchatka depleted the supply of fur-bearing animals and forced the Russians farther east. This necessitated longer voyages, which tied up capital for a longer time. In turn it became necessary to gather larger cargoes, which meant larger vessels and larger crews. This development gave the advantage to merchants with larger amounts of capital. By 1780 the smaller venture was becoming obsolete. Thereafter the fur hunting and America-finding activity of the Russians fell into the hands of five big merchant capitalists.

Most notable was the first permanent company in the North Pacific fur trade, organized by the Irkutsk merchants Grigorii Shelikhov and Ivan Golikov in 1781. By 1799 it had absorbed, driven off, or combined with its competitors to form the Russian-American Company, upon which Tsar Paul conferred a state-ordained monopoly of the Russian North Pacific fur trade. It was the employees of these companies who, during the last two decades of the eighteenth century, explored or surveyed the Alaska Peninsula, Cook Inlet, the Kenai Peninsula, the shores of Prince William Sound, the Pribilof Islands in the Bering Sea, the breeding grounds of the fur seal, and the islands of the Alexander Archipelago, along which Chirikov had sailed after his landfall in July 1741. By the end of the eighteenth century most of southern and southeastern coastal and insular Alaska had been found.

In the post-Bering period until the end of the century, the role of the state in searching for hitherto unknown or unseen parts of America was minimal. Only Catherine II showed some interest. In 1764 she dispatched a supposedly secret expedition to the North Pacific under Captain Petr Krenitsyn and Lieutenant Mikhail Levashev to obtain more information about the islands already discovered, to annex them formally, and to impose some control over the *promyshlenniki*. The expedition's efforts focused mainly on Unimak and Unalaska islands, providing more accurate information about them, but discovering no new areas. Later Captain Cook, who sailed into the Chukchi Sea in 1778–79 and surveyed the American coast from Bristol Bay to Icy Cape, stirred Catherine into commissioning the Joseph Billings expedition of 1785–92 into the Arctic Ocean and Bering Sea. It brought back accurate charts of the areas it surveyed, of value to the navy in particular; but, again, no new parts of America were found. By the end of the eighteenth century most of Russian America had been found. The vast interior of Alaska, however, remained mostly unexplored until the next century.

As we review in our minds the finding of America in the three-quarters of a century after 1720, we see that it was the state's effort, a transoceanic leap, that first found northwestern America. The state chose not to follow up on that discovery, but Bering's voyage opened the way to island-hopping by private entrepreneurs in pursuit of the valuable sea otter, and these men by incremental steps revealed the land and islands not seen by Vitus Bering and Alexeii Chirikov on their epoch-making voyages of 1741. It was a two-phase process that put Russia in America.

"Russian America" was the term used by the Russians to refer to their colonies in America, and it is so used in the title of the exhibit of which this volume is a part. By Americans at least it has been an oft-forgotten frontier, but what has also been little appreciated is that it became an American as well as a Russian frontier. To be sure, the Russians were the first to find the path to northwestern America, to Alaska, as its new owners called it, in pursuit of fur-bearing animals. But the Americans found a path there, too, in pursuit of fur-bearing animals. Both paths were encumbered by the same disadvantage, separation from the center by a continent and an ocean or oceans, making Russian America a distant frontier for each. It became the area of convergence of Russia's overextended imperial expansion and of the United States' commercial imperialism. After its acquisition by the United States, it became for a long time "Alaska: The Forgotten Frontier."

NOTES

1. This voyage is the subject of a study I made several years ago: *The Voyage of Semen Dezhnev in 1648: Bering's Precursor* (London: The Hakluyt Society, 1981). See esp. chapters 7–9.
2. Raymond H. Fisher, *Bering's Voyages: Whither and Why* (Seattle and London: University of Washington Press, 1977), p. 160.
3. The nautical day began at noon and was half a day ahead of the civil day.
4. Until the Russian Revolution of 1917 the Russians continued to use the Julian calendar while most other western countries had converted to the Gregorian (present) calendar. To Julian dates in the 18th century 13 days must be added to equal the Gregorian date.
5. Quoted in Fisher, *Bering's Voyages,* p. 94.
6. Arkadii A. Sopotsko, *Istoriia playaniia V. Beringa na bote,* "Sv. Gavriil" *v Severnyi ledovityi okean* [History of the voyage of V. Bering in the boat *St. Gabriel* to the Arctic Ocean] (Moscow, 1983), p. 129; Vasilii V. Vakhtin, *Russkie truzhenik moria. Pervaia morskaia ekspeditsiia Beringa dlia resheniia voprosa, soediniaetsia li Aziia s Amerikoi* [Russian toilers of the sea. Bering's maritime expedition to decide whether Asia is joined to America] (St. Petersburg, 1890), p. 57.
7. Quoted in Fisher, *Bering's Voyages,* p. 112.
8. Ibid., p. 131.
9. Ibid., p. 186.
10. This instruction was discarded the next year in favor of a more southerly route south of the yet-to-be-discovered Aleutian Islands.
11. Fisher, *Bering's Voyages,* p. 128; O. W. Frost in Georg W. Steller, *Journal of a Voyage with Bering, 1741–1742* (Stanford: Stanford University Press, 1988), p. 18.

Russian Dependence on the Natives of Alaska

JAMES R. GIBSON

James Gibson of the Geography Department at York University near Toronto has devoted much of his career to the study of Russia's involvement in the North Pacific maritime fur trade. His early book Imperial Russia in Frontier America *(New York: Oxford University Press, 1975) addressed the problem of supplying Russian America, a problem the Russians never adequately solved. His most recent work, a monumental study,* Otter Skins, Boston Ships and China Goods: The Maritime Fur Trade on the Northwest Coast, 1785–1841 *(Seattle: University of Washington Press, 1992), provides comprehensive detail on the economic and social aspects of the fur trade and explores the complex relationships between its various players: Native hunters, American, English, and Russian merchants and seafarers, and Chinese traders and wholesalers.*

In the article reprinted here, Gibson delineates the high degree of dependence of the Russians both on the Aleut people of the "Eastern" Islands, as the Russians knew the Aleutians, and on the Tlingit Indians of the Alexander Archipelago. For most of the 20th century, historians of Russian America, with historians of European settlement elsewhere in the Americas, have either ignored the Native populations or have based their analyses on a presumption of European self-sufficiency and Native helplessness. Gibson demonstrates that such presumptions clearly are inappropriate. The Russians depended on the Natives for food, for technology, for labor, and for companionship and sex. Gibson goes so far as to say that the Russian occupation of the Northwest coast would have been impossible without Native support, for the Russians were undermanned and overextended. Both the Spanish and the French also were dependent on the Native populations, although in quite different ways from the Russians. Only the English arrived in such numbers as to become within a generation virtually independent of the aborigines. Gibson's article represents an important formative

This article appeared originally in S. Frederick Starr, ed., *Russia's American Colony* (Durham: Duke University Press, 1987), 77–104; it is reprinted here by permission.

perspective for readers developing a realistic understanding of the European-Native encounter in America. Portions of the original text of this article have been omitted by the editors.

In the literature on the early relations between the Native occupants and the European colonizers of North America, the former have commonly been seen as rather helpless dupes who were manipulated almost at will by the latter; many observers have held, moreover, that the Natives soon became dependent upon European trade goods, particularly guns, liquor, tobacco, metalware, textiles, and even foodstuffs. Recently, however, this characterization of the contact period has been called increasingly into question.[1] This paper carries the revisionism further by trying to show that in the case of Russian America—or, more accurately, the insular and coastal margins to which the Russian presence was largely confined—the traditional characterization is not only oversimplified but downright erroneous, for in fact virtually the opposite situation obtained, with the Russians being dependent upon the Aleuts, Kodiaks, and Tlingits for such basics as furs, provisions, labor, and sex.

The fur trade was, of course, the raison d'être of Russian America, just as it had been of Siberia. Russian eastward expansion from the Urals was really a rush for "soft gold"—principally sables in Siberia and sea otters in America. The latter succeeded the former as the world's most valuable furbearers, and the resultant overhunting took the Russian *promyshlenniki* ever eastward—from the basin of the Ob' [River] to the Enisei and Lena, then to the peninsula of Kamchatka, along the Aleutian archipelago to the Gulf of Alaska, and finally down the Northwest Coast. The depletion of sea otters was especially rapid because of the creatures' low fertility (one offspring per year per dam) and high value (of the dam in particular). Thanks to the high luster, dark color, large size, and durability of sea otter pelts, they were the most prized of all furs, especially by the Chinese. In the 1810s a prime adult female pelt could bring the Russian-American Company up to 1,000 rubles, as much as the total annual salaries of three *promyshlenniki*. Other furbearers, particularly fur seals, were hunted in Russian America, but none approached sea otters in value.[2]

Although the Russians were primarily interested in sea otters, they themselves did not actually hunt them. In the continental fur trade of Siberia the *promyshlenniki* were able to bag sables as readily as the Samoeds, Buriats, Iakuts, Koriaks, and other Natives, but the maritime fur trade was quite another matter. Pelagic hunting was foreign to the Russian landsmen. So they became abjectly dependent upon the Native hunters' traditional expertise in the killing of sea animals, especially sea otters, which were the most elusive. As Governor Ferdinand von Wrangell (1830–35) noted, "Of all hunts, the sea otter hunt requires the most experience, skill, and patience. Fur seals, sea lions, and walruses, despite their strength and size, are caught more easily and more quickly." Moreover, the sea otter chase was "very toilsome, and sometimes dangerous," according to the Russian navy's Captain Otto von Kotzebue, who twice visited the colony.[3] The inexperienced Russians were reluctant to exert their brawn and risk their lives, particularly when highly skilled and largely defenseless Native hunters were readily available. Besides, the hunting of nimble sea otters in the open sea from flimsy kayaks with short harpoons was a formidable task that the Natives practiced from childhood and took years to master. It was an integral component of Aleut and Kodiak culture. The German naturalist and physician Georg von Langsdorff, who accompanied the first Russian circumnavigation in 1803–6, found that "scarcely has [an Aleut] boy attained his eighth year, or even sometimes not more than his sixth, when he is instructed in the management of the canoes [kayaks], and in aiming at a mark with the water javelin."[4] In the same year Captain Iurii Lisianskii, one of the commanders of the circumnavigation, remarked that the Kodiaks (Koniaga Eskimos), "exercised from their childhood to this sort of hunting, are very expert at it." And in 1820 on Unalaska Island Lieutenant Aleksei Lazarev of the Russian navy observed that "an Aleut is, so to speak, born in a kayak, skillful in all forms of hunting, and familiar from childhood with winds and currents."

Furthermore, according to Father Ivan Veniaminov, who spent a decade (1824–34) among the Aleuts as a missionary, they were physically superior to the Russians as hunters. He pointed out that the Aleuts were solidly built and broad-shouldered and hence made strong, tireless workers.[5] Veniaminov concluded bluntly that "Russians . . . will never be sea otter hunters."

The Aleuts were better sea otter hunters than the Kodiaks, too. They even liked to hunt sea otters, or so it was alleged by their Russian masters. One of them, Kiril Khlebnikov, who probably knew Russian America better than any other colonial official, having served fifteen years (1817–32) there, declared that the Aleuts were the only Natives with an innate passion for hunting sea otters. Similarly, Warrant Officer Friedrich Lütke of the Russian navy observed in 1818 that the Aleuts were as fond of catching sea otters as cats were of catching mice. More importantly, the Aleuts were better kayakers than the Kodiaks (or any of the coastal Natives of the Gulf of Alaska for that matter), probably because they had better craft. Light, fast, and maneuverable, with a shallow draught, kayaks were admirably suited to the pursuit of sea otters in the kelp and shellfish beds of the rocky and shallow coastal waters. They weighed less than thirty-six pounds and could be carried by a seven-year-old boy, and in a "moderately smooth" sea they could easily do ten miles per hour.[6] Veniaminov asserted that "it seems to me that an Aleut kayak is so perfect in its type that not even a mathematician could add very much, if anything, to the perfection of its nautical qualities."

So the Aleuts, as Governor von Wrangell acknowledged, were the most skillful hunters of sea otters. In fact, their expertise with kayaks and harpoons was such that under Russian pressure it contributed to the rapid diminution of the sea otter population.[7] It was also such that the Russian *promyshlenniki* became totally dependent upon the Aleuts, not even bothering to learn how to hunt "sea beavers" themselves. Martin Sauer, secretary to the Billings expedition (1785–94), observed on Kodiak Island in 1790 that foxes and ground squirrels were the only animals that the Russians were capable of killing. Lieutenant Lazarev noted on Unalaska Island in 1820 that the Russians were less competent kayakers than the Aleuts, so much so that if the latter were to refrain from hunting the Russian-American Company would be deprived of sea otters. He explained that "if the company should somehow lose the Aleuts, then it would completely forfeit the hunting of sea animals, for not one Russian knows how to hunt the animals, and none of our settlers has learned how in all the time that the company has had its possessions here." And in 1830 the colonial administration admitted that the Aleuts' skill in sea otter hunting was irreplaceable. Little wonder that Governor von Wrangell referred to the Aleuts as the "sole miners of the company's wealth."[8]

They also dominated the hunting of fur seals. The principal fur sealing grounds were the Pribilof Islands of St. George and St. Paul, where, from 1786 through 1830, 3,144,494 fur seals (an average of nearly 70,000 every fall) were killed. In 1810, 200 Aleuts were sent from Unalaska to the Pribilofs; in 1814, 300 Aleut men with their wives and children worked on the islands under the supervision of several Russian *promyshlenniki* and clubbed 70,000 to 80,000 fur seals; and in 1820 the Pribilof fur seal hunt was carried out by 380 Aleuts and only 10 Russians. Not surprisingly, the essential Aleuts constituted nearly one-third of company employees in 1832.[9]

Because their expertise was so necessary to the prosecution of the maritime fur trade, the Aleuts were severely exploited by the Russians. At first, sea otter pelts were exacted from the islanders as tribute, and hostages were taken to ensure payment. This practice was banned in 1788 but in fact lasted until 1794; it was replaced by compulsory labor, with the Aleuts becoming, in effect, serfs, who were paid in kind (clothing, tobacco, food). All Aleut males between the ages of fifteen and fifty had to work for the Russian-American Company, which monopolized the administration and exploitation of the colony from 1799 to 1867. They were forcibly separated from their families, moved to new hunting grounds, subjected to arduous labor, and exposed to cold, hunger, accidents, disease, and Indian enemies. By 1790, following fifty years of Russian contact, the Aleut population may have decreased by as much as two-thirds. On the Fox Islands, the most densely populated of the Aleutians, the number of Natives fell from 1,904 in 1806 to 1,046 in 1817—a decline of almost 50 percent in a dozen years. Surely, the impact of the Russian maritime fur trade on the Aleuts belies the "enrichment" thesis, which contends that the fur trade was more beneficial than detrimental to Native culture and caused minimal cultural change that the Natives were able to control.[10]

This decimation of the colony's best sea otter hunters prompted the Russians to use more and more Kodiaks or, as they were known to the Russians, *Koniaga,* whose ability with kayak and harpoon was second only to that of the Aleuts. Already by 1790, for instance, 600 two-hatched kayaks with 1,200 Kodiaks were hunting sea otters around Kodiak Island for the Golikov-Shelikhov company. And in 1830, 880 Kodiak kayaks were hunting sea otters in the Gulf of Alaska for the Russian-American Company; one group of 500 was supervised by fewer than 10 Russians. Such exploitation quickly began to affect Kodiak numbers, too. Their population fell from 5,700 in 1792 to 1,500 in 1834, a decline of 75 percent. From 1792 through 1805, 751 Kodiaks were killed in accidents alone, including 350 from drowning in 1805. One-third of the Kodiak population succumbed to smallpox during the last half of the 1830s. Fortunately, for the Russians, the rate of decrease of the Aleuts and Kodiaks was exceeded only by that of the sea otter, so a shortage of expert sea otter hunters did not arise.[11]

The Russians even relied upon the Aleuts and Kodiaks to hunt land furbearers; otherwise they were bartered from independent Natives. On Unalaska Island the Aleuts trapped foxes during the fall for the Russian-American Company. In the Kodiak district in the last half of the 1790s, an average of 250 Natives and only 25 Russians hunted land furbearers. "Very few" Kenais (Tanaina Indians) of Cook Inlet were employed by the company, probably because they were not considered good sailors; but they hunted and traded land furs and skins (marten, lynx, bear, wolverine, river otter, beaver, muskrat, mink, caribou) for the company, whose Fort St. Nikolai [present-day Kenai] derived most of its business from these Natives. And most of the land furs produced by the Novo-Arkhangel'sk district (Sitka and the Alexander Archipelago), especially mink, beaver, and river otter, were obtained for the company by the Tlingits. In 1821, for example, the company procured 150 river otters and 100 beavers, as well as 50 sea otters, from the Tlingits.[12]

The insular and coastal Natives of Russian America were not only the providers of the Russians' peltry but also the suppliers of their very sustenance. The colony suffered from a chronic problem of supply, particularly food supply. The shipment of provisions over land and sea from Siberia via Okhotsk and from European Russia via Kronstadt and the Cape [of Good Hope] or the Horn [Cape Horn] was prolonged and expensive, as well as subject to considerable loss. Importation from nearby foreign countries, colonies, and companies brought better provisions more rapidly and more cheaply but made the Russians precariously and embarrassingly dependent upon their American, British, and Hispanic rivals for control of the Northwest Coast. Farming in Russian America itself was unproductive, owing mainly to the raw climate and inexperienced manpower. During a stopover at Novo-Arkhangel'sk in 1837, a young British midshipman explained, "I should think there was not a single spot in the whole world where so much rain falls during the year; at Sitka, a fine day is really a perfect rarity." Only certain vegetables, chiefly potatoes, succeeded. Aleuts worked the vegetable gardens at the colonial capital, but not with spectacular results. Nevertheless, potatoes fared better there than anywhere else in the colony. They were fertilized with kelp, and yields averaged seven and one-half-fold increases in the 1820s. Six hundred 145-pound barrels of potatoes were produced at Sitka in 1821, one hundred fifty barrels in 1825; and in some years a hundred barrels were sold to visiting American and Russian ships. The potatoes were tasty and nourishing and rivaled bread as a staple.[13]

It was, however, the unruly Tlingits or *Kolosh,* as they were called by the Russians, not the placid Aleuts, who became the principal growers of potatoes. Relations between the Russians and the Tlingits contrasted sharply with those between the Russians and the Aleuts and Kodiaks. The *promyshlenniki* failed to subjugate and pacify the Tlingits, who consequently retained their culture longer than the islanders, and always remained suspect. The hapless Aleuts and Kodiaks were subdued quickly and easily, but the Tlingits, who were not encountered by the Russians until 1783, were able to resist them much more successfully. Described by Russian observers as strong, agile, hardy, brave, and clever, the Tlingits had a richer environment (more timber, fish, and land animals) and a larger territory (including a continental interior) to exploit, and they were less essential to the acquisition of sea otters than the Aleuts or Kodiaks. Without control of the Aleuts and Kodiaks the Russians would have had to either do their own hunting or, more likely, resort to barter, whereby the supply of pelts would undoubtedly have been less regular and more expensive. For example, the Russians had to pay the intransigent Tlingits three to five times as much as they did the enserfed Aleuts for the same furs. The Tlingits were also more numerous, numbering 10,000 in 1805, including 2,000 Sitka Tlingits. In 1818 on Baranof (Sitka) Island alone there were 1,000 Tlingits, whose number doubled during the spring herring run. The Tlingit population still totaled 10,000 in 1835, although by 1838 it had been reduced to 6,000 by smallpox. Furthermore, the Tlingits were better organized than the Aleuts or Kodiaks, thanks partly, at least, to their more abundant food supply, which left them more time to create a more elaborate social system. They lived in large dispersed villages, each consisting socially of several independent clans whose intervillage allegiances overrode all intravillage ties; the Aleuts, by contrast, lived in more numerous and smaller villages closer to scarcer food sources, each village consisting socially of one autonomous extended family ruled by one man, with weak intervillage loyalties. Among the Tlingits, clan identity and solidarity were accentuated by the restriction of inheritance to the female line and by the imposition of phratric exogamy. This cohesiveness enabled the Tlingits much more effectively to resist Russian control. As von Langsdorff noted in 1805, "Single families, as well as single tribes (clans) have contentions sometimes with each other . . . but if attacked by a common enemy, suppose the Russians, they unite for their common defense." Consequently, as Khlebnikov warned, "to kill several hundred of them would be to instill a tribal vengeance into several thousand men." The Russian naval captain Vasilii Golovnin, who made a tour of inspection of Russian America in 1818, recognized the Tlingit problem at Sitka:

> But because the local Natives do not constitute one single tribe under one chief but are divided into various clans who live or roam as they please, quite independent of one another (often one of them even fights another), it is not possible to take revenge on them, for one cannot tell to which clan the guilty belong, unless one were to make it a rule to take revenge indiscriminately. But in that case they would all unite to attack the company's settlement.

Golovnin added:

> The Aleuts and Kodiaks had permanent dwellings in villages and did not have firearms, so the company with a handful of *promyshlenniki* easily kept them in subjection; but the inhabitants of the Northwest Coast of America . . . are strong, patient in their work, and extremely bold . . . ; they love independence so much that they would rather part with life than freedom, and to subjugate them is not only difficult but impossible, for they do not have permanent dwellings but roam the channels from island to island and live in huts; they build their boats so well that no European rowed vessel, except a whale boat, is able to overtake them . . . ; in battle they are so courageous that they are rarely captured alive, and they have learned quickly to use firearms, and they shoot very accurately.[14]

The Tlingits' adoption of firearms was yet another advantage. In this they were abetted by American traders, whereas the Aleuts and Kodiaks, being completely under Russian control, were unable to turn to foreign vessels. Yankee "coasters" plying the "straits" that fragmented the Alexander Archipelago supplied the Tlingits with powder, shot, and guns, including falconets, instructed them in their use, and incited them against the Russians. In the process the Americans deprived the Russians of many furs; in 1805, for instance, Captain Lisianskii found that Novo-Arkhangel'sk could be getting 8,000 instead of 3,000 sea otter pelts annually but for American traders. Lisianskii and von Langsdorff also found that the Tlingits had virtually abandoned their spears and bows and arrows in favor of the best English guns, which could be purchased more cheaply on the Northwest Coast than in England itself. The Sitkan Tlingits had muskets and small cannons, as well as iron breastplates, and Chief Kotlean owned no fewer than twenty of the "best" muskets and was an "excellent" marksman. At this time Count Nikolai Rezanov, who was inspecting the colony, reported to the directors of the Russian-American Company that "they [the Tlingits] are armed by the Bostonians [Americans] with the very best guns and pistols and have falconets too." In 1825 Captain von Kotzebue observed that "no Kalush is without one musket at least, of which he perfectly understands the use." And in 1860 another colonial inspector, Captain Pavel Golovin, found that "they [the Tlingits] always go armed with knives and often with revolvers and rifles, which are supplied to them nearby by the English and the Americans. They are very good shots and are bold . . . and *Novo-Arkhangel'sk is constantly in a state of siege."* Golovin's fellow inspector, State Councillor Sergei Kostlivtsev, was likewise impressed by the military strength of the Tlingits. He reported that "when at our request the Kolosh living near the port were invited to show us how they warred against other savages . . . we noted with no little surprise that the Kolosh [who] assembled on that occasion were all armed with rifles and pistols and fired rapid volleys, like the firing of regular infantry."[15]

No wonder that the Russians treated the Tlingits gingerly and respectfully, so much so that during the first fifty years of Russian contact, which reduced the Aleut population by two-thirds, the Tlingit population remained undiminished. And little wonder that the Tlingits impressed Captain von Kotzebue as a "warlike, courageous, and cruel race." They hated the Russians for having seized their ancestral lands, occupied their best fishing and hunting grounds, desecrated their burial sites, and seduced their women.[16]

The colonial capital was precariously situated, for it was in fact a double settlement—a Russian fort with a Tlingit village just outside the walls. The former contained 1,230 souls in 1845 and 988 in 1860, when it comprised more than a hundred houses, three churches, two schools, two mills, two warehouses, and a two-storey governor's mansion. The latter contained 500 to 600 Indians in the middle 1820s, 700 to 750 in 1837–38, and 600 to 700 in 1860. Governor Nikolai Rosenberg (1850–53) reported in 1851 that "no fewer than 500 well-armed savage Kolosh, who are always ready to take advantage of our negligence, live right by our settlement." Furthermore, every spring the two-to-three-week herring run brought even more Tlingits; in the early and middle 1820s up to 2,000, and in the early 1860s more than 1,000, assembled in Sitka Bay every March and April to obtain herring. Inspectors Golovin and Kostlivtsev, who reconnoitered Russian America for six months in 1860–61, reported that Novo-Arkhangel'sk's fort contained 55 cannons mounted and 87 stored, as well as 1,170 other guns, and 147 soldiers and 39 sailors, most of whom, however, were "ailing" and "badly" trained in gunnery; they faced up to 1,000 Tlingit males in the spring and the fall and 500 at other times—all "cunning and fearless" and "well-armed with pistols and rifles." So many hostile and well-armed Indians so close to the capital endangered its residents and restricted their activities. Everything company employees did outside the fort's walls—hunting, fishing, gathering, felling, watering, ballasting—was imperiled. As late as 1860, only half a dozen years before the sale of Russian America, Captain Golovin asserted that "no Russian dared to go 50 paces from the fort" for fear of the Tlingit. He added that the Tlingits, in their own words, "tolerate the Russians."[17]

Although the Tlingits had, according to Captain Golovin, an innate passion for petty trading, at first they were understandably reluctant to trade with the Russian invaders. By 1805 the Tlingits at Sitka had largely discarded their fur and hide garments for woolen clothes, but American and British traders, not Russias, were undoubtedly responsible. At this time the Tlingits even refused Russian offers of liquor, fearing that it would render them easier prey. In 1821 Lieutenant Lazarev found that trade between the Russian-American Company and the Tlingits was "very insignificant" because American traders paid higher prices. Thereafter, however, the Indians turned increasingly to the Russians for trade goods as their Yankee suppliers gradually disappeared from the coast with the decline of the fur trade and as the Muscovites under the post-1818 breed of governors (naval officers) permitted closer but stricter contact. Mostly land furs and provisions, including potatoes, black-tailed deer, halibut, salmon, shellfish (especially crabs), wildfowl (grouse, ducks, and geese), birds' eggs, berries, roots, herbs, and even snails (or marine slugs), were provided by the Tlingits. By 1830 traffic had increased to the point where Governor von Wrangell was moved to complain that "we buy much of our food every year on the Kolosh market, in spite of the ever increasing prices, which are now extremely high."[18]

That the Russians were willing to pay the mounting prices indicates that the Tlingit provisions played a vital role. In 1831 the company traded 29,100 rubles' worth of goods (mainly blankets, cloth, iron utensils, axes, tobacco, and paper) for Tlingit furs (chiefly beaver, mink, fox, and land otter), provisions, bark (for siding), clay (for bricks), and fat (for candles); the provisions accounted for 8,000 of these rubles, and they consisted mostly of black-tailed deer, halibut, salmon, birds' eggs, grouse, ducks, geese, and berries. In 1832 the Russians introduced liquor into the "Kolosh trade," probably in order to meet increasing competition in the "straits" from the Hudson's Bay Company's new coastal posts. The explorer Lieutenant Lavrentii Zagoskin reported from Novo-Arkhangel'sk in the spring of 1840 that "the Kolosh . . . daily bring the food we eat in return for much tobacco and rum." The trading was done every day at a special bazaar inside the fort. It was described in 1842 by Dr. Alexander R. Rowand, who visited the colonial capital with Governor George Simpson of the Hudson's Bay Company: "Their market, which is held within the Russian settlement, appeared to me quite extraordinary, presenting to view a goodly supply of deer carcasses, with salmon, cod, red-rock fish and herrings, together with abundance of wild fowl, partridge and woodcock. The women are the sellers; their husbands considering them far more successful in driving a bargain than they could be."[19]

From 1841, Russian-Tlingit relations improved. By then the last of the Indians' American suppliers had withdrawn from the coastal trade, so the Russian-American Company and the Hudson's Bay Company were the only sources of trade goods. Tlingit resistance had been further weakened by smallpox in the last half of the 1830s; in 1836 alone, 400—almost one-half—of the Tlingits living at Novo-Arkhangel'sk had succumbed. The smallpox epidemic broke the back of Tlingit resistance because: 1) it killed so many Tlingits (nearly half of their number perished in the first two months of 1836); 2) it particularly affected the elderly, who were the most hostile to the Russians and the most influential among the Tlingits; 3) it convinced the Tlingits of the efficacy of vaccination and consequently of the superior knowledge of the Russians, and 4) having changed their opinion of the Russians, the Tlingits lost faith in their shamans. Perhaps the missionary zeal of the astute Ivan Veniaminov, at Novo-Arkhangel'sk, 1834–38 and 1841–50, also served to pacify the Tlingits, and perhaps, too, they were mollified by the abolition of the liquor traffic in 1842 by the two companies.[20]

Whatever the reasons, from the early 1840s, Russian-Tlingit contact increased and the "Kolosh trade" boomed, mainly on the strength of potatoes, black-tailed deer, and halibut. By 1860 the Tlingits were accustomed to flour, rice, molasses, tobacco, and vodka; they were obtaining more than 3,600 pounds of flour per month from the company at Sitka. The Kolosh bazaar was now held outside the fort and the trading was done with caution, as Captain Golovin found:

> The Kolosh are not allowed inside the settlement, and trading at the bazaar is conducted in the following way: alongside the battery there has been erected a building, which contains all of the goods that are usually needed by the Kolosh; behind this building toward the Kolosh village, there is a small parcel of land enclosed by a high palisade—this is the bazaar. The Kolosh are admitted through a portcullis, which, if necessary, can be lowered instantly. In the wall of the building or storehouse there is a window, which is closed from the inside with a thick shutter. When the Kolosh arrive at the market in the morning with provisions, consisting of deer, wildfowl, fish, and potatoes, the window in the shop is opened and the company agent accepts the provisions from each Indian in accordance with fixed prices and gives in return scrip or goods also at fixed prices. . . . When trading with the Kolosh has finished, the residents of New Archangel come to the shop and get the necessary amount of venison, potatoes, and fish at fixed prices, paying in scrip.

The Russians had shown the Tlingits how to plant and use potatoes, probably in the late 1810s or early 1820s. This cultigen is well suited to the cold, damp summers and the light, well drained soils of the Northwest Coast, and adoption was undoubtedly facilitated by the existence of a root-collecting tradition and of more or less permanent camps among the Tlingits. They were selling potatoes to the Russian-American Company as early as 1841 (when an annual fair was inaugurated at the capital to facilitate the Indian trade), and thereafter almost every year until at least 1861, but particularly during the 1840s. In 1843 the Kaigani Tlingits-Haidas of Prince of Wales Island accepted the offer of Governor Adolph Etholen (1840–45) to bring potatoes to Novo-Arkhangel'sk every fall. In October 1845 more than 2,000 Tlingits in 160 to 250 boats, many of them from as far away as the Queen Charlotte Islands, assembled at Novo-Arkhangel'sk to sell potatoes. This traffic allowed the company to ship 200 barrels of the tubers to Kodiak Island that year. It also provided the Russian residents of Novo-Arkhangel'sk with their principal fresh vegetable.[21]

More important to the sustenance of the Russians, however, than Native farming were hunting, fishing, and gathering on the part of the Aleuts, Kodiaks, and Tlingits, and even the Kenais of Cook Inlet and the Chugach Eskimos of Prince William Sound. Native hunting, which was dominated by the Tlingits, provided virtually the only fresh meat in winter, since colonial stock raising did not thrive. The chief game were Sitka black-tailed deer, Dall or Big Horn sheep, and mountain goats, all found in the coastal mountains, including Baranof Island. The black-tailed deer and the mountain goats had "very tasty" flesh, and one of the species of sheep had thick, smooth wool. The Kenais and Chugaches bagged some of these animals for the Russians, but the Tlingits were the main suppliers. They hunted mountain goats and deer with bows and arrows, usually from November to May, when the animals were driven to lower ground by deep snow. Sometimes, when the black-tailed deer were driven right down to the coast by heavy snow (as in the winter of 1859–60), the Tlingits used clubs. From the "whitish, fine, and very long" goat hair or wool, which rivaled silk "in the delicacy and softness of its texture," the Tlingits wove their very handsome Chilkat dance blankets, which were "as soft and fine as the Spanish merino." From the same fiber the Russians knitted stockings and hats, and from the skins they made leather; from the horns the Tlingits also carved spoons. It was as a source of venison that the black-tailed deer became important to the Russians. During the 1820s the company's Aleuts at the capital were bagging as many as 200 animals in a good year, but as early as 1824 the Tlingits were furnishing the settlement with a "sufficient number" of black-tailed deer, ducks, and geese. From 1844 they supplied a remarkable average of more than 500 deer annually. During the 1850s the capital consumed an average of up to 400 black-tailed deer (and up to 1,000 wildfowl) yearly, thanks to the Tlingits.

Fishing was even more important than hunting as a source of food for the Russians. Owing to the difficulties of colonial agriculture and the irregularity of importation, as well as the "superfluity" of fish in colonial waters, the diet of the Russians and Natives alike was dominated by fish. As Lieutenant Lazarov noted at Novo-Arkhangel'sk in 1821, "fish . . . are to this place what bread is to Russia." Even the opening of trade with California in the late 1810s brought little relief. In 1824 Zavalishin found that there was barely enough beef and milk at Novo-Arkhangel'sk for the governor himself. And in 1831 Governor von Wrangell reported that company employees at the capital were buying fish, wildfowl, and snails (or marine slugs) from the Tlingits at high prices for want of salted beef and cow's butter.[22]

Fish, supplemented by some flour and meat, remained the dietary staple. Officials and officers ate better than laborers, getting more and fresher food, as well as some luxuries, like tea, wine, and sugar. For all, fish was the main source of protein and vitamin D. The most common food fish were salmon, halibut, herring, and cod, with halibut being preferred by the Natives. Halibut and cod were abundant year round, although the former were caught mostly in winter; herring peaked in spring and salmon in summer. Shellfish, especially crabs, were also eaten. . . .

The company's head office acknowledged the contribution of the Tlingits, telling its stockholders in 1845 that "the Kolosh abundantly supply the Novo-Arkhangel'sk market with fresh provisions and firewood, giving the colonial authorities the means for rendering more assistance to company employees and for making life in New Archangel more economical." And in 1860 Dmitrii Nedel'kovich, a young naval officer in the company's service, recorded:

> Every day from 8 in the morning until 4 in the afternoon they [the Tlingits] come to the bazaar to sell *iamany* (a combination of wild goats and deer), which replace meat here for want of livestock, and the Kolosh also bring fish, primarily halibut and various shellfish, wildfowl, other products, and berries. In this respect the Kolosh are essential to the Russians, since employees in the colony for want of free time cannot procure their own food; moreover, all of the Kolosh are excellent hunters and are used to the climate and the country.

This dependency was confirmed that same year by Captain Golovin: "Fearing the Kolosh, [the Russians of Novo-Arkhangel'sk] have long contemplated driving them from the settlement, but they are afraid that then there will be no fresh provisions because *the Russians do not go into the woods to hunt, there are few gardens, and there are no livestock except pigs. On the entire island there are five or six cows and four horses.*" Noting that the Tlingits supplied the capital with more than 1,000 black-tailed deer annually, Golovin's colleague, State Councilor Kostlivtsev, added that "all of the inhabitants of Novo-Arkhangel'sk, for the want of cattle there, are provisioned with the fresh meat of deer and fresh fish by the Kolosh, and that is why every time that the Kolosh quarrel among themselves or for some reason are displeased with the Russians, the entire fort is left with old salted meat and salted and dried fish." Kostlivtsev concluded:

> Although in the company's current charter, as well as in the one being re-drafted, these Natives are considered to be completely dependent on the colonial authorities and to be residing in the colonial territory, I for my part would deem them more correctly to be completely independent. In no respect whatever can the Kolosh be considered dependent on the company; rather, it can be said that the company's very set-

> tlements on the American coast depend on them. The latter have only to make a noise, as is said here, and the port of Novo-Arkhangel'sk and its entire population is deprived of all fresh food and even the opportunity of showing itself a few yards outside the palisade.

Finally, the Russians were dependent upon the Natives of the Russian-American colony—again primarily the Aleuts, Kodiaks, and Tlingits—for labor and sex. One of the main reasons the Russians relied so heavily upon the Natives for so many goods and services was the shortage of Russians themselves. The legal bonds of serfdom immobilized most of the inhabitants of Russia, and for those not tied to a landlord (or for those who simply fled) Siberia was a more attractive alternative than Russian America because it was less distant and more tamed. So few Russians went to "barbarous, desolate Sitka," as it was described by Governor Semën Ianovskii (1818–21); during his stay at the colonial capital in 1861 Captain Golovin found that "here it is just as if we were in a kind of wasteland where the voice of cultured people is rarely heard . . . if it were not for the isolation from the rest of the world and such a foul climate, it would be possible to live here . . . thank God that I do not." Those who did reach the colony tended not to stay long (unless they had to stay in order to work off debts to the Russian-American Company). Of 35 families of settlers sent to Alaska in 1784, only 4 individuals remained in 1818, whereas they should have multiplied to at least 175 souls by then (assuming that every family had stayed and had grown to 5 persons). In 1838 Governor Ivan Kuprianov (1835–40) bemoaned the "utter shortage at present of workers in the colony." The company was often simply unable to replace employees who died or quit. From 1838 through 1842, 101 laborers left Russian America for Russia proper, and 80 died in the colony, but only 67 recruits arrived from the motherland, for a net loss of 114. In 1839 the colonial administration reported that the colony lost about 40 laborers annually, and the company's head office in St. Petersburg resolved to send 40 replacements every year; in fact, 70 were needed yearly, but instead 40 arrived in 1825, 81 in 1827, 50 in 1828, 30 in 1829, 33 in 1830, 40 in 1833, 55 in 1837, 31 in 1838, and 42 in 1839. In 1846 Governor Teben'kov complained that "there is much work but no men." In 1849, when the colony was short 100 men, he declared that "the shortage of laborers in the colony greatly influences everything and, incidentally, is very unfavorable." In the spring of 1851 Governor Rosenberg reported that there were 426 adult male employees of the company at the colonial capital but that there should be 638. From 1854 through 1858, 131 laborers (plus 202 soldiers) reached Russian America, but 176 departed for a net loss of 45. And in early 1865 Governor Dmitrii Maksutov (1863–67) bewailed the "extreme shortage of workers in the colony" and requested a reinforcement of 100 men, but instead their number was allowed to decrease from 381 at that time to 299 in early 1867, leaving a shortfall of nearly 200 men.[23]

Such labor deficits obviously weakened Russian occupancy, particularly in the face of Tlingit hostility and American rivalry. For example, until the arrival of the Russian navy's 83-man *Loyal* and 74-man *Discovery* in the fall of 1820, Governor Murav'ev's force of some 200 Russians at Sitka was insufficient to allow the sending of any men outside the palisade to cut timber for a new fort (the old structure being so dilapidated that it had begun to collapse), for this would have left the post without enough defenders.

Russian America's image was tarnished not only by its remoteness and savagery. The foul climate, heavy work, low pay, and spare diet further sullied the colony's reputation; hence a deacon's remark that "it is better to go into the army than to go to [Russian] America." Moreover, these punitive conditions—plus negligence (there was no doctor or infirmary at Novo-Arkhangel'sk, for instance, before 1820)—debilitated the few Russians who did go there. Sickness and death rates were high. In the spring of 1819 Governor Ianovskii reported that one out of every six men in the capital was sick on account of the unhealthfulness of the climate and the scarcity of fresh food, and in 1829 Governor Petr Chistiakov (1825–30) asserted that one-third of the laborers in Novo-Arkhangel'sk were usually incapacitated by illness. Captain Edward Belcher put in to the colonial capital in the fall of 1837 and found that "the total number [population] is about eight hundred, but of these many, if not the greater part, are invalids; but few able-bodied men were visible." The smallpox epidemic of the last half of the 1830s especially reduced colonial manpower, Native in particular. But the most common afflictions, according to Alexander Rowand, the Scottish physician who visited in 1842, were hemoptysis, typhus, pulmonary disorders, and venereal diseases. During the 1850s a Russian doctor found that rheumatism and catarrh predominated, owing to the changeable weather and the excessive drinking. It took Russian newcomers two years to become "creolized," that is, acclimated to the colonial seat; in the meantime they were "constantly" ailing. No wonder that the number of deaths not infrequently exceeded the number of births at the colonial capital.

The disease-ridden labor force was further handicapped by drunkenness and incompetence, both of which were chronic problems in Russia proper. In 1805 Count Rezanov reported to the directors of the Russian-American Company from the colonial capital that "most of the men who come here are depraved, drunk, violent and corrupted to such an extent that any society should consider it a great relief to get rid of them." He added that "they drink two or three bottles of vodka every day" in this "drunken republic," and "the depravity and wildness of the hunter threaten this country with ruin." In 1815 the commandant of Okhotsk, where the company had an agency, complained that most of the company's laborers were drunkards and ruffians. In 1842 Simpson rated Novo-Arkhangel'sk the most drunken and dirtiest place that he had ever visited. His companion, Dr. Rowand, agreed, stating that the company's employees were a "drunken and dissolute set." Little wonder that 150 of the company's laborers on Baranof Island in 1846 were considered "useless." In 1860 Captain Golovin found that drunkenness, carousing, violence, illness, and insubordination were "extremely common," especially among soldiers and laborers. He added that "in general rum and vodka play an important role here . . . the creoles [halfbreeds] and common people are all generally given to drunkenness . . . and work here is valued in vodka." . . .

Not surprisingly, then, the Russian-American Company hired many Native workers. The use of Aleut and Kodiak hunters has already been detailed. Eventually even Tlingits were employed, mainly from the early 1840s, when the company was particularly desperate for recruits and the Tlingits were seeking new trading partners in the aftermath of the departure of American vessels from the Northwest Coast. In 1842 for the first time the company hired some Tlingits at Novo-Arkhangel'sk (at one-half of the cost of Russian laborers, incidentally). Every summer from 1842 through 1846 fifty Tlingits, and from 1847 twenty, were employed as sailors, woodcutters, stevedores, and fishermen. According to Father Veniaminov, who ministered to the Tlingits in the 1840s, they were by nature "energetic and industrious," particularly the women, "who learned Russian very quickly." By contrast, the Aleuts (whom the Tlingits regarded as cowards and slaves of the Russians) were characterized by Veniaminov as being lazy, gentle, peaceable, and patient. To him the Tlingits were the most capable of all of the Natives of Russian America. In the 1850s a number of Kenais and Kodiaks were employed in, respectively, coal mining and ice cutting but they soon became exhausted or sick and were deemed "hopeless."

Not only was there a want of Russians in general but also a lack of Russian women in particular. The colony had even less attraction for Russian females than males, and females were less mobile anyway, apart from the loyal and daring wives of some officials. For example, Russian males outnumbered females twenty-nine to one in 1819, fourteen to one in 1820, nine to one in 1833, and eight to one in 1836 and 1860. So the Russian men turned to Native women—mostly Aleuts and Kodiaks but also Pomos and eventually Tlingits—for sex. The offspring of these liaisons were termed creoles, the counterparts of New France's métis and New Spain's mestizos and mulattos. Most creoles were illegitimate, their fathers not wanting to legalize the alliances because they already had wives in Russia proper. Considered to be "handsome and intelligent" by Lieutenant Zagoskin and generally capable, especially in mechanics, by Captain Golovin, creoles were educated at company expense as prospective employees. In 1817 there were up to eighty creole pupils on Kodiak and at Novo-Arkhangel'sk. And about the same time a dozen creoles were sent to St. Petersburg to be taught technical skills, especially navigation and shipbuilding; they learned quickly, but only two returned to the colony, the rest dying in Russia of consumption and melancholy. Upon graduation most creoles became artisans or laborers for the company; under the company's second twenty-year monopoly charter (1821) creoles educated at the firm's expense became, in effect, temporary serfs, having to serve the company for ten years (with compensation).

As employees the creoles helped to offset the shortage of Russian manpower, particularly skilled manpower. But they were not without disadvantages. Captain Golovin found that they led a dissipated life, being inclined to debauchery, wildness, irresponsibility, and idleness; drunkenness in particular was their undoing. Also, by the age of thirty or thirty-five nearly all creoles suffered from chest ailments, especially tuberculosis, so that few of them reached old age. Moreover, many shunned company service, preferring to live like their maternal relatives. Generally they were poor substitutes for Russians, Governor Teben'kov asserting in 1846 that one Russian was worth three creoles. By 1818 there were already one-half as many creoles (280) in Russian America as there were Russians (450), and at the colonial capital there were just as many creoles (206) as Russians (204). In 1832 152 of the company's 1,025 colonial employees, or 15 percent, were creoles. Creoles outnumbered Russians 2 to 1 by 843 and 3 to 1 by 1860.

Clearly, then, the Russians became very dependent upon the coastal Natives of Russian America for essential goods and services, just as they likewise became dependent upon American, British, and Hispanic rivals for such necessities as grain, beef, salt, and manufactures. This dependency, which reflected the cultural versatility and resilience and commercial acumen of the Natives, as well as the small numbers and limited skills of the Russians, was both a serious economic drain and a major geopolitical weakness. Lieutenant Lazarev noted in the early 1820s that the "upkeep of this colony costs the Company very dearly." It was to cost even more. Annual upkeep rose from between 150,000 and 175,000 rubles during the first half of the 1820s to between 250,000 and 300,000 rubles during the last half of the 1830s, thanks to the construction of new posts inland, the depletion of furbearers near old posts, the raising of the salaries of employees, and the expansion of various services (churches, schools, hospitals, charities). Between 1824–25 and 1838–39, when the Russians were becoming increasingly reliant upon the Natives for food and labor (and when furbearers were becoming increasingly scarce), colonial expenses rose 91 percent, from 337,000 to 645,000 rubles, while colonial revenues rose only 13 percent, from 1,189,000 to 1,341,000 rubles.

The dependency made Russia's imperial position in the North Pacific tenuous, and it suggests that in the New World, at least, Russia's imperial system, traditionally continental in disposition, was simply no match for those of the maritime European colonial powers. The only reason Alaska remained in Russian hands as long as it did was the absence of any serious foreign competition for the land; there was such competition for the maritime resources, but the mainland was not a necessary adjunct to the acquisition of those resources. So the Russians were able to persevere, just as they had in Siberia in the face of minimal aboriginal resistance and virtually no foreign rivalry; being largely unopposed, Russia had been able to move eastward successfully with limited manpower. No other great power really coveted the forbidding spaces of Siberia and Alaska. If they had, Russia probably would not have been able to acquire, let alone hold, the two territories, for her eastward drive was too undermanned and too overextended, especially in Russian America, where Native support was consequently crucial.

NOTES

1. For example, Robin Fisher, "Indian Control of the Maritime Fur Trade and the Northwest Coast," in *Approaches to Native History,* ed. D. A. Muise (Ottawa, 1977), 65–86; and Arthur J. Ray, "Fur Trade History as an Aspect of Native History," in *One Century Later,* ed. Ian A. L. Getty and Donald B. Smith (Vancouver, 1978), 7–18.

2. In 1834, for example, sea otter pelts and fur seal skins, respectively, fetched an average of 561 rubles and 32.5 rubles each at Kiakhta on the Russian-Chinese frontier (in terms of tea) and 600 rubles and 23 rubles each in St. Petersburg and Moscow; United States National Archives, file Microcopies of Records in the National Archives, no. 11, "Records of the Russian-American Company, 1802–1867: Correspondence of the Governors General" (hereafter USNA), roll 9, pp. 110v, 135v.

3. Otto von Kotzebue, *A New Voyage Round the World in the Years 1823, 24, 25, and 26* (London, 1830), 2:47.

4. G. H. von Langsdorff, *Voyages and Travels in Various Parts of the World. . . .* (London, 1813–14), 2:41.

5. Veniaminov voyaged in kayaks with Aleuts for fourteen to twenty hours at a time with no more than one stop for no longer than fifteen minutes—and that break was taken at sea, not on shore.

6. It took an Aleut a year or more to build a kayak, largely from driftwood and hide, so it was very expensive. Martin Sauer, *Expedition to the Northern Parts of Russia* (Richmond, England, 1972), 159.

7. Capt. Lisianskii had warned that "the Aleutians . . . from their skill, are sure to commit dreadful depredations wherever they go," and he was right; Iurii Lisianskii, *A Voyage Round the World* (London, 1814), 242.

8. Sauer, *Expedition,* 179; USNA, roll 33, p. 169v.

9. James R. Gibson, trans., "Russian America in 1821," *Oregon Historical Quarterly,* 77 (1976): 187.

10. Richard A. Pierce, ed., *The Russian Orthodox Religious Mission in America, 1794–1837,* trans. Colin Bearne (Kingston, 1978), 55. As an example of native mortality, 165 Aleuts were killed by Tlingits in 1802, and 300 Aleuts were drowned in 1805. By 1815, there were 150 Aleuts at Sitka, and in 1821 one-third of the town's residents were Aleuts. Capt. Pavel Golovin, who inspected Russian America in 1860–61, alleged that the Aleut population may have been halved by Russian contact between the middle and the end of the eighteenth century.

11. Sauer, *Expedition,* 171; G .I. Davydov, *Two Voyages to Russian America, 1802–1807,* trans. Colin Bearne (Kingston, 1977), 194–95.

12. Davydov, *Two Voyages,* 196. Every April during the 1820s, 400 to 600 Kenais gathered at Fort St. Nikolai to trade.

13. James R. Gibson, *Imperial Russia in Frontier America: The Changing Geography of Supply of Russian America, 1784–1867* (New York, 1976). Only in Russian California (Fort Ross) did grain growing and stock raising meet with some success. Even that, however, was wrought largely by Pomo Indian laborers; they, with some Aleuts, did most of the farm work. In 1838 at Kostromitinov Rancho, for example, four Russians supervised 250 Pomo laborers.

14. Richard A. Pierce and John H. Winslow, eds., HMS *Sulphur on the Northwest and California Coasts, 1837 and 1839* (Kingston, 1979), 105–6. Potatoes also did fairly well in the Kodiak District, where yields averaged eightfold in the 1860s. According to Father Veniaminov, in 1840 the Tlingits numbered 5,000 to 5,850, the Aleuts 2,380, the Kodiaks 1,508 to 1,719, and the Kenais 1,606 to 1,628.

15. According to the political radical and naval officer Dmitrii Zavalishin, at first up to six sea otter pelts fetched one ordinary musket, which the Indians "quickly learned to use well." In 1815 a Russian observer contended that if the Russian-American Company had competed with the Americans by offering the Tlingits "realistic" prices "without deception," it would have been able to get another 8,000 to 10,000 sea otter skins yearly. The Americans paid (in goods) from two to three times as much as the Russians for Tlingit furs, as did the British in the early 1830s. In 1837 Midshipman Francis Simpkinson of the HMS *Sulphur* noted that, although the Russian-American Company theoretically monopolized the fur trade of Russian America, "they (the Tlingits) are glad however at any time to get an opportunity of smuggling them (furs) for barter as they in general make a great deal more by the foreign vessels than by the Russians who only give them a certain price for their furs." On arms, see Richard A. Pierce and Alton S. Donnelly, eds., *A History of the Russian-American Company,* trans. Dmitri Krenov (Kingston, 1979), 2:156. In addition to guns and ammunition, incidentally, American skippers dealt in blankets, tobacco, rum, rice, and molasses, which the Tlingits then traded to interior Indians at a profit of 200 to 300 percent.

16. The Tlingit attacked and captured the Russian post at Sitka three years after its founding; the Russians recaptured it in 1804. When they did so they destroyed at least one hundred totems, each topped with a box of human ashes.

17. Occasionally, too, several Tlingit groups gathered at Sitka for talks, as in mid-March of 1831, when up to 2,000 congregated at the colonial capital.

18. Lisianskii, *Voyage,* 237–38; von Langsdorff, *Voyages and Travels,* 2:111, 131.

19. Sir George Simpson, *Narrative of a Journey Round the World, During the Years 1841 and 1842* (London, 1847), 2:2; Henry N. Michael, ed., *Lieutenant Zagoskin's Travels in Russian America, 1842–1844* (Toronto, 1967), 73; Alexander Rowand, *Notes of a Journey in Russian America and Siberia, During the Years 1841 and 1842* (Edinburgh, n.d.), 7.

20. No sooner had American fur trading vessels disappeared from Russian-American waters than they were replaced by American whaling ships. Already in 1842 up to 200 Yankee whalers were plying the far North Pacific.

21. At the end of 1841 a company agronomist, Egor Chernykh, reported from Sitka that the Tlingits had "recently" begun to cultivate potatoes and now grew them in "large numbers"; he added that in the fall of 1841 the company steamer *Nikolai I* bought up to 100 barrels of potatoes from the Tlingits while trading in the straits. Right up to the sale of Russian America in 1867 the company was still sending a ship into the straits once or twice every fall to buy potatoes (and black-tailed deer and, from 1862, turnips as well) at 5 rubles per barrel. In October of 1861, for instance, the steamer purchased 260 barrels. The fair which the Russian established commonly lasted two days in the middle of April. In 1851 up to 2,000 Tlingits, plus slaves (paddlers), attended.

22. George Simpson of the Hudson's Bay Company found in 1841 that the British Fort Taku (Durham) just south of Sitka was maintained chiefly on venison; Simpson, *Voyage,* 1:214.

23. In 1806 Count Nikolai Rezanov, who was making a tour of inspection of the colony, recommended to the minister of commerce that anyone who wanted to go to Russian America be allowed to do so and that 150 to 200 exiles be sent there; P. Tikhmenev, *A History of the Russian-American Company,* trans. Richard A. Pierce and Alton S. Donnelly (Seattle, 1978), 95. In 1808, however, the State Council announced it had rejected the minister's suggestion that "free persons" be permitted to settle in Russian America for fear that the state would lose taxpayers and conscripts.

Ivan Pan'kov

Architect of Aleut Literacy

LYDIA T. BLACK

Professor Lydia Black of the Anthropology Department at the University of Alaska Fairbanks has devoted her academic career over the last two decades to questions relating to contact between Russians and the Aleut and Eskimo people of Alaska and to the Russian Orthodox mission in Russian America. A prolific writer and thorough researcher, she has opened this particularly rich aspect of Alaska history to students and other scholars and has dispelled many false and damaging myths.

Working with Professor Richard A. Pierce, the eminent bibliographer of Russian America, she has published numerous articles on Aleut and Eskimo history and prehistory and on art and artifacts. Her work on the Orthodox missionary Hiermonk Gideon was published by The Limestone Press in 1987. She edited the Yukon journals of the Aleut Orthodox priest Iakov Netsvetov, published by Limestone in 1984, and helped prepare the Limestone edition of Ioann Veniaminov's Notes on the Islands of Unalaska District, *also in 1984.*

In the article reprinted here, Professor Black discusses Veniaminov's work among the Fox Island Aleut, the people of Unalaska and vicinity, in the 1820s. Father Veniaminov is usually credited with developing a Fox Aleut alphabet in which Orthodox liturgical works could be written, a monumental achievement equal to the development of a Cherokee alphabet by the warrior-scholar Sequoyah in 1821. Creation of an alphabet in one's mother tongue would seem to have profound implications for the preservation of cultural integrity. Black finds that an Aleut headman, Ivan Pan'kov, played a central role in helping Veniaminov in his work of bringing literacy to the islands, a role which Veniaminov did not want forgotten.

Veniaminov has long been recognized as an exceptional man, noted particularly for his advocacy of Alaska Natives. He was appointed the first Bishop of Alaska in 1841, and after returning to Russia rose eventually to the highest position in the

This article appeared originally in *Arctic Anthropology* 14 (1977): 94–107; it is reprinted here by permission.

Russian Orthodox church; he was canonized in 1977 as St. Innocent, the name he had taken as bishop. While Lydia Black, along with other writers, has emphasized the beneficence of the Orthodox mission in Alaska, others, including James Gibson, have emphasized the toll of Russian exploitation on the Natives of Alaska, while at the same time documenting Native accommodations and adaptations.

This paper is about an Aleut chief who lived over 150 years ago, at a time when his people faced one of the most difficult periods in their history: adjustment to a new social, economic, and ideological order imposed by invading Russians. Soon after Russian entry into the Aleut area, the Aleuts became converted to Orthodox Christianity. The Orthodox Church became a vehicle for maintenance of group identity and group solidarity, replacing the aboriginal religion. Less well known is the fact that literacy was a concomitant introduction: Aleuts became literate in their own language. I shall attempt to demonstrate that at least in the Fox Islands this change was facilitated by the activity of Ivan Pan'kov, the Aleut chief of Tigal'da Island, and that he was an active participant in the events that made the Orthodox Church in a very deep sense the Aleut Church and Aleut literacy a heritage of the Aleut people.

The Aleuts, a Native American group inhabiting the Aleutian Islands since prehistoric times, are known in ethnological and anthropological literature primarily as representatives of an ancient population of the Bering land bridge. Very little has been written about the modern Aleuts, and nothing about their recent history. Yet, as of February 1976, there were 3,060 registered shareholders in The Aleut Corporation[1] and during the 1972 U.S. Census, 6,352 Alaska citizens identified themselves as Aleut.[2]

Reams of paper have been devoted to bemoaning the demise of the Aleuts, postulated to have occurred with the Russian invasion of the 18th century:

> Aleuts now might raise potatoes (as many of them did) and cattle (occasionally), but there evidently was not much pride in the new life. . . . The burning of tobacco was no substitute for the inner fire that had gone out of them.[3]
>
> Today there are fewer than 800 Aleuts left! Furthermore, the decline is continuing despite U.S. Government reports to the contrary. This demise of a race and its culture is a sorry testimonial to our own inability to cope with complex factors that are responsible for such a tragedy. . . .

> Today only a few older Aleuts remember any details concerning the former customs and beliefs of their people. Young Aleuts seldom even express an interest in the past. In another thirty or fifty years, it will be too late to look for Aleut informants, or to help them.[4]

It is true that in the course of the last two centuries Aleut culture has changed. Aleuts are predominantly members of the Orthodox branch of the Christian Church, are participants in the modern economic and political order, and have been *literate in their own language for over 150 years.* The Aleuts are concerned with their heritage; they take great pride in their literary legacy.[5] As far as the alleged lack of interest in history is concerned, the problem may lie not among the "young Aleuts" but among the investigators who look for the wrong kind of history—a history that is no longer pertinent to the Aleuts.[6] Aleuts want to know about themselves as people—about their ancestors and about their political and spiritual leaders. They want to know about persons and the events in which these persons acted. Most Aleut tradition which relates the events of the recent past remains to be published. I have recently begun to focus on information about the conversion of the Aleuts to Christianity and the creation of Aleut literacy, although this was originally tangential to my research interests.[7] Gradually, I formed a mental picture of several Aleut leaders who were active at various times in the last two centuries. One man stands out, and it is clear that his role in the conversion process and in the creation of Aleut literacy was very important. He was a close associate of the great missionary priest Ioann Veniaminov (Innokentii),[8] and because of this association, his life can be reconstructed from the records in considerable detail.

The name of this Aleut leader was Ivan Pan'kov. Specialists know him as Veniaminov's collaborator in the translation of various Church publications into the Aleut language. I assert that he was much more than that: that it was through his efforts that literacy "took hold" and spread fast and that the new faith grew to be identified as the "Aleut faith" or "Aleut Church" by Aleuts and non-Aleuts alike.[9] I believe that the rapid change in the realm of ideology and spiritual culture, which occurred in less than half a century, was the direct result of support by influential Aleut leaders of the time.[10]

Veniaminov came to the Aleutians from Irkutsk. He accepted the Bishop's call for missionary duty after a meeting with Ivan Kriukov—a Russian settler in the Fox Islands. Ivan Kriukov, an "Old Voyager"—that is, someone who participated in the early Russian exploration and exploitation of the Aleutians prior to the establishment of the Russian-American Company in 1799—spent over 40 years in the islands, and was married to an Aleutian woman, presumably of Umnak Island. He was probably the founder of the first chapel in the Fox Islands (St. Nicholas at the Village of Nikol'ski) in 1806. His son, Stefan Kriukov, built the new chapel in 1826–28 and was the manager of the Russian-American Company at Umnak. He was also in charge of sealing operations in the Pribilofs. Both father and son presumably were the leaders in the local "Church."[11] Later, in his old age, the son, is styled in various records as the Chief of Nikol'ski. To this day, direct descendants hold both the offices of lay readers and chiefs. Ivan Kriukov passionately pleaded with Veniaminov to come to the Aleutians. Veniaminov responded.[12] He came, accompanied by his wife, Katherine, three small children (the youngest was born en route at Sitka; four more were born to the Veniaminovs at Unalaska), his brother, Stefan, aged 18, who was later to marry an Unalaska girl, and his aged mother, Fekla. At the time of his arrival, Veniaminov was 27 years old. Though he began the study of the Aleut language while on the way to the Aleutians (at Sitka), he did not speak it. However, he planned to establish a school for the Aleuts to be conducted both in Aleut and Russian. This he accomplished, and the school continued to exist in accordance with the lines he laid down until the middle 1920s.

At the time of Veniaminov's arrival in the Aleutians, Ivan Pan'kov was 46 years old, so that a birth date of 1778 may be postulated.[13] He was married[14] and had children, among them at least one adult son, Semen,[15] and possibly others.[16]

Ivan Pan'kov was at that time the chief *(toion)*[17] of the Island of Tigal'da, one of the most populous Fox Islands at the time, which together with the island of Akun accounted for a large proportion of Aleut population in the District.[18] He apparently was influential as far as the Alaska Peninsula and the Shumagin Islands. Only a generation earlier, in the 1760s, the Krenitzyn Islands, notably Akutan, Akun, and Tigal'da, provided the leadership and organizational talent for Aleut "war" against the Russian intruders.[19] Aleut tradition records that the Akun and Tigal'da chiefs, famed throughout the archipelago, ruled with an iron hand.[20]

There is no question that Pan'kov was an important leader of the Aleut community. Moreover, he also acted as the representative of the Russian-American Company in the area where there were no Russian settlers.[21] He was well known to the General Management of the Russian-American

Company in St. Petersburg.[22] His rank in the community, however, may be judged on the basis of more direct evidence. On August 1, 1824,[23] immediately upon arrival, Veniaminov was presented, by his parishioners-to-be, with a written address and a sum of money, designed to ease his adjustment in the unfamiliar situation and to help him establish his household.[24] Two hundred three persons donated.[25] The list is headed by Rodion Petrovsky, the General Manager of the Russian-American Company of the District, who gave the largest donation of 30.00 rubles, and Semen Petelin, company clerk, who gave the second largest donation of 15.00 rubles.[26] Stefan Kriukov (see previous discussion regarding his status in the Aleut community of the time) also gave 15.00 rubles. Five Aleut *toions* are listed as contributors. The minimum contribution was 1.00 ruble; the average was 4.36 rubles; very few contributions, by Russians or Aleuts, exceeded 5.00 rubles. Of the five Aleut *toions* who contributed, only one, Vassilii Davydov of Umnak, contributed 10.00 rubles. Other *toions* donated in the range from 2.00 to 3.00 rubles. Ivan Pan'kov gave 11.00 rubles and his son Semen 10.00 rubles, well in excess of other *toions* and Russian settlers. Four other Pan'kovs contributed 11.00 rubles total and a Cherepanov, for whom a link to the Pan'kovs may be postulated (see below), gave a donation of 7.00 rubles—well above the average.

Ivan Pan'kov was bilingual and literate. He knew and understood Orthodox theology. There is evidence that he preached Orthodox tenets to the Aleuts on his own.[27] The entry in Veniaminov's journal for April 24, 1828, reads: "Though there is no need to reiterate the story of the reception of myself and of my teachings by the Aleuts, as it would only constitute useless repetition, I cannot omit to mention the inhabitants of the islands [Krenitzyn] I just visited. They are very diligent and attentive to the word of God and appreciative of instruction. I must witness, though, to the work of Ivan Pan'kov. He instructs the most respected men in Christian Law on many feast days. This they told me themselves."

Toward the end of his life, Pan'kov was instrumental in the establishment of two chapels, one built in 1842 on the island of Akun and consecrated to the Assumption of the Holy Mother of God in 1843, and one on Tigal'da, built and consecrated in 1844 in the name of St. Ioann (John) Lestvinnik.[28] According to the Annual Reports on the Status of the Church,[29] these chapels were "created by the care, effort and diligence" of Toion Ivan Pan'kov. The same documents note that these chapels were constructed by Aleut workmen, that the services were conducted by laymen, and that the iconostasies (the altar screens) were of "fine Aleut workmanship." There is some indication that these chapels might have been located at or near places sacred to the Aleuts in pre-contact times.

Ivan Pan'kov died presumably near the end of the decade or possibly in the beginning of the next, certainly prior to 1855.[30] Until the 1880s his descendants seemed to be important in Aleut affairs.[31] Today, to my knowledge, the name Pan'kov does not appear on the rolls of the shareholders in The Aleut Corporation, though several descendants linked to the Pan'kov family through women still are resident in the islands.[32]

It is not known when Veniaminov and Ivan Pan'kov met for the first time or under what circumstances the meeting occurred. Nothing indicates the impression the meeting must have left on both men. It is apparent, however, that their association began not too long after Veniaminov's arrival in the islands, continued until his departure ten years later, and probably was not forgotten when Veniaminov became Bishop of the Aleutians. The character of this association may be deduced on the basis of frequent references in the documents; it is clear that in Veniaminov's communication with the Aleuts, be it propagation of the Word of God, discussions with the "knowledgeable men," visits to remote areas of his parish, or simply a "celebration," Pan'kov was Veniaminov's constant companion, mentor, guide, interpreter, and sponsor. Often they traveled together. There are mentions of trips in *baidarka* (the kayak) or on foot, of treks across mountains, overnights on deserted islands; sometimes danger and privation, and sometimes pleasure. One can only surmise the conversations carried on and the relationship that must have grown between the older Aleut and much younger Russian.[33]

It is pertinent, at this point, to reiterate the fact that Pan'kov was literate and knowledgeable in the tenets of the Orthodox faith. The question then arises: when and how did he gain this knowledge? The official record is silent, but inferences are possible. Of the several possible explanations, I think the most likely relates to Pan'kov's father, Gavriil Pan'kov, who, judging by his name of record, was already baptized a Christian. We must look at the events that took place in the lifetime of the previous generation, in the early Russian-Aleut contact situation, and at the identity and character of the individual Russian *promyshlenniki*.[34] Some of them—Glotov, Druzhinin, Soloviev—are well known to historians and to the Aleuts; they are associated with the brutal breaking of the Aleut resistance to the Russian invasion. Such men are detested by the Aleuts. The role of some (e.g., Glotov, Korovin) is ambivalent. The names of others either have passed out of history or are known only to specialists, but many survive as the surnames of modern Aleuts. Careful attention to historical detail, Aleut traditions, and localization of surnames in the islands permits us to postulate certain activities of the individual *promyshlenniki* in the islands. There is no doubt that some of the *promyshlenniki* established and maintained cordial relations with the Aleuts; still others settled among them. (It is even possible that in the conflicts that raged in the 1760s some of the *promyshlenniki* might have aided the Aleuts.)[35]

I suggest that two of the *promyshlenniki*, Merchant Stefan Cherepanov and Navigator Dimitrii Pan'kov, might have belonged to the latter class; that the two were familiar with, and at various times called to, the Krenitzyn Islands; and that both men formed personal links with some Aleuts in that area. It is notable that the names Pan'kov and Cherepanov have been localized in the Krenitzyn Islands. Members of the Cherepanov family still reside on the island of Akutan and are very influential members of that community.

There is a record of two voyages by Stefan Cherepanov (1759 to 1762 and 1768 to 1773) and of three by Dimitrii Pan'kov (1758 to 1763; 1770 to 1774; 1780 to 1786). However, this record does not indicate the total time spent by the men in the islands. Many a man who outfitted a ship or became skipper, so that his name appears in the historical record, first sailed as a member of the crew. If financial success may be taken as an indication of diplomatic skill, Cherepanov and Pan'kov were, indeed, first-rate diplomats: in the years when their fellow hunters were attacked by the Aleuts, their ships burned, and the crews killed throughout all the Fox Islands, from Unimak to the Four Mountains, Cherepanov and Pan'kov, operating in the same area, brought home the richest cargoes, and there are no published reports of encountered violence.[36] Cherepanov's report (giving his location as Andreanof Islands) indicates that his relations with the Aleuts were good, that he was sympathetic to Aleut religious expressions, and that through spontaneous sharing of food at meals with Aleuts who happened to come by at such times, he and his crew came to be considered "kinsmen by affinity."[37] Similar conduct could be postulated for Cherepanov when he hunted in other areas. Pan'kov, of course, reached Unimak on his first voyage, and is credited with the discovery of that island by Russian historians.[38] He operated in the Fox Islands and in the Krenitzyns in the years 1761 to 1763—the years when Druzhinin, Medvedev, Korovin, and others suffered gravely. It is known that at least once D. Pan'kov and S. Cherepanov became partners: they joined forces on Pan'kov's second voyage (1770 to 1774).

It is well known, too, that some *promyshlenniki* acted as missionaries, and many administered baptism (in Orthodox religion laymen may baptize). As a rule, the newly baptized Aleut was given a Christian name (quite often the name of the saint whose feast fell on that day) and the surname of the Russian who stood as his sponsor—as godfather. Further, apparently on the basis of such ritual link, economic partnerships were created. It is well within the realm of probability that Navigator Dimitrii Pan'kov formed such a relationship with either Ivan Pan'kov's father, Gavriil, or one of his senior kinsmen. If Pan'kov, like his friend and partner Cherepanov, was a religious man, he would have taken his role as godfather very seriously indeed. In Russian ideology, godparents are responsible for spiritual and educational needs of their godchildren. This obligation would extend to the children of an Aleut with whom such a ritual connection was formed. It is possible to postulate that Pan'kov urged education of Gavriil's son and that he (or another skipper whom Gavriil trusted) was charged with the supervision of Ivan's schooling. Ivan, who at the time of the conclusion of Pan'kov's last voyage of record in 1786 would have been about eight years old, probably was taken to Russia.[39]

I see, then, a very small Aleut boy, possibly a hostage, perhaps a godson, taken on a Russian ship to one of the ports on the Pacific and possibly traveling to a Russian town. I see him sent to school, surely at his sponsor's expense, perhaps living in his sponsor's household, a literate and religious household.[40] I see a young man returning to the islands to assume his position in the Aleut social order as chief or chief-to-be, trying to make sense out of his experience in two different and conflicting worlds. And I see a mature man seizing the opportunity, provided by his meeting with Veniaminov, to reconcile these worlds. Did Pan'kov discern the parallels in the Aleut and Russian world view?[41] Did he discuss them with Veniaminov? This we shall never know, but we do know that Pan'kov engineered a meeting between Veniaminov and an Aleut shaman and that at the end of that meeting, with Pan'kov translating the dialogue, the priest proclaimed the shaman a Man of God. I shall let the words of Veniaminov speak for themselves.[42]

> By nature and upbringing I am very far from believing various superstitions and still less inclined to invent false miracles. Yet, I have no wish to hide from your Grace anything, including my weaknesses, and therefore I want to [apprise] Your Grace of the following occurrence, which is not impossible, as the ways of the Lord are unfathomable and the

strength of His mercy does not diminish, but nevertheless an event most rare and unheard of in these our times.

During my stay in April of 1828 on the island of Akun and the other three islands belonging to the former, I learned through the interpreter Ivan Pan'kov that the resident of the village Recheshnoye on the island of Akun, on its SE side, about 10 *versts* [a *verst* is equal to 1.0668 km. or 0.6629 miles. 500 sazhen' make up one *verst*. (*Sovetskaia Entsiklopediia*, 3rd ed.) L.B.] from the main settlement on the island, Ivan Smirennikov, an old man of about 60 years of age, is regarded by the local inhabitants and by many others as well, as a shaman, not an ordinary person, at least.

1) The wife of the Toion of the village Artelnovskoye, one Fedor Zhirov, on October of 1825 was caught in a fox trap, and her leg was badly hurt. There were no means to help her, and she was expected to die momentarily. The trap hit her at the kneecap by all three iron teeth, about two *vershok* [a *vershok* is equal to 44.45 mm. or approximately 1.75 inches (*loc. cit.*) L.B.] in length. Her kinsmen secretly asked the said old man Smirennikov to cure her. After thinking the matter over, he said that the patient will be well by morning. And, indeed, the woman rose in the morning from her deathbed, and is even now entirely well, not suffering any pain;

2) In the winter of the same year, 1825, the inhabitants of Akun suffered great lack of food, and some of them asked Smirennikov to pray for a whale to be washed ashore. After a short time the old man instructed the people to go to a certain place, where they indeed found a fresh whale carcass—precisely in the spot designated;

3) Last fall I planned to visit Akun, but because of the arrival of state ships from Russia, I had to postpone the trip. Yet, the Akun people sent an escort and all expected my arrival. Only Smirennikov boldly asserted that I would not come that fall, but should be expected next spring. And so it happened, contrary winds did not permit my departure, then the cold weather set in, and I was forced to delay my visit until spring.

There are many additional instances which prove his gift of clairvoyance, but I shall omit them here.

Such tales, confirmed by trustworthy informants, convinced me that I should meet Smirennikov in person and personally inquire how is it that he knows the future and what means does he employ to learn it? He thanked me for my interest and told me the following:

Soon after being baptized by Hieromonk Makarii[43] there appeared to him first one, later two spirits, not to be seen by any other man. The spirits had the appearance of humans, light of face, dressed in white robes and, according to his description, these robes resembled church vestments and were trimmed with rose bands. 1) They told him they were sent to him by God to instruct, teach, and preserve him, and they continued to appear to him for thirty years almost daily. The spirits instructed him in Christian teaching. 2) They granted his requests, and through him requests of others (though pretty seldom); they repeated to him my own teachings and told him not to confess his sins to anyone, listen to my teachings and not to listen to *promyshlenniki*, that is the Russians. Even this very day, as he was *en route*, they appeared and told him that I am calling him and for what reason, and instructed him to tell me all, not to be afraid, that no evil shall befall him.

I asked him, what did he feel when the spirits appeared—sorrow or joy? He said that only if he was conscious of having done something bad did he feel a twinge of conscience, but otherwise he did not experience any fear. Moreover, as the people regard him as shaman, and he does not want to be a shaman, he asked the spirits to leave him alone; the spirits replied that they are not demons and cannot leave him. To his question, why they do not appear to others, the spirits replied that they were so ordered.

It is possible to suppose that this man has heard from me or from somebody else the teaching of our faith he recounted and only for effect or out of vanity invented the appearance of the spirits. Yet, I must state that Aleuts do not fall prey to pride, vanity and empty bragging. Moreover 1) I, when preaching, for the sake of brevity and in order to avoid complications, omitted the story of creation, the fall of angels, of the tree of knowledge of good and evil, of the first murderer, of Noah, Abraham and John the Baptist and usually also the story of the Annunciation of the Birth of Christ. But he, Smirennikov, told me these stories in detail. When I preached, he was the first to confirm the truth of my words in the tone of a person conversant with the Holy Writ; 2) Aleuts who live here, all except the interpreter Pan'kov and very few others, even though they had Faith and prayed prior to my arrival, had little knowledge to whom they pray. Hieromonk Makarii, my predecessor here in 1794 and 1795 did not instruct the people here for lack of any kind of interpreter. It is only very recently that interpreters are on hand and among them Pan'kov is the best and most intelligent. But he, Pan'kov, afraid to fall into error, and having firm faith in the One

God, never entered into any conversations with the old man and he also protested and tried to restrain others when they called on the help of Smirennikov. This fact was attested by many Aleuts, and therefore there was no one from whom Smirennikov could have learned in the matters of Church teaching; 3) He himself is illiterate and does not know any Russian; therefore, he could not have read about it and finally, 4) I asked him if I could meet with his protectors—the spirits. He replied that he does not know, but that he will ask. Shortly thereafter, in about an hour, he came and told me their answer: What does he want? Does he consider us demons? If he insists, he can see and converse with us. And then they said something very flattering to me, which I omit here. But I refused the meeting with the spirits. One could ask why did I do so? My answer is that there was no need for me to meet them. Why should I want to see them personally when their teaching is Christian teaching? Out of curiosity, to learn who they are? For this I should ask the blessing of my Archbishop, to avoid the pitfall of error, should I meet those spirits.

All of the above is attested to by Smirennikov under oath, and transmitted by me not word for word but true to the meaning, without additions or omissions. Moreover, the freedom, fearlessness and even pleasure of his discourse, and above all his clean manner of life, convinced me and confirmed me in the conviction that the spirits which appear to this old man (if they appear) are not demons. Demons may sometimes assume the image of Angels of Light, but never for the purpose of instruction, teaching and salvation of human beings, but always for their perdition. As the tree of evil cannot bear the fruit of good, these spirits must be the servants sent to those who seek salvation. Therefore, in order not to weaken (among the people) the faith and hope in the One Omniscient God, I, until I receive instruction from Your Grace, determined to render the following decision: "I see that the spirits which appear to thee are not demons and therefore I instruct thee to listen to their teachings and instructions, as long as these do not contradict the teachings I deliver in the assembly; just tell those who ask your advice about the future and request your help, to address themselves directly to God, as He is common Father to all. I do not forbid thee to cure the sick, but ask thee to tell those thou curest that thou doest so not by thy own powers, but by the power of God and to instruct them to pray diligently and thank the Sole God. I do not forbid thee to teach either, but only instruct thee to confine this teaching to

> the minors." I told the other Aleuts who were present not to call him a Shaman, not to ask him for favors, but to ask God.
>
> In reporting to you, Your Grace, I deemed it necessary to ask Ivan Pan'kov who translated my words and those of the Old Man Smirennikov, to sign this statement, in witness of the truth of my story and the correctness of his translation. I also requested him to keep this matter secret for the time being. I beg your Grace to let me know if my decision was right and if there is any need for me to meet with the spirits which appear to the old man, and if so, what precautions I should take. If I erred, forgive me.
>
> Signed: Your Grace's Priest Ioann Veniaminov, of the Church of Ascension in Unalashka, June 1828;
>
> Signed: below by interpreter Pan'kov as follows:
>
> To the truth of the words of Priest Ioann Veniaminov and the accuracy of translation of the words of the old man Ivan Smirennikov attests Tigal'da Toion Ivan Pan'kov.
>
> True copy of the original, Tobol'sk, 5 November, 1829.

Strange, indeed, this acceptance of the Aleut shaman on the part of the priest, but not so strange if one considers the implications of his relationship with Ivan Pan'kov: the age differential mentioned previously, the obvious ability to converse on an equal level, the role of Pan'kov as his companion and sponsor in the strange, new Aleut world. When one reads the terse scattered remarks in Veniaminov's official papers one cannot escape the impression that there was trust, friendship, respect. A glimpse is afforded by Veniaminov's letter to Archbishop Michael requesting a reward in recognition of Ivan Pankov's aid. Noteworthy is the suggestion that the most suitable gift for Pan'kov, in his opinion, would be a book:

> I should like to draw your Grace's attention to the diligence of the Toion Ivan Pan'kov in the matters of the propagation of the faith. As you know, he helped me consistently with the catechism. He responded with pleasure to my invitation, and continued to work with me, sometimes at cost and inconvenience to himself. Prior to my visits to the Aleuts under his jurisdiction, he—often, as I was told—on every conceivable occasion taught the Faith to the leading men. Such constant effort deserves recognition, and therefore I ask Your Grace to send at the most pleasing and suitable gift, a book possibly inscribed in your own hand.[44]

By 1828, when Veniaminov went on his first extended visit to the Krenitzyn Islands, the two men were close friends indeed. An escort was sent for Veniaminov from Akun; they traveled in five *baidarkas*—one three-hatch *baidarka* and four two-hatch ones. Throughout the trip Ivan Pan'kov was at his side. It is through Pan'kov that Veniaminov addressed the leading men on Akun,[45] then on Tigal'da (where, as Veniaminov notes, were also assembled the residents of the Island of Ugamak), and on Avatanok, then returning to Akun to celebrate the feast of St. Alexander Nevsky.[46] On April 23, 1828, Veniaminov did not go to the bedside of a dying woman because Pan'kov was not able to come along, having developed trouble in one of his legs. Instead, the ailing person was brought to their camp.[47] It is on this day that Pan'kov arranged the meeting between Veniaminov and the shaman Smirennikov "locally known as a sorcerer,"[48] cited above, and on Akun he was introduced to the old woman who told him the story of Aleut defeat and destruction by Soloviev. Pan'kov must have been very sure of his man to have risked these meetings. Indeed, by that time the two men had shared two years of collaboration on the first book in Aleut—the Catechism—and on the design of an Aleut alphabet. By March 1826 the following entry is made in Veniaminov's journal:

> In the beginning of this month arrived the Tigal'da Toion Ivan Pan'kov at my invitation and respectful plea.[49] Together *we* checked my translation of the catechism up to the Creed and began work on further chapters.[50]

And further: "By Easter *we* finished the work on the catechism, and during Easter checked it over."[51] That Pan'kov helped Veniaminov with Aleut phonology is clear from Veniaminov's note that in the course of the work on the catechism he corrected the diacritical marks over letters designed to represent sounds of the Aleut language. Thus, Pan'kov participated in the design of the alphabet itself.

By May of 1826 Veniaminov made a clean copy of the catechism and sent it to Archbishop Michael of Irkutsk for submission to the Synod and permission to print. The copy of the catechism was accompanied by a petition signed by several Aleut leading men who understood Russian. The list was headed by the name of Ivan Pan'kov and in the covering letter Veniaminov wrote:

> Not trusting to my own knowledge I called upon the aid of Toion Ivan

> Gavriil Pan'kov, the best interpreter in the entire Chain. He is a Native born Aleut, but knows Russian language well, speaking it without any accent and he is literate. He is forty nine years of age, lives in a settlement where reside only Aleuts, so that there can be no doubt about his perfect knowledge of his own language. The catechism was translated with his help, but I, not deeming the work yet finished, did the following: I read from this work in Aleut assemblies throughout my voyage through the Eastern part of my parish [Krenitzyn Islands. L.B.]; I discussed the text with the wisest among the Aleuts and solicited their opinions on the merit of the work; they approved the text and expressed the wish to have it.[52]

The letter, the petition, and the manuscript were forwarded to St. Petersburg, where on 19 November 1829, the Synod rejected it. The reason for rejection was the fact that in the meantime a new, abridged catechism was approved in Russia as a text for religious instruction, that is, the Russian text used by Veniaminov as the basis for the first Aleut catechism was superseded. The Synod instructed Veniaminov to proceed immediately with translation of the new text and a copy was sent to him for this purpose. Once again, Veniaminov called on Ivan Pan'kov and by July 1830 the new translation of the catechism, still in use today, was well under way.[53] But this task receives bare mention in Veniaminov's journal of the time, because in the meantime the two men were busy on a matter they considered of much greater significance: they were engaged in the translation of the Gospels into Aleut. This time they worked on Akun, where Veniaminov traveled to join Pan'kov, traveling to that island at least two times, and continued to work into the fall of 1829. Into that period falls the time of most intensive effort, when the Gospel of St. Matthew was translated into the Aleut language. The work did not go on when Pan'kov was absent. Once Veniaminov missed him, and the work had to be postponed until Pan'kov's return. Interruptions, when one of the men was called to attend to his other duties, as for example, when Veniaminov had to visit the sick, were kept to a minimum: "In response to a call from a sick Aleut who lived at about fifteen *versts'* distance, Pan'kov and I went to him, first traveling in *baidarka*, then on foot, and having administered the rites, we returned immediately to our task."[54] They began this, what they considered their most important task, on September 10th: "Having called on the aid of God-the-Word . . . and this day translated the first two chapters."[55] It was literally, as Veniaminov tells us in his Journal, the product of "sleepless labor."

> We worked in the following manner: from early morning till nightfall we worked on the translation; evenings, in the assembly of the most intelligent of the Aleut, and in the presence of all those who wished to come, we read aloud what has been translated during that day.[56]

Veniaminov notes that news of their enterprise traveled through the villages and that many Aleuts were coming from outlying settlements to listen and to watch.[57] Toward the end of the task, they worked around the clock:

> We finished at nine o-clock in the morning with the Lord's help, through the prayers of the Holy Apostles and Evangelist Matthew, the translation of this Gospel, to the very end, except two verses: to wit, VII-17 and IX-17. The first we omitted because in the local language there are no names for any items mentioned therein, the second, because the essence of its meaning appears obscure to many. We supplemented instead with verses from other Gospels on the subject of suffering of Our Lord.[58]

On Sunday, October 6th, in Unalaska, a service of thanksgiving was held to mark the completion of the task.[59] A clean copy was made, distributed to several bilingual and literate persons, and then sent to St. Petersburg. After some delays, the first Gospel printed in Aleut was published in 1840. In the Church of the Holy Ascension of Christ in Unalaska is presented a first edition of this work. It is beautifully bound in a silver cover, decorated with miniature icons on enamel insets, and annotated in the hand of Veniaminov marking chapters to be read in the course of the annual ritual cycle. It is today an Aleut treasure. On its title page, as on the title page of the first 1826 catechism, next to the name of Ioann Veniaminov appears the name of "Toion Ivan Pan'kov," an Aleut Chief.

Veniaminov never intended Pan'kov's name to be forgotten. In his "Introduction" to the Gospels (see edition of 1898, page III), and in the "Introduction" to the *Catechism*, he gives Pan'kov full credit. Without his aid, Veniaminov's message hardly would have been made intelligible to the Aleut so effectively and so soon.

I believe it is no exaggeration to say that Ivan Pan'kov, Chief of Tigal'da, was instrumental in creating Aleut literacy and making Orthodoxy the "Aleut Church."[60]

NOTES

I am deeply grateful to His Grace, Gregory, Bishop of Sitka and Alaska, for permission to use the original manuscript of Veniaminov's papers and to Father Paul Merculief and his wife, Elizabeth, originally from the island of St. George, in whose hospitable home in Kodiak I worked on these manuscripts.

Thanks are also due to Phyllis Nottingham, Librarian, and the entire staff of the State Historical Library at Juneau, Alaska, and to the staff of the Manuscript Division, Library of Congress, Washington, D.C., for unfailing help in locating archival materials which enabled me to piece together the story presented in this article.

I am also indebted to the following persons with whom I have discussed some of the points mentioned in this paper: Dr. William S. Laughlin, Department of Biobehavioral Sciences, University of Connecticut; Rev. Innokentii (Gordon H. Marsh); Dr. Dorothy M. Jones, University of Alaska, Anchorage; Dr. Michael Krauss, Director, Native Languages Program, University of Alaska, Fairbanks; Mrs. Beverly Holmes, Department of Biobehavioral Sciences, University of Connecticut. All generously shared their knowledge, which I have put to use in marshalling my arguments. The interpretations presented here, however, are my own and no one shares any blame for any shortcomings or errors of fact or opinion.

1. *The Aleutian Current* (Aleut Corporation newsletter), February 1976, 4: 2.

2. The discrepancy between the enrollment in The Aleut Corporation (established under Alaska Native Claims Settlement Act of 1971) and the U.S. Census Bureau data must be understood in the light of the fact that many Alaskans other than the descendants of the aboriginal occupants of the Aleutian Archipelago *per se*, and some who are technically not eligible for enrollment under the Act, identify themselves as Aleuts to outsiders. This problem merits special attention by social anthropologists.

3. Margaret Lantis, ed., *Ethnohistory in Southwestern Alaska and the Southern Yukon, Method and Content* (Lexington: University of Kentucky Press, 1970), p. 291.

4. Ted Bank II and R. Williams, "Urgently Needed Research on Aleut Culture," *Bulletin of the International Committee on Urgent Anthropological and Ethnological Research*, No. 17 (Vienna, Austria), p. 7.

5. The only published work on the importance of Aleut literacy is that by J. E. Ransom. [See Jay Ellis Ransom, "Writing as a Medium of Acculturation among the Aleut," *Southwestern Journal of Anthropology* 1, no. 3 (1945): 333–344.] Gerald D. Berreman, "Inquiry into Community Integration in an Aleutian Village," *American Anthropologist* 57 (1955): 49–59, noted the importance of Aleut literacy and identified the Orthodox Church as the mechanism of social solidarity in modern times, but treats the subject only in passing. William S. Laughlin and G. H. Marsh, "A New View of the History of the Aleutians," *Arctic* 4, no. 2 (1951): 87, identified the importance of written Aleut for language maintenance and published a sample of printed Aleut. However, their discussion on this point is very brief.

6. Cf. Joan Chandler, "Anthropologists' Perceptions of U.S. Indians in the Southwest, 1928–1966," paper presented at the 73rd annual meeting of the American Anthropological Association, November 19–24, 1974, Mexico City, for the dis-

cussion of the effect on the structure of research design pertaining to the Native Americans of the prevailing ideology held by investigators as to what is and what is not "Indian." Chandler convincingly demonstrates for her area (American Southwest) that groups which early adapted to the Western impact received little or no attention in American anthropology of the late 19th and, until recently, 20th centuries. The Aleut case is most blatant; their very existence is frequently denied.

7. Several Aleuts asked me to provide precise data on the establishment of the Church of the Holy Ascension of Christ in Unalaska, founded by Veniaminov and considered the Mother Church of the Aleutians. Its 150th anniversary is being celebrated in 1975–76, and recently the Church has been declared a National Historic Landmark (Site).

8. Ioann Veniaminov (later Innokentii, Bishop, then Archbishop, of Kamchatka, the Kuriles, and the Aleutian Islands, and finally Metropolitan of Moscow and Kolomna, the head of the Russian Orthodox Church) is known worldwide as a scholar and churchman. His authoritative ethnography of the Aleutian peoples, *Zapiski ob ostrovakh Unalashkinskogo otdela* [*Notes from Unalaska District*] (1840, St. Petersburg) has never been superseded. His analysis and command of the Aleut language stands up today as the best extant (Dr. Michael Krauss, Director, Native Language Program, University of Alaska, personal communication). His *Indication of the Way to the Kingdom of Heaven*, originally composed in the Aleut language in 1833 and first published in Aleut in 1840, was translated later into Russian (and in 1952 into English) and is used as an instructional text in Orthodox communities throughout the world. Veniaminov's parish comprised the Fox Islands, the Krenitzyn Islands (the largest of this group being Akun, Akutan and Tigal'da), the Shumagin Islands, the Alaska Peninsula, and the Pribilof Islands in the Bering Sea. The Andreanof Islands, the Rat and Near Islands (Atkha, Amlia, Adak, Attu, etc.), together with the Kommandor Islands (within the jurisdiction of Russia) and the Northern Kuriles comprised the Atkha District of the Russian-American Company administration and constituted a separate parish. In 1828 Yakov Netzvetov, son of a Russian settler and an Atkha Aleut woman, became the first priest of the Atkha District. Netzvetov adapted the texts Veniaminov worked out as well as the alphabet to the Atkha dialect.

9. Such identification is apparent through perusal of the official reports, travel and memoir literature for the American period (post-1867), and persists to this day (field data 1975 obtained from various residents in Unalaska, and personal communication by Beverly Holmes, formerly a long time resident of the Aleutians).

10. A role analogous to that of Pan'kov seems to have been played in the Andreanof Islands by Amlia Chief Vassilii Dediukhin (Yakov Netzvetov journals, Alaska Church Collection, Manuscript Division, Library of Congress, Washington, D.C.).

11. Aleut tradition, Gordon H. Marsh, personal communication.

12. Ivan P. Barsukov, *Innokentii, Mitropolit Moskovskii i Kolomenskii, po ego sochineniiam, pis'mam i rasskazam sovremennikov* [*Innokentii, Metropolitan of Moscow and Kolomna, as Reflected in His Works, Letters and the Recollections of His Contemporaries*] (Moskva: Synod, 1883).

13. In various documents Pan'kov's age is given as 46 (in 1824); 48 (in 1828); and 49 (in 1827).

14. In the index to correspondence in Veniaminov's archive Pan'kov's "marriage case" is listed separately in the register for July 1825, relatively soon after Veniaminov's arrival. See Innokentii (Ioann Veniaminov), *Bumagi* [Papers] (including journals), MS. holdings, St. Herman Pastoral School, Kodiak, Alaska, Folio 263. [This collection is hereafter cited as *Bumagi*.] It is possible to postulate that Pan'kov was anxious to solemnize and "regularize" his marriage. While baptisms and burial services could be conducted by laymen, marriages could not be, and the rite had to await the presence of a regular consecrated priest. Marriages in those times were solemnized *post factum* and often *en masse*: Veniaminov records up to twenty per day.

15. Semen's age is given as 39 for 1833, making his year of birth 1794. He became Veniaminov's official interpreter in 1832 (toward the end of the latter's stay in the islands when he had no functional need for an interpreter). This birthdate would account for 16 years' age differential between Ivan Pan'kov and Semen. However, Aleut men married early (between the ages of 16 and 18, when they achieved the status of hunters; William S. Laughlin, personal communication), and a potential chief would have been expected to marry earlier than his peers. That a father/son relationship existed between Ivan and Semen Pan'kov is stated in correspondence between the Priest of Unalaska Sizov (or Sizoy) with Bishop Innokentii. Sizoy rejected the aid of the Pan'kovs in the work on Gospel translations. Soon thereafter, this priest was replaced (presumably on further orders of the Bishop Veniaminov) by Innokentii Shaiashnikoff, who was a Fox Island "creole." The gospels Sizoy translated were not published. (Manuscript in Alaska Church Collection.)

16. In 1824 at least six male adult Pan'kovs were present in the District. In addition to Ivan and Semen, Mitrofan, Luka, Prokopii, and Yakov Pan'kov are listed. Their relationship to each other is not known at this time (*Bumagi*, Folios 134–135).

17. *Toion*—a term of Siberian origin, possibly Yakut, applied by the Russians to designate native leadership positions (frequently anglicized as "toyon").

18. In 1824, of the total Aleut population of 1509 (*Bumagi*, Folio 171), the Krenitzyn Islands accounted for 451—a number equaling Unalaska's population and far exceeding that of Umnak. It should be kept in mind that Unalaska, by that time, as center of the Russian-American Company activities in the Fox Islands and Pribilofs, experienced some growth through immigration and resettlement from other areas in the Archipelago.

19. A. Sokolov, "Expedition to the Aleutian Islands by the Captains Krenitsyn and Levashev, 1764–1769," *Notes on the Hydrographic Department* (St. Petersburg) 10 (1852): 88; A. I. Andreyev, ed., *Russkiie otkrytiia v Tikhom okeane i Severnoi Amerike v XVIII v. Sbornik materialov* [*Russian Discoveries in the Pacific Ocean and North America in the 18th Century. Collection of Materials*] (Moscow-Leningrad: Akademiia Nauk, 1948).

20. William S. Laughlin, personal communication.

21. *Bumagi*, Folio 359.

22. *Bumagi*, Folio 276 and 359 verso.

23. All dates are in Julian calendar. To translate 19th century dates into Gregorian calendar, 13 days should be added to the date as given.

24. Russian priests normally received minimal salaries from the Church and were supported mainly through parishioners' contributions. The missionary priests in Alaska constituted an exception in that their salaries, very substantial for the times, were paid by the Russian-American Company. Veniaminov was to reject any contribution by his parishioners and to refuse payment for life crisis rites. At the time of his arrival, however, his parishioners' gesture reflected their recognition of the normal situation as well as of the difficulty a person faced in adjusting to life in the Aleutians.

25. The donors represented fewer than one-fifth of the Districts' population, including Aleuts, Russians, and Creoles (persons of Russian ancestry). Extensive population data are available in Veniaminov's "Papers" (*Bumagi*) and in Alaska Church Collection.

26. Veniaminov's eldest daughter, Katherine, later married Semen Petelin's son (by an Aleut woman), Ivan Petelin. Ivan Petelin, one of the first students in Veniaminov's school in Unalaska, became a priest and served as missionary in the Eskimo area of Alaska.

27. *Bumagi*, Folios 190, 276v, 359, 360; Ivan P. Barsukov, *Pis'ma Innokentiia, Metropolita Moskovskogo i Kolomenskogo, 1828–1878* [*Letters of Innokentii, Metropolitan of Moscow and Kolomna, 1828–1878*] (St. Petersburg: Synod, 1897–1901), p. 5.

28. The date of construction of these chapels is interesting. It is the time when Veniaminov had returned to Alaska as Bishop. Previous to that time, the only chapel in the Eastern Aleutians, aside from the authorized church in Unalaska, was one at Umnak built originally in 1806; a new building was erected in 1826–28 by Stefan Kriukov (see above) according to Veniaminov's design. The Church administration at that time discouraged what was considered unnecessary proliferation of churches and chapels which could not be staffed by clergy. It was possible to rebuild the chapel at Umnak in 1826 only because Archbishop Michael of Irkutsk, in ruling on Veniaminov's request to permit such construction, while ostensibly prohibiting it, left a carefully constructed loophole for independent local action (*Bumagi*, Folio 158). In the 1840s, as Bishop, Veniaminov had the authority to permit chapel and church construction. The name of the saint to whom the Chapel on Tigal'da has been dedicated, is, of course, Veniaminov's (and Pan'kov's) given name.

29. *Vedomost' o Tserkvi*, Alaska Church Collection, Box 249, 1st set.

30. Annual Report on the Status of the Church for 1855 lists the Tigal'da and Akun chapels as having been built by "the *late* Toion Ivan Pan'kov" (Alaska Church Collection, Box 249, 1st set).

31. Monetary contributions toward the maintenance of the symbolic system may indicate relative status. In the 1880s the Aleut community was building the new Church in Unalaska (the present building). The actual construction was carried out under the auspices of the Alaska Commercial Company, but the funds for construction, in very large measure, were donated by the parishioners. Donations, as preferred by the Alaska Commercial Company, were mostly in sea otter skins. The Pan'kovs of Tigal'da contributed several choice pelts. This information is contained in a handwritten ledger, property of Mr. L. Shaishnikoff of Unalaska. The ledger was kept by Mr. Shaishnikoff's kinsman, Vassilii, who at that time was the

harbor chief at Unalaska. I am indebted to Mr. Shaishnikoff for showing me the ledger in the summer of 1975.

32. There are persons bearing the surname Pan'kov living in the Kommandor Islands. They must have moved there sometime in the last decade of the 19th century or at the beginning of the 20th.

33. Very little of Veniaminov's private correspondence has been published. I doubt that it has survived. Barsukov (1897–1901) apparently selected from Veniaminov's private letters only those addressed to or dealing with affairs of his two children who entered the ecclesiastical life (the younger son became a missionary priest in the Amur region; one daughter entered a convent). Veniaminov's "Journals" in *Bumagi* are not a private diary, but an official record kept for presentation to ecclesiastical superiors. Only occasionally does a personal note creep in.

34. *Promyshlennik* (plural *promyshlenniki*) is a term which entered American historical literature to designate the Russian commercial fur hunters of the period. The term is largely untranslatable, connotes a hunter, a provider, and a commercial entrepreneur simultaneously.

35. In this conflict Aleuts used firearms. It is generally assumed that those were captured weapons. I have very tenuous evidence that some might have been acquired by other means. That some *promyshlenniki* aided Aleuts in their own conflicts is mentioned by Veniaminov in his *Notes of Unalaska District*. He states that according to Aleut tradition Glotov wiped out the Four Mountains and adjacent islands' population on behest of Umnak Aleuts, who were in a conflict of long standing with the former.

36. R. V. Makarova, *Russkiie na Tikhom okeane vo vtoroi polovine XVIII v.* [*Russians on the Pacific, 1743–1799*] (Moscow: Nauka, 1968), pp. 56–59, 70–71, 79; Vassilii Berkh, *A Chronological History of the Discovery of the Aleutian Islands or the Exploits of Russian Merchants*, trans. Dimitri Krenov, ed. Richard A. Pierce (Kingston, Ont.: The Limestone Press, 1974), p. 21.

37. Andreyev, *Russkiie otkrytiia*.

38. Makarova, *Russkiie na Tikhom okeane*.

39. Since the earliest contact, *promyshlenniki* brought young Aleuts to home ports, and some were educated in Russian schools. Initially, many of these were hostages—*amanats*. As a rule, *amanats* were sons or close kinsmen (male) of the Aleut chiefs and leading men, and the preferred age was from 8 to 14 years. Younger children were difficult to care for; the older teenagers, too dangerous to keep, demanding constant watch. By the 1780s numerous young Aleuts, sons of leading citizens, were sent by their fathers to Russia for schooling, along with the *amanats*. Moreover, *promyshlenniki* who spent many years on a single voyage sometimes became personally attached to their small hostages. There is some evidence that occasionally some of these men instructed the Aleut hostages in language and religion. I reject the possibility that Ivan Pan'kov was a Russian hostage in the islands because he, evidently, was relatively well educated and spoke Russian without any trace of an accent—residence in Russia seems much more likely. For the same reason, I reject the possibility that he traveled to Russia as an adult. Hostage status is possible but seems unlikely because of Pan'kov's obvious sympathy for the Russian

culture and his loyalty to Orthodoxy. For these reasons I postulate a sponsorship and young age as well as residence in Russia.

40. Both Cherepanov and Pan'kov were literate men. Cherepanov's report (in Andreyev) was signed in his own hand; Pan'kov's literacy is inferred from the fact that he was a navigator (*shturman* not a *morekhod*), that is, he must have been a graduate of Navigators' School. Cherepanov's piety was referred to earlier and is based on close reading of his report cited above; Pan'kov's attitudes may be only guessed.

41. The existence of such parallels has been discussed informally by W. S. Laughlin, Gordon Marsh, and myself in recent conversations and correspondence. In the summer of 1975, an Aleut informant brought up the subject in conversation.

42. The letter was published by Barsukov (1897–1901) with the additional commentary indicating that Veniaminov was so impressed by the meeting that he recounted the incident to Governor-General Muraviev. In the summer of 1975 I identified a handwritten copy of the original letter in the "Miscellaneous Papers," Russian Church, in the archival holdings of the Alaska Historical Library. This copy was used for the translation offered here.

43. Hieromonk Makarii, member of the first Orthodox mission (the Kadiak Mission) to Alaska, arrived in the Aleutian Islands in 1795. He traveled widely through the islands, from Unga to the Four Mountains Islands, he baptized many, without instruction, as he did not speak Aleut, left the island in 1796 accompanied by several important Aleut men, for Irkutsk and hence for St. Petersburg, to present a case against *promyshlenniki's* treatment of the native inhabitants. He perished in the wreck of *Phoenix*, presumably off the coast of Unalaska, in 1799, on his return voyage. See Michael George Kovach, "The Russian Orthodox Church in America" (Ph.D. thesis, University of Pittsburg, 1957), p. 80.

44. *Bumagi*, Folio 208–209 verso.

45. Ibid., Folio 359.

46. It is interesting to note that the chapel on the island of Akutan, the most recent of all Aleut chapels, is dedicated to St. Alexander Nevsky. Akutan was resettled by Aleuts from Akun and other Krenitzyn Islands. One wonders if there is any connection between the first service held in Akun by Veniaminov in 1828 and eventual dedication of the chapel to this saint.

47. *Bumagi*, Folio 360.

48. Ibid.

49. Russian expression used by Veniaminov reads "po moiemu priglasheniiu i moiemu prosheniiu"—the element of supplication is emphasized. The entire tone of the passage is one of respect.

50. *Bumagi*, Folio 338v; emphasis mine.

51. Ibid., Folio 340; emphasis mine.

52. Ibid., June 21, 1827.

53. The new Aleut version was approved by the Synod by 1832. This indicates the speed with which the two friends worked by now, especially if one takes into account the enormous time it took to communicate with St. Petersburg. Four hundred copies were printed by 1837, and sent to Alaska, but printing errors were so

numerous that Veniaminov did not deem it fit for distribution. He determined to supervise a new printing himself. The situation was enough to try the patience of the Man of God—and his correspondence indicates the fact. The new corrected edition done under Veniaminov's personal supervision appeared in 1840 and is known under the title *Nachatki Christianskogo Ucheniia ili Kratkaia Sviashchennaya Istoriia i Kratkii Christianskii Katechisis* [Beginnings of Christian Teaching or the Short Sacred History and Short Christian Catechism]. No copies of the faulty edition have been located. The original 1826 manuscript survives and is located at the St. Herman Pastoral School, Kodiak, forming part of Veniaminov's *Bumagi*.

54. *Bumagi*, Folio 378, entry for Monday, September 16, 1829.

55. Ibid., 377 verso.

56. Ibid., Folio 378, entry for September 24, 1829.

57. Ibid., footnote, Folio 378.

58. Ibid., Folio 378.

59. Ibid., Folio 379.

60. That the Church served as the vehicle for maintenance of group identity and group solidarity among the Aleuts has been noticed by several investigators, notably Berreman, "Inquiry into Community Integration" and "A Contemporary Study of Nikolski, an Aleutian Village" (Master's thesis, University of Oregon, 1953) and Dorothy Jones (personal communication). BIA teachers were aware of the fact, and were, as a rule, hostile to the Church. A notable exception is Phoebe West, "An Educational Program for an Aleut Village" (M.S. thesis, University of Washington, 1938). The best evidence, however, is the negative one originating from persons who economically exploited the region. I cite but from one example of many: Knut B. Birkeland, *The Whalers of Akutan: An Account of Modern Whaling in the Aleutian Islands* (New Haven: Yale University Press, 1926), pp. 79–85:

> It was natural for me to think that the natives would come around looking for jobs, but they did not do so. Evidently they expected us to go to them. I did not know at the time that the Russian system of village administration was so methodically carried out in any part of America as I later found it to be at Akutan.
>
> If anyone is in need of workers from one of the small villages in the Aleutian Islands, he will first have to consult with the village chief, who will call his men together and discuss the matter with them. It is for the members of his council to decide which ones shall go to work and at what wages. Once when we were in need of men I went to the little village of Bjork, on the island south of Unalaska. I stayed on board the *Kodiak* while the captain went ashore with the interpreter to find out from the chief if any men were to be had. I could see the villagers assembling in consultation, and pretty soon the meeting broke up and everybody went into the church. After a brief service all the able bodied men of the village came on board, ready to start work. . . .
>
> At the time the United States bought Alaska, together with the Aleutian Islands, from Russia, the latter reserved a right the scope of which the purchaser probably did not understand at that time. Russia obtained a guarantee

from the United States that it would not in any way interfere with the religion or the religious customs and practices of the natives. . . .

After Alaska was deeded to the United States, the priests, as officials of the Russian government, continued to govern the natives in accordance with the orders of Russian government, and pictures of the czar remained over the altars in native churches. The Russian system of village administration could not be interfered with by the United States, because it was part of the religious customs. . . .

Until the recent revolution, Russia consistently made use of the privilege which it had reserved at the time of transferring Alaska to the United States. This made it impossible to do efficient missionary work among the natives, and the same may be said of the attempt to make them learn the English language. These natives call themselves Christians, but it is my opinion that their religion is nothing but plain paganism. They have a number of holy days which are rigorously observed. . . .

The natives were never able to work much on the day following a celebration, which, of course, interfered considerably with our work at the station. It was especially annoying that they should be celebrating one of their holy days on the other side of the bay when the weather was fine and the whales were coming in regularly; for such a practice greatly hampered the progress of our work. I wondered for some time if we could not eliminate a few of their holy days during the whaling season, making up for lost pleasures during the wintertime.

Astor and Baranov

Partners in Empire

JAMES P. RONDA

James Ronda of the History Department at the University of Tulsa has written on various aspects of exploration and development in the Pacific Northwest. His major work Lewis and Clark among the Indians *(Lincoln: University of Nebraska Press, 1984) reinterpreted the relationship of the two captains with the Natives they encountered while venturing west as agents of empire and capitalism. Spanish and French traders and settlers had, from the beginning of the 17th century, already drawn the Natives into the world market system. At the start of the 19th century the American John Jacob Astor sought to organize the interior and maritime fur trade into a unified system, which, had it been successful, would have changed the nature of the economic history of North America.*

In his book on Astor and his imperial idea, Ronda explores what he calls the "Russian Connection." Astor sought to make an ally of Aleksandr Baranov, chief manager of the Russian-American Company and Governor of the colony of Russian America. Knowing that the Russians were dependent on external sources of supply, Astor suggested to Baranov that he, Astor, become the Russians' sole colonial supplier. In exchange, he asked that Baranov grant him exclusive non-Russian trading privileges along the coast. In a period when the Europeans still were vying for sovereignty along that coast, this was a daring proposal; Astor sought to become the dominant power in the continental West, a role which later the Hudson's Bay Company would fill, though to a lesser degree, for half a century.

In the piece reprinted here, written for the Anchorage symposium "Russian America: The Forgotten Frontier," Ronda examines the details of Astor's proposed contract with Baranov and the motivations of each party to the agreement. Baranov achieved the success he did with the Russian-American Company through shrewd judgment and ruthless control. His involvement with Astor was much to

This article appeared originally in *Pacifica* (Pacific Rim Studies Center, Alaska Pacific University) 2 (1990): 104–14; it is reprinted here by permission.

his and Russia's advantage and, in the end, the more so, since John Jacob Astor gave up his imperial design while Baranov solidified the Russian hold in the Northwest. In this volatile period before the lines of sovereignty were drawn, any one of the contenders for imperial control might have succeeded: Spain, Britain, Russia, or the United States. Had Astor and Baranov successfully concluded their negotiations, the map of the Northwest would likely be considerably different today.

The name John Jacob Astor has come to symbolize the single-minded pursuit of profit. Astor seems to us the archetypal moneygrubber whose life was defined by ledger lines and the bottom line. Alexander Baranov, governor of the Russian empire in America, suffers an even worse fate. He has simply become the invisible man on a frontier so distant as to be unimportant. From the pen of Washington Irving, Baranov emerges as a brawling, profane, hard-drinking tyrant. The moneygrubber and the tyrant are easy stereotype descriptions that mask a complex reality and a fascinating although brief relationship.

Contemporaries knew better. They understood what latter-day commentators sometimes overlook—that both Astor and Baranov possessed powerful, audacious plans for empire in the far Northwest. Thomas Jefferson recognized the imperial dimensions of Astor's plans. Writing in 1813, he likened Astor to Columbus and Raleigh, and portrayed Astoria as the "germ" of a great western empire.[1] Baranov's impressive plans for exploration and expansion might have prompted Jefferson to put him in the pantheon of empire builders as well. Because the Astor and Baranov visions crossed paths here in the north Pacific, it is even more important that we take the measure of each dream and then plot their crossing.

John Astor's western dream first sprang to life in late 1807. It was then that Astor first mentioned his western ideas to DeWitt Clinton. Clinton was an ideal sounding board. Mayor of New York and sometime lieutenant governor of the state, he had important political friends and considerable business savvy. And it was not lost on Astor that Clinton's uncle George was Jefferson's vice-president. No direct record of those earliest talks between Astor and Clinton survives, but it is clear from later correspondence that the mayor urged his friend to pursue the Pacific enterprise.[2]

Astor's flash of imagination took written shape in January 1808. In a private letter to DeWitt Clinton, Astor carefully drew the outlines of what he hoped would become the first American empire west of the Rockies. In this and subsequent letters to President Jefferson and Secretary of the Treasury Albert Gallatin, Astor proposed a vast trade network extending from western Europe and the American Great Lakes to the Pacific Northwest and on to Russian America and China. He envisioned a complete land and sea transportation system shifting trade goods, pelts, information, and employees around a global marketplace. The vehicle for this enterprise would be the Pacific Fur Company, a private venture with close ties to the federal government. In Astor's scheme, company posts would occupy sites from the Missouri to the Columbia. Fur and the flag would join forces to plant American sovereignty along the Great River of the West.[3]

Alexander Baranov's expansionist strategies were no less audacious or visionary. Driven by the need to expand hunting territories and locate suitable sites for agricultural settlements, Baranov undertook an impressive exploration program. The 1808 Kuskov expedition, the founding of Fort Ross, and tentative moves toward Hawai'i represent a kind of national-corporate expansionism that Astor would have readily grasped. Working from opposite sides of the continent, Astor and Baranov shared a common passion—the drive for empire.[4]

Astor's plans were prompted neither by the journeys of American explorers like Lewis and Clark nor by the western vision espoused by Jefferson. Rather, it was his connection to Canadian promoters—especially the North West Company—that gave both form and substance to the design. Astor's tutors in empire were Peter Pond, Alexander Mackenzie, and his own Montreal partner, Alexander Henry the elder. By the fall of 1809, Astor was busy turning his Canadian lessons into American reality. In August, there had been a hasty and ultimately unsuccessful trip to Montreal for discussions with the North West Company on the joint Pacific venture. Now back in New York, Astor was busy with final preparations for his first voyage in the northwest maritime fur trade. His ship *Enterprise* under Captain John Ebbets, was soon to sail for the Pacific.[5]

What played now was a diplomatic ballet of exceptional delicacy. Sometime during September 1809, Astor was approached by Andrei Dashkov, a Russian diplomat and commercial agent of extraordinary skill and energy. Dashkov represented not only the Russian government but also the Russian-American Company. The company had been trying for some time to negotiate a diplomatic arrangement with the United States to restrain weapons trading along the Northwest coast. Once in the United States, Dashkov was to press for a commercial treaty. That treaty was to contain an especially deceptive provision virtually forcing the United States to halt the weapons trade. If such diplomatic maneuvers failed, Dashkov was instructed to negotiate with an American merchant who could deliver provisions on a regular schedule to Russian America. But the company wanted no ordinary entrepreneur with modest Pacific experience. Dashkov had to find someone with solid credentials and contacts in Canton.[6]

Dashkov's diplomatic efforts proved fruitless. American officials seemed quite uninterested in the problems of one Russian company on so remote a frontier. By the end of August 1809, the Russian agent had abandoned diplomacy and was busy seeking a private American ally. That search brought Dashkov to Astor. Every crossing of dreams needs a broker, an intermediary; Dashkov was now to be a midwife for Astor and Baranov.

The conversations between Astor and Dashkov changed the course of Astoria's history and the history of the greater Northwest. Dashkov explained Russian needs and problems, suggesting "a direct and permanent trade with our settlements." When he asked Astor about his western plans, the merchant confided that the Pacific Fur Company intended to establish a colony on the north bank of the Columbia River. Astor consistently told the Russians that his post was planned for the north bank of the river. Astoria was, of course, built on the south bank. Astor may have purposely misled Dashkov as part of his scheme for a joint Russian and American presence to squeeze out the Canadians. Warming to the benefits of cooperation between the two companies, Astor suggested that if the Russians moved south while American traders headed north, the British would be eliminated as a power in the Northwest. Dashkov was taken aback by such a daring proposal and gave only the vaguest of replies. But the Russian was impressed with Astor's capital, spirit of enterprise, and business acumen.

Finding that Astor was well disposed toward a venture in Russian America, so much so that it seemed to Dashkov "as if he had had this same thought before," the two men fashioned a proposal for Pacific Fur Company–Russian-American Company cooperation. Their plan called for both companies to sign a three-year agreement. The pact made Astor sole supplier of all goods to Russian America. He would be required to send at least two or three ships each year. Payment for these goods could be in cash, fur, or bills of exchange. Astor's ships would then be chartered by the Russian company to transport furs to Canton. Astor promised that the Russian furs would be sold to the Chinese by his commercial agent, thus concealing their true origin. Dashkov believed that a deal with Astor would achieve both company and national goals far quicker than any tedious negotiations with American diplomats. He was convinced that once other American merchants learned of Astor's monopoly to provision the Russian settlements all incentive for northern voyages would vanish. The deadly weapons trade would promptly collapse. The settlements would be fed, furs would be sold in Canton at good prices, and the Russians might feel more secure in Alaskan waters.[7]

Any plan as ambitious and far-reaching as this needed approval from both the Russian-American Company and the imperial government. But Astor and Dashkov were unwilling to wait for so lengthy a process to take its course. Sometime in October 1809, they decided to change sailing plans for Captain Ebbets and the *Enterprise* to include a long stay at Sitka. If this voyage proved successful, it would provide solid experience for future journeys from both New York and Astoria. All this meant a flurry of work for everyone from Astor and Ebbets to the *Enterprise* crew and dock hands. New supplies had to be found, some Indian trade items off-loaded, and cargo manifests rewritten. The *Enterprise* had originally been loaded with cargo suitable for the maritime fur trade. Using a list supplied by Dashkov, Astor and Ebbets were able to reload the ship with items more suited to the Sitka market. Notes from Captain Ebbets reveal the sorts of things destined for the Russian colony. The *Enterprise* cargo hold was crammed with everything from twenty dozen empty bottles and countless strings of blue beads to barrels of molasses and bolts of canvas cloth. Dashkov's original list suggested one thousand gallons each of rum and brandy. Perhaps because he had made earlier voyages to Alaska, Ebbets knew better. The Captain doubled the amounts and ordered that "the liquors must be as strong as *Aqua Fortis* if possible."[8]

Having the right cargo for Russian needs was essential for this first venture and subsequent success. Because Ebbets was to be Astor's initial contact with Baranov, the captain's detailed instructions occupied much of Astor's attention. During the first week of November, with the *Enterprise* nearly ready to sail, Astor drafted two sets of orders for Ebbets. One set, enclosed in Astor's November 4 letter to Dashkov, presented in straightforward terms how Ebbets was to deal with the Russian company. The captain was told to sail for the Russian settlements without delay, trade at the best and fairest terms, and then take on Russian furs for Canton. Ebbets was granted full authority to make a binding contract with Baranov.[9] These bland instructions were meant for Dashkov's eyes. A rather different set went directly to Ebbets. Astor and Dashkov had agreed that if necessary the *Enterprise* could deliver her cargo on the Siberian mainland. What Astor feared was that the *Enterprise* and future ships might be ordered by Russian officials to sail throughout the North Pacific as something of a private company navy. The Russian part of Astor's western design was important, but it could not be allowed to dominate the entire venture. Ebbets was privately told that he was not obligated to go to more than one post in addition to the call at Sitka.[10]

During that busy first week of November, Astor made room for an important letter to Baranov. Good relations with the governor were essential, not just for this voyage, but for Astoria's future. Astor recited a brief history of his dealings with Dashkov and the subsequent changes in the *Enterprise*'s lading. "Nothing would be more gratifying to me," wrote Astor, "than to be in a small degree useful in assisting in the establishing a trade on such a footing between us as would secure stability and success to a trade, the importance of which is as yet known only to yourself." Knowing that details of the pending arrangement between the Pacific Fur Company and the Russian-American Company were to be spelled out by Dashkov, Astor saw no reason to repeat such items. But he did want to reassure the governor about the weapons trade. If American ships were denied a place in the lucrative provisioning trade because Astor had a monopoly, far fewer Yankee ships and Boston skippers would trouble Alaskan waters.[11]

Once the *Enterprise* sailed at the end of November, Astor had to face far more complex diplomatic challenges. From the time he first laid western plans, Astor knew that his dream would be hostage to the shifting winds of international diplomacy. Now the twists of national policy—Russian and American—threatened to sever Astor's ties to Baranov. Dashkov had been ordered to make a commercial treaty with the United States, and despite his dealings with Astor, the Russian diplomat was intent on pursuing that goal. Astor, on the other hand, hoped he would fail. Any commercial treaty with the United States was sure to touch on the weapons trade, thus making any private arrangement with Astor much less attractive. Throughout the early months of 1810, Astor seemed to have little to fear. Dashkov's meetings with Secretary of State Robert Smith produced no immediate progress.[12] Astor's confidence that the talks were going nowhere suddenly vanished in the light of two unexpected events. In early May 1810, the State Department decided that John Quincy Adams, American ambassador to the Russian imperial court, might well begin informal talks with Russian officials regarding a commercial treaty. If those consultations produced a treaty, Astor had no deal.

And now there was a new complication. Astor had long depended on Andrei Dashkov for both information and direction. But in the spring of 1810, Dashkov suddenly became only the second most important Russian official in the United States. His new superior and the first fully credentialed Russian ambassador to the American republic was Count Fedor Pahlen. Now Astor had to watch events in St. Petersburg while courting a new ally in Washington.[13]

Like his predecessor Dashkov, Ambassador Pahlen hoped to strike a deal with State Department officials. Secretary of State Smith had decided to let John Quincy Adams do the negotiating in St. Petersburg, and Pahlen soon found himself as frustrated as Dashkov.[14] Astor heard about that frustration and decided to play on it. His chosen performer in this diplomatic dance was Adrian Benjamin Bentzon. Bentzon, a former Danish diplomat, was rapidly becoming Astor's most adept agent. And it did not hurt that he was married to Magdalen Astor, John's eldest daughter. Astor now dispatched Bentzon to Washington, and the agent made sure he and the ambassador were soon fast friends. Pahlen found Bentzon an easy listener, and the Russian promptly poured out his bitterness at American indifference. Rebuffed, Pahlen vowed that he would never again call at the State Department. Once Pahlen made that promise, Bentzon made his move. He laid out in careful detail the proposed arrangement between Astor and the Russian company, dwelling on the obvious advantages to both the company and the empire. Pahlen was quickly sold and suggested that Astor send Bentzon to St. Petersburg for direct talks with the government.[15]

Astor must have been delighted with this response. With work going forward on other aspects of his western design, he did not want to lose his Russian chance. The problem now was to organize an unofficial diplomatic mission to St. Petersburg without running afoul of either the State Department or Ambassador John Quincy Adams. Throughout the fall of 1810, Astor used every bit of influence he could muster. There were hurried talks with his long-time Washington confidant, Secretary of the Treasury Albert Gallatin, and through Gallatin, contacts were made with President James Madison.[16] All of this produced no results. And with Astor's overland and seaborne expeditions to the Pacific already under way, something had to be done. That something was the kind of personal influence peddling few did as well as Astor. In December 1810, he heard that the naval frigate *John Adams* was preparing to sail, carrying on board the American diplomat George W. Erving. Turning to Gallatin, Astor asked why not slip Bentzon and his wife on board. Astor and Gallatin had become increasingly close personal and political friends. Those connections now paid off, and by mid-January 1811, the names of Adrian and Magdalen Bentzon were on the *John Adams* passenger list.[17]

With the thorny transportation question resolved, Astor and Bentzon met in New York at the end of January 1811 to plot their final Russian strategy. They knew they could depend on Pahlen to pave the way with officials at the foreign ministry. Bentzon and Astor now reviewed the proposals to be offered to the Russian company. Astor recognized that the greatest advantages to the Russians were in regularly scheduled supply shipments and the sale of furs at Canton. Astor gave Bentzon two different supply schedules, suggesting that the Russians could select the one best suited to their needs. While these arrangements were sure to bring Astor some profit, he wanted Bentzon to press for Russian acceptance of two additional demands. The first was economic. Astor wanted duty-free access to the Russian domestic fur market. This demand was closely linked to a second geopolitical request. Bentzon was to recruit the Russians for joint action against Anglo-Canadian activities in the Northwest.[18]

Adrian Bentzon reached St. Petersburg in the late summer of 1811. For once, the winds of diplomacy were blowing in Astor's direction. In early August just as Bentzon arrived, talks between Ambassador Adams and Foreign Minister Nikolai Rumiantsev on a possible commercial treaty broke off. Adams was convinced that war between the United States and Great Britain was imminent. In a period of such uncertainty, Adams thought talk of commercial treaties was senseless. If the Russians wanted their Pacific problems resolved, they would have to turn to Astor.[19]

Adrian Bentzon was ready. Formal talks with the company's chief director Michael Buldakov began in September 1811. While Buldakov was eager to sign an agreement on supplies and markets, Astor's other demands met with considerable resistance. The Russian-American Company was not about to be drawn into Astor's skirmish with the Canadians. And there was an equally strong rebuff to Astor's request for special privileges in the Russian domestic fur market. Bentzon pressed his case, the company refused to budge, and there were endless consultations with imperial government officials. It was not until early May 1812 that Bentzon and company agents finally signed an agreement.[20] A month later the War of 1812 stormed into the Atlantic. Its tidal motion would eventually capsize Astoria and sink Astor's grand western design.

In the midst of these complex diplomatic events, we need to recall that Astor's vessels did make calls at Sitka. The *Enterprise* reached the Russian settlements in the summer of 1810. More important was the journey of the ship *Beaver.* In early August 1812, the *Beaver,* her captain Cornelius Sowle, and Astor's chief western agent Wilson Price Hunt left Fort Astoria on the Columbia bound for the Russian settlements. Hunt, a mild-mannered St. Louis merchant, was no match for Baranov. The Russian subjected Hunt to an endless round of hard bargaining, punctuated by boisterous drinking sprees. Throughout September, Hunt struggled to hammer out an arrangement with Baranov. When terms were finally settled on, Baranov announced that he would pay in seal skins. Since the warehouses at New Archangel currently held none of those skins, Hunt and Sowle were obligated to sail to St. Paul in the Bering Sea. It was not until the end of October 1812 that the *Beaver* could begin loading at St. Paul. In the first week of November, fortune turned against Hunt and the *Beaver.* A fierce storm severely damaged the ship making repairs necessary before any trip to Canton.[21]

This broken voyage and the larger events of the War of 1812 put a stop to any thoughts of linking a Russian empire in the north Pacific to an emerging American one in the Northwest. By 1814, Astor knew all the grim details—Astoria sold, ships lost, and chances beyond grasp. Writing to his old ally Andrei Dashkov, Astor reported that the post on the Columbia was in British hands and "the whole property gone." With remarkable equanimity, Astor reminded the Russian of a timeless proverb: "This makes good the saying that one misfortune seldom comes alone." Officials in St. Petersburg were not nearly so eloquent. "That is the end of it" was their blunt announcement.[22] The winds of war had switched about and changed courses for both Astor and Baranov. For one imperial moment partners, now their empires seemed bound for separate ports.

NOTES

1. Jefferson to Astor, Monticello, November 9, 1813, Jefferson Papers, Library of Congress, Washington, D.C.

2. The fullest discussion of Astor's plans is in James P. Ronda, *Astoria and Empire* (Lincoln: University of Nebraska Press, 1990), ch. 1.

3. Astor to Clinton, New York, January 25, 1808, DeWitt Clinton Papers, 4: 5–6 Butler Rare Book and Manuscript Library, Columbia University, New York.

4. James R. Gibson, *Imperial Russia in Frontier America* (New York: Oxford Uni-

versity Press, 1976), 3–23. See also Basil Dmytryshyn, E. A. P. Crownhart-Vaughan, and Thomas Vaughan, eds., *To Siberia and Russian America: Three Centuries of Russian Eastward Expansion, 1558–1867,* 3 vols. (Portland: Oregon Historical Society, 1985–89), especially vol. 3.

5. Ronda, *Astor and Empire,* ch. 2.

6. Russian-American Company to Dashkov, St. Petersburg. September 1, 1808, Nina Bashkina, Nikolai N. Bolkhovitinov, and David F. Trask, eds., *The United States and Russia: The Beginnings of Relations, 1765–1815* (Washington, D.C.: Government Printing Office, 1980), 523. Hereafter cited as *Russ. Docs.*

7. Dashkov to Baranov, Philadelphia, November 7, 1809, *Russ. Docs.,* 608–13. See also Dashkov to Rumiantsev, Philadelphia, November 18, 1809, ibid., 614–15.

8. John Ebbets, Notes on *Enterprise* cargo, late October 1809, John Jacob Astor Papers, Baker Library, Harvard University Graduate School of Business Administration, Boston, Massachusetts. Hereafter cited as Astor Papers, MD-BA.

9. Astor to Ebbets, New York, November 4, 1809, *Russ. Docs.,* 601–603.

10. Astor to Ebbets, Philadelphia, November 4, 1809, Astor Papers, MD-BA. There is some confusion over Astor's whereabouts on November 4. The document in Russian archives is datelined in New York; that in the Astor Papers was drafted in Philadelphia.

11. Astor to Baranov, New York, November 4, 1809, *Russ. Docs.,* 603–604.

12. Dashkov to Rumiantsev, Philadelphia, November 15, 1809, *Russ Docs.,* 614–17, The fullest account of United States–Russian diplomacy in this period is Nikolai N. Bolkhovitinov, *The Beginnings of Russian-American Relations, 1775–1815* (Cambridge: Harvard University Press, 1975).

13. Smith to Adams, Washington, May 5, 1810, Diplomatic Instructions, All Countries, 7: 91, RG 59, National Archives, Washington, D. C. Hereafter cited as DNA.

14. Pahlen to Rumiantsev, Philadelphia, July 29, 1810, *Russ. Docs.,* 677–79.

15. Bentzon to Astor, Washington, July 9, 1810, Astor Papers, MD-BA. See also Pahlen to Rumiantsev, Philadelphia, July 21, 1810, *Russ Docs.,* 675–76, and Pahlen to Rumiantsev, Philadelphia, October 26, 1810, ibid., 677–79.

16. Gallatin to Madison, Washington, September 5, 1810, and Madison to Gallatin, Montpelier, September 12, 1810, James Madison Papers, Library of Congress.

17. Astor to Gallatin, New York, December 27, 1810, including Gallatin's marginal notes, Albert Gallatin Papers, New York Historical Society, New York.

18. Astor to Bentzon, New York, January 21, 1811, Astor Papers, MD-BA.

19. Adams to Monroe, St. Petersburg, August 9, 1811, Diplomatic Despatches, St. Petersburg, 2, RG 79, DNA.

20. These negotiations are discussed in Ronda, *Astoria and Empire,* 83–86.

21. Ronda, *Astoria and Empire,* 283–84.

22. Astor to Dashkov, New York, September 26, 1814, Astor Papers, MD-BA; Russian-American Company

Two Missions to Alaska

RICHARD L. DAUENHAUER

Richard Dauenhauer, a trained anthropologist, is a director of the Sealaska Heritage Foundation, a cultural resource agency established by the Sealaska Corporation, one of the Native regional economic development corporations provided for and capitalized by the Alaska Native Claims Settlement Act of 1971. Richard and Nora Marks Dauenhauer have devoted much of their careers to the translation and preservation of Tlingit songs and texts and to the publication of other materials related to the Indian cultural heritage in southeastern Alaska, including biographical sketches of the founders and leaders of the Alaska Native Brotherhood, the principal Indian social, self-help, and political organization in Alaska before statehood in 1959.

In the work reprinted here, written while he was teaching at Alaska Pacific University in Anchorage, Dauenhauer, who is Russian Orthodox, compares the two giants of Alaska mission work, Father Ioann Veniaminov (St. Innocent) and the Presbyterian Dr. Sheldon Jackson. Part of Veniaminov's work in the Aleutian Islands is interpreted by Professor Lydia Black in her article in this volume. In 1834 Veniaminov was transferred to Sitka and in 1841 appointed Bishop of Sitka and Alaska; his see actually included Russian-American Company lands in Kamchatka and Siberia. In the late 1850s he became Metropolitan of Moscow and the leading Patriarch of the Church.

Graduating from Union Theological Seminary, Jackson served briefly in the Civil War before becoming a missionary among the Indians in the West and eventually head of the Rocky Mountain District of the Presbyterian Board of Foreign Missions, from which post he began missionary work in Alaska in 1877. Dauenhauer finds that Veniaminov and the Orthodox mission were much more flexible and culturally sensitive than Jackson and the Protestant missions. The Orthodox tradition was to build on culture, while the Protestant agenda was to supplant one culture, aboriginal, with a new one, American. Evidence for the comparison is seen in the adaptation of ritual on the one hand, and its suppression on the other, and even

This article appeared originally in *Pacific Historian* 26 (Spring 1982): 29–41; it is reprinted here by permission.

more clearly in the use of Native languages by the Russians and the insistence on only English by the Americans.

In assessing Dauenhauer's stimulating and insightful comparison, readers should keep in mind two important mitigating factors. Other traditional churches, most particularly the Catholic, also built upon Native customs in their missionizing efforts. More important, at the time when the Protestant missions entered Alaska, Progressive thinkers in America were convinced that the only alternative to acculturation for American Indians was extermination, either through war in the West, or through disease and attrition. The notion that one could be American and Indian had not yet been accepted in American culture. The Protestant missionaries were confident, naively so, that through education they could acculturate, and save, the Indian populations in a single generation.

Ted Hinckley's article later in this anthology examines more closely the work of Jackson's Presbyterian predecessor, the Reverend Samuel Hall Young.

Sheldon Jackson is a name well known in the history of education in Alaska, which is as it should be. But how about John Veniaminov, Archbishop (now Saint) Innocent. Metropolitan of Moscow? Hardly a household word, but in fact Veniaminov also deserves to be well known as a missionary to Alaska, a visionary, and a remarkable force in education in his own time. It is instructive to look at the careers of both of these leaders and especially to compare their approaches to educating children from the Native cultures, which demanded much of their time, energy, and inspiration. Late twentieth-century controversies over bilingual education are simply a continuation of the major distinction between Jackson and Veniaminov: their radically differing attitudes toward religion and culture in general, and toward Alaska Native language and culture in particular. What is happening in Alaskan education today stems in considerable measure from the successive influences of Veniaminov and Jackson.

The first was born Ivan (John) Popov in 1797 in a small town in the Siberian district of Irkutsk. While he was in his teens all persons in the area named Popov were requested to adopt new surnames because there were too many Popovs and the record-keeping was getting difficult. John Popov accepted the special honor of receiving the name Veniaminov after the late Bishop Benjamin (Veniamin).

Intelligent and talented, John Veniaminov excelled in his studies. In 1817 he married and was ordained a deacon. Four years later he was ordained into the priesthood and in 1823 accepted an invitation to work in Alaska. Wintering in Sitka with his family, 1823–24, he recorded in his journals his first study of the Aleut language, with the aid of bilingual helpers. Planning the church he wished to build in Unalaska, he had the needed timbers cut to measure at Sitka. The church was constructed in Unalaska after his arrival there on July 29, 1824. In this period he also began a years-long practice of observation and note-taking. The breadth of his interests became manifest when his notes were published in 1841, encompassing aspects of geology, botany, anthropology, meteorology, and other sciences.

Veniaminov opened a bilingual school in which both Aleut and Russian were taught, evidence of his major effort in promoting bilingual education, our concern here. With Ivan Pan'kov, an Aleut leader, he designed the Aleut alphabet, and the two men worked at translating scripture. Both were influential in spreading literacy in Aleut. By 1840 Veniaminov had translated and published several books in Aleut and had composed some original works in the same language. Nor was he alone in this. Other clergy were also engaged in translating, and some Aleuts were themselves undertaking creative writing in their newly written language. There are extant biographies and bibliographies for over a dozen Aleut nineteenth-century writers.

Veniaminov traveled extensively. In 1832 he went by kayak to Bristol Bay and Nushagak. While assigned to Sitka, 1834–38, he traveled as far as Fort Ross in California. In 1838–39 he returned to Russia via Hawaii, Tahiti, and Cape Horn. In Saint Petersburg he met with company officials, government leaders, and of course the holy synod. One purpose of his journey was to lobby for additional support for the Alaska mission as well as for publication of books in Alaska Native languages.

In addition to his work in the Aleut language, Veniaminov also devoted much attention to the Tlingit language during his Sitka years. He developed a writing system for Tlingit and composed original works in that language. He is recorded as having prepared bilingual textbooks for Tlingit children with his own hand, with parallel texts in Tlingit and Russian.

A British visitor to Sitka in 1837 has left an impression of Veniaminov which helps in understanding his role and importance in Russian Alaska. Captain Edward Belcher was commander of HMS *Sulphur* and wrote that Father Veniaminov,

> who officiated in his splendid robes, was a very powerful, athletic man, about forty-five years of age, and standing in his boots (which appear

> to be part of his costume) about six feet three inches: quite Herculean and very clever. I took a very great liking to him, and was permitted to examine his workshop, in which I noticed a good barrel-organ, a barometer, and several other articles of his own manufacture. He was kind enough to volunteer his services on one or two of our sick barometers, and succeeded effectually. Notwithstanding he spoke only Russian, of which I know nothing, we managed to become great allies.

While still in Russia in 1839, Veniaminov learned of the death of his wife. Assured of excellent care for his children, he agreed to become a monk and was elevated to Bishop of Kamchatka, the Kuriles, and Aleutian Islands in December 1840. He took the name Innocent (Innokentii) after the famed missionary bishop of Irkutsk, Saint Innocent. Before the end of 1841 he was back in Alaska to begin a new phase of his career.

The following years were characterized also by education, building, and travel. He designed and supervised the construction of Saint Michael's Cathedral in Sitka, consecrated in 1848. It was primarily a local project made with local wood. The Bishop himself made the clock, and in his new residence he personally built much of the furniture, including the organ. In November 1845 the Petropavlovsk Seminary in Kamchatka was relocated in Sitka and called the New Archangel Seminary. It opened with fifty-four students, three teachers, and a library. Twenty-three of the students were Alaska Natives and the curriculum included six years of Native languages—Aleut, Tlingit, and Yupik. In 1858 the seminary was transferred to Yakutsk to strengthen the missionary effort in that area.

Bishop Innocent had meanwhile been elevated in 1850 to Archbishop and transferred to Yakutsk. His work continued much as before, including translating scripture into the Yakut language, and on July 19, 1859, he read the Gospel in Yakut for the first time. But his long years in missionary work were drawing to a close. In 1868, the year following sale of Alaska to the United States, Archbishop Innocent was appointed Metropolitan of Moscow, the highest position in the Russian Orthodox Church. Aged seventy-two, nearly blind, and extremely weary, he nevertheless undertook his new responsibilities with as much vigor as his health permitted, and served until his death in 1879. A significant postscript: on October 6, 1977, he was canonized as a saint of the Orthodox Church, equal to the apostles, the enlightener and apostle of America.

With this brief overview of the highlights of John Veniaminov's remarkable career in mind, it will be useful to comment on the cultural and religious values he bore with him, which were those also of many other Orthodox priests and teachers. To understand the flowering of Alaskan Native literature in the nineteenth century, and the rationale behind Veniaminov's enlightened educational methodology, some further knowledge of Russian Orthodoxy will help.

One important concept of Orthodoxy is capsulized in a famous saying attributed to St. Athanasius, that God became man so that man might become God. This statement is interpreted to imply that each person contains within himself or herself the potential of divinity. Such an interpretation directly influences the church's official view of human dignity and respect for the individual. Specifically, the Orthodox tradition has maintained great respect for the language and culture of the individual, frequently using local languages in its liturgy. For example, one of the first tasks of Saints Cyril and Methodius, early missionaries to the Slavs, was to design an alphabet and translate the liturgy and scriptures. Similarly, the first major project of the Russian Orthodox mission in the Aleutians was to design a writing system and to translate scriptures and liturgy into Aleut.

The schools were designed to train bilingual Native lay readers to help conduct church services, of course, but they were also consciously intended to instill in the people a sense of pride. From the very beginning, use of the vernacular was encouraged. Even today, on Sundays and feast days, the divine liturgy and other services are sung in combinations of English, Church Slavonic, and one or more of the Native languages, depending upon the ethnic composition of the congregation. Rather than attack Native culture and substitute their own, the church leaders supported a program which reinforced local customs and increased popular literacy, while simultaneously winning converts and building up a strong Native clergy, who would assure continued church vitality.

The Orthodox missions' stress on literacy was successful to the point that an estimated one-sixth of the total Aleut population could read and write. In Siberia, under Veniaminov's jurisdiction as bishop, the Native people attained a higher literacy rate than that of resident Russians.

The Orthodox vision of education continued intact for some time after the sale of the colony in 1867. The Americans, for their part, proceeded to ignore their vast new acquisition for almost twenty years; a governor was not appointed until 1884. For a number of years there was little or no civil law or government: the rough and tumble environment attracted an inordinate number of "hard cases," giving rise to a society far from genteel. In the capital of Sitka tensions between Tlingits and white settlers resulted in street fighting and random killings. In 1879 an English warship "came to the rescue" of the town. The next five years became known as the period of Navy Rule.

Into this scene of instability stepped the American clergyman Sheldon Jackson, and with him, the vision and concepts of American Protestant Christianity, specifically Presbyterianism. Like Veniaminov, Jackson was a missionary, founded schools, and at the time of his death occupied the highest position in his church. Thus he is at least an appropriate figure against whom to draw contrasts and parallels with Veniaminov. For the latter, the question of religion and culture had been settled in apostolic times: one *could* be socially, linguistically, and ethnically different from other members of the church locally, nationally, or world-wide, and still participate in the liturgical fullness of the church through its sacraments. For Jackson and most American Protestants, on the other hand, the social unit was the base for church membership and organization. There was and is emphasis on group participation in a shared cultural background, including language and attitudes. Jackson and many other American leaders, religious or not, earnestly and honestly believed that only through massive conversion to Christianity *and acculturation* could Alaskan Natives be spared the military defeat and tragic poverty and exploitation of the reservation system befalling Native Americans. Alaska was to become a battleground between strikingly different viewpoints, and the confrontation has not been fully resolved even in the present day.

In physical contrast to John Veniaminov, whom one writer called "Paul Bunyan in a cassock," Sheldon Jackson was barely over five feet tall. He suffered from weak eyes and frequent illness, but was equally as well known as his Russian predecessor for his energy, drive, and determination. The Alaska historian Ted Hinckley has described him as having "a personality and philosophy that matched those of John Calvin himself, Sheldon Jackson hated sin and loved work." Born in New York State on May 18, 1834, he graduated from Union College in Schenectady in 1855. He was ordained and married the same year. Initiating his missionary career in a school for Choctaw boys in 1858, he spent most of the next twelve years in Minnesota. He then became active in the

Board of Home Missions, blazing a path of church-founding from the Canadian border to the Rio Grande. His activity brought him north to Alaska in 1877.

Sheldon Jackson's efforts took several directions. Not only was he concerned about educating and converting Native Americans—actions he felt would serve to protect them from white exploitation—but he also favored either controlling or banning the manufacture and sale of liquor. In this he had the cooperation of U.S. Navy authorities on hand. As conditions changed, the various tensions lessened, and schools were constructed, Presbyterian concern became directed more and more toward protecting Native women from various elements of white male society—the military, miners, and merchants—as well as continuing the control of the flow of cheap rotgut whiskey which was devastating entire villages. Many mission schools—"Protestant Forts"—were constructed to implement these programs.

Jackson's influence on the course of events in Alaska grew with his arrival in Washington, D.C., as business manager of the Board of Home Missions in 1883. From this base he was very active and powerful in affairs dealing with the far northern territory. Pressure from the Alaska lobby to replace the military jurisdiction of the territory with civil government resulted in the passage of the Organic Act in 1884, with Jackson a major contributor to the writing of this legislation. On July 4, 1884, President Chester Arthur appointed Alaska's first U.S. territorial governor. Less than a year later, Jackson was himself appointed the First District General Agent of Education. His office remained in Washington.

With the organic act Jackson had killed the proverbial two birds with one stone; he combined his own proposals for civil government with those for Alaskan education into a single act. Among other things, the latter aspect of the bill called for "proper provision for education of children of school age . . . without reference to race." Public schools were set up in conjunction with the various missions. This arrangement, of very questionable constitutionality, lasted into the mid-1890s. It was defended by the argument that missionary-teachers were the only ones available. Although the mission schools were designed to be integrated, Jackson soon found he had to retreat from intense white community pressure and to start separate Native public schools. With this, segregated schooling began in Alaska. The territory witnessed the beginning of parallel school systems that exist to the present day.[1]

With both his political and philosophical bases firmly established,

Jackson laid the framework for a movement in education away from the system of Veniaminov and the Orthodox. The critical feature of this movement—the insistence on English-only instruction—led to suppression of Native cultural development. Generations of teachers dating from this time have convinced Native parents that use of Native languages results in stupidity and difficulty in learning English; this is still the case in many areas.

Jackson himself lived long enough to instill this policy but was not around to witness the dismal consequences, the legacy of linguistic insecurity which serves as a psychological roadblock in contemporary life for many Native Americans. Elected Moderator of the General Assembly of the Presbyterian Church in May 1897—the highest honor conferred by the Church—Jackson died shortly before his seventy-fifth birthday on May 2, 1909, in Asheville, North Carolina.

The implementation of such a regimen of instruction brought forth a number of policy directives offering suggestions for proper instruction of Native pupils. This particular example appeared in the February 1888 issue of the *North Star,* co-edited by Sheldon Jackson:

> The Board of Home Missions has informed us that government contracts for educating Indian pupils provide for the ordinary branches of an English education to be taught, and that no books in an Indian language shall be used, or instruction given in that language to Indian pupils. The letter states that this rule will be strictly enforced in all government Indian schools. The Commissioner of Indian Affairs urges, and very forcibly too, that instruction in their vernacular is not only of no use to them but is detrimental to their speedy education and civilization. It is now two years and more since the use of the Indian dialects [was] first prohibited in the training school here. All instruction is given in English. Pupils are required to speak and write English exclusively: and the results are tenfold more satisfactory than when they were permitted to converse in unknown tongues.

U.S. Bureau of Education Commissioner William Torrey Harris, reflecting attitudes espoused by Jackson, felt that "we have no higher calling in the world than to be missionaries of our ideas to those people who have not yet reached the Anglo-Saxon frame of mind," and ordered all teachers to "take with them such books of literature as portray in the most powerful form the ideas and convictions of the people of England and the United States." The works of Shakespeare, Dickens, Walter Scott, and their like, he added, "furnish exactly the material to inspire the teacher and to arouse and kindle the sluggish minds of the Natives of Alaska with sentiments and motives of action which lead our civilization."

These official statements from the policy makers were reinforced by the unofficial attitudes shared by many teachers in classrooms across the territory. "The Tlingit language is doomed to speedy extinction, the sooner the better for the Natives," wrote the missionary instructor Livingston Jones in 1914. "There is little in their language to merit perpetuation." Other opinions expressed by Jones reflect a lack of understanding of the linguistic and cultural phenomena he was observing at the time and illustrate clearly the American attitude toward Native language and culture. For Jones, Tlingit was a "stunted and dwarfed language," one inadequate for widening intellectual horizons and useless for communicating with whites. The Tlingits "have no written language. Their totemic emblems are the nearest . . . to it." He admits that the language does get passed on orally, concedes that "the Native is never at a loss to express himself in his own tongue," but feels that scarcely a sentence is spoken "in which a peculiar and distressing guttural does not appear."

It is not necessary to debate the merit of these arguments, which were widely shared among American educators in Alaska at the time, and still are, for that matter, in some areas. The important point is that the *bilingual* option was never raised as a viable alternative—that is, *adding* English to the Native language and striving for dual competence. There is no evidence at all that Russian was ever forced upon Alaska Natives at the expense of or to the exclusion of their own language. Obviously there was "Russification." Many Natives learned Russian and some still speak it fluently. But the educational policies were bilingual. Many homes were bilingual (through intermarriage) but most were probably Native-language only.

The consequences of such a drastic revision in public policy toward the Native people of the territory may best be understood in terms of the effect on the Aleuts. During the height of John Veniaminov's work among these people a flowering of local culture had taken place, stemming in large measure from the emphasis placed on Native language literacy in the Russian Orthodox missionary effort. Yakov Netsvetov, for example, was an Aleut born in Atka, where he began to serve as a priest in 1828. In 1842 he was transferred to the Central Yupik area, where he designed a Yupik writing system and translated the first church books into Yupik.

Netsvetov was not only bilingual in Russian and Aleut but learned Yupik as well. Primarily known as an author and translator of Yupik books, he also wrote some Atkan texts and is probably the author of an anonymous Russian-Aleut dictionary, the largest Alaska Native language dictionary of the nineteenth century. Netsvetov's work is indicative of the vitality enjoyed by Native languages during the period of Russian control. Sheldon Jackson himself noted in 1886 that half the population of Unalaska was literate in Aleut. Around the turn of the century, there was even a trilingual newspaper published in Unalaska, with articles in Aleut, Russian, and English.

The experience of the Aleuts epitomized what happened to other Alaskan Native groups after the coming of the Americans. American missionaries embarking upon the great crusade of conversion and education discovered the Aleuts to be not the anticipated stereotype but highly literate Christians with a longstanding tradition of Native clergy. Unfortunately, it was the wrong kind of Christianity and the wrong (Cyrillic) alphabet.

Attempts to suppress Russian and Aleut met with limited success, in fact. Contemporary reports touching upon the progress in promoting English sound a consistent theme, namely that the policies weren't working. Instructors attacked various attempts at reinforcing the Aleut and Russian their students already knew, efforts they held responsible for the lack of progress:

> There has been one day of each week devoted to the Russian school which, in my opinion, has a bad effect upon the children in their attempt to master the English tongue, and I therefore, respectfully suggest that the practice of teaching Russian to the school children be abolished.

Or:

> One of the most serious obstacles in the way of American schools has been and is now, the demand by the church that all her children learn Russian so as to understand the church services. Consequently, a great deal of time is wasted in teaching or attempting to teach, the children two languages. . . . It is not that the average native child is dull or stupid, for he is not, but is because the child never hears English spoken except what he hears in the school.

Language suppression was enforced by many means. There are numerous accounts of physical punishment for speaking Aleut. Mouths were taped, knuckles rapped; one teacher reportedly swabbed students' tongues with a stinging solution. Even adults were verbally reprimanded for speaking Aleut in the presence of whites.

The immediate results were no better. The following is a typical report: "It seems incredible but it is true that young men and women who have been to school here for several years do not know how to speak or read a sentence of the English language. . . ."

Although these policies met with limited success at the start, the cumulative effects over the following sixty to one hundred years were disastrous to Native self-image and language survival. Where Russian culture and Orthodoxy led to a flowering of the literary arts, American culture and Calvinism had led most of the Native languages along the path of extinction beyond the point of no return. As for self-image, one often hears Natives say, "I'm just a dumb Native."

It is important to note two things here: many of the teachers could not tell the difference between Aleut and Russian, especially in written form, so discriminated against both languages. Around 1921 the U.S. government closed the Orthodox Church school on St. Paul Island by force. This was a significant act in what the Orthodox perceive as a government-sponsored and -supported campaign against Orthodox and Native culture in Alaska. The dark ages had settled over Alaska Native language and culture, and the suppression would continue without letup until the 1970s.

The Presbyterians and other American groups were not without scholars and translators who valued and studied Alaska Native languages. William A. Kelly and Frances H. Willard wrote a Tlingit grammar book that was fine by the standards of their day (1905), for example, and hymns were translated into Native languages in a number of instances. However, their efforts had no effect on general educational policy.

All Alaska Native peoples and languages have been subjected to the kinds of pressures and circumstances described above, with devastating results. The legacy is one of linguistic and cultural insecurity. In Alaska and nationwide, we are fighting the same issues we fought a hundred years ago. Irreparable damage has been done to the mental health of the Native communities and many individuals, and in fact to the white community as well, as all function in a very intricate language community.

Although the present format does not allow greater documentation and discussion of the intellectual history involved, this essay will serve its purpose well if it calls attention to choices at hand and points to the existence of values that modern western, secular culture may wish to emulate, not eradicate.

NOTE

1. Use of federal funds to bolster the budgets of mission schools was a common if questionable practice by the Bureau of Indian Affairs on Indian reservations in the American West, as was the hiring of missionary-teachers for government schools. Jackson imported this system into Alaska, although there were no traditional Indian reservations in the territory. The Department of the Interior ended the practice in response to Congressional pressure. See Francis Paul Prucha, *American Indian Policy in Crisis: Christian Reformers and the Indian, 1865–1900* (Norman: University of Oklahoma Press, 1976), 17, 247–49, 253. Segregation of public facilities for different races was institutionalized in the United States in the 1880s, a practice confirmed by the Supreme Court in *Plessy v. Ferguson* in 1896. Alaska's remoteness did not insulate the territory from this social development. As in the contiguous states, many schools in Alaska were integrated by the 1940s. In 1945 the territorial legislature passed an antidiscrimination act, barring discrimination on the basis of race (see the article by Terrence Cole in this anthology). In the 1980s, the State of Alaska agreed to provide high schools in all Native villages with a student population of fifteen or more, and state regulations provide for local school boards to develop policy for village schools. [Ed.]

SOURCES

For information on Veniaminov, see A. P. Kashevaroff, "Ivan Veniaminov, Innocent, Metropolitan of Moscow and Kolmna," *Orthodox Alaska* 6 (October 1977); R. N. DeArmond, ed., *Early Visitors to Southeastern Alaska* (Anchorage: Alaska Northwest Publishing, 1978); Paul D. Garrett, *St. Innocent: Apostle to America* (New York: St. Vladimir's Seminary Press, 1979).

I have traced the development of Aleut literacy in some detail in "Spiritual Epiphany of Aleut," *Orthodox Alaska 8* (January 1979): 13–42; see also the article by Lydia Black in this anthology. For more on Aleut, see Barbara Torrey, *Slaves of the Harvest* (St. Paul Island: Tanadgusix Corp., 1978); David Starr Jordan, *Seal and Salmon Fisheries and General Resources of Alaska. Reports on Conditions of Seal Life on the Pribilof Islands by Special Treasury Agents in Charge and Others from 1868–1895* (Washington, D.C.: Government Printing Office, 1898).

Authoritative and broadly useful is Ted C. Hinckley, *The Americanization of Alaska* (Palo Alto: Pacific Books, 1972); see also Hinckley's article on S. Hall Young in this anthology; a primary source on Jackson's thinking is his 1886 report, *Education in Alaska* (Washington, D.C.: Government Printing Office); for a devastating account of ethnocentrism in Alaska Native education, see Glenn Smith, "Education for the Natives of Alaska: The Work of the United States Bureau of Education, 1884–1931," *Journal of the West 6* (July 1967): 445–50.

The best general information to date for Alaska Native languages is Michael E. Krauss, *Alaska Native Languages: Past, Present and Future* (Fairbanks: Alaska Native Language Center Research Papers, No. 4, 1980).

For more on the development of parallel school systems, see Krauss, and also David S. Case, *The Special Relationship of Alaska Natives to the Federal Government* (Anchorage: Alaska Native Foundation, 1978); David H. Gretches, *Law and Alaska Native Education* (Fairbanks: CNER, University of Alaska, 1977), and Louis Jacquot, *Alaska Natives and Alaska Higher Education, 1960–1972: A Descriptive Study* (Alaska Native Human Resources Development Program, July 1974).

The Sale of Alaska in the Context of Russian American Relations in the Nineteenth Century

NIKOLAI N. BOLKHOVITINOV

Nikolai Bolkhovitinov is the dean of Russian historians who have studied interaction between Russia and the United States in the 19th century. In the 1970s and 1980s he headed a team of Russian historians who worked with American scholars to publish a multivolume documentary record of Russian American contacts.

The history of Russia's colony in America is a particular interest of Bolkhovitinov's. In 1991 he traveled to Anchorage to present the following paper at the symposium "Russian America: The Forgotten Frontier." Bolkhovitinov interprets the history of Russian American relations in the period as basically congenial. The sale of Russian America, he asserts, took place in an atmosphere of mutual friendship and support. Russia's need for currency and American goodwill were, according to Bolkhovitinov, important factors in the exchange.

Not all historians agree. Foremost among those who do not is Howard Kushner, who in his study, Conflict on the Northwest Coast: American Russian Rivalry in the Pacific Northwest, 1790–1867 *(Westport, Conn.: Greenwood Press, 1975), argued that persistent interloping by American fur traders along the coast, and particularly their penchant for trading rum and firearms to the Natives, soured contacts between the two contestants for sovereignty in the Northwest. Relations never recovered, Kushner asserted, from the American refusal to accept the czar's* ukase *of 1821 prohibiting foreign trading in Russian-claimed lands.*

While earlier historians of Russian America highlighted signs of friendship, including the visits of the Russian fleet to New York and San Francisco during the Civil War, more recent writers have emphasized America's economic imperialism, manifested not only in Seward's desire for Alaska, but in his interest in Hawaii and Greenland and the Virgin Islands as well. Bolkhovitinov's argument here offers a

This article appeared originally in *Pacifica* (Pacific Rim Studies Center, Alaska Pacific University) 2 (1990): 156–71; it is reprinted here by permission.

useful comparison with the conclusions of the current generation of North American scholars.

Portions of the original text of this article have been omitted by the editors.

The sale of Russian America has attracted the attention of both Soviet and foreign researchers for a long time. In 1939, the now deceased Professor S. B. Okun' published a monograph in which he gave, for the first time in Soviet literature, an adequately detailed and documented account of the general history of the Russian-American Company and the 1867 sale of Alaska. "It was impossible to preserve our colonies in case of war, it was impossible to protect them from the consequences of widespread rumors concerning the presence of gold there . . . and finally, there was a transfer of Russian interests to the Asian mainland —these were the reasons that nudged the tsar's government toward selling Alaska." The most significant factors, in Okun's opinion, were the awkward position of the Russian-American Company, which "was able to exist only with the support of the government," the serious financial problems of that government, and several international considerations. "Attempting to strike a blow against English power in North America and to force a collision between the United States and the British Empire, Russia decided to put Alaska up for sale. Yet, it was this drive for supremacy on the American continent that compelled the United States to acquire it."[1]

Later on, in a fundamental work, A. L. Narochnitskii offered a detailed interpretation of the expansion of European powers and the United States in the North Pacific, specifically the active involvement of the American traders, whalers, and smugglers in Russia's American possessions in the 1800s and 1860s. A small, and unfortunately, rather tendentious work about the American expansion into the North Pacific and the sale of Alaska was published by T. M. Batueva, while R. V. Makarova devoted an article to the history of the liquidation of the Russian-American Company.

A significant number of books and articles about Russian American relations and the sale of Alaska have been published outside the Soviet Union, particularly in the United States and Canada, as well as in Mexico and Japan.[2] As a result of successful international collaboration, a collection of articles was published in 1987 under the title, *Russia's American Colony,* which included papers by N. N. Bolkhovitinov, J. R. Gibson, and H. I. Kushner. This book contains a useful survey of new literature about the whole history of Russian America.[3]

Along with these serious works by scholars, unfortunately, there have also appeared derivative works frequently using invalid hypotheses and assumptions. For example, M. I. Belov published a jubilee article in 1967. Among the author's bold and interesting ideas, he suggests that "Alaska was sold by Russia fifty years before its official sale." However, he does not go so far as to provide detailed support for this assertion. He simultaneously offers overemotional and inadequately supported conclusions. He asserts, for example, that several people "within the tsar's entourage" had been bribed, that the Russian government "got involved in a dishonest deal" on account of the danger of war with the United States, and, finally, that "the initiative for selling Alaska, if one can put it so mildly, belonged completely to the United States of America."[4]

A weak acquaintance with the literature and sources is reflected in the popular works of A. I. Alekseev, particularly in the book *The Destiny of Russian America:* "neither notes nor preliminary protocols of the discussions have reached us," the author categorically asserts.

> We have found them neither in the personal archives of the Tsar nor in the archives of the chancellor, A. M. Gorchakov, who carried on negotiations regarding the sale of Alaska, one on one, eye to eye, without leaving any official documents. . . . Certainly, to reach such a decision was not at all simple: yet right up until the actual deed of sale, none of the government officials, nor any of the heads of the Russian-American Company had raised the question of selling Russian territories. But as with all these foreign policy affairs, the shortsighted tsarist government, pushed by the governments of the United States, England and France, arrived at this shameful decision.[5]

It is not at all clear in which archives Alekseev was working. If he had turned to the principal archives which preserve material on the Russian-American Company and Russian foreign policy, then without too much difficulty he would have discovered documents in the tens and hundreds. Among them are numerous documents concerning preliminary discussions on just this issue which occurred within the highest governmental circles of St. Petersburg and Washington, beginning as early as the 1850s, continuing throughout the course of the negotiations, and concluding with the signing of the treaty dated April 11 (March 30), 1867, in the American capital.

In addition, to comprehend the actual circumstances which led up to the conclusion of the 1867 treaty, it is not necessary to turn exclusively to archival documents. A large amount of important material has already been used by S. B. Okun' and Victor J. Farrar. Many documents have been introduced into scholarly circulation, published either in whole or in part, and are accessible to researchers on microfilm.

A weak knowledge of the sources, inaccuracies, which may at first glance seem harmless, mistakes, and unfounded assumptions, all lead the reader to an incorrect and even distorted understanding of the essential interrelationship between Russia and the United States in the North Pacific. It might even seem that informed people sometimes "construe" that the United States "actually forced" the tsarist government to conclude the treaty of 1867, and that "the doubtful character of the act is confirmed by archival material which points to bribery of several people having an influence on the tsar and all sorts of encouragements to conclude this treaty."[6] More than this, in the weekly publication *Abroad* (published in Moscow), A. Sergeev wrote about the 1867 treaty as an "act of thievery," concluded by a Belgian baron Stoeckl. "Opposed to this shameful and dishonest act was the eminent Russian navigator, Ferdinand Petrovich Wrangell."[7]

It is hardly worthwhile to consider similar pearls of bold journalistic opinion if they did not create completely distorted assumptions, about not only the fate of Alaska but all the history of Russian American relations. It is not mere chance that the editorial sections of newspapers and journals contain letters received from readers with questions. "When will it be time to take Alaska back?" "Will it be taken back gradually so that over the course of time 'the loan' will revert this territory?" [i.e., Russia's "loan" of Alaska will run out; ed.] Assertions also appear: "The treaty is a 'loan' that expires in the year 2000"; "it has a 'temporary character,'" and so on.

It turned out that the press was not entirely precise with the details but essentially gave a correct reply. "Russian America (now the state of Alaska) was sold by the tsarist government and not loaned; the treaty was not signed with a temporary intent but 'for all time.'"[8]

The clamor over this "act of thievery," in my opinion, not only distorts the character and sense of the events during the last century, but may also inflict direct damage on current relations between the Soviet Union and the United States.[9] An American journal has already published an article by M. I. Belov which cannot help but arouse distrust of the Soviet Union.[10]

At the same time, a completely objective and documented study of the history of the sale of Russian America could contribute to a mutual understanding and trust between both countries. It was with this particular aim in mind that I began the research on this problem in the early 1980s.

The academician, A. A. Guber, correctly identified the major difference between western European and imperial Russian colonial policy: the former was maritime, the latter was continental. The Far Eastern and the Pacific interests of Russian politics accordingly played an immeasurably lesser role at this time [i.e., 1867] and were subordinated to the general political situation in Europe. The influential tsarist expert, Count Ia. O. Lambert, emphasized as early as 1817 that, "in consequence of her geographic location, Russia was not destined to be a large developed marine power." She should treat the notion of increasing trade in the outlying areas, away from her main ports, with great circumspection. The conservative character of Russia's feudal-serf policies toward the Pacific and northwest America at this time is manifested in a number of ways: by the skeptical reaction toward P. Dobell's projects concerning the growth of trade ties between Kamchatka, Russian America, the Philippines, California, and Canton; by the refusal of a request by the "owner of the Sandwich Islands" Kaumuali'i, for Russian citizenship, and by the categorical refusal to support Georg A. Schaffer's proposal to annex the Hawaiian Islands in 1818 and 1819.

Those supporting the expansion of Russian influence in the Pacific basin and North America at the beginning of the 1820s (N. P. Rumiantsev, N. S. Mordvinov, I. B. Pestel', and others) gradually began to lose ground. On the opposing side were the more influential figures like K. V. Nesselrode and Ia. O. Lambert. Accordingly, conservative and protective tendencies began to dominate the Russian policy in northwest America, and for the most part, complaints from the Russian-American Company were given little attention.

The tsarist government and the Russian-American Company strongly disagreed during the signing of the conventions of 1824–1825, when the company, strengthened by the influence of Decembrists, specifically K. F. Ryleev, openly quarreled with the Department of Foreign Affairs. Numerous notes and protests were sent to the government, pointing out that the convention of April 5 (17), 1824, by granting the Americans free trade and fishing rights in the Russian possessions for a period of ten years, not only violated the privileges of the company but threatened its welfare and its very existence. In the summer of 1826, the leadership of the Russian-American Company once again requested intercession by asserting that "the company finds itself in such a dubious and even unfortunate position that not only its own existence is threatened but all the local areas mentioned above would face certain destruction."

All these protests and complaints encountered the resistance of the Department of Foreign Affairs, particularly K. V. Nesselrode, who maintained that the conventions of 1824–25 actually benefited the company because they established recognized borders for Russian possessions in America by international agreements. Free trade and navigation by foreign competition was limited to the ten-year period. Nesselrode reiterated this opinion in a wordy report to the tsar in the autumn of 1826. According to the agreement, the Americans themselves recognized that "over the course of several years, we will have the legal power to effectively prevent them from trading and fishing in this whole area," wrote the Minister of Foreign Affairs. To change the text of the conventions and "have it out politically" with the United States and England, Nesselrode not only considered premature, but thought it contrary "to the dignity of our court and to all the interests of the company itself."

As we see, despite the repeated complaints and protests, the Russian-American Company did not succeed in obtaining a reconsideration of the 1824–25 conventions. However, the company's firm position did have some impact. After the ten-year period expired, the unfavorable free trade conditions for the United States and England in Russian America were not continued. This occurred in the mid-1830s, after a lengthy, but ineffectual diplomatic correspondence that led to the well-known (although not very prolonged) reorientation of the Russian-American Company's relations with its foreign competitors.

One of the results of my research is the corroboration of a thesis regarding the expansionist character of United States politics (similar, by the way, to those of tsarist Russia), about which Soviet specialists were already writing in the 1950s, and which was developed in the works of radical American historians in the 1960s and 1970s.[11] Numerous documents in AVPR, the Central Archives in Moscow and Leningrad; material in the [U.S.] National Archives and the Library of Congress in Washington, D.C.; the papers of W. Seward, W. Gwin, and other American political figures; and representatives in business circles—all explicitly testify to

American expansionism in the North Pacific and Russian America's opposition to it.

But this is only one side of the question. The same archives and libraries contain many documents that demonstrate the mutually advantageous business ties between Russia and the United States and the cooperation of Russian *promyshlenniki* with the Boston whalers delivering American provisions to Russian America.

Which of these tendencies prevailed? There does not seem to be a single answer to this question. At the beginning of the 1820s and in the mid-1830s, opposition and rivalry intensified, threatening at times to seriously affect the relations between the two governments. During the mid-nineteenth century, United States whaling reached its height in the North Pacific. With the beginning of the Crimean War, on the other hand, fruitful business contacts and joint ventures were enriched and intensified. Americans brought war munitions, provisions, sea vessels, and a variety of equipment to Russian America, to Kamchatka, and to the Amur region. During the years of the American Civil War (1861–65), the United States was not particularly interested in foreign expansion. G. V. Fox's triumphant mission to Russia in the summer of 1866 was the culmination of Russian American rapprochement. It was during this time that Alaska and Siberia entered into a joint venture to construct a telegraph line to connect Europe and America. It was precisely at this time that the decision was made to sell Russian possessions in America to the United States, during a special meeting which took place on December 16 (28), 1866, and in which Emperor Alexander, I. A. M. Gorchakov, Grand Prince Konstantin, M. Kh. Reutern, H. K. Krabbe, and E. A. Stoeckl participated.

When discussing the reasons for the sale, allusions are often made to the difficult situation of the Russian-American Company. Documents testify that the company's position was indeed difficult but not critical. The decision to prolong the company's period of operation had essentially been made, and the government decided to accept the responsibility of providing it financial assistance. More important, though not the deciding factor, was the external threat to the colony and the impossibility of defending it in the event of war.[12] Although United States expansion was more a potential threat than a real one, Russia undoubtedly took this into account.

From these documents, it is obvious that the main reasons were to eliminate a potential hotbed of future conflict, to consolidate a true alliance between the two countries, and to redirect Russian attention to strengthening its position in the Far East (particularly in the Amur River region).

Other more general causes which were closing the future of Russian America: the remnants of a serf system, the smallness of the Russian population in the colonies (maintained at between six hundred and eight hundred people), the Indian factor, the independence of the Tlingits, and so forth. These general causes, however, are not specifically discussed in the documents of the "special meeting."

Neither contemporary nor earlier researchers have turned their attention to the fact that Russia, by yielding its ownership to the United States, turned out to be the first European power to actually relinquish its overseas colonies voluntarily. In connection with this, it is interesting to recall that in 1780, Catherine II, while rejecting a request from G. Shelikhov and I. Golikov, had emphasized, "The examples of American settlements were not flattering, and moreover not advantageous for the motherland. . . . A great dispersion into the Pacific will not be beneficial." To trade is one thing, "but to take possession is another." The long-held idea of a continental and not a maritime future for Russia, the rejection of annexation of distant overseas territories, and the concentration on strengthening her position in the Far East, Siberia, and Central Asia acquired, in the long term, a greater meaning. In the mid-1860s, these ideas found expression in the decision to sell Russian America to the United States.

The mission of G. V. Fox to Russia in the summer of 1866 and the subsequent sale of Alaska in the spring of 1867 gave rise to many rumors about the unusual Russian American rapprochement, even suggestions of an alliance. In Russia, delays in the United States payment temporarily cooled the ardor of the overenthusiastic proponents of such an alliance. Speculation about an alliance soon resumed. During the course of debates in Congress, there were many allusions to the friendly position of Russia during the years of the American Civil War. In July of 1868, almost simultaneously with the disbursement of the funds for the purchase of Alaska, the imperial palace decided to ask the president to hasten the revocation of all obstacles "for the passage of trade and war vessels through the straits."[13] (This was one of the main goals of Russian foreign policy after the Paris Peace Conference in 1856.)

In August of 1867, the visiting United States squadron, commanded by Admiral David Farragut, was joyously welcomed in St. Petersburg. Within one year, Admiral Farragut, on the flagship *Franklin,* received permission to cross the Black Sea straits. It is interesting that the American sailors greeted the Russian ambassador in Constantinople, Count N. P. Ignattev, with particular affection. He, in turn, held a reception in honor of the famous American admiral. It was precisely these events (the decision of the House to grant the request for free passage through the Bosphorous and Dardanelles and the visit of Admiral Farragut to Constantinople) that the American consul in Moscow, E. Schuyler, singled out when he mentioned the growth in Russian amicability toward the United States.[14] Once again, articles appeared in the press about a Russian-American alliance.

It is significant that, in its September 1868 issue, the magazine *Dirzhevye Vedomost* (*Exchange Gazette*) featured a comprehensive article about the traditions and perspectives of Russian American relations. Reviewing the fundamental landmarks of the two countries' relations since the Crimean War, this influential organ of Russian business circles came to the conclusion that "rapprochement between Russia and North America, these two colossi on either side of the ocean, was not only possible but also in both their best interests."

The magazine ranked the "goodwill concession" of the sale of Russian possessions to the United States "the most important and successful act by our government in the area of external politics." As a result, Russia "lost little of her political importance, her prestige," but took the "first step toward a Russian-American alliance," a step which "eliminated every cause for future conflict which might have arisen between Russia and the United States." The article concludes, "In the whole world we know of no other two governments which would be able to arrive at a means for promoting coexistence between themselves, in friendship and in union, as Russia and the United States of North America and for this reason, this union serves with a guaranty of true civilized progress for each of these powers."[15]

Now it is hardly necessary to argue with the optimistic evaluation and charitable hopes of the *Exchange Register* editorial. A more sober judgment was expressed by one of a few principal opponents to the sale of Russian America, P. N. Golovin: "Regarding the strengthening of friendly relations between Russia and the United States, it can be said positively that the sympathy of Americans toward us will continue as long as they are not obliged to do something and it continues to be advantageous; the Americans will never sacrifice their interests for simple convictions."

Although the old myth about the existence of a Russian American alliance is longstanding, it seems necessary to reject it decisively, since I do not agree with the widespread opinion in the literature about the serious break which allegedly occurred in Russian American relations after 1867.[16] Professor Gaddis, the father of contemporary postrevisionists, characterizes the period after 1867 as a time of intensification of opposition and "diverging interests" in contrast to the "heritage of harmony" of 1781 to 1867. He observes that "the good relations" during the first half of the nineteenth century were determined by "the absence of conflicting interests" and the existence of a common competitor, Great Britain; these gave way to an intensification of competitiveness in the Far East and Manchuria. "Ideology began to make a difference; questions began to be raised as to whether democracy could, or should, maintain friendly relations with the most autocratic nation in Europe."[17]

So it was that in the last years of the nineteenth century the general arrangement of powers in the international arena began to change, and there can be no doubt that disagreements between Russia and the United States began to intensify gradually. Incidentally, the period before 1867 was not only characterized as a time of "harmony," but also one of colliding interests, disagreements, and even conflicts (specifically in the northwest of America). Even the sale of Alaska was partly a result of these disagreements. For a time, at least, it had eliminated or assuaged these difficulties (if the whole of the North Pacific is taken into consideration). In any case, it is quite impossible to assert that after 1867 these conflicts grew. Ideological conflicts had existed for a long time before 1867. The reforms of the 1860s to some extent mitigated them but they were not eliminated.

In his book, G. P. Kuropiatnik demonstrates that the relations between Russia and the United States remained highly favorable in the 1870s, particularly during the period of the eastern crisis and Russo-Turkish war of 1877–78.[18] At the turn of the 1870s to 1880s, in the opinion of the author,

> The active cooperation of the two countries came to an end. It was no longer possible to overshadow the differences, pretensions and series of unpleasant incidents. Another phase had begun, when the growth of Russian American relations was, for the most part, determined by, the new social strengths of the two bourgeois governments, gradually transforming them into imperialist powers.

Quite definitely, revived conflict between Russia and the United States, first in Manchuria and then in the Far East, was already apparent at the end of the nineteenth century and the beginning of the twentieth.

But even during these years, both countries retained old features in their relationship. They continued successfully to develop social-political, trade, scientific, and cultural contacts. In the last ten years of the nineteenth to the beginning of the twentieth, there was a sharp increase in emigration from Russia to the United States, but all this is too far removed from our theme to deal with it effectively at this time.

The historic significance of the 1867 treaty rests first in the fact that it served as a basis for the formation of Russia's Asiatic–Pacific Ocean borders, which are roughly unchanged to this day. The treaty eliminated any foundation for claims or disagreements regarding territorial questions and established a basis for cooperation and not conflict in the North Pacific.

The timeliness of the study of the Pacific Ocean aspect of Russian American relations is also connected with one more event—the 500th anniversary of the discovery of America by Columbus (1492). It should be kept in mind that representatives of various countries have participated in the discovery and opening up of America—Spain, Portugal, England, Holland, and France. To Russia belongs the credit of discovery and penetration into the northwest part ot the American continent. Incidentally, 1991 marks the 250th anniversary of the V. Bering–A. Chirikov expedition (1741) that, in effect, began the actual opening up of the northwest part of North America. Outer space is being studied today through international efforts. In a similar way, American mainlands were also opened up and made known by representatives of various countries and peoples; it is not chance that on the ground of North America, in its time, there existed New Spain, New England, New France, and, subsequently, Russian America. The discovery and colonization of America was not a single event, but a lengthy process.

The final stage of this process began at the end of the eighteenth and the first part of the nineteenth century when, on the western shores of North America (California and Oregon), several colonizing clans met—the Russians from the North, the Spanish from the South, the Americans and English from the east. This powerful process was completed when the United States claimed the firmest position on the Pacific seacoast of North America.

NOTES

1. Translated from the Russian by Mina A. Jacobs, Anchorage, Alaska. The basis of this paper is taken from the book by the author entitled *Russian-American Relations and the Sale of Alaska, 1834–1867* (Moscow: Nauka, 1990); S. B. Okun', *Rossiisko-amerikanskaia kompaniia* (Moscow and Leningrad, 1939), 234–35, 242; and others.

2. R. J. Jensen, *The Alaska Purchase and Russian-American Relations* (Seattle, 1975); H. I. Kushner, *Conflict on the Northwest Coast: American Russian Rivalry in the Pacific Northwest, 1790–1867* (Westport, 1975); D. H Miller, *The Alaska Treaty* (Kingston, 1981).

3. S. Frederick Starr, ed., *Russia's American Colony* (Durham: Duke University Press, 1967); see also the proceedings of the 2nd International Conference on Russian American History (Sitka, 1988), *Russia in North America* (Kingston: Limestone Press, 1988), ed. Richard A. Pierce, and papers from the Anchorage symposium, *Russian America: The Forgotten Frontier* (Tacoma: Washington State Historical Society, 1990), ed. Barbara Sweetland Smith and Redmond Barnett, and *Pacifica* 2 (November 1990), ed. Robert D. Craig.

4. Belov's study was published in Moscow in 1982; it has not been translated into English.

5. This work of Alekseev, published in Magadan in 1975, has not been translated into English.

6. That the U.S. forced the treaty was suggested in a 1986 work by G. Voitolovskii, published in Moscow. On charges of bribery associated with the passage of the treaty and the appropriation of the funds for it by Congress, see Paul S. Holbo, *Tarnished Expansion: The Alaska Scandal, the Press, and Congress, 1867–1871* (Knoxville: University of Tennessee Press, 1983).

7. Eduard von Stoeckl was the Russian (not Belgian) minister to the United States who negotiated the treaty with U.S. Secretary of State William Seward. Baron Ferdinand von Wrangell served as governor of Russian America, 1830–35; though a naval officer, he was not known particularly as a navigator.

8. Readers might compare these populist assertions in the Russian popular press with claims in the Alaskan press that Alaska was taken from Alaskans by the federal government in violation of the U.S. Constitution, or that the federal government does not have the constitutional authority to establish environmental regulations for Alaska, or that Congress has broken the "statehood compact" with Alaska.

9. This article was written before the dissolution of the former Soviet Union.

10. M. I. Belov, "Sale of Alaska," *Alaska Review* (Spring-Summer 1967): 3–19; H. R. Huttenbach, "Sale of Alaska: Reply to a Soviet Commentary," *Alaska Review* (Spring-Summer 1970): 33–4. *Alaska Review* was published at Alaska Methodist University, 1967–70. Belov's article argued that the United States threatened war if Russia did not sell Russian America, an assertion not supported by the documentary record.

11. William Appleman Williams, *The Roots of Modern American Empire* (New York, 1964); Walter LaFeber, *The New Empire: An Interpretation of American Expan-*

sion, 1860–1898 (Ithaca, 1963); E. V. Paolino, *The Foundation of the American Empire: William Henry Seward and U.S. Foreign Policy* (Ithaca, 1973); and Kushner, *Conflict on the Northwest Coast.*

12. In addition it became known that gold had been discovered in northwestern North America. The Russian-American Company was left with practically no means to protect its posssessions from the invasion of foreign adventurers. See Okun', 230–34.

13. *Congressional Globe* (the official U.S. Congressional record), 40th Congress, Second Session (July 6, 1868), 3764.

14. R. J. Jensen, 133–34; E. Schuyler to W. Seward, September 19, 1868, No. 39, NARS (National Archives and Record Service, Washington, D.C.) RG 59. CD (Diplomatic Correspondence), 1867, Central State Archives, Moscow, roll 1.

15. E. Schuyler was particularly interested in this article. He had an English translation made of it and sent it to W. Seward. See E. Schuyler to W. Seward, September 29, 1868, No. 39, NARS, RG 59, Moscow, r. 1.

16. E. H. Zabriskie, *American-Russian Rivalry in the Far East* (Philadelphia, 1946); E. J. Carrol, "The Foreign Relations of the United States with Tsarist Russia, 1867–1900," doctoral dissertation, Georgetown University, 1953); J. L. Gaddis, *Russia, The Soviet Union and the United States: An Interpretive History* (New York, 1978); and others.

17. Gaddis, *Russia,* 27.

18. Kuropiatnik's book was published in Moscow in 1981 and has not been translated into English.

American Public Opinion and the Purchase of Russian America

RICHARD E. WELCH, JR.

It has been accepted as axiomatic by writers of American history that the purchase of Alaska was unpopular. Terms such as "Icebergia," "Walrussia," and "Seward's Folly" have been repeated from newspapers of the time to suggest that Americans thought the territory was a land of perpetual ice and snow and that it was worthless. Several often-reprinted editorial cartoons of the era have contributed to the familiar interpretation.

There is significant evidence that the purchase was not as unpopular as the traditional interpretation holds. There was in fact a considerable body of accurate information on Alaska available in 1867, collected by observers and scientists from several nations over the years, including the U.S. Moreover, Alaska was purchased by treaty. A treaty does not become law under the U.S. Constitution unless ratified by a two-thirds majority of the Senate. Supporters of the Alaska Treaty, most particularly the chairman of the Senate Foreign Relations Committee, Charles Sumner of Massachusetts, obtained the necessary vote on the first try, when the count was 27 to 12. The final official tally was 37 to 2. Sumner's speech to the Senate on the day of the vote shows that he was quite familiar with real Alaska conditions. America was in an expansionist mood at the time, and William Seward was a generally popular Secretary of State. It should not be surprising, therefore, that despite the fact that Alaska was the first noncontiguous acquisition of the U.S., the two-thirds majority was fairly handily obtained.

Why, then, has the myth of unpopularity been so persistent? It is partly because of a general ignorance about Alaska on the part of most Americans, including the writers of general textbooks. But also, there was considerably more enthusiasm in Congress for the notion of purchasing Alaska than there was for spending the money necessary to administer it, to which there was significant opposition. Also, at the very time of the purchase, Congress was involved in two of

This article appeared originally in *American Slavic and East European Review* 17 (1958): 481–94; it is reprinted here by permission.

the most significant constitutional crises in American history, southern Reconstruction and the impeachment of Andrew Johnson, leading to much acrimonious criticism of the executive branch.

Over three decades ago Professor Richard Welch of the History Department at Lafayette College in Pennsylvania surveyed the major newspapers in the U.S. at the time of the purchase. He found that nearly all of them either supported the purchase editorially or at least did not oppose it. We reprint Welch's article here, as Morgan Sherwood did in 1967, in the hope that it will raise awareness concerning the complex nature of the reaction to the Alaska Purchase and lay to rest "once and for all" the traditional myth.

Students should note also a more recent analysis of the charges of bribery associated with the Alaska purchase, Paul Holbo's Tarnished Expansion: The Alaska Scandal, the Press, and Congress, 1867–1871 *(Knoxville: University of Tennessee Press, 1983).*

The American purchase of Alaska from Russia in 1867 is often cited today as an example of providential intervention in behalf of America's national security. Commentators shudder at the thought of Soviet air bases in what was once Russian America and praise the near-miraculous foresight of Secretary of State William Seward.

Constituting as it does the only real estate transaction ever completed by Russia and America, Seward's annexation of Alaska properly holds a rather unique place in the diplomatic annals of both countries. The tendency of textbook writers to overdramatize the role of Providence and to imply that Seward alone saw the value of Russian America is, however, both mistaken and unfortunate.[1] It tends to make the Alaska Treaty of 1867 the mysterious property of a single individual, a thing foisted on the American people and accepted by them, reluctantly, only from a sense of obligation to Russia for her supposed aid to the Union government during the Civil War. It is possibly congenial to our current self-esteem to believe that only in our generation have Americans appreciated the value of American ownership of Alaska. Such a view, if gratifying, is incorrect. Contemporary public opinion—as reflected in the newspapers of the day—was far from universally opposed to our purchase of Alaska.[2]

The initial response of certain newspapers, upon hearing of the unexpected transaction, was one of some bewilderment. But the editorial mind of many journalists was soon affected by the March 30th dispatch of the Associated Press, by the quantities of information eagerly supplied by the State Department, or by a reasoned weighing of the increasingly available evidence. Each of these influences requires perhaps a brief explanation.

The March 30th dispatch of the Associated Press was a lengthy account, relating the existence of the treaty, its chief provisions, and its supposed origin.[3] It was not dictated by Secretary Seward, but he was certainly its anonymous, responsible source. The dispatch implied that the Johnson Administration, inspired by a concern for the economic welfare of our citizens in Washington Territory, was solely responsible for initiating the treaty. The implication was clear. If this treaty was rejected, the innocent and obliging Russian Emperor would consider himself insulted and betrayed, and let all remember that Alexander II was the one European monarch who had "befriended" the United States during the Civil War.

The influence of the State Department on the American press, in general, though apparent, was not conclusive. Surely Secretary Seward "planted" some information and made available to the press certain letters he had received,[4] various official scientific reports, and copies of Charles Sumner's eloquent speech in the Senate; surely all the information so distributed was favorable to the purchase. This need neither surprise the historian, however, nor give rise to the assumption that the press was bribed or controlled by Secretary Seward. Charges current at the time, and later, that vast sums of government money were expended by Seward to subsidize large portions of the press seem definitely unfounded. What Seward termed his "education campaign" was neither extravagant nor illegal; indeed, it has perhaps been rather overemphasized by certain writers. Indirectly, this educational campaign influenced both congressional approval and the acquiescence of a large part of the articulate public. It did not alone create this approval and acquiescence. Any belief in Seward's omnipotence is perhaps disproved by the fate of the Secretary's West Indian project.

For the purpose of this paper the *extent* of Seward's influence on the press is somewhat irrelevant. It is with the opinions and given reasons of American journalists that we are concerned; whether they obtained these opinions and reasons from prepared releases or original research is relatively unimportant.

The press was not dependent for information on Alaska solely from Secretary Seward, in any case. It is quite erroneous to believe that Alaska was *terra incognita* for all Americans in March 1867. Not only had New England whalers brought back news of seal furs and walrus ivory, as well as sperm oil and ambergris, but the mishaps of the Perry Collins–Western Union Telegraph project, and the exploits of the "Rebel pirate" *Shenandoah* had acquainted various Americans with Alaska's existence. Moreover, after March 1867, information on Alaska increased considerably, thanks to the reports of the combined coast survey–scientific expedition sent out by the government in 1867; the research efforts of Professors Baird, Bannister, and Henry of the Smithsonian Institution; the literary labors of Fredrick Whymper, artist of the ill-fated "Telegraph Expedition"; and the "Alaskan lectures" of the indefatigable William H. Dall.

Editors would also, of course, consult local leaders whose views would reflect local economic interests. New England papers, for example, mentioned the whalers of New Bedford; West Coast papers, the needs and desires of Louis Goldstone and the California fur traders.[5]

Because the initial bewilderment of many papers was overcome by second thoughts and growing information, one must not accept the first editorial comment as the considered judgment of a paper; neither must one confuse a touch of good-natured raillery with confirmed antagonism. The walrus and the polar bear lent themselves to jest and remarks of supposed wit, and even many pro-Alaska editors could not resist a facetious comment or two. James Gordon Bennett of the New York *Herald* favored the treaty but could not forbear to print certain editor-manufactured advertisements to the effect that any impoverished European monarch who wanted to sell worthless territory "should apply to W. H. Seward, State Department, Washington, D.C."[6]

The forty-eight newspapers consulted (for the months of April 1867 and July 1868) constitute, it is believed, a reasonably representative sample, geographically and politically. Most of the quotations will be found to carry an April 1867 dateline. Very few editors seem to have taken the trouble to express any real interest in the House proceedings of July 1868, when the appropriation bill was debated. This can perhaps be accounted for on the grounds that the physical transfer of the territory was then an accomplished fact and the presidential campaign of 1868 well under way.

The papers consulted will be divided geographically. Chief concentration will be placed on the Eastern newspaper capitals of Boston, New York, and Philadelphia, and for all sections only those papers will be mentioned which offered opinionated editorial comment concerning the Alaska Purchase.

The Boston press was almost uniformly favorable to the purchase, evincing no trace of fear that the Alaskan fishing grounds would affect adversely New England interests in the North Atlantic fisheries. The Boston *Herald* (moderate Republican) of April 11, 1867, declared, regarding Alaska, that

> those who know most about it, estimate it most highly. The climate on the Pacific side [at that latitude] is not to be compared to that on the Atlantic side of the continent. . . . The country is reported to abound in furs, forest, and minerals, while its rivers and bays on its coast swarm with as fine fish as ever were caught. [Alaskan timber] will be particularly valuable in the development of our domain on the Pacific coast and the commerce of the Pacific which has just been entered upon. As to the price, there can be but one opinion—it is dog cheap.

The Boston *Daily Evening Transcript* (April 3, 1867) emphasized "the great value and growing importance of our fisheries, both for whale and cod, in the waters of the North Pacific." Though by no means ardent in its favor of the purchase, the *Transcript* seemed to think Alaska a reasonably good buy at $7,200,000. It had not changed its mind fifteen months later, though it expressed shock at the rumors that only four of the seven millions would reach Russian soil.[7]

The Boston *Advertiser* (Democratic) warned that the "treaty is not a matter to be dismissed lightly in ignorance." There was involved "the great whale fishery of the Northern Pacific and of Behring Straits, in which Massachusetts is so deeply interested." The western tip of Alaska, moreover, would provide a commanding naval station (April 6). A letter to the editor (April 9) declared that the Aleutian Islands would make fine coaling stations between our country and China, and that the products of India would soon be flowing across the Pacific to America, in ever-mounting quantities.

The Republican *Daily Evening Traveller* gloated over the supposed excitement the purchase had caused among the British, and editorialized to the effect that Alaska's "chief value is now its fur trade and its fisheries; but . . . of vastly more importance than all other things, will be the command it will give us of the western and the northwestern territory of this continent." This paper could not resist mocking (April 12) the "great change [that] has come over the American mind with respect to Russian America. Everybody is looking at Russian America, and it is discovered that that country, which *once* was scarcely supposed fit for the presence of civilized men, is one of the finest parts of the globe." The *Traveller*, however, by no means condemned the turn the public mind had taken. "It deserves praise rather than censure." Whether the bargain would be a good or bad one would depend in the final analysis on the use that should be made by America of the acquisition. "The change in Russian America, there is reason to hope and expect, will prove as great as that which within living memory has taken place in the country purchased from Napoleon."

The Boston *Journal* (Republican) made little editorial comment on the purchase, but its Washington correspondent proclaimed that Sitka would follow the example of San Francisco, and in ten years would be a city of 50,000 persons.

The leading northern New England papers of the period were the Bangor (Maine) *Daily Times* and the Manchester (New Hampshire) *Daily Union*. Though for a time rather neutral, both finally concluded that the purchase was a good thing. In the opinion of the editor of the *Daily Union* (Democratic), it was well worth seven millions "to get good boundaries like the Pacific and Arctic Oceans" (April 10). Of the seven New England papers consulted not one may be classified as an opponent of Alaskan annexation.

Among New York papers was the great journalistic opponent of the treaty, Horace Greeley's New York *Tribune* (then radical Republican). It opened fire on April 1 with a charge that the Administration was trying to divert attention from its domestic difficulties by plunging the country into foreign complications. Americans had no use for this territory and were putting "ourselves in the attitude of seeking ostentatiously the friendship of a power not friendly to England, and of contracting what is tantamount to an alliance for the sake of an affront."

By April 8 the *Tribune* was complaining that "national good will does not usually extend so far that one nation will sacrifice its interest merely to oblige another," and warning that Alaska was "territory on which Great Britain holds a virtual mortgage, and in which her fishermen and hunters will have equal rights with ours." On the following day the *Tribune* printed a story to the effect that Admiral Fox had once been told by Prince Gortchakoff that Russia would gladly *give* Alaska to the United States, just to be rid of it. The lobbying activities of Seward and his "Esquimaux ring" were steadily criticized by Greeley, and the Senate, when it ratified the treaty, was accused of land mania—"if it is at the North Pole, no matter" (April 10).

The *Tribune* initially expressed the hope that the House would refuse to appropriate the money to effect this hideously expensive and tax-burdensome folly, this acquisition of impossible "deserts of snow" (April 11); but by July 16, 1868, the paper was grandly conceding: "We have not felt justified in urging the House to refuse the acquisition appropriation. We believe it was advisable to pay the money. Having received it, we wish Russia would consent to receive back the territory as a free gift from the Republic."

Of the other New York papers only the *Independent* (April 18, 1867) and the *Sun* (July 1, 20, 1868) joined the *Tribune* in real opposition to the acquisition of Alaska. The *World, Commercial Advertiser, Times,* and *Herald* were all on the other side of the fence.

The New York *World* (Democratic) was increasingly favorable to the acquisition as the first week of April 1867 wore on. In its first editorial (April 1), it asked: "But have we done wisely in buying it? If estimated by what it is now, certainly no; if by what the purchase may hereafter lead to, perhaps yes." As an advocate of expansion the *World* was inclined to favor the treaty because, "it is an advancing step in that manifest destiny which is yet to give us British North America."

Twenty-four hours were sufficient to evoke other arguments in the treaty's favor. "The whaling merchants of New England and settlers in Oregon and California will no doubt find some way of profiting by the annexation. . . . Our commerce . . . ought pretty certainly to be benefited by the opening of ports along this extreme verge of the continent, and by the attendant expansion of the fur trade and the fisheries."[8]

The New York *Commercial Advertiser* (Democratic) was both pro-Seward and pro-treaty, and in the New York *Times* the purchase had one of its most influential advocates.

> While narrow minded political bigots have been exhausting all their resources in branding him [Seward] as a traitor to his party, he has been quietly pursuing great objects of permanent and paramount interest for his country. The main importance of this acquisition grows out of its bearing upon our future trade with Japan, China, and the other countries of Eastern Asia. . . . Reluctant as that body [the Senate] may be to accept even so great a boon as this from the hands of the President and Mr. Seward, its sense of public duty will constrain its ratification. (April 1)

With its next issue the *Times* was ready boldly to declare that the purchase was "a natural though perhaps unexpected consummation of negotiations dating back to the time of Monroe, and its tendency is to lessen the likelihood of 'further entanglements' by removing Russia from the diplomatic area so far as the future policy of this continent is concerned."[9] In later editorials it mentioned the undeveloped coal seams of the new territory, spoke of the possibilities of the Aleutian Islands as a naval station, and declared that seven million "was a mere bagatelle compared with the magnitude and importance of the acquisition" (April 8, 10).[10]

The New York *Herald* (Republican) favored the treaty mainly on grounds of international policy:

> Politically considered, however, this cession of Russian Alaska becomes a matter of great importance. It indicates the extent to which Russia is ready to carry out her "entente cordiale" with the United States . . . it places British possessions on the Pacific coast in the uncomfortable position of a hostile cockney with a watchful Yankee on each side of him. . . . [It is a] flank movement for this greater object [Canada] . . . we are satisfied that the proposed purchase from its political bearings will be at once approved by the public sentiment of the country and will, perhaps, be considered a bargain at seven million, simply as a speculation in fish oil and the fur business. (April 1)

The *Herald* was a sharp critic of the "pushing" tactics of Mr. Seward, however, and with reference to Seward's "promotional" dinner parties declared: "But with his Pennsylvania roast beef, his Virginia oysters, his smoked walrus from Bering Strait, his Esquimaux stews and ice, his California wines and Kentucky Bourbon, his seven million and the lobby, the undaunted Seward, perhaps, will best them yet" (April 9).

Despite such exercises in literary irony, the *Herald* was a treaty advocate. The leading paper in extracting names and quotes from the executive sessions of the Senate, and the first paper to publish the treaty text, the *Herald* was sure that this new empire, "in area more than twice the size of France," would prove valuable as a factor in the international scene and valuable, too, for its fisheries, whales, fur trade, and coal (April 12).

The New York Evening *Post* demonstrated an inexplicable example of editorial indecision. In its first edition of April 1, it declared that the territory was a "frozen, sterile, desert region . . . of no value present or prospective." In its second edition of the same date, it asserted: "The purchase of the Russian Territory is a step towards the retrieval of this blunder [the Oregon "Compromise" of 1846] not only by giving us the undisputed prominence on the American coast of the Pacific, but by pushing it out of the power of England to extend her territory in that quarter." The forests there were immensely valuable, its agricultural capabilities had never been developed, and, as for its fisheries, "the advantage of our whaling and fishing interest in these northern seas, in having always ports of their own country to run into, will develop its value with the advance of our population in the Pacific."

On April 8, however, the *Post* declared, "We hope the Senate will reject the proposed purchase." The next day it spoke in resigned tones of the acquisition and, on April 19, went so far as to make plans for the future of the various areas of Alaska when "the increase of population and of trade requires a division of the territory." The only thing that seems certain about the attitude of the *Post* is that it was neither decisively for or against the treaty. Of the seven New York papers which took a definite stand, four were, on balance, favorable to Alaskan annexation.

In Philadelphia the editor of the *Inquirer* (Republican) was a most ardent advocate of the purchase:

> [Alaska] might become very useful to any power having naval interests in the Pacific. . . . A time may come, when the possession of this territory will give us the command over the Pacific, which our extensive possessions there require. (April 1)
>
> If there is any value in the timber, furs, and fisheries of that region, and it must be great, the consideration of the cost of the territorial government is not worthy of a moment's thought. (April 8)

The *Inquirer's* Washington correspondent was equally enthusiastic over the territory's possibilities and spoke of the Pacific Coast's desire for Alaska and of the treaty's value in preserving the Union Party in the Far West. Numerous letters to the editor were published, all of them favorable to the purchase.

The Philadelphia *Ledger* (Democratic) was less decided in its support of the treaty but, despite some merriment over the possibilities of political elections among the polar bears (April 11), offered no real objection to the treaty. The expansionist-minded *North American Gazette* (Republican) also favored the results of Seward's latest project. Philadelphia, indeed, produced little or no journalistic opposition to Seward's treaty.

Moving South, the press of Washington, D.C., was generally favorable. The Washington *Evening Star* scouted the opposition to the treaty, jibing that it paralleled the foolish reluctance of some in 1803 to accept the Louisiana Purchase. It viewed the treaty as a proper piece of expansionism and dogmatically pronounced: "There are few full-blooded Americans who do not devoutly believe in the doctrine that this country is to absorb not only Russian America, but all the British possessions in North America" (December 21).

The *National Intelligencer* was equally convinced:

> The Russian possessions will secure us furs, fish and lumber in the greatest abundance to say nothing of the undisputed route of an overland telegraph. The fisheries, in the hands of our hardy seamen, would be of priceless value, and, as we are soon to have the Pacific railway, which will give an extraordinary impetus, we wonder that American statesmen should hesitate. (April 5)

The *National Republican* voiced its support in turn. In an editorial entitled, "Now is the Day and Hour for the Confirmation of the Treaty with Russia" (April 6), it lectured to the following effect: "American civilization has pushed itself through to the Pacific sea, where a commerce is growing up . . . which demands that the United States have absolute sovereignty over the entire coast from California to Bhering [*sic*] Straits." In listing various reasons for desiring the territory, the *National Republican* mentioned the protection it would afford U.S. fisheries and fishermen there, the splendid nature of the rivers and harbors of Russian America, the territory's use as a broad base of trade with Japan and China, and the chance it gave to fill out and protect the Continental Republic. The friendship of Russia was noted by way of further justification, and the warning given that "if we shall ever need the aid of any foreign power . . . it will be the immense and almost immaculate power of Russia" (April 8).

Whatever might have been the case when the purchase was before the House, it is most likely that John Forney's *Daily Morning Chronicle* was a free and unbribed agent in April 1867, quite uninfluenced by the labors of former Senator Robert Walker or the purse of Minister Stoeckl. In this early and "amateur" phase, the *Chronicle* heartily applauded the treaty, if not with the violence it was to exhibit later: "Our people have faith in the manifest destiny of the nation. They look to the eventual absorption of the whole North American continent, and the Senate has undoubtedly gratified a national instinct in ratifying the treaty" (April 11). The favor with which the *Chronicle* received this treaty is indicated by its quoting in full—and with marked approval—an editorial in the Rochester (New York) *Democrat,* which virtually eulogized the possibilities of the Alaskan territory.

The Wilmington (Delaware) *Daily Commercial* favored the acquisition of the territory, but opposed its purchase: "It seems to us the worst of policies, for it . . . is certainly to become ultimately the property of our Yankee nation, and we consider it fair to presume at a price next to nothing at all. If this were our last chance, and the lowest offer likely to be made, we might urge its acceptance" (April 4).

The Baltimore *Sun* (Democratic) and *American and Commercial Advertiser* (Republican) were not so economy-minded. The latter printed the highly favorable and nationally quoted Associated Press dispatch of March 31 as its first news of the treaty, and followed this up with a pair of editorials in which the value of the area's fisheries and fur trade was discussed at great length.

The *Daily Journal* of Wilmington, North Carolina approved the purchase only "in view of ulterior events." The expansion of the fur trade and whale fisheries on the Pacific Coast and the increased likelihood of garnering the British possessions in North America furnished such "events" (April 4).

The Louisville (Kentucky) *Daily Journal* favored the treaty, observing: "The great commercial advantages secured by it are universally admitted" (April 3). The Memphis *Daily Post* (moderate Republican) urged the purchase in these terms:

> In view of our growing commerce in the Pacific, the establishment of lines of steamers to run regularly between China, Japan, and Australia, the increase of the coastwise trade, the completion of the Pacific Railroad and the Russo-American telegraph . . . the acquisition of this vast possession is desirable, and seven millions of dollars is a small consideration to pay for it. (April 5)

The Memphis paper, however, reviled the manner in which Seward had "unscrupulously urged" the treaty and insisted that the actions of the Secretary and the President in this connection would further damn them in the eyes of the public (April 15).

The Washington dispatches of both the Savannah *Daily Republican* and the Augusta *Daily Press* included press releases, telegrams, and Seward-inspired "reports from Washington" highly favorable to the purchase.

Of the New Orleans papers the *Commercial Bulletin* seems to have been the most enthusiastic, virtually urging an alliance between the now-enlarged Northwest and the South:

> The demands for cotton goods in the new region of the Northwest will be enormous, and there is no reason why these goods should not be manufactured in the South, thereby employing our poor and industrious population, and adding greatly to our resources . . . it will be seen that the South will be greatly advanced by the acquisition and settlement of the Russian American possessions. (April 15)

The New Orleans *Times* and the newborn New Orleans *Republican* contained a large number of dispatches and letters favorable to the purchase, but *La Tribune de la Nouvelle-Orleans* had mild doubts about the value of the territory. It suspected that if the Russians were willing to shed the territory it must be of little value ("evidemment inutile aux Russes, elle ne peut pas etre d'un bien grand profit pour les Americains") (April 3).

The Galveston *Republican*, though making no editorial comment, printed at considerable length the panegyric on Alaska delivered by Representative Banks during the debate in the House (July 13). Of the sixteen Southern newspapers consulted, only two may be labeled outright opponents of the Alaska Purchase.

In the Middle West, the city of Chicago saw its two leading papers somewhat divided on the desirability of Alaska. The *Evening Journal* cheered the purchase without qualification of any kind, but the reaction of the *Republican* was less clear. The Washington correspondent of that paper was vehemently anti-treaty; its editor, tepidly favorable. The same issue of the *Republican* that found the correspondent calling the treaty a "huge farce" found the editor pontificating that it was "very natural that Russia and the United States should form an alliance. . . . Russia has demonstrated her good faith in this matter by ceding to our Government all her possessions on the American continent" (April 1). Even though the editor jocosely declared some four days later that the real reason for the purchase was to give the Fenians a base of operations, and even later (April 13) spoke of the danger of soon seeing in the House a representative from Sitka "dressed in a grizzly bear–skin overcoat and seal-skin unmentionables," the attitude of the paper seems to have been, on the whole, one of hesitant favor. "As evidence of the good will of the Russian Government toward the United States, this treaty has its chief significance. Future explorations may prove it to be rich in mines, while it will undoubtedly prove of increasing value to the Pacific states for its fisheries" (April 10).

The Cincinnati *Daily Gazette* rather opposed the purchase, but its sister paper, the *Commercial*, favored it. Other affirmative voices were those of the Detroit *Free Press* and the St. Louis *Times* and *Daily Missouri Democrat*. The latter stressed the wonderful effect of the Japanese current on the climate of Alaska and asserted that the acquisition "affords another perspective of Uncle Samuel's 'manifest destiny' to absorb the continent" (April 11).

The Alaska Treaty does not seem to have interested Midwestern editors to the extent it did those on the East and West coasts, but even the few examples given show that the press of this section was in no sense solidly opposed to the purchase.

What then can be said of the reaction of the press as a whole?[11] First, that all statements to the effect that the newspapers were uniformly unfavorable to the treaty are erroneous. Second, that, though the sample of newspapers consulted is perhaps too small to support any sweeping generalizations, it can be suggested that a majority of the American press seems either to have favored the treaty or at least not to have been opposed to it.[12] Third, that neither the political allegiance nor the geographic location of a newspaper was usually decisive in determining its stand. Finally, that the main arguments advanced by the press in support of the purchase, listed perhaps in order of increasing importance, were: the propriety of maintaining the friendship of Russia; the possibility that the purchase would facilitate the acquisition of British Columbia and generally promote our predestined expansion and power; and the probability that we should derive great economic benefits from the purchase.[13] "Russian friendship" and the "assistance" Russia gave the federal government during the Civil War was often mentioned by the American press, though usually as an auxiliary argument.[14]

Contemporary press opinion indicates that there was a good deal of latent expansionism in the United States in 1867. The Civil War had caused certain Americans to think for the first time of the desirability of such objects as naval and commercial bases, and that quasimystical doctrine Manifest Destiny had still its supporters. Belief in the inevitable and benevolent assimilation of North America by the politically and morally superior United States was nurtured in many an editorial heart and column. In so far as Manifest Destiny was basically an agrarian movement, the desire of certain Americans for Alaska was not an offshoot of Manifest Destiny. But Manifest Destiny also had its commercial side, and in this sense, the purchase was the vestigial remain of that nation-shaping doctrine. Certain papers emphasized the importance of Alaska's harbors for our Oriental trade, and more spoke of the necessity of checking British expansion and securing a favorable balance of power for the United States in the Pacific West. Various editors on the Pacific Coast went to far as to express hope that the purchase of Alaska, by putting British Columbia in "an American vice," would mean the ultimate acquisition of that choice and strategic area by the United States.[15]

The chief argument of those members of the press who supported the purchase, however, was that, in economic terms, Alaska was worth the purchase price. Because of its supposed resources in fish, whales, furs, timber, and minerals, because of its very real commercial value, Alaska was thought a good bargain.

Those were arguments and motives that could have clear appeal for the average educated American. Surely they were such as to deter press or public from howling in united chorus, "Seward's Folly!"

NOTES

1. One receives from many secondary accounts the impression that virtually the only American who did not think the acquisition a complete folly was Mr. Seward. That gentleman by lobbying and legerdemain somehow forced the United States to accept his treaty despite a solid hoot of derision from the American public. See, for example: Hubert Howe Bancroft, *History of Alaska* (San Francisco, 1890), vi; Henry Wadsworth Clark, *History of Alaska* (New York, 1930), 78–81; Asa E. Martin, *History of the United States* (Boston, 1931), II, 334; Foster Rhea Dulles, *America in the Pacific: A Century of Expansion*, 2d ed. (Boston, 1938), 83–88; R. E. Riegel; D. F. Long, *The American Story* (New York, 1955), I, 423; Oscar Handlin, *Chance or Destiny* (Boston, 1955), 119; H. U. Faulkner, *American Political and Social History*, 7th ed. (New York, 1957), 626. The last four works cited testify to the persistence of this view despite the provocative article by Thomas A. Bailey, "Why the United States Purchased Alaska," *Pacific Historical Review* 3 (1934): 39–49. Bailey sampled contemporary editorial opinion in six Pacific Coast newspapers and reached the conclusion that these newspapers were definitely favorable to the Alaskan Treaty. He admits, however, that geographic proximity and special commercial interests could have made opinion in the Far West a rather special case.

2. The measure to which newspaper opinion reflects public opinion must always be a point of dispute. It is surely a component part of the public opinion of

a period, and, to a degree, usually both influences and mirrors general contemporary opinion.

3. See in this connection Victor J. Farrar's excellent monograph, *The Annexation of Russian America* (Washington, 1937), 56–57.

4. U.S. Congress, 40th Cong. 2nd Sess., *House Exec. Doc.* #117, 6–109.

5. A group of California fur traders headed by Louis Goldstone had for some years envied the favored position which the Hudson's Bay Company enjoyed under charter in Russian America. Using Senator-elect Cornelius Cole of California as intermediary, they began in 1866 to negotiate with the Russian minister Stoeckl for the expiring rights of the British company. Baron Stoeckl led them on and, after they had made a formal request, made his refusal the opening wedge in his March 1867 talks with Seward.

6. New York *Herald*, April 12, 1867.

7. This is a reference to the old "mass bribery charge" that was well disposed of by William A. Dunning in 1912, but which still crops up on occasion. For the origins of this charge see the New York *Sun* of November 30, 1868, the Worcester *Spy* of December 4, 1868 (Worcester, Massachusetts), and Reports of the Committee on Public Expenditures, *House Reports* (40th Cong., 3d Sess.), #35; #1388. Dunning's article, "Paying for Alaska," is to be found in *Political Science Quarterly* 27 (1912): 385–98. See, also, Ellis P. Oberholtzer, *A History of the United States since the Civil War* (New York, 1917), I, 556; Reinhard L. Luthin, "The Sale of Alaska," *Slavonic and East European Review* 16 (1937): 168–82.

8. Though the *World* favored this extension of our boundaries, it was sufficiently anti-Seward to mock the arguments and methods used by the Secretary to help effect the purchase, and to mock the self-conflicting extravagances of the treaty advocates. "Tropical Disadvantages Offset by the Value of the Ice Trade—Secretary Seward's New Ice-othermal Line—A Great Opening for Soda-Water Fountains and Skating Ponds" ran the headline of April 9.

9. Like many Eastern papers, the *Times* printed large sections from Charles Sumner's famous and scholarly address in the Senate. Sumner's speech, incidentally, was most influential in producing the large pro-ratification majority in the Senate, and had probable influence as well on American press opinion.

10. The *Times* still strongly favored the purchase fifteen months later, but on abstract constitutional grounds agreed with the pretensions of the "House Constitutionalists" (July 15). A group of "House Constitutionalist" or "House Rights Men" succeeded initially in attaching to the Alaskan Appropriation Bill the Loughridge Amendment. By this amendment the House of Representatives asserted its right to be "previously consulted" respecting any future purchase of territory. It was but an exhibition of jealousy by the House over senatorial prerogative in treaty making, similar to that demonstrated in connection with the Jay Treaty. In both cases, the House had finally to give way. For the views of the House Constitutionalists see *Congressional Globe*, 40th Cong., 2d Sess., IV, 3621–25, 4052–55; V, 4392–94.

11. The writer has not made a sufficient study of contemporary periodical literature to warrant any overall conclusions in that area. Of the fifteen "national" periodicals consulted, however, only three expressed an editorial opinion adverse to the Alaska Purchase: *Leslie's Weekly*, the New York *Nation*, and *Harper's Weekly*.

12. Though there was much initial hesitation on the part of many editors to express a definite opinion, the statement of Theodore Clark Smith that "the bewildered comments of the newspaper press during the week when the treaty was pending indicate clearly the absence of any popular feeling for or against annexation" is a statement of doubtful validity. T. C. Smith, "Expansion After the Civil War, 1865–1871," *Political Science Quarterly* 16 (1901): 415.

13. These arguments were interestingly enough almost identical to those made in Congress during the ratification and appropriation debates. All can be found in Senator Sumner's speech (*House Exec. Doc.* #177, 124–88). In the House of Representatives see the speeches of Representatives Schenck and Banks on "Russian Friendship"; Representatives Orth, Donnelly, Maynard, Myers, Spalding, and Munger on "Expansion and British Columbia"; and Representatives Munger, Higby, Johnson, and Banks on "Economic Value." *Congressional Globe*, 40th Cong., 2d Sess., IV, 3625–27, 3659–60, 4054; and V, Appendix, 386–432. These arguments and motives also appear prominently in the private letters received by Senator Sumner in 1867 from such correspondents as Spencer Baird, G. V. Fox, John Rodgers, Major General Meigs, W. Beach Lawrence, John M. Forbes, and Louis Agassiz. Sumner Correspondence for the year 1867, *Sumner Papers*, Widener Library, Harvard University.

14. It was an argument and "motive," however. The statement of John G. Latane to the effect that the research of Frank A. Golder in the Moscow archives "leaves one with the impression that Russian friendship can no longer be considered an important factor in the purchase of Alaska" is erroneous. Golder's concern was the motives of Seward and the Johnson Administration, not public opinion and its inspiration. Myths have as much influence on public opinion as facts. Latane, *A History of American Foreign Policy* (New York, 1927), 424–25. Golder, "The Purchase of Alaska," *American Historical Review* 25 (1920): 411 ff., "The Russian Fleet and the Civil War," 20 (1915): 801 ff.

15. Bailey, "Why the United States Purchased Alaska." See, especially, Sacramento *Daily Union*, April 1, 1867; Seattle *Puget Sound Gazette*, April–May, 1867. See, too, Chicago *Evening Journal*, April 1, 1867.

"Hemmed In"

Reactions in British Columbia to the Purchase of Russian America

RICHARD E. NEUNHERZ

As Richard Welch noted in his work on the popularity of the purchase of Alaska, American newspapers which favored the purchase often suggested that the acquisition of Alaska might facilitate U.S. acquisition of British Columbia as well. Soon after the Alaska Purchase, William Henry Seward did in fact attempt to buy British Columbia, though unsuccessfully, motivated by his expansionist vision of America's future. The fact that many residents of British Columbia also favored annexation of the province to the United States is less well known.

Richard Neunherz received his Ph.D. at the University of Washington in 1975. In the following article, based on his dissertation, "The Purchase of Russian America: Reasons and Reactions," he examines the short-lived but strong annexationist movement in British Columbia. Not surprisingly, Neunherz found support for annexation to be strongest among United States citizens living in B.C. But economic hardship there and British Columbia's distance from other British North American colonies generated support among other people as well, particularly those who lived on Vancouver Island. Yet, as Neunherz demonstrates, the true extent of that support remains problematical.

The cession of Russian America to the United States in 1867 placed British Columbia in a precarious position. Flanked by Washington Territory to the south and Alaska to the north, the colony blocked direct land access between the U.S. and its new possession. The American republic, which had a deserved reputation for territorial aggression, had never before included noncontiguous continental lands within its domains. Consequently, many people assumed that British Columbia would soon be the target of Yankee expansion.

This article appeared originally in *Pacific Northwest Quarterly* 80 (July 1989): 101–11; it is reprinted here by permission.

Such a possibility had been foreseen by czarist advisers who had counseled Alexander II to sell Russian America. As an imperial rival of Great Britain in the Pacific, Russia would benefit from England's expulsion from British Columbia and its regional naval headquarters at Esquimalt on Vancouver Island. Edouard de Stoeckl, Russian minister to Washington and negotiator of the 1867 cession, had argued as early as 1860 that if the U.S. owned Russian America "British Oregon would be crowded on the northern side and on the southern side by the Americans and would escape with difficulty from their aggressions." The minister of finance, Mikhail Reutern, assured the czar that the sale would increase "the chances for a disagreement between the States and England." Prince Aleksander Gorchakov, minister of foreign affairs, believed that Britain had long feared such cession. In December 1866, he suggested that "this consideration is perhaps motive for us to cede our Colonies to the United States:—it is undoubtedly one for the Americans to acquire them."[1]

Numerous American journalists and politicians, unaware of the Russian view, came to similar conclusions. Approximately 45 percent of the newspapers that endorsed the purchase of Russian America expressed the belief that the acquisition would increase the probability of obtaining British Columbia. No records exist of the Senate's executive session deliberations on the treaty, but notes from the meetings of the Committee on Foreign Relations indicate that members discussed the possible impact on the colony. In the House of Representatives the topic repeatedly arose in the debate on the appropriation bill for the Alaska Purchase; 13 of the 31 addresses considered the effects of the purchase on British Columbia, and several speakers asserted that the transaction would hasten its annexation. Such expectations coincided with the territorial ambitions of William H. Seward, secretary of state, who for some months after the Russian treaty intrigued to acquire the English colony.[2]

Considering the belief held by many American and Russian leaders that the cession of Russian America had compromised British Columbia, questions naturally arise about what the colonists thought. How did British Columbians, particularly government officials and the press, react to the sale? Did they interpret the transaction as a menace to their British community? If so, did residents oppose the idea of an American absorption of their settlements, or did some view the possibility with ambivalence, even enthusiasm? Historians have largely ignored such questions and have failed to consider the existence of an annexation movement in 1867. Instead, they have focused on agitations in 1866 and especially

1869. Consequently, examination of the colonial response to the cession of Russian America should provide a fresh perspective on the annexation movement in British Columbia, as well as new information on the foreign impact of the American expansion.[3]

British Columbia, in the spring of 1867, faced serious problems that had clouded its future even before the announcement of the cession of Russian America. Not the least of these difficulties was the colony's physical isolation from other British territories. Bordered on the west by a vast and often violent sea and on the east by towering mountains, separated from the nascent Dominion of Canada by hundreds of miles of fortress escarpments, vacant plains, dense forests, and muskeg swamps, British Columbia occupied a vulnerable position because of its proximity to U.S. possessions. Great Britain, furthermore, lay too distant to provide effective military protection or economic support.

Confounding the problems of isolation, once prosperous British Columbia, by 1867, was mired in an economic depression companioned by a declining population, a growing discontent with the colonial government, a widening internal division between the island and mainland communities, and a deepening crisis of confidence. Gold production, the basis of the colony's economy, had decreased significantly, bank exports of the metal having fallen from $2,801,888 in 1864 to $1,996,580 in 1866. Other commercial activities—the fur trade, farming, fishing, coal mining, and lumbering—had failed to replace this loss. The dearth of exportable products meant that two of every three ships clearing colonial ports sailed in ballast. Other signs of the faltering economy were declining government revenues and consistently increasing expenditures. As a result, the colonial debt had risen steadily since 1860.[4]

As economic conditions worsened, hundreds of people emigrated. The non-Indian population, estimated at 13,624 in 1861, fell to 8,631 in 1866, as miners left to seek opportunities elsewhere and merchants who had supplied them shipped south in quest of new customers. The *Daily British Colonist and Victoria Chronicle,* the leading colonial newspaper, bemoaned the situation in a gloomy editorial in January 1867: "All leaving for other parts—mark! not by choice, but by the stern decrees of necessity, unable longer to find a living here."[5]

The government of British Columbia, both unpopular and largely undemocratic, lacked the resources and direction to combat the depression or stay the flight of discouraged people. Characterized as "a well-meaning, easy-going mediocrity," Governor Frederick Seymour, a crown officer, had neither the vision nor the energy to lead effectively. An appointed Executive Council and a partially elected Legislative Council rounded out a government thought by citizens to be wasteful, excessively bureaucratic, opposed to change, and dependent on burdensome taxes.[6]

An internal rift that set island against mainland exacerbated these problems. Joined in November 1866 by imperial fiat, the two portions of the colony remained suspicious of each other and especially antagonistic over the issue of the site of the capital. Although New Westminster on the mainland currently had the privilege, Victoria on Vancouver island had not given up agitating for a change.

In this season of discontent, some new course for the colony seemed mandatory. Since Great Britain had no intention of providing substantial economic assistance, only two viable options existed: annexation to the United States or confederation with Canada. Territorial proximity, the presence of many Americans in the colony, and trade and communications advantages made the first alternative attractive. Nevertheless, annexation had won few adherents. Instead, confederation had been gaining converts, despite the manifest geographic impediments; and on March 18, 1867, the Legislative Council unanimously endorsed the idea of union with Canada. At this moment, when a new direction had been charted, news of the Alaska Purchase arrived.[7]

The report reached Victoria by telegraph during the night of April 1, 1867, and it received a few lines in the next day's issue of the *Colonist.* On April 3, the editor, David Higgins, commented, "From a commercial point of view the establishment of a colony of energetic, go-ahead people . . . would certainly prove beneficial to us." He was less sanguine, however, in reviewing the political implications of the Russian cession, confessing alarm over "the strides that our American neighbor is making on all sides to hem in and cut off" the British North American possessions.

Other colonial journals also responded. The Nanaimo *Tribune* seized the moment to criticize England's treatment of British Columbia. An April 6 editorial described the colony as "struggling for a doubtful existence under the tutelage of a haughty dame, too proud and inattentive to consider our juvenile wants." The editor cautioned English officials that "our colony will be bounded north and south by a . . . people, whose protection and affiliation we may by and by prefer." The Victoria *Morning News,* edited by James McMillan, warned that the purchase was more important than people suspected, because it would lead to difficulties between the U.S. and Great Britain. Of the leading newspapers, only the

New Westminster *British Columbian,* mainland rival of the *Colonist* and acid critic of Vancouver Island politics and journals, initially ignored the cession except to print relevant dispatches.[8]

News of the treaty, Governor Seymour reported to the Colonial Office in London, had caused considerable excitement, especially in Victoria. U.S. citizens living there hailed the purchase, and on Tuesday, April 16, American merchants and tavern owners displayed their national flag to celebrate. A letter dated April 20 congratulating Seward on his achievement bore 22 signatures. In his own letter to the secretary of state, the United States consul in Victoria, Allen Francis, explained that every American offered the chance had signed.[9]

If the American residents were jubilant over the treaty, the English settlers were, according to Seymour, "somewhat despondent as to their future condition." Having United States territory north and south of the colony, he warned the home government, would "tend to strengthen the American sympathies felt by a considerable number of persons in Victoria." On the mainland, however, he believed that goodwill toward England predominated and that no excitement over the purchase existed, although the population was half foreign. An April 4 letter from Edward G. Alston, later a magistrate and member of the Legislative Council, reflects the concerns of some in the colony. Writing to a correspondent in eastern Canada, Alston confided that British Columbians felt "isolated from British sentiments"; having American territory "within ten miles of us to the south" and now to the north made them "feel more solitary and unprotected." William F. Tolmie, a chief factor of the Hudson's Bay Company (HBC) at Victoria and temporarily in charge of its Western Department, admitted in a dispatch to his superiors in London that the news "to us has been very unwelcome intelligence."[10]

Some people blamed Great Britain for the predicament in which the colony now found itself. John Etheridge, an HBC officer writing to London headquarters on April 2, observed that if the information about the cession proved reliable "it is a fitting consummation to the gross neglect and misgovernment which the British possessions here have received at the hands of the Imperial authorities." Later that month, Dr. John S. Helmcken, chief trader and surgeon for the company, stated that "Her Majesty's Government not only does not assist, but is believed to take no interest in this colony or pay any attention to its representations." Even the colonial attorney general, Sir Henry Crease, voiced frustration over England's neglect, asking, "How Cd. England let the States get Russian America?"[11]

The cession, according to the American consul, "may have created distrust" among British subjects, "but I do not think enmity." Within two weeks Francis noted that early doubts had given way to feelings of despair. The American expansion, he reported to Seward, had

> still further paralyzed their hopes and prospects,—and the poeple [sic], those claiming to be loyal subjects included, are now urging with great unanimity annexation to the United States, as the only solution—as the only means of retrieving the Colonies from their present embarrassment and decline. The spirit of annexation, with the exception of the officials and a solitary Press in the colonies favoring Confederation with the Canadas, is general and earnest.[12]

W. Carey Johnson of Oregon City, Oregon, noted similar reactions to the purchase. An attorney who specialized in land disputes, he was in Victoria as legal representative of Caleb Cushing, a prominent Republican and chief counsel for the U.S. government on the British and American Joint Commission on the Hudson's Bay and Puget Sound Agricultural Companies Claims. Returning home on April 24, Johnson informed the local newspaper that the treaty had been well received and the colonists "were more disposed to favor annexation . . . than ever." He also wrote Seward:

> I found that all the Irish, Germans, and other naturalized subjects of Her Majesty were most decidedly in favor of annexation. . . . The English and Scotch are extremely careful not to say or do anything which would subject them to imputations of disloyalty. But if . . . an expression could be called for with the consent of Her Majesty's Government, I have no doubt that a majority—of Englishmen and Scotchmen, resident in the Colony would vote directly in favor of annexation to the United States.[13]

These descriptions of the popular mood in British Columbia may appear exaggerated. Yet, though the two Americans hardly qualify as disinterested witnesses, both had access to prominent people, particularly those in government, Victoria businesses, and the HBC. Some of these individuals could have confided feelings about the cession and about annexation that they would not have expressed in public. When, on April 25, the *Colonist* reported more disturbing telegraphic news, Francis's and Johnson's assessments were soon verified. From New York came a report that the United States was negotiating for the purchase of the western part of British Columbia, including Vancouver Island. Only the American insistence that the *Alabama* claims be used to offset part of the price seemed to be delaying the bargain.

Reactions in the colony came swiftly and encompassed a variety of emotions. Some people were incredulous, even amused; they dismissed the story as rumor or wishful Yankee thinking—and time would prove them correct. Others were angered by the effrontery of the proposal but apprehensive, nonetheless, that it might be in earnest. A final group responded enthusiastically, believing annexation to be the best course for the future of the colony. If the American acquisition of Alaska had sown in British Columbia the seeds of interest in a union with the United States, news of an attempt to purchase the colony made the idea bloom.

Although the colonial press once more led in the public discussion of the issue, an immediate personal reaction can be found in the comments of Helmcken of the HBC, who was an elected member of the Legislative Council. In a note of late April he remarked on "the ever growing idea, that this Colony would soon prosper and flourish, if it were a portion of the United States of North America." Years later Helmcken recalled that "there sprang up afresh an agitation in which many joined, that annexation to the U. States would be more beneficial than Confederation with Canada." Americans naturally held this position, and "many Britishers agreed with them." As a result, he observed, "Victoria and B. Columbia became a political boiling cauldron."[14]

Of the colony's six major newspapers the three on Vancouver Island endorsed annexation; mainland journals rejected the idea. McMillan of the Victoria *News,* for example, was confident that a transfer of the colony "would be received by a majority . . . of every nationality, with . . . unmingled satisfaction . . . if not loud demonstrations of joy." The colony, he asserted, had no real value for England, and the connection provided neither profit nor population for British Columbia. The editor of the Nanaimo *Tribune* agreed, adding that annexation had long been the obvious solution to the colony's many problems. Loyalties to Great Britain ran deep, but the advantages of union with the United States outweighed such sentiments.[15]

Like its two Vancouver Island counterparts, the *Colonist* appraised the current state of affairs as unsatisfactory, the colony being "hemmed in" and left defenseless by the "extraordinary indifference and apathy" of the home government. Claiming that it spoke for 90 percent of the population, the paper next reported that talk of annexation was "heard at every street corner . . . in the saloons—in all places . . . and the feeling is growing and spreading." However, having flirted with the annexation idea, Higgins finally endorsed confederation as "the only course that will preserve the loyalty of this people or save the country from falling into a condition of hopelessness." Thereafter, he argued frequently and forcefully for union with Canada. Perhaps to offset his earlier editorials, Higgins announced on May 2 that "the COLONIST has not expressed itself in favor of annexation," an idea he later called "a myth—a delusion."[16]

As for the mainland press, there never existed any doubt that it opposed union with the United States. Although slow to respond, the biweekly *Cariboo Sentinel* of Barkerville consistently advocated confederation and attacked "annexation bunkum" and its Vancouver Island supporters. John Robson's twice-weekly *British Columbian,* however, took up these themes most effectively and persistently. An elected member of the Legislative Council from New Westminster, Robson ridiculed the American attempt to buy British Columbia and reported that all colonists "indignantly protested against being sold . . . to a foreign power like so many slaves." Chiding island newspapers for succumbing to the annexation "myth," he wondered: "Have these people, child-like, cast away the Federation toy for the hobby-horse of Annexation so soon?" The *British Columbian* repeatedly counseled that the future lay with Canada.[17]

The heated press debate about annexation versus confederation blazed through May, June, and early July. The vehemence of the editors' polemics may well testify to the significance and persistence of the controversy in the public mind, as well as to the depth of the rivalry among the colonial papers. Discussion of the annexation issue, however, went beyond the journalists. Governor Seymour, writing from Victoria to the Colonial Office on June 26, stated that "there is a systematic agitation going on in this town in favor of annexation to the United States" and that financial support for the movement allegedly came from San Francisco. On the mainland, he reported, he had been met "everywhere with salutes & other expressions of loyalty to the government.[18]

Further evidence of the "agitation" is found in a frank report by William Tolmie to William G. Smith, governor of the Hudson's Bay Company. On July 12 Tolmie warned his superiors that the annexation idea was "still entertained by some British, but by more foreign-born residents of Victoria." The Alaska Purchase had touched off debate about British Columbia's union with the United States, but the controversy was fueled by "the discontent universally felt here with the form and manner of government in the Colony." Some residents succumbed to "captivating assertions" that annexation would bring American investments in real estate and natural resources and would make Victoria a "city second only to San Francisco."[19]

No doubt both Seymour and Tolmie knew of efforts under way to draft and circulate a petition for annexation. The suggestion for such a document seems to have originated in a letter to the *News* in mid-May from a "correspondent" widely believed to be the editor, McMillan, himself. Admitting that the proannexation meeting held the previous fall had been "premature," the writer proposed another. If no remedy other than annexation could be found for "the miserable, heart-rending, deplorable condition" of the country and its people, "Let a petition arising from the public meeting be freely circulated, and . . . nine out of every ten of the British inhabitants throughout the Colony will sign it."[20]

Despite such exaggerated predictions of support, the proposal failed to produce an immediate public initiative, but it did engender a swift reaction from the rival *Colonist.* Higgins printed a letter on May 18 that denounced the petition idea as an "absurd proposition" inspired by "renegade Englishmen in San Francisco" and "American greenbacks." Annexation, it continued, would ruin British Columbia, and Victoria would "be snuffed out like a candle." Two days later, Higgins, who may have written the letter, editorialized confidently that "the thinking portion of our readers [knows] . . . that no movement of that kind will meet with the smallest amount of success," for Great Britain would never permit it.

Accusations about foreign support may have done more damage to the annexation movement than the counterarguments of the *Colonist.* McMillan departed Victoria on May 21 aboard the steamer *Active* bound for San Francisco. What business drew him to the American port is unknown, but the timing of his journey favored his opponents and seemed to verify their suspicions. Two letters to the editor of the *Colonist* condemned the trip, one predicting that "American gold" and the meddling of "outsiders" in the affairs of British Columbia would defeat annexation, "unite the people as one man and make the Government popular."[21]

Because neither public meeting nor petition had materialized, on May 27 the *Colonist* gloatingly commented that the annexation movement's plan was a "miserable failure." Early in July, however, a petition finally surfaced. Addressed to Queen Victoria, the appeal enumerated the now familiar litany of real and embellished calamities that had befallen the colony. The authors "humbly" asked Her Majesty either to see to the colony's needs—"population from England, a direct British steam-line from Panama, a cheap system of government, and an overland road from Canada"—or to do whatever "your wisdom will deem proper for the speedy transfer of this colony . . . to the United States."[22]

The summer of opportunity was passing, however; although the annexation movement was apparently at its zenith, and an appeal to the mother country supposedly under way, the controversy had already begun to cool. Several considerations suggest this view. In a July 2 dispatch, the American consul, Francis, stated that influential citizens had signed the petition and that it would attract the "signatures of three-fourths of the loyal citizens of this Colony." The *Colonist* seems to have been closer to the truth when it announced with satisfaction, the "Petition has proved a complete fizzle," adding that "we trust that we have heard the last of this cry for Annexation." How widely the document was circulated, how many names the promoters obtained, and whether the appeal was ever sent to the British government are not known. It appears significant, however, that the press did not mention the petition again.[23]

The loss of newspaper support damaged the cause. The Nanaimo *Tribune,* once a leading voice for union with the United States, ceased urging this course, and in August it ceased altogether. In July, the *News,* the remaining press advocate, ended daily publication and became a weekly. McMillan faulted the depression and also the fears of those in government who privately favored annexation but believed that support for his newspaper would "lead to the forfeiture of their situations." Robson of the *British Columbian,* however, offered an alternative explanation, suggesting that the problems of the *News* stemmed from its "advocacy of treason and the promulgation of misrepresentation." Whatever the reasons, the last press voice for annexation had been largely stilled.[24]

Despite the obvious abatement of sentiment favoring union with the United States, some members of the colonial government remained nervously alert to the possible danger. For example, the attorney general wrote on July 17 to the bishop of Columbia and two naval officers "to learn if there were any truth in the rumor brot. by Admiral Hastings that England was going to sell B.C. to the Yankees." Although all answered in the negative, proannexationist feeling remained alive in the colony.[25]

Late in September, Governor Seymour reported to the duke of Buckingham that six American warships, enroute to Sitka, currently rode at anchor in the capital's harbor and that numerous officers, including two generals, had stopped at the port. "I need not conceal from Your Grace that the energetic efforts being made by the Americans to garrison the miserable territory . . . and develop its meagre resources, causes, with some, a feeling of repining at their connection with a far distant country which does . . . but little for them." In a more pointed dispatch, one marked "Secret," Seymour bemoaned the colony's financial problems at the very moment when the U.S. was expending so much effort to the north. "I fear," he conceded, "that the annexation feeling prevalent in Victoria will be stimulated by the contrast of the total self-reliance imposed upon us and the absence of all assistance from Home."[26]

It was this American effort to occupy Alaska, in fact, that produced the most intriguing account of the annexation movement in British Columbia and the best evidence that it remained alive in the fall of 1867, when the leading journals no longer mentioned the subject. Among the officers who descended on Victoria in September were Brevet Lieutenant Colonel Robert W. Scott and Brevet Major James T. Hoyt, assigned to discuss with colonial leaders both Indian affairs in British Columbia and matters concerning the supply of the troops to be stationed in Alaska. Scott and Hoyt remained in the colony for nearly two months, during which time they visited the major communities, traversed the territory from its southern to northern borders, and were, they later wrote, "in constant communication with citizens of all classes, including Government officers, Legislators and other officials."[27]

Hoyt and Scott returned to San Francisco in November convinced that a majority of British Columbians favored annexation. They shared these views with their superior officer, Major General Henry W. Halleck, commander of the Military Division of the Pacific, who asked them to detail their opinions and evidence in writing. Their report, accompanied by Halleck's own assessment of the situation in British Columbia, his analysis of the geopolitical conditions in the Pacific Northwest, and his own statement of support for annexation, was forwarded to the War Department.[28]

The account submitted by Scott and Hoyt consisted of two parts, a description of the annexation sentiment that they had encountered in British Columbia and an overview of the financial and commercial conditions that had created a climate favorable to such opinions. This second portion, comprising nearly three-quarters of the report, gives the entire document credibility. Its detailed and generally accurate information on population, government revenues, and debt, including incomplete but plausible figures for 1867, could have been obtained only through frank and revealing discussions with highly placed individuals privy to such data. Those people also would have had a reasonable grasp of the actual extent of the annexation movement, and they apparently shared this knowledge and their personal views. Scott and Hoyt certainly suggest that they did so.

The American officers left British Columbia, they explained, "satisfied beyond any question" that two-thirds of the inhabitants "consider[ed] annexation the only possible relief from the utter prostration of business and certain destruction of all their material interests." Among this large majority, they found the foreign population unanimously in favor of annexation" (p. 2). Especially impressive to the American officers was the fact that "it did not become necessary in a single instance to broach the subject of the cession of that territory to the United States, for it was the constant theme of conversation—obtruded upon us everywhere, and upon nearly all occasions when we came in contact with the people, either officials or citizens" (p. 3).

As for negative views, they reported anew. Antiannexationists were invariably individuals whose connection with the government made it apparent that they would personally benefit from continued affiliation with Great Britain. "Even among the higher government and colonial officials," Scott and Hoyt "heard very candid expressions on the subject, to the effect that if it was for the best interests of the people, and their desire [was] that the colony should be ceded to the United States, such a cession should be made" (p. 3).

Perhaps the strongest advocates of the idea, according to Scott and Hoyt, were members of the Hudson's Bay Company, although these men—and many others—preferred not to make their views public for fear of negative reactions from London. The small group that strenuously fought annexation had made "a reputation for superior loyalty by denouncing all who entertain[ed] sentiments in favor of such a measure." According to the report, many "prominent and leading business men" (p. 4), people commonly believed to be opposed to union with the United States, actually favored the movement but did not want to be openly identified with it. They explained to the American officers that Englishmen were so sensitive about their loyalties as British subjects that many would vote against a cession even if a referendum were held.

As evidence for this claim, Scott and Hoyt related the fate of the July annexation petition, a document they clearly had examined. Its originators had been "furiously assaulted . . . with epithets charging them with disloyalty, unfaithfulness to their Government, and denouncing their conduct as treasonable." Such virulent attacks had effectively stopped the petition effort, but that did not negate the true feelings of the majority. Scott and Hoyt concluded that "if the cession of the country to the United States was proclaimed as a fact," thus sparing people from having to express their views openly, "the rejoicings of that colony would be most enthusiastic and general" (p. 5).

By October, the issue of union with the U.S. was no longer mentioned in the press, government documents, or any other colonial source. If people still discussed it privately, local newspapers took no notice, and no information arrived from the States or Britain to fuel a new public debate or suggest that American interest in acquiring British Columbia was anything more than idle rumor or wishful thinking. Under these circumstances, whatever survived of annexation sentiment became quiescent.

The swift fading of support for union with the United States raises questions concerning the seriousness and scope of the movement. Only the *British Columbian* and the *Colonist* provide significant documentation refuting the reality of any annexation spirit in the colony in 1867. The latter journal, moreover, took up the cudgel of denial only after first trumpeting the existence of strong annexationist feelings in its late April editorials. Both editors, Robson and Higgins, may have had personal convictions opposing union, but they had other motives as well. Both newspapers, for instance, contracted for a time to print official notices of the colonial administration and the debates and laws of the legislature. Robson, furthermore, was an elected member of that body. In addition, both men favored, to varying degrees, confederation with Canada, and neither would be likely to benefit from U.S. annexation. Finally, only one thing is certain about the printed positions taken by newspapers generally: they represent the views of the editor or owner, but not necessarily anyone else. For several reasons, therefore, the negative stance of the *British Columbian* and the *Colonist* is not very convincing.[29]

In contrast, the sources that recognize the existence of annexation sentiment are numerous and diverse. They include two lesser colonial papers and individuals whose ranks encompass a private American businessman and the U.S. consul, three HBC officials—one a member of the Legislative Council—the governor and the attorney general of the colony, a private citizen, and two U.S. Army officers. Clearly, they could not all have been equally and simultaneously deluded in their perceptions of the state of affairs in British Columbia, nor is it likely that all could have had personal reasons for fabricating or grossly exaggerating conditions.

These people instead were reporting on an annexation movement they believed was under way. The evidence that their eyewitness accounts represent, in tandem with the reports in the *News* and the *Tribune,* is not conclusive, but it is more persuasive than that presented by the editorials of the *Colonist* and the *British Columbian.*

Although the actual breadth, depth, and strength of the 1867 annexation movement in British Columbia remain uncertain, some aspects of the episode can be determined. It is clear that many residents and most of the press reacted with varying degrees of anxiety, anger, and acquiescence to the cession of Russian America to the United States, which they recognized as a threat to the future of their colonial community. The menace designed by influential Russians and perceived by many Americans, therefore, was also apparent to British Columbians.

Reactions to the treaty can be divided into two phases separated by the cable that on April 24 brought news of an American offer to buy British Columbia. The rumor shook the confidence of colonial residents. Annexation became an open topic of conversation in the press and in public, and the relative merits of union with the United States and confederation with Canada were aired. The response proved more intense, and support for annexation most avid, on Vancouver Island; mainland residents took less notice and expressed little interest.

As a result of the news of the cession and the rumor of an American attempt to acquire British Columbia, a spontaneous and significant annexation movement appeared in the colony in the late spring and early summer of 1867, and it continued into the early fall.

Although the extent of this sentiment remains unknown, historians of British Columbia have hitherto failed to recognize the vigor of this movement. Furthermore, their failure seems particularly curious. If annexation ever had a chance for success, it was that year, following the Alaska Purchase. That nothing came of the opportunity and British Columbia eventually joined the dominion does not mean the annexation movement lacked substance. It indicates, rather, that the rise of such a movement may be local but the resolution is determined by attitudes held elsewhere and decisions made in distant capitals.

NOTES

1. Edouard de Stoeckl to Aleksandr Gorchakov, Dec. 23, 1859–Jan. 4, 1860, Annex 6, and draft of report by Gorchakov, December 1866, Annex 13, Papers Relating to the Cession of Alaska. 1856–67," T495, roll 1, General Records of the Department of State, RG 59, National Archives (NA) (1st, 3d qtns. translated from the French by R. Neunherz); S. B. Okun, *The Russian-American Company,* ed. B. D. Grekov, trans. Carl Ginsburg (Cambridge, Mass., 1951), 262 (2d qtn.).

2. Richard E. Neunherz, "The Purchase of Russian America: Reasons and Reactions," Ph.D. dissertation (University of Washington. 1975), 152, 164–71 (subsequent research, now encompassing 320 newspapers, has substantiated the original findings), 364; "Beamon Memorandum," April 1, 1867, Charles Sumner Manuscripts, Massachusetts Historical Library, Boston, consists of notes on meetings of the Senate Committee on Foreign Relations; also see David E. Shi, "Seward's Attempt to Annex British Columbia, 1865–1869," *Pacific Historical Review* 47 (1978): 217–38, which, though flawed, has a plausible thesis.

3. Donald F. Warner, *The Idea of Continental Union: Agitation for the Annexation of Canada to the United States, 1849–1893* (Lexington, Ky., 1960), 127–41; Margaret A. Ormsby, *British Columbia: A History,* rev. ed. (Toronto, 1971), 235–36, 243–44; Willard E. Ireland, "The Annexation Petition of 1869," *British Columbia Historical Quarterly* 4 (1940): 267–87; Alvin C. Gluek, Jr., *Minnesota and the Manifest Destiny of the Canadian Northwest: A Study in Canadian-American Relations* (Toronto, 1965), 193–219.

4. Paul A. Phillips, "Confederation and the Economy of British Columbia," in *British Columbia and Confederation,* ed. W. George Shelton (Victoria, B.C., 1967), 56, [61–62].

5. Ibid.; 58–59, *Daily British Colonist and Victoria Chronicle,* Jan. 16, 1867.

6. F. W. Howay, W. N. Sage, and H. F. Angus, *British Columbia and the United States: The North Pacific Slope from Fur Trade to Aviation* (Toronto, 1942), 180.

7. Walter N. Sage, "The Critical Period of British Columbia History, 1866–1871," *Pacific Historical Review* 1 (1932): 433.

8. *Morning News* (Victoria), n.d., quoted in *San Francisco Bulletin,* April 12, 1867.

9. Frederick Seymour to the duke of Buckingham, April 17, 1867, "Despatches, 1867 April–August," 79, Original Correspondence—Secretary of State, C.O. 60, vol. 28, British Columbia, Public Records Office, London (hereafter cited as PRO CO 60-28); Americans in Victoria to William Seward, April 20, 1867, enclosure in Allen Francis to Seward, April 23, 1867, "Despatches from United States Consuls in Victoria, Canada, 1862–1906," T130, roll 1, RG 59, NA.

10. Seymour to Buckingham, April 1867; *Examiner* (Charlottetown, Prince Edward Island), June 26, 1867 (reprint of E. G. Alston letter); William Tolmie to W. G. Smith, May 21, 1867, A 11/81, fol. 1–4, Hudson's Bay Company Archives (HBCA), Provincial Archives of Manitoba, Winnipeg.

11. John Etheridge to governor and committee, April 2, 1867, and John Helmcken to Etheridge. n.d., enclosure in Etheridge to governor and committee, April 29, 1867, A 11/81, fol. 1–4, HBCA; Henry Crease to C. W. Franks, April 22, 1867, Henry Pering Pellew Crease Manuscripts, "Misc. Letters. Private, January 1, 1866–December 31, 1867," Provincial Archives of British Columbia (PABC), Victoria.

12. Francis to Seward, April 13–23, 1867, "Despatches from U.S. Consuls in Victoria."

13. W. Carey Johnson to Tolmie, April 13, 1867, to Caleb Cushing, Oct. 4, 1867, and Feb. 14, 1868, Caleb Cushing Manuscripts, Library of Congress; Oregon City *Enterprise,* April 20 and 27, 1867 (see any issue for professional status of Johnson, under "Business Cards"); Johnson to Seward, April 29, 1867, "Miscellaneous Letters," M179, roll 256, RG 59, NA.

14. Helmcken to Etheridge, n.d.. enclosure in Etheridge to governor and committee, April 29, 1867, and *idem,* "Reminiscences," vol. 5, p. 67, Helmcken Papers, PABC.

15. *News,* April 25, 1867 (qtn), clipping from Scrapbook, James E. McMillan Manuscripts, PABC, and April 27, 1867, quoted in *Pacific Commercial Advertiser* (Honolulu), June 1, 1867 (extant copies of the *News* contain no McMillan material: the Scrapbook contains clippings of some McMillan editorials, a few of which were quoted by West Coast newspapers and rival colonial journals); Nanaimo *Tribune,* May 4, 1867.

16. *Colonist,* April 25 (1st, 2nd qtns.), 29 (3rd, 4th qtns.), May 27 (last qtn.), 1867.

17. *Cariboo Sentinel* (Barkerville), June 24, 1867; *British Columbian* (New Westminster), April 27 (slaves), May 1 (last qtn.), June 1, 1867.

18. Seymour to Buckingham, June 26, 1867, no. 7989, B. Columbia, 134–39, PRO CO 60/28.

19. Tolmie to Smith, July 12, 1867, A 11/82, fol. 118–26, HBCA.

20. *News,* May 17? 1867, quoted in *Daily Alta California* (San Francisco), June 2, 1867.

21. *Colonist,* May 22, 23 (qtns.), 1867.

22. Copy of petition, enclosure in Francis to Seward, July 2, 1867, "Despatches from U.S. Consuls in Victoria."

23. Ibid.; *Colonist,* July 13, 1867. No mention of the petition has been found in the records of the Colonial Office, nor did Seymour mention it in his communications.

24. McMillan quoted in *British Columbian Examiner* (New Westminster), June 29, 1867. Opponents had announced in early July that the *News* had ceased publication on June 29, but clippings in the Scrapbook, McMillan Manuscripts, bear dates through September 1867 and carry a heading stating that the *News* was printed weekly, on Sunday morning. *British Columbian,* June 29, 1867.

25. Crease to bishop of Columbia, July 17, 1867, and reply note, July 27, 1867, "Misc. Letters, Private—January 1, 1866–December 1867," Crease Manuscripts.

26. Seymour to Buckingham. Sept. 24 and 25, 1867, pp. 207–10, PRO CO 60/29.

27. Robert Scott and James Hoyt to James B. Fry, Nov. 20, 1867, "Miscellaneous Letters," M179, roll 271. This letter is known as the Scott-Hoyt report.

28. Ibid.; Henry Halleck to adjutant general, Nov. 21, 22, 1867, ibid. The following paragraphs are based on the Scott-Hoyt report.

29. Madge Wolfenden, "The Early Government Gazettes," *British Columbia Historical Quarterly* 7 (1942): 171–90.

The Early Ministry of S. Hall Young, 1878–1888

TED C. HINCKLEY

American missionaries first arrived in Alaska 10 years after its purchase by the United States. It is apparent today that the missionaries' own cultural and intellectual heritage led many of them (although not all) to view all cultures as either superior or inferior to their own. They simply had no concept of the value of cultural diversity. Their own culture, they believed, was undeniably superior; "inferior" societies, including those of Alaska's Native inhabitants, had merely not yet evolved from hunting and gathering through herding and then agriculture to reach the most fully "civilized" form, that of industrial democracy. One of their tasks, the missionaries felt, was to assist this evolutionary process so that Alaska Natives (but not necessarily their cultures) might survive into the 20th century. Thus, they were assimilationists as well as Christianizers.

One is most likely to think of the Presbyterian leader Sheldon Jackson when one hears the word missionary. *But Jackson never engaged in parish work in Alaska at all. Instead, he organized missionary activity, directed the acculturation of Alaska Natives, and raised public and private funds for both purposes from the contiguous United States. From 1885 until 1906 Jackson also served as General Agent of Education in Alaska, a position established by the Organic Act of 1884. To accomplish his goals, Jackson maintained residency in Washington, D.C., and traveled extensively throughout the rest of the country, visiting Alaska each summer.*

The historian Ted C. Hinckley, Professor Emeritus at San Jose State University, has written a number of articles about Jackson and his contemporaries. Hinckley's research extends to other aspects of Alaskans' experiences during the early American period as well. His publications include accounts of William Seward's only visit to Alaska, of the U.S. Navy's shelling of the village of Angoon in 1882, and of the Tlingits' concerns about non-Native encroachment onto their lands and traditional fishing sites. Hinckley's major books include The Americanization of Alaska,

This article appeared originally in *Journal of Presbyterian History* 46 (September 1968): 175–96; it is reprinted here by permission.

1867–1897 (Palo Alto, Calif.: Pacific Books, Publishers, 1972) and a biography of the gold rush era governor Alaskan John G. Brady: Missionary, Businessman, Judge, and Governor, 1878–1918 *(published for Miami University by Ohio State University Press, 1982). Hinckley presently is preparing a history of the Tlingit people following United States acquisition of Alaska.*

In the following selection, Hinckley discusses Samuel Hall Young, the resident Presbyterian leader in Alaska for many years. The article suggests that the missionary experience in Alaska was more varied than readers familiar only with Jackson might suppose. It also demonstrates that Jackson had both rivals and critics.

The survival and durability of the Puritan tradition into nineteenth- and even twentieth-century America is a remarkable phenomenon. A splendid example of this legacy in action is the career of Samuel Hall Young. An evaluation of his early Christian labor in and for Alaska is particularly valuable as the forty-ninth state celebrates its 1867–1967 centennial.

Samuel Hall Young was born in Butler, Pennsylvania, on September 2, 1847. Young's parentage was of solid Calvinist persuasion. His mother, Margaret (Johnston) Young, was particularly proud of one extension of the family tree—none other than Oliver Cromwell's eldest daughter. Typically independent-minded, her American forebears had come to represent every type of Presbyterianism: Seceders, Oldside Covenanters, Newside Covenanters, United Presbyterians, *ad infinitum*. Sectarian divisiveness was no less evident on S. Hall Young's father's side.

The Young and Johnston families, like their Puritan ancestors, seem to have respected the power of a formal education. At the dawn of the nineteenth century, after the New England grandfather Robert Young had moved his family into western Virginia, he served as a part-time teacher. One of his sons, S. Hall's father, Loyal Young, completed his education at Allegheny's Western Theological Seminary. His graduation occurred in 1832. That same year America's western champion was triumphantly reelected, and Andrew Jackson's "Democracy" revealed a nation burgeoning with unpredictable confidence. Many years later Loyal's son reflected how well the young Republic's amazing social mix had diluted Puritan predestination. "I would not emphasize heredity too strongly," S. Hall Young wrote. "We are what we are. Our blood may have power to sway us this way or that, and environment is still more potent; but every strong man is 'captain of his soul.'"[1]

Samuel Hall Young grew up in the penury familiar in a rural manse. Whether it was Scotch-Irish testiness, or simply boyish embarrassment over initials that spelled SHY, the youth chose Hall as his name, and it stuck. The deprivations of a rural ministry in western Pennsylvania do not seem to have injured seriously the happiness of Hall Young and his seven brothers and sisters. But there is no mistaking the sacrifice and spartan simplicity which guided their home life. Hall's grammar school education was spotty, partially because his affection for outdoor romps would not surrender to the confinement of a one-room schoolhouse. Severe discipline was meted out to him. Unfortunately this liberal application of the rod plus his rather poor health resulted in much of his boyhood education being of the "Lincoln home study" type: the Bible and *Pilgrim's Progress*. The recently published historical poems of Longfellow, such as "Hiawatha" and "The Courtship of Miles Standish," provided entertaining dinner recitations.

In later years Young expressed his relief that the hellfire ideology to which his youth had exposed him was balanced by the ever-present sweetness of his parents' love. One experience during his teens had made him understand that love was not simply happiness: the sight of his parents literally risking their lives as conductors on the underground railroad. Very likely the fear written on the faces of the runaway slaves frightened the youth more than the very real hazards confronting his parents.

Adolescence and poor health kept Hall from joining his brothers in the ranks of the Union Army. Nonetheless, the monumental humanitarian issues which exploded in the Civil War were ever present in the sensitive lad's mind. After the war Young joined two of his brothers in Michigan. He had planned to study law. Like many a minister's son, Young had carried his religion rather automatically. Now, suddenly, unexpectedly, the twenty-year-old, whose constitution had been toughened by demanding physical labor, was converted. "I joined the Church . . . and the whole tide of my life flowed towards the Christian ministry and evangelization of those who 'sat in darkness'; I was a missionary from the moment of my conversion."[2]

Further education was therefore mandatory, and in 1871 Young entered Wooster College. Founded only five years before, Wooster faced considerable collegiate competition and was not reluctant to promote its virtues. One blurb ran: "It is better to give a son a complete education than to give him a farm. He will then be able to earn far more in a year than a farm could produce, and he may besides wield a great influence for good."[3] It was the latter wish that Young sought to fulfill, but due to "constant poverty," he finished at Wooster one year late. Eager to sit at the feet of Princeton Theological Seminary's esteemed Dr. Charles Hodge, Young traveled to New Jersey. One year was enough. Hodge was far more interested in his Greek Testament than his students, and, Young later declared, he got "more good" from New York City's Madison Square meetings of Moody and Sankey than he got from his whole seminary year.[4] He finished seminary at Western Seminary, Allegheny, Ohio. Sandwiched between his studies were valuable preaching and teaching experiences.

No different from hundreds of other ministerial novices, Young had frequently dreamed of foreign service. The achievements of nineteenth-century missionaries in Africa, Asia, and America's Far West were immensely challenging. Men like David Livingstone, Adoniram Judson, and Marcus Whitman enjoyed a fame and public acclaim that went far beyond sectarian or even Christian circles.[5] But Young's poor health record seemed to disqualify him for harsh missionary rigors. His reservations vanished, however, when he encountered another minister who years before had also been told to seek a comfortable eastern parish because of weak physique, and who had subsequently become the Presbyterian Church's Far Western "Rocky Mountain Superintendent."

It was just before Christmas in 1877 when this popular home missionary organizer, Dr. Sheldon Jackson, spoke at Western Seminary. The pint-sized Jackson declaimed on the needs of America's most recent territorial acquisition—giant-sized Alaska.[6] In his inimitable way ramrod Jackson quickened a mandate for Christian service. As Young later recalled, "Alaska became a land of enchantment. . . . Its heathen multitudes were a reproach to Christendom." Forthwith Young volunteered himself to the Board of Home Missions.[7]

Alaska in 1878 was badly in need of dedicated Americans who would assume responsible civilizing roles. During the preceding year the United States Army had withdrawn its forces from the northern territory, and only the thinnest veneer of either government or American society existed there. Here was a country one-fifth that of the contiguous United States, inhabited by some thirty thousand natives, many of whom had never heard of the Christian faith—for a tyro minister it posed a tremendous challenge.

Sparked by the "Rocky Mountain Superintendent," who would himself in a few years devote his entire attention to the Far Northern frontier, Young sought the facts.[8] From Aaron L. Lindsley, pastor of the First

Presbyterian Church of Portland, Oregon, and from Mrs. Amanda R. McFarland, the pioneer Presbyterian missionary to Alaska, he obtained additional information about what would be required. Mrs. McFarland's replies were strong medicine. The harsh picture which she painted of indigenous social disintegration in Wrangell, Alaska, left no doubt that evangelization there must be coupled with, if not preceded by, social action.[9] Despite her sobering accounts, Hall Young was impatient for his last year of seminary to end. His impatience with a student's life only grew when soon after the New Year of 1878 he heard that John Green Brady, a graduate of Union Theological Seminary, and Miss Fannie E. Kellogg, Lindsley's niece, had already reinforced Mrs. McFarland in Alaska. In the spring of 1878, the Board of Home Missions commissioned him to Alaska. Sheldon Jackson editorialized: "The action of the Board is none too soon, as the Jesuits are also entering the field."[10]

Before Young left for his new assignment in late spring of 1878, Dr. Henry Kendall, Secretary to the Board of Home Missions, told the ministerial recruit half jestingly, half seriously, "If those Indians scalp you, we will canonize you as a martyr, but don't let them do it if you can help it." Young docked at Fort Wrangell on July 10, 1878.[11] To welcome him was a crowd of two: an ex-soldier who had fallen in love with the misty, mountainous Alexander Archipelago, and an Indian covered with lampblack. Prior to his departure, Kendall had urged Young to "find a wife." Upon disembarking at Wrangell, a Hudson's Bay agent counseled him, "Don't become an Indian." Within a few days Young had found his wife, and a distinguished fifty-year career would testify that he never "went native." Yet, like almost every other educated man or woman who dared the Alaskan frontier, Young found intervals of stateside service indispensable. Alaska was beautiful but it was also brutal and barbarous.

Before commencing his work as Mrs. McFarland's co-worker, the apprentice had to satisfy his curiosity about his Presbyterian peers at Sitka. Continuing aboard the steamer, he journeyed up the Inside Passage to the District capital. Sitka, Young discovered, had changed little since Russian days. He soon met John G. Brady and Miss Fannie Kellogg; the former proved to be quite as industrious as Young, while the latter proved to be most charming. Certainly Miss Kellogg wasted no time. She took the missionary novice on a tour of historic "Lovers' Lane" to Indian River, and, as Young later confessed, "the stately trees of hemlock and spruce impressed me much less than the lively young lady at my side."[12] Miss Kellogg had already built a mission school with over fifty students, although their attendance was about as predictable as a Sitka sunbeam. In age they ranged from six to sixty. Her enthusiasm and capabilities, not to mention her feminine attractiveness, were what Young had hoped to find—but never in Alaska. On December 15 Fannie became his wife and joined him at the Wrangell mission.[13]

A worthy career had begun, but as fate would have it, it had been flawed even before it began. The controversial place of Aaron L. Lindsley, Fannie's uncle and pastor of Portland's First Presbyterian Church, still needs to be evaluated. Regrettably, both he and Sheldon Jackson, for all their abilities, unabashedly scrambled after the historic distinction of having pioneered the Presbyterian Church in Alaska. When their respective partisans got into the unseemly quarrel, their contest became more than a case of two egos in collision. In the author's opinion, and in the view of Dr. Charles A. Anderson, one-time Secretary of the Presbyterian Historical Society, Lindsley bungled much of what he attempted in Alaska.[14] To call him the "Father of Alaska Missions," as Young later did, is historically incorrect.[15] And to describe Lindsley as the "loving and bountiful parent of all the early missionaries" is laughable. Alaska's first Presbyterian missionary, Mrs. Amanda McFarland, thoroughly distrusted Portland's eminent divine. Young's superior, Dr. Henry Kendall, surely had no doubt about Lindsley's troublesome role.[16] The only substantial aid which his church seems to have rendered Alaska missions during the 1880s was to the Wrangell mission, and it was minimal compared with the support forwarded by the New York Board. Whatever the verdict of history, Young unsuccessfully tried to remain neutral in the Jackson-Lindsley feud.

Presbyterians are everything but neutral. By 1884 Lindsley was of no real significance to Alaska missions, while Jackson's territorial role, both in and out of the Church, had skyrocketed. Because of the success of his spreading mission school system, Jackson in 1885 was appointed, under the United States Bureau of Education, General Agent for Education for all of Alaska. Unlike Young, John G. Brady had been an unqualified pro-Jackson man from the outset. Blessed by a warm personality, a quick mind, and legal training, Brady would ultimately become Alaska's governor. He would achieve the high office on his own merits, but Jackson's political leverage at the nation's capital certainly did not hurt him.

Jackson never broke with his younger fellow missionary, S. Hall Young. Yet they never achieved the mutual confidence and deep friendship which Jackson and Brady came to enjoy. Many years later Young made various invidious comparisons between himself and Jackson's protégé—especially how he had remained a minister while Brady had abandoned the cloth.[17] Clearly it was a case of sour grapes, for Young also suffered from the political itch, and if fate had afforded him a chance to substitute the gavel for the collar, he would probably have done so.

By the fall of 1878, Young was totally immersed in educational work with Mrs. McFarland and the Wrangell mission. His correspondence bubbled with the optimism of the tyro. "Six tribes look to us for light." The Indians "learn rapidly and are delighted with the school. . . . I preach twice every Sabbath to the Indians and once to the whites. We have Sabbath School after the morning service. Our congregations are large and orderly. . . . Wrangell's future is assured and its rapid growth is certain." Young was wrong about a Wrangell boom. Yet his approach to founding a church was completely practical. "We cannot think of organizing a church yet . . . I am about organizing a catechetical class of men. I wish to train material for elders, deacons, and private members."[18] In less than a year, on August 3, 1879, to be exact, Wrangell had its Presbyterian Church with "eighteen Native and five white communicants." Present to honor the occasion were Messrs. Kendall, Jackson, and Lindsley, and their wives.[19] Despite the tension between Lindsley and Jackson, everyone could rejoice at the mission station structures: a church 35 by 55 feet and a two-story girls' industrial school 40 by 60 feet.[20]

During 1879 Young had done considerably more than teach, preach, and pound nails. Drawn by the challenge of Archipelago "pagans" outside the mission's influence, he took to the water. Accompanying him was none other than the California naturalist John Muir. Muir recalled how "even those chiefs who were not at all inclined to anything like piety were yet anxious to procure schools and churches that their people should not miss the temporal advantages of knowledge which . . . they were not slow to recognize." At the meeting with the Chilkats an old chief patiently listened to the young minister and then replied:

> I might say that through all my long life I have never until now heard a white man speak. It has always seemed to me while trying to speak to traders and those seeking gold mines that it was like speaking to a person across a broad stream that was running fast over stones and making so loud a noise that scarce a single word could be heard. But now for the first time, the Indian and the white man are on the same side of the river, eye to eye, heart to heart.[21]

Young not only had many chances to explore the hearts of men, but in company with Muir he explored regions not previously investigated by white men.[22] Later, without Muir, Young made two "long voyages of discovery and missionary work": one a four-hundred-fifty-mile circuit of Prince of Wales Island and another southward to the Cape Fox and Tongass tribes.[23]

One thing Young had quickly discovered in Alaska was the latent immediacy of violence. Murderous altercations occasionally erupted among the white miners who crowded into Wrangell during the winter months. And if the usual forms of civil justice were lacking, prompt legal decisions were not. One time Young found himself officiating at a funeral which laid to rest both the victim and the murderer.[24] The local aborigines spared white men, at least near the settlements, but not each other. One of the worst blows which befell Young was the loss of two of his Christian Indians, Moses and Tow-a-att. The quarrel which claimed their lives had begun over the destruction of some native hoochinoo, or hooch.[25] From the very first the American military as well as the later Christian teachers had struggled to separate the indigenes from all forms of liquor. In Alaska as in other regions of the Pacific and Far West, "fire water" reduced to rubble certain native societies.

On his famous canoe voyage with John Muir, Young had encountered a whole village "afire with bad whiskey." As the naturalist later commented, "This was the first time in my life that I learned the meaning of the phrase 'a howling drunk.'"[26] In conjunction with the United States Navy, Young did everything he could to beat back the flow of rotgut. Illustrated classroom lectures on the evils of drink, actual physical destruction of stills, and a whole battery of efforts were fired at the beverage nemesis. Around the zones of settlement, at least, the dry campaign accomplished some good.[27]

Another campaign in which Young involved himself was the Juneau meeting of Alaskans "for the purpose of taking some action toward procurement of recognition and representation of this Territory by the United States Government." Juneau, in July 1881, had not yet been named, and its population was largely itinerant miners. In fact, the rush to this remote site was hardly a year old, but with typical western impatience, residents called a territorial convention. S. Hall Young came as one of the Wrangell delegates and was elected secretary of the one-day convention. As the Juneau historian Robert N. De Armond has noted, the popular vote that seated Young and his fellow delegates was ridiculously small. Understandably Congress did not take their demands for increased civil government very seriously. But for Young, no doubt, the convention was a heady affair.[28]

That spring Young escorted twelve Archipelago boys and girls to the United States Indian Training School at Forest Grove, Oregon. This institution had copied some features of Captain Richard H. Pratt's Carlisle establishment and taught a similar polytechnical curriculum with a heavy emphasis on English-language instruction. Inspection of the Forest Grove plant stimulated Young's hopes for a similar school at Wrangell.[29] Before returning home, he made some public addresses and met with the Presbytery of Oregon. A. L. Lindsley's duchy endorsed his work. Because he had earlier complicated the work of the Board of Home Missions, neither Jackson nor Kendall wanted any further involvement with the Portland pastor. Indeed, in the preceding year, Jackson had requested the General Assembly either to organize a Presbytery of Alaska or to place the missionaries under the Presbytery of Puget Sound.[30] Although an attempt by the Presbytery of Oregon to lay claim to Alaska was blocked, it was not until May of 1883 that the Presbytery of Alaska was constituted. By that time Young's territorial duties had undergone a marked change.[31]

Certainly the mission personnel perplexities which beset Young were not the product of his sloth or lack of imagination. A sample of his nonteaching, nonpreaching tasks included: substituting for the local Wrangell Customs Officer; writing copy for the *Evangelist;* trying to outbluff a native shaman "doctoring" a sick native; and "logging in the mission's winter supply of salmon." As if all this were not enough, he urged his seniors to forward a boat so that the mission's evangelizing radius might be expanded. "Such a boat as I contemplate would need only three men or at most four." Dollar-conscious Home Board secretaries could only shake their heads. What he "contemplated" would have doubled the Wrangell staff.[32]

Certain factors appear to have injured S. Hall Young's early ministry. His very enthusiasm intimidated those with less drive; overwhelmed by his exuberant loquacity, tact occasionally fled. Alaska, like all remote missionary fields, was an inviting preserve for gossip. Fannie Young's aggressive abilities, plus the link with her uncle's Portland church, did not help mend this affliction. During the early 1880s the Young team irritated virtually every missionary working at Sitka and Wrangell.[33] A letter from Captain Henry Glass, commanding officer of the U.S.S. *Wachusetts*, clearly reveals how difficult it was for Young to restrain both tongue and pen.[34]

The truth was, notwithstanding his ambition to move large groups of men, Young had been cast as a vivacious Christian whose triumphs would lie in the small-scale, person-to-person realm. In the full vigor of early manhood he could not know this.

On February 9, 1883, the Home for Wrangell's Indian girls which Mrs. McFarland had labored so hard to build burned to the ground. One year earlier, the mission structure at Sitka had met a similar fate. The result was that in 1884 the McFarland Home was moved to Alaska's capital. Well before the Wrangell conflagration Young had pressed upon the Home Board the desirability of an agricultural school for boys. With typical ebullience, and confidence that it could be made self-supporting, he inquired of Jackson, "Can't you do something for our boys? This farm scheme is not visionary for it is simply business. The chance seems providential. It would be a saving to our outlay. We could keep fifty head of cattle there without more work than the labor of one or two more."[35] No less than her husband, Fannie wanted a speed-up in social amelioration. During October of 1881 she had commenced to agitate for a hospital. Wrangell's medical needs were publicized in the *Presbyterian Home Missions*, and by November Young boasted, "Mrs. Young's hospital gets along well and the Lord keeps ahead of her all the time in money and Indian Food. . . . The place looks very tidy and neat."[36]

Shortly after the destruction of the McFarland Home, Young steamed southward for aid. Actually by this time the Wrangell mission's day school and the coeducational boarding facilities had received additional personnel. The Sitka station, as well as other new Panhandle mission posts, was thriving. Almost all of this had been accomplished under the authority and with the support of the Church's Board of Home Missions. Young must have made quite a plea to the Presbytery of Oregon. Food, money, and nine cases of clothing were promptly dispatched as succor.[37]

In his pocket Young carried a petition from the five Alaska missionaries (Sheldon Jackson, J. Loomis Gould, J. W. McFarland, Eugene Willard, John G. Brady, and himself) urging the 1883 General Assembly to create a Presbytery of Alaska.[38] Recognizing the handwriting on the wall, the Presbytery of Oregon not only seconded the action of their northern colleagues but elected Young Commissioner to the General Assembly.[39] To help assure that the Youngs arrived at the Saratoga Springs, New York, General Assembly, Jackson secured them half-rate ministerial railway tickets.[40] Young described the Saratoga Springs gathering as "a momentous one for Alaska." An Alaska Presbytery was officially instituted at this General Assembly. The really momentous part for Young was the aftermath. He had a wonderful time showing off his attractive wife and talking Alaska before eastern church groups.

> A constant whirl of social and church activities kept us busy; a series of missionary conventions in New York, Pennsylvania and New Jersey, with trips as far east as Rhode Island and as far west as Chicago, and south to West Virginia and Kentucky, kept us speaking almost daily.

Young further commented that the "response of the churches was more than we anticipated. The Board had to put on the brakes."[41]

What in fact had happened was that he and his eager wife had gone considerably beyond what their Home Board employers had expected. It was not their having raised money to build an independent boarding home for Wrangell natives that was so disconcerting, but that the Portland church once again appeared to be competing with the Church's Home Board. The Church's governing bodies rightly wanted Sheldon Jackson to win any prospective federal appointment for administering Alaska mission schools. Lindsley, however, lobbied for the partially experienced S. Hall Young. The Portland pastor, no doubt, believed he could have some control over Young.[42] Predictably it was asked, "Why start another boarding school when the Sitka Industrial School and its unification with the late McFarland Home already left everything in such an embryonic state?" Members of the Wrangell day school staff were no less perplexed and a bit angry.[43]

Fannie Kellogg later claimed that she founded her Tlinkit Training Academy in 1882. If she meant that she and Hall informally adopted some youngsters into their home in 1882, this is correct.[44] Actually the academy seems to have been born in 1884 when the United States government authorized a free lease of some old abandoned garrison buildings for sleeping quarters and classrooms, and even permitted service rifles to be issued for hunting purposes.[45] Aided by his brother, James W. Young, and his Indian students, Hall transformed the barracks into a carpenter-cabinet-shoe shop and dormitory for boys and girls. A farm nine miles from Fort Wrangell in the Stickeen River delta was purchased for five hundred dollars, in order that the Academy might meet its own food requirements.[46] Fannie told how "Our aim from the first has been to make the institution as nearly self-supporting as practicable." By November of 1885 the Tlinkit Training Academy boasted nineteen boys and eight girls.[47] James Young worked as farm foreman and mechanic while Young's cousin from West Virginia, Miss Lydia McAvoy, assisted as teacher. It appears the Youngs eventually planned to have boy boarders only.

Fannie and Hall were in full earnest when they spoke of a "self-supporting" institution. In the spring and summer months the native lads applied themselves to farm chores during the morning, while the afternoon was spent in study. As Young described it for the *Presbyterian Journal*, there was plenty to do:

> They are putting in sixty bushels of potatoes, besides plenty of oats, buckwheat, peas, turnips and garden seeds. Foragers are sent out every day for a supply of game and fish. Ducks, geese, grouse, and bears are abundant and close at hand. Then the supply of salt salmon and trout, dried small fish and dried berries will be put up for the winter.

To further assist the school, each student would be given a "Christian name" by "some individual or society" which promised to donate sixty dollars a year for his support. What would the boys receive for their labor? Young summed it up, "We are protecting these promising boys from temptations which would else surely prove their destruction, keeping them busy, pushing forward their English, Christian education, and striving to 'thoroughly furnish' them for the future."[48]

Throughout 1885 and 1886 the Youngs really threw their hearts into the Tlinkit Academy effort. Principal Young also sought to maintain his work as Home Board preacher-teacher at Wrangell; inevitably there were Sundays when the ranch chores kept him from his village pulpit.[49] Concerned over inadequate mission communication, Jackson encouraged him to initiate a needed United States mail link. For a period Young assisted as Wrangell's unofficial postmaster.[50] In 1885 Governor A. P. Swineford visited the Tlinkit school and reported that the "training academy . . . had effected a great deal in the civilization and Christianization of the Indians."[51] One tourist noted that the ranch had "fifteen hundred acres . . . raising potatoes, turnips, etc. Mr. Young informed us that one thousand acres could be cut with a mower. They intend to demonstrate that there is good soil in Alaska for farming purposes." Stock was brought in to supply both power and food; indeed, Fannie's team of horses may have been Wrangell's first.[52]

At approximately the same time that Sheldon Jackson received his appointment as General Agent for Education in Alaska, Congress began to authorize funds for native education in Alaska. By 1885 Jackson had begun to coordinate (in a loose fashion) the Moravian, Episcopalian, Methodist, and Congregational high commands in a common assault on Alaska. Each was to assume a special region in which to labor. Naturally General Agent Jackson would do all he could to abet church missions with federal aid.[53] This problematically constitutional design had been adumbrated by President U. S. Grant's earlier, well-publicized Peace Policy for the Far West Indian population.[54] Although Jackson's scheme was better organized, it was not without its deficiencies. Among the incipient common schools now funded by Uncle Sam (and in which the precursor missionaries understandably would have a major role) was the Home Board's Wrangell Day School now transformed into a Government Common School. Young's cousin, Lydia McAvoy, assumed this billet in mid-1885, and a year later Hall ejaculated, "We have had the best day-school this year ever held in Wrangell. . . . the progress of the children has been remarkable."[55]

It was not all triumph. A building fire proved too much for one girl and she "jumped through a window and cut her hand dreadfully . . . three girls . . . took their chances to run off." Indian boy-girl relations frequently horrified the Victorian mission staff. Once Fannie had to expel some boys for "insubordination and impudence," and to keep them fed was a herculean labor. One year's larder required the killing of "one hundred and twenty-one deer, eleven seals, one bear, about one hundred fifty wild geese, over three hundred ducks, and numerous other grouse, porcupines, marmots . . . they caught all the salmon, halibut, codfish, trout, herrings, flounders, crabs, clams, etc. needed."[56] Costs always outran income. To expand their public relations, hoping to enlarge donations, Fannie and Hall initiated a school newspaper, *The Glacier*. The monthly ran from December 1885 to May 1888. *The Glacier* was a one-page sheet; an annual subscription was fifty cents; and its copy was local chit-chat, mission happenings, and the progress of Christianity among the natives. What was not reported were the sexual propensities of the young student body that kept the missionaries in "constant trouble both at Wrangell and Sitka."[57]

In order to balance their constant expenses, Young had early attempted to barrel and ship salmon.[58] With the initiation of federal support, he no doubt hoped that Jackson would exert himself in support of the Tlinkit Training Academy as he had for the Sitka Training School. Jackson did not do so. In fact he actually discouraged what money might have been forthcoming. In answer to an inquiry from the Commissioner of Indian Affairs, the newly appointed General Agent for Education replied, "There is already one [Training School in Alaska]. . . . And instead of having two starved ones in the same region of the country it is better to have one well sustained and efficient."[59] Fannie took the bit in her mouth and protested directly to the Secretary of the Interior, Honorable L. Q. C. Lamar.

> Of the appropriation, voted by Congress of Fifteen Thousand Dollars for Industrial Schools in Alaska, for the fiscal year ending June 30th, 1885, Eleven Thousand was given to the Sitka Training School, and our application for the unexpended balance sent on in May with the endorsement of the Civil Officers . . . was stated by the Department to have been received too late, the balance having been already paid back into the Treasury.[60]

It seems highly doubtful that the parsimonious Jackson permitted a single penny of any appropriation to go unspent. Whatever the case, the Academy's costs continued to mount, and reality demanded an economic answer. On October 15, 1885, Hall wrote to Oregon's Senator J. N. Dolph. He admitted the school was in serious financial trouble and that the farm "on which we based our principal hope of self-support failed to realize these hopes." His solution was to let "the Government take up this school, using the shops, farm, printing press and supplies on hand."[61] Unfortunately Congress' ridiculously small allocation for Jackson's expanding school system precluded another training school 150 miles from Sitka. However, in 1887–88, the Bureau of Indian Affairs' budget did supply some temporary relief: for her twenty-five students the government promised $167 per annum.[62] Alaska's capital newspaper rejoiced at the news. Declared *The Alaskan*: "Heretofore this school has been supported by voluntary contributions, and the donation to it of a large part of Mr. Young's salary as a missionary, and a person of less indomitable will and energy than good Mrs. Young is possessed of would have abandoned the work long ago."[63]

Certainly Fannie had given her best. On January 1886, her husband reluctantly reported to *Glacier* readers:

> Our institution is now motherless. Mrs. Young has been doing the work of three. Our funds were not sufficient to warrant the employment of the needed assistants. Mrs. Young was not very strong to begin with; and the constant strain upon bodily and mental powers told severely upon

> her health and developed a heart trouble that was growing to dangerous proportions. So we sent her down to Portland by this month's steamer, for the double purpose of obtaining medical advice and giving her a much needed rest.[64]

Fannie recovered, but a year later the Youngs suffered the tragic loss of their youngest daughter, Fannie Louise, because, as her sorrowing father wrote, "The delicate health of this little one could not be recruited amidst the rigors of the Alaskan climate." Both the Reverends Lindsley and Jackson participated in the funeral ceremonies.[65]

The 1887 government aid was just not enough to sustain the Academy's momentum. Despite Fannie's will and Hall's industry, the institution's end appeared in sight. In the fall of that year the United States Commissioner James Sheakley visited the Wrangell School.

> In the conscientious discharge of my official duties I had to decide a case against Mrs. Young and her so called Training school; and the facts developed by the investigation proved that she had no training school at all and that she was keeping nothing but an Indian boarding house of rather inferior grade. I have the kindest of feelings toward the Young family and have put myself to some inconvenience to assist and accommodate them and will do so still but the facts and the law are against her and I could not decide otherwise.

The upshot was that the Commissioner (later to become Governor Sheakley) strongly urged the Youngs "to abandon their effort . . . and seek some employment better adapted to their capacity." He reported they had "decided to act upon [his advice] and will make ready to leave this place by early spring."[66] The following spring Sheakley was surprised to discover that Fannie "was making a determined effort to continue the so-called training school." "The farm," he insisted, "is of no value. It has never produced anything but debts and an annual loss of about a thousand dollars." One good training school in the Territory is all that is required and the one at Sitka now in successful operation is sufficient to accommodate all who need such educational advantages."[67]

Aware that the Young enterprise was about to collapse, Jackson sent Mr. and Mrs. H. F. Lake to salvage enough for a far simpler mission school operation. The transition was understandably not always pleasant for either Mrs. Clara Lake or Fannie Young. "It is indeed very fortunate," penned Mrs. Lake, "that Mr. Lake and I are not troubled with being sensitive—those that are she worries the life out of."[68] Clearly Fannie and Hall had exhausted themselves. No doubt they accepted the news that the Office of Indian Affairs had not renewed their contract less as a *coup de grace* than as a reprieve. Hall felt the lack of civilization was deteriorating him "mentally and spiritually." He had grown to loathe preaching in Chinook and Tlinget.[69] By July, Young was on his way to scout out a California parish assignment, and faithful Fannie labored to close down the late Tlinkit Academy. Writing to the Commissioner of Education, Sheakley commented "that the closing of Mrs. Young's 'so called training school' is a good thing for all concerned." To Jackson he wrote a laconic "All is well that ends well."[70]

Regrettably it was not that graceful. Before Fannie could disengage herself from Wrangell, she got into a legal battle with a petty representative, spiteful, it would appear, of the United States Government. To hasten her departure, the officer placed six locks on her home, commenting, "Won't that old hairpin be surprised when she comes home and finds her doors locked." The "old hairpin" was furious, and both the frontier press and the Sitka Judge, none other than her old co-worker John G. Brady, heard about "A LADY MISSIONARY PERSECUTED." Flemming, the government official, beat a hasty retreat.[71]

Happily Fannie and Hall enjoyed their own well-earned retreat. His new ministry took him to the Southern California coastal community of Long Beach. With the old enthusiasm he informed Jackson, "I am well suited in my location here—am by the sea, in a delightful climate and a beautiful country. Am 22 miles from Los Angeles with Railroad connection. The town is rapidly growing and the church which was only organized in June has excellent prospects."[72] But the Golden State could not match Alaska. Neither could subsequent pastorates at Cedar Falls, Iowa, and Cabery, Illinois, nor a college pastorate at Wooster, Ohio. The Great Land was in his blood, and in another ten years S. Hall Young would again be in the north, but serving a new role and in a completely different part of Alaska.[73]

It seems rather obvious why S. Hall Young's Wrangell efforts did not produce the result for which he and his loyal wife labored so assiduously. First of all, their sweat and vivacity could not outweigh lack of money, lack of Home Board support, and a farming operation for which neither Wrangell's soil nor settlement was adapted. If Wrangell had been a thriving town everything would have been stimulated. As it was, the place by

1888 was a haunt of its former self. One visitor referred to it as a "ghost town," with its main street covered by knee-high grass.[74] Furthermore, Jackson was right about an ill-advised training school duplication. There is no way to prove that Jackson's *bête noir,* Aaron L. Lindsley, kept encouraging Young's institution to spite the Church's Home Board leadership, but circumstantial evidence is tantalizing. Surely if he had wanted to promote the Presbyterian Church in Alaska he should have told the exuberant and naive Pennsylvania novice to play the team game, that is, to keep his shoulder behind one of the regularly constituted Panhandle missions.

But maybe this does Lindsley a grave injustice. Possible he did attempt to restrain Young and his dynamic wife in their academic independence. To judge from Young's later career, in which he lunged from one assignment to another, the man's impetuosity was very unpredictable. Young was never one to soft-pedal his achievements. But then neither was he incapable of admitting his deficiencies. Gazing back on his Wrangell ministry from the perspective of the 1920s, the grey-haired Young declared, "My mistakes were many, and I regret them, both those mentioned, and more of which I cannot tell."[75]

Any fair-minded student who seeks to evaluate the early 1878–88 career of S. Hall Young and/or his Alaska co-workers must admit that, equipped with all the money in the world, the missionaries' goals were next to impossible to fulfill. An age which is a bit wiser in the enormous variables and complexity of acculturation can either scoff at their temerity or express respect for their steadfast sacrifices. Estimating a missionary's worth, like measuring the successful teacher, is largely impossible; one must weigh *future* achievement. In 1893 the Reverend Clarence Thwing, Presbyterian minister in charge at Wrangell, wrote, "In spite of any irregularity about the latter enterprise, [the Tlinkit Academy] and its unfortunate (almost ignominious) termination, there are twenty or more fine young men, now just entering manhood, who were more or less educated or trained in the Academy. Mr. Young's works do follow him."[76] Add to these visible signs S. Hall Young's countless words and deeds for his Native, as well as white, parishioners. Surely the verdict must be that he left Alaska a better place in which to live.

NOTES

1. The best source of information of S. Hall Young's family background is his autobiography, *Hall Young of Alaska, "The Mushing Parson": The Autobiography of S. Hall Young* (New York, 1927). Both the Presbyterian Historical Society in Philadelphia and the San Francisco Theological Seminary contain documents of his life's story.

2. Ibid., p. 52.

3. Frederick Rudolph, *The American College and University: A History* (New York, 1962), p. 65.

4. Young, *Hall Young*, p. 59.

5. Clifton E. Olmstead, *History of Religion in the United States* (Englewood Cliffs, N.J., 1960), p. 496; William Warren Sweet, *The Story of Religion in America* (New York, 1930), p. 357.

6. Still the only really complete biography of the remarkable Sheldon Jackson is the biography which he authorized Robert Laird Stewart to write, *Sheldon Jackson: Pathfinder and Prospector of the Missionary Vanguard in the Rocky Mountains and Alaska* (New York, 1908). For Jackson's Rocky Mountain achievements see also the pamphlet, *An Historical Sketch of the Presbyteries, Church and Mission Work of the Synod of Colorado*, and the articles by Andrew E. Murray in the *Journal of the Presbyterian Historical Society* 27 (March, June, and September 1950).

7. S. Hall Young to Sheldon Jackson, Dec. 15, 1877. Jackson Correspondence Collection, Presbyterian Historical Society, Philadelphia, Pennsylvania. Vol. 7, p. 199. Hereafter this collection referred to as J. Corr.

8. Along with a study of medical books, the book on Alaska which Young promptly turned to was the pioneer work by William H. Dall, *Alaska and Its Resources* (London, 1870).

9. Jackson gave maximum publicity to her heart-rending descriptions in his own newspaper, *The Rocky Mountain Presbyterian*. Most of her letters are available in Charles A. Anderson (ed.), "Letters of Amanda R. McFarland," *Journal of the Presbyterian Historical Society* 34 (June and Dec. 1956): 83–102; 226–44.

10. *The Rocky Mountain Presbyterian*, April 1878. A complete file of Sheldon Jackson's monthly is now available on microfilm from the Board of Microtext, Dr. Raymond P. Morris, Yale Divinity School Library, 409 Prospect St., New Haven, Conn. 06511.

11. Young, *Hall Young*, p. 66. Young formally began his work at the Wrangell mission on August 8, 1878. Sheldon Jackson, *The Presbyterian Church in Alaska: An Official Sketch of Its Rise and Progress 1877–1884* (Washington, D.C., 1886), p. 4.

12. Young, *Hall Young*, p. 78.

13. Ivan Petroff referred to her as a "highly intelligent lady." Ted and Caryl Hinckley (eds.), "Ivan Petroff's Journal of a Trip to Alaska in 1878," *Journal of the West* 5 (Jan. 1966): 23. Sheldon Jackson, *Alaska, and Missions on the North Pacific Coast* (New York, 1880), p. 215.

14. Conversations with author, July 1959, Philadelphia, Pa. For details of Jackson-Lindsley feud see: Ted C. Hinckley, "The Alaska Labors of Sheldon Jackson, 1877–1890" (unpublished Ph.D. dissertation, Indiana University, 1960), pp. 23–39.

15. Young, *Hall Young*, p. 69. See also: National Archives Microfilm Series No.

430, Interior Dept., Alaska. Roll 1, Young to President Rutherford B. Hayes, Dec. 24, 1880.

16. Thomas Stratton Goslin, "Henry Kendall and the Evangelization of a Continent" (unpublished Ph.D. dissertation, University of Pennsylvania, 1948), p. 337.

17. S. Hall Young, *What Every Presbyterian Should Know about Alaska* (n.p., n.d.). Young, *Hall Young*, p. 79.

18. *The Rocky Mountain Presbyterian*, February, 1879; Young to Sheldon Jackson, Nov. 11, 1878, J. Corr., Vol. 9, p. 3.

19. Jackson, *The Presbyterian Church*, p. 4. It was the first and apparently the last time Lindsley visited Alaska. Jackson would make, with a few exceptions, an annual tour of the Far North frontier until after the turn of the century.

20. *The Alaska Appeal*, Sept. 15, 1879.

21. John Muir, *Travels in Alaska* (Boston, 1915), pp. 127 and 172.

22. Morgan Sherwood, *Exploration of Alaska, 1865–1900* (New Haven, 1965), p. 74.

23. S. Hall Young, *Alaska Days with John Muir* (New York, 1915), pp. 126–127.

24. Young, *Hall Young*, pp. 163–64.

25. Newspaper clipping by Young in Sheldon Jackson Scrapbooks, Presbyterian Historical Society, Philadelphia, Pa., Vol. 8, pp. 29 and 59–61. Hereafter collection referred to as J. Scrap.

26. Muir, *Travels*, pp. 131–33.

27. On the Presbyterian battle to separate Alaska's native population from liquor see: Morgan B. Sherwood, "Ardent Spirits: Hooch and the Osprey Affair at Sitka," *Journal of the West* 4 (July 1965): 301–344; Ted C. Hinckley, "Punitive Action at Angoon," *Alaska Sportsman* 24 (Jan. and Feb. 1963): 8ff and 14ff; and "Sheldon Jackson and Benjamin Harrison: Presbyterians and the Administration of Alaska," *Pacific Northwest Quarterly* 54 (April 1963): 66–74.

28. Robert N. De Armond, *The Founding of Juneau* (Juneau, 1967), pp. 118–22.

29. Young, *Hall Young*, pp. 255–57; Young to S. Jackson, March 24, 1881; J. Corr., Vol 11, p. 105; Young to S. Jackson, March 8, 1881, ibid., p. 8D. *Annual Report of the Commissioner of Indian Affairs to the Secretary of the Interior—1881* (Washington, D.C., 1881), p. xxxvii.

30. Young to S. Jackson, May 16, 1881, J. Corr., Vol. 11, p. 164; *Minutes of the General Assembly, 1880* (New York, 1880), p. 44.

31. Jackson, *The Presbyterian Church*, p. 8; *Minutes of the General Assembly*, p. 590.

32. J. S. Oakford, Deputy Collector, to William G. Morris, April 26, 1882, Alaska Custom House Records, Alaska State Historical Library, Juneau, Vol. 22. Hereafter collection cited as Custom House. Young to S. Jackson, Aug. 15, 1882, J. Corr., Vol. 12, p. 258; Young to S. Jackson, Jan. 9, 1882, ibid., p. 48.

33. Young to S. Jackson, June 4, 1881, J. Corr., Vol. 11, p. 186; H. Kendall to S. Jackson, June 10, 1881, ibid., p. 195; Mrs. E. S. Willard to S. Jackson, June 29, 1881, ibid., p. 241; Eugene S. Willard to S. Jackson, Oct. 29, 1881, ibid., p. 282; S. Jackson to Mrs. Jackson, July 10, 1881, ibid., p. 219; Young to S. Jackson, Dec. 14, 1881, ibid., p. 48; Maggie McFarland to Mrs. McFarland, Sept. 17, 1883, J. Corr., Vol. 13, p. 204; A. E. Austin to S. Jackson, Nov. 19, 1883, ibid., p. 240; Maggie McFarland to Mrs. McFarland, April 15, 1884, ibid., p. 336.

34. Henry Glass to S. Jackson, Nov. 14, 1882, J. Corr., Vol. 12, p. 291; Young to S. Jackson, Nov. 15, 1882, ibid., p. 305.

35. *Presbyterian Home Missions*, Nov. 15, 1880, p. 227; Young to S. Jackson, Nov. 22, 1880, J. Corr., Vol. 10, p. 358.

36. Jackson, *The Presbyterian Church*, p. 4; Young to S. Jackson, Nov. 15, 1881, J. Corr., Vol. 11, p. 305.

37. Young to S. Jackson, March 12, 1883, J. Corr., Vol. 13, p. 60.

38. J. Loomis Gould arrived in Alaska in 1882; he was Young's second cousin and took over the Howkan Mission Station. J. W. McFarland arrived in Alaska in 1880; he was a nephew of Amanda McFarland's late husband. After marrying Maggie Dunbar of the Wrangell staff, he joined the Wrangell team. Rev. Eugene S. Willard arrived in Alaska in July 1881 and commenced work at Portage Bay. Jackson, *The Presbyterian Church*, pp. 4–6.

39. Young, *Hall Young*, p. 267.

40. Young to S. Jackson, March 12, 1883, J. Corr., Vol. 13, p. 60.

41. Young, *Hall Young*, p. 269.

42. O. D. Eaton to H. Teller, June 24, 1884, J. Corr., Vol. 13, p. 384.

43. Maggie McFarland to S. Jackson, Aug. 13, 1883, J. Corr., Vol. 13, p. 194; Maggie McFarland to S. Jackson, Feb. 25, 1884, ibid., p. 309.

44. Fannie E. Young to Hon. L. Q. C. Lamar, Secretary of the Interior, Nov. 7, 1885, Miscellaneous Correspondence, National Archives, Washington, D.C., Bureau of Education. Hereafter cited as National Archives.

45. H. F. French to Collector of Customs, Dec. 8, 1883, Custom House Records, Vol. 26; C. J. Folger to Collector, June 12, 1884, ibid.; Thomas A. Willson to Peter French, April 20, 1886, ibid., Vol. 30; *Juneau City Mining Record*, October 4, 1888.

46. Young, *Hall Young*, p. 271; *The Evangelist*, Aug. 9, 1884. A contemporary, the missionary John W. McFarland, stated that the farm was acquired "for 400. also oxen and farming implements." John W. McFarland to S. Jackson, April 15, 1884, J. Corr., Vol. 13, p. 334.

47. F. Young to L. Q. C. Lamar, Nov. 7, 1885, National Archives. This is the way the school's name was spelled in the Academy's newspaper, not the way Young spelled it in his autobiography. There he identifies the institution as the Thlingit Training Academy for Boys. Young, *Hall Young*, p. 269.

48. *The Presbyterian Journal*, June 12, 1884. While there were to be a number of fine products of the Presbyterian missionary institutions in Alaska, the most outstanding was Edward Marsden. For his life story see: William Gilbert Beattie, *Marsden of Alaska: A Modern Indian* (New York, 1955).

49. Francis C. Sessions, *From Yellowstone Park to Alaska* (New York, 1890), pp. 58–59.

50. Hinckley, "The Alaska Labors," pp. 188ff. The excellent compilation by Melvin Ricks, *Directory of Alaska Post Offices and Postmasters* (Ketchikan, 1965) does not list Hall; however, his wife, Fannie, is credited as Sitka's postmistress July 1878–November 1878, p. 58.

51. *The Alaskan* (Sitka), Jan. 16, 1886.

52. Sessions, *Yellowstone*, pp. 58–59.

53. For background details of this enterprise see: Hinckley, "Alaska Labors," Chapter 10, and the *Annual Reports of the Commissioner of Education* for the 1880s (Washington, D.C.).

54. Two extremely useful books for understanding this phase of Indian history are: Loring Benson Priest, *Uncle Sam's Step-Children: The Reformation of the United States Indian Policy, 1865–1887* (New Brunswick, N.J., 1942); and Henry E. Fritz, *The Movement for Indian Assimilation, 1860–1890* (Philadelphia, 1963).

55. S. Hall Young to S. Jackson, May 13, 1886, J. Corr., Vol. 14, p. 210.

56. Maggie D. McFarland to Mrs. Jackson, April 15, 1884, J. Corr., Vol. 13, p. 336; *The Alaskan*, Feb. 20, 1886; John McFarland to S. Jackson, April 15, 1884, J. Corr., Vol. 13, p. 334.

57. *The Alaskan*, Jan. 30, 1886. The author possesses some *Tlinkit* fragments but knows of no full-run file of this useful publication. James Wickersham, *A Bibliography of Alaskan Literature: 1724–1924* (Cordova, 1927), p. 260; Young, *Hall Young*, p. 309.

58. *The Presbyterian*, June 12, 1884.

59. S. Jackson to D. C. Atkins, July 20, 1885, "Alaska Schools," Vol. I, p. 248, Sheldon Jackson Manuscripts Collection, Princeton Theological Seminary, Speer Library, Princeton, N.J. Hereafter this manuscript collection referred to as PTS.

60. F. Young to L. Q. C. Lamar, Nov. 7, 1885, National Archives.

61. Young to Senator J. N. Dolph, Oct. 15, 1885, Miscellaneous Educational Materials in Sheldon Jackson Collection, Presbyterian Historical Society. A. B. Upshaw to N. H. R. Dawson, Aug. 8, 1888, National Archives.

62. S. Jackson to H. Kendall, July 31, 1886, "Alaska Schools," PTS, Vol. 4, p. 175.

63. *The Alaskan*, Dec. 18, 1886.

64. *The Glacier*, Jan. 1886.

65. *The Glacier*, June 1887; *The Occident*, June 8, 1887; and Clipping, J. Scrap, Vol. 18, p. 20.

66. James Sheakley to S. Jackson, Oct. 31, 1887, J. Corr., Vol. 14, p. 137.

67. James Sheakley to S. Jackson, May 23, 1888, J. Corr., Vol. 15, p. 124C.

68. J. F. Lake to S. Jackson, June 20, 1888, ibid., p. 67; Mrs. (J. F.) Clara Lake to S. Jackson, April 7, 1888, ibid., p. 15.

69. D. C. Atkins to N. H. R. Dawson, May 11, 1888, National Archives; S. Jackson to Mrs. C. E. Walker, July 11, 1888, J. Corr., Vol. 26, pp. 238–41; Young, *Hall Young*, p. 312.

70. James Sheakley to N. H. R. Dawson, June 16, 1888, National Archives; James Sheakley to S. Jackson, July 7, 1888, J. Corr., Vol. 15, p. 75.

71. William Irwin to S. Jackson, Sept. 10, 1888, ibid., p. 93; James Sheakley to S. Jackson, Sept. 29, 1888, ibid., p. 97; *Juneau City Mining Record*, Oct. 4, 1888.

72. Young to S. Jackson, 1888, J. Corr., Vol. 15, p. 103.

73. *New York Times*, Sept. 4, 1927; and Young, *Hall Young*, Chapter 31ff.

74. Septima M. Collis, *A Woman's Trip to Alaska . . . 1890* (New York, 1890), pp. 78–79.

75. Young, *Hall Young*, p. 313. The statement in the *Dictionary of American Biography*, Vol. 20, p. 20, that, "By 1888, when Young resigned his place at Fort

Wrangell, Christian missionary work was proceeding in all the principal tribes of Southern Alaska largely because of his initiative," exaggerates his fine work.

76. Dr. Clarence Thwing to Mr. Boyd, Feb. 24, 1893, Thwing Letter Book, San Francisco Theological Seminary, San Anselmo, California. An edited version of this letter book is: Ted C. Hinckley, ed., "Excerpts from the Letters of Dr. Clarence Thwing, Presbyterian Missionary to Wrangell, Alaska, during the Mid-1890's," *Journal of Presbyterian History* 41 (March 1963): 37–55.

Female Native Teachers in Southeast Alaska

Sarah Dickinson, Tillie Paul, and Frances Willard

VICTORIA WYATT

Not all those who worked to educate and convert southeastern Alaska natives were Caucasian. Some Natives, convinced that accommodation offered the best alternative available in a rapidly changing world, did the same in an effort to insure their people's survival.

Victoria Wyatt, who holds a Ph.D. from Yale, is Associate Professor in the Department of History in Art at the University of Victoria, British Columbia. She has written Images from the Inside Passage: An Alaskan Portrait by Winter and Pond *(Seattle: University of Washington Press, 1989),* Shapes of Their Thoughts: Reflections of Culture Contact in Northwest Coast Indian Art *(Norman: University of Oklahoma Press, 1984), and several articles on Northwest Indian art and oral history.*

In the following selection, Wyatt examines the careers of three Alaska Native women who became Christian educators: Sarah Dickinson, Tillie Kinnon Paul, and Frances Willard. Although they are not mentioned in Ted Hinckley's article, both Sarah Dickinson and the young Tillie Kinnon served for a time as translators for S. Hall Young. And, while working together at the Sitka Industrial Training School, Tillie Kinnon Paul and Frances Willard devised a Tlingit dictionary. Wyatt describes well the difficult decisions these women faced in a time of change, noting that their acceptance of Christianity forced them to reject certain elements of their traditional culture. However, as she also points out, all three also fought against those aspects of the newly imposed American culture which they deemed undesirable.

As Wyatt's insightful analysis demonstrates, culture change is a complex phenomenon which cannot easily be categorized. Determining motivation is a difficult challenge for the historian, for why people act can never be known with cer-

This article appeared originally in Margaret Szasz, ed., *Between Indian and White Worlds: The Cultural Broker* (Norman: University of Oklahoma Press, 1994), 179–96; it is reprinted here by permission.

tainty; most of us as individuals often have difficulty identifying our own motivation clearly and coherently. Natives made choices regarding acceptance or rejection of Western beliefs and ideas though, as Richard Dauenhauer's article emphasizes, their choices were often highly circumscribed by the control and pressure brought to bear by the government and the mission societies. Part of the significance of Wyatt's work is her understanding of the active role of Natives in defining the parameters of change in their world. She has particularly emphasized the role women played in the accommodations made by Natives.

In the late nineteenth and early twentieth centuries, Tlingit and Haida Indians in Southeast Alaska faced tremendous challenges as non-Native settlers moved into their region. Even more than the Russians who had previously occupied Native lands in Alaska, the American settlers appropriated traditional fishing and hunting areas and imposed new economic, religious, legal, and political systems.

Native people had to develop strategies quickly to respond to these changes and to the political and cultural oppression they brought. U.S. naval gunboats discouraged Native peoples in coastal Alaska from using force to oppose the foreign invasion. Almost certainly, too, Native leaders there got news of the very violent federal policies toward Indians in other areas of the United States in the 1860s and 1870s and wanted to avoid similar experiences in Alaska. Thus, leaders sought ways to help their people survive and cope with the new developments.

As elsewhere in the United States, different individuals chose different methods of achieving this end, and opinion was divided—then and now—about the desirability of each strategy. Many of the choices involved a considerable amount of accommodation and either the appearance or the reality of adopting the value system of the foreign culture.

This was certainly true of the many Native women and men who worked among their own people as Christian lay workers and educators. They accepted a new form of spirituality and a new type of educational system and sought to use them as a vehicle to help their peers. Their mission was to educate their people about the non-Native society that was growing around them and to prepare the coming generation to function and compete successfully in the new system.

Like all Indians in Southeast Alaska at the time, they faced hard choices. Often white prejudice, cultural oppression, and harsh economic realities forced them to relinquish time-honored customs to maximize chances for survival. Given these grim circumstances, they did not necessarily reject their ethnic identity when they chose to counsel change. They turned from their past so as to turn toward their people.

Native women, as well as men, chose to be Christian lay workers and educators. Women traditionally were both influenuial and respected in Tlingit and Haida society, both of which are organized by matrilineal descent. The churches established by missionaries generally did not give women the same opportunities as men to hold church offices or to be ordained, either in Alaska or elsewhere. However, there were opportunities for Native women to work actively as educators, and many did. Trained and employed by missionaries, they taught about Christianity as well as about secular matters, and the distinction between educator and lay worker is a fine one indeed. Their activities went far beyond classroom teaching: missionaries expected them to devote enormous energies to their role, to be available at all times, and to model and encourage a very specific way of life.

This chapter explores the activities of three women who chose to be Christian educators so as to help their people face the challenges visited on them. Sarah Dickinson assumed that role as an adult. Tillie Paul developed the wish to do so as a girl in an Alaskan mission school. Frances Willard was sent to a seminary in New Jersey and returned eager to teach. The decision each made to embrace this work was only one of many difficult options various Native leaders explored to try to help their people. It is not my intent to suggest that their decision was any more or less laudable than those of their peers who chose other routes. I do suggest that, no matter what methods Native people chose, their determination to ensure that their people survived is a testimony to cultural strength under adversity. Whatever they were forced to relinquish then, they helped lay the foundation for the cultural revival occurring in many places in Southeast Alaska today.

Unfortunately, very little information is available in written sources about the lives of Native lay workers, whether female or male. Oral history would certainly reveal more information about some of the woman discussed below and would be an essential component of any comprehensive study. The discussion here must be restricted to written sources—most left by non-Native missionaries. These records are usually episodic: I have recounted some seemingly mundane incidents to convey the range of activities the women's work entailed. However, the sources provide little insight about the thoughts and feelings of the individuals discussed.

Indeed, even the descriptions of their activities contain large chronological gaps; and often the women abruptly drop altogether from the record. Also, it is important to remember that missionaries had a vested interest in portraying their work as successful and may have deliberately or unknowingly misrepresented the Native educators.

However, as western historians have recently pointed out, we cannot omit peoples or genders from the historical record because the sources about them are incomplete. Even scant written records may provide a basis for some understanding of their lives and work and give a good foundation with which to approach the oral history that could project Native voices more directly. The discussion below must be restricted to those ends.

Often Native lay workers and educators started their careers as interpreters for missionaries. Women who had married non-Native men were prime candidates for such work, for they already knew both languages and both cultures. Sarah Dickinson was one such woman. As in most cases, there is little written information on her life, but enough exists to piece together a biographical sketch and gain some insight into her experiences.

Sources disagree about Dickinson's exact ethnic background. One white commentator described her as "a woman of great personality and devotion who was of mingled Thlingit, Tsimpshean and white blood."[1] However, the Presbyterian missionary S. Hall Young, for whom she worked as interpreter and who knew her more closely, referred to her as "a full-blood Tongass Native," explaining that "her tribe was the most southern of the Thlingits, living just across Dixon's Entrance from the Tsimpsheans of Port Simpson and Metlakalaa." Young added that she had "early acquired the Tsimpshean language as well as her own."'[2]

In any event, Dickinson had been educated by the missionary William Duncan at his first "model village" of Old Metlakatla in British Columbia and reportedly was converted to Christianity there.[3] Undoubtedly, she learned some English at the time, and she also spoke Tsimshian and Stikine, the dialect of the Tlingits living near Wrangell.[4] She married George Dickinson, an American fur trader. They may have met in Wrangell; at any rate, she was living there, where he worked, by 1877. When Young arrived in 1878, she had two children—a son, Billy, who was then fifteen, and a daughter, Sarah. The children had learned to read and write English, which the family spoke at home. Young's impression was that they "held themselves rather aloof from other natives, speaking of them as 'they' and of the whites as 'we.'"[5]

Sarah Dickinson was already helping in a Native-run school in Wrangell at that time.[6] Tlingit Indians in Wrangell became interested in a mission when Christian Tsimshian Indians began worshipping there in 1876, and in the absence of an ordained minister, a Tsimshian man known as Clah began giving instruction. This indication of interest eventually led the Presbyterian Board of Home Missions to send a white lay worker, Mrs. Amanda R. McFarland, to Wrangell to start a school in 1877.[7] The Rev. Sheldon Jackson, who brought Mrs. McFarland there, described his meeting with Dickinson as follows. "When we reached Wrangel this woman was a hundred miles up the Stickeen River gathering the winter supply of berries. Learning from a passing steamer that the missionaries had come, she placed her children, bedding, and provisions in her canoe, and paddled home, against heavy head winds, to give us a welcome."[8]

Leaving Mrs. McFarland in Wrangell, Jackson asked Dickinson to become her interpreter. McFarland opened a school and reported that the Native people were "very much interested in it" and that the class averaged thirty students. Sarah Dickinson was one of them; McFarland made a special note that she and Clah were in a class together. "They study reading, spelling, geography, and writing." McFarland taught in the morning, and Clah took over a "short session" in the afternoon. McFarland explained, "Since Mrs. Dickinson came home, Clah preaches in Tsimpsean, and Mrs. D. interprets his sermon into Stickeen."[9]

When the Presbyterian minister the Rev. S. Hall Young arrived in Wrangell in 1878, he immediately made Dickinson his "official translator." Her son, Billy, also served as an interpreter, and Young trained him "for prayer-meetings and conferences."[10] Dickinson's influence in prayer meetings extended beyond translating. Young wrote, "Mrs. Dickinson must be given credit for checking the practice of entering complaints against and berating one another in these prayer-meetings and confessions."[11]

Dickinson also played influential roles outside formal gatherings. She was the voice through which McFarland and Young spoke in a wide range of situations in which they represented mission interests to the Native community. Thus, in a sense, she acted as an advocate for the mission. On at least one occasion and possibly more, she helped McFarland and Young persuade reluctant parents to allow their daughter to be placed in the mission's residence for girls.[12]

Dickinson's responsibilities led her into extremely tense situations, sometimes reluctantly. Young determined to stop certain Tlingit practices that he and other missionaries felt were incompatible with Christianity, and he relied on Dickinson to act as translator when he intervened in Native affairs. Much more than Young, Dickinson was in a position to understand the anger his actions would generate and to appreciate the potential consequences.

Particularly trying for Dickinson were the times when Young opposed shamans, or spiritual healers (known in Tlingit as *ixts*). Young and other missionaries in Southeast Alaska were particularly offended by *ixts,* who derived their power through communication with spirit helpers. Shamanism represented a competing belief system that threatened missionaries' success, and missionaries claimed *ixts* accused people of witchcraft and promoted their torture. Young waged an ongoing battle with them and on several occasions called on Dickinson to translate. He reported that she was very fearful of his actions, in part because of the power of the *ixts* and in part because she thought people were so angry at Young that they might use violence. During one incident, he threatened to fire her as interpreter if she refused to accompany him, and he implied it was only that threat that made her cooperate.[13] He claimed his success in that incident increased her confidence, and she was more willing to cooperate later.[14] However, it may be that this statement was merely an attempt to vindicate his actions and perhaps should not be accepted at face value.

In being asked to help fight shamanism, Dickinson faced a dilemma she shared with many Native people in Alaska and elsewhere who worked with non-Native authorities. Young, who liked his writing to be dramatic, may have exaggerated her reactions, but without question she was in a situation that many other Native people also found tense. In the early 1880s, L. Beardslee, the naval commander, established a Native police force in Sitka and reported that the only instance in which these policemen failed to cooperate with him was a case involving shamanism.[15] Similarly, Indian agents on reservations in the contiguous United States also found that the Native police forces there were often reluctant to become involved in cases concerning accusations of witchcraft.[16]

Dickinson's own work with Clah and her diverse services as interpreter in Wrangell made her well suited to assume primary teaching responsibilities elsewhere on her own. The Presbyterian Board of Home Missions was quick to take advantage of her skills and her willingness to teach. When her husband was transferred to the Chilkat region in 1880 to run a store that was opening there, the board commissioned her to start a school for Chilkat Tlingits. She helped lay a foundation for the Presbyterian missionaries the Reverend and Mrs. E. S. Willard, who arrived a year later to open Haines Mission. They employed her as a teacher and an interpreter. Mrs. Willard's first impression of Dickinson was tinged with the condescension characteristic of the period. She wrote, "She is a very good woman, I think, and has done well under the circumstances. We shall soon need a teacher of larger scope."[17]

Besides helping locally, Dickinson sometimes accompanied the Reverend Willard when he traveled to more distant villages in the Chilkat country. She went with him and his wife on the first of these trips, shortly after the Willards arrived in the Chilkat region. As Mrs. Willard described it, the trip was not without dangers, including crossing rapids in a canoe. She explained, "I sat with my back to the head of the canoe, and saw the dangers only to be thankful that we had escaped them, while Mrs. Dickinson, turned the other way and seeing always the rock we were to split upon, kept uttering little cries of alarm."[18]

Dickinson was generous with her time, and she also used her ties with the trading post store to help the Willards. During their first Christmas in the Chilkat country, Mrs. Willard held out the promise of Christmas presents as an incentive to encourage children to attend school. Thus, she had to "grade every child and make every present," a task involving some sixty-nine children. She reported that Dickinson "knit several little collars of yarn and two small scarfs, and gave me about a dozen tiny dolls out of the store, which helped a good deal."[19]

At times, Dickinson and her husband were the only other people near the mission who spoke English, and thus her company was important to the Willards psychologically as well as practically.[20] She was also their source of information when they were absent. In the summer of 1882, the Willards both suffered dangerously poor health and made an emergency trip to Sitka.[21] Dickinson sent them news before leaving for a two-month vacation in Oregon.[22]

If Sarah Dickinson had initially been reluctant to participate in Young's campaign against *ixts,* her actions were different in the Chilkat country. During the Willards' absence in Sitka, she heard of an elderly Tlingit woman who had been accused of killing a small boy through witchcraft. Indian leaders from the mission freed her with the help of Dickinson's husband. When the Willards returned to the mission in spring 1883, they found that Sarah Dickinson was sheltering the woman in her home. The woman had admitted using witchcraft but was still given protection.[23]

Caroline Willard's published letters conclude in November 1883, and information about Dickinson after that time becomes more scarce. In

1886, she was still teaching in the school at Haines and had an average of seventy students.[24] By June 1887, she had resigned that position.[25] Oral history or written sources unavailable for this study might give more information about her life and her activities after that year.

Sarah Dickinson devoted at least a decade of her life to missionary and educational work among her own people. Despite Young's impression that she held herself aloof from Native people, she clearly cared deeply about them and acted in ways she felt would help them. As noted, her work involved episodes of considerable tension exacerbated by the fact that she did not choose when to intervene in Native affairs but was expected to cooperate nonetheless. Her services were tremendously important to Young and the Willards, who could not have functioned without an interpreter with a clear understanding of their teachings and a willingness to help promote their goals. Considering her importance to them, she appears very much in the background in their writings, primarily mentioned only in passing. It is impossible to know whether this reflects the way she was treated by them or simply the particular focus of their accounts.

Sarah Dickinson must have been at least in her thirties when she became a teacher. Some other Native women and men in Southeast Alaska were encouraged from the days of their mission schooling to become teachers among their own people. This was an explicit goal of the missionaries. They felt that converted Indians could be good role models for other Indians; they hoped that converts who taught themselves would develop a stronger commitment to Christianity; and they also faced a shortage of non-Native workers. Caroline Willard expressed her views in an article written in 1888 entitled "Native Sabbath School Teachers." By that time, she and her husband were working in Juneau and had established a weekly class for the training of teachers. She wrote,

> When we started the Sunday School of the Juneau Thlingget Presbyterian Church it was with the determination of making it a Christian Training School, that is, of bringing into activity our whole Christian force among the Natives . . . . Realizing that inactivity was full of danger for these young Christians, and that the best means of growth was labor for the bringing-in of others, we made them teachers in the school.[26]

This same philosophy undoubtedly informed missionary goals for some years before Caroline Willard described it; and students in mission schools had shown an interest in becoming teachers before such formal classes were formed. Tillie Kinnon Paul is one such student. She was born around 1864. Her mother was a Tlingit woman from the Wrangell area, and her father, a Scotsman, was a factor for the Hudson's Bay Company in Victoria.[27] She spent her early years among her mother's people. When she was about twelve, she was briefly in the Methodist mission in Port Simpson and then returned to Wrangell and entered Mrs. McFarland's Home for Girls.[28]

The girls at the school were expected to help with chores and to take classes in domestic work. Mary Lee Davis, a white writer who knew Paul later, suggested that this took a real adjustment, for she was from a high-ranking Tlingit family. Davis observed, "It often seems to me that even the best of our missionaries have not quite realized or given all the credit that they should to the stout-hearted perseverance shown by many a high-caste Thlingit girl, in going through with courses that meant manual labor." She added that most of the first girls at the McFarland home were of lower rank and that it would be difficult for someone of higher rank to work side by side with them.[29]

Whether or not this is true, Kinnon seems to have become committed quickly to her life at the home. In November 1879, she was the oldest girl there and was a leader among the other students. A teacher wrote that she had become a Christian, that she "expresses a great desire to be trained for a teacher. She is already quite a help in teaching the younger children. She is a girl of much promise and decision of character."[30]

When Sarah Dickinson left Wrangell, Tillie Kinnon started working with S. Hall Young as interpreter. Davis suggests that this was a complicated responsibility for a young girl, for she had to adapt the images in the Bible to make them meaningful to her own people. Davis explained,

> You may catch a notion of all the latent lurking difficulty, when you recall how very many choicest sections of our scripture deal with the symbolism of the shepherd, the lore and feeling of a long-time pastoral people, and of men as sheep that wander from the fold—sheep that are timid, frightened, lost. But the Thlingit word for sheep refers to mountainy, wild creatures . . . skilful in defence with their sharp horns and hoofs against even the most powerful prey–[beasts]. All the rich color and the connotation of Bible story are quite lost, if this word sheep should be translated literally.

Davis concluded, "You will guess the struggles this young girl must make, using an art so alien to her nature, to turn such themes into intelligible Thlingit."[31]

Tillie Kinnon married Louis Francis Paul, a man of Tlingit and white ancestry. In 1882, the couple was commissioned by the Presbyterian Board of Home Missions to open a school in Klukwan, some thirty miles from the Willards' mission.[32] They arrived in Klukwan in late May, stopping first at the Willards' mission, where they were given slates and other supplies.[33] Davis points out that the fact that they were both from high-ranking families may have helped open doors for them among the Chilkat people.[34] Louis Paul reported that the Indians said they were sorry a teacher had not come sooner, "that by this time they would know more about God." Thirty-seven men and twenty-seven women attended the school with just twelve primers among them. The Pauls made regular circuits of the village, visiting each house three times weekly.[35]

Like Sarah Dickinson, the Pauls tried to decrease the practice of shamanism. Without providing details, Davis implies that this proved difficult and dangerous work for them, too. She suggested that their ties to both the Wrangell and the Tongass tribes helped protect them, since any harm done to them would have offended these powerful groups.[36]

The Pauls also opposed the manufacture of alcohol, a technique Indians had learned from whites. Tillie Paul suggested that drinking caused fights to break out between Indians. She sent an appeal that was quoted later, unedited, by Julia McNair Wright. "I would like if there were law to restraint those Indians from making liquor, for there is plenty of it in this place, for it is the root of all evil amongst them. If the liquor was taken from them, the [sic] would be peaceable Indians."[37]

Tillie and Louis Paul returned to Wrangell early in the summer of 1883, possibly in part because they were expecting their first child. Caroline Willard was pleased with what they had achieved. She stated, "The experiment has been well tried." Presumably she meant the "experiment" of sending Native teachers to a remote location on their own. She added that "good work has been done . . . . The people have learned to want education, and now will be more ready to receive it."[38]

The Pauls' first son, Samuel, was born in Wrangell. They then moved to the Tongass region and opened a school among Louis's people. Their second son, William, was bom in 1885.[39] Louis and Samuel Saxman, a white government teacher, drowned in 1886. Shortly thereafter, Tillie Paul gave birth to her third son, whom she named for his father.[40] She moved to Sitka and started teaching at the town's Native school and at the Sitka Industrial Training School (later called the Sheldon Jackson Institute), a Presbyterian residential school for Native students. When her oldest son was four, she allowed Sheldon Jackson to take him east to live with Mrs. Saxman, who had moved there.[41] Saxman later went to Ashland, Oregon, and joined the staff of the Sitka Industrial Training School late in 1890.[42]

Tillie Paul played a variety of roles in Sitka. As in Dickinson's case, serving as a teacher meant a commitment of time and energy that extended far beyond the formal classroom. In 1889, a listing of the staff of the school gives her title as "General Worker and Interpreter."[43] The *North Star,* the school's publication, mentions her from time to time, and occasionally she contributed articles to it. The April 1889 edition notes that she was in charge of a "Sabbath School class" of about fifty "untutored natives."[44] Around that time, one of her duties at the Sitka Industrial Training School was to supervise sewing classes.[45]

In October 1889, Paul traveled to Oregon to visit her eldest son and Mrs. Saxman. It was the first time she had traveled outside Alaska. She later published an account of the trip in the *North Star,* noting that she had never before seen "the cars" (presumaby streetcars) or ridden in a horse-drawn buggy. "It is wonderful the works of man!" she wrote. "When you compare the works of God and man how wonderful the world seems!"[46]

Paul returned from Oregon in spring 1890 and was immediately commissioned assistant matron at the Sitka Industrial Training School. The *North Star* reported that she conducted a temperance meeting in the Native village; by the beginning of 1891, she was the president of the Native temperance society in Sitka.[47] She still served as interpreter when needed for classes in the Native village.[48] For a six-month period in 1890 when the matron of the girls' department was absent, Paul acted in that position. Late in 1890, she was placed in charge of the Boys' Hospital and became the attendant nurse there.[49] The physician in charge, Clarence Thwing, wrote that she was "very devoted to her work and untiring in her attention to the sick."[50]

The Sitka Industrial Training School strongly emphasized English; children were not expected to use their Native language. In 1891, Jackson reported that for five years English had been the sole language at the school.[51] However, Paul and other Native workers at the school did not reject their heritage; in fact, they found ways to express it and preserve it which were acceptable to school officials. Paul published articles in the

North Star on Native "folklore." One article, recounting a myth, concluded with the comment, "Old customs have bound us like chains of steel, but the missionaries have brought us a light—God's Word—which will yet save the remnant of our race."[52] It is unclear whether these words were written by Paul or by William Kelly, the principal of the school and an editor of the paper, whose name is written in by hand on the by-line as coauthor with Paul. What is clear is that whatever denunciation was added at the end, Paul was interested in publishing detailed accounts of Native mythology.

Similarly, Paul helped to preserve the Tlingit language by working with Frances Willard to prepare a Tlingit dictionary and a means to put the language in writing.[53] Further, although students were prohibited from speaking Tlingit, there were special contexts in which the language was celebrated, and Paul took part in that celebration. Thus, on May 13, 1890, when the Sitka Industrial Training School sponsored an evening of "school entertainment," Paul and two other Tlingit women sang a hymn in Tlingit. They were followed by some Tsimshian students who sang in their language.[54]

The written record thus reveals a few ways in which Paul showed a strong interest in helping to preserve her culture. Undoubtedly, there were other occasions that have gone unrecorded. In the work she chose, Paul clearly had to distance herself from her Native language and mythology most of the time, but these few glimpses from the written record suggest that she did not reject her heritage.

Davis reports that eventually Paul was promoted to the position of girls' matron; she claims the salary offered was $250 per year, half that paid to white women in the same post. Reportedly, Paul decided to move to Wrangell because of the salary injustice and the jealousies her promotion had generated, but Jackson persuaded her to remain and increased her salary to $400 per year.[55] In 1903, the Presbyterian Board of Home Missions asked her to move to Wrangell to help resolve a problem that had caused some of the Native Presbyterians to leave the church there. She moved to Wrangell and in 1905 married William Tamaree, who like Paul, was of Tlingit and white ancestry. She served as organist in the church, acted as interpreter for ministers, and translated Christian hymns into Tlingit. After the Presbyterian General Assembly held in Cincinnati in 1930 declared women eligible to be elected church elders, the Native Presbyterian Church of Wrangell made Tillie Paul Tamaree an elder. Thus she became one of the first women in the United States to hold such a position.[56]

From her early years, Paul was encouraged and perhaps groomed to become a teacher among her own people. She must have been quite conscious of the fact that she and her husband were the first Native couple to be sent by the Presbyterian Board of Home Missions to a post alone, and it may well have generated a considerable amount of pressure on people so young to live up to the hopes and expectations of their mentors. Clearly, though, Paul's devotion to her work went far beyond a desire to meet others' expectations. She was sincerely committed to her roles as teacher, interpreter, nurse, administrator, and temperance worker—and these responsibilities made up much more than a full-time job. At the same time, she cared about presenting knowledge of her Native language and mythology, and made opportunities to help do so. The work she chose in no way implied a lack of pride in her heritage.

Missionaries in Southeast Alaska sent some Native children to Eastern institutions for training. Just as they hoped the children in the Alaskan missions would grow up to be teachers and lay workers, they hoped the students they sent East would return with those aspirations. One who did was Frances (Fannie) Willard, a Tlingit woman whom missionaries named for the famous Presbyterian worker active in the Woman's Christian Temperance Union. She spent about five years at a young ladies' seminary in Elizabeth, New Jersey.[57] Graduating in June 1890, she took an appointment as an assistant teacher at the Sitka Industrial Training School. The *North Star* commented, "Miss Willard is the first Alaskan with sufficient training and education to be considered competent to take charge of a school."[58] A later edition commented at more length.

> Miss Frances Willard, who has been East for five years, returned and will assist in the work of the school. We are highly pleased with the education and the culture which she has acquired in the short space of five years. A debt of gratitude is owing the ladies who so generously and kindly provided and cared for her, and we trust that they may in a measure be recompensed by her life of usefulness. Miss Willard shows a commendable spirit and a sincere desire to help to elevate her people.[59]

The paper added that it was "most essential" that she learn "the art of housekeeping in all its departments" so that she could be ready for "successful missionary work and for making her life most useful."[60]

Willard's career exemplified the path missionaries hoped their Native students would choose, and she was often cited by missionaries and their supporters as a model. One writer commented in the *North Star* in April 1891: "If you doubt the intellectual capacity, capabilities, or possibilities of the Native girl, I advise you to become acquainted with Miss Willard."[61] Clearly, this writer defined these qualities in ethnocentric terms, measuring potential by the extent to which a person chose particular missionary-approved goals; Willard was probably surrounded by white contemporaries who did the same. Nevertheless, she did not sever her ties with her own heritage; like Tillie Paul, she wrote about Tlingit mythology for the *North Star.*[62]

Willard maintained contact with missionary supporters outside Alaska, contributing notes about her activities to the *Home Mission Monthly.* The *North Star* reproduced one of her reports in that journal.

> Nine of my little ones have been advanced to the First Reader. It would have done you good to have looked in upon us in our school rooms the morning that I announced the important fact of their raise in the intellectual world—nine pairs of shining black eyes looking so eagerly and delightedly into mine; all so overjoyed to have a book all their own to study. I expect great things from this class.[63]

This suggests that Willard derived much pleasure from her work in Sitka. Nevertheless, she aspired to go outside Alaska for more training, as she felt it would enable her to help her people more. The *Home Mission Monthly,* hearing her plans, wrote, "She will be warmly welcomed by many who have learned to love her for her work's sake."[64]

These aspirations played a major role in her personal life. When she first arrived at Sitka, Fannie Willard may have met Edward Marsden, a Tsimshian man from William Duncan's mission at New Metakatla who served as the band teacher and the organist at the Sitka Industrial Training School.[65] Marsden's choices were similar to Willard's, but as a male he had more opportunities available to him within the Christian church systems. He attended Marietta College in Ohio and became ordained as a minister in 1897, after which he returned to work in Southeast Alaska. Like Willard, he broke new ground and was held up by his missionary mentors as a model. Since they had such similar experiences and goals, a union between the two probably seemed logical to many people who knew them, and at some point Willard became engaged to Marsden. White missionaries were encouraged to work as couples, and it is possible this proposed marriage may have been one of convenience.

At any rate, Willard found she wanted a different kind of life. In 1898, she broke the engagement and left Alaska temporarily to continue her schooling. Writing to Jackson from Seattle, she explained, "If I had become Edward Marsden's wife, that would have been the end of my ambition." Her ambition was to return to Alaska "not only as a teacher but as a trained nurse." She wanted to enroll in a three-year nursing course in San Francisco. Using self-deprecating humor to emphasize her determination, she implored Jackson to support her plans. "Did you ever hear of a Tlingit who never begged? I am not an exception you see. I *beg* you to help me in this manner."[66]

It is not clear whether Willard pursued more training, but she returned to Alaska and continued to teach at the Sitka Industrial Training School. It was then that she and Tillie Paul wrote a Tlingit dictionary.[67] Unfortunately, like so many of her people, she died early of tuberculosis.[68]

Like Paul, Frances Willard broke new ground in the eyes of her missionary mentors and must have lived most of her life knowing she was considered a model on display for others. Having been educated in the East, she had experiences very different from those of her contemporaries in Alaska; even Paul, with whom she worked and whose goals she shared, traveled outside Alaska for the first time only in 1899. Willard seemed strongly committed to working for her people, but she also kept ties with the country outside, hoped to spend more years in school there, and rejected the life of a minister's wife in a small Alaskan village. Possibly her interest in spending more years outside the region reflected a certain restlessness with life in Alaska after her five years in the East, as well as her wish to be better prepared to help her people. While her experiences must have distanced her to some extent from her own people, she was dedicated to them.

Sarah Dickinson, Tillie Paul, and Frances Willard chose similar routes to help their people. Each felt that an education in English and Christianity would prepare their people to face the changes to which they had to adapt and would help them survive economically and spiritually in the new society growing around them. They must have felt that this education had benefited them personally, given the circumstances, for each tried to make it possible for other Native people to have the same sort of training they had received. Studying in non-Native schools, adopting a new language, converting to a non-Native religion—even, in Willard's case, studying in the East for five years—did not cause these women to lose their commitment to their own people.

From the records cited here, it is impossible to tell whether these women identified primarily with their Native communities or with the non-Native missionaries whose work they made their own. Often those determinations are difficult for an individual to make about herself or himself; they are certainly inaccessible to historians almost a century later. These women's contributions to the *North Star* were written for (and possibly edited by) a missionary publication and may reflect the genre encouraged or dictated by the editors; at best, they were not intended as personal testimonials and do not reveal much about identity.

In fact, the choices Dickinson, Paul, and Willard made were extremely complex. Converting to Christianity certainly meant giving up (or never accepting) certain beliefs of their people, but their choices were much more complicated than neatly rejecting one cultural package and adopting another. They devoted their energies to their own people and maintained an interest both in Native oral traditions and in the Tlingit language. They opposed some indigenous practices such as shamanism, but many of their efforts were spent fighting the negative effects of white presence—effects such as alcoholism and the white exploitation of young women. They certainly did not view all aspects of white culture as desirable, and they certainly did not reject all aspects of Native culture. Despite common assumptions today about missionary activities, these women's choices were simply not that clear-cut.

What is clear is that they were eager to help their own people and believed that the work they did would have that effect. They lived in a time of painful choices; theirs were probably often very difficult. However, in embracing Christianity, in adopting English as their language, in teaching in mission schools, they did not reject their own people. Rather, they viewed this route as the best way to help, given the roles open to women at the time, and they devoted enormous energies toward that end.

All three of these individuals appear to have been independent women with strong determination. Obviously, they were greatly influenced by missionaries, but they made their choices freely. And while they were leaders, they were not alone: around the turn of the century, many Native people in Southeast Alaska, women and men, took similar options. In addition to Edward Marsden, these include individuals such as Frederick Moore, a Tlingit graduate of the Sitka Industrial Training School who continued his education in the East and later became a schoolteacher and interpreter;[69] Samuel Davis, a lay worker who taught and led a Presbyterian congregation at Howkan;[70] Mr. and Mrs. James Newton, Robert Harris,

Charles Gunnock, John Howard, Dick Smith, and Sam Williams, who worked as lay preachers for the Friends Church;[71] and William Benson, George Demmert, and George Field, who worked with the Salvation Army.[72] And while men are mentioned much more often than women in the written record, there were undoubtedly many women who also worked in similar ways and who might be more present in oral history.

In retrospect, some people may applaud their work and commitment, while others may question their degree of accommodation. Such judgments are difficult in hindsight and not particularly useful. These Native educators worked as they did in a sincere and earnest attempt to help their people survive the changes forced on them. Their choice to work with non-Native missionaries does not reflect passivity. Rather—like other leaders who made different choices—they showed great will and determination in facing the adversity of the times.

NOTES

1. Mary Lee Davis, *We Are Alaskans* (Boston: W.A. Wilde Co., 1931), 246.
2. S. Hall Young, *Hall Young of Alaska, "The Mushing Parson": The Autobiography of S. Hall Young* (New York and Chicago: Fleming H. Revell Co., 1927), 92.
3. Caroline Willard to friends, August 23, 1881, in Eva McClintock, ed., *Life in Alaska: Letters of Mrs. Eugene S. Willard* (Philadelphia: Presbyterian Board of Education, 1884), 49.
4. Mrs. A. R. McFarland to Sheldon Jackson, September 10, 1877, in Sheldon Jackson, *Alaska and Missions on the North Pacific Coast* (New York: Dodd, Mead & Co., 1880), 151.
5. Young, *Hall Young of Alaska,* 92.
6. Caroline Willard to friends, August 23, 1881.
7. For a detailed account of these developments from Sheldon Jackson's point of view, see his description in Jackson, *Alaska,* 128–47.
8. Jackson, *Alaska,* 144.
9. Mrs. A. R. McFarland to Sheldon Jackson, September 10, 1877, pp. 148–51.
10. Young, *Hall Young of Alaska,* 92.
11. Ibid., 165.
12. Amanda McFarland to Sheldon Jackson, April 6, 1879, in Sheldon Jackson Correspondence, Presbyterian Historical Society, Philadelphia, Pa.; and Jackson, *Alaska,* 219. These accounts differ both in chronology and in details and may describe two different episodes. Young and McFarland wanted girls placed in residence so they would not become concubines of non-Native miners.
13. Young, *Hall Young of Alaska,* 130–31.
14. Ibid., 150.

15. L. A. Beardslee, Reports of Captain L. A. Beardslee, U.S. Navy Relative to Affairs in Alaska, and the Operations of the USS *Jamestown* under His Command, while in the Waters of that Territory, January 24, 1882, 47th Cong., 1st sess., 1882, Sen. Ex. Doc. 181.

16. William T. Hagan, *Indian Police and Judges: Experiments in Acculturation and Control* (Lincoln: University of Nebraska Press, 1966), 72–74.

17. Caroline Willard to friends, August 23, 1881, p. 49.

18. Ibid., 57.

19. Caroline Willard to the Little Mission Band of the Second Presbyterian Church, New Castle, Pennsylvania, February 3, 1882, in McClintock, ed., *Life in Alaska,* 158–59.

20. Caroline Willard to Sheldon Jackson, September 26, 1882, in McClintock, ibid., 93.

21. Caroline Willard to parents, August 14, 1882, ibid., 231–32.

22. Caroline Willard to the Sabbath-School of the Presbyterian Church of East Springfield, New York, November 17, 1882, ibid., 248.

23. Caroline Willard to the Sabbath-School of the Presbyterian Church of East Springfield, New York, May 8, 1883, ibid., 300–305.

24. *North Star,* Sitka, Alaska, vol. 4, no. 11 (October 1891): 4. (As reproduced in facsimile by the Shorey Book Store, *The North Star: A Monthly Publication in the Interests of Schools and Missions in Alaska; The Complete Issues from December 1887–December 1892* [Seattle: Shorey Book Store, 1973], 188).

25. Sheldon Jackson, Report of the General Agent, Office of the General Agent of Education in Alaska, Sitka, June 30, 1887, to the Territorial Board of Education. Schools in Alaska. In Bureau of Education, Report of the Commissioner for 1886–1887, 50th Cong., 1st sess., H. Ex. Doc. 1, pt. 5, v. 2, serial 2545.

26. Carrie M. Willard, "Native Sabbath School Teachers," *North Star,* vol. 1, no. 9 (August 1888): 4 (reproduced in Shorey, 36).

27. Davis, *We Are Alaskans,* 247–48.

28. Ibid., 240–45.

29. Ibid., 245–46.

30. Maggie J. Dunbar to Sheldon Jackson, November 29, 1879, in Jackson, *Alaska,* 250–51.

31. Davis, *We Are Alaskans,* 247–48.

32. Florence Hayes, *A Land of Challenge: Alaska* (New York: Board of National Missions of the Presbyterian Church of the United States of America, 1940), 16.

33. Caroline Willard to Sheldon Jackson, May 24 and June 1, 1882, in McClintock, ed., *Life in Alaska,* 215–17; and Correspondence, Caroline Willard to friends, June 30, 1883, ibid., 317–18.

34. Davis, *We Are Alaskans,* 252–53.

35. Clipping of unidentified newspaper article written by Louis Paul from Chilkat mission, probably in 1882, in Jackson Scrapbook Collection, vol. 5, Prebyterian Historical Society.

36. Davis, *We Are Alaskans,* 254.

37. Julia McNair Wright, *Among the Alaskans* (Philadelphia: Presbyterian Board of Home Missions, 1893), 342.

38. Caroline Willard to friends, July 16, 1882, in McClintock, ed., *Life in Alaska,* 318.

39. Davis, *We Are Alaskans,* 254–55.

40. Ibid., 256.

41. Tillie Paul, "My First Trip," in *North Star,* vol. 3, no. 7 (June 1890): 3 (reproduced in Shorey, 123).

42. *North Star,* vol. 3, no. 12 (November 1890): 4 (reproduced in Shorey, 144).

43. Ibid., vol. 3, no. 1 (December 1889): 2 (reproduced in Shorey, 98).

44. Ibid., vol. 2, no. 5 (April 1889): 2 (reproduced in Shorey, 66).

45. Ibid., vol. 2, no. 9 (August 1889): 3 (reproduced in Shorey, 83).

46. Paul, "My First Trip."

47. *North Star,* vol. 3, no. 10 (September 1890):1 (reproduced in Shorey, 154).

48. Ibid., vol. 4, no. 1 (December 1890): 3 (reproduced in Shorey, 135).

49. Ibid., 4 (reproduced in Shorey, 148); ibid., vol 4, no. 2 (January 1891): 4 (reproduced in Shorey, 152).

50. Ibid., vol. 4, no. 4 (March 1891): 2 (reproduced in Shorey, 158).

51. Sheldon Jackson, Education in Alaska, 1890–91. Reprint of chap. 25, Bureau of Education, Report of the Commissioner of Education for 1890–91. (Washington, D.C.: Government Printing Office, 1893) (also in 52nd Cong., 1st sess., H. Ex. Doc. 1, pt. 5, v. 5, pt. 2, serial 2939).

52. *North Star,* vol. 2, no. 4 (March 1889): 4 (reproduced in Shorey, 64); ibid., vol. 2, no. 4 (March 1889): 2–3 (reproduced in Shorey, 66–67).

53. Sheldon Jackson, Education in Alaska, 1890–91.

54. *North Star,* vol. 3, no. 6 (May 1890): 2 (reproduced in Shorey, 118).

55. Davis, *We Are Alaskans,* 262ff.

56. Ibid., 273ff.

57. *North Star,* vol. 4, no. 6 (May 1890): 1 (reproduced in Shorey, 161); ibid., vol. 3, no. 10 (September 1890): 2 (reproduced in Shorey, 134).

58. Ibid., vol. 3, no. 10 (September 1890): 2 (reproduced in Shorey, 134).

59. Ibid., vol. 4, no. 2 (January 1891): 4 (reproduced in Shorey, 152).

60. Ibid.

61. Ibid., vol. 4, no. 5 (April 1891): 1 (reproduced in Shorey 161).

62. Ibid., vol. 4, no. 12 (November 1891): 2–3 (reproduced in Shorey, 190–91).

63. *North Star,* vol. 5, no. 3 (February 1892): 4 (reproduced in Shorey, 204).

64. As quoted in *North Star,* vol. 5, no. 5 (April 1892): 1 (reproduced in Shorey, 209).

65. *North Star,* vol. 3, no. 1 (December 1889): 2 (reproduced In Shorey, 98); ibid., vol. 4, no. 4 (March 1891): 3 (reproduced in Shorey, 159). For a biography of Edward Marsden, see William Gilbert Beattie, *Marsden of Alaska, A Modern Indian: Minister, Missionary, Musician, Engineer, Pilot, Boat Builder and Church Builder* (New York: Vintage Press, 1955).

66. Fannie Willard to Sheldon Jackson, May 23, 1898, Sheldon Jackson Correspondence, Alaska State Historical Library, Juneau.

67. Sheldon Jackson, "Alaska," in Lake Mohonk Conference, Friends of the Indian, Report of the 20th Annual Meeting (Philadelphia, 1902): 31–38.

68. Undated obituary, John Green Brady Papers, Beinecke Rare Book and Manuscript Library, Yale University, New Haven, Conn.

69. Sheldon Jackson, Education in Alaska, 1896–97, reprint of chap. 35, Bureau of Education, Report of the Commissioner for 1896–1897 (Washington, D.C.: Government Printing Office, 1898): 1608 (also in 55th Cong., 2nd sess., H. Doc. 5, pt. 2, serial 3650); *Assembly Herald* 6 (June 1902): 240.

70. David Waggoner, "In the Land of the Hydahs," *Assembly Herald* 13 (June 1907): 252–54.

71. Charles Replogle, *Among the Indians of Alaska* (London: Headley Bros., 1904): 144–49, 177–78; Arthur O. Roberts, *Tomorrow Is Growing Old: Stories of the Quakers in Alaska* (Newberg, Oreg.: Barclay Press, 1978): 43, 48–53, 60–66, 81.

72. Sallie Chesham, *Born to Battle. The Salvation Army in America* (New York: Rand McNally, 1965): 105–7, 197; and Arch R. Wiggins, *The History of the Salvation Army,* vol. 4: 1886–1904 (London: T. & A. Constable, 1964): 90.

Chief Sesui and Lieutenant Herron

A Story of Who Controls the Bacon

WILLIAM SCHNEIDER

Morgan Sherwood asserted in Exploration of Alaska, 1865–1900 *(New Haven: Yale University Press, 1965) that the United States government did not ignore Alaska during the early American period, contrary to the charges of the several hundred non-Native inhabitants who regularly sought some form or another of federal assistance. In fact, Sherwood found that the federal government rather generously funded research and exploration by such institutions as the United States Geological Survey, the Smithsonian Institution, and the United States Army. These activities were documented by those who undertook them, and the accounts understandably reflect the Western culture's point of view.*

William S. Schneider has examined exploration and initial contact between Natives and non-Natives from the Native point of view. Schneider, who received a Ph.D. in anthropology from Bryn Mawr in 1976, is Curator of the Oral History Collection in the Alaska and Polar Regions Department of the Elmer Rasmuson Library, University of Alaska Fairbanks. Schneider helped to create that collection and implemented the first systematic statewide oral history indexing system. His research projects have included an oral history of the Alaska Steamship Company and interviews for the Alaska Statehood Commission. The bulk of his work, however, has been with Native Alaskans. He initiated the Life History Series, which resulted in the publication of Moses Cruikshank's The Life I've Been Living *(Fairbanks: University of Alaska Press, 1986), and he is presently working through that program on a biography of Waldo Bodfish, an Inupiat whaling captain.*

In the following article, which first appeared in the Alaska Historical Society's journal, Alaska History, *Schneider describes Lieutenant Joseph Herron's 1899 expedition to the Upper Kuskokwim and explains that Herron and his men probably would have perished had they not been rescued by the Athabascan Chief Sesui and his people. Schneider concludes that the incident is an example of pos-*

This article appeared originally in *Alaska History* 1 (Fall/Winter 1985): 1–85; it is reprinted here by permission.

itive cultural adaptation among the members of Chief Sesui's band and suggests that because of their location Upper Kuskokwim Athabascans were able to maintain an unusually high level of cultural integrity following contact with non-Natives.

In 1899 Joseph Herron, a First Lieutenant in the 8th Cavalry, United States Army, led a small detachment of soldiers through the Alaska Range into the Upper Kuskokwim drainage. Enroute to the Yukon, this party became lost in the broad flatlands of the Upper Kuskokwim and was rescued by the Athabascan Chief Sesui (Shesoie or Shesuie) and his followers. The soldiers were cared for and then led to Tanana on the Yukon, where a new military post had just been established.[1]

The story of that extraordinary rescue is dramatic, but the events leading up to the rescue and the conditions of the rescue provide fascinating clues to the successful cultural adaptation of the Natives in the Upper Kuskokwim. Examples of positive cultural adaptation by Native peoples in times of rapid change are few. The usual pattern is marked by disruption of the seasonal cycle of hunting and fishing, strains on the social system, and curtailment of culturally valued activities. That does not seem to have happened in the Upper Kuskokwim. Indeed, the Upper Kuskokwim Natives, living in an area remote from outside supply and maintaining a high level of flexibility and trading options for much of their history, were able to sustain cultural integrity and to take advantage of economic opportunities which finally developed in their region.

For years the Native population of the Upper Kuskokwim had engaged in limited contact with traders, missionaries, and perhaps the lone prospector. But the Natives had not, until Herron's expedition in 1899, experienced prolonged interaction with a non-Native population in the heart of their homeland. Because 1899 is a comparatively late date in the history of white-Native contact in Alaska,[2] the event therefore provides a good setting for evaluating the ways that Native people at the local level learned about outsiders before they actually arrived and how they selectively incorporated the foreigners' goods and way of life. The expedition reports and Native oral accounts which persist even today provide rich detail on the response of the Upper Kuskokwim people to Herron and his men. And the circumstances surrounding the expedition help to explain the history of exploration in Interior Alaska.

These circumstances gain added significance because rather shortly after

Herron's trip, the Upper Kuskokwim was traversed by the two major trail systems which brought prospectors and employment opportunities for the Native population. The Natives' success in exploiting these opportunities stands in marked contrast to the dislocation and disruption, particularly of subsistence pursuits, that development brought to many other parts of Alaska. A consideration of developments in this area can therefore provide insights on the effects of culture contact and change in general.

For many years, the U.S. government showed little interest in governing the territory of Alaska. The military, in name, was to provide the major federal presence, but it was not until a large influx of gold seekers occurred in the 1890s that the Army gained authority and resources to play an active role in the Territory. The gold seekers were headed for the Yukon, to rich proven ground on the upper river, or downriver to new prospects on the tributaries. The prospectors expected to find supplies plentiful enough to support their needs, and they assumed there would be law and order. Often they were disappointed on both counts. They found that the transportation companies which ran the steamboats on the Yukon River could not be depended upon; shallow water and limited service meant few goods and exorbitant prices.

In addition, as gold mining developed, Americans became concerned that Canadians might seek to control access to the goldfields of the Upper Yukon in Alaska. In the 1890s access to the Upper Yukon was by three basic routes. Each had particular problems. One route led over the Chilkoot and other passes from tidewater at Skagway and Dyea into the Yukon Territory of Canada and then down the Yukon River. Another way was by the Old Hudson's Bay Company route through northern Canada and down the Porcupine River to Fort Yukon. The third way was by ship to St. Michael and then by steamboat up the Yukon. This route, while avoiding the Canadian problem, was blocked in winter by sea ice, and in summer, shallows on the river created special problems for supply.

These were the conditions that finally prompted the government to action. In 1897, Captain P. H. Ray of the U.S. Army was sent to Alaska under special assignment by the president of the United States to report on conditions in the Interior. Ray was a keen observer, an extremely competent leader under pressure, and he had influence back in Washington.[3] In the fall of 1897, Ray experienced problems of supply firsthand, and soon after his arrival he formulated recommendations for alternative routes in Interior Alaska, overland "All-American" routes from tidewater to the Yukon River.

Ray made his recommendations on hearing of Native trails from the mouth of the Tanana River to the Copper River, Cook Inlet, and the Upper Kuskokwim River. Ray reported on these trails and urged military exploration from Cook Inlet or Valdez Inlet to the mouth of the Tanana.[4] The War Department accepted his proposals, and in the summers of 1898 and 1899, the Army mounted expeditions from Prince William Sound and Cook Inlet. While Ray's report provided the principal justification for Lieutenant Herron's expedition in 1899, additional support for the Upper Kuskokwim route to the Yukon was provided by a United States Geological Survey geologist, Josiah Edward Spurr. During the summer of 1898, Spurr led a geological expedition from Cook Inlet up the Susitna River and through the Alaska Range to the Upper Kuskokwim, down that river and thence across the Alaska Peninsula. This journey marked the first scientific investigation of the Upper Kuskokwim, but Spurr's trip is noteworthy because of his observations on the potential for a transportation route from Cook Inlet to the Upper Kuskokwim and thence to the Tanana drainage. This may very well have added fuel to Ray's plea for an "All-American" route and certainly influenced the plans for Herron's expedition the following year. Spurr wrote:

> From the shores of Cook Inlet to the Tordrillo Mountains the way lies over a comparatively level plateau with practically no irregularities and the Tordrillo Mountains themselves offer convenient passes near the place where they were crossed. . . . On the Kuskokwim side of the mountains the same low, level plateau reaches down to the perfectly flat country through which such a large portion of the Upper Kuskokwim flows. Thus for a wagon road or a railroad there are few engineering difficulties to surmount. From the Upper Kuskokwim communication with neighboring districts is easy. The divide between the Upper Kuskokwim and the Lower Tanana consists of low mountains which offer few obstacles; indeed, a well-known native route to the Kuskokwim is by way of the Toclat River, which enters the Lower Tanana and which communicates with a tributary of the Kuskokwim. It is probable that a wagon road or railroad across the divide would also be a very simple matter.[5]

Spurr's enticing description had appeal, but the "well-known native route" was to prove elusive for Herron.

In 1899, Herron led his expedition from Cook Inlet through the Alaska Range and into the Upper Kuskokwim in search of an "All-American" route from tidewater to the Yukon. Joseph Herron was a graduate of the U.S. Military Academy, class of 1891. Eight years later, he found himself the leader of a major expedition which, by the standards of the military of his day, was a success. He traversed over five hundred miles of unknown territory, experienced tremendous hardships, and produced a detailed map and description of the country.[6] In October 1901, two years after the trip, he was advanced to the rank of captain.[7]

Like many other expeditions of 1898 and 1899, Herron and his party of eight men were heavily loaded for extensive overland travel in dense forest cover. They began with, among other items, six hundred pounds of bacon and a thousand pounds of flour. Fifteen horses and eight men carried a total weight of 3,300 pounds.[8] The previous year there had been considerable trouble acquiring trained horses for explorations because military horses were in demand for the Spanish-American War. Whether this was also true of Herron's expedition is not clear. What is evident is the unsuitability of horses for the traverse. The animals became bogged down in the heavy brush; there were difficulties in finding sufficient graze; and the animals were not suited for the swift streams that had to be crossed. The animals were finally abandoned. The expedition was forced to cache many of its foodstuffs, a decision that ironically aided their eventual rescue.

Herron's destination was Rampart on the Yukon River, the site of prospecting activities and near the location where John Mynook had discovered gold in 1893.[9] By this time, the Yukon was well known; Captain Charles Raymond's trip up the river by steamboat in 1869 had demonstrated its navigability by steamer, and by the mid-1870s traders such as Arthur Harper, Jack McQuesten, and Al Mayo had carried on a lively trade for furs. McQuesten was instrumental in broadcasting the gold-mining potential of the streams. He grubstaked some of the early prospectors working in the Yukon Valley.[10]

Lieutenant Herron acquired two Native guides at Susitna station, an Alaska Commercial Company trading post on the Susitna River. The party did not get started until June 27th when the season was quite advanced.[11] They traveled up the Susitna to the Yentna, up the Yentna to the Kichatna, then through Simpson Pass to the Upper Kuskokwim where they eventually became bogged down. The Upper Kuskokwim is complicated and provides unusual challenges. The numerous tributaries and the broad expanse of the lowlands create a veritable maze to the uninitiated. The two guides, Slenkta and Stepan, abandoned the party before they reached

Egypt Mountain, a landmark and traditional Native trading site. The expedition was in serious trouble. The reasons for the Natives' desertion are unclear. Perhaps they lacked knowledge of the country beyond that point, or they may have feared reprisal from Upper Kuskokwim people who would recall unfavorable treatment they had received from Tanaina traders at an earlier time.[12] The expedition continued without Native guides. Floundering in an area near Telida, the men cached supplies and abandoned the remaining horses.

Both written and oral accounts tell of the rescue. Herron's report tells how a bear broke into their cache and consumed bacon they had put there. The bear was killed by the Telida Indians, and upon discovering the bacon in its stomach, the Indians backtracked its trail to Herron's cache and then were able to track the soldiers. Herron reported: "September 19 we found an Indian, who, I learned later, was the one who had killed the bear that had robbed our cache; or rather, the Indian found us."[13] Judge James Wickersham has also provided a written account of the rescue which he undoubtedly gathered from oral accounts while in the Kantishna. He wrote:

> Shesoie, the chief of the Telida (Tena) village was out hunting one day and ran across and followed a bear's trail until he found the animal and killed it. He ascertained the bear had been eating bacon; and being interested in learning where it had obtained this white man's food he followed on its back track, which finally led him to one of Lieutenant Herron's caches at which the bear had obtained the bacon. Until that moment the Indian had not known there were white men, or bacon, in his country. He immediately set out to follow the white man's trail, and so found Lieutenant Herron and his soldiers afoot, lost and starving, in the maze of the Kuskokwim marshes. He took them safely to his village where he sheltered them and fed them for two months, and then guided them over his Cosna trail to the Tanana River and put them on that highway to Fort Gibbon.[14]

Oral accounts of the rescue tell how Carl Sesui, son of Chief Sesui, saw horse tracks and droppings. He asked his father what they were. Chief Sesui told him that was the white man's dog, his way of describing the horse. One version of the story tells how Carl Sesui and his father saw the tracks and droppings which Chief Sesui identified for his son. They went on and shot a bear. They discovered the bear had bacon in its stomach and then they went back to the horse tracks and followed them until they came to Herron's camp. They found Herron and his men there.[15] Charlene LeFebre, an anthropologist who met Carl Sesui while looking for archaeological sites in the Upper Kuskokwim, was told by him:

> My father went down with a canoe and he took me down below my place. We see on other bank some kind of track there. He says "horse." That summer he been to Tanana and he see white man and horse. That what he know. And he talk me that is white man and I don't believe it because I don't see that kind of track . . . nails and funny thing stick out behind . . . heel. I don't believe it. I don't know that game. That is some kind of animal. Go down 4–5 mile and see horse and my father told me we see horse. Still alive. And few miles further father find men. Thought this was Tanana. Make raft. Find this neck and make fire and my father show them how the Kuskokwim and Tanana and Cochaket and Kantishna meet. Got down to old village and put him in cabin—don't know how long he stay there. An[d] started to get cold and my father and mother make moccasins, mits, fur cap and father make snowshoes for those fellow. An[d] started to walk and went thru to Minchumina and Cochaket and don't cost nothing. Just help that guy that all.[16]

Herron's account also told how they were taken to Telida and housed, fed, and clothed for their trip to the Yukon:

> I proceeded to go into camp there for two months, until we could get winter clothes and socks made of our horse blankets, procure mits, fur caps, moccasins, and snowshoes for the party from the Indians, and to wait until conditions were favorable for snowshoe travel.[17]

On November 25th, they were guided by four Telida Natives to Tanana following the Native trail to Lake Minchumina, and the Cosna River trail to the Tanana, and downriver to Fort Gibbon, the newly established army post at Tanana. They had expected to proceed to Rampart, but Fort Gibbon had been built that summer (1899) and therefore became their immediate destination.[18] News of their pending arrival was passed through local groups, but their appearance at the post created quite a stir. Robert Farnsworth, son of Captain Farnsworth, the post commander, reported:

> Arriving at our cabin they could hardly walk. We asked them in, but Lieutenant Herron refused to even shake hands, saying they were cov-

> ered with lice. So they were taken to the post laundry, which was only partly finished. Their clothes were soaked in the much valued kerosene, then the men were shaved and had haircuts and baths. . . .
>
> The Indians also got cleaned up and came to the cabin for a recommendation and money for supplies. . . . A recommendation was written out for them on the typewriter and also an order for some food, but they refused to take either, saying they were no good. The documents had to be written in longhand before they would accept them.[19]

The Herron expedition marked a major achievement in the description and mapping of an uncharted portion of the Interior. Portions of the route would be retraced by gold seekers in the years that followed, on routes such as the Iditarod Trail. Besides describing unrecorded country, Herron's expedition demonstrated that the western slope of the Alaska Range was not the best "All-American" route to the Yukon. The Valdez Trail to Eagle and the Fortymile proved to be a more appropriate route, because of the distances involved and because of the economic opportunities for miners which continued to be available in the Upper Yukon.

Herron's expedition marked the end of an era, the end of large overland military expeditions in Alaska. The attention of the Army shifted to the posts on the Yukon. The role of exploration and description of Alaskan territory was inherited by the United States Geological Survey. It employed quite different methods. It sent out small parties of professional geologists equipped with lighter outfits. They were unhampered by the formal chain of command which typified the Army expeditions.[20]

Herron's rescue stands out in the record of Native-white relations because Chief Sesui and his followers demonstrated so much knowledge of white men and their ways. Native assistance to military expeditions in the Interior was not unique—Lieutenant Henry Allen was guided on the upper Copper River by Chief Nikolai, and Lieutenant J. C. Castner depended upon Native assistance, particularly on the Volkmar.[21] However, the Herron rescue is notable because of the many details which Sesui noticed and used in finding and assisting Herron. The discovery of foreign food (bacon), the tracking process, knowledge of horses, and the preparations for the trip to the Yukon point to the very sophisticated knowledge that these people had of white men.

Considering that this was the first intrusion of white men into the heartland of their territory, it would seem that the Upper Kuskokwim people must have traveled extensively beyond the upper river and relied upon a wealth of detail about white men gleaned from accounts from neighboring groups. Both of these assumptions are substantiated by the historical record going back to the period of Russian and British traders, before the Treaty of Cession in 1867.

In the early years of the nineteenth century, Russian traders extended their search for profitable furbearers, entering the Interior and finally establishing a post at Kolmakovsky (Kolmakov Redoubt) on the Kuskokwim River in 1841. From there the Russian-American Company maintained a seasonal trading site at Vinasale in the 1850s, some twenty river miles below present-day McGrath.[22] Vinasale became a trading focus for some Upper Kuskokwim people, although they also met Tanaina Athabascans from Cook Inlet at trading sites close to the place Medfra called Itstynoo[23] and near Egypt Mountain on the north side of Rainy pass.[24]

Russian expansion on the Yukon River was from St. Michael up the Yukon to Nulato where a post was established in 1839. The Hudson's Bay Company, also in search of fur, gradually extended a network of posts across Canada, finally entering Alaska and establishing Fort Yukon in 1847. From this post, its traders sometimes made the trip downriver after breakup to the confluence of the Tanana and the Yukon where they traded with the Native groups gathered there.[25] The Russians also made spring trips to trade, but they had to wait until the ice cleared Nulato and rarely went further upriver than the mouth of the Tanana.[26]

Some of the trade goods from the Yukon-Tanana trade must certainly have made their way to the Upper Kuskokwim people, although we do not have much information on this critical question. However, by Herron's time, the Upper Kuskokwim people had an established route to the Tanana River and were familiar with the settlement of Tanana, having been there to trade.[27]

The importance of trade and travel to Tanana deserves some additional consideration. The newly established post there, Fort Gibbon, was near the location of the traditional spring gathering where Athabascan groups came to trade,[28] a gathering enriched by the Hudson's Bay and Russian-American Company traders before the American purchase of Alaska. The location continued to be important after the purchase when the Church of England established St. James Mission at the mouth of the Tozitna, some eighteen miles from the confluence of the Yukon and the Tanana, near a trading post called Fort Adams. The mission was taken over by the Episcopal Church in 1891,[29] and this is where the Indians of the Tanana, Koyukuk, and surrounding Yukon drainages went for religious and trading purposes. The church's influence extended as far as Lake Minchumina where the Natives held allegiance to the Episcopal Church, but the Upper Kuskokwim people were Russian Orthodox and maintained religious connections downriver. However, in the last quarter of the nineteenth century, their trading allegiances may have been oriented toward Tanana. As noted, the Upper Kuskokwim people's trade with the Tanaina of Cook Inlet was interrupted sometime late in the century, largely as the result of a serious incident involving Diqelas Tukda, a Tanaina trader who allegedly deceived them.[30] After this incident, the Upper Kuskokwim people turned to other sources of trade,[31] and it is likely that the trading posts on the Yukon and specifically at Tanana increased in importance. Genealogical work with the residents of Telida and Nikolai may indicate kinship and other social ties at this time with the Yukon people. On the Kuskokwim River, after the Treaty of Cession, the Russian-American Company was replaced by independent traders, and eventually by the Alaska Commercial Company. White traders did not pursue trade on the Upper Kuskokwim River as vigorously as on the Yukon, where there was a larger population and concentration of activity, until the development of gold mining on the Lower and Middle Kuskokwim after the turn of the century.[32]

The Upper Kuskokwim people were ready to assist Herron on his way through, and they were ready to assist the hundreds of others that came in the early years of the twentieth century on their way to gold strikes farther downriver and at Nome. This readiness is unique for Indian groups which experienced gold rush activities and can be credited to a number of factors. A prolonged period of indirect contact facilitated cultural integrity. The Upper Kuskokwim is geographically distant from the major western supply lines; therefore, Native services were vital to travelers. The Upper Kuskokwim Natives had flexibility to develop culturally appropriate and economically remunerative roles in activities of the gold rush—activities such as running roadhouses, supplying fish and game, and serving as dog team mail carriers.

In 1908 the Iditarod Trail was surveyed and became a winter route of travel for prospectors headed for Southwest and Northwest Alaska. In 1923, with the completion of the Alaska Railroad, the Kantishna–Upper Kuskokwim trail also became an important winter travel route. These two trails crossed the Upper Kuskokwim and were traveled by many people headed for the distant gold-mining areas.[33]

Strikes in Fairbanks in 1902 and Kantishna in 1905 also brought gold seekers who spilled over into the Upper Kuskokwim. To support the newcomers, roadhouses were built along the trails, and Upper Kuskokwim Natives were employed to work at these sites and to provide food for the travelers and their dog teams. Some Natives were employed to carry the mail. In some cases the roadhouses were run and owned by Natives.[34]

The introduction of fishwheels by 1918 on the upper river signaled a major technological advance that permitted Upper Kuskokwim people to catch large quantities of salmon on the main river. Fish were also caught in traps in the streams and sold to the roadhouses to feed travelers and their dog teams.[35] The dramatic picture that emerges is of a small Native population which very quickly and effectively provided basic services on the trails and at the roadhouses. The services involved some skills that they had used all of their lives: hunting, fishing, and dog team driving. The introduction of fishwheels was advantageous and, along with the traditional fish traps, provided a ready source of fish near the main travel routes. The ownership of roadhouses and the entrepreneurial skills that this demanded are of considerable interest.

The Upper Kuskokwim presented unique problems of supply. In summer, river steamers could operate dependably as far upriver as McGrath,[36] but the roadhouses farther on had to depend on shallow-draft boats and, of course, winter supply over the trails. One suspects that for these roadhouses, local—meaning Native—supply was very important, more important than where white traders could depend upon steamboats for supply. The geographical remoteness from outside supply necessitated a dependence on local resources and therefore permitted a relatively high degree of local control, paralleling in some respects the situation Herron found himself in during his stay at Telida.

Unfortunately, the period of employment and entrepreneurship was short-lived, lasting only until the 1930s when the airplane signaled an end to dog team mail delivery. Many of the roadhouses and even the trails ceased to be important.[37] The employment opportunities decreased dramatically. By then, the hordes of prospectors were gone. Those who had found paying quantities of gold were established in a few locales, most outside the Upper Kuskokwim. The traffic had decreased, the wage labor opportunities were few, and people returned to the trapping life that they had had before, only now the area was less isolated and white trappers shared in the rich fur resources.

Reflecting on the historical events surrounding Herron and the gold seekers, we are left with the strong feeling that the Upper Kuskokwim Natives not only culturally survived but thrived during the early phases of direct contact. In at least one important respect, the situation is reminiscent of descriptions of the "Dawson Boys," the Peel River Kutchin from Canada, who participated in the Klondike gold rush of 1897–99.[38] In both cases, the Natives were able to contribute culturally valued skills in demand by the prospectors—most notably hunting and guiding travelers. Some Peel River Natives left their homeland temporarily in order to participate in the gold rush, whereas the Upper Kuskokwim Natives experienced large numbers of people traveling through their country. But, in both cases, the important point that emerges is that the Native group was able to control the type and amount of interaction. For the Peel River people, there was the chance to decide if they wanted to go to Dawson or to the mining camps. And for the Upper Kuskokwim people, control came from their unique position along a major route which was isolated from the centers of Western supply.

The Herron expedition demonstrates that the Upper Kuskokwim people were also well prepared to meet these opportunities. Years of indirect contact from many different directions provided opportunities for these people to gain a very sophisticated knowledge of white civilization and to incorporate this information into their own lives. When the prospectors came, the Indians relied upon their traditional skills to fill the needs of the travelers, and they expressed a willingness to do so. Therefore a very special situation was created for the traveler and for the Natives. The willingness and interest of the Upper Kuskokwim people to capitalize on the opportunities which came with the trails is of particular interest, and it is suggested here that the Natives' ability to provide locally available services on their own terms created a favorable situation for cultural contact between the two groups.

Unlike Native Alaskans whose direct contact in a home territory followed rather quickly after indirect contact and necessitated immediate change, the Upper Kuskokwim people maintained insulation for a long time, absorbing what they wanted and declining what they did not want. For many years they dealt with strangers on their own terms, and that may have influenced their willingness to exploit the opportunities that finally developed. The people who entered their territory had destinations elsewhere. They sought gold outside that territory and did not provide direct competition for the employment opportunities. A contact situation was thus created which permitted the resident population ample opportunity to maintain its integrity and to benefit from a geographically remote location.

NOTES

1. Joseph S. Herron, *Explorations in Alaska, 1899, for an All American Overland Route from Cook Inlet, Pacific Ocean to the Yukon* (Washington, D.C.: Government Printing Office, 1909).

2. The lower reaches of their homeland were visited by Russian traders and explorers, but the middle and upper reaches remained insulated from prolonged contact with outsiders until Herron's expedition in 1899. Josiah E. Spurr, a United States Geological Survey geologist, conducted a reconnaissance of the Kuskokwim in 1898, descending the river after portaging to the headwaters from the Susitna. That party made no prolonged stops once they reached the Kuskokwim. However, Spurr's report provides some specific information on prospectors and traders who had traveled through the Upper Kuskokwim country. See Josiah Edward Spurr, "A Reconnaissance in Southwestern Alaska in 1898," in *Explorations in Alaska in 1898,* pt. 7 of *Twentieth Annual Report of the United States Geological Survey to the Secretary of the Interior, 1898–99* (Washington, D.C.: Government Printing Office, 1900), 95. For further discussion of the territory, see Edward H. Hosley, "Kolchan" in *Handbook of North American Indians,* Vol. 6: *Subarctic* (Washington, D.C.: Smithsonian Institution, 1981), 618–22; and Wendell H. Oswalt, *Historic Settlements along the Kuskokwim River, Alaska,* Alaska State Historical Monograph No. 7 (Juneau: Alaska Division of State Libraries and Museums, 1980), 81. The present paper defines the Upper Kuskokwim Natives' territory differently from Hosley's more expansive definition of the territory before 1900. The restrictive use of the term here is not meant to contradict Hosley but to focus the discussion on the middle and upper reaches of the Upper Kuskokwim Natives' traditional territory.

3. For a more detailed discussion of P. H. Ray and his assignment in Alaska, see William Schneider, "P. H. Ray on the Alaskan Frontier in the Fall of 1897" (1985). Manuscript available from the author.

4. See Ray's letters of September 15 and November 15, 1897 to the Adjutant General in *Compilation of Narratives of Explorations in Alaska* (Washington, D.C.: Government Printing Office, 1900), 525–28, 544–45. Further reference can be found in a telegram from Brigadier General Merriam to Adjutant General, (summarizing Ray's letters), February 1, 1898, Record Group 107, National Archives and Records Service.

5. Spurr, 96.

6. Herron, 7–8.

7. Francis B. Heitman, *Historical Register and Dictionary of the United States Army from its Organization, September 29, 1789 to March 2, 1903* (Washington, D.C.: Government Printing Office, 1903), 526. (Republished by University of Illinois Press, 1965).

8. Herron, 24–27.

9. Alfred Hulse Brooks, *Blazing Alaska's Trails* (Caldwell, Id.: Caxton Printers, for the University of Alaska and the Arctic Institute of North America, 1953), 332.

10. Charles P. Raymond, "Reconnaissance of the Yukon River," in *Compilation of Narratives of Explorations in Alaska,* 23. Discussion of the pioneer traders Harper, McQuesten, and Mayo can be found in Brooks, 316–20.

11. Herron, 20–21, 27.

12. For many years the Tanaina Athabascans enjoyed an advantageous trading position with the Upper Kuskokwim Natives. But when the Upper Kuskokwim people discovered that the Tanaina were becoming rich off their trade, they became angry. This point is made in the oral account of Diqelas Tukda, a Tanaina who was forced to flee from a trading session when it was discovered that he was charging exorbitant prices for trade goods. The Upper Kuskokwim people said, "He took too much from us . . . let's throw him in the river." This story is found in Shem Pete, *Diqelas Tukda, the Story of a Tanaina Chief* (Fairbanks: Alaska Native Language Center, 1977), 25–26.

13. Herron, 38–42.

14. James Wickersham, *Old Yukon: Tales, Trails and Trials* (Washington, D.C.: Washington Law Book Co., 1938), 259.

15. Leonard and Hazel Menke, personal communications, 1980 and 1983. The account of this story was collected at Lake Minchumina from the Menkes who had heard the story from Carl Sesui. It was told again for the author in 1983 with elaboration on the tracking process. Hazel Menke recalled that Carl Sesui said he was about twelve years old when the rescue was made.

16. Charlene LeFebre, Field Notes, July 7, 1949, 3.

17. Herron, 42.

18. Captain P. H. Ray suggested the site of the Tanana post, Fort Gibbon, in a letter to the Adjutant General dated September 15, 1897 in *Compilation of Narratives of Explorations in Alaska*, 525. Subsequent letters also mention the desirability of this location, so the establishment of the post probably came as no surprise to Herron and his men.

19. Robert J. Farnsworth, "An Army Brat Goes to Alaska: Conclusion—Building Fort Gibbon," *Alaska Journal* 7 (Autumn 1977): 216.

20. Morgan B. Sherwood, *Exploration of Alaska, 1865–1900* (New Haven: Yale University Press, 1965), 167–68, 181–82; Jonathan Nielson, "Soldiers on a Northern Frontier: The Military in Alaska's History, 1867–1983," *Report to the Alaska Historical Commission* (1980), 89.

21. Henry T. Allen, "Military Reconnaissance in Alaska," in *Compilation of Narratives of Explorations in Alaska*, 432–37; J. C. Castner, "A Story of Hardship and Suffering in Alaska," ibid., 691–92.

22. Oswalt, 47, 86.

23. C. M. Brown, "Navigable and Non-navigable Waters in the Upper Kuskokwim River Basin," Bureau of Land Management, Anchorage, May 6, 1980, photocopy, 7.

24. Personal communication from Nikolai elder Bobby Esai, 1980.

25. Brooks, 175.

26. Ibid., 233; see George R. Adams, *Life on the Yukon, 1865–67* (Kingston, Ontario: Limestone Press, 1982), 73.

27. Charlene LeFebre's field notes indicate that Chief Sesui had been to Tanana before Herron arrived. LeFebre, Field Notes, July 7, 1949, 3.

28. The exact location of the post is described in "Copy of a Military Historical Sketch of Fort Gibbon, Alaska," Box 1, Folder 1, Major General C. S. Farnsworth Papers, University of Alaska Archives, Fairbanks.

29. Hudson Stuck, *The Alaskan Missions of the Episcopal Church* (New York: Domestic and Foreign Missionary Society, 1920), 41–44.

30. Pete, 25, 27, 30.

31. James Fall recounts the story of Diqelas Tukda and also indicates the break in trading relations which undoubtedly occurred after 1877. James Arthur Fall, "Patterns of Upper Inlet Tanaina Leadership, 1741–1918" (Ph.D. Dissertation, University of Wisconsin, 1981), 207–9.

32. L. D. Kitchener, *Flag over the North* (Seattle: Superior Publishing Co., 1954), 176; Oswalt, 11, 86.

33. Oswalt, 14–15. See also William Schneider, Dianne Gudgel-Holmes, and John Dalle-Molle, "Land Use in the North Additions of Denali National Park and Preserve: An Historical Perspective," 24–26, 1985 Draft Report available at Denali National Park.

34. Schneider et al., 26.

35. Jeff Stokes, "Subsistence Salmon Fishing in the Upper Kuskokwim River System, 1981–82," Juneau, Department of Fish and Game, Division of Subsistence, 1982, 1–29. For the introduction of fishwheels on the Kuskokwim, see Hosley, 550–51. As noted, fish fences and traps were used on the clear water, up river tributaries until the mid-1960s. Stokes claims that most salmon were taken with this method up to that date. I suspect that this was a localized take; the introduction of fishwheels along the main rivers must have greatly facilitated fishing while the roadhouses were in operation and had a large demand for fish.

36. Oswalt, 55.

37. Brown, 89; and Schneider et al., 27.

38. Richard Slobodin, "The Dawson Boys—Peel River Indians and the Klondike Gold Rush," *Polar Notes* 5 (June 1963): 24–36. I am very appreciative of the assistance of many people who read earlier drafts of this paper. Particularly I would like to thank Dianne Gudgel-Holmes, Joan Antonson, Lyman Woodman, Jon Nielson, Barbara Smith, Marvin Falk, Paul McCarthy, Doug Best, Jeff Stokes, Charlene LeFebre, and Morgan Sherwood.

Controlling the Periphery

The Territorial Administration of the Yukon-Alaska, 1867–1959

KEN COATES

Ken Coates, formerly of the University of Victoria and the University of Northern British Columbia, now teaching at Hamilton, New Zealand, has been a prolific contributor to analysis of the Canadian and American North. With William Morrison of UNBC he has published a score of important books and articles on various aspects of northern development.

One of the persistent myths of the North has been that the Canadian government exerted early and consistent control in the Northwest Territories (which originally included all of Canada west of Ontario) and the Yukon, and that the American government, on the other hand, neglected Alaska, which was thus denied its democratic rights and was at the same time characterized by lawlessness. In the following article Coates turns that mythology on its head. Canadian administrators considered the Canadian North too unpromising and too expensive for much investment of time, resources, or energy, he asserts. The American government was much quicker to extend its authority to Alaska, the "neglect" thesis notwithstanding, and has consistently invested federal resources to encourage and sustain settlement and economic development there.

With other mythologies, the notion that Alaskans stood on their own without government help has astounding staying power, perhaps because it fits so well with the American commitment to individuality and the American love of freedom. Readers can gain insight into the nature of Alaska mythology by studying the Canadian example. Canadian northerners seem to have much less ambivalence than their American counterparts toward their federal government. Whereas Americans have complained both that the federal government did not do enough for Alaska and, at the same time, that the heavy hand of federal administration restrained and inhibited development and freedom, the Canadians have complained throughout the 20th century of being ignored and abandoned

This article appeared originally in *Pacific Northwest Quarterly* 78 (October 1987): 141–51; it is reprinted here by permission.

by the central government in Ottawa. "Damned if you do and damned if you don't" must be the feeling of any federal official who has attempted to deal with the North.

Historians of the Canadian and American Northwest have been mesmerized by the image of the Mounties. Standing tall and straight at their border posts, serge-coated and honest to a fault, the men of the North West Mounted Police symbolize Canada's active involvement in the governance of its northern territories. In contrast, the famous Skagway duo, the villainous Soapy Smith and the virtuous vigilante Frank Reid, suggests that the American governmental presence on the northern frontier was negligible.

These contrary images reflect much about national mythology and character and have become firmly entrenched in the historiography. The Alaskan historian William R. Hunt observes that during the Klondike gold rush the "few miles of mountain pass" between Alaska and the Yukon Territory "gave striking evidence of the difference between the rule of Canada's government and the neglect of that of the United States." Northern Canada's foremost historian, Morris Zaslow, echoes that view:

> Hence the Yukon was the locale of a fascinating contrast between two different North American political philosophies. The American version stressed local autonomy and the right of settlers to establish their own system of government and frame their own regulations. In the territories of the United States, federal government authority was asserted diffidently and always was likely to be challenged. . . . [F]ew regulations were imposed from outside to check the triumph of the most efficient producers or the speedy reorganization of industry to maximize profits.
>
> Against this stood the tradition of Canadian administration, sprung from British roots—a tradition of authority, of rules and regulation established from outside, of development controlled and directed in the presumed general or national, rather than the particular local or regional interest. . . . Thus the frontier tradition of Canada was one of unspectacular, orderly, solid development under external guidance, characterized by fewer abuses and injustices than its American counterpart pehaps, but also by little of the obsessive, all consuming drive to speedy, efficient development and exploitation of natural resources, of which the United States is mankind's supreme exponent.[1]

A comparative review of northern territorial administration offers a unique opportunity to consider what is truly northern about the pace, scale, and direction of Alaskan and Yukon development. The nature of government on the northernmost Canadian and American frontiers reveals how politicians and businessmen viewed the potential of their newly acquired lands. Second, the response of people in the territories to the government there indicates a great deal about northern frontier society and its perceptions of its place in the larger nation.

Historians have much to learn from such a comparison. Those studying Canada's North have been preoccupied with government activities, a reflection of their belief that federal policies and officials played a major role in determining the nature of northern development. Given the generally active federal role in more southerly districts, the assumption seems relatively safe. Even a preliminary comparison with government activities and attitudes in Alaska, however, reveals the comparatively modest hand of the Canadian government in the Yukon and the exceptionally minor role ascribed to the territory in national development schemes. Conversely, it also shows the surprising degree of activity and direct intervention in northern affairs by the American government.

Both approaches to territorial administration lay rooted in the process by which Canada and the United States separated from England. The violent breach between Britain and the 13 colonies, which originated in a confrontation over colonial administration, influenced subsequent U.S. policy toward peripheral territories. It proved difficult, if only because it seemed incongruous, for the new republican state to be devising a means of colonial control. But the Northwest Ordinance of 1787 codified a commitment to a progressive assumption of power for the periphery. Newly settled territories were to be ruled initially as colonies but were promised eventual statehood and full participation in the union. This administrative arrangement offered a peaceful, systematic evolution from colonial status to political equality, and it reflected the values of the founding fathers and their determination not to repeat the mistakes of the British.[2]

Canadian politicians adopted a markedly different approach to their periphery, one rooted in affinity for the British Empire, a hatred of American republicanism, and a fear of American expansionism. The desire of the dominant provinces, Ontario and Quebec, to extend their control to the western periphery set the terms for territorial administration. While the U.S. constructed its continental empire through purchase, war, occupation, and negotiation, Canada gained its colonies through the acquisition of Rupert's Land from the Hudson's Bay Company in 1870. The territories spread across the western plains, reached to the Arctic coast, and included land surrounding Hudson Bay. Faced with the daunting prospect of administering so vast an area, and in the absence of a specific Canadian political ideology that might have guided them to a different approach, the Canadian authorities followed the British colonial model. Red River, the only settled part of the new territories, bitterly resented the imposition of Canadian control. Forced by angry métis and Indians to alter its plans, the government allowed the Red River region to enter the Dominion as the Province of Manitoba, although control over natural resources remained in federal hands.[3]

Concessions to Manitoba notwithstanding, the rest of the Northwest Territories continued to be administered by appointed federal officials and provided with only the most rudimentary of political institutions. Although granted their Legislative Assembly in 1888, residents got no assurance that they would eventually receive their full rights as Canadian citizens. In 1905, the federal government created two new provinces, Alberta and Saskatchewan, out of the southerly (below the 60th parallel) sections of the Northwest Territories. But these new entities, like Manitoba, lacked control over their own resources until 1930, and their inhabitants were not politically equal to other Canadians.[4]

The political machinery employed in the Canadian and American Northwest reflected different national attitudes toward the territories. When William Seward negotiated the purchase of Alaska, Americans immediately saw promise in the new land. Despite public portrayals of the acquisition as "Seward's Folly," most people welcomed the opportunities that national expansion provided. The government quickly made Alaska a military district and imposed laws regulating customs, commerce, and navigation.[5]

The U.S. military was not in Alaska purely for symbolic purposes. The mere existence of army posts helped to stifle smuggling, kept foreign competitors out of American markets, and preserved valuable resources (like the Pribilof Islands) for American business interests. Speculators, developers, settlers, traders, and frontiersmen went north. Although the territory did not immediately match its promoters' dreams, the scale and majesty of the land instilled confidence that the future held better prospects. Government interest in the region lagged somewhat behind that of northern visionaries, but officials were prepared to offer modest assistance to regional development.[6]

While Americans occupied and developed their new possession, Canadians paid scant attention to the far corners of their territories. The region was, after all, still a fur trade preserve and under the practical, if no longer the legal, control of the Hudson's Bay Company. Furthermore, settlement of the southern prairie required most of the country's meager resources. Although intellectuals pontificated about Canada's salubrious climate and location, and about the firm, aggressive national character being molded in the North, the rhetoric of nationalism bore little relationship to reality.[7]

By 1870 Canadians had come to view the prairie West as a veritable garden. Perceptions of the North, however, shifted much more slowly. In the 1880s, a small group of promoters circulated laudatory descriptions of the Mackenzie River valley and praised the short-term prospects of northern development. Such efforts had little effect on government policy. Canadian authorities, like most Canadians, knew little about their northern posessions. The government's commitment to the Yukon River valley consisted, until the mid-1890s, of several brief attempts to identify its resources and describe its geography.[8]

Businessmen and missionaries asked that measures be taken to protect Canadian business from American competitors and Canadian natives from Yankee miners. Only after years of effort, particularly by the Anglican bishop William Carpenter Bompas, did the federal government finally send a member of the North West Mounted Police to investigate conditions in the region. Inspector Charles Constantine's 1894 expedition, which revealed that the Yukon was largely occupied by Americans and that Canada was losing thousands of dollars in potential customs duties each year, led to the government's decision to establish a formal police presence there. The Mounties—only 20 men initially—undertook to supplant the libertarian traditions of American frontier jurisprudence, particularly the miners' meeting, and to enforce Canadian mining regulations. They did little else, for the government saw scant promise in the North and hence no justification for incurring substantial costs.[9]

Clearly, Canadians and Americans had different attitudes toward the frontier. The periphery had a valued place in the American psyche; it was synonymous with richness, potential, and personal opportunity. U.S. law encouraged settlement, providing that when population and development warranted the frontier would gain full statehood. But the frontier held no mythical place in the Canadian mind. Although a few citizens toyed with the idea of a Canadian "empire," most recognized the climatic, demographic, and geographic limitations of their sprawling and comparatively poor nation. The Yukon Territory was yet another region Canada was incapable of developing, and the interests of those on the frontier had to be subordinated to the "purposes of the Dominion." Canadian politicians, therefore, viewed their northland as a responsibility, one reluctantly accepted, and a fiscal burden.[10]

The difference in perception had its clearest manifestation in the area of resource management. Alaska and the Yukon faced common economic problems, including isolation, high transportation costs, lack of local capital, and an insufficient regional labor force. U.S. lawmakers passed a series of measures in order to overcome these difficulties. Perhaps the most telling evidence of federal commitment to Alaskan development was the Alaska Railroad. After several private attempts to build a line from the coast to the interior had failed, Congress in 1914 authorized construction of the first government-financed and -operated railroad in the nation. Other legislation, like the law providing navy support for coal mining, followed, allowing the government to encourage and to regulate the pace of resource development.[11]

Disposition of forests is a further indication of government faith in the long-term prospects of Alaska. In the southern states, forest lands had typically passed quickly from the public domain into the hands of individual timber operators. Anger at rapacious resource exploitation led to gradually increasing federal intervention and control. In Alaska, Lawrence Rakestraw argues, "the system was turned on its head. Acquisition was soon followed by reservation and custodial management, with a limited amount of disposal." Federal control of the forest reserves indicated the pervasiveness of progressive ideology in government planning; the political isolation and weakness of Alaska made such control possible in a way it was not in the states. Ironically, Alaskans envied the *laissez-faire* policy operating in Canadian territory, a policy that placed few restrictions on Yukon timber operations.[12]

U.S. government resource planning and development left little room for local involvement. Alaskans found much to protest in the federal programs but had few avenues of recourse. In 1920, for example, a territorial appeal for equal treatment under the Maritime Act was rejected by the U.S. Supreme Court. The court acknowledged overt discrimination against Alaska but held that colonial dependencies were not guaranteed the same treatment as the states. Contrary to common belief, the northern frontier was not lawless and unregulated; American authorities played a substantial role in Alaska's economic development.

Canadian authorities, on the other hand, basically surrendered to the economic problems of the Yukon Territory. Although the government underwrote much westward expansion, it did not support northern development. Even the Klondike gold rush, which proved beyond doubt the existence of abundant mineral resources in the territory, generated minimal federal response. Besides increasing the police force and enforcing Canadian laws, the government attempted to exact rents from the gold-mining sector but backed down when the largely American mining constituency objected. Clifford Sifton, minister of the interior, saw little future in the Yukon. The district, he wrote, "'is not the same as any other gold mining country in the world'. . . 'and the difference consists in the fact that it is good for nothing except mining, which in all probability will be temporary.'"[13]

Not totally oblivious of the short-term potential, however, Sifton proposed several measures designed primarily to give southern Canadian businesses greater access to Yukon markets. The cornerstone of his program, an all-Canadian railway that would free the Yukon from its dependence on Alaskan ports, fell before concentrated American protest, but he arranged for the gradual take-over of the Klondike gold creeks by large concessionaires. After the rush ended, Dawson City became a small-scale government center and a company town.[14]

Canada's pattern of neglect and indifference toward northern economic expansion continued into the 20th century, the myth of the government-dominated frontier notwithstanding. The federal government provided modest subsidies to the territorial government for road construction, and it lent some assistance for the Keno Hill silver mines. There was no federal effort to diversify the Yukon economy, no Canadian equivalent of the U.S. Navy's underwriting coal production, no Canadian version of the Alaska Railroad to subsidize and encourage development of timber, farming, fisheries, and minerals.[15]

The manner in which the two countries dealt with agriculture in the territories provides further evidence of American interest and Canadian neglect. To Americans, the frontier homesteader was an irreplaceable component of hinterland development. The imminent disappearance of homestead land in the American West would, many believed, encourage the rapid settlement of Alaska. Despite obvious climatic and locational problems that limited the appeal of the region for homesteading, government agents promoted agricultural settlement, surveyed lands, established experimental stations, and erected grandiose displays at the

Lewis and Clark Centennial Exposition in Portland and at the Alaska-Yukon-Pacific Exposition held in Seattle in 1909. Such efforts were renewed during the depression, when environmental calamities in the Midwest and West and a new level of government interventionism led to federally sponsored settlement in the Matanuska Valley. The poorly conceived scheme foundered, but it underscored both America's commitment to frontier settlement and its ignorance of agriculture in the North.[16]

In the Yukon Territory, private producers, particularly during the gold rush, discovered that agriculture (including stock raising) was financially viable, but they received little federal encouragement. The Canadian government reserved its support—subsidies, cheap freight rates, even access to land—for prairie farmers. Because prospects for export agriculture in the Yukon were nonexistent, Ottawa withheld assistance, thus hampering regional attempts to achieve partial self-sufficiency in farm products.[17]

Before the 1950s, the administration of Native affairs on the northern periphery followed a similar pattern: Canadian neglect and American involvement. Canada's Indian policy was formally aimed at the protection, civilization, and assimilation of its aboriginal citizens. The fine rhetoric of national politicians and Ottawa civil servants did not, however, translate into appropriate action on the frontier. Believing that the Yukon had negligible prospects for development, Indian affairs officials felt no compulsion to start the long and expensive process of integration.[18]

When Inspector Constantine of the North West Mounted Police left for the Yukon in 1894, the government directed him with regard to the Indians, "not to give encouragement to the idea that they will be received into treaty, and taken under the care of the government." Reluctance to assume responsibility characterized Canadian Indian affairs practices for three-quarters of a century. In the fields of health and education, the government made some efforts, and its agents provided relief supplies to Natives who could prove utter destitution. But the belief that Indians would "if left as Indians earn a better living" dominated federal Native policy in the Yukon. Accordingly, the government attempted, after a fashion, to protect Native access to resources since it considered a harvesting economy the Indians' sole option in the territory.[19]

After 1945, the new policies of the emerging welfare state, which included renewed commitment to the country's Native people, were gradually applied in the Yukon. Civil servants often did not tailor national policies to the northern setting. Housing provided for Natives, for example, was not designed for the arctic climate, making the already difficult transition to village life even more troubling. In the postwar period the federal government was determined to bring the Indians under the umbrella of national programs.[20]

The U.S. government took a far more active interest than the Canadian government in Native affairs. Under the Alaska Organic Act of 1884, Indians remained on the land, subject to future legislative initiatives. Through the Bureau of Education, led by the dynamic Sheldon Jackson, the federal government provided schools and established several cooperative stores. To encourage Indian self-sufficiency, it devised programs that introduced reindeer herding, allowed Natives to own land, and increased regulation of the salmon industry.[21]

During the 1930s, when financial exigency forced the Canadian government to limit its already parsimonious spending for northern Natives, the American government initially excluded Alaskan aboriginal people from New Deal legislation. Under pressure from the Alaska Native Brotherhood, which wanted financial assistance and secure title to its lands, the politicians changed direction and, in 1936, passed the Alaska Reorganization Act. This law encouraged Native organization, village incorporation, and individual loans. Indian life under the new legislation was not without its troubles; title to aboriginal lands, for example, remained in question. The problems, however, were caused by activity and government initiative, forces that bypassed the Yukon Indians until the 1950s.[22]

In contrast to these long-term concerns about the northern periphery, the onset of World War II (and particularly the attack on Pearl Harbor) provided a test of national resolve under crisis conditions. Although they clearly overestimated the Japanese threat and acted contrary to the advice of their military advisers, American officials decided in February 1942 to build a defense and supply road from Edmonton, Alberta, to Fairbanks, Alaska. The Canadian response to the perceived military threat and resulting American activity was predictable. Canadian authorities did not believe that a highway, associated airfields, and pipeline were required; not until 1943, and then only at the urging of the British high commissioner to Canada, did the federal government send a special commissioner for Northwest defense projects to function as liaison with American officials.[23]

Even the Americans soon realized that the Alcan project was unnecessary and a colossal waste of money. The Canadian government reluctantly assumed responsibility for maintaining the highway after the war. Ignoring pleas from Yukoners and Alaskans, it spent little for necessary construction and improvements. The Yukon now had a long-desired road, but it followed the wrong route, was not up to proper standards, and did not have the positive economic effect that many in the territory had hoped for. Nor did it signal a new federal commitment to northern development.[24]

Wartime projects did, however, bring a brighter future to Alaska. Although the American government had long maintained a small military presence in the territory, the war and subsequent cold war tensions stimulated a major expansion. New bases were built, and thousands of military personnel arrived to man the stations. The economy of the region surged to meet the military's needs for housing, goods, and services. In the postwar period, the Alaska Highway—paved in Alaska but largely gravel-surfaced in Canada—symbolized the different national attitudes toward the northern territories. The gap between the Yukon and Alaska, growing since the Klondike gold rush, grew wider still.[25]

Constitutional and political changes also mirrored the different approaches to economic development. Yukoners and Alaskans alike resented the dominance of their colonial parent. They fought against the external control, the lack of local democratic institutions, and the slow progress toward meaningful political reform. The results of those protests differed greatly.

Yukoners expected, and wanted, little from the Canadian government before the gold rush. Most people in the region were Americans, working on Canadian soil and benefiting from the nonenforcement of Canadian customs duties and mining law. With the discovery of gold and the arrival of thousands of would-be miners, local needs changed dramatically. Yukon residents now demanded local autonomy. The federal government refused, providing instead a small civil service, a greatly expanded police contingent, and the Yukon Field Force (200 Canadian army regulars) to maintain order in the goldfields.

Concessions came grudgingly. The Yukon was made a separate territory in 1898; residents were allowed to elect two members to the Territorial Council in 1900, and three more after 1902. In that year as well, the government permitted the Yukon one elected member in the federal House of Commons. In 1908, the Territorial Council became a wholly elected body, although still subservient to the federally appointed commissioner, who could dissolve the council if it disagreed with him. The largest community, Dawson City, was incorporated in 1902. The territorial population did not handle its new duties well. Local politics was characterized by patronage, partisanship, and corruption.[26]

The gains of the gold rush period proved illusory. Over the next 20 years Yukoners lost virtually all influence over their political affairs. A declining population, especially during World War I, provided the government and its territorial officials with a rationale for rescinding Dawson City's municipal charter, reducing the civil service, and restricting elected representation on the Territorial Council. It was, as Jim Lotz commented, "a withering away of the state in a way in which Marx never envisaged. One man [the commissioner of the Yukon, George Jeckell] wore many hats, and the Commissioner was a virtual dictator, ruling the Territory on behalf of the federal government." In 1937 the government came close to turning over responsibility for the Yukon to British Columbia, despite protests from northern residents; even later it argued that the territory's small population base and nationally important resources precluded local control. Substantial change, as a result, was delayed until the 1970s.[27]

Alaskans were decades ahead of Yukoners in achieving political power. Like the Canadian government, various U.S. administrations used population and cyclical economy to justify limited self-rule in the North. Not until 1884 (more than a decade before the Yukon) did federal law grant Alaska proper civil and judicial authority. Improvements came slowly. The district received congressional representation in 1906, but it struggled six more years for a territorial legislature, which the Second Organic Act authorized.[28]

Conditioned by the American expectation of evolutionary self-rule, Alaskans soon set about gaining full autonomy. As early as 1916, the territorial delegate James Wickersham introduced a statehood bill. It failed, partly due to Alaskan indifference. Despite complex problems within the region, particularly taxation, Alaskan politicians continued to pressure their stateside counterparts about entry into the Union. By the early 1950s the battle was sustained by the "Little Men" of Alaska, a grass-roots group dominated by many newly arrived northerners who demanded their full rights as American citizens. Innovative measures like drafting a state constitution and submitting it to the people for ratification gave the states' rights movement notable vitality. Finally, after much opposition and debate, Alaska gained admission as the 49th state on January 3, 1959. Alaskans had fought longer for their rights than did most territorial residents, but they did so confident of their ultimate success.[29]

The comparison of the Alaskan and Yukon experiences is instructive in many ways. Although popular myth and historical convention suggest that the Canadian government exercised far more control over its frontier than the American authorities exercised over Alaska, the truth is otherwise. The U.S. government was active, building railways, regulating resources, and rushing to the defense of its periphery. Canada saw expense, not opportunity, on its northwestern frontier, and it did its best to limit its financial and political obligations there.

Historians should scrutinize the differences between the Canadian and American governmental roles in the North. Federal neglect of territorial needs went a long way toward shaping the Yukon's destiny. The search for an explanation of the Yukon's evolution clearly must shift to new topics. Historians have not, for example, examined the effect of the White Pass and Yukon Route or the large Klondike mining concerns on Yukon society. No one has yet attempted study of mine workers, the Keno Hill mines, or such important themes as transiency and seasonality in the North. The historians' current emphasis on government policy and territorial administration in the Yukon Territory, while instructive, must be balanced by a close examination of the northern society and economy.

American mismanagement and "neglect" in Alaska take on a different hue when compared with the Canadian handling of the Yukon. Although Alaska historians have preferred to contrast the development of Alaska with that of the American West, ignoring the special limitations imposed by the far northern location, they can gain perspective from studying the Yukon experience. Residents of the Canadian North could not overcome isolation, government neglect, and a boom-and-bust economic base; a comparative study indicates how the U.S. used its wealth and power to overcome many of these barriers to regional development and stability.

Finally, studying the administration of the Yukon Territory and Alaska reveals just how much is national, and what is northern, in their development. In each case, development followed a pattern determined by traditional national attitudes toward peripheral territories. Americans assumed that the frontier meant wealth and opportunity and acted on that assumption even when faced with contrary evidence. Canadians waited for proof, and even when the Klondike gold rush showed that the region possessed untold riches, the government held back, firm in its belief that such discoveries would prove transitory. The problems faced by Yukoners and Alaskans were northern and similar; the resolution of those problems was specific to Canada and to the U.S.

NOTES

1. William R. Hunt, *North of 53: Wild Days of the Alaska-Yukon Mining Frontier, 1870–1914* (New York, 1974), 246; Morris Zaslow, *The Opening of the Canadian North, 1870–1914* (Toronto, 1971), 139; also see: R. C. Macleod, "Canadianizing the West: The North-West Mounted Police as Agent of the National Policy, 1873–1905," in *Essays on Western History: In Honor of Lewis Gwynne Thomas,* ed. Lewis H. Thomas (Edmonton, 1976), 101–10, and Melody Webb, *The Last Frontier* (Albuquerque, 1985), which attempts to apply Turner's ideas to the history of the Yukon River basin.

2. Robert F. Berkhofer, Jr., "The Northwest Ordinance and the Principle of Territorial Evolution," in *The American Territorial System National Archives Conferences, Papers and Proceedings of the Conference on the History of the Territories,* ed. John Porter Bloom (Athens, Ohio, 1973), 45–55.

3. The administrative evolution of the Northwest Territories is traced in Lewis Herbert Thomas, *The Struggle for Responsible Government in the Northwest Territories, 1870–97,* 2nd ed. (Toronto, 1978).

4. Ibid., 265.

5. Richard E. Welch, Jr., "American Public Opinion and the Purchase of Russian America," in *Alaska and Its History,* ed. Morgan Sherwood (Seattle, 1967), 273–90 (and reprinted in this anthology). See also William R. Hunt, *Alaska: A Bicentennial History* (New York, 1976), 33–37.

6. On Canada as a northern nation, see Carl Bergen, "The True North, Strong and Free," in *Nationalism in Canada,* University League for Social Reform, ed. Peter Russell (Toronto, 1966), 3–26, and Louis-Edmond Hamelin, *Canadian Nordicity: It's Your North, Too* (Montreal, 1979), 3–13.

7. In 1869, acting on requests from American traders, Captain Charles Raymond of the U.S. Navy visited Fort Youcon (Yukon) and ordered the Hudson's Bay Company to stop trading on American soil. American traders took over the post and used it as a base from which they expanded into Canadian territory. Kenneth Coates, "Furs along the Yukon: Hudson's Bay Company–Native Trade in the Yukon River Basin, 1830–1893," *BC Studies* (1982), 50–78.

8. Zaslow, 94–100.

9. William R. Morrison, "Showing the Flag: The Mounted Police and Canadian Sovereignty in the North, 1894–1925" (Vancouver, B.C., 1985), chapter 2. See also Thomas Stone, "The Mounties as Vigilantes: Perceptions of Community and the Transformation of Law in the Yukon, 1887–1897," *Law and Society Review* 14 (1979), 83–114.

10. Welch, 289, and W. L. Morton, "The North in Canadian Historiography," in *Contexts of Canada's Past,* ed. A. B. McKilloy (Toronto, 1980), 229–39.

11. William H. Wilson, *Railroad in the Clouds: The Alaska Railroad in the Age of Steam, 1914–1945* (Boulder, Colo., 1977); *idem,* "The Alaska Railroad and Coal: Development of a Federal Policy, 1914–1939," *Pacific Northwest Quarterly,* 73 (1982), 66–77. On the Canadian railway, the White Pass and Yukon Route, see Roy Minter, *White Pass: Gateway to the Klondike* (Toronto, 1987).

12. Lawrence Rakestraw, "Forest History of Alaska: Four Approaches to Two

Forest Ecosystems," *Journal of Forest History* 23 (1979), 70; William H. Wilson, "Developing Central Alaska's Forest Resources: The Alaska Railroad, 1923–1941," ibid., 25 (1981), 26–35.

13. D. J. Hall, *Clifford Sifton*, Vol. 1: *The Unsung Napoleon, 1861–1900* (Vancouver, 1981), 166.

14. Hal Guest, "A History of Dawson City, Yukon Territory, 1896–1920," Microfiche Report Series No. 7 (Ottawa. 1984), *Sifton*, Vol. 2: *The Lonely Eminence, 1901–1929* (Vancouver, 1985).

15. K. J. Rea, *The Political Economy of the Canadian North* (Toronto, 1968), 67–196; Kenneth Coates, *Canada's Colonies: A History of the Yukon and Northwest Territories* (Toronto, 1985), 94–99.

16. James R. Shortridge, "The Alaskan Agricultural Empire: An American Agrarian Persuasion, 1898–1929," *Pacific Northwest Quarterly* 69 (1978), 45–58, and William H. Wilson, "The Alaska Railroad and the Agricultural Frontier," *Agricultural History* 52 (1978), 263–79.

17. C. S. Mackinnon, "The Rise and Decline of Agriculture and Horticulture in the Mackenzie District and the Yukon," *Musk-Ox* 30 (1982), 48–63, esp. 51–56.

18. John L. Tobias, "Protection, Civilization and Assimilation: An Outline History of Canada's Indian Policy," *Western Canadian Journal of Anthropology* 6 (1976), 13–30.

19. For Constantine's instructions, see Public Archives of Canada, Department of Indian Affairs, RG 10, Vol. 1115, Deputy Superintendent's Letterbooks, April 27, 1894–November 16, 1894, H. Reed to Charles Constantine, May 29, 1894; Yukon Territorial Archives, Anglican Church Records, New Series, file 2, Notes of interview with Mr. Pedley and Mr. Oliver, Feb. 26, 1909 (2d qtn.).

20. Ken Coates, "Best Left as Indians: The Federal Government and the Indians of the Yukon, 1894–1950," *Canadian Journal of Native Studies* 4 (Fall 1984), 199.

21. Glenn Smith, "Education for the Natives of Alaska: The Work of the United States Bureau of Education, 1884–1931," *Journal of the West* 6 (1967), 440–50.

22. Kenneth R. Philp, "The New Deal and Alaskan Natives, 1936–1945," *Pacific Historical Review* 50 (1981), 309–27, reprinted in this anthology.

23. M. V. Bezeau, "The Realities of Strategic Planning: The Decision to Build the Alaska Highway," Richard J. Diubaldo, "The Alaska Highway in Canada–United States Relations," and Curtis R. Nordman, "The Army of Occupation: Malcolm MacDonald and U.S. Military Involvement in the Canadian Northwest," in *The Alaska Highway : Papers of the 40th Anniversary Symposium,* ed. Kenneth Coates (Vancouver, 1985), 25–35, 102–15, 83–94. Bezeau's article is reprinted in this anthology.

24. Cf. Richard Stuart, "The Impact of the Alaska Highway on Dawson City," ibid., 188–204.

25. On the early period, see Webb, 143–70; Hunt, *Alaska,* 110–15. To contrast American activity with the modest Canadian interest in the defense of the Yukon, see Stephen Harris, "'Really a Defile throughout Its Length': The Defence of the Alaska Highway in Peacetime," in *Alaska Highway,* ed. Coates, 119–32.

26. Thomas, *Responsible Government,* chap. 10; W. R. Morrison, "The Politics of the Yukon Territory, 1898–1909," *Canadian Studies in History and Government* 12 (Toronto, 1968), 40–41, 46–47.

27. Jim Lotz, *Northern Realities: The Future of Northern Development in Canada* (Toronto, 1972), 80; Richard Stuart, "Duff Pattullo and the Yukon Schools Question of 1937," *Canadian Historical Review* 64 (1983), 25–44, describes the struggle over the Yukon. Not until 1977 did elected representatives gain control of the executive committee of the Territorial Council; two years later, the government reduced the authority of the commissioner and gave elected officials greater autonomy. Gordon Robertson, *Northern Provinces: A Mistaken Goal* (Ottawa, 1985), 1–80.

28. Pat McCollom "Alaska's First Delegates, Waskey and Cale," *Alaska Journal* 3 (1973), 50, 55.

29. Gerald E. Bowkett, "The Alaska Constitutional Convention,"' *Alaska Journal* 6 (1976), 154–60. Alaska adopted the so-called Tennessee plan, which involved organizing for self-rule and presenting the *fait accompli* to Congress in order to force a decision on statehood. On the broader statehood process, see Claus-M. Naske, *A History of Alaska Statehood* (rev. ed.) (Lanham, Md., 1985). The chronology used here is summarized from Hunt, *Alaska,* 117–34.

Gold Rushers North

A Census Study of the Yukon and Alaskan Gold Rushes, 1896–1900

JAMES H. DUCKER

United States census figures show that the population of Alaska roughly doubled beween 1890 and 1900, rising from 32,052 to 63,592. The Native population rose from 25,354 to 29,542, although some of that increase may be the result of more accurate reporting. The greatest growth occurred among non-Natives, whose numbers jumped from 4,298 in 1890 to 30,450 in 1900. One can plausibly assume that most of those came to search for gold or to provide goods and services to the gold seekers. But who exactly were they?

James Ducker works as a planner for the Bureau of Land Management in Anchorage. His doctoral dissertation at the University of Illinois was published under the title Men of the Steel Rails: Workers on the Atchison, Topeka & Santa Fe Railroad, 1869–1900 *(Lincoln: University of Nebraska Press, 1983). He has been the editor of* Alaska History, *the scholarly journal of the Alaska Historical Society, for over a decade.*

In the following article Ducker used material from the census of 1900 to examine the demographics of Alaska in the gold rush era. Some of his findings can be anticipated. For example, many more men than women came to Alaska, and those men who came were generally young. But Ducker finds much else of interest as well. The principal significance of his work is documenting what is often taken as fact but is based essentially on anecdote.

Men from the sands of the Sunland;
men from the woods of the West;
Men from the farms and the cities,
into the Northland we pressed.
Graybeards and striplings and women,
good men and bad men and bold,

This article appeared originally in *Pacific Northwest Quarterly* 83 (July 1994): 82–92; it is reprinted here by permission.

Leaving our homes and our loved ones,
crying exultantly, "Gold!"

Never was seen such an army,
pitiful, futile, unfit;
Never was seen such a spirit,
manifold courage and grit.
Never has been such a cohort
under one banner unrolled
As surged to the ragged-edged Arctic,
urged by the arch-tempter—Gold.[1]

On July 15, 1897, the *Excelsior* steamed into San Francisco. Two days later, the *Portland* reached Seattle. The two ships, fresh from Alaskan waters, carried the first miners returning from an obscure northern river called the Klondike. There had been rumors of a gold strike in the Far North. The mining frontier always generated rumors, which wise men treated with skepticism. But the bundles of bullion that the prospectors hauled down the gangplanks in their suitcases, chests, and bags confirmed earlier stories of the discovery made by George Carmack, Skookum Jim, and Tagish Charlie. The 68 miners aboard the *Portland* alone carried nearly two tons of gold worth well over a million dollars.[2]

The magnitude of the find sent some men north immediately, but due to the lateness of the season, the surge of gold seekers did not reach flood tide until 1898. By then all the best ground near Dawson had been claimed, so many of the prospectors overflowed into Alaska, floating down the Yukon in search of their own Eldorado. In the next two years they found a series of moderately successful fields and the bonanza at Nome. Consequently, the territory's population continued to boom. Alaska's population doubled from 1890 to 1900; most of the growth occurred during the summers of 1898, 1899, and 1900.

The 1900 U.S. census provides an extensive look at the Alaskans of that year. Published census statistics illustrate the district's demographics. For example, there were 63,592 inhabitants; 46 percent were Indians, Eskimos, or Aleuts. Detailed analysis of census manuscripts, however, permits a much more comprehensive understanding of the characteristics of the men and women who partook of the gold rush. Probing the manuscripts is especially valuable because the 1900 census in Alaska was unique.

The Census Office was interested in the rush north and asked questions it had never asked during other censuses. In addition to their age, sex, marital status, birthplace, and occupation, Alaskans were to state the month and year they arrived in the district, their "Post Office Address at Home," and their job at home. The answers to these questions not only add depth to a knowledge of Alaskans, but they also are of interest to those studying geographic mobility.[3]

This computer-assisted study of the non-Native population of nine communities—six towns, a heavily industrialized hard-rock mining camp, a placer district at the peak of its activity, and an area on the prospecting frontier—portrays the people who came north. The nine communities offer a variety of environments experienced and created by Alaskans in 1900.[4]

Sitka, the old Russian town and turn-of-the-century district capital, was the most settled Euro-American community in Alaska and the least touched by the gold mania. Juneau, Douglas, and Treadwell were established in the 1880s. The first two were market towns for the nearby mines, including the Treadwell quartz gold operation, which boasted of being the largest of its kind in the world. Skagway, a town born during the Klondike rush, was the southern terminus of the Yukon & White Pass Railway, by which most miners reached the Klondike and the upper Yukon River. Eagle, on the Yukon just west of the Canadian border, was founded in 1898 by gold rushers who turned to the older fields in Alaska when they found little opportunity on the Klondike. Mining activity on the Fortymile River and American Creek helped sustain the supply center of Eagle. Nome was the site of one of America's greatest gold rushes in the early summer of 1900. The Tanana Valley was on the cutting edge of the mining frontier. In 1900 a couple of dozen prospectors panned its gravel; not until 1902 would Felix Pedro discover the gold that started the stampede to which Fairbanks owes its origins.[5]

Nome, Skagway, and Juneau were easily the largest cities in Alaska. The Census Office counted more than 12,000 people at Nome. Most of them rushed into the muddy streets of the city or out to the placers from ships that arrived as the Bering Sea ice retreated. The best the census takers could do was record names from passenger lists. Good demographic data, therefore, are available for only 1,733 adults. The census takers listed 2,012 people in Skagway and 1,456 in Juneau. There were 465 in Treadwell, 441 in the Fortymile, 369 in Douglas, 279 at Sitka, 274 at Eagle, and 29 in the Tanana Valley.[6]

The basic facts derived from the census reveal the differences and similarities among the nine communities. Whether or not women brought "civilization" to a settlement, it is clear that they were very rare on the prospecting frontier. All of the non-Natives in the Tanana Valley were males, as were 90 percent of the newcomers to Nome, Eagle, and the latter's surrounding placer country. Women accounted for only 7.5 percent of the population in Treadwell, where many mining company workers lived. The combined population for Treadwell and nearby Douglas was about three-quarters male. So was that of Juneau and Skagway. Sitka, because of its maturity and because it witnessed much less mining-induced growth, had the most balanced gender breakdown: 43 percent of its residents were female.

Similarly, marital statistics reflected the cultural and economic development of these communities. The newer, more rugged areas had few married men; one-fourth or fewer of the men in Nome, Eagle, and the Fortymile district were married, and fewer than a quarter of those had their wives with them. Eight of the twenty-nine men in the Tanana Valley were married, but none was living with his spouse. Juneau and Skagway had diversified economies and more settled environments, thus attracting greater numbers of married men and their wives—more than a third of the men in each town were married and well over half of their wives accompanied them. In Sitka nearly half the men were married, and almost all of these lived with their wives. Because Treadwell was a company town with few family dwellings, many married men working in the mines made their homes a mile away in Douglas. More than 50 percent of the men in Douglas were married, compared to 25 percent in Treadwell.[7]

Women's marital status was more uniform than the men's. Generally two-thirds to three-quarters of the women in each locality were married. The exceptions were at Eagle and in the Fortymile, where 16 of 19 and 14 of 14, respectively, were married. Evidently, little except marital bonds could persuade women to venture into interior Alaska. Examination of the arrival dates of married couples in Nome, Skagway, and Douglas indicates that most wives waited from several months to a couple of years before following their husbands north. Thus, the story of women and the gold rush includes not only the women who ventured north but also those who stayed behind, maintaining homes and families while their husbands shipped off to vast, distant Alaska.[8]

Not surprisingly, the ruggedness of the interior and Nome dissuaded many married couples with children from venturing there or at least discouraged them from bringing their children. Nearly 80 percent of Sitka couples had children; in the other southeastern communities, the percentage ranged from 62 percent in Juneau to 73 percent in Treadwell. In contrast, 41 percent of couples in Eagle, 28 percent in the Fortymile, and 14 percent in Nome had children.

Those who sought gold, or at least a job, in the Far North had to be able to move quickly with news of a gold strike. Single men and women, men who left their wives behind, and couples without children were free to pull up stakes at the latest rumor of a new prospect. They dominated the mining frontier of northern Alaska. They were not the sort of people to build up all the institutions of a well-rounded community. The demographics of these mining settlements weighed heavily against townspeople who wanted a community that offered more than the essentials of life and business.

The census revealed two other indicators of Alaskans' domestic arrangements—it listed individuals together who lived in the same house, and it gave their relationship to the head of the household. Some enumerators, particularly those in Skagway and Nome, did a poor job of recording this information, and subtle differences in the others' practices make comparisons of the communities only suggestive.

Between 12 and 15 percent of residents in the southeastern towns of Sitka, Douglas, and Juneau lived alone, compared to almost 25 percent in the Fortymile country and 38 percent in Eagle. Southeasterners were far more likely to live with kin than those in the interior. Two-thirds of adults in Juneau who did not head a household, three-fourths of those in Douglas, and more than 90 percent of those in Sitka lived in the home of a relative. The figures for Eagle and the Fortymile were much lower: less than 20 percent and less than 10 percent, respectively. In the latter two communities, most of those who did not head households were lodgers or partners.

The census enumerator recorded more than three of every four people in Treadwell as lodgers. Two company lodging houses held 175 and 199 men, 87 percent of all the men in town. The impermanent nature of Nome's population was evident: more than 50 percent of its residents were transients, lodgers, boarders, or tenants. In Skagway the enumerator decided that virtually everyone who was not related to the head of a household was a head of a household. Thus, he recorded that more than three-fourths of the town's adults were household heads. Doubtless, the enumerator found much of Skagway's transient population in what he referred to as the "tent town" near Moore's Wharf.

Census takers also recorded home ownership. Such an endeavor was somewhat farcical in that, except for townsites and mining claims, legal private appropriation of federal lands in Alaska was almost impossible. Possibly, this difficulty helps to explain why only in Juneau, Douglas, Treadwell, and Sitka do the enumerators seem to have done an adequate job. In Sitka and Juneau, homeowners headed more than half of the households. But the company town aspect of Douglas and Treadwell is apparent: two-thirds of the homes in Douglas and 16 of the 17 family residences in Treadwell were rented.[9]

Differences in the age distributions of the men in the communities again point out that Sitka and Treadwell were unusual cases. Nearly equal numbers of Sitka men were in their twenties, thirties, and forties, and more than a fourth were 50 or older. Sitka was more representative of California and Washington, the states from which nearly half of Alaska's men came, than of gold rush Alaska. In contrast, Treadwell's population was skewed toward youth—46 percent of its residents were under age 30.[10]

Generally, the men who moved north to Alaska were youthful. Only 10 percent were age 50 or older, but in the national population 22 percent of men were at least 50. Sixty-eight percent were age 18 to 39, in contrast to 60 percent in the nation and 55 percent and 60 percent, respectively, in California and Washington. Yet Alaskan men were not as youthful a group as many might presume. Pierre Berton, in *The Klondike Fever*, states that "the great majority [of those stampeding to the Klondike] were young men in their mid-twenties." Such youth had been a hallmark of the California gold rush of the late 1840s. Ralph Mann discovered that over 60 percent of those who came to two of California's important mining camps were in their twenties. But the Alaskan gold rushers were more likely to have been in their thirties than in their twenties. In Alaska in 1900, 38 percent of the Caucasian men were in their thirties, and 29 percent were in their twenties.[11]

Nor does an examination of men's ages at the time of their arrival in Alaska bolster the image of the youthful gold rusher. Nearly 6 out of every 10 men in the nine communities arrived in Alaska when they were age 30 or older. This ratio increases if only those who reached the district at the height of the rush in 1898 are studied.

Nevertheless, if the men who came north were not particularly young, they did have the independence of youth. Not only had many left their wives behind, but Alaskan men as a whole were remarkably adverse to nuptials. Nationally, 64 percent of men age 20 or older were married. Barely a quarter of white males in Alaska were married, and fewer than a third in the nine communities. Significantly, although in the rest of the country 22 percent of men in their younger twenties were married and most of those older than 24, in Alaska only 21 percent of white men in their early thirties were married, and in no age group were there more men married than not. Thus, though the male gold rushers had reached or were nearing middle age, they were as free of family responsibilities as most of the country's young.[12]

American-born residents outnumbered others in all the communities except Douglas and Treadwell. Women were especially likely to be native Americans. Half of the women in Douglas, Treadwell, and the Fortymile were American-born; in the other towns more than two-thirds were. Twenty-five percent of Sitkans had their origins in Alaska. Almost none of the Euro-American residents of the other communities were born in the territory. This reflected the territory's status as America's last frontier. In 1900, 78 percent of all Americans born in the United States lived in their state of birth. The proportion dropped to one-half in the West. Only 3.7 percent of Alaska's non-Native residents, however, were born in the territory. The North Central states (from Ohio to the Dakotas) provided approximately half of the American-born inhabitants in the nine areas studied. Between a sixth and a third of American-born Alaskans in each community were from the north Atlantic states. Most of the rest came from the West; very few were born south of the Mason-Dixon line. This distribution of birthplaces was roughly similar to that found in the western states and territories.[13]

The Chinese were by far the largest foreign-born ethnic group in Alaska in 1900, numbering more than 3,000. They were on both the social and geographic fringe of the territory, engaged almost entirely by canneries; they did not inhabit the settlements in this study. In most of these communities, Canadians were the largest foreign-born group, with Germans, English, and Irish not far behind. The exceptions were Sitka, where Russians were the largest group of foreign born, and Douglas and Treadwell. In Douglas, Canadians were the largest group, but they were followed by Swedes and Finns. Austrians composed 15 percent of the men at Treadwell followed by Swedes, Finns, and Norwegians.

Nearly all of the foreign born had established some roots in the contiguous states and territories or Canada before coming to Alaska. More than 95 percent of the residents of all but Treadwell and Sitka claimed a hometown in the United States or Canada. In most of the communities in the study, a majority of residents had arrived in Alaska from the American West. The striking exceptions to this generalization were the least and most established areas. Of the 29 men prospecting on the Tanana, 10 told the census taker that their homes were in the north Atlantic and 10 the North Central states. In Sitka, 30 percent of the population came from the West, 15 percent each from north Atlantic and North Central states, and a little over a third from foreign countries, led by Russia, Canada, and England. Between 53 and 60 percent of the residents of Nome, Douglas, Treadwell, and the Fortymile listed homes in the West; in Juneau and Skagway the figure was 75 percent. Washington and California provided the vast majority of those from the western states and territories.[14]

Examination of the years in which the Alaskans of 1900 first came north not only points to varying stages of settlement but also to the phenomenal impact of the recent gold discoveries on the peopling of Alaska. Between 1890 and 1900, the district's population grew from 32,000 to 63,600. Most of the increase came in the three years prior to the turn of the century, spurred by voluminous writings on Alaska in the national and international press following the Klondike discovery. Of all the non-Native men in the communities under study, 80 percent arrived in 1897 or later. The "ninety-eighters" were especially prominent; most of the non-Native males in the Tanana Valley and in the Fortymile mining district entered Alaska in 1898. Nearly half of the men in Eagle, more than a third in Skagway and Nome, and between 17 and 22 percent of those in Juneau, Douglas, Treadwell, and Sitka also came that year.[15]

Identifying the former homes of those coming to Alaska in different years reveals some interesting trends. The numbers of men arriving from Canada prior to 1890 reflect the mining frontier's gradual movement northward. In the mid-1890s westerners made up more than 70 percent of those traveling north. But the Klondike excited the entire U.S., and consequently more gold seekers came from distant parts of the country in 1898 and 1899 than previously. These results coincide with two tenets of migration theory. That Canadians played a significant role in early migration to Alaska and that those from the American West dominated the flow of men to the North throughout the late 19th century corroborate the theory that most migrants traveled short distances. And the principle that migration to a region increases as information about its promise spreads finds support not only in the stampede of the late nineties but also in the somewhat more widespread origins of the migrants of 1898 and 1899.[16]

Quite understandably, there was a sharp distinction between the arrival dates of residents in the older communities of Sitka, Douglas, and Juneau and those of Skagway, Nome, and the interior. A quarter of the surveyed residents in Sitka came to Alaska before 1890, as did 20 percent and 12.5 percent, respectively, of the inhabitants of Douglas and Juneau. In contrast, fewer than 6 percent of those in Skagway had been in the district before 1897, and that figure was no higher than 17 percent for the more northerly mining areas.

Treadwell was an exception among the southeastern communities. Its largely single, young, foreign-born, and unskilled population evidently was also quite transient. Only 20 percent had been in the district since 1896. It was the only community in which a plurality of residents did not arrive in 1898. Rather, 38 percent came in 1899, 22 percent in 1898, and 16 percent in 1897. Apparently, many men stayed at Treadwell for a year or two before moving on. Evidence on the number of years the foreign born had been in the United States further indicates the transiency of Treadwell's population. More than 14 percent of Treadwell's males had been in the country less than a year. In nearby Douglas the figure was 9 percent, but elsewhere it fell to 5 percent or lower. In Treadwell, 35 percent of the men had been in the United States fewer than five years, compared to only 15 percent in most of the other communities. The large number of recent arrivals made Treadwell the only community in which most of those who were foreign born were aliens rather than naturalized citizens, which was the case in the other settlements.

Men and women from occupations as diverse as sailors and salesmen, ranchers and railroaders, and preachers and prostitutes ventured north in the late 19th century. In order to distinguish occupational groups and their distribution in the nine Alaskan communities, this study divides jobs into 16 categories. The categories include mining as well as other callings common in any community, such as business (both mercantile and craft oriented), the professions, the building trades, clerical work, and those jobs associated with restaurants and taverns. Some categories represent fields that many people worked in before coming to Alaska and which were almost nonexistent there, such as agriculture. Others, such as government service, land transportation, and railroading, are included because of their importance in some Alaskan communities.[17]

More than three-fourths of the nearly thirteen hundred women surveyed listed no occupation. Married women were least likely to be employed. Fewer than 1 in 10 of them worked. Of the employed women, 20 percent were housekeepers, domestics, or servants. Other prominent occupations were dressmaker and seamstress (15 percent); cook, boardinghouse keeper, and waitress (12 percent); and stage performer (9 percent). Others were teachers, laundresses, clerks, missionaries, merchants, nurses, or ran or worked in rooming houses and hotels. Undoubtedly, not all prostitutes were counted. The census taker in Juneau described one woman as "sporting," and there were 10 prostitutes listed in Douglas. The enumerators in the other towns were more circumspect in classifying prostitutes, presumably listing them in other occupations or as unemployed.[18]

The men who came north were not a cross-section of those they left behind. Farmers, ranchers, and others engaged in agricultural pursuits were greatly underrepresented on the ships bound from Seattle, Portland, and San Francisco. In 1900, 39 percent of all males over age 10 in the contiguous United States were engaged in agriculture, yet barely 11 percent of the Alaskan men examined in this survey claimed to have been agriculturists before heading to Alaska.[19]

Relatively few professionals ventured to Alaska. Because of the vast underrepresentation of former farmers in the mining-oriented and agriculturally inhospitable North, however, men in virtually all other occupations made up a greater proportion of the population in Alaska than elsewhere in the nation. Not surprisingly, miners were especially prone to head north. Only 2.4 percent of the men in the contiguous states and territories were miners in 1900; 15 percent of the men in the nine communities had been miners before traveling to Alaska.

Different communities attracted men from different occupations. Former farmers avoided the commercial centers. They composed a disproportionately large segment of Eagle, the Fortymile, Douglas, and Treadwell. Few miners went to Sitka. Fewer than 3 percent of the men in Sitka had been miners, compared to 9 percent in Eagle and Skagway and 23 percent in Treadwell. The mines at Treadwell and the railroad at Skagway employed large numbers of unskilled workers. As a result, these towns had a percentage of former laborers two and one-half to five times as high as the other communities.

Professionals tended to make their way to the capital, Sitka, or to the large and established town of Juneau. Comparisons of the nearly contiguous communities of Juneau, Douglas, and Treadwell suggest that migrants matched their occupational backgrounds to the opportunities offered by these equally accessible settlements. Former professionals made up nearly 10 percent of the men in Juneau, a proportion three times larger than that for Douglas and Treadwell. Treadwell also had far fewer men who had been businessmen or clerks than Douglas, and Douglas had a smaller proportion than Juneau. In contrast, Treadwell had a far larger group of former laborers and a slightly higher proportion of miners.

After the Klondike discovery, the North was increasingly attractive to men of all occupations, but the proportion of miners and seamen and fishermen declined after 1896. Seamen and fishermen were prominent among the earlier arrivals because, when few land-bound Americans knew much about this distant possession, seamen and fishermen had greater opportunity to learn of and use Alaska's resources. Miners, of course, followed the mining frontier. But after 1896 the gold mania stirred amateurs to head north to try their luck. Thus, the proportion of immigrants in almost all occupations besides mining, seafaring, and fishing increased slightly after the Klondike discovery, and laborers increased from less than 8 percent of all migrants through 1896 to more than 15 percent of those arriving later.

Published census statistics reveal that the percentage of men in mining in Alaska was 10 times that in the rest of the United States. Of the men in Alaska, 24 percent were miners, compared to 16 percent in both Arizona and Montana, the regions with the next highest concentrations of miners. Eliminating Natives from the count would have greatly increased the proportion of those engaged in mineral activity in Alaska.[20]

More than half the men surveyed in the nine communities examined here were miners. There were twice as many miners than men in any other occupation in all but Sitka and Skagway. In Sitka, government was as important as mining, and, though mining on the Klondike and other Yukon tributaries explained Skagway's existence, mining's impact on the town was largely felt through the employment of common laborers at that entrepôt and on the railroad.

An examination of those not employed as miners highlights the differences between the communities. The sole white on the Tanana who was not a miner was a trapper. The Fortymile district had advanced well beyond the Tanana's frontier prospecting stage. Miners there (91 percent of the total male population) furnished a demand for 17 roadhouse keepers and nine freighters; these two occupations accounted for more than three-quarters of the jobs not held by miners in the area. The census taker found other freighters who supplied the Fortymile in Eagle, where they made up one-quarter of the nonmining population. Excluding the soldiers at Fort Egbert adjacent to Eagle, this border town still had a disproportionate number of government workers, including such officials as a U.S. deputy marshal, postmaster, and customs collector.

Nome had few men earning a livelihood as laborers, craftsmen, or freighters. Rather, the inhabitants of this boom town were prepared to sell goods and professional services to the gold rushers. A third of its men not engaged in mining were businessmen or clerks, nearly a fifth dispensed food and drink, and 15 percent were professionals.

Treadwell was thoroughly working class. It had no doctors, lawyers, or ministers, and it had the smallest percentage of businessmen of any of the examined towns. The largest groups of nonminers in Treadwell were laborers, railroaders, craftsmen (primarily mining-related machinists and blacksmiths), and cooks and waiters in the company lodging houses. Treadwell miners patronized saloons and restaurants in Douglas and Juneau—dispensers of food and drink made up nearly 20 percent of the nonminers in the former and 13 percent in the latter—and the needs of the mines and miners helped support business owners who made up more than a fifth of these two towns' nonminers.

Comparing the ages and marital status of men in the various job categories produces some predictable results. In most job groups, the older the workers, the greater the tendency toward marriage. Thus men in the professions, in business, and in the building trades were as a body both older and more likely to be married than other nonaboriginal Alaskans; clerks and laborers generally were young and single. Miners, railroaders, sailors, and fishermen were exceptions. They were neither markedly older nor younger than men in most other occupations, but they were considerably more likely to be single. This may be a result of the peripatetic ways of men in these occupations.[21]

Except for the Japanese, men of all ethnic backgrounds were nearly equally likely to engage in mining. Ethnicity had a striking impact, however, on the other types of work Alaskans did. American-born Alaskan men were overrepresented among professionals, clerks, and businessmen (but not among craft-oriented businesses). Although 57 percent of Alaskan men in this study were born in the United States, two-thirds of the businessmen, more than three-quarters of the professionals, and nearly 80 percent of the clerks were born in the States. Canadians and men born in England, Scotland, or Wales were overrepresented or modestly underrepresented within the professions, noncraft businesses, and clerical occupations. Germans were slightly overrepresented among businessmen and were heavily overrepresented among craft shop businessmen. Irishmen and all those born in non-English-speaking nations other than Germany were dramatically underrepresented among businessmen, professionals, and clerks.[22]

The jobs Americans did not take in the food industry or as railroaders, seamen, and fishermen went to men of specific ethnic backgrounds. Forty-six of the sixty Japanese males in this study worked in the food and drink occupations; all were cooks or waiters, not saloonkeepers. Although the Japanese represented barely 1 percent of the men recorded in the census of the nine communities, they provided more than 17 percent of those engaged in food and drink work. The Irish were slightly overrepresented among laborers, but they contributed hugely disproportionate numbers to the unskilled work force of the White Pass & Yukon Railway in Skagway. Irishmen made up 22 percent of the railroad's employees, though less than 5 percent of the men studied. Scandinavians contributed the same proportion of Alaska's fishing and sailing fleets, though they constituted less than 12 percent of the men in the communities. Scandinavians were also overrepresented in the physically demanding fields of common labor, building trades, and, to a smaller extent, mining. Their impact on mining was strongest in Nome and Treadwell. More than 90 percent of the Scandinavians in each of these two towns engaged in mining. Similarly, about 95 percent of Austrians in both of these communities were miners.

The Alaskan census offers a unique opportunity to compare occupations before and after migration. This study shows in very striking terms that, except for the large numbers who put aside their former jobs to take up mining in Alaska, most men continued in the same type of work they had pursued prior to coming north. Predictably, the vast majority of former miners in every community continued to mine. Even in Skagway, where only 20 percent of the men said they were miners, nearly three-fourths of those who had been miners in their former hometowns remained so in Alaska.

Farmers, ranchers, and lumbermen had little opportunity to continue their work in Alaska; mining attracted them north. To a lesser extent this was the pattern for railroaders, seamen, and fishermen. White-collar workers, especially professionals such as doctors and lawyers, were particularly likely to continue their former trade. Among the blue-collar groups, only food and drink establishment owners and employees did not transform themselves into miners in large numbers; the large proportion of Japanese in this group, who were largely absent from mining, accounts for the exception.

Like all mining rushes, Alaska's was an overwhelmingly male phenomenon. Those men who came to the territory were generally Americans nearing middle age, often sons of the Midwest, and chiefly recent residents of the Rocky Mountain or Pacific Slope states. Unlike their countrymen of similar ages, most were single. Their chances of marrying someone of their own race in Alaska were minimal; those women who came to mining outposts were almost all married to men who had arrived months or years earlier.

Many of the men who came north may have been spurred by a general desire to try their luck in the diggings. But their movement was not wholly random. Those with skills useful in the territory were most likely to come north. A far greater proportion of the nation's miners than farmers left their homes to come to Alaska. Moreover, Alaska was large and diverse enough to offer a variety of attractions. Married men found the southeastern towns more congenial to family life than the more rugged Nome and interior. Professionals and businessmen saw their greatest opportunities in Nome and the southeastern towns. Unskilled laborers could most readily find employment in the large Treadwell mines or at the shipping and railroad town of Skagway. And those inexperienced in commercial or professional ventures were most likely to head for the more isolated mining areas.

The discovery of gold on the Klondike resulted in a population tidal wave that rolled across the northwest corner of the continent, dramatically altering Alaska north of Juneau, a vast region largely unvisited, much less inhabited, by non-Natives. In the decade after the gold rush, people from the far points of the globe made their way to Alaska and built new towns, established a transportation network, and developed a society built on the unique conditions of the North.

The 1900 census was well timed and, with its special questions, well designed to capture an invaluable picture of the demography of those who built the new Alaska. The census does not tell us all we might like to know about these people. It does not tell us about their politics, religion, personal goals, or moral beliefs. But by providing us with some of the basic information about the newcomers' backgrounds, occupations, marital status, and family situation, the census can suggest the raw material with which Alaskans fashioned their new communities and society.

NOTES

1. Robert Service, *Best Tales of the Yukon* (Philadelphia, 1983), 28.

2. Pierre Berton, *The Klondike Fever: The Life and Death of the Last Great Gold Rush* (1958; rpt. New York, 1977), 99–108; Terrence Michael Cole, "A History of the Nome Gold Rush: The Poor Man's Paradise," Ph.D. dissertation (University of Washington, 1983), 6; David Wharton, *The Alaska Gold Rush* (Bloomington, Ind., 1972), 86.

3. U.S. Department of the Interior, Census Office, *Twelfth Census of the United States: Population*, II (Washington, D.C., 1902), ccxv.

4. Native when capitalized in this article refers to Indians, Eskimos, and Aleuts. When uncapitalized, native refers to any person born within American boundaries. Because this survey describes the gold rushers and their communities, it does not include Natives.

5. Henceforth, reference to residents of the Fortymile should be understood to include those the census taker recorded in the Fortymile River drainage and the nearby American Creek valley.

6. Alaska's vastness and the difficulties of travel dictated that the enumerators conduct their work at different times through the winter and early spring, rather than on a few days clustered around the official census day of June 1. Travel was generally easier in winter than in summer, especially in the Tanana Valley and the Fortymile mining district. Consequently, the Alaskan census takers gathered most of their data between January and May. The timing of the census resulted in an inaccurately low count of whites in the district in July.

7. H. R. Shepard to collector of customs, Sitka, April 10, 1903, in *Annual Report of the Governor of the District of Alaska to the Secretary of the Interior, 1904* (Washington, D.C., 1904), 123.

8. Only couples who listed the same hometown are assumed to have been married at the time they came to Alaska.

9. The microfilm of the census for Juneau, Douglas, Treadwell, and Sitka crops the home ownership column on every other page. The data that are available, however, can be used as a sample of home ownership in these settlements.

10. *Twelfth Census: Population*, II: 14–15, 102–3.

11. Ibid., 2–5, 8–9, 14–15, 102–103; Berton, 431; Ralph Mann, *After the Gold Rush: Society in Grass Valley and Nevada City, California, 1849–1870* (Stanford, Calif., 1982), 17. Statistics obtained from the published census returns are for Caucasian men over 18 in order to represent the non-Native gold rushers. Alaskan women in the surveyed communities were younger than their male counterparts. Nearly 45 percent were younger than 30.

12. *Twelfth Census: Population*, II: 254, 257. Of all Alaskan men, including its Natives, 39 percent were married. Of the contiguous states and territories, only Wyoming (41 percent married), Montana (42 percent), and Nevada (44 percent) came close to this percentage. Ibid., 283, 285, 307.

13. Ibid., cxliv–cxlvi; U.S. Department of the Interior, Census Office, *Twelfth Census of the United States: Population*, I (Washington, D.C., 1901), cxxxii.

14. *Twelfth Census: Population*, II: ccxvi.

15. In all the settlements, the women's arrival dates paralleled men's.

16. Everett S. Lee, "A Theory of Migration," *Demography,* 3 (1966), 47–57; Aba Schwartz, "Interpreting the Effect of Distance on Migration," *Journal of Political Economy,* 81 (1973), 1153–69.

17. The published census classified only 367 Alaskans as engaged in agricultural pursuits. Of these, all but 123 were woodchoppers, lumbermen, or raftsmen. *Twelfth Census: Population,* II: 510. The categories used in this study and some examples of occupations within the categories are: agriculture (farmer, rancher), building trades (carpenter, painter, plasterer), business (merchants and store owners in businesses that did not require a craft skill, such as banker, merchant, roadhouse keeper), clerk (clerk, bookkeeper, accountant), craft (machinist, surveyor, dressmaker), craft shop business (craftsmen whose skill was frequently associated with running one's own shop or store, such as jeweler, baker, photographer), food and drink (barkeeper, cook, boardinghouse keeper), government (police, postmaster), labor (laborer, stevedore, janitor), land transportation (freighter, livery stable worker or owner), log and lumber (logger, wood dealer), mining (miner, prospector, assayer), nontraditional professions (teacher, engineer, actress), railroading (conductor, boilermaker, section worker), seafaring and fishing (sailor, fisherman), traditional professions (doctor, lawyer, clergy).

18. Catherine Holder Spude identifies at least two prostitutes in the Skagway census—one listed as a singer and the other as a dancer. "Bachelor Miners and Barbers' Wives: The Common People of Skagway in 1900," *Alaska History,* 6 (Fall 1991), 25. Some women engaged in mining, but their numbers were small. The published census records only 5 women miners in Alaska in 1900, and 7,072 men. *Twelfth Census: Population,* II: ccxvi.

19. *Twelfth Census: Population,* II: 508–509.

20. Ibid., 508, 514, 534.

21. The geographic mobility of railroaders is discussed in James H. Ducker, *Men of the Steel Rails: Workers on the Atchison, Topeka & Santa Fe Railroad, 1869–1900* (Lincoln, Nebr., 1983), 75–77, and H. Roger Grant, ed., *Brownie the Boomer: The Life of Charles P. Brown, an American Railroader* (1930; rpt. DeKalb, Ill., 1991), ix–xii. The former study's quantitative analysis, however, did not reveal that marital status affected mobility.

22. Only 1 of the 60 Japanese recorded in this study listed himself as a miner.

Sourdough Radicalism

Labor and Socialism in Alaska, 1905–1920

JOSEPH SULLIVAN

More and more of the nation's resources fell under the control of large corporations during the late 19th century and early 20th centuries. And more and more workers found employment with these corporate giants, whose owners often ignored workers' demands for higher wages, shorter hours, and better working conditions. When workers unionized, some corporations refused to recognize union legitimacy. Frequently, company officials fired union organizers as well as any employees who had ventured to join the union. In response to corporate intransigence, radicalism among workers gradually increased, especially in the western United States. Membership in the Industrial Workers of the World, a syndicalist union preaching revolution, peaked in the years just prior to World War I, as did membership in the Socialist party. Running for President in 1912, the Socialist candidate Eugene Debs garnered nearly one million popular votes, about 6 percent of the total number cast.

But political and labor radicalism declined rapidly during and after World War I. Analysts differ about the reasons for this, although most agree that workers in the United States never developed the class consciousness necessary for successful radical action. The "American dream" remained too persistent. American workers did not want the working class to take over; rather, they aspired to rise out of it. Scholars find other reasons for the decline of radicalism as well. The Socialists' continual bitter infighting seriously weakened their movement. The anti-foreign, anti-radical Red Scare following World War I dealt a death blow to both socialism and labor radicalism.

While the image of the lone sourdough has persisted in popular representations of the gold rush, in fact most gold occurred in lode deposits which were developed only through intensive labor by wageworkers in a corporate, capital-intensive context. The chief worker in the goldfields was not a sourdough, but a

This article appeared originally in *Alaska History* 7 (Spring 1992): 1–16; it is reprinted here by permission.

miner. Most miners in Alaska were unionized, as were most miners in the American West.

Joseph Sullivan, who conducts ongoing research into radicalism in the American West, describes socialism in Alaska in the piece reprinted here. He finds Alaskan Socialists' experiences to be similar to those of party members in other parts of the nation. Perhaps this suggests stronger similarities between economic development in Alaska and that in the "lower 48" than many historians have recognized in their accounts of the gold rush era.

For many Americans, mention of the Socialist Party of America conjures up images of a brief, eccentric movement among urban ethnic industrial workers alienated from the mainstream of American values by the avarice of plutocratic employers. One reason cited to explain why American socialism failed to maintain its early momentum and gain the scope of support that it did in Europe is that the possibility of a fresh start on the western frontier simply neutralized the frustration and desperation of urban Americans. The rise of socialism in Alaska, however, highlights the inadequacies of these views. During the Socialist Party's heyday, 1910 to 1920, it was the West that gave the party a disproportionately large measure of support, evincing much concern and dissatisfaction with the continuing erosion of popular control over the nation's economy and resources.[1] Alaskans, living in the last of American frontiers, shared this rage. Socialists maintained a vigorous presence, organizing locals of the Socialist Party, publishing a party newspaper, organizing labor unions, winning some local offices in Nome and Fairbanks, and running strong races for Congressional delegate.

Eastern emigrants who uprooted themselves to find a new life and new hope in the West came within a short time to face the same eastern villain: the profit-gorged capitalist with his tentacles of monopoly. This was especially so for the new settler who dreamed of owning the means of production, particularly, the homesteader or the miner who, after a period of intense effort, bad harvests, learning he could extract no further minerals by hand, or any number of misfortunes, was forced to sell or otherwise abandon his claim and be reduced to the level of an employee. Thus were Oklahoma Sooners transformed within a decade to tenants and sharecroppers on what had been their own land, and thus too did many Alaskan frontiersmen soon find themselves working for the

Morgan-Guggenheim Alaska Syndicate. While many people understand the term "radical" as meaning a dramatic or even excessive move forward, for western socialists the concept had a classical meaning: a return to the economic roots of the western frontier, that is independent ownership coupled with social cooperation and responsibility.

An excellent example of a pioneer-turned-socialist is Frank Buteau. Born in Quebec in 1860, Buteau settled in the North in 1887, prospecting and mining near Fortymile a decade before the Klondike discoveries. A sourdough before the term was invented, Buteau was the quintessential Alaskan prospector and one of the few white men who knew anything about Alaska's frontier freedom and solitude prior to the gold rush. When he retired to Fairbanks in 1911, Frank Buteau became a charter member of the community's Socialist Party local and in 1914 was one of the party's candidates for city council.[2]

The change from independence to "wage slavery" was eloquently lamented in the Alaska Socialist Party's 1914 platform preamble: "Alaska, the last of the great American frontiers, the home of the pioneer, is rapidly becoming a thing of the past. The dreams of the lonely prospector are giving way to the ugly realities of wage slavery and job hunting. The nightmare of Capitalism already haunts the workers of Alaska. It is only a matter of time until all the accompanying evils of this system will be rampant in the Golden North."[3]

Amid this gloom, the Socialist Party's program of worker ownership and management of the means of production offered some appeal to Alaskans, who had since 1906 seen the Alaska Syndicate consolidate its hold on mineral lands, salmon canneries, and steamships. Other targets of the Socialists were the commercial monopolies, such as the Northern Commercial Company.

Organized nationally in 1898, the Socialist Party of America caught the public eye with a series of unexpected victories in shoe- and textile-manufacturing towns in eastern Massachusetts. Composed of ex-Populists, former members of the largely German-speaking Socialist Labor Party, remnants of the American Railway Union, and the Nationalist Club followers of Edward Bellamy, the Socialist Party's membership grew from 10,000 in 1900 to 108,000 in 1912. Running the former American Railway Union founder and Pullman Strike hero Eugene V. Debs for president, the party gathered 916,000 votes, 6 percent of the total, in the 1912 campaign.[4]

Between its founding and the outbreak of World War I, the Socialists won two seats in Congress, garnered a score of state legislative seats, and elected the mayors of over eighty cities and towns, including Milwaukee, Minneapolis, Butte, Berkeley, Flint, Schenectady, and Canton. Preaching the "Cooperative Commonwealth," the party attracted a smorgasbord of celebrities and reformers. Among those who prefaced their signatures with "Yours for the Revolution," were the millionaire Los Angeles real estate developer Gaylord Wilshire, Buffalo Bill Cody, Carl Sandburg, Helen Keller, and, popular among readers of Klondike adventure stories, Jack London.[5]

The rising tide of socialist sentiment and ideas washed Alaska's shores and crept inland. Organizational efforts by the Western Federation of Miners in Nome, the Tanana Valley, and Juneau provided Alaskans with their first notable taste of radical politics. Between 1906 and 1908, the WFM led strikes for better pay and working conditions in Alaska's mines. Founded in 1893, the WFM went on record in 1902 as a socialist union advocating worker ownership and management of the means of production. In May 1905, the WFM became a charter member of the syndicalist Industrial Workers of the World at that union's founding convention in Chicago. In Nome, the Western Federation's members were officially known as Local 240, Nome Mine Workers Union.

Since no formal Socialist Party local existed in Nome at this date, the WFM fulfilled the function of a worker's political organization. In a rare show of cooperation, the Nome Mine Workers collaborated with the more conservative American Federation of Labor in support of a "Nome Labor Party" ticket which, in April 1906, won five of seven at-large seats on the city council and the mayoralty in a campaign directed more against municipal corruption than for socialism. The Labor Party again won a majority of the seats in the 1907 elections. Leading the majority on the council was a socialist miner-turned-merchant named Joseph Chilberg. In addition to being a member of Local 240, Chilberg was the proprietor of a local delicatessen. Chilberg's leadership on the council resulted in fiscal responsibility and a graft-free administration. Encouraged by these successes, the WFM throughout Alaska organized a campaign for Chilberg's election to Congress in 1908. In a field of five candidates, Chilberg finished second with an impressive 25 percent of the vote. His best showing was in his own Second Division where he won 31 percent of the vote. In a presidential straw poll taken by the Nome Chamber of Commerce that November, Eugene Debs won second place with an identical percentage.[6]

In May 1909, following Chilberg's campaign, L. S. Coleman, writing to the *International Socialist Review*, noted a failed Interior strike the previous year and predicted that Alaskan workers would endure more misery before they avidly adopted the socialist cause. Coleman reported that in 1908 "hundreds of strikebreakers were shipped up to Valdez and 'mushed' in over the trail to Fairbanks to break the strike, and they succeeded in doing so." Unemployment in the Tanana Valley and Cordova was blamed on the "extravagant offers made by employment agencies" who deliberately maintained an oversupply of labor to depress wages and discourage strikes. The jobs these Cordova workers sought were on the Syndicate's railway project to the Kennecott Mine and Copper River, by which it would "gain control of the riches of the interior and force the poor prospector to give up his holdings to capital." Coleman added that "in a few years, when the monied interests own all of Alaska, and the people have nothing to hope for but jobs, they will begin to take an interest in socialism."[7]

With Chilberg's defeat and the crushing of the WFM Fairbanks local in the strike, the union's interest in political action flagged. A half-hearted campaign for the WFM organizer William O'Connor in the 1910 Congressional race netted 15 percent of the vote.[8] But as the 1912 Congressional race approached, Socialist Party organizers, to fill the vacuum of working-class politics left by the collapse of the Labor Party, descended upon the territory with evangelical fervor. First among these was Lena Morrow Lewis, the first woman elected to the Socialist Party's National Executive Committee. Born in Illinois of a Presbyterian minister father, Lewis graduated from Monmouth College and spent six years as a paid lecturer for the Woman's Christian Temperance Union, after which she joined the Socialist Party. Arriving in Fairbanks, she set up headquarters in a donated cabin and began publishing a semimonthly newspaper, the *Alaska Socialist*.[9] The same year another Seattle Socialist named John McGivney landed in Nome where he edited the *Industrial Worker*. Born in Ireland, McGivney trained for the role of labor organizer and Socialist spellbinder in a Jesuit seminary.[10]

Lewis and McGivney's backgrounds were indicative of the variety of people who came to Alaska and took a role in the socialist movement's leadership. When McGivney retired in 1916, he handed his editorial duties to Bruce Rogers, who had fled Oklahoma after being implicated in a murder, joined the army during the Spanish-American War, and eventually made his way to Seattle where he propounded the ideas of industrial socialism as an organizer for the IWW.[11] In 1912 socialist teachings reached the miners on both sides of the border with Canada through lectures and social events by the Alaska Socialist Educational Society, of which Swedish-born Gustave Sandberg, who had rushed to the Klondike in 1898, served as secretary.[12] And Kazis Krauczunas, a native of Lithuania and former federal official, was the standard-bearer for the party in the territory in the 1912 election.

Krauczunas's campaign for territorial delegate came at a period of growing support for socialism across the nation and in Alaska. The Socialist Party at the time of the election had locals in at least ten Alaskan communities—Juneau, Nome, Valdez, Fairbanks and four smaller Interior mining camps, and the fishing towns of Ketchikan and Seldovia. Krauczunas had some name recognition. In 1909, as Chief U.S. Immigration Inspector for Alaska, he had used his power to round up foreign-born prostitutes in Fairbanks and elsewhere for deportation hearings in Seattle. Since then he had taken up a law practice in Ketchikan.[13]

The state party's platform, besides advocating the usual national issues of unionism, child labor laws, and collectivism, contained specifically "Alaskan" planks calling upon the federal government to build public highways and railroads in the territory, eliminate absentee claim-staking, operate all coal mines for public use, and make and enforce laws against anti-union blacklisting. Additionally, the Socialists demanded a mechanic's lien law, a strengthened home rule legislature, an eight-hour day, election of judges and mining inspectors, an assessment of five dollars per acre on all corporate mining property, the Australian ballot, and initiative, referendum, and recall powers for voters.[14]

While some partisans were enthusiastic about Krauczunas's campaign, some Socialists understood the difficulties his candidacy faced. When John C. Chase, who had been elected the first Socialist mayor in the country at the turn of the century and who subsequently stumped the nation for the party, visited Juneau in the summer of 1912, he rendered a pessimistic prognostication for the party's chances at the polls that "very much disappointed" the Juneau local.[15]

Chase was proven correct, though. When the votes were counted, the Socialist Krauczunas received 1,688 votes to the Republican William A. Gilmore's 1,726 and the winning incumbent James Wickersham's 3,335. The "regular" and "progressive" Democratic candidates occupied fourth and fifth places with 1,174 and 281 votes, respectively.[16] The Socialists might have won more votes had it not been for Wickersham. Seeking his third term, the incumbent was viewed by many as a Teddy Roosevelt progressive who stole the Socialists' thunder by attacking the venality of the "Morganheim" Syndicate and by patiently striving to educate a lethargic and misinformed Congress about Alaska's needs. His record of integrity combined with his campaign slogan of "Alaska for Alaskans" made him a nearly irresistible candidate.

That the Socialist campaign appealed chiefly to mining camp sourdoughs is evident in the voting results. Krauczunas received vote percentages greater than his territorial average in the remote mining precincts, while the maritime communities of the Panhandle and the "electric light" towns all but ignored him. In the First Division, which encompassed southeastern Alaska, Krauczunas ran uniformly poorly except in his home town of Ketchikan, where he won first place with 43 percent of the vote. In the Third Division (southcentral Alaska), only the community of Copper Center gave him any notable support, 29 percent, a plurality. In the Second Division, the territory's west, Krauczunas's popularity among miners may have been eclipsed by the even greater popularity of his Republican opponent, Mayor William Gilmore of Nome. The Socialist did well, however, in two outlying mining precincts, Jesse Creek (67 percent) and Shovel Creek (33 percent).[17]

It was in the Fourth Division, the Interior, that the Socialists won their greatest support, garnering 30 percent of the vote and second place. Although the relatively metropolitan Fairbanks gave him a bare 19 percent, Krauczunas ran exceedingly well on the creeks, winning eleven of the nineteen precincts. If nothing else, the 1912 campaign revealed the uneven, nonurban landscape of Socialist strength. With Ketchikan the lone exception, the party failed to win fifteen of the territory's sixteen incorporated municipalities, and nearly half of Krauczunas's votes were won in just the Fourth Division, particularly in the sourdough mining camps and hamlets where mineral extraction was still performed by individual claim holders owning the means of production. Socialist candidates for Alaska's first territorial legislature likewise polled a large vote in the Fourth Division, though none were elected. In April 1913, the party scored a victory in the Interior when J. E. Moody was elected treasurer of the Fairbanks School Board.[18]

The Socialists' showing in these campaigns was the catalyst for the consolidation of the party in Alaska. Prior to Lena Lewis's arrival, the party consisted of several unaffiliated locals governed by the national office in Chicago. In March 1914, a mass convention at Fairbanks resulted in a formal territorial organization with headquarters there. On June 17, the Socialist Party of Alaska elected Mrs. M. L. Gerth Territorial Secretary and nominated John M. Brooks of Wade Creek to run for delegate to Congress in the 1914 campaign, as well as a slate of candidates for the territorial legislature. Brooks was a prospector and may have been the first Socialist elected in Alaska, having served two terms on the Juneau city council in the early 1900s. Brooks moved to Fairbanks in 1904 where he joined the WFM and won election to the city council during the 1907–1908 strike of mine workers in the Tanana District.[19]

No sooner was the party organized, however, than a major rift occurred in the Fairbanks local. A divisive atmosphere had begun forming as the Socialists entered the April 1914 Fairbanks elections. In its municipal platform, the Socialist Party promised to eliminate graft in city hall and embark upon several public works projects, including razing or removing the city's tenderloin district. The party also railed against price gouging by the Northern Commercial Company, which had developed a near commercial monopoly in the creek camps and dominated the city's electrical and telephone utilities. The real issue among the Socialists, however, was the party's endorsement of certain candidates of questionable ideological purity. The Socialist city council candidates R. P. McGowan, a miner; James T. Morgan, a chicken peddler; and Andrew Knowles, a printer, bolted the party and ran as independent socialists in protest over the party's support of the school board member Moody.[20]

With twenty-one candidates for the seven at-large seats advocating much the same thing, the Socialists' effectiveness was somewhat diluted. Moreover, Alaska's local and territorial politics were not rigidly partisan. Candidates often ran without any formal party distinction, and the propensity of all the candidates to attack the monopoly of the Northern Commercial Company, plus the division within the Socialists' own ranks, deprived the party of a potential domination of the pro-labor, pro-working-class vote. On election day, the Socialists—official and insurgent—failed to win a seat on the council. N. R. King, a miner, was the front runner among the eight socialist candidates with 20 percent of the vote. The *Fairbanks News-Miner* opined that "the Socialists themselves were surprised" at the low returns.[21]

After the city election, Andrew Knowles wrested the editorship of the *Alaska Socialist* from Lena Lewis and split the party by denouncing John Brooks as a traitor to the party who conspired with Lewis to dominate the Alaska Socialist movement. According to Knowles, the "Lewis-Brooks Machine" denied the party's candidacy to the miner Dan McCabe who, it turned out, had allegedly won most of the votes cast at the nominating convention. Referring to Brooks as a "Seattle carpetbagger," the *Alaska Socialist* continued its excoriation of the party's territorial leadership. Brooks's biggest offense was his support for William "Scab" O'Connor, the 1910 Socialist Labor candidate for delegate. In fact, Brooks was no newcomer to Alaska, having arrived in Juneau in 1897, and the "scab" charges against O'Connor had no basis. Lena Lewis was said to have "sneaked into Fairbanks" uninvited by the Alaskan comrades to seize control of the party apparatus. Lewis and several Socialist allies had "abandoned the principles of Socialism and worked political tricks that would shame a bunch of Tammany politicians." Lewis was also accused of failing to organize more than a single local in one year while dunning Fairbanks comrades for her organizational expenses. The Socialist local at Olness, a mining camp north of Fairbanks, lent its voice to these charges, denouncing the Brooks nomination and demanding that McCabe be chosen to run.[22] In the midst of this bickering, the *Alaska Socialist* deleted the words "Socialist Party of America" from its masthead and proclaimed itself an "independent Socialist paper devoted to political and industrial action." Clear of official party constraints and the "Lewis-Brooks Machine," the *Alaska Socialist* was free to pursue the principles of socialism. This it chose to do by accepting a campaign advertisement for the incumbent congressional delegate Wickersham and five legislative candidates of sundry political affiliation.[23]

The factionalism that split the Fairbanks local was typical of the Socialist Party elsewhere in the nation. Friction between left and right, opposition by eastern members against the westerner Big Bill Haywood and the Industrial Workers of the World, accusations of political opportunism in quest of public office weakened the party and brought about more electoral defeats than the combined efforts of the Republican and Democratic parties. Corrupt election officials and company goons were never able to surpass the Socialists in their ability to wreck their own party.

In the territorial elections in November, the Fourth Division Socialist legislative candidates ran well ahead of the Brooks campaign, Dan McCabe receiving 735 votes for the territorial legislature and Brooks 548 votes for Congress. Since no Socialists won, the only thing the McCabe faction might have gained from these returns was a certain amount of gratification. Overall, Brooks garnered 1,107 votes, 10 percent, and only two-thirds of Krauczunas's tally of 1912.[24] Although Brooks carried several mining precincts in the Fourth Division, the returns pointed to a distinct decline from the 1912 election. In 1915, the demoralized Fairbanks comrades did not bother to offer a municipal ticket.

While the Fairbanks local disintegrated, Socialist organizers encountered different frustrations to the west and south. In Nome, Bruce Rogers shared the editorship of the *Nome Industrial Worker*, the official organ of Local 240, with the miner Martin Kennelly. The *Industrial Worker* seconded the national Socialist Party's April 1917 declaration against American involvement in World War I with articles attacking war profiteers and the British. The news of the Bolshevik revolt in Russia was hailed by Local 240. According to unverified stories, several Nome comrades sailed to Siberia to meet with representatives of the new regime, and Rogers and Kennelly toyed with the idea of creating a "soviet" in Nome. Amid such activities and the nationwide jingoistic and antiradical sentiment, Kennelly was indicted for sedition in the spring of 1918, just as a similar trial for Eugene V. Debs was ending in his conviction in Cleveland. Kennelly's jury was discharged after jurors failed to agree on a verdict and the district attorney recommended that the government drop the matter. Judge William A. Holzheimer, nevertheless, persisted in the prosecution until a second jury acquitted Kennelly.[25]

Rogers did not fare so well. After Kennelly's acquittal, the *Industrial Worker* amplified its opposition to the Wilson administration's curbs on civil rights. "We must make the world safe for Democracy," Rogers sarcastically wrote, "no matter if we have to bean the Goddess of Liberty to do it." For these criticisms and some irreverent remarks made at a Local 240 meeting, Rogers was convicted in the summer of 1918 under a recently enacted Alaskan sedition law. Sentenced to three years' imprisonment at McNeill Island, Rogers was pardoned along with Debs and several other war protesters in 1921. Although Nome's radical leadership was not an important electoral force in the Second Division anyway—despite the Labor-Socialist municipal victory a dozen years before—Judge Holzheimer's repression of it effectively stifled whatever electoral support the Socialists might have attracted or revived, while weakening the miners' unionization efforts by associating them with disloyalty and treason.[26]

In Anchorage the Socialist presence was manifested not through electoral action, but through the organization of an industrial union. In May 1915, the government began construction of the Alaska Railroad to link the ocean with the Interior. Ideally, Socialists preferred a government-built and operated railway to that of a Morgan-Guggenheim system, and indeed the nationalization of railroads, banks, and mines was called for in successive Socialist Party platforms. Uncle Sam, however, proved to be as stingy and difficult an employer as any capitalist. Low pay and unsanitary conditions in the ramshackle tent city that later became Anchorage were the chief causes of workers' dissatisfaction. Track gangs working for 37 1/2 cents per hour struck on February 7, 1916, for 50 cents. Shut out by management, 1,200 workers formed the Alaska Labor Union headed by the Socialists Frank Hanson, James A. Wilkinson, Jack Sutherland, and Charles Peters, the latter two members of Nome's WFM Local 240. After a lengthy delay, the strike was settled in the spring, and the ALU triumphantly constructed a fifty-by-one-hundred-foot union hall in Anchorage. Lena Lewis officiated at the hall's dedication and edited the union's newspaper, the *Alaska Labor News*. More than a union hall, the ALU's "Labor Temple" served as the center for civic entertainment in Anchorage. In addition to dances and games of whist, the Temple also sponsored a variety of fraternal activities such as the Italian Red Cross Relief Committee Dance, the Masonic Washington's Birthday Celebration, and the St. Patrick's Eve Entertainment and Hop, as well as vaudeville troupes from Seattle and San Francisco. The ALU also constructed the Union Hotel—for ALU members only—which boasted steam heat, hot baths, and electricity.[27]

Yet despite these civic successes, complaints continued regarding the poor quality of the government beef used to feed the workers and the inadequate health care that resulted in ruined constitutions. In December 1917, as the railway reached Nenana, the government arrested Robert Smith, an IWW member working for the ALU, and several others for inciting a work stoppage. Since the country was at war, the district attorney charged Smith with treason and sedition. When it was learned that Smith was an unnaturalized German alien, he was incarcerated in Utah until war's end. In fact, the coming of the First World War revealed that, although the ALU's leadership trafficked in radical ideas, its membership was quite conventional. Tired of its antiwar diatribes, a conservative faction within the ALU overthrew the left-wing editorial board of the *Alaska Labor News* in June 1917, incorporating the paper into the politically innocuous *Anchorage Weekly Times*, where it ceased to be a radical voice for labor.[28]

Socialist union leadership did not translate into worker support for socialist candidates at the polls. For a labor union reputed to contain half of all the workers in Anchorage, the ALU sponsored candidates who did remarkably poorly in the congressional and legislative races. In 1916 the workers of Anchorage proved that they liked Lena Lewis far more as a labor organizer than as a delegate to Congress. She received a mere 10 percent of the vote in Anchorage. One of the best socialist showings in a legislative race was that of the ALU leader James A. Wilkinson in his 1918 campaign for the territorial senate. Out of 681 votes cast in Anchorage, Wilkinson received 191 votes, or 28 percent, losing to the Democrat Thomas Price.[29]

Socialist organizing among railway workers in Alaska might have resulted in strong locals as it did in other American communities where the cause of labor was closely identified with the cause of socialism. But the tensions between the workers and the railroad were resolved with the completion of the railroad. From an estimated 6,000 persons during the height of the construction boom, Anchorage counted fewer than 2,000 residents when the town incorporated in 1920. Few discharged employees chose to remain in the territory, and as the work force melted back to the states in search of jobs, the Socialist Party's chances of establishing a toehold in Anchorage melted too. The ALU's remaining members disbanded and the Labor Temple fell into receivership. Toward the end of the world war, the remaining ALU radicals reorganized into the Alaska Industrial Union in a last effort to keep socialism alive. Even this final spark was stamped out by official repression when the government indicted its leader, Jack Sutherland, for refusing to allow uniformed soldiers to attend an otherwise public social function at the Anchorage Labor Temple. Sutherland's unplanned departure from Alaska was hastened by a mob from Hyder that tarred and feathered the hapless organizer. Alaska Industrial Union organizing among fishermen in Juneau and miners in Fairbanks kept Justice Department agents and informers busy throughout the Red Scare summer of 1920.[30]

The Socialists' fate at Anchorage was, in microcosm, the Socialist Party's fate throughout Alaska. The territory's unstable, boom-and-bust economy militated against a stable worker-based political organization. Never particularly popular in the towns, the Socialists garnered most of their support from the scattered mining camps which, while numerous, contained a small electorate. In 1912, 58 percent of the Fourth Division's precincts cast only 30 percent of the votes. Alaska's at-large system of legislative representation made it less likely that Socialist candidates could win seats in Juneau without capturing the larger towns in each division. In one exceptional case, the Nome Mine Worker's Union president, Philip

Corrigan, won election to the legislature by a slim margin in November 1916. Corrigan's campaign, which oddly enough received little mention in his union's own newspaper, adopted the strategy of the 1906 Labor Party; he emphasized his working-class status, refrained from any overt mention of socialism, and accepted support from the Democratic Party.[31]

Where corporate absorption of individual mining properties drove many sourdough prospectors into unemployment or exile, large-scale enlistments into the First World War depleted Alaska of still more laborers and mechanics. Finally, the postwar recession further reduced the work force in other Alaskan industries, such as timber and canning. Caught between corporate consolidation and nationwide recession, the Socialists' potential electorate quickly evaporated. What potential remained was harassed during the wartime hysteria or the subsequent Red Scare. By 1918 John McGivney, Lena Lewis, Kazis Krauczunas, and Bruce Rogers, four of Alaska's most important socialist figures, had left the territory either for greener pastures or, as in the case of Rogers, for prison.[32]

Unemployment and emigration, however, were not the only reasons for the party's decline. Labor's support of the socialists was fickle. Joseph Chilberg's 2,383 votes in his 1908 campaign for Congress fell well below the Alaska WFM membership of 6,000. Even though Nome's Labor-Socialist government provided honest administration, it failed to receive the sustained support of union rank and file. And despite the alliance in 1906 between the socialist WFM and the American Federation of Labor in Nome, or between the party and the Alaska Labor Union, Lena Morrow Lewis received a bare 9 percent of the vote in her 1916 congressional race. In the same election, the Eight Hour Day referendum passed with 80 percent of the vote. Clearly, most Alaskan workers wanted shorter hours and better pay, not socialism.[33]

Finally, what the vicissitudes of capitalism and war failed to do to the party, the party did to itself. The endless internal struggles among shrinking factions in the Interior, the locus of its largest electoral support, undermined whatever strength the Socialist Party might have mustered. By refusing to work with Lena Lewis and John Brooks in 1914, Andrew Knowles and Dan McCabe squandered valuable resources and sacrificed rare opportunities to demonstrate to Alaskans what had been successfully demonstrated elsewhere: that Socialists can be a constructive force in government. For all their talk of cooperation, the chief impediment to an Alaskan Socialist victory may have been the Socialists's failure to practice the cooperation and solidarity they preached.

NOTES

1. For example, Eugene V. Debs received 6 percent of the vote nationally in his 1912 presidential campaign. His percentage in the West, however, was typically higher. Oklahoma and Nevada led the nation, giving him 17 and 16 percent of their votes, respectively. One can only surmise Debs's popularity in Alaska, since the territory was not part of the Electoral College. The Socialist candidate for Alaska's Congressional delegate that year won 20 percent of the vote. See David Shanon, *The Socialist Party of America: A History* (Chicago: Quadrangle Books, 1967); Harvey O'Connor, *Revolution in Seattle* (New York: Monthly Review Press, 1964); Jerry W. Calvert, *The Gibraltar: Labor and Socialism in Butte, Montana* (Helena: Montana Historical Society Press, 1988); John McCormick, "Hornets in the Hive: The Socialist Party of Utah," *Utah Historical Quarterly* 44 (Spring 1988): 236–46; James Hulse, "The Socialist Party of Nevada," *Nevada Historical Society Quarterly* 31 (Winter 1988): 129–40; Joseph W. Sullivan, "Rising from the Ranks: Socialism in Nye County, Nevada," *Nevada Historical Society Quarterly* 34 (Summer 1991): 340–49. Harvey O'Connor, whom the author was pleased to meet, edited newspapers for the Industrial Workers of the World in Seattle and Tacoma.

2. For more on Oklahoma socialism, see James R. Green, *Grassroots Socialism: Radical Movements in the Southwest, 1895–1943* (Baton Rouge: Louisiana State University Press, 1982). The existence of a socialist mentality in preindustrial frontier Alaska is discussed by an anonymous "Alaskan Miner" in "The Growth of Socialist Sentiment in Alaska," *International Socialist Review* 12 (January 1912): 405–6. The Syndicate's dominion over Alaska is discussed in Harvey O'Connor, *The Guggenheims: The Making of an American Dynasty* (New York: Covici, Friede Co., 1937). On Frank Buteau, see Melody Webb, *The Last Frontier* (Albuquerque: University of New Mexico Press, 1985), 79.

3. "Preamble and Platform, Socialist Party of Alaska, Campaign 1914," MS 4, Box 7, 2–4, Papers of the Socialist Party of Alaska, Juneau Local (hereafter cited as Papers of the SPA), Alaska Historical Library, Juneau. I am indebted to Gladi Kulp of the Historical Library and Dean Dawson of the Alaska State Archives for their generous work in locating materials relating to this topic.

4. For an excellent survey of the Socialist Party's general history, see Shannon, *The Socialist Party of America*. The Socialist Labor Party was founded in 1891 but quickly became an elitist, ideology-obsessed clique dominated by its irascible leader, Daniel DeLeon. By 1900 most SLP members had joined the Socialist Party of America.

5. James Weinstein, *The Decline of Socialism in America, 1912–1925* (Chicago: Monthly Review Press, 1978), 91.

6. *Nome Nugget*, April 4, 1906, November 5, 1908; James C. Foster, "AFL, IWW and Nome: 1905–1908," *Alaska Journal* 4 (Spring 1975): 72–73; *Nome Industrial Worker*, August 10, 1908; Jeannette Paddock Nichols, *Alaska* (Cleveland: Arthur H. Clark Co., 1924), 316. The Nome Labor ticket consisted of three miners, an assayer, a boat captain, an engineer, and a blacksmith. Like Socialist municipal campaigns around the country, the party's Nome campaign emphasized local issues of honesty and efficiency, rather than socialist ideology. The Nome Laborites lost their majority in 1908.

7. L. S. Coleman, "Conditions in Alaska," *International Socialist Review* 9 (May 1909): 918. For details of this strike, see James C. Foster, "Syndicalism Northern Style: The Life and Death of W.F.M. No. 193," *Alaska Journal* 4 (Summer 1975): 130–41.

8. Nichols, *Alaska*, 358.

9. O'Connor, *Revolution*, 106. Lewis's progress from the WCTU to Socialism was not unusual. A strange affinity existed between many Socialists and the prohibition movement reflecting the homespun, undoctrinaire nature of an American socialist ideology that bestowed equal blame on John Barleycorn and John Rockefeller for the workers' wretched condition. That Alaskan Socialists shared this quirk is indicated by Local Valdez's 1915 resolution favoring a dry territory. "Prohibition Resolution of Local Valdez," February 20, 1915, Socialist Party of America Papers (Alaska), Duke University Collection, Durham, North Carolina. Alaskans voted for prohibition the following year.

10. O'Connor, *Revolution*, 103.

11. Ibid. In 1916, Rogers campaigned for Congress from Washington.

12. "News and Reviews," *International Socialist Review* 12 (November 1912): 261.

13. Krauczunas's diligence was somewhat offset by the uncooperativeness of the Fairbanks police, who exacted monthly fees from the pimps. Claus-M. Naske, "The Red Lights of Fairbanks: Prostitution in Alaska in 1909," *Alaska Journal* 14 (Spring 1984): 28–32. Krauczunas later became a judge in Seattle. Evangeline Atwood and Robert N. DeArmond, *Who's Who in Alaskan Politics* (Portland: Binford & Mort, 1974); "News and Reviews," *International Socialist Review* 12 (November 1912): 261.

14. "Socialist Party Platform [1912]," MS 4, Box 7, 2–4, Papers of the SPA.

15. H. J. Lorenzen (Secretary) to John M. Work, July 24, 1912, ibid.

16. *Daily Alaskan Dispatch* (Juneau), November 19, 1912.

17. Ibid., November 10, 1912.

18. *Daily Alaska Dispatch*, August 16, 1912; *Fairbanks Daily News-Miner*, April 10, 1913; *Report of the Governor of Alaska to the Secretary of the Interior, 1921* (Washington, D.C.: GPO, 1921), 66. Two-thirds of the party's membership lived in the Fourth Division. *Alaska Socialist*, June 30, 1914.

19. Lena Morrow Lewis to Comrades, June 22, 1914, MS 4, Box 7, 2–4, Papers of the SPA; *Tewkesbury's Who's Who and Alaska Business Index* (Juneau: Tewkesbury Publishing Company, 1947). Local Juneau was chartered in July 1911.

20. *Alaska Socialist*, March 31, 1914. Despite his protest of party support for Moody, Knowles praised his performance on the school board. Later Moody and other school board members took out personal loans to pay schoolteachers after the city council refused. Ibid., January 31, 1915.

21. *Fairbanks Daily News-Miner*, April 4, 1914; *Alaska Socialist*, April 18, 1914.

22. *Alaska Socialist*, June 30, August 31, 1914; Atwood and DeArmond, *Who's Who in Alaskan Politics*.

23. *Alaska Socialist*, June 15, 1914.

24. *Fairbanks Daily News-Miner*, November 9, 1914.

25. O'Connor, *Revolution*, 270; William R. Hunt, *Distant Justice: Policing the Alaskan Frontier* (Norman: University of Oklahoma Press, 1987), 224–25.

26. Hunt, *Distant Justice*, 225; Special Agent Heard McClellan to Bureau of In-

vestigation, Nome, December 1, 1917, Bureau of Investigation Case Files, OG, Record Group 60, National Archives.

27. Frank Hanson, "Building a Union at 40 Degrees Below," *International Socialist Review* 16 (November 1916): 292; *Nome Industrial Worker*, October 26, 1916; Mari Jo Buhle, "Lena Morrow Lewis: Her Rise and Fall," in *Flawed Liberation: Socialism and Feminism*, ed. Sally M. Miller (Westport, Conn.: Greenwood Press, 1981), 78–83; *Alaska Labor Union Bulletin*, February 15, 1918.

28. "News from Alaska," *International Socialist Review* 19 (April 1917): 601–2; Pat Lawler, "Railroad Workers Battle 'Capitalist Wage Slavery,'" *Alaska Journal* 10 (Summer 1980): 22–27; Hunt, *Distant Justice*, 222–23. Charles Herron, the *Times*'s editor, was a Republican.

29. Lawler, "Railroad Workers Battle," 27; "Official Returns of the Election of Delegate from Alaska, Members of the Fourth Territorial Legislature and Road Commissioner Held November 5, 1918," Box 106–7, File 61, RG 101, Alaska State Archives.

30. Lawler, "Railroad Workers Battle," 22; Lieutenant Thomas Saugre (Commander, 14th U.S. Infantry) to Commanding General, Western Department, March 3, 1918, and reports of Special Agent N. H. Castle, June 25, August 17, September 2, 1920, Bureau of Investigation Case Files, OG, Record Group 60, National Archives; *Alaska Labor Union Bulletin*, February 25, 1918.

31. Fairbanks, with five thousand people, had a Socialist Party membership of twenty-seven in 1914, while Olnes, a mining camp of fewer than a thousand persons, counted fifty members. *Alaska Socialist*, June 30, 1914.

32. Buhle, "Lena Morrow Lewis," 80; Hunt, *Distant Justice*, 221; *Fairbanks News-Miner*, November 9, 1916; "Official Returns of the Election . . . Held November 5, 1918," Box 106–7, File 61, RG 101, Alaska State Archives. In the Fourth Division, Lewis received 10 percent where Brooks had received 17 percent in 1914. The party's final Congressional candidate, Francis Connolly, received even fewer votes—4 percent—in 1918.

33. Foster, "Syndicalism Northern Style," 140.

The Pacific Salmon Fisheries

A Study of Irrational Conservation

JAMES A. CRUTCHFIELD and GIULIO PONTECORVO

From modest beginnings in 1878, the Alaska salmon-canning industry became the most important economic enterprise in the territory in the first half of the 20th century, outdistancing gold and copper mining, timber, and tourism in value of export, number of people employed, and the scope of the activity. The industry, headed by the Alaska Packers' Association, was the most significant absentee investment in Alaskan resources and one of the most powerful political forces both within Alaska and in Congress and the federal executive agencies which managed Alaska's resources. The industry's considerable lobbying effort often had a major effect on legislation and policy concerning Alaska. Many Alaskans found the effect to be detrimental to the interests of self-government and economic independence.

Overfishing during World War I, when the U.S. military purchased much of the annual salmon pack, and subsequent depletion of salmon stocks led to a debate within the territory and among federal bureaucrats over regulation of the fishery. The result was major regulatory legislation by Congress, the 1924 White Act, which set the pattern for fisheries regulation virtually until statehood.

Professor Giulio Pontecorvo of the Graduate School of Business at Columbia University and Professor James Crutchfield, now retired from the School of Finance at the University of Washington, undertook a study of the regulation of the fishery while they were at the University of California in 1969. Their study was supported by Resources for the Future, a conservation research group funded by the Ford Foundation. Pontecorvo has since written several articles dealing with management of maritime resources, and in 1974, with John King Gamble, Jr., he edited the proceedings of the eighth annual Law of the Sea Conference, Law of the Sea: The Emerging Regime of the Oceans *(Cambridge, Mass.: Published for Law of the Sea Institute by Ballinger Publ., 1974).*

This article appeared originally in *The Pacific Salmon Fisheries: A Study of Irrational Conservation* (Baltimore: Published for Resources for the Future, Inc., by Johns Hopkins University Press, 1969), 95–103; it is reprinted here by permission.

In their study of the Alaska salmon industry, Pontecorvo and Crutchfield found that the new fisheries regulations of the 1920s did not adequately curtail overfishing. Nor did they save the resource from eventual severe depletion.

In the broadest sense, the White Act was the product of three forces: the biological state of the salmon resource; the economic condition of the Alaska fishing industry; and political attitudes in Washington, D.C. In the summer of 1919, C. H. Gilbert and Henry O'Malley carried out an investigation of the fishery. Their report summarized and stated forcefully the feelings of some biologists concerned with the Alaska salmon stocks. They charged that the evidence pointing to overfishing was clear and that rapid increase in inputs of men and equipment with no corresponding increase in the yield made evident the necessity for economic regulation. This perceptive report indicated a partial understanding of the need to formulate a regulatory program consistent with both biological constraints on output and the price-profit-motivated reactions of fishermen and processors. While biologists were by no means unanimous in their evaluation of the state of the salmon stocks or of the measures required to protect them, there was general concern for the future.

The industry had expanded rapidly during World War I. In 1915 there were some 86 canneries operating in Alaska, and by 1920 this number had jumped to 143. Almost 6.7 million cases were packed in 1918. After the war, in 1919, the government canceled its contracts and returned its unused supplies to the packers. These heavy inventories presented difficult financial problems for the overexpanded industry, and prices broke sharply as dumping developed. In 1919 the opening price for red salmon (per dozen one-pound cans) was $3.35, up $1.00 from 1918. In 1920 the market opened at $3.25, down $0.10, and by 1921 it had fallen to $2.35.[1] The general economic depression which began in January 1920 complicated the problems of the industry, and a number of failures occurred among the canning firms. These economic pressures altered industry attitudes sharply, and conservation suddenly became good business as well as good biology.[2] This position relaxed somewhat as prices stabilized in 1922 and 1923, but at least part of the impetus for legislation reflected the weak economic position of the industry. Finally, Secretary of Commerce Herbert Hoover was favorably disposed toward the conservation issue and was prepared to accept the increase in the regulatory powers of his Department required to mount a more effective program.

The legislation that emerged in 1924 was a compromise between economic interests and biological necessity. With two major exceptions the Act represented an extension of the existing pattern of regulation. The first change, in Section 6, involved the scope of federal authority and penalties for violation of regulations. As had been suggested by Gilbert and O'Malley, this change put the regulatory process more on a par with that in the continental United States by giving the Bureau [of Fisheries] the legal power to arrest and also to seize gear. The latter was a more serious threat to fishermen and canners than the usual small fines, and its implementation caused widespread resentment against the Bureau.

The most striking innovation, however, was in Section 2 of the Act, which required not less than 50 percent escapement in most streams. This meant that the commercial fishery had to be regulated in such a manner as to allow 50 percent of the fish in any given stream to escape the fishery. Unfortunately, the application of a rigid percentage escapement rule, like almost all other inflexible regulations, is not well adapted to the peculiar characteristics of the Pacific salmon. Depending on the size of the returning run, a 50 percent harvest could easily be either too large or too small for optimal escapement.

More interesting are the implications of the rule for the regulatory agency. A policy aimed at maintenance of maximum sustained yield through assurance of adequate escapement requires the regulatory agency to mount a research and enforcement effort sufficient for the task. At the time the White Act was passed, only a few persons had any real grasp of the complexity of the regulatory problem. The development of an organization capable of carrying out the requirements of the Act would have taken many years in the best of circumstances. In the face of subsequent congressional neglect, partisan sniping, and conflicting pressures from vested interests, only very modest results could have been expected. The lack of general recognition of the difficulties became a source of disappointment and disillusionment with the results achieved under the Act.

At first, however, the industry thought highly of the Act, and this opinion was reflected in the trade journals. Some 15 years later, Gregory and Barnes, without adequate knowledge of the biological situation, could regard the Act as "making possible greater production of salmon than previously, yet this has taken place despite the restrictions imposed to insure proper escapement, and therefore presumably without jeopardizing the future."[3] Writing in the late 1930s, they could not foresee the catastrophic decline in the fishery that was to come, nor could they appreciate the inadequacy of both the research and the enforcement capabilities of the regulatory agency.

Other authors were critical of the Act for other reasons. Writing in the 1950s, Ernest Gruening emphasized what eventually was recognized as a key omission in the Act from the standpoint of the emerging regional consciousness of the Territorial residents: "By the White Act of 1924, Congress had foreclosed Alaskans' principal aspiration—control of their fisheries."[4]

By any reasonable standards the program developed under the Act of 1924 must, in retrospect, be judged a failure. Certainly it did not prevent depletion of the fishery. Yet, once the delusion about the status of the resource had been dispelled in the 1950s, the Act became the basis of a greatly expanded federal program of research and enforcement. In spite of the provision about escapement and the penalties provided for enforcement, however, the Act did not change *de facto* conditions in the fishery. The status quo was maintained.

After the contraction in the fishery in the early 1920s, the industry began to expand again in the latter part of the decade. New firms entered and some mergers occurred. The most important entrant was Nakat Packing (A&P) and the key merger, the creation of the Alaskan Pacific Salmon Company, in 1928. After 1924, prices rose sharply, fluctuated around those higher levels until 1928, then began to decline again. The entries and mergers that took place, in part as a result of financial speculation, did not change the basic structure of the industry.

There were other changes, perhaps the most significant being the introduction of high-speed canning lines in 1926 and extension of the market by vigorous national advertising. The level of industry activity continued to respond to market conditions, with heavy pressure to pack as much as possible as long as price expectations were firm and to curtail operations (as in Bristol Bay in 1935) when they were not. Prices showed severe cyclical variations. The opening price for reds (per dozen one-pound cans) dropped from $3.10 in 1930 to $1.45 in 1932. Thereafter it recovered, and the industry began another period of expansion.

During the initial stages of the depression, economy measures in the federal government curtailed the already slender enforcement capability in Alaska. The aerial survey program was cut back, and the number of stream guards reduced. There was some increase in enforcement later in the decade, but expenditures for research were minimal, averaging less than $25,000 per year until 1939.

With the outbreak of war in 1939, price increases put more and more pressure on the resource. The price of salmon rose 63 percent from 1940 to 1942—an increase of 25 percent even after adjustment for changes in the general price level. At this point, the catch began to decline, a development that simply intensified the industry's efforts to obtain relaxation of regulations.

During the 1930s a more cohesive and vocal Alaskan position on regulation was developing.[5] This position gradually polarized around two central issues: opposition to outside interests and dissatisfaction with federal control. Public concern with both matters increased in the later 1930s and came to a head in 1939. Early in that year the Commissioner of Fisheries resigned. In May the Bureau of Fisheries was transferred to the Department of the Interior and became part of the Fish and Wildlife Service, and in July the House of Representatives passed a resolution calling for a congressional investigation of the administration of the Alaska fishery. The principal result of the investigation was to break down some of the isolation surrounding the industry. For the first time Congressmen were exposed to a full airing of the divergent interests in the Alaska fisheries: the complaints of Alaskans, mostly directed against traps and absentee administration; the attitudes of the canners; and the actual operating conditions in Alaska. Despite evidence of congressional dissatisfaction with (and confusion over) the situation, American entry into the war in 1941 prevented any major overhauling of administrative programs.

There was a strong tendency to rationalize the economic structure of the fishery during World War II. Regulations were relaxed, the fishery moved further inshore, fishing was permitted in areas previously restricted, and canners were required to consolidate operations in a limited number of joint units. For example, in 1942 the Bristol Bay season was allowed to open two weeks earlier than usual and the midweek closing was suspended, and in 1943 only 83 canneries operated in all of Alaska. Military security requirements and the drain on manpower in the fishery reduced the number and range of operating units to a point at which relatively full and efficient utilization of gear became possible.

The trend of output continued downward, however. Landings of salmon averaged 560 million pounds during the 1935–39 period. During the war (1940–44), despite curtailment of the number of operating units, the catch had dropped to 453 million pounds, and in the immediate postwar period (1945–49) it was only 381 million pounds—a 32 percent decline over the decade. In the 1950s, the catch declined further to a 259 million pound yearly average for the next five years, and only moderate recovery in the 1960s seems indicated. These aggregate figures conceal great variation in both the catch by species and in the finer detail of yield by species, by area, or by particular race of fish.

This was the pattern predicted in 1919, when Gilbert and O'Malley had written (in reference to the Kvichak-Naknek area in Bristol Bay):

> The sequence of events is always the same. Decreased production is accomplished by increase of gear. Fluctuations in the seasons become more pronounced. Good seasons still appear in which nearly maximum packs are made. But the poor seasons become more numerous. When poor seasons appear no attempt is made to compensate by fishing less closely. On the contrary, efforts are redoubled to put up the full pack. The poorer years strike constantly lower levels, until it is apparent to all that serious depletion has occurred.[6]

This behavior hypothesis was supported by the investigations of Rich and Ball and was consistent with the general decline in the fishery.[7]

In addition to the decline in abundance, the postwar period produced a shift in the political situation in Alaska. In [1939] Ernest Gruening was appointed Governor. One of his proposals involved a basic tax reform program that was bitterly opposed by the Alaska fishing and mining industries. The ultimate passage of this program in 1949 marked, in the opinion of one observer, the end of effective opposition by the salmon lobby in the Territory.[8] In 1949 the Territorial legislature also established a Department of Fisheries. This was a shadow department, assisting and supplementing by means of Territorial appropriations the work of the U.S. Bureau of Commercial Fisheries. It also provided the training ground necessary for eventual assumption of control by the state.

As indicated above, production fell sharply in the 1950s to the level of output prevailing before World War I. Specific areas were very hard hit, and political pressures increased further. In a statewide referendum in 1952 Alaskans voted 20,500 to 5,500 to request Congress to turn control of the fisheries over to the Territory on the grounds that local management would be better management.[9] The publication of Gruening's book in 1954 restated the Territorial version of the history of congressional neglect, the power of the lobbies, and the case for statehood. From that time, given the level of economic development reached in Alaska and the hardening of political attitudes, it seems probable that a shift to state control was inevitable, especially since no rehabilitation program for the fishery, no matter how well conceived, could be effective in the short run.

There were two other structural changes of great importance in the overall salmon management program. The decline in landings forced the government and the industry to turn to a greatly expanded program of biological research. Expenditures on research by the Bureau of Commercial Fisheries were less than $100,000 per year until 1948. By 1956 they had reached almost a quarter of a million, and in 1958, the last year before statehood, they exceeded $900,000. In addition, the industry supported the formation, in 1947, of the Fisheries Research Institute at the University of Washington, largely because of dissatisfaction with the level and orientation of the federal program. Today the Institute, in cooperation with federal and state programs, provides for a broad-based attack on the complex biological problems of the fishery. The Institute has been supported financially by both the industry and the Bureau of Commercial Fisheries, and the latter is currently the major contributor.

Fully as important as the biological factors, and largely misunderstood or ignored in the political debate, were the massive economic problems of the fishery. In addition to the core problems of inefficiency and the stifling effect of regulation on innovation and technical progressiveness, the specter of unemployment in the precarious Alaskan economy and the special role of the immobile Native fishermen have exerted constant pressure on fishery administrators.

The problems posed by the economics of the fishery have been as ubiquitous as the problem of depletion. Pre–World War I proposals for economic controls included suggestions that both fishing units and the number of canneries in an area be limited. After the war Gilbert and O'Malley emphatically stated the need for economic control, and during World War II, in a proposed revision of the White Act, detailed legislation was presented that included direct measures for economic regulation.[10] Finally, the problem of the amount of fishing effort and its regulation weighed heavily on the minds of those who formulated the revised federal regulatory program in the 1950s. All these efforts suffered from the same deficiency that had plagued those charged with formulation of meaningful biological regulations: the lack of detailed empirical and theoretical economic knowledge of the fishery, which made it impossible to specify the implications and costs of unrestricted entry.

In spite of the long history of bad feelings, the transfer of regulatory authority over the fisheries to the state was accomplished smoothly. The

Alaskan department already in existence had established its competence. Its much greater public acceptance made its task easier, and thus far it has retained this respect. Operating details of the conservation problem are obviously easier to administer from Juneau than from Washington, although today there are many issues, primarily international, that are basically beyond the capacity of any state to handle in a satisfactory manner, and some critical potential conflicts between state and national interest are yet to be faced.

Within the existing framework, the question of economic performance of the industry under regulation remains the overriding issue. The furor over the Japanese high-seas fishery and the recent mild upturn in the catch have tended to obscure this question, but the state can ill afford, either in terms of its own needs or as an instrument in international bargaining, to let the fishery dissipate millions each year in manifestly inefficient operations.

NOTES

1. *Pacific Fisherman Yearbook*, 1918–22.

2. For a detailed account of these attitudes see Richard A. Cooley, *Politics and Conservation: The Decline of the Alaska Salmon* (New York: Harper & Row, 1963), 109 ff.

3. Homer E. Gregory and Kathleen Barnes, *North Pacific Fisheries, Studies of the Pacific*, No. 3 (San Francisco: American Institute of Pacific Relations, 1939), 178.

4. Ernest Gruening, *The State of Alaska* (New York: Random House, 1954), 282.

5. George W. Rogers, *The Future of Alaska* (Baltimore: The Johns Hopkins Press, 1962), chapter 5.

6. C. H. Gilbert and Henry O'Malley, "Special Investigations of the Salmon Fishery in Central and Western Alaska," *Alaska Fishery and Fur-Seal Industries in 1919*, Bureau of Fisheries (Washington: U.S. Government Printing Office, 1920), 151.

7. Willis H. Rich and Edward M. Ball, *Statistical Review of Alaska Salmon Fisheries*, Bureau of Fisheries Document No. 1041 (Washington: U.S. Government Printing Office, 1928), 65.

8. Rogers, *The Future of Alaska*, 255 ff.

9. Gruening, *The State of Alaska*, 406.

10. U.S. Cong., 78th Cong., 2nd Sess., House Committee on Commerce, Hearings on S.930, January 20, 1944. See the U.S. Cong., 78th Cong., 2nd Sess., House, Annual Report of the Secretary of the Interior and amendments, House Doc. 746, 97–98.

Anthony J. Dimond and the Politics of Integrity

MARY CHILDERS MANGUSSO

*Mary Childers Mangusso has taught in various capacities at the University of Alaska Fairbanks since 1966. She earned her doctoral degree at Texas Tech University in 1978 with a dissertation on the career of Anthony J. Dimond, Alaska's delegate to the U. S. Congress from 1933 to 1945. She has published articles on Dimond (*Alaska Journal*, 1982) and on the Nome gold rush (*Pacific Northwest Quarterly*, January 1982, with Andrea R. C. Helms), as well as numerous reviews and has presented many papers at professional conferences.*

In the article reprinted here, taken from a chapter of her dissertation, Mangusso discusses territorial political issues in the 1920s and Dimond's role as senator in the territorial legislature. Alaska politics depended much more on dynamic personalities and the loyalty they could command than it did on party organization and discipline. Dimond was a major figure in territorial politics and earned a reputation for ethical conduct and intelligent investigation of issues.

Salmon canning was the economic mainstay of Alaska in the 1920s, and the question of territorial regulation and taxation of the industry occupied much political attention. For the most part regulation stayed with the U.S. Commerce Department despite territorial protestations that the fisheries should be controlled by the territory.

Another issue was the organization of territorial government. Many Alaskans resented the power of the "federal brigade," which included the Governor, a presidential appointee, as well as the heads of the district offices of federal agencies with jurisdiction over Alaska affairs, such as the Bureau of Fisheries, the U.S. Forest Service, the Bureau of Education, and the judges in the court system, among others. But attempts to invest with substantive power officials who were elected in the territory did not succeed.

This article is adapted from "Anthony J. Dimond: A Political Biography" (Ph.D. dissertation, Texas Tech University, 1978), chapter 2, 44–110; it is reprinted here by permission.

Dimond was involved in these battles as well as in the fight over the Literacy Act of 1925. Throughout, Mangusso found, he supported Progressive social legislation and tried to set a high ethical standard in the practice of territorial politics.

When the sixth session of the Alaska legislature convened in March 1923, a squabble concerning selection of a permanent secretary delayed organization of the Senate. Anthony J. (Tony) Dimond and his fellow senator from the Third Judicial Division (south-central Alaska), backed by one member from the Second Division (north-western Alaska) and another from the Fourth (the Interior), supported Miss Selma N. Scott of the Third Division for the position, while the other four senators favored Will Steel of the First (the Southeast). Three of the four men who supported Steel described themselves as Republicans; one, as an independent. Scott had the support of Dimond (a Democrat), two Republicans, and an independent. A deadlock ensued until Steel solved the problem by withdrawing from consideration.[1] Obviously, neither party affiliation nor geographic origin necessarily determined how a senator might vote on a question of patronage, and the same held true for many other issues.

When Congress established the Alaska legislature in 1912, only the most rudimentary party organizations existed within the territory. Parties consisted of shifting coalitions with no specific programs and no Alaska-wide machinery. This condition resulted in part from the absence of firmly established political traditions, since territory-wide politics had come into existence only in 1906, when voters had been empowered to send a non-voting delegate to Congress. However, absence of strong party systems also may be attributed to the character and personality of Alaska's major political figure, James Wickersham.[2]

Wickersham had come to Alaska in 1900 as a federal district judge and had entered politics in 1908, when he ran for the delegateship as a self-designated "Independent Republican" and defeated four opponents (a Republican, a Democrat, an independent, and a laborite). Vigorous and flamboyant, he dominated Alaskan politics for the next quarter century. No one could ignore him; individuals either supported him enthusiastically or abhorred him. His followers praised his energy, his combative style, and his courage. He hurled imaginative oratorical insults at his adversaries, who in turn accused him of self-aggrandizement and opportunism, often referring to him gleefully as "Flickering Wick." That appellation was not unearned, for Wickersham placed little apparent value upon political consistency. He won reelection as delegate in 1910 as an insurgent Republican and in 1912 as a Progressive. In 1914 he again ran successfully, describing himself throughout most of Alaska as an independent supporting Democratic President Woodrow Wilson's politics. However, in some parts of the territory he called himself a Progressive Democrat. After 1916 he always identified himself as a Republican, although other Republicans did not necessarily agree. Since he was the only politician whose influence and reputation extended throughout the whole territory, his party hopping produced considerable turmoil. Political alliances formed and disintegrated according to their members' opinions of Wickersham's activities. Both major parties split into pro- and anti-Wickersham factions, and these factions attacked each other with an intensity rivaling that of their attacks upon members of the opposing party.[3]

Internal party divisiveness also resulted from differing economic interests and local and regional jealousies. Many voters, their loyalties shaped by place of residence and means of livelihood, distrusted any office seeker from another area. Alaska's size and the lack of adequate transportation made it difficult for anyone to campaign in all regions, and voters' sources of information often proved unenlightening. Newspaper publishers, for example, frequently demonstrated greater creativity than objectivity. As a result, misunderstandings, misinformation, and sectional rivalries contributed to a tendency among Alaskans to support a person rather than a party or a platform.[4]

Substantive issues existed, and often opposing candidates held remarkably similar views about them. However, the territorial legislature had no power to deal with many of these issues. In the Organic Act of 1912, which created the Alaska legislature, Congress imposed restrictions upon its powers greater than those imposed upon any other territorial law-making body in the United States. The legislature possessed limited power to tax and could not alter the existing system of license fees on business and trade or the federal laws allocating revenue from such fees. Legislators could not amend or alter those acts of Congress which established Alaska's executive and judicial departments, could not allocate land, and could not change, amend, or repeal federal laws relating to fish, game, fur seals, or fur-bearing animals. Neither the territory nor its incorporated municipalities could incur bonded indebtedness. While many of these limitations applied to all territorial legislatures, the sections which prevented creation of a territorial judicial system and which retained federal control over fish, game, and fur-bearing animals were unique to Alaska.[5]

While election to the Alaska legislature certainly represented more than the "empty and profitless honor" that Dimond once described it to be, the Organic Act severely limited legislators' abilities to address many of Alaska's problems. In areas where action could be taken, inadequate revenue often restricted their options.[6] The legislature's weakness contributed to petty quarreling and to perpetuation of the cult of personality in territorial politics.

The cult of personality probably contributed to Dimond's political successes during the 1920s. Perhaps the best evidence of this can be found in letters from friends who urged as early as 1912 that he run for one or another office. Such suggestions sometimes included offers of money but never mentioned party affiliation, possibly because friends knew him to be a Democrat but more likely because they regarded party identification as relatively unimportant.[7]

Dimond first entered territorial politics in 1922, running for a Third Division territorial Senate seat. He faced no opposition in the primary. Republican Thomas A. Wade of Anchorage ran against him in the general election. A resident of Valdez, Dimond had earned a reputation as a formidable defense lawyer throughout southcentral Alaska. However, by 1922 Anchorage had grown into the largest town in the division, and Dimond expected Wade to receive a majority of the votes cast there. Because of limited funds and uncompleted legal business, Dimond did not campaign extensively. But Wade proved to be an unexpectedly weak opponent, and Dimond won easily, carrying even the Anchorage precincts and receiving 1,406 votes to Wade's 872.[8]

As a freshman senator in 1923, Dimond served on the Committee on Mining, Manufacturing, and Labor and the Committee on Engrossment and Enrollment, Per Diem, and Mileage. He chaired the Committee on Judiciary and Federal Relations. The judiciary committee assignment took most of his time, for Alaska's attorney general inundated the Senate with forty-seven proposed bills intended to bring territorial law into conformity with recommendations made by federal judges in Alaska and by the United States Commission of Uniform Laws. Dimond himself proposed additional bills intended to regularize and strengthen existing laws.[9]

The mining committee undertook a general revision of territorial mining law, but after much discussion members could not agree upon the extent of the legislature's authority under the terms of the Organic Act and gave up their attempt. Dimond did introduce a bill to clarify the time limit for filing the affidavits of annual labor required on mining claims; this measure passed and received the governor's signature.[10]

Dimond generally supported progressive or reform legislation. In the 1922 general election, voters had approved, by slightly more than two to one, a referendum which proposed that women be allowed to serve on juries. Dimond supported that measure[11] and introduced his own bill designed to insure that jurors would be chosen fairly. Formerly marshals or deputies had selected jurors for commissioners' courts, marshals had selected jurors for special venires, and in district courts the names of jurors had been drawn from a box containing the names of 300 persons eligible to serve. Dimond felt that the existing procedure could be abused too easily, especially in the case of commissioners' courts where juries could be virtually handpicked. The "Dimond Jury Law" provided that in all courts jurors would be chosen by drawing from a box containing the names of three-fourths of the persons in the area who had voted in the previous general election.[12]

Dimond also supported an act which permitted a married woman to dispose of her property without authorization from her husband[13] and an act giving fishermen and cannery workers preferred liens on property owned by the company employing them in case of nonpayment of wages.[14] He drafted and voted for an act which increased workmen's compensation benefits by thirty percent and extended coverage to more workers.[15]

All of the acts described above passed the Senate unanimously. Senators also accepted without dissent a bill intended to help fur farmers by raising the existing territorial bounty on eagles from fifty cents to one dollar per bird.[16] Obviously members shared certain assumptions, for each backed some types of social and legal reform, and all proved eager to reduce predation which seemed to threaten an infant industry. However, the legislators did not concur on all proposals; measures relating to regulation of commercial fisheries, reorganization of the executive branch of the government, and a literacy test for voters provoked spirited debate and revealed profound differences of opinion.

By the 1920s the annual value of Alaska's salmon pack had begun to decline sharply, falling from about $50 million in 1918 to roughly half that amount in 1921. The drop in part reflected a postwar decline in prices, but also it resulted from overfishing and consequent depletion of supply.[17]

Responsibility for regulating the Alaska salmon industry rested with

Secretary of Commerce Herbert Hoover, whose purview included the Bureau of Fisheries. At Hoover's suggestion the Warren G. Harding administration attempted to halt the decline by creating two fish reserves to be administered by the Bureau of Fisheries, one located in the Aleutians and the other encompassing Bristol Bay and the Kodiak area. About forty percent of Alaska's commercial salmon fisheries fell within the reserves.[18]

Major corporations based outside the territory dominated the salmon industry and consistently blocked efforts to secure strict and effective regulation of fisheries by either federal or territorial authorities. Alaskans strongly resented both continued federal control of Alaska's resources and the powerful economic and political influences which the salmon packers undeniably exercised. Accordingly, most of the territory's residents interpreted establishment of the fish reserves as an effort to protect the interests of the large corporations at the expense of resident fishermen.[19]

A memorial to Congress introduced in the Alaska House by Representative William D. Grant of Wrangell expressed this common belief:

> Irrespective of the good intentions of present officials, the privileges upon a reserve must, in the very nature of things, go to those who maintain the strongest lobby. It cannot be presumed that before the Bureau of Fisheries, any more than before a tribunal primarily created to administer justice, a claimant who can neither appear in person nor by counsel can possibly have an even chance with one who is constantly represented by men specially skilled in presenting facts.[20]

The memorial reportedly had been written by Dan Sutherland, then Alaska's delegate, Wickersham's protege, and a vigorous foe of Hoover's policy. Dimond felt the memorial to be weak because it suggested no remedy for the existing situation, but he viewed it more favorably following House adoption of an amendment which requested abolition of the reserves and establishment of territorial control over Alaska fisheries. When the Senate considered the proposal, Dimond and E. E. Chamberlain, the Third Division's senior senator, framed a somewhat more tightly worded substitute, which the Senate rejected. Both men eventually joined in approving the memorial as it had come from the House.[21]

Rejection by the Senate of the substitute memorial prepared by Chamberlain and Dimond probably resulted from a natural preference among Wickersham/Sutherland supporters for a draft reportedly written by Sutherland instead of a similar measure drawn up by someone else. But all members of the Senate certainly agreed on the undesirability of fish reserves and the desire to protest such a policy.

However, a controversy soon arose regarding the means and extent of an effective protest. Senator Forest J. Hunt of Ketchikan introduced a resolution at Sutherland's request authorizing Alaska's attorney general to test the validity of the fish reserves. One section of the resolution instructed that official

> to protect and defend any private citizen or corporation of the United States against any charge of the violation of any rules or regulations promulgated by the secretary of commerce or bureau of fisheries attempting to deny to any person or corporation any right which in the opinion of the attorney general is vouchsafed to such person or corporation by the constitution or the laws of the United States, and, to that end, to defray the necessary expenses connected with his or its defense, including the engaging of attorneys to assist whenever he shall deem the same necessary.[22]

In considering the resolution Dimond acknowledged the need for conservation of salmon but questioned both the intent and the potential effectiveness of the reserve system. He disagreed with those who believed creation of the reserves to be unconstitutional, but he expressed willingness to have their validity tested in court. He refused, however, to support the resolution as written, objecting vehemently to the portion which directed the attorney general to defend and pay the legal expenses of anyone accused of violating federal fishing regulations. He contended that passage of such a resolution would be futile at best and, at worst, might encourage and abet open, violent rebellion against the government of the United States.[23]

During the discussion of Hunt's resolution, no one mentioned either the possible expense to the territory or the potential benefit to any corporation which might take advantage of the provision for territorial financing of a legal defense. Apparently everyone expected the governor to veto the measure if it passed, and it seems to have been introduced merely to lay a foundation for its sponsors' future partisan appeals. Dimond must have recognized the resolution's political origin and purpose. Yet he could not question the propriety of using territorial funds in such a manner without implying that his opponents had sold themselves to the cannery lobbyists, a move his belief in political fair play would not allow him to make. Instead, he attacked indirectly, stressing the danger of insurrection,[24] a point not entirely improbable when one considers the acknowledged magnitude during the 1920s of fish piracy (theft of fish from traps owned by major packers by Alaska residents, who then sold the fish to the packers from whom they'd been stolen).

The Senate considered an alternate resolution containing less explicit language than the original, but Dimond believed that the meaning remained essentially unchanged and refused to vote for the substitute. The Senate passed the alternate proposal by a five-to-three vote, with Dimond, Chamberlain, and Fred M. Ayer of Nome in the opposition. The House also adopted the substitute, which the governor vetoed.[25]

In addition to pushing through the fish reserve resolution, the Sutherland faction in the Senate proved strong enough to defeat a bill which would have required all voters to be able to read and write the English language. Proponents of the literacy qualification intended it as a means by which to restrict voting by Indians, thereby breaking the political power of Native leader William L. Paul. Paul, a Tlingit who had studied and traveled extensively in the contiguous United States, had politicized the Alaska Native Brotherhood and by 1923 reportedly controlled a bloc of about one thousand Native votes in southeastern Alaska, which he used in Sutherland's behalf. Many of Paul's followers were believed to be illiterate; at election time he allegedly supplied them with stencils to be placed over the official ballot and instructed them to mark an "x" in each cutout. Although hoping to eliminate Paul's political base and undercut Sutherland, the literacy test's backers described it as a reform designed primarily to reduce corruption.[26]

Dimond supported the measure, stressing that voting should be regarded as a privilege, not a right automatically accorded to every citizen. A working democracy, he argued, depended upon the participation of an enlightened electorate; voting by persons presumably unable to inform themselves adequately about public affairs perverted democratic ideals. He admitted that the proposal would affect Indians almost exclusively. The responsibility for educating Indians lay with the federal government, and properly qualified Alaskan voters should neither accept blame nor suffer inequities because the federal government had failed to fulfill its obligations. He noted that Paul openly admitted that the bill could deprive Sutherland of one thousand potential votes and characterized that admission as "an abject confession" of political impropriety.[27]

Had the literacy measure passed, it would have reduced somewhat the influence of the First Division in territorial affairs as well as undermining Republican support there. The boundaries of Alaska's four judicial divisions had been determined for the geographical convenience of the territory's four federal district judges. In the Organic Act of 1912 Congress made no attempt to provide proportional representation in the legislature but simply established four election districts, each coinciding in area with one of the judicial divisions.[28] The population of the four districts differed greatly. In the election of 1922 a combined total of 3,002 votes had been cast in the First Division for the two major candidates for the delegateship. The Second Division's vote for the two men together totaled 704; the Third Division's, 2,297; and the Fourth's 1,805.[29] While these numbers obviously represent only politically active adults, they also reflect the relative size of the population in each of the four divisions. Those differences in population accounted for some of the interdivisional rivalry that existed.

Disproportionate representation did not bother most politicians of the 1920s nearly as much as did the dominant position of the First Division in territorial affairs. In 1923, 53 (48.2 percent) of Alaska's 109 appointed and elected officials came from the First Division. George J. Love, United States Commissioner at Valdez, expressed an opinion typical of non-southeasterners when he wrote Dimond following the Senate dispute over selection of a secretary to congratulate him upon his victory over "those grafters in Juneau and southeastern Alaska."[30] Besides distrusting a relatively remote government and resenting the extent to which it was run by southeastern Alaskans, persons from other regions disliked the fact that the First Division could cast a larger vote than any other district in territory-wide elections. Since the Third Division (Dimond's) contained the second largest number of voters, elimination of one thousand First Division votes would have given to the Third the chief role as a makeweight in territorial politics.

In 1923 the only territory-wide elections consisted of those held to choose a delegate to Congress and a territorial attorney general, but in that year the Senate considered transferring most of Alaska's executive authority from the presidentially appointed governor to a territorial Board of Control composed of officials elected at large throughout Alaska. The Wickersham/Sutherland faction strongly backed this "controller bill." Since the proposal raised the possibility that elected officials actually might possess power and exert increased control over patronage, some politicians from northern, central, and western Alaska became even more eager than before to restrict the First Division's role in territorial affairs.

Some also opposed the measure because they feared that, if it passed, Wickersham/Sutherland forces would dominate the Board of Control.[31]

Neither the literacy test nor the controller bill passed the Senate in 1923, both meeting defeat by four-to-four ties. Dimond voted against the controller bill and for the literacy test. Although the author of the literacy bill advanced frankly racist arguments in its favor, Dimond's support apparently did not stem from racial prejudice. On one occasion he expressed shock and disgust when informed of a rule barring persons of Indian descent from membership in the Elks, and his oldest daughter recalled that he had taught his children to be unprejudiced.[32] Probably his votes best can be explained as compatible with his own and his division's political interests.

In 1925 William Paul, a newly elected member of the Alaska House of Representatives, proposed expansion of Alaska's pension system to cover Natives as well as non-Natives. Many politicians and some newspapers opposed the suggestion, angrily decrying the expense involved in adding to territorial pension rolls persons who already received federal aid. Paul's presence in the legislature, the furor over his pension proposal, and the 1924 federal act declaring Indians to be citizens of the United States led to renewed controversy over the literacy bill. For example, the *Alaska Daily Empire* of Juneau, staunchly anti-Sutherland and therefore anti-Paul, editorialized:

> If anyone ever had any doubts about the need for a literacy test for voters in the election laws of Alaska, the attempt of Mr. Paul, leader of the organized Indian voting bloc in southeastern Alaska, to open . . . the Territorial pension list to Indians ought to clear away the doubt. . . .
>
> Above all, the Legislature should pass the literacy test measure and alleviate the harm that is being done to both whites and Indians through political demagoguery that has created a race problem in Alaska and threatens to wreck our territorial government.[33]

The literacy bill proposed in 1925 included a clause exempting from its provisions all voters who had cast ballots legally in any prior election. Dimond twice tried to eliminate this exemption, but both attempts failed. He and three like-minded Senators then joined the other four to approve the measure unanimously.[34] As finally adopted, the Voter's Literacy Act of 1925 represented a hollow victory for those legislators who favored a literacy test, since it left Paul's political base intact.

The controller bill also resurfaced in 1925. It again failed when Dimond and the same three colleagues who had attempted unsuccessfully to amend the Voter's Literacy Act voted against it.[35]

During 1925 Dimond again chaired the Committee on Judiciary and Federal Relations and also served on the Finance and Corporations Committee and the Committee on Education. He introduced thirteen bills, eleven of which passed the Senate unanimously and received the approval of the House of Representatives and the governor's signature. Most involved amendments to clarify or improve existing laws. One measure, for example, slightly modified the process of jury selection prescribed by the Dimond Jury Law of 1923. It provided that jurors had to be able to read, write, speak, and understand the English language; those who could not do so might be dismissed for cause. Another of his bills authorized diversion of some of the money originally appropriated for road construction in the Third Division into a fund for construction of airfields.[36]

Although for the most part the 1925 session proved unusually harmonious, Dimond once again tangled with the Sutherland faction. Amidst a patronage battle during which he attempted to discredit and dislodge several federal appointees in Alaska, most of whom happened to be Dimond's friends, Delegate Sutherland asserted in the United States House of Representatives that some regions of the territory suffered from a breakdown of law and order due to the incompetence of resident legal and judicial officials. His remarks apparently furnished the basis for statements made at a press conference by Supreme Court Justice Harlan Fiske Stone, who, according to the Associated Press, characterized Alaska as an uncivilized frontier where unruly citizens lacked respect for the law. Understanding that Sutherland had portrayed Alaska in strident, inaccurate tones to strengthen his hand in the patronage fight, Dimond and Representative Joseph H. Murray, Dimond's former prospecting partner, introduced identical memorials in the territorial legislature denouncing Stone's reported remarks as untrue and demanding the name of the person from whom Stone obtained such an impression so that the informant "might be branded from one end of Alaska to the other as the liar that he is." Sutherland's followers retaliated; Paul introduced a resolution condemning the Dimond/Murray memorial in highly emotional terms as an unjustified, politically motivated attack upon Sutherland by the Democrats. His argument, although partially correct, ignored the fact that Murray belonged to the Republican party, albeit not the Sutherland wing. Both the resolution and the memorial failed to pass, but the dispute increased the enmity between Dimond and the Sutherland camp.[37]

Several Democrats urged Dimond to run for the delegateship in the 1924 and 1926 elections, but he declined. In August 1923, he and T. J. Donohoe, his longtime mentor and Valdez law partner, had accepted a retainer from the Alaska Syndicate. The syndicate, a consortium formed by J. P. Morgan, the Guggenheim brothers, and other eastern investors, owned the Kennecott copper mines, the Copper River and Northwestern Railroad, a steamship line, and assorted salmon canneries and gold mines. His relationship with the syndicate, a favorite target of anti-monopolists, made Dimond vulnerable politically. It required no special astuteness to recognize that an attorney for the "Guggies" had little hope of winning a territorial election given existing anti-syndicate sentiment throughout much of Alaska. Following the 1925 Senate session, Dimond apparently intended to retire from politics, for he informed a friend, "I am glad that the session is over, and that I can do something else for awhile, being the last time that I shall ever appear in any legislative body. I thought it would be interesting, but it has been instead an awful bore."[38]

By 1926, however, Dimond had changed his mind, and he filed as a candidate for reelection to the Senate. Unopposed in the primary, he faced Republican nominee Arthur Frame in the general election. Frame, also a lawyer, had come to Alaska in 1905 and worked for several years in a Fairbanks law firm staffed by friends of James Wickersham before moving to Anchorage.[39] Frame did not campaign extensively. Instead Sutherland, a candidate for reelection to the delegate's seat, led the opposition to Dimond.

Wickersham's role in the 1926 campaign seems unclear, although in the past he had shown a pronounced tendency toward vindictiveness, neither forgetting nor forgiving anyone who disagreed with him on any issue. As Wickersham's protege, Sutherland may have acquired some of his patron's less endearing traits; certainly he adopted some of Wickersham's techniques. In the territorial Senate Dimond had opposed the controller bill, attacked the wording of the Sutherland faction's resolution protesting the fish reserves, and attempted to undercut the delegate's political base by advocating a literacy requirement for voters. Dimond had affronted Sutherland particularly by cosponsoring the memorial denouncing Justice Stone's allegations. In addition, several prominent Cordovans had retained Donohoe and Dimond to institute a libel suit against Sutherland, who had accused them of belonging to a bootleggers' ring during the 1925 patronage battle.[40] Although protected from the lawsuit by congressional immunity, Sutherland had ample reason to promote Dimond's defeat.

Even so, the delegate seems to have devoted a surprising amount of effort exclusively to attacking Dimond. Frame was not a dynamic speaker, so he doubtless needed help. Sutherland's opponent for the delegateship, Thomas Marquam of Fairbanks, had entered the race as an independent. Although the Democratic candidate had withdrawn to avoid splitting the anti-Sutherland vote, Marquam generated little enthusiasm outside the Fourth Division.[41] Sutherland remained popular throughout the territory and therefore could spare the time to concentrate upon Dimond, whom he seems to have regarded as a potentially dangerous rival as well as an effective opposition leader.

In a series of addresses given in the Third Division, Sutherland concentrated upon Dimond's connection with the Alaska Syndicate. Dimond's three children innocently attended a Republican rally in Valdez while their parents were out of town because they wanted to see the free movie which preceded the speeches. They then listened while Sutherland denounced their father as a tool of the "fish trust," a man who represented the salmon packers rather than the people both off and on the Senate floor. Dimond's oldest daughter later recalled, "And he banged and banged, and he said all those things, and here we were sitting there just kind of open-mouthed . . . I heard afterwards . . . he was terribly embarrassed.[42]

Sutherland wrongly charged Dimond with obstructing all proposals to authorize a test of the validity of the fish reserves. He attacked Dimond for opposing a bill to tax the fishing industry by means of a graduated tax on the number of salmon taken in fish traps rather than by a set fee per trap. He also charged that Donohoe and Dimond had engineered the selection of Marquam as the anti-Sutherland candidate and suggested that Dimond ran Marquam's campaign. The latter assertion may have hurt Dimond's chances with Native voters, since Marquam viewed the literacy test as a major issue and campaigned as an avowed racist, promising to save Alaska from "the menace of Indian controlled government."[43]

Sutherland's assertions contained just enough truth to put Dimond on the defensive. He would have been less vulnerable had voters been better informed about public affairs, but press coverage of legislative sessions ranged from the very spotty to the completely nonexistent. Only the Juneau *Empire* attempted complete coverage, and its editor's blatant anti-Sutherland bias made its accounts highly suspect. Hence, many voters accepted half-truths or plausible falsehoods because they had no factual basis for comparing the candidates' records. Dimond patiently tried to sort out Sutherland's allegations and to explain those charges he regarded as false or misleading. He acknowledged that he favored Marquam for delegate but denied organizing or administering Marquam's campaign. Indeed, prior to 1926 Dimond seems to have had no contact with Marquam, whom he apparently supported without great enthusiasm as the only alternative to Sutherland. Dimond explained in great detail his opposition to fish reserves and his votes on the legislative protests against them. He noted that Sutherland had described the existing fishery taxes erroneously, outlined his own attitude regarding the best system of taxation, and pointed out that both taxes on fisheries and appropriations for the relief of aged citizens and for the Alaska Agricultural College and School of Mines had more than doubled since 1919, the last year during which Sutherland had served in the territorial legislature. He affirmed that he had supported the higher taxes and the larger appropriations, although he had voted against a proposal to tax fisheries solely by graduated fees on numbers of fish caught because he believed such a system impossible to enforce. He compared his own record in favor of territorial control over Alaskan resources to Sutherland's record, pointing out the delegate's undeniable ambiguity about whether or not the territory should be allowed to regulate its own fisheries. He admitted acting as an attorney for the syndicate but stoutly denied representing any "fish trust." He asserted that in his capacity as a senator he always had sought to represent the people, not his corporate clients. Even Abraham Lincoln, he protested, once had performed legal work for corporations.[44]

Although his temper became frayed by election day, Dimond concluded his campaign on an ethical level unusually high by prevailing standards. Refusing to employ the opposition's tactics, he attempted to counter inaccurate, emotionally charged attacks calmly and logically. He received endorsements from the *Cordova Daily Times* and the *Anchorage Daily Times*. However, many voters clearly believed Sutherland, and Dimond lost to Frame.[45]

Still not satisfied, Sutherland Republicans struck at Dimond again in 1927 when Governor George A. Parks appointed him to the Board of Regents of the Alaska Agricultural College and School of Mines. Four senators successfully blocked his confirmation because of his prominence in the Democratic party. They likewise rejected Dr. J. H. Romig of Fairbanks for membership on the Board, reportedly because he had played a major role in Marquam's campaign. As if to emphasize the point, the four voted to accept as regent a less politically active Fairbanks Democrat.[46]

Undaunted, Third Division Democrats nominated Dimond for a Senate seat again in 1928. Although unopposed in the primary, he once more found himself confronted by charges that he represented the "fish trust."[47] William Paul's monthly newsletter, *The Alaska Fisherman*, circulated distorted allegations similar to those made by Sutherland two years earlier:

> You have it in your power to elect men who will represent you and not the steamship company or the Kennecott Mine. You can put an end to the government of Alaska by carpet-baggers who look to Washington, D.C.
>
> But you cannot do so if you elect Tony Dimond, senator. . . .
>
> Tony Dimond is the man who engineered the joker law that successfully tied the hands of our own attorney general and prevented this elected official from testing the infamous FISH RESERVATIONS.[48]

Voters responded less sympathetically to Paul than they had to Sutherland two years earlier. Dimond won.

During the ninth session of the Alaska legislature (1929), Dimond introduced nineteen bills, fourteen of which passed. The governor vetoed one of these, the so-called "poor convict bill," which would have provided for the release of persons imprisoned solely because they could not pay a fine or a fine plus court costs. Dimond intended it, he said, to "put the poor man on the same footing with those who have money." The governor felt that the bill endangered effective law enforcement, and lawmakers failed to override the veto.[49]

The acts which Dimond sponsored successfully included one which authorized refunding the license fee required by law for each fish trap if the trap later could not be operated because of new government restrictions,[50] a second providing for creation of a public school teachers' pension fund,[51] and another, cosponsored by Senator John W. Dunn, designed to revise and codify all laws regarding Alaska's public schools. Dunn and Dimond proposed substituting a nonpartisan, appointed territorial Board of Education for the existing board, by law composed of the governor and the four senior senators and therefore necessarily politically oriented. The Senate deleted this reform before passing the bill.[52]

The perennial controller bill became the chief issue facing the 1929 legislature, precipitating a dispute which remained unresolved until the clock had been stopped to keep the session from exceeding its sixty-day limit. Introduced by Senator Will Steel, now from the First Division, the bill provided for creation of a Board of Control to assume all territorial executive duties, for the election of Alaska's Treasurer, and for the establishment of an elective office of Auditor. The bill passed the Senate over negative votes cast by Dimond, Dunn, and Luther C. Hess of the Fourth Division. Although supporters touted the measure as a method for increasing Alaskans' control over their territorial government, the Senate minority feared creation of a potentially powerful executive board at a time when political trends indicated that it would be staffed by Wickersham/Sutherland men.[53]

The territorial House amended the Senate version beyond recognition, eliminating the Board of Control entirely and passing only the sections relating to the positions of Auditor and Treasurer. The Senate majority refused to concur with the House amendments, while the House refused to rescind them. The conference committee deadlocked. The five pro-controller senators retaliated against House intransigence by holding a number of House bills in committee. Dimond led an unsuccessful effort to pry these bills loose. As part of a compromise settlement on the final day of the session, the Senate majority finally released a veritable flood of measures voluntarily.[54]

The version of the controller bill finally adopted contained no Board of Control. The act made the territory's Treasurer an elected rather than an appointed official. It created the new elective office of Auditor and gave that official many responsibilities, including most duties formerly performed by Alaska's Secretary, an appointed gubernatorial assistant.[55] Other acts originating in the House provided for election rather than appointment of the Commissioner of Education[56] and created the elective office of Highway Engineer.[57] Thus the legislature achieved the aim of the controller bill, increasing the power of elected officials and decreasing the influence of appointees, without enacting the entire measure. Both sides could express satisfaction.

Compared to the 1929 session, the 1931 legislative session proved tranquil. Dimond introduced twenty-eight of the eighty-two Senate bills considered. More of his proposals than before involved local improvements to benefit Third Division constituents. These measures included requests for territorial funding of repair work upon the dike which protected Valdez from spring flooding and for money to build or repair schoolhouses at Longwood, Afognak, Oozinkie, and Matanuska. Of seven such bills, only the Valdez dike repair measure passed.[58]

The Territory of Alaska faced extraordinarily severe fiscal problems in 1931. The governor recommended strict austerity. In an effort to organize finances better, he asked the legislature to establish a Board of Budget. Dimond drafted the act which did so.[59] In another attempt to improve administration, Dimond successfully proposed creation of the office of Superintendent of Public Works. The Highway Engineer would also act as Superintendent, coordinating and supervising construction of all public buildings.[60] Dimond also convinced the legislature to remove the few remaining restrictions on married women's property rights.[61]

The 1931 legislature repealed Alaska's "Bone Dry Law," a stringent prohibition act which Wickersham had sponsored and vigorously defended through the years. Legislators also repealed the "Wickersham Mining Act" of 1912, which limited the size and number of placer claims that prospectors could stake. (Since both were federal laws, neither repeal could become effective without congressional assent. Both repeals simply constituted efforts to win sympathy in Washington, D.C.) Dimond introduced the act repealing the 1912 mining law as well as a companion measure which abrogated a similar territorial statute.[62]

By 1931 Dimond had begun to consider running for delegateship in 1932.[63] Wickersham/Sutherland influence had begun to wane, and 1932 promised to be a good year for Democrats. Dimond had proven his popularity with voters by returning from his 1926 defeat to weather a second attack by the Sutherland forces two years later. Fellow legislators had come to respect his ability and energy, and he had become something of a public figure throughout the territory. Despite allegations by political opponents, his legislative record indicated no favoritism for his corporate clients. Instead, he had consistently supported reforms of a progressive nature, measures designed to promote economic development in the territory, and proposals to insure equal rights and fair treatment to all citizens. From a present-day viewpoint, his support for a literacy qualification for voters may be interpreted as a smudge on his record; however, he seems to have been motivated by political considerations rather than by prejudice. In retrospect his record reveals almost none of the stains acquired by those involved in the grubby territorial political battles of the 1920s.

On March 16, 1931, Dimond gave a public lecture on the Declaration of Independence and the Constitution of the United States to Juneauites as part of a series of presentations sponsored by the local Order of Moose. He cautioned that "tyranny was to be feared not only through the accumulation of all power in one officer, but also through the operation of temporary majorities; that 'democracy has its own capacity for despotism.'" These remarks doubtless reflected his own recent political experiences. However, the speech also may well have marked the opening of his campaign for the delegateship, which he was to win in 1932, for he also stressed a favorite Alaskan theme: "When the speaker dwelt upon the necessity of self-rule in all local matters rather than a concentration of all power in the hands of the national government at Washington, he was enthusiastically applauded."[64]

NOTES

1. Alaska (Ter.), *Senate Journal of Alaska 1923,* pp. 9–13, 344.

2. Ernest Gruening, *The State of Alaska*, rev. ed. (New York: Random House, 1968), p. 158.

3. Jeannette Paddock Nichols, *Alaska: A History of Its Administration, Exploitation, and Industrial Development during the First Half Century under the Rule of the United States* (Cleveland: The Arthur H. Clark Company, 1924), pp. 358–62, 395–98; Gruening, *State of Alaska*, pp. 158, 186–87; William R. Hunt, *North of 53°—The Wild Days of the Alaska-Yukon Mining Frontier, 1870–1914* (New York: Macmillan Publishing Co., Inc., 1974), pp. 281–85; William R. Cashen, *Farthest North College President: Charles E. Bunnell and the Early History of the University of Alaska* (Fairbanks: University of Alaska Press, 1972), pp. 39–60, 76.

4. Gruening, *State of Alaska*, p. 158; Cashen, *Farthest North College President*, p. 76; Hunt, *North of 53°*, pp. 266–73.

5. *An Act To Create a Legislative Assembly in the Territory of Alaska . . . ,* U.S. Statutes at Large 37: 512–18 (1912); Gruening, *State of Alaska*, pp. 151–53; Melvin Crain, "Governance for Alaska; Some Aspects of Representation" (Ph.D. dissertation, University of Southern California, 1957), pp. 179–86; George Washington Spicer, *The Constitutional Status and Government of Alaska* (Baltimore: The Johns Hopkins Press, 1927), pp. 73–81.

6. Anthony J. Dimond to A. F. Hoffman, 18 August 1914, T. J. Donohoe–John Y. Ostrander–Anthony J. Dimond Papers, Alaska and Polar Regions Collection (Archives), Elmer E. Rasmuson Library, University of Alaska Fairbanks. [Hereafter, this manuscript collection will be cited as "DOD."] Also see Gruening, *State of Alaska*, pp. 283, 285.

7. For example, see Peter S. Erichsen to Dimond, 16 October 1912; telegram, R. F. Isaacson to Dimond, 19–21 [sic] October 1912; telegram, "Nizina, Kennecott Bunch" to Dimond, 22 October 1912; Isaacson to Dimond, 31 October 1912; Bill Salonka to Dimond, 5 November 1914, DOD.

8. Dimond to Thomas C. Price, 20 January 1922; to L. Leo Wardell, 27 May

1922; to Joseph Murray, 2 and 14 November 1922, DOD. *Valdez Miner*, 28 January 1922, p. 1; 25 February 1922, p. 4; 29 April 1922, pp. 1–2; 11 November 1922, p. 1; 17 February 1923, p. 3. *McCarthy Weekly News*, 21 October 1922, p. 1.

9. Senate Journal 1923, pp. 8, 22–28, 36–37, 41–43, 84, 156, 242; *Alaska Daily Empire* (Juneau), 8 March 1923, p. 8.

10. Dimond to E. S. Larson, 30 March 1923, DOD; *Senate Journal* 1923, pp. 103–104, 132, 181; Alaska (Ter.), *Session Laws of Alaska 1923*, Chapter 43, p. 53.

11. *Senate Journal 1923*, pp. 35, 66, 85, 291; *Laws of Alaska 1923*, Chapter 68, pp. 106–107.

12. *Senate Journal 1923*, p. 138; *Alaska Empire*, 21 April 1923, p. 8; *Seward Weekly Gateway*, 10 October 1926, p. 11; *Laws of Alaska 1923*, Chapter 91, pp. 160–65.

13. *Senate Journal 1923*, pp. 24, 50, 84, 101; *Laws of Alaska 1923*, Chapter 20, p. 28; Chapter 40, p. 51.

14. *Senate Journal 1923*, pp. 23, 160–61; *Laws of Alaska 1923*, Chapter 53, pp. 70–79.

15. *Seward Weekly Gateway*, 10 October 1926, p. 2; *Senate Journal 1923*, pp. 261, 268; *Laws of Alaska 1923*, Chapter 98, pp. 235–63.

16. Dimond to W. C. Snook, 31 March 1923, DOD; *Alaska Empire*, 23 March 1923, p. 8; *Senate Journal 1923*, pp. 43, 94; *Laws of Alaska 1923*, Chapter 34, pp. 39–41.

17. Gruening, *State of Alaska*, pp. 245–63; Henry W. Clark, *History of Alaska* (New York: The Macmillan Company, 1930), p. 182.

18. Gruening, *State of Alaska*, pp. 263–64.

19. Ibid.

20. House Joint Memorial No. 1, *Laws of Alaska 1923*, pp. 319–20 (quotation, p. 319).

21. *Anchorage Daily Times*, 29 October 1926, p. 3; Dimond to Larson, 30 March 1923; DOD; *Seward Weekly Gateway*, 10 October 1926, p. 11; *Senate Journal 1923*, pp. 129–30; *Laws of Alaska 1923*, pp. 320–21; *Alaska Empire*, 6 April 1923, p. 2.

22. *Senate Journal 1923*, p. 138; Senate Joint Resolution No. 2 as quoted in *Anchorage Daily Times*, 29 October 1926, p. 3.

23. *Alaska Empire*, 18 April 1923, pp. 1, 8.

24. Ibid.

25. *Alaska Empire*, 18 April 1923, p. 8; 2 May 1923, p. 4; *Anchorage Daily Times*, 29 October 1926, p. 3; *Senate Journal 1923*, pp. 137–38, 144, 148, 166, 170–71, 177, 184, 231.

26. *Alaska Empire*, 3 April 1923, p. 3; 4 April 1923, p. 8; William L. Paul, Sr., "The Real Story of the Lincoln Totem," *Alaska Journal* 1 (Summer 1971): 3, 5; Stephen Haycox, "William Paul, Sr., and the Alaska Voter's Literacy Act of 1925," *Alaska History* 2 (Winter 1986/87): 19–20.

27. Dimond to Larson, 30 March 1923, DOD; *Alaska Empire*, 3 April 1923, p. 3 (quotation); 4 April 1923, p. 8.

28. Spicer, *Status and Government of Alaska*, pp. 74–75; Crain, "Governance for Alaska," pp. 188–90.

29. *Valdez Miner*, 17 February 1923, p. 3.

30. Officeholders listed in *Laws of Alaska 1923*, pp. 5–8. The figures given ex-

clude the governor, usually someone from outside of Alaska, and the two senators and four representatives from each division. Quotation from George J. Love to Dimond, 15 March 1923, DOD.

31. *Senate Journal 1923*, p. 41; *Alaska Empire*, 16 March 1923, p. 4.

32. *Senate Journal 1923*, pp. 121, 176; *Alaska Empire*, 3 April 1923, p. 3; Dimond to I. D. Bogart, 22 July 1925, DOD; Sister Marie Therese, Notre Dame de Namur, interview with Claus-M. Naske, Washington, D.C., 20 April 1975 [transcript in author's possession].

33. *Alaska Empire*, 6 March 1925, p. 4; 7 April 1925, p. 1; 8 April 1925, p. 4 (quotation); 21 April 1925, p. 4.

34. *Senate Journal of Alaska 1925*, pp. 119, 143; Alaska (Ter.), *Session Laws of Alaska 1925*, Chapter 27, pp. 51–54.

35. *Senate Journal 1925*, pp. 88–89, 164, 183, 190.

36. *Alaska Empire*, 28 March 1925, p. 1; *Senate Journal 1925*, pp. 61–62, 73, 102, 104–106, 141–42, 171, 186, 192, 217, 231, 235, 272–84; *Laws of Alaska 1925*, Chapter 16, pp. 29–38 (jury selection); Chapter 62, pp. 106–107 (airfields).

37. James Wickersham to J. W. Keith, 6 April 1925, Daniel Sutherland Papers, Alaska and Polar Regions Collection, Elmer E. Rasmuson Library, University of Alaska Fairbanks; *Alaska Empire*, 15 April 1925, pp. 1, 3 (quotation, p. 3); 17 April 1925, p. 1; 18 April 1925, pp. 1–2; 23 April 1925, pp. 1, 8; 1 May 1925, pp. 1–2; *Senate Journal 1925*, pp. 81, 172–73; *Valdez Miner*, 31 July 1926, p. 3; 2 October 1926, p. 2.

38. Emmet Egan to Dimond, 10 November 1922; Dimond to Murray, 11 August 1923; Dimond to J. C. Murphy, 16 August 1923; John F. Coffey to Dimond, 28 June 1925, 7 August 1925; Dimond to Coffey, 18 July 1925; Dimond to Mrs. Agnes W. B. Shepard, 2 May 1925 (quotation), DOD; *Valdez Miner*, 1 September 1923, p. 2.

39. *Valdez Miner*, 13 February 1926, p. 2; "Arthur Frame," *Alaska-Yukon Magazine*, January 1909, p. 317.

40. *Cordova Daily Times*, 4 February 1926, p. 1.

41. *New York Times*, 11 July 1926, p. 6.

42. Sister Marie Therese interview, 20 April 1975.

43. *Valdez Miner*, 9 October 1926, p. 2; *Anchorage Daily Times*, 27 October 1926, p. 3; 28 October 1926, pp. 4–5; 29 October 1926, pp. 3, 6. For examples of Marquam's campaign: *Seward Weekly Gateway*, 10 October 1926, p. 9; *Anchorage Daily Times*, 27 October 1926, p. 1 (quotation); *Fairbanks Daily News-Miner*, 29 October 1926, p. 4.

44. *Seward Weekly Gateway*, 10 October 1926, p. 2; *Anchorage Daily Times*, 28 October 1926, pp. 4–5; 29 October 1926, pp. 3, 6; *Fairbanks Daily News-Miner*, 29 October 1926, p. 4.

45. *Valdez Miner*, 9 October 1926, p. 2; 6 November 1926, p. 1; *Anchorage Daily Times*, 28 October 1926, p. 4; *Cordova Daily Times*, 30 October 1926, p. 4; 1 November 1926, p. 4.

46. *Alaska Empire*, 4 May 1927, p. 8; 5 May 1927, p. 4; *Valdez Miner*, 21 May 1927, p. 2.

47. *Valdez Miner*, 10 December 1927, p. 2; 28 April 1928, p. 1; 13 October 1928, p. 2.

48. *The Alaska Fisherman*, October 1928, p. 2.

49. Alaska (Ter.), *Senate Journal of Alaska 1929*, pp. 45, 57–58, 62, 67, 70–71, 88, 93–94, 98–99, 106, 115, 122–23, 148, 152, 163, 168–69, 172, 174–76 (governor's veto message), 179, 223, 232, 262, 273, 306, 320, 350–76; *Alaska Empire*, 2 April 1929, p. 8 (quotation).

50. *Senate Journal 1929*, pp. 70, 172, 273; Alaska (Ter.), *Session Laws of Alaska 1929*, Chapter 54, p. 123.

51. *Senate Journal 1929*, pp. 163, 223, 306; *Laws of Alaska 1929*, Chapter 83, pp. 172–78.

52. *Senate Journal 1929*, pp. 93, 186, 189, 194–95, 199, 202, 207, 218, 224, 228, 232, 249, 251, 274, 286, 291, 320; *Laws of Alaska 1929*, Chapter 97, pp. 194–233; *Alaska Empire*, 29 March 1929, pp. 1, 8; 22 April 1929, p. 8.

53. *Senate Journal 1929*, pp. 49, 83; *Alaska Empire*, 25 March 1929, p. 2; 26 March 1929, p. 2.

54. *Senate Journal 1929*, pp. 185–87, 203–204, 213–14, 225, 236–37; *Alaska Empire*, 20 April 1929, p. 8; 26 April 1929, p. 1; 27 April 1929, p. 1; 2 May 1929, p. 1.

55. *Laws of Alaska 1929*, Chapter 118, pp. 279–94.

56. *Laws of Alaska 1929*, Chapter 115, pp. 274–75.

57. *Laws of Alaska 1929*, Chapter 114, pp. 272–73.

58. Alaska (Ter.), *Senate Journal of Alaska 1931*, pp. 16, 49, 69, 83–84, 154, 161, 191–92, 203, 248, 272, 312, 317, 420–43; Alaska (Ter.), *Session Laws of Alaska 1931*, Chapter 10, pp. 55–57.

59. *Alaska Empire*, 4 March 1931, p. 1; 5 March 1931, p. 1; *Senate Journal 1931*, p. 184; *Laws of Alaska 1931*, Chapter 72, pp. 128–30.

60. *Senate Journal 1931*, pp. 184, 231, 363; *Laws of Alaska 1931*, Chapter 91, pp. 168–69.

61. *Senate Journal 1931*, pp. 54, 90, 197; *Laws of Alaska 1931*, Chapter 16, p. 64.

62. *Laws of Alaska 1931*, Chapter 95 (repeal of the "Bone Dry Law"), pp. 173–74; Chapter 65 (repeal of the Wickersham Mining Act), pp. 117–18; Chapter 64 (repeal of Alaska's mining act based upon the Wickersham law), p. 117; *Senate Journal 1931*, pp. 173.

63. Sister Marie Therese interview, 20 April 1975.

64. *Alaska Empire*, 17 March 1931, p. 2.

The New Deal and Alaskan Natives, 1936–1945

KENNETH R. PHILP

The Indian Reorganization Act of 1934, passed in the early years of Franklin Roosevelt's New Deal, represented a dramatic change in American Indian policy. The IRA recognized the legitimacy of Indian self-determination by permitting Indian businesses to be incorporated, establishing Indian credit agencies, protecting some forms of Indian land title, and granting limited power of self-government to Indian reservations. It was a reversal of the highly destructive Indian policies of the late 19th and early 20th centuries.

The IRA was not immediately applicable to Alaska because there were no tribes in Alaska as that term was understood in the continental states. Alaska's congressional delegate Tony Dimond and the Tlingit lawyer William Paul, Sr., worked with Interior Department officials and congressional leaders to amend the IRA for extension to Alaska, and Congress passed a bill for that purpose in 1936.

In this article Professor Kenneth Philp of the University of Texas at Arlington discusses the Alaska Reorganization Act (as the amended IRA was called) and some of the struggles of Alaska's Tlingit and Haida Indians which followed. Having earned his doctorate at Michigan State University, Philp published an important study on the New Deal Indian Commissioner John Collier, John Collier's Crusade for Indian Reform, 1920–1954 *(Tucson: University of Arizona Press) in 1977. He has published a number of articles on 20th-century Indian affairs, including "Dillion S. Meyer and the Advent of Termination, 1950–1953" (*Western Historical Quarterly, *January 1988) and "Stride toward Freedom: The Relocation of Indians to Cities, 1952–1960" (*Western Historical Quarterly, *April 1985).*

In the article reprinted here, Philp discusses the attempt of the Secretary of the Interior Harold Ickes to persuade Alaska's Tlingit and Haida Indians to accept the establishment of reservations in Alaska to protect Native land title. Some Southeast villages did vote to create small reservations, but these were declared

This article appeared originally in *Pacific Historical Review* 50 (1981); it is reprinted here by permission of the author.

invalid by court action in the 1950s. Governor Gruening opposed the creation of Indian reservations as discriminatory toward Alaska Natives and detrimental to the statehood movement.

On April 21, 1933, President Franklin D. Roosevelt appointed John Collier commissioner of Indian affairs. During the previous decade Collier had been executive secretary of the American Indian Defense Association, an organization that opposed the Dawes General Allotment Act of 1887.[1] This legislation had destroyed much of the reservation system in the United States by abolishing tribal governments and providing the Indians with 160-acre, or smaller, homesteads. The Dawes Act was part of a broader effort by nineteenth-century Indian reformers to promote the objective of assimilation. Collier believed that the Dawes Act and similar efforts had led to poverty, landlessness, and the general social disorientation of Native Americans. Shortly after taking office, he met with officials in the Department of the Interior and formulated a new federal Indian policy based on the concept of cultural pluralism. The centerpiece of this policy—the Indian New Deal—was the Indian Reorganization Act of 1934, which encouraged the use of reservations as homelands where tribes could engage in self-government and cooperative economic activity.[2]

Historians have recently provided new insights concerning the Indian New Deal, but they have neglected to analyze carefully how it affected the Eskimos, Aleuts, and Indians who resided in the territory of Alaska.[3] The Alaska Reorganization Act of 1936 allowed Natives to establish village self-government and borrow money from a federal credit fund in order to combat the effects of the Great Depression.[4] The Interior Department used this legislation to create five reservations, and it held hearings to determine the extent of Haida and Tlingit claims to fishing rights and land in southeastern Alaska.

The Alaska Reorganization Act provided the Natives with needed financial assistance, but it was poorly administered and inadequately funded by Congress. More important, the policy of setting aside reservations met opposition from white settlers and Natives who had become assimilated after Alaska came under the jurisdiction of the United States in 1867.[5] Rather than listen to their critics, New Deal officials in the Interior Department pushed ahead with plans to establish reservations and determine the validity of Native claims. They neglected, however, to consult with Congress or gain needed grass-roots support. The result was further delay in securing social justice for Alaska's Native inhabitants.

After the purchase of Alaska, the United States did not sign treaties with the Natives and provide them with reservations in return for ceded land rights. Instead, Congress passed the Alaska Organic Act of May 17, 1884, which allowed the Natives to remain undisturbed on the land they occupied until their title was confirmed by future legislation. After 1890, some 126 reserves containing 1,338,700 acres for 2,063 Natives were created by executive order. Most of these reserves were not bonafide reservations. Except for areas devoted to the grazing of reindeer, they consisted of forty-acre or smaller plots set aside for federal schools and hospitals. In 1898 and 1906, Congress permitted the Natives to apply for homesteads, but the absence of surveyed land made it impossible to confirm land claims.[6]

The federal government had been concerned about the welfare of Alaska's Natives long before the New Deal. Beginning in 1884, the Bureau of Education in the Interior Department provided the Natives with schools, founded cooperative trading stores, and helped the Eskimos herd reindeer.[7] In 1905, President Theodore Roosevelt had requested an investigation of conditions among the Eskimos, Aleuts, and Indians of Alaska. This led to a report which recommended improved health and educational facilities, the development of Native arts and crafts, the right of Natives to own real estate and hold mineral claims, and increased federal supervision over the salmon industry.[8]

During the next four years, Congress passed legislation which implemented many of these recommendations. It regulated the fisheries of Alaska, established a school system for Native children which included medical care, and in 1906 authorized the Secretary of the Interior to grant homesteads to Alaskan Indians and Eskimos. The Natives were not given rights to mineral claims under this homestead law.[9]

The federal government in subsequent years demonstrated little concern for Alaska's Natives until 1931, when the Bureau of Education was transferred to the Bureau of Indian Affairs in order better to coordinate federal programs. Before turning over his responsibilities, William Cooper, the U.S. Commissioner of Education, had obtained money from the Carnegie Foundation in order once again to survey the social status of Alaska's Native inhabitants. This study rejected proposals to set aside large Native reserves similar to those in Danish Greenland. It did, however, encourage the government to increase financial aid to Native economic enterprises, use village councils for citizenship training, and take steps to end racial discrimination.[10]

Commissioner John Collier hoped to implement many of these recommendations when he included the Natives of Alaska under the Indian Reorganization Act (IRA) of 1934. The IRA abolished future land allotment, permitted tribal self-government, provided money for Native educational loans, and authorized $2 million annually for the consolidation of checkerboarded reservations or the establishment of new homelands for propertyless Indians. It also set up a $10 million credit fund to encourage tribal economic development.[11] These steps were opposed by Anthony J. Dimond, an Alaska politician, who believed that Collier had made a mistake by including Alaska's Natives under the Indian Reorganization Act. Prior to his election in 1932 as a delegate to Congress, Dimond had been a member of the Alaska Territorial Senate and served as mayor of Valdez.[12] Before the IRA passed, he convinced a congressional conference committee to exclude Alaska from several of its provisions. The committee omitted Alaska from sections of this legislation that ended the issuing of land allotments, allowed tribes to incorporate for business activity, and permitted the Secretary of the Interior to create new reservations.[13]

Dimond was convinced that the IRA did not meet the needs of the 4,462 Tlingit, 588 Haida, and 466 Tsimshean Indians located in southeastern Alaska, or the 4,028 Aleuts, 4,935 Athabascan, and 15,000 Eskimos who resided on the Aleutian Islands, in the interior, and along the coastal regions of the territory.[14] Except for the Metlakatla Tsimshean Indians, who had established a prosperous reservation on Annette Island in 1891, most of Alaska's aboriginal population consisted of small family groups which resided on town lots in villages. They lacked the tribal cohesiveness found in many parts of the United States.[15] Dimond's position on the IRA also reflected the hostile attitude of the Alaska Native Brotherhood toward the creation of reservations. The ANB had been founded at Sitka in 1912 by acculturated Natives. They patterned the brotherhood after white fraternal lodges and local church societies. By the 1920s, almost every community in southeastern Alaska had established a local branch of this organization.[16]

Most of the founders of the Alaska Native Brotherhood had attended the Sitka Training School, where they were influenced by Sheldon Jackson, a Presbyterian missionary. An active participant in the Lake Mohonk Conference, Jackson was one of the humanitarian reformers who worked feverishly to Christianize and assimilate Native Americans in the decades after the Civil War. Jackson established church-state contract schools, secured reindeer to improve the Eskimos' economic status, and fought attempts to set aside reservations in Alaska. He feared that reservations would only promote segregation and lead to Native dependence on government annuities.[17] Another influential person was Richard Henry Pratt. Several leaders of the ANB had also attended boarding schools in the United States where they learned the philosophy of Pratt, the director of the Carlisle Indian School. Pratt insisted that the reservation system and tribalism had to be eliminated before the Natives could become first-class citizens. The leaders of the ANB promoted Pratt's and Jackson's assimilationist ideas by advocating equal citizenship rights, educational opportunities, and the abolition of what they considered to be outmoded aboriginal customs.[18]

William L. Paul, Sr., an officer in the ANB, had told Dimond about the Natives' objections to the reorganization act. Paul, a mixed-blood Tlingit, had attended the Chemewa and Carlisle boarding schools. He had later studied law and in 1926 was elected to the territorial legislature as a Republican.[19] Although Paul favored loans from the IRA's credit fund to individual Native fishermen, he argued that new reservations in Alaska administered by government bureaucrats would undermine principles of sound Americanism. Paul and many other Natives were disappointed when the solicitor of the Interior Department ruled that tribal organization was a necessary prerequisite to securing federal money.[20]

Because the Natives desperately needed financial help and secure title to their homesteads, Dimond agreed to support the passage of the Alaska Reorganization Act (ARA) in 1936. This measure enabled Alaska's Natives to enjoy most of the benefits of the IRA. Groups of Natives not previously recognized as bands or tribes, but having a bond of common occupation or association, could adopt constitutions for self-government and receive charters of incorporation required for federal loans. The ARA authorized the Secretary of the Interior to designate as reservations land previously set aside for the Natives by executive order or congressional legislation, adjacent nearby public lands, and land actually occupied by Eskimos, Aleuts, and Indians. Congress required the Secretary of the Interior to secure Native approval for any new reservations at special elections where thirty percent of the population would have to turn out.[21]

After the passage of the Alaska Reorganization Act, employees of the Indian Bureau persuaded 10,899 Natives, out of a population of over 29,000, to draw up constitutions and charters of incorporation.[22] The constitutions drawn up by the forty-nine villages that organized under the ARA varied, but most allowed the formation of an elected municipal council. Many of these councils had been in existence since the passage of the Indian Village Act of 1915, which authorized settlements with more than forty members to establish self-government.[23] The councils had authority in all matters not prohibited by federal law, the right to employ legal counsel, and jurisdiction over any adjacent reservation set aside for Native use.[24] But the refusal of Congress to appropriate the $200,000 needed to operate these village governments limited their effectiveness.[25]

Natives who adopted charters of incorporation could organize business corporations with the power to manage property of every description, make contracts, sue and be sued, and borrow money from the IRA's credit fund.[26] Members of chartered village credit associations and business cooperatives secured approval for 383 individual loans worth $604,158. Most of these loans were confined to southeastern Alaska where the Indians purchased new boats and fishing gear, repaired old equipment, and financed home payments at the village of Hoonah.[27] In 1939, the Haida Indians on Prince of Wales Island established the Hydaburg Cooperative Association and borrowed $142,000 for the construction of a new salmon cannery building, dock, and related equipment. W. A. Pries, a white businessmen from Ketchikan, received a contract from the Interior Department to construct and operate this cannery. He received twenty-four percent of its profits until 1944, when an additional loan of $280,000 enabled the Haidas to assume complete financial control.[28] But they still had to pay a white manager to operate the cannery, because members of the village had little financial experience. A decline in the salmon run also made it difficult for the cooperative to repay the government.[29]

The Natives received important benefits from the Alaska Reorganization Act, but inept administration within the Interior Department caused numerous problems. The Indian Bureau had only three people to process loan applications. When Congress refused to provide money for field workers to supervise the loans, the bureau had to rely on thirty-three untrained schoolteachers for this important task. They often approved unsecured loans. Unfortunately, the educational loans authorized by the IRA were not used to train Alaska Natives to become managers of their credit associations and business cooperatives. Seventy-seven students received over $34,500 for tuition and related expenses, but they used this money to become clerical workers or to enroll in liberal arts and teacher-training programs rather than to study business administration.[30]

There were other problems. The Eskimos, Aleuts, and Indians needed a secure land base in order to take full advantage of the Alaska Reorganization Act. For various reasons, plans for reservations failed to materialize until after the loans were made. Field studies of Alaska were virtually nonexistent and the Indian Bureau had to start from scratch in the compilation of the essential economic and human data necessary for the creation of reservations. When Indian Bureau officials finally submitted concrete proposals, they discovered that many Natives and interested agencies in the Interior Department refused to cooperate.[31]

Commissioner Collier's own special efforts were often unsuccessful. During July 1937, he used section two of the ARA to withdraw extensive areas of land and water for the Natives near Anchorage. His goal was to guarantee Native fishing rights on water frontage adjacent to the Eklutna school site. He also requested a 1.6 million-acre reservation on the west side of Cook Inlet and an expanded reservation of nearly 1.5 million acres for the 106 Athabascan villagers at Tyonek, with fishing rights three miles into the east side of the inlet and 100 miles along the shore.[32] Collier's proposals were never implemented because of legal objections raised by Nathan R. Margold, the solicitor of the Interior Department. In a ruling issued on September 14, 1937, Margold held that Congress never intended "to permit immense areas of land to be tacked upon existing reservations" when it passed the Alaska Reorganizition Act.[33] The two reservations under consideration, argued the solicitor, were illegal because the Natives did not actually occupy all of that land as stipulated in the ARA. Margold also blocked the withdrawal of water frontage at Eklutna for nearby Native fishermen because the adjacent land was a school site rather than a bonafide reservation.[34]

Officials in the General Land Office, who defended the interests of non-Indians, were pleased with Margold's decision. They had contributed to this impasse by raising difficult legal questions that caused endless debates among Interior Department lawyers. The General Land Office wanted to know how Native claims would be affected by the creation of reservations, who would control subsurface mineral deposits, and whether proposed Native fishing rights might interfere with federal authority to improve and regulate navigable waters.[35]

Margold's ruling forced Secretary of the Interior Harold L. Ickes to intervene in the reservation controversy. Before joining the Roosevelt administration, Ickes had supported liberal causes. As a lawyer in Chicago, he had accepted civil liberty cases without compensation, taught classes at Hull House, and fought against Samuel Insull's utility company. During the 1920s, he had joined Collier's American Indian Defense Association and criticized the Republican-run Indian Bureau.[36] As head of the Interior Department, Ickes was determined to confirm Native title to reservation land and to help the Natives defend their hunting and fishing rights. But he had other motives as well. Native control over waters adjacent to reservations would enable him to gain more leverage over the powerful Alaska salmon industry. Ickes also favored reservations as a way of implementing conservation policies that would prevent the depletion of the country's natural resources. He was especially interested in preventing the Forestry Service from overcutting timber on the mountain slopes in the Tongass National Forest in southeastern Alaska.[37]

In order to secure the necessary legal authority to carry out his plans, Ickes asked Solicitor Margold to consult with Felix S. Cohen, an associate solicitor in the Interior Department, on whether he had the power to close down the fish traps of non-Indians who were threatening the operation of Native canneries and the livelihood of individual seiners. Cohen, who had a doctorate in philosophy from Harvard and a law degree from Columbia University, was one of the main architects of the IRA and a militant defender of Native rights. His interest in applied anthropology and the philosophy of law eventually led to the publication of his *Handbook of Federal Indian Law*, which upheld both tribal sovereignty and the principle of federal jurisdiction in Indian affairs.[38]

Cohen made his influence felt on Margold, who used a legal brief compiled by the associate solicitor as the basis for a sweeping opinion issued on February 13, 1942. Margold upheld the Natives' aboriginal claims to extensive areas of land and nearby fishing grounds. He based the reversal of his 1937 opinion on the U.S. Supreme Court decision of 1941 in the so-called Walpai case (*United States* v. *Sante Fe Pacific Railroad*) in which the court had recognized aboriginal possessory rights. According to Margold, the Supreme Court had held that aboriginal occupancy established rights of possession; that this possessory right extended to land under the prior sovereignty of European nations; that tribal right of occupancy need not be based upon a treaty or statute; and that extinguishment of occupancy rights could not be inferred from existing legislation or administrative action.[39] The use of waters or submerged lands by Alaska Natives, concluded Margold, was similar to the Walpais' use of their lands for "agriculture, hunting, and seed-gathering."[40] Thus section two of the ARA could be invoked to set aside traditional lands and fishing areas of the Alaska Natives.

Ickes used Margold's ruling to set aside four large reservations, in addition to the small one he had established in December 1941 at the Eskimo village of Unalakleet.[41] They were part of an overall plan to create twenty-five extensive reservations to protect the Natives in central and northern Alaska who subsisted on a game and trapping economy.[42] During May and June 1943, Ickes reserved 72,000 acres for sixty-eight natives at Akutan; 32,200 acres and adjacent tidelands for the 185 villagers at Karluk on Kodiak Island; 1,408,000 acres for the 202 Athabascan inhabitants at Venetie, Arctic, and other Christian villages north of the Yukon River in the Brooks mountain range; and 7,200 acres of land and 14,000 acres of water for the 194 Eskimos at Wales on the Seward Peninsula.[43]

Two additional reservations that Ickes established in 1943 were rejected by the Eskimos at elections required by the ARA. These reserves included 3,000 acres for the residents at Shishmaref on the north side of the Seward Peninsula and 1,200 acres of land and water for the White Mountain village on Norton Sound.[44] The Eskimos feared that fixed reservation boundaries might limit their hunting and fishing rights. They were also upset that the mineral rights to this land belonged to the United States pending future determination by the Interior Department. These Eskimos, who were converts to the Norwegian Lutheran and Catholic churches, agreed with the contention of the ANB that reservations would turn back the clock and promote racial segregation.[45] The Eskimos also remained suspicious of the government because it had mismanaged their reindeer herds. In September 1937, Congress had passed the Alaska Reindeer Act which placed the entire reindeer industry under Native control.[46] While officials in the Interior Department carried on lengthy legal negotiations to compensate non-Native owners for their reindeer and range equipment, thousands of reindeer were left to roam on an overgrazed, unsupervised range. The Eskimos became embittered as they watched thousands of their animals die from starvation and attacks from predators.[47]

The objections raised by the Eskimos did not prevent Ickes from imposing his reservation policy on the Haida and Tlingit Indians of southeastern Alaska. Ickes paid little attention to complaints by leaders of the Native American Brotherhood that reservations would result in the loss of their citizenship rights. Instead, he sought the support of elderly and less acculturated Indians who had concluded that reservations would offer them security. Many Haidas and Tlingits also believed that reservations were the best way to guarantee ownership of large areas of land and nearby fishing grounds.[48]

Ickes wanted to help the Haida and Tlingit Indians regain control over their fishing economy. The P. E. Harris Company, Pacific American Fisheries, Libby, McNeill and Libby, the Nakat Packing Company, the New England Fish Company, and several other absentee packing companies operated over fifty-six percent of the 434 fish traps granted by the War Department under legislation enacted in 1899. Each year they harvested salmon and herring worth over $60 million, which made it difficult for many Natives who fished in nearby streams to improve their economic condition.[49] Also a source of resentment was job discrimination. Under pressure from the Alaska Fisherman's Union, the canning companies had given preferential treatment to 17,398 whites, most of whom were nonresident unionized fishermen from Seattle and San Francisco. During the peak season harvest in 1937, the canneries employed 3,908 Filipinos, 967 Japanese, 634 Mexicans, and 556 Chinese aliens, who were viewed as a source of cheap labor.[50] The Alaska Native Brotherhood had bitterly complained to officials in the Interior Department about this type of employment discrimination, which resulted in only 6,600 Natives being hired.[51]

One month after Margold's 1942 legal opinion upholding Native occupancy rights, Ickes amended Alaskan fisheries regulations to prohibit fish traps on the Indians' property without their consent. Although he lacked authority from either Congress or the court system, Ickes invited the Natives to request departmental hearings where they could present claims to land traditionally used for hunting and fishing and now used by non-Indians who had installed fish traps. If the Interior Department recognized these claims, the Indians could lease valuable fishing areas to the canneries, establish a Native-run fishing industry, and request large reservations under the provisions of the ARA.[52]

The critical military situation in Alaska during the Second World War delayed hearings requested by the Natives until 1944. During June of that year, Ickes sent the associate solicitor Felix S. Cohen and other attorneys to Alaska to persuade the Tlingit and Haida Indians that reservations were necessary in order to protect their hunting and fishing rights. They succeeded in bringing many Indians around to their point of view and also helped the villagers at Hydaburg, Klawock, and Kake to prepare witnesses and legal cases for the hearings scheduled for September.[53]

Ickes tried to insure a fair hearing of the Indians' claims by persuading the Department of Justice to allow Richard Hanna, a special assistant to the Attorney General, to act as the presiding chairman at the hearings. Hanna had had a distinguished career on the New Mexico supreme court and during the 1920s had earned a reputation as a champion of Indian rights by helping the Pueblos to defend the title to their lands.[54] Though Hanna's temporary transfer was secured, some officials in the Department of Justice feared that it constituted a conflict of interest.[55] Hanna had been working on two cases pending in the court of claims that concerned the Haidas and Tlingits. After the passage of the Haida and Tlingit Claims Act of 1935, these Indians had sued the government for a cash settlement of all aboriginal rights destroyed with the tacit approval of the U.S. government. Hanna had prepared a legal brief for the Haida and Tlingit Indians at the Justice Department, and some government attorneys questioned whether he could impartially judge the validity of similar claims presented at Interior Department hearings.[56]

Hanna opened the hearings during the last two weeks of September 1944 in the federal schoolhouses at the villages of Hydaburg, Klawock, and Kake.[57] The Indians' attorneys argued that neither Russia nor the United States had extinguished the aboriginal possessory rights to land and water used by the Haidas and Tlingits from time immemorial. The area that the Indians claimed included 3,339,000 acres in southeastern Alaska, including submerged land and water 3,000 feet from the shoreline, lakes and streams that emptied into the ocean, and nearby unpatented lands drained by these watersheds.[58]

Individuals, organizations, and corporations challenged the Indians' position. W. C. Arnold, an attorney from Ketchikan, represented the salmon-packing industry and trap operators and argued that, if the government recognized the Haida and Tlingit claims, it would have to confiscate a substantial portion of the salmon industry and turn over a third of the Alaska panhandle to fewer than a thousand Natives. This would deprive the territory of needed tax revenues, threaten public navigation of waters, and overturn legislation that had opened the resources of Alaska to all citizens. Only Congress or "a court of competent jurisdiction," Arnold insisted, could determine possessory rights on the public domain.[59] This view received the endorsement of Stephen Carey, a lawyer representing the Pacific American Fisheries, and J. F. Jurich, a spokesman for the 22,000 International Fishermen and Allied Workers of America. The closing of the fish traps operated by the Pacific American Fisheries and Fidalgo Packing Company at Kasaan, claimed Carey, would jeopardize the $1.5 million investment of these canneries and lead to widespread unemployment.[60] Jurich feared that the Indians' claims would eliminate future job opportunities by ending the development of Alaska's mining, lumber, oil, and power resources.[61]

The Juneau and Ketchikan chambers of commerce also opposed the Haida and Tlingit claims. Juneau's representative stated that, contrary to Margold's ruling, Native families had never established a right of occupancy except for small fishing villages.[62] The delegate from Ketchikan argued that the petitions presented by the residents of Hydaburg, Klawock, and Kake threatened the free enterprise system that had contributed to his community's steady growth. Furthermore, the government had not explained how the areas claimed by the Indians would be administered. If reservations were established, the Indians would lose their citizenship rights and face "Jim Crow" segregation.[63]

While Ickes waited for Hanna to rule on the conflicting testimony, he received criticism from Ernest Gruening, governor of Alaska. Gruening was considered a liberal; he had supported Robert La Follette, the Progressive party candidate in 1924; criticized U.S. military intervention in Latin America; and worked for *Nation* magazine. He had joined the Roosevelt administration in 1934 as director of the Division of Territories in the Interior Department. Five years later, when the president had appointed him governor of Alaska, Gruening had demonstrated his New Deal credentials by proposing a corporate income tax designed to retain wealth previously taken from the territory by absentee business corporations.[64]

Gruening believed that Ickes's attempt to create reservations in Alaska was a reactionary move that would promote racial disharmony. In December 1944 he wrote Ickes a bitter letter, warning him that the policy of setting aside reservations "on a gigantic scale" not only threatened the economy of Alaska but would also "set the Natives back a full generation."[65] Gruening believed that Ickes had violated the spirit of the Alaska Reorganization Act which, he believed, only permitted the establishment of townsite reservations as a device for qualifying the Natives to borrow money from the IRA's credit fund. The Indian Bureau, he complained, had pressured reluctant Natives to accept large reservations in 1943, and this tactic savored "strongly of Hitlerism."[66]

Ickes was unmoved. He accused the governor of failing to distinguish between the attempt to determine Native claims under the Supreme Court's doctrine of aboriginal occupancy rights and the Interior Department's authority to create reservations. The hearings, Ickes stressed, were merely a forum to give the Natives an opportunity to present their claims so the government could determine their validity. The next step would be to decide what to do about these claims. Perhaps Congress would authorize negotiations with the Natives that would determine "whether a given area should be set aside as a reservation or whether title to all or a portion of it should be extinguished."[67] In any event, the Secretary concluded, the Native population was entitled to receive land on which it had lived for generations as well as adjacent areas necessary for "economic security."[68]

Ickes's problems multiplied when Richard Hanna submitted his report on March 7, 1945. Hanna rejected most of the Indians' claims because of deficiencies in the evidence provided by Interior Department lawyers. They had relied on the "diffuse and vague" oral testimony of Natives over eighty years old.[69] Moreover, the claims to lands in the interior were contradicted by reports of anthropologists who testified that Haidas and Tlingits seldom ventured inland because of religious taboos and because virtually all their economic activity was confined to the coast. Conflicting statements by older and younger Indians also made it difficult to determine changing concepts of land use and those areas that had been held in common by villages.[70] Hanna also seriously undercut the Interior Department's plans to establish large reservations in southeastern Alaska. The inhabitants of Hydaburg, Klawock, and Kake, he concluded, had failed to present "substantial evidence" that they had exclusively used tidal ocean waters 3,000 feet from the shoreline except for "some small areas adjacent to the mouth of the salmon streams."[71] These Indians had also abandoned fishing rights to most of the salmon trap sites by not objecting to the construction and operation of non-Indian canneries. Similarly, Hanna decided that the Haidas and Tlingits had, for the most part, abandoned their aboriginal rights to streams flowing into tidal waters, inland lakes, forests, and uplands used for hunting and trapping. The reduction in the Native population in recent years, he concluded, had prevented use of much of this disputed area which white settlers had acquired in good faith under Alaska's homestead laws. Furthermore, the Indians had forfeited their claim to many towns and villages when they moved to different locations and accepted the "larger benefits of gainful employment in the new commercial fishing industry."[72] Hanna agreed that the claimants owned those lands that had been held for generations by Indian families, but the evidence presented at the hearings made it difficult to "measure or even approximate" the exact boundaries of these holdings.[73] Hanna recommended that Congress investigate the validity of Indian land titles and authorize cash compensation for property lost to white settlers through government neglect. If Congress failed to act, Ickes should set aside a reasonable portion of land where continuous Indian occupancy was apparent.[74]

Fowler Harper, the solicitor of the Interior Department, disagreed with Hanna's assertion that a congressional investigation was necessary.[75] Instead, he urged Ickes to use the factual data found in the 2,700 pages of testimony obtained at the hearings to establish administratively the precise boundaries of Indian possessions. Ickes's determinations could then be forwarded to Congress which could create reservations and provide compensation for the "cession of any areas in excess of those reserved for Indian occupancy.[76] The Secretary decided to follow Harper's advice because the Hanna report was "much less favorable to the Indians" than he had expected.[77]

On July 27, 1945, Ickes released a legal opinion (prepared by the associate solicitor Felix S. Cohen) which held that the evidence presented at the hearings made it possible for the government to recognize as valid eight percent of the Indians' land claims.[78] He reserved 101,000 acres for Hydaburg; 95,000 acres for Klawock; and 77,000 acres for Kake. These lands, he ruled, could be set aside by "mutual consent" of the Indians and the federal government.[79] While the Indians had failed to prove exclusive possession to ninety-two percent of their claims, Ickes acknowledged, they had not abandoned the right to hunt, fish, and trap in those areas so long as the lands remained part of the public domain. Ickes promised to decide in the future whether the inhabitants of Kake and Klawock owned 2,008,000 acres, including all of Kuiu Island, after nearby Indian bands who were not represented at the departmental hearings presented their claims. Nor did these adjudications prevent the Indians from asking the Court of Claims for compensation due to "past invasions of their property rights."[80]

The Haidas and Tlingits of Hydaburg, Kake, and Klawock were not entirely satisfied with Ickes's decision, and in September 1945 they petitioned the Interior Department for a rehearing of their claims. At the new hearings they argued that the government had erred in not confirming their possessory rights to 1,120 acres of gardens, smokehouses, homes, cemeteries, and cannery facilities at Hunters Bay and Rose Inlet. In January 1946, Ickes agreed that most of their claims were justified, and he awarded them an additional 800 acres.[81] He also concluded that the three villages owned nearby beaches down to the low-tide mark. This meant that fish traps which were anchored on Indian land could be operated only "with the consent" of the Natives.[82]

Ickes did not succeed in establishing reservations on the land he had awarded to the Indians of southeastern Alaska before he resigned from office in February 1946.[83] The effort had never gained widespread Native support because government officials underestimated the extent of the Americanization of Alaska's aboriginal inhabitants. Christian missionaries and educators had successfully changed the lives and thought of many Natives.[84] Moreover, the imbalance between white males and females on the Alaska frontier accelerated the process of acculturation. As early as the 1930s, every fourth individual in the Native population had mixed blood.[85]

Instead of carefully studying the social implications of contemporary Native culture, New Deal reformers imposed their ideas of social justice on the Aleuts, Eskimos, and Indians. The Alaska Reorganization Act was drafted without Native input, and when many Natives resisted the creation of reservations, the Interior Department issued legal rulings that enabled the Secretary of the Interior to set aside extensive areas of land and water. This well-intentioned policy led to confusion within the Roosevelt administration, a premature dismissal of Haida and Tlingit claims, and increased tension between the territory's Native and white residents.

In retrospect, it seems to have been a mistake to attempt a settlement of Native hunting and fishing rights without the full cooperation of Congress and the Justice Department. Whites refused to accept the validity of Interior Department rulings which threatened the economic development of the territory and its progress toward statehood. They continued to oppose the creation of reservations through complicated litigation in the federal courts.[86] In 1946, Congress undercut the authority of the executive branch of the government to determine Native claims when it authorized the establishment of the Indian Claims Commission.[87] The Natives of Alaska would have to wait another twenty-five years before the Claims Commission and Congress resolved the questions that had surfaced during the New Deal debate over aboriginal rights.

NOTES

1. The activities of John Collier before he became commissioner are discussed in Kenneth R. Philp, *John Collier's Crusade for Indian Reform, 1920–1954* (Tucson, 1977), pp. 1–112.

2. William Zimmerman, Jr., "The Role of the Bureau of Indian Affairs since 1933," *Annals of the American Academy of Political and Social Science* 311 (May 1957): 31–32.

3. See Angie Debo, *A History of the Indians of the United States* (Norman, 1970), pp. 322–23; Lawrence C. Kelly, "The Indian Reorganization Act: The Dream and the Reality," *Pacific Historical Review* 44 (1975): 291–312; Philp, *John Collier's Crusade*, pp. 183–84; Graham D. Taylor, "The Tribal Alternative to Bureaucracy: The Indian New Deal," *Journal of the West* 13 (1974): 128–42; and Michael Smith, "The Indian New Deal," *Journal of the West* 10 (1971): 521–34.

4. Throughout this essay the term *Native* is used to include the Eskimos and Aleuts who are distinct from the Athabascan, Tlingit, Haida, and Tsimshian Indians. Felix S. Cohen, *Handbook of Federal Indian Law* (1942; reprint ed., Albuquerque, 1972), p. 401.

5. June Helm, *The Indians of the Subarctic: A Critical Bibliography* (Bloomington, 1976), pp. 1–91, and Ted C. Hinckley, "Researching Alaska's Pioneer Years, 1867–1912," *Journal of the West* 16 (1977): 52–62 provide bibliographical information about the impact of white settlement in Alaska.

6. U.S. Congress, Senate, Subcommittee of the Committee on Interior and Insular Affairs, *Hearings on S. 2037, Repeal Act Authorizing the Secretary of Interior to Create Indian Reservations in Alaska*, 80th Cong., 2d sess. (1948), pp. 44, 53–56; Ernest Gruening, *The State of Alaska* (New York, 1954), pp. 355–63; and Ted C. Hinckley, "Presbyterian Leadership in Pioneer Alaska," *Journal of American History* 52 (1966): 751.

7. Glenn Smith, "Education for the Natives of Alaska: The Work of the United States Bureau of Education, 1884–1931," *Journal of the West* 6 (1967): 440.

8. David E. Conrad, "Emmons of Alaska," *Pacific Northwest Quarterly* 69 (1978): 54, 57–58.

9. Ibid., pp. 59–60.

10. H. Dewey Anderson and Walter Crosby Eells, *Alaska Natives: A Survey of Their Sociological and Educational Status* (Stanford, 1935), pp. 5–6, 211–12.

11. Philp, *John Collier's Crusade*, p. 159.

12. *New York Times*, May 30, 1953, p. 15.

13. William Zimmerman, memorandum for Secretary Harold L. Ickes, Nov. 16, 1944, Commissioner's Files, 1933–1953, National Archives, Record Group 48, Washington National Records Center, Suitland, Md. (hereafter referred to as RG 48, NA).

14. Merle Colby, *A Guide to Alaska: Last American Frontier* (New York, 1942), p. 44.

15. Ibid., pp. 126–27; and Rita Singer, memorandum for Felix S. Cohen, Nov. 11, 1944, Records of the Solicitor's Office, Alaska Native Rights, RG 48, NA.

16. Philip Drucker, *The Native Brotherhoods: Modern Intertribal Organizations on the Northwest Coast* (Washington, D.C., 1958), pp. 16–22.

17. Useful accounts of Sheldon Jackson's work among the Natives of Alaska are Ted C. Hinckley, "Sheldon Jackson as Preserver of Alaska's Native Culture," *Pacific Historical Review* 33 (1964): 411–24; Hinckley, "Presbyterian Leadership in Pioneer Alaska," pp. 742–56; Dorothy Jean Ray, "Sheldon Jackson and the Reindeer Industry of Alaska," *Journal of Presbyterian History* 43 (1965): 71–99; and Glenn Smith, "Education for the Natives of Alaska," pp. 440–45.

18. Drucker, *The Native Brotherhoods*, pp. 41, 51–57.

19. Ibid., pp. 34–39.

20. William L. Paul to John Collier, April 1, 1935, Interior Department, Records of the Solicitor's Office, Alaska Native Rights, RG 48, NA.

21. Theodore H. Haas, *Ten Years of Tribal Government under I.R.A.* (Washington, D.C., 1977), p. 42

22. Ibid., pp. 29–30.

23. Senate Subcommittee on Interior and Insular Affairs, *Hearings on S. 2037*, pp. 146–49.

24. Ibid., pp. 75–79; *Constitution and By-Laws of the Native Village of Barrow, March 21, 1940* (Washington, D.C., 1941), pp. 1–3.

25. U.S. Congress, House, Committee on Appropriations, *Hearings on the Interior Department Appropriation Bill for 1941*, 76th Cong., 3d sess. (1940), pt. II, p. 191.

26. *Corporate Charter of the Village of Barrow, March 21, 1940* (Washington, D.C., 1941), pp. 1–2.

27. Senate Subcommittee on Interior and Insular Affairs, *Hearings on S. 2037*, pp. 110, 190–91.

28. Ibid., pp. 92–95.

29. Gruening, *State of Alaska*, p. 400.

30. Senate Subcommittee on Interior and Insular Affairs, *Hearings on S. 2037*, pp. 74, 110–11, 200–209.

31. Nathan Margold, memorandum for Ickes, Sept. 14, 1937, Interior Department, Solicitor's Office, Administrative Correspondence Files, RG 48, NA.

32. Ickes, memorandum to the Commissioner of Indian Affairs, Sept. 16, 1937, ibid.

33. Margold, memorandum for Ickes, Sept. 14, 1937, ibid.

34. Ibid.

35. Warner W. Gardner, memorandum for the Assistant Secretary, Jan. 23, 1943, ibid.

36. Maxine Block, ed., *Current Biography* (New York, 1941), pp. 426–28; and Ickes, "The Federal Senate and Indian Affairs," *Illinois Law Review* 24 (1930): 577.

37. *New York Times*, Oct. 20, 1953, p. 29; "Felix S. Cohen," *Nation* 177 (Dec. 19, 1953): 538; and Cohen, *Handbook of Federal Indian Law*, pp. vii–xi.

38. Paul H. Douglas, "A Sharp Tongue, a Hot Temper and a Tender Heart: A Recollection of Harold L. Ickes," *New Republic* 129 (Dec. 21, 1953): 14–15; Claude R. Wickard to the Secretary of the Interior, Feb. 5, 1945, office files of Oscar L. Chapman, 1933–1953, Alaska, RG 48, NA.

39. Senate Subcommittee on Interior and Insular Affairs, *Hearings on S. 2037*, pp. 415–16.

40. Ibid.

41. Ibid., p. 13.

42. Ibid., pp. 9–13; Oscar L. Chapman, memorandum for the Secretary, April 27, 1943, office files of Oscar L. Chapman, 1933–1953, Indians-Alaska, RG 48, NA.

43. Senate Subcommittee on Interior and Insular Affairs, *Hearings on S. 2037*, p. 13.

44. Ibid.

45. Ibid., pp. 50, 371; and Anderson and Eells, *Alaska Natives*, pp. 206–207.

46. For background material on the reindeer controversy, consult James and Catherine Brickey, "Reindeer: Cattle of the Arctic," *Alaska Journal* 5 (1975): 16–24; Hinckley, "Sheldon Jackson as Preserver of Alaska's Native Culture," pp. 411–24; Carl J. Lomen, *Fifty Years in Alaska* (New York, 1954), pp. 275–98; James R. Shortridge, "The Alaskan Agricultural Empire: An American Agrarian Vision, 1898–1929," *Pacific Northwest Quarterly* 69 (1978): 153–55; Ray, "Sheldon Jackson and the Reindeer Industry of Alaska," pp. 71–99; and Ray, *The Eskimos of the Bering Strait, 1650–1898* (Seattle, 1975), pp. 226–40.

47. House Committee on Appropriations, *Hearings on the Department of Interior Appropriation Bill for 1941*, Pt. II, pp. 465–66.

48. Drucker, *The Native Brotherhoods*, p. 52.

49. Gruening, *State of Alaska*, pp. 395–96; and Jonathan M. Steere, ed., "Alaska Natives Seek Justice," *Indian Truth* 21 (1944): 1.

50. Colby, *Guide to Alaska*, p. 49.

51. Ibid.; Matthew K. Sniffen, ed., "From Alaska," *Indian Truth* 9 (1932): 3.

52. Fowler Harper, memorandum for Chapman, April 27, 1944, office files of Oscar L. Chapman, 1933–1953, Indians-Alaska, RG 48, NA.

53. Felix S. Cohen, "Report to the Commissioner of Indian Affairs," July 10, 1944, ibid.

54. Press release (undated), Interior Department, Solicitor's Office, Alaska Native Rights, RG 48, NA.

55. Fowler Harper to George W. Folta, Sept. 2, 1944, ibid.

56. Ibid.; Senate Subcommittee on Interior and Insular Affairs, *Hearings on S. 2037*, pp. 459–60.

57. Harper, memorandum for Ickes, March 10, 1945, Interior Department, Solicitor's Office, Alaska Native Rights, RG 48, NA; and Senate Subcommittee on Interior and Insular Affairs, *Hearings on S. 2037*, pp. 434–35.

58. George W. Folta, Theodore H. Haas, and Kenneth R. L. Simmons, "Legal Brief, Proposed Findings of Fact, Conclusions of Law, and Recommendations of Petitioners," Sept. 1944, Interior Department, Solicitor's Office, Alaska Native Rights, RG 48, NA.

59. W. C. Arnold, "Supplemental Objection in the Matter of Hearings upon Claims of the Natives of Alaska Pursuant to the Provisions of Sections 201.21b," Sept. 15, 1944, ibid.

60. Stephen Carey, "Protest on Behalf of the Pacific Fisheries," Sept. 16, 1944, ibid.

61. J. F. Jurich, "Statement of the International Fishermen and Allied Workers of America," Sept. 16, 1944, ibid.

62. Homer Garvin, "Protest of the Juneau Chamber of Commerce against the

Establishment of Fishing Reservations Based on Aboriginal Claims," Aug. 31, 1944, ibid.

63. A. M. Spaeth, "Protest by the Ketchikan Chamber of Commerce to the Granting of Exclusive Use and Occupancy of Lands and Waters to Certain Indian Tribes," Sept. 28, 1944, ibid.

64. *New York Times*, June 27, 1974, p. 48; Charles Moritz, ed., *Current Biography* (New York, 1966), pp. 144–46; and Gruening, *The Battle for Alaska Statehood* (Seattle, 1967), pp. 1–2.

65. Gruening, memorandum for the Secretary of the Interior, Dec. 11, 1944, Interior Department, Central Files, 1937–1953, RG 48, NA.

66. Ibid.

67. Ickes to Gruening, Dec. 14, 1944, ibid.

68. Ibid.

69. Harper to Folta, Nov. 6, 1944, Solicitor's Office, Interior Department, Alaska Native Rights Hearings, RG 48, NA.

70. Haas to Zimmerman, Aug. 13, 1945, ibid.; Rita Singer, memorandum for Felix S. Cohen and Theodore H. Haas, Nov. 3, 1944; and Singer, interview with Father Cooper, Nov. 11, 1944, Solicitor's Office, Interior Department, General Correspondence Alaska, RG 48, NA.

71. Senate Subcommittee on Interior and Insular Affairs, *Hearings on S. 2037*, pp. 426–29.

72. Ibid.

73. Ibid., p. 431.

74. Ibid., pp. 432–33.

75. Harper, memorandum for Ickes, March 10, 1945, Interior Department, Solicitor's Office, Alaska Native Rights Hearings, RG 48, NA.

76. Ibid.

77. Harold L. Ickes, Diary, July 28, 1945, p. 9907, Library of Congress.

78. Senate Subcommittee on Interior and Insular Affairs, *Hearings on S. 2037*, p. 447; U.S. Dept. of the Interior press release, July 29, 1945, Interior Department, Solicitor's Office, Alaska Native Rights, RG 48, NA.

79. Senate Subcommittee on Interior and Insular Affairs, *Hearings on S. 2037*, pp. 436, 439.

80. Ibid., pp. 436, 440.

81. Ibid., p. 451.

82. Ibid., p. 452.

83. Ickes resigned because of a dispute with President Harry S. Truman over the appointment of Edwin Pauley as Under-Secretary of the Navy. Harry S. Truman, *Memoirs, 1945: Year of Decisions* (New York, 1965), pp. 608–609.

84. Hinckley, "The Presbyterian Leadership in Pioneer Alaska," pp. 749–50; Hinckley, *The Americanization of Alaska* (Palo Alto, 1972), pp. 113–17, 245–48; and Ray, *The Eskimos of the Bering Strait*, pp. 205–206, 241–53.

85. Anderson and Eells, *Alaska Natives*, pp. 105–106.

86. Haas to Assistant Secretary William Warne, June 28, 1949, Central Files, Interior Department, Alaska Native Rights, RG 48, NA.

87. The operation of the Indian Claims Commission is discussed in Ralph A.

Barney, "Some Legal Problems under the Indian Claims Commission Act," *Federal Bar Journal* 20 (1960): 235–39; Sandra C. Danforth "Repaying Historical Debts: The Indian Claims Commission," *North Dakota Law Review* 49 (1973): 359–403; Thomas Le Duc, "The Work of the Indian Claims Commission under the Act of 1946," *Pacific Historical Review* 26 (1961): 1–16; and Nancy Oestreich Lurie, "The Indian Claims Commission," *Annals of the American Academy of Political and Social Science* 436 (1978): 97–110.

Governor Ernest Gruening's Struggle for Territorial Status

Personal or Political?

CLAUS-M. NASKE

Professor Claus-M. Naske, senior member of the History Department at the University of Alaska at Fairbanks, has written a number of important studies furthering the understanding of Alaska history. His Interpretive History of Alaskan Statehood, *published in 1973, was republished in a revised edition in 1985 as* A History of Alaska Statehood *(Lanham, Md.: University Press of America). His biography of Delegate Bob Bartlett,* Edward Lewis "Bob" Bartlett of Alaska: A Life in Politics, *was published in 1980 (Fairbanks: University of Alaska Press). His popular text,* Alaska: A History of the 49th State, *written with Herman Slotnick and originally published in 1979, was published in a revised edition in 1987 (Norman: University of Oklahoma Press). He has published numerous articles on Alaska history.*

In the article reprinted here, Naske finds that Ernest Gruening was very concerned about demonstrating his administrative abilities when he first came to Alaska Territory as Governor in 1939. Gruening, who died in 1974, had been a journalist before he was appointed by Franklin Roosevelt as head of the new Division of Territories and Island Possessions in 1934. By 1939, it was clear to Roosevelt and other national leaders that the drive for Alaska statehood was not far off, and the President wanted a strong figure who could help lead the territory toward full self-government. Governor Gruening would serve with distinction during the war and through the turbulent postwar period of unprecedented population growth, stepping down in 1953. In 1958 he was elected one of the first U.S. Senators from Alaska and served until 1968.

This article appeared originally in *Journal of the West* 20 (January 1981): 32–40; it is reprinted here by permission.

In May of 1934, President Franklin D. Roosevelt by executive order created a new agency in the Department of the Interior, the Division of Territories and Island Possessions. This agency would supervise federal relations with outlying and dependent areas and also assist them in every possible way to compensate for their lack of voting representation in Congress.

After the agency was created, the President appointed Ernest Gruening to be the director. Gruening brought an impressive background to his new job. Graduated from Harvard Medical School in 1912, instead of practicing medicine, he pursued a career in journalism. After various newspaper jobs, he became editor and managing editor of *The Nation*. In his capacity as newspaperman, Gruening became acquainted with various New Deal personalities, including President Roosevelt. He caught the President's eye and in 1933 was appointed to serve as an adviser to the United States delegation at the Seventh Inter-American Conference at Montevideo. There he had a hand in fashioning the New Deal's policy toward Latin America.[1]

In his new position, Gruening quickly came into conflict not only with his superior, Secretary of the Interior Harold L. Ickes, but also with Rexford Guy Tugwell, who in 1934 had gone to Puerto Rico on orders from the President and formed a committee of local leaders, which became known as the President's Policy Committee on Puerto Rico. Tugwell was involved in setting up Puerto Rico development programs. Gruening was doing the same thing in his agency.[2] At that point the President, disliking conflict, apparently decided to kick Gruening upstairs and make him governor of Alaska.

It was not surprising that Gruening, with his background and ambition, came to Alaska determined to make something out of the territory, to demonstrate to the President his capabilities. Arriving in Alaska early in December of 1939, he took the oath of office in Juneau, the territory's capital, on 5 December. Almost immediately he discovered that the governor "has really very little power: that he may be able, if he handles himself correctly, to exercise a good deal of influence and leadership which apparently has been lacking." Gruening then and there determined to supply that leadership. There was no question at all that a man of his talents, ability, determination, drive, and ego would throw himself into his work—and lead Alaska superbly. It was equally clear that, in the process, he would disrupt established relationships, generating both intense dislike and admiration.[3]

Gruening also very soon discovered a number of Alaskan realities with which he had to deal. The first, and perhaps the most important, was the fact that Alaskans considered him an "Outsider." Although few whites had been born in the territory in those days, Alaskans carefully reminded each other of their length of residency in the North. The longer the stay, most believed, the more genuine was the honored term *pioneer* or *sourdough*. Alaska's Indians, Eskimos, and Aleuts were collectively known as Natives, but apparently could not become pioneers or sourdoughs, on the assumption, perhaps, that you cannot be either on your native ground. More basically, most white Alaskans shared American racial attitudes of the day, considering Natives to be inferior to whites.

The governor also quickly discovered Alaska's intense regionalism, fostered by vast distances and different modes of making a living. Gruening determined to do his part to break down this regionalism. He found that until his arrival, most governors, either by choice or necessity, had been content to stay in Juneau. Gruening decided to make the governor's office a highly visible one throughout the territory. He traveled widely and incessantly and interested himself in small as well as large problems, tackling all of them with singular gusto and enthusiasm. The governor, one acquaintance recalled, operated like a "trip hammer, he broke up everything that was in his way, he bored through, he had the determination of sixteen men, and a mind that was sharp and quick and ruthless." Once Gruening had made up his mind, he seldom changed it. He was a very athletic individual who, at times, exerted himself physically to the point of collapse, almost as if "to show his strength" to prospective opponents.[4] Gruening's swimming stunts in cold mountain lakes, his hiking expeditions with a string of panting and exhausted bureaucrats trying to keep up, and his fast tennis matches soon became legend in Alaska.

One of the first problems the governor tackled involved the discriminatory hiring practices of U.S. Navy defense contractors who engaged their labor through Seattle unions to the virtual exclusion of resident Alaskans. Gruening eventually carried his complaints to Secretary of the Navy Charles Edison, who ordered that contractor employment managers visit territorial towns at six-week intervals and hire Alaskans on the same basis as men from Seattle. Gruening then successfully persuaded the Army to forgo discriminatory practices in its defense construction program.[5]

Next the governor looked at municipal government management and finances and found both to be lacking. He convinced the Juneau City Council to contribute $2,400 in matching funds for the construction of a swimming pool financed by the Works Progress Administration. Gruening counseled the Sitka municipal government to reassess all property adequately in order to stave off financial collapse and purchase the city light and water services, a private monopoly which, although charging exorbitant rates, did not meet expanding needs.[6]

One of the governor's chief concerns was the modernization of the outdated and inadequate tax system. Gruening's predecessor, John W. Troy, had asked the territorial planning council to make a tax study in the late 1930s. The research was not completed until the fall of 1940. The authors of the report concluded that an annual revenue of $10 million was entirely feasible. They recommended the adoption of a modern tax system and urged that the revenue obtained be invested in a soundly planned and economically executed program of permanent improvements such as roads, schools, hospitals, and public buildings. Gruening enthusiastically endorsed these proposals, made them his own, and fully intended to push them through the legislature. The plan the governor presented to the 1941 legislature for adoption would abolish all obsolete mercantile taxes and license fees, imposing instead a very moderate income and profits tax, plus a nominal levy on property outside incorporated towns.[7]

Governor Gruening, however, had waded into deep water with his proposal for a streamlined tax system. The scheme immediately mobilized the ever-alert economic interests, such as the canning and mining industries, who were in no mood to relinquish their privileged status in Alaska. Many residents, depending for a livelihood on these industries, were unwilling to antagonize them. These feelings were reflected in the mood of the legislature which flatly rejected the governor's tax proposals in every legislative session between 1941 and 1947.

Although Gruening made many enemies in the territory rather quickly, he also won numerous friends. When renominated for another term in 1944, he was readily confirmed. When Harry S. Truman succeeded to the presidency after the death of Roosevelt, talk about a replacement for Gruening began to circulate in Washington. Two men were mentioned, both close Truman associates. Walter Walsh, who had received a Marine Corps commission at the beginning of the war with Truman's help, and Fred Canfil, a U.S. marshal in Kansas City who had actively worked in one of the new President's senate campaigns.[8]

In the meantime, Gruening called a special session of the legislature to convene in March of 1946. The purpose was to have measures enacted designed to aid Alaska's veterans. Meeting for thirty days, the legislators passed most of Gruening's proposals. And although the governor was pleased, he was alarmed by a senate memorial which asked the President and the new Secretary of the Interior, Julius A. Krug, "to remove the present governor from office with all possible dispatch." It passed the senate by a vote of nine to six. Thereupon Steve McCutcheon, a Gruening supporter in the Alaska house, introduced a long memorial praising Gruening unqualifiedly. It passed by a vote of sixteen to seven. "The opposition," Gruening confided to E. L. (Bob) Bartlett, Alaska's delegate to Congress, "are going to do everything to smear me in Washington." Bartlett, however, reassured the governor that he "should not attach any particular importance to any Senate memorial so far as its influence here [in Washington, D.C.] is concerned."[9]

Complaints about the governor, however, trickled into Washington. Walter P. Sharpe, the territorial commissioner of the Department of Labor told Robert E. Hennegan, the chairman of the Democratic National Committee, that the governor had done everything to split the Democratic Party in Alaska. "Put in anyone, but get rid of this 'pinko' who has no ties in Alaska," Sharpe counseled. The commissioner essentially resented the fact that Gruening made appointments based on ability rather than party affiliation. But despite sniping from various quarters, the governor survived in office. When talk about his replacement once again revived late in 1947, Bartlett persuaded Robert S. Allen of the *Boston Daily Globe* to analyze Gruening's predicament. Such an article, Bartlett hoped, might help to force the President's hand. On 30 January 1948 the *Globe* carried the piece entitled "Next on List of New Dealers to be Dropped by Truman?" Allen stated that Gruening, one of the few Roosevelt appointees still holding high office, had only an outside chance of being reappointed for another term. "As of now," Allen claimed, "President Truman does not intend to rename Gruening." That could change, he continued, because the governor had strong Alaskan backing as well as powerful administration support both in and out of Congress, including "equally powerful Democratic opposition," most of it centered in Washington State, particularly in Seattle. For years the governor had been at loggerheads with Seattle business and transportation interests, accusing them of exploiting the territory as if it were a colonial possession. Washington's Governor Mon Walgren and Seattle shipping and fishing magnate Nick Bez, both Truman cronies, led the opposition to Gruening. The President faced a dilemma, Allen concluded, for he needed West Coast support in the upcoming election. Replacing Gruening, however, would upset the New Dealers whose support he needed as well.[10]

It may have been the piece in the *Globe* which prodded Secretary Krug to see the President and urge the reappointment. In any event, on 12 March, Truman sent Gruening's name to the Senate Interior and Insular Affairs Committee for confirmation. Bartlett was happy. "I won't forget ever," he told Krug, "that you went to the White House today and successfully urged President Truman to reappoint our friend, Ernest Gruening, as Governor of Alaska. It was a noble stroke of work." Unhappily, however, an informal poll of the committee revealed that the Republican majority favored "pigeonholing action until after the November election." One Republican member of the committee succinctly summed up majority opinion. "Why should we give a Democrat—and an ardent New Deal Democrat at that—a four-year term when after the Presidential election we could put in a good Republican?"[11]

Territorial Republicans were not satisfied with mere delays. The *Fairbanks Daily News-Miner,* owned by Alaska's foremost entrepreneur "Cap" Austin E. Lathrop, long a Gruening opponent, urged that the governor be denied a third term. Lathrop argued that Gruening had enjoyed ample opportunities to prove himself as governor of Alaska, yet he had failed. Instead of fostering a sound legislative program for Alaska during the last five sessions, he had "tried to promote tax legislation which was not acceptable" to the lawmakers. As a result, the territory's finances "are now as near [to] complete disorganization as they have ever been." Even more disturbing, biennial territorial appropriations had increased from a modest $3,511,510 in the 1939–40 period, the last before Gruening took office, to a record $8,476,309 appropriation passed by the last legislature. In short, Gruening had attempted "to use the power and prestige of his office and the resources of the federal government to transfer to himself the initiative and law-making powers of the citizens."[12] Lathrop left unclear how the governor had appropriated to himself all of these powers. In fact, Lathrop's editorial was transparently self-serving, for he was a chief beneficiary of Alaska's totally inadequate tax system. His many enterprises, ranging from banks to motion picture theaters, and from construction companies to a coal mine, paid only negligible taxes to the territory.

In any event, the anti- and pro-Gruening forces quickly lined up for battle. While Lathrop urged his friends and associates to communicate their opposition to the Senate committee, the pro-Gruening forces similarly gathered support. Lathrop, for example, praised territorial senator Chas. D. Jones for the fine letter he had written to U.S. Senator Arthur H. Vandenberg, a member of the committee considering Gruening's confirmation. Lathrop was convinced that a sufficient number of protests had reached the Senators to convince them that "right or wrong, he [Gruening] has engendered so much bitterness and dissension in the Territory that very little of a constructive nature can be expected until there is a new governor." Foremost among Gruening's friends, Bartlett solicited support. Among many others, for example, he asked the Right Reverend John S. Bentley of the National Council of Protestant Churches to lend his help in the impending confirmation struggle.[13] Despite all the efforts, Senator Hugh Butler (R., Neb.) decided to allow Gruening's unconfirmed nomination to die.

In the meantime, however, territorial finances had run into trouble. On 31 December 1948 the general fund contained only $6,289.40, and the auditor held legitimate claims against the territory amounting to $758,209.59. It was only through individual and corporate pledges of $200,000 of interest-free loans, for example, that the doors of the University of Alaska had been kept open. Earlier on, the governor had rejected pleas for a special legislative session, hoping that angry citizens would vote delinquent legislators out of office. Gruening's hopes were largely fulfilled when Alaskans trooped to the polls in October and "threw the rascals out." At that point, the governor summoned the newly elected body, not the lame-duck legislature, into special session. Its only task was to consider the tax bills which territorial Attorney General Ralph Rivers had prepared in his capacity as legislative counsel. From the extraordinary session which convened on 6 January 1949 and the regular one which followed on 24 January there emerged, at long last, a basic tax system.[14]

The first element of the new system consisted of a territorial income tax based on ten percent of the federal tax. A property tax of one percent was credited against the municipal and school district assessments, thus avoiding duplication. At the same time the territorial legislature took over and streamlined the old system of license fees from the federal government. For each separate business an initial application fee of $25 was charged. Beyond the initial fee, a sum equal to one-half percent above $100,000 received during the income year was to be remitted to the territory. This levy applied to those concerns which, so far, had paid no monies whatever to the Alaska territorial government. These included steamship companies, air and bus lines, lighterage companies, banks and motion picture theaters, oil and construction companies, garages and service stations, newspapers, radio stations, and logging operations. Professional registration, examination and insurance levies were to be collected by the various professional boards. The legislature changed the tax on the fishing industry from a case tax to one based on the wholesale value of the pack, amounting to four percent of the value of the raw fish processed for salmon cannieries to one percent of the value of raw fish for herring-processing plants. Fishermen's license fees increased from $1 to $5 for residents, and from $25 to $50 for nonresidents. Fishing gear, such as traps, gill nets, and seines, was also taxed. Excise taxes on liquor were raised, and establishments serving alcohol were regulated by fees which varied from $75 to $5,000, according to the type of business, the size of the town, or the volume of the business. In addition, the usual motor fuel taxes, vehicle and drivers' licenses, and tobacco and various other miscellaneous taxes were modernized.[15]

Gruening was jubilant, and understandably so. It had been a long battle, finally crowned with victory. The special interests were furious. When word reached Alaska that Senator Joseph O'Mahoney (D., Wy.), the new chairman of the Committee on Interior and Insular Affairs, intended to hold hearings on Gruening's confirmation, a number of former legislators asked the committee to postpone any action until the territorial legislature had adjourned. Residents of Alaska, they telegraphed, should be given an opportunity "to present evidence and data supporting contention of many substantial citizens of territory that present governor's policies are not only definitely destructive to territorial development but will almost stop flow of badly needed investment capital from stateside sources." These disgruntled ex-legislators also asserted that the "present session being quarterbacked by governor is travesty of American tradition and legislative procedure."[16]

In the middle of March, the U.S. Senate appointed a subcommittee, headed by Clinton Anderson (D., N.M.) to investigate the various charges against the governor which had been accumulating in committee files. These charges ranged from bossism to the misuse of public funds, and from the refusal to permit an audit of territorial offices to furthering the spread of communism. Hearings on Gruening's confirmation were to be held on 1 April 1949. Cap Lathrop decided to charter a plane and take a number of witnesses to Washington, D.C., to oppose the governor. When this mission became known, Stanley McCutcheon, legislator, Gruening friend, and Anchorage attorney, gathered 44 individuals sympathetic to the governor and also chartered a plane so they could testify at the Washington hearings as well.[17]

Reactions to McCutcheon's flight were immediate. One Gruening foe advised the Senate committee to "carefully screen the bunch of political dregs named as holding reservations" and not to "let this lot of grafters stay in Washington too long because it will be shameful to stink up the atmosphere by their presence." The critic had unkind words for most of the pro-Gruening witnesses, alleging that one, for example, supported the governor only because he had a persecuted anti-Jewish feeling and was Jewish, while another was nothing more than a plain thief, another a tin-horn lawyer, a third a labor racketeer, while a fourth was a nice Eskimo who would vote for the governor if he could be kept sober that long, and the like.[18]

According to the *Washington Evening Star*, Gruening's supporters "whooped" into D.C. "aboard a giant airliner, dubbed 'Ship of State, our Skipper Gov. Gruening' to break the glad tidings that everything's fine up their way, that the territory has launched a great development program and is preparing to realize its manifest destiny." Despite the hoopla, the delegation did not make a ripple, there were no pictures in the papers, no names, in part because of competition from the cherry blossoms and the eleven delegations from overseas in town to sign the Atlantic Pact.[19]

When the hearings opened, all the prior publicity had filled the large caucus room in the Old Senate Office Building to capacity, including eleven out of the thirteen committee members. The anti-Gruening witnesses were the first to be heard. Frank Angerman, Fairbanks machinist and member of the territorial house, accused the governor of buttonholing legislators and trying to convince them to support his program. Senator Eugene Milliken (R., Colo.) asked if Angerman charged Gruening with corruption. Angerman replied in the negative. Was there any charge that Gruening lacked intelligence for the job, Milliken persisted? Again, the witness replied no. Was there any charge that the governor attempted to influence legislators other than by talk, Milliken persisted? "No, not to my knowledge," Angerman stated. Milliken asked the same or similar questions of the next two witnesses and received the same answers.[20]

George Miscovich, house member and a Fairbanks placer gold miner, accused the governor of building the most powerful political machine ever seen in Alaska. Through his appointive powers, Gruening doled out territorial jobs and promised political favors "to selected individuals irrespective of party." This had practically destroyed the two-party system in Alaska. Perhaps worse, Gruening was attempting to establish a planned economy and was also encouraging radical elements. Milliken asked if Miscovich challenged Gruening's patriotism. Miscovich replied that he "certainly would like to, although I am not familiar with the routine procedure, and I do not know that it would be my duty to do it." Senator Bert Miller (D., Idaho) thereupon admonished witnesses to confine themselves to facts about Gruening's fitness for office.[21]

Charles D. Jones of Nome charged the chief executive with lobbying for his legislative program, and when that failed, "he plies the legislators with cocktails and cultured conversation in the Governor's Mansion amid surroundings more luxurious than most of these unpretentious Alaskans from mining and fishing communities and Eskimo villages have ever seen before." Jones then discarded his prepared statement and told the committee that this language was not his own, that the testimony had been prepared for him by Lathrop's secretary, and that he would "like to talk just as I talk." Encouraged by Senator Anderson, Jones stated that Gruening "takes them up and gives them plenty of booze and lots of conversation. Let me tell you, brother, the way he is throwing it out, you know, we have an expression, that what he peddles makes the grass grow green on the Kougarok. He's got it. Dairy farmers know what it is."[22]

Lathrop testified that Gruening had failed miserably as governor. "Never in my fifty-three years in Alaska have I seen the strife between parties and within parties, the friction between labor and capital, and the class and racial hatred that exists today—largely because of Gruening's leadership." Lathrop charged that the governor's policies, "almost without exception, have been motivated by personal or political considerations—certainly not by a constructive and sincere interest in Alaska." Lathrop stated that Gruening was a very intelligent and fine man, "I like Governor Gruening in many respects. I like him because I get ideas as well by talking with him." The rest of the opposition witnesses elaborated on various points, contending that the governor's opposition to absentee ownership and vested interests had prevented risk capital from coming into Alaska; that he used dictatorial methods; and that he campaigned with Alaska Native Service officials among the Natives, asking them to support his favored candidates for the territorial legislature. To a man, the seven witnesses asked the committee not to inflict Governor Gruening on Alaska for yet another term.[23]

Nine out of the forty-four Gruening supporters next testified. Their spokesman, Stanley McCutcheon, claimed that his group represented a cross-section of Alaskan citizens. All asserted that Gruening had been a good, progressive governor who had the interests of the people at heart. They all approved of the tax program which just had become law. The added revenue was urgently needed for the rehabilitation of the school system and public health program and the expansion of various other vitally needed territorial activities. In short, the governor had transformed Alaska from a wilderness to a thriving and progressive community in the brief span of nine years.[24]

The opposition witnesses had been given the lion's share of the available time, but they had not used it to advantage. The seven were frequently put on the defensive chiefly by the Republican members of the committee. Impatient at times because of the piddling criticism offered, Senator Milliken repeatedly had asked if there had been any corruption in the Gruening administration? The answer had always been negative. Bartlett, although he did not speak, "spiritually rallied" to Gruening's side when the opposition testified, but then "became almost acutely ill to [my] stomach when the proponents had their turn," because they were so lavish and uncritical in their praise of Gruening. Nothing the proponents could have done, however, could have been "so infantile as the opposition," Bartlett remarked, for "they were stupid, no less."[25]

After the witnesses had been heard, the committee asked the governor to take the stand. Gruening denied all charges. He stated that he had pressed for the enactment of his program for the development of Alaska but that he had much less influence over the legislature than was generally assumed. In fact, Alaska's appointed governor had less power than even his Hawaiian counterpart. All important territorial officials were elected, not appointed, and therefore wholly independent of the governor. Finally, Gruening stated that it was his duty to tell Alaskans what he thought. The legislature had the responsibility to modify, adopt, or reject his views. With that, the hearings concluded late in the evening.[26]

The following Monday, 4 April, the territorial house representative Robert Hoopes, a Fairbanks filling station operator, filed a statement with the committee accusing Governor Gruening of having gone to England in the 1920s at the behest of the Mexican government to stir up British miners in the interest of world revolution. On his return from England, Hoopes asserted, Gruening again visited Mexico City and reported to President P. Elias Calles. Shortly thereafter, according to documents in Hoopes's possession, the Mexican government transmitted some $350,000 in two payments to England to aid the cause of communism. Hoopes also asserted that Gruening had received $10,000 from the Mexicans for his services.[27]

The committee thereupon decided to hold an executive session on 6 April to give Gruening an opportunity to respond to these new charges.

The governor told the senators that the document was a forgery and had been exposed as such. Gruening admitted that he had gone to Mexico in the fall of 1922 assigned to write articles for *Collier's* and other magazines. He had stayed in Mexico about six months and had become very interested in the country. Realizing that no book existed which answered all of his questions, he therefore decided to write such a volume and began the project after returning to the United States. Soon aware, however, that he had insufficient materials, he laid aside his notes and did not start again until 1924 when President-elect Calles had returned from Europe to Mexico and made an official visit to Washington, D.C. Calles invited Gruening and others to attend his inauguration. Gruening went, and his interest in the country was rekindled. During the next three years he spent approximately a year in Mexico working on his book. In 1927 Gruening had completed his research and went to Portland, Maine, where he started a daily newspaper and wrote the book in his spare time. In the late fall of 1928 a friend told him that the New York Hearst papers had published on their front pages a photostatic reproduction of the letter Hoopes had given to the committee. Gruening immediately contacted Hearst and the editor of the *New York Evening Journal* and pointed out that the document was a forgery and grossly libelous and demanded a retraction. No retraction was forthcoming, however, and a few days later the paper published a series of photostatic letters purporting to show that four United States senators had received $25,000 each for conducting propaganda in favor of the Calles government.[28]

Thereupon the United States Senate of the day ordered an investigation which showed the documents to be forgeries. The Hearst press, however, did not retract in Gruening's case, whereupon he sued. After some time, Hearst settled out of court, paid Gruening $75,000, and published retractions in his papers. Furthermore, Gruening told the senators, he never went to England on an assignment for President Calles or anyone else—he merely went to Europe in 1926 to join his wife and three sons.[29]

It did not take the committee very long to recommend Gruening's reappointment by unanimous vote, and the Senate confirmed it by a voice vote. As noted, the opposition to the governor had brought no substantial charges; in fact, his opponents had made fools of themselves. But Gruening's supporters were far too lavish in their praise of his performance. The governor, however, acquitted himself superbly before the senators. An eloquent speaker and a man of substantial achievements, Gruening totally demolished his opposition with his arguments. He had pointed out to the committee that many of the people who protested his confirmation had been retired from public life only because they had opposed his program—a decision made by the voters. Furthermore, the principal issue of the 1948 campaign in Alaska had involved the adoption of a tax program which the governor had urged since 1941. In 1948 Alaskans had decided the issue in favor of the governor by electing a legislature which had enacted the Gruening tax program.

Jack E. Eblen, a student of territorial government, has stated that the job of territorial governor was a difficult one in "which success might assure a bright future, and failure, oblivion." Territorial governors symbolized an often detested system of colonial government and had very limited powers. A governor's ability to adapt and succeed in the office, Eblen asserted, could be "measured roughly by the length of his tenure. It took an unusually capable man to be effective, either as a leader or as an administrator." Gruening held office for more than thirteen years, from 1939 to 1953. Only Benjamin F. Pott, governor of Montana from 1870 to 1883, equaled that.[30] Gruening presided over a complex and difficult territory during a crucial period in its development. By any test, he was a very competent administrator and capable leader. Alaskans rewarded his service when they elected him one of their two United States senators after the territory had become the 49th state in 1958.

In conclusion, Gruening's quest for territorial status was both political and personal. He certainly wanted to demonstrate his capabilities as an administrator to his superiors. At the same time, as the Alaska statehood movement gained momentum in the postwar period, the governor probably had his heart set on a U.S. Senate seat from Alaska.

NOTES

1. Sherwood Ross, *Gruening of Alaska* (New York: Best Books, Inc., 1968), pp. 77–89.
2. Rexford Guy Tugwell, *The Stricken Land: The Story of Puerto Rico* (New York: Greenwood Press, Publishers, 1968), pp. 5, 71.
3. Ernest Gruening Diary, December 5, 1939, Ernest Gruening Papers, University of Alaska Archives, Fairbanks.
4. Interview with Doris Steward, April 6, 1975, Sequim, Washington.
5. Ernest Gruening, *Many Battles: The Autobiography of Ernest Gruening* (New York: Liveright, 1973), pp. 278–90.
6. Ibid., pp. 288–94.

7. Gruening to John F. Wiese, October 4, 1944, General Correspondence File, 1909–53, Alaska Territorial Governor, Federal Records Center, Seattle.

8. E. L. Bartlett to Gruening, May 26, 1945, E. L. Bartlett Papers, General Correspondence File, Ernest Gruening, 1944–45, box 11, UA Archives.

9. Gruening, *Many Battles*, pp. 334–41; Gruening to Bartlett, March 29, 1946, Bartlett to Gruening, April 1, 1946, Bartlett Papers, General Correspondence File, Gruening, 1946, box 9.

10. Bartlett to Gruening, February 5, 1948, Bartlett Papers, General Correspondence File, Gruening, 1948, Box 10; *Boston Daily Globe*, January 30, 1948.

11. Bartlett to Julius Krug, March 12, 1948, Bartlett Papers, General Correspondence File, Gruening, 1948, box 10; *Daily Alaska Empire*, March 15, 1948.

12. *Fairbanks Daily News-Miner*, March 15, 1948.

13. A. E. Lathrop to Chas. D. Jones, March 29, 1948, Correspondence 1948, Jan.–June, File 8, box 1, Chas. D. Jones Collection, UA Archives; Bartlett to John S. Bentley, April 2, 1948, Bartlett Papers, General Correspondence File, Gruening, 1948, box 10.

14. Alaska Legislature, House, *Journal*, 1949, p. 49: Gruening, *Many Battles*, p. 348; *Daily Alaska Empire*, June 24, 1949; *Anchorage Daily Times*, December 18, 1948.

15. 63 Stat. 694; 62 Stat. 302: Alaska, *Session Laws*, 1949, Extraordinary Session, pp. 54–56, Regular Session, pp. 136, 30–33, 205–206, 254.

16. Joe Coble to Hugh Butler, March 7, 1949, Gruening Papers, File Pearson, Drew, 1949, box 11-A.

17. Memorandum to Senators Anderson et al. from S. French, counsel, Interior and Insular Affairs Committee, March 22, 1949, in author's files; Bartlett to Gruening March 21, 1949, Stanley McCutcheon to Bartlett, March 28, 1949, Bartlett Papers, General Correspondence File, Gruening, 1949, box 10.

18. Anonymous to Hugh Butler, March 24, 1949, Gruening Papers, box 34-A, UA.

19. *Washington Evening Star*, April 5, 1949.

20. *Nomination of Dr. Ernest Gruening to be Governor of Alaska, April 1, 1949, Hearings held before the U.S. Senate Committee on Interior and Insular Affairs* (Washington, D.C.: Ward & Paul, 1949), vol. 1, pp. 2–15. Hereafter referred to as *Hearings*.

21. *Hearings*, pp. 16–28.

22. Ibid., pp. 65–85.

23. Ibid., pp. 98–140; *Ketchikan Daily News*, April 14, 1949.

24. *Hearings*, pp. 141–99.

25. Bartlett to Hugh Wade, April 7, 1949, to Herb Hilscher, April 5, 1949, Bartlett Papers, General Correspondence File, Hugh Wade, 1945–51, Herb Hilscher, 1949, boxes 25 and 10.

26. *Daily Alaska Empire*, April 2, 1949.

27. Ibid., April 5, 1949.

28. *Hearings*, vol. 2, pp. 277–311.

29. Ibid.

30. Jack Ericson Eblen, *The First and Second United States Empires* (Philadelphia: University of Pennsylvania Press, 1968), pp. 271–85.

The Realities of Strategic Planning

The Decision to Build the Alaska Highway

M. V. BEZEAU

In 1982, while serving as Head of the Directorate of History for the Canadian defense ministry, M. V. Bezeau participated in a 40th Anniversary Symposium on the Alaska Highway at Northern Lights College in Fort St. John, British Columbia, near the beginning of the highway. The symposium, organized by Curtis Nordman, presented papers by a number of scholars on all aspects of the history of the road that connects the North with the Outside.

Bezeau challenged a particularly tenacious northern misconception in his article dealing with the decision to construct the road—that it was a supply road needed by the military to support the defense of the North. The prewar British Columbian Premier T. D. Patullo had for many years pushed for a northern road as a way to encourage development in the northern tier of his province. But he had met with a cool reception both in Ottawa and in Washington, D.C., where he also went to enlist support. The Ottawa government was not eager to spend the money which such a venture would cost and not happy about the implications for Canadian sovereignty of a road across Canada to connect two U.S. areas. On the other hand, while some officials in Washington were enthusiastic, the American military saw the project as unnecessary and too far outside its defense mission to be justifiable.

The onset of World War II changed some minds. But as Bezeau points out, the road was not intended as a supply route; it was too primitive, problematical, and unreliable for such use. Moreover, the American military only grudgingly gave approval to the project, and then only on the condition that its construction would divert no military resources needed for the war effort.

At first glance, the strategic reasons for building the Alaska Highway appear obvious. On December 7, 1941, the Japanese attacked Pearl Harbor, Hawaii,

This article appeared originally in Kenneth Coates, ed., *The Alaska Highway: Papers of the 40th Anniversary Symposium* (Vancouver: University of British Columbia Press, 1985), pp. 25–35; it is reprinted here by permission.

and destroyed a large part of the U.S. Navy's Pacific Fleet. American territorial vulnerability immediately increased, especially in the North. Although the Great Circle route, the shortest distance linking Tokyo with the west coast of the United States, passed through the Aleutian Islands, American military planners earlier had concluded that a road to Alaska had little military value. Now, facing a greatly increased threat, they declared that a land link was imperative. Both American and Canadian authorities approved the construction of a highway as a defensive measure. These facts seem to indicate that the military recommendation to build the road stemmed from a careful strategic reassessment of changing defense requirements under wartime conditions. In reality, it did not.

For many years prior to the outbreak of the Second World War, various Canadians and Americans advocated construction of a road to Alaska. They stressed economic and developmental advantages but also noted the possible value of such a road for defense.[1] In response, the United States War Department repeatedly examined these suggestions and rejected them. From a military point of view, the strategic areas of Alaska were the Panhandle, the south coast, the Alaska Peninsula, and the Aleutian Islands. These all lay near ocean transport and probable air routes. Other areas had low temperatures and poor communications which made year-round operations difficult. The sea lanes connecting all the valued areas were shorter in both time and distance than any highway route. Moreover, the proposed roads did not provide links to such areas as the Alaska Peninsula and could not do so to Kodiak, Unalaska, and other islands where important installations were located. Thus, sea transport would be required in any case. The navy saw little likelihood of any permanent interruption to sea communications in the event of war with Japan. Shipping could be in short supply in an emergency, but this was more quickly corrected by new marine construction than by building a road. Hence, the defensive value of a highway to Alaska was "negligible," and construction on the basis of military necessity alone was unjustified and unsupportable.[2] The Canadian-American Permanent Joint Board on Defense (P.J.B.D.) reached similar conclusions on 15 November 1940.[3]

Of course, military communications to Alaska could not be, and were not, ignored. Primary reliance was placed on the sea, but air routes were developed along the coast and from the prairie interior. The prairie link, the Northwest Staging Route, was especially important since it avoided the poorer coastal weather, was removed from potential enemy interruption, and was connected to the continental heartland. The staging route originated in 1935 with a Canadian Department of Transport survey for a Great Circle air route to the Orient. The line from Edmonton to Alaska was chosen, and airfield sites were selected at Grande Prairie, Fort St. John, and Fort Nelson, B.C., and Watson Lake and Whitehorse, Yukon. Survey parties were in the field when the European war broke out in September 1939. With the British Commonwealth Air Training Plan and other expanded air force construction about to begin, consideration was given to ending the program. It was decided, however, that if the U.S. were to enter the war, the strategic value of the airfields would increase, so work continued. By September 1941, the route was considered usable in daylight, and radio range stations were operational along its Canadian length by the end of the year.[4]

During this construction, but unrelated to it, a new move was launched in the U.S. House of Representatives to build a highway north. On 5 February 1941, Delegate Anthony J. Dimond of Alaska introduced Bill HR 3095 to construct a road along a route to be selected by the president.[5] The army's War Plans Division was asked to examine the issue once more, and it concluded that there still appeared to be little military justification for constructing a land route to the north. The division recommended, as it had before, that the bill not be considered favorably in the interests of national defense.[6] This staff work took time, however, and was not finished until early June. By then the strategic balance was about to undergo a dramatic change.

On 22 June 1941, Hitler launched a massive invasion of the U.S.S.R., slicing easily and deeply into Soviet territory, and the great Russian empire trembled. In the Far East, Japan was an Axis power, allied with Germany and Italy for mutual aid and assistance since the previous September. Although Japan had also signed a neutrality treaty with the Soviet Union in April 1941, the United States had no guarantee that the German attack would not ultimately lead to a Japanese presence in Siberia if the Soviet armies collapsed. Prudence seemed necessary, at least until the situation became clearer.[7]

Two days after the German invasion, the American chief of staff, Gen. Marshall, returned the War Plans Division's report. "In view of recent developments in the international situation," he advised, a highway was "desirable as a long range defense measure, providing this construction is controlled so as not to delay or interfere with other more pressing military construction requirements." Marshall directed that the report "be rewritten to interpose no objection to the passage of the authorization bill."[8] This new War Department position was subsequently passed to the House Committee on Roads. A recommendation which mentioned "certain military limitations" which justified only "a low priority" and merely interposed "no further objection" was scarcely a ringing endorsement of quick construction.[9] Nonetheless, it was a significant shift from clear opposition to gentle support and helped ensure that the issue did not die.

A few short months later, the Japanese attacked Pearl Harbor, and the United States was at war. Delegate Dimond and others now pressed William Cartwright, the chairman of the House Committee on Roads, to give active consideration to the bill. In turn, Cartwright solicited departmental views and on 6 January asked the War Department if the changing international situation now increased the military importance of the road.[10] The War Plans Division referred the request to the G-4 staff, responsible for logistics, noting in passing that the division now felt that conditions justified more active support than before.[11]

Meanwhile, other departments were also concerned with the highway proposal. On 16 January, Secretary Ickes of the Department of the Interior raised the issue at a cabinet meeting. President Roosevelt, who had previously gone on record as favoring an early route survey, was interested, and cabinet sentiment was generally favorable. Roosevelt appointed Secretaries Stimson (war), Knox (navy), and Ickes as a committee to "agree on the necessity for a road and the proper route."[12] Since the matter was then being studied by the War Department, a meeting of the committee was delayed until the army's in-house assessment was complete and its expert opinion obtained.[13]

The critical moment for a professional military contribution had arrived. Soldiers are carefully trained to make staff estimates—"appreciations of the situation" in Canadian terminology—and to weigh all factors, such as the enemy threat and considerations of time and distance, before giving their balanced conclusions. The G-4 staff's procedure was less dispassionate but perhaps more interesting.

The House Roads Committee's request, with the War Plans Division's note, went to the Transportation Branch, which would be responsible for the effective use of the highway if built. The branch disagreed with giving more active support to the bill. To do so without also giving funds, manpower, and other resources, it argued, would be ineffectual, while allocating these would only divert scarce assets. The branch strongly suggested that the immediate needs of higher priority projects meant that more support was unjustified.[14]

This advice led to some soul-searching within the G-4's staff. The War Department, it felt, was now forced to take a definite stand on the issue. The Transportation Branch's opinion, if accepted, would reverse the chief of staff's 1941 position, repeated by the secretary of war, that highway construction should no longer be opposed, and this in spite of the fact that the international situation had since deteriorated. On the other hand, it was argued, a road would eventually have to be built to Alaska anyway, and "it could be started now in the interests of the national defense," even if this meant "diverting materials and machinery from other necessary important road projects." Under the current wartime circumstances, Canada could be expected to look favorably on the project but might not do so later. Accordingly, it was recommended that the War Department "take advantage of the present war to secure the necessary agreements from Canada to start work now and finish perhaps many years to come."[15]

Col. A. R. Wilson, the author of this recommendation, drafted a carefully worded reply, which was repeated to the War Plans Division.[16] He wrote:

> It is believed that hearings should be scheduled on this Bill as early a date as practicable . . . construction of a highway to Alaska . . . is a desirable undertaking to initiate. However, the amount of work to be undertaken at the present time or in the immediate future depends upon a careful evaluation of the amount of machinery, material, engineering talent, labor and funds which can be diverted from other national defense projects which may be more important.
>
> The Bill should provide that no unit of work should be started or no funds appropriated . . . until approval has been obtained from the War and Navy Departments and the necessary priorities board.[17]

This reply seemed "generally favorable" to the division, which had a predisposition toward more active support. To the chief of staff, the division noted that increased Alaskan garrisons and the possibility of enemy interference with water routes indicated a greater need for an alternate land route for supplies and reinforcements. The road should follow the line of the Northwest Staging Route airfields in order to supply them and to support additional airfield construction.[18] The proposal now had a life of its own.

A subsequent War Plans Division draft paper clearly spelled out the army's position. It acknowledged that the cost of the highway in man hours, equipment, and supplies would be greater than the same expenditure for an equivalent amount of transport ship building; that the estimated construction time of two years made the road "unavailable in the present emergency"; and that the road would not reach vital installations such as Kodiak, Dutch Harbor, and Sitka—all of which would still need sea transport. Nevertheless, the division concluded, somewhat unconvincingly, that the security of a supply line to the central portion of Alaska outweighed all disadvantages. It recommended that the highway be authorized.[19] The gist of this paper was passed orally to the secretary of war on 2 February.[20]

By then, both Stimson and Knox had also received the State Department's opinion. They were told that the highway would have to be negotiated with Canada, but "if the United States Government really wanted it, Canada would accede." Route selection was left to the expert opinion of the army engineers, but since a road would be needed to ease northwest airfield supply difficulties, that route seemed logical: a choice, it was noted, which would "break the hearts of the politicians in our Pacific Northwest." The State Department deliberately refused to advise on whether or not the highway was important enough to justify immediate construction.[21] The army, of course, had already recommended that it was.

Armed with this information, the American cabinet committee decided to obtain engineer surveys of the highway route and reports on the availability of road-building equipment and to commence the survey work before the spring thaw in the north.[22] Brig.-Gen. C. L. Sturdevant, assistant chief of engineers, was immediately given this task. He was told that the decision was to build the highway via the airfield line and was ordered to submit a survey and construction plan within a few days.[23] Sturdevant's report was ready two days later, on 4 February 1942.[24]

Although Knox, the secretary of the navy, was a member of the special cabinet committee, the chief of naval operations had not yet been formally asked for his opinion, in spite of recommendations to consult him and the persistent concern over the security of sea links. On the day that Sturdevant returned his outline plan, Gen. Marshall finally signed a letter to Adm. King. He asked for "a brief statement as to the ability of the Navy, considering all its commitments and probable future requirements, to maintain, under all circumstances, uninterrupted communications" to Alaska. King replied immediately. Guarantees of uninterrupted communications were impossible, but he assured Marshall that the navy would provide adequate protection for the garrisons and civilian population. King believed it improbable that the enemy could gain any foothold in Alaska which would make the communication links dangerous. Specifically, he rejected the thesis that a road to Alaska was necessary because the navy could not afford adequate shipping defense.[25] By now, however, this opinion was irrelevant.[26] Plans were already being made. On the 11 February, President Roosevelt approved the project and authorized the army to proceed immediately.[27]

Canadian permission to build was still necessary, but the State Department's confidence that American approval would gain Canadian concurrence was firmly based. Such support had been all but guaranteed previously when American officials visited the Canadian Department of External Affairs in mid-1941. Canada, then already at war, made it clear that the primary consideration in such matters was national defense, but the Permanent Joint Board on Defense had downplayed the highway's importance in 1940. If the board now recommended construction, however, Canada would do its share. It was strongly implied that, if the United States put up the bulk of the money, it could probably choose the route. After the meeting, Norman Robertson, the Canadian under-secretary of state for external affairs, conferred further with J. Pierrepont Moffat, the U.S. representative in Ottawa. Robertson said that he was personally sympathetic to the project, but that the government would agree to it only if it were really needed for the war effort. He assured Moffat that if the United States Army "really went to the mat for it in the Permanent Joint Defense Board . . . then . . . any opposition at this end would automatically disappear."[28] The U.S. Army was now quite prepared to take such action. Shortly after the initial plans were ready, the army's senior member on the joint board, Lieut.-Gen. S. D. Embick, took steps to ensure that the American army and navy representatives would speak with one voice favoring the project. Presidential approval assured that this would be so.[29]

There was still some reason to expect opposition from Canada. After all, the Canadian members of the board had joined in the 1940 judgment that the military value of such a road was negligible. There was no reason for them to have reversed their opinions. As late as 4 February 1942, the Canadian chiefs of staff considered the question and decided that, from their point of view, a highway to Alaska would only indirectly affect the defense of the west coast, even if it could be completed during the war. Canadian construction of the road, therefore, was unwarranted.[30]

American construction for American purposes, however, was another question.

On 10 February, the secretary to the Canadian Cabinet War Committee noted that Canada was about to receive a request to allow American army engineers to survey a highway route via the Peace River to Whitehorse. The matter was discussed at a meeting two days later. The committee agreed to allow the survey. Such permission, noted C. D. Howe, the minister of munitions and supply, would in any event not commit Canada to actual construction.[31]

The American request was formally presented by Moffat the next day. It asked for permission both to make a survey and to construct a pioneer road, noting that four regiments of engineers were scheduled for employment on the project and that the United States would defray all associated costs. In reply, Norman Robertson passed on the Cabinet War Committee's approval of the survey but queried the definition of "pioneer road." Specifically, he wished to know if, by approving it, the Canadian government would be automatically committing itself to the construction of the entire road. This, he said, would require further cabinet consideration, since only the survey had been approved so far. Moffat sought clarification from Washington and reported back the same day that a commitment for the final road would be sought later through the joint board. As for the pioneer road, he defined it as "a rough working road . . . considered part of the survey . . . [which] would be in part the site of an eventual road." Robertson was satisfied with this explanation and was pleased that Canada and the United States had come to a mutual understanding about limiting Canadian liability.[32]

The United States War Department now directed its chief of engineers to proceed with the project. Robertson may have visualized the pioneer road as a rough trail for survey parties, but the American army engineers were under no such delusions. Orders were given for a corridor thirty-two feet wide, subsequently much enlarged, with log bridges and culverts, to provide complete access for the whole distance for civilian contractors who would build the permanent road.[33] The United States Army's official historical chronology rightly regards 13 February, the day Robertson and Moffat met, as the date that Canada approved construction.[34]

In Canada, discussion continued. It was decided that the Canadian members of the board would agree to a proposal to build the highway if the Americans asked for it for defense reasons and accepted all construction and maintenance costs. Subsequently, the board formally advocated this proposal on 25–26 February 1942. The Canadian chiefs of staff still did not think the road warranted by Canadian defense standards but were willing to accept American reasons for justifying construction at their own expense.[35]

Others were more frank. H. L. Keenleyside, the Canadian assistant under-secretary of state for external affairs and the secretary of the joint board's Canadian section, noted before final Cabinet approval that the board's recommendation should be accepted, but not for defense reasons. The military arguments advanced were questionable, especially since the road was not expected to be finished until 1944, and adequate ship construction and other plans would obviate its requirement by then. Nonetheless, he concluded, "the United States Government is now so insistent . . . that the Canadian Government cannot possibly allow itself to be put into the position of barring . . . land access to Alaska." Canada "should agree," he declared, "but this agreement should be recognized, in our own minds at least, as being based on political and not on strategic grounds. The political argument, given the attitude of Washington, is inescapable; the strategic argument, in my opinion, is a most dubious egg."[36] To this Norman Robertson could add only: "I agree that on political grounds we cannot be put into the position of blocking its construction."[37]

Whatever the value of the arguments, the board had supported the proposal, and now the Canadian government prepared to do its part. On 5 March 1942, the Cabinet War Committee approved the recommendation.[38] The last legal obstacle to construction had been passed.

We now know that the Japanese never intended to invade mainland Alaska. Planners in 1942 did not, and they had to be prepared to respond to any reasonable enemy capability. Still, it is fair to assess both the actual and perceived strategic requirements for building the highway during the war. Two issues stand out: the ability of the U.S. Navy to protect the sea lanes of communication north, and the availability of sufficient sea transport to handle all the foreseeable supply and reinforcement requirements of Alaska.

Prior to Pearl Harbor, the U.S. Navy's ability was virtually unquestioned. With the destruction of a large part of the American Pacific fleet, however, it was reasonable for the issue to be reexamined. The U.S. Army certainly voiced some doubts about the navy's capability to maintain sea communications to Alaska but carried out no detailed assessments to see if they were valid. The navy was not asked for its opinion until after all vital decisions had been made. Its rejection of the idea that it could not provide adequate protection was then no longer relevant. Beyond this general point, there are two additional significant facts. There always was a reasonably secure route along the Inside Passage as far north as Skagway—and the Americans took steps to increase the Passage's defenses—with only the few hundred additional miles of open sea to Seward remaining.[39] From there, sea transport was required, highway or no highway, to the important forward installations on Kodiak Island and points west. Navy protection had to be relied upon at these advanced locations in any case.

Sea transport required ships, and these were the Allies' most critical logistical resource. Losses were then far exceeding new construction, and the highway could have been justified on the basis of freeing a depleting resource for other uses. Plans were already under way for massive new shipbuilding programs, however, and from the summer of 1942, the Allies experienced a net gain, not loss, in available cargo space. Military shipping requirements to destinations other than Alaska had a much higher priority, but there was no reason to suspect such a severe shortage of ships in 1944—the planned highway completion date—that the essential maintenance of the Alaskan garrison and population would be prevented. Indeed, the road at first contributed to existing shortages, since a great deal of construction material in the critical summer of 1942 was transported by water to Skagway and mainland Alaska.[40]

There were other opportunity costs as well. Despite assurances that sufficient men and material were available, resources sent to Canada reduced those available elsewhere.[41] In early 1942, it was already clear that the U.S. Army did not have enough engineers to handle all its tasks. To provide them for the highway required breaking an existing policy not to send black troops to extreme northern climates.[42] Demands for heavy transport trucks led to shortages and shipping difficulties as far away as the Persian Gulf, while later reallocations of road-building machinery designated for British use led to controversy and compromise in the Allied Munitions Assignments Board.[43] All this would have been justified, of course, if it had been needed to meet real or perceived strategic requirements. But it was not.

With hindsight, one can see that the highway never really contributed much to Alaskan supply even after its completion. Although the first trucks from Dawson Creek rolled into Fairbanks on 21 November 1942, in essence the territory remained an "island" for military transportation purposes throughout the war.[44] When Gen. DeWitt, the commanding general of the U.S. Western Defense Command, was informed at the end of October 1942 that the opening of the highway would lead to a curtailment of available shipping, he took immediate steps to stop such action. Completion of the highway, he pointed out, did not alleviate the need for shipping during the westward movement to the Aleutians.[45] As a strategic measure for the direct support of Alaska, therefore, the highway's impact was, as previously assessed, virtually negligible.

But as a construction project, it was a great success. It captured the public imagination as few things did in those dark and forbidding midwar years. Work on it had a frontier spirit on a scale which seemed to typify the best in American pioneering tradition: men and machines against the wilderness in a race against time.[46] It was a magnificent achievement carried out as a military project in time of war. But it was not needed for defense. The highway was actually planned and built for other reasons.

NOTES

1. Karl C. Dod, *The Corps of Engineers: The War against Japan*, United States Army in World War II (Washington: United States Army, 1966), p. 299; C. P. Stacey, *The Military Problems of Canada* (Toronto: Ryerson, 1940), pp. 36–37.
2. Secr. of War Henry Stimson to Maj. Gen. J. Cartwright, 2 August 1940, Lt. Gen. J. McNarney to Assist. Secr. A. Cofs, 24 April 1941, Nat. Archives Records Serv., RG 165, War Plans Division (WPD) 4327.
3. Army Service Forces, "The Alaska Highway," May 1945, exhibit B (Gen. Somervell's desk file), NARS, RG 160.
4. Stanley W. Dziuban, *Military Relations between the United States and Canada 1939–1945*, United States Army in World War II (Washington: Department of the Army, 1959), pp. 201–2; C. P. Stacey, *Arms, Men and Governments: The War Policies of Canada, 1939–1945* (Ottawa: Queen's Printer, 1970), pp. 379–80.
5. Army Service Forces, "The Alaska Highway," exhibits B and E.
6. Gerow to Cofs, 9 June 1941, NARS, RG 165, WPD 4327-11.
7. See, for example, warnings to Western and Alaska Defense Commands in early July 1941, in U.S. Army, Western Defense Command (WDC), "History of the Western Defense Command," MS (1945), I: ch. 1, p. 6, ch. 2, pp. 5–6, copy in U.S. Army Military History Institute, Carlisle Barracks, Carlisle, Pa.
8. Ward to Cofs, 24 June 1941, NARS, RG 407, WPD, AG 611.
9. Gerow to Cofs, 30 June 1941, NARS, RG 165, WPD 4327; Stimson to Cartwright, 6 October 1941, in Army Service Force, "The Alaska Highway," exhibit E.
10. Cartwright to Stimson, 6 January 1942, NARS, RG 407, AG 611.
11. Gerow to Cofs, 19 January 1942, NARS, RG 165, WPD 4327-25.
12. "Notes on Cabinet Meeting of January 16, 1942," in Army Service Force, "The Alaska Highway," exhibits B and F.

13. Smith to Cofs, 19 January 1942, Stimson to Ickes, 21 January 1942, NARS, RG 165, WPD 4327-25, 26.

14. Hamblen to Construction and Real Estate Branch, 17 January 1942, NARS, RG 407, AG 611.

15. Wilson to chief, Construction and Real Estate Branch, 18 January 1942, ibid.

16. Ibid.

17. Somervell to WPD, 20 January 1942, ibid.

18. Gerow to Cofs, 23 January 1942, ibid.

19. Draft Gerow to Cofs, n.d., NARS, RG 165, WPD 4327-27.

20. Tully minutes, n.d., ibid.

21. Hickerson to Berle, Berle to Knox, 31 January 1942, Knox to Berle, 3 February 1942 (Knox Office File 4-1-2), NARS, RG 80.

22. Gerow to Cofs, 6 February 1942, NARS, RG 165, WPD 4327-27.

23. Excerpt from Sturdevant's notes, in Army Services Force, "The Alaska Highway," exhibit F.

24. Gerow to Cofs, 6 February 1942, NARS, RG 165, WPD 4327-27.

25. Marshall to King, 4 February 1942, memo for record, 21 February 1942, ibid.

26. The navy did not really seem to care and in the future treated the highway with some indifference. See Knox to Cartwright, 9 March 1942 (Knox office file 4-1-2), NARS, RG 80; and lack of correspondence on CNO Confidential 1942 file on highways, ibid.

27. Crawford minutes, 11 February 1942, on Gerow to Cofs, 6 February 1942, NARS, RG 165, WPD 4327-27.

28. "Memorandum of Conversation," 6 August 1941, enclosed with Hickerson to Embick, 11 August 1941, ibid.

29. Senior army representative to A. Cofs, 8 February 1942, memo for record, 21 February 1942, ibid.

30. Stacey, *Arms, Men and Governments*, p. 382.

31. Cabinet War Committee minutes, 12 February 1942, in Canada, External Affairs, *Documents on Canadian External Relations, 9: 1941–1943*, ed. J. F. Hilliker (Ottawa: Minister of Supply and Services, 1980), p. 1175 (hereafter cited as *DCER 9*).

32. Minister of United States memorandum on conversation with Robertson and Hickerson, 13 February 1942, ibid., pp. 1176–78.

33. Dod, *Engineers*, pp. 300, 307.

34. Mary H. Williams, *Chronology, 1941–1945*, United States Army in World War II (Washington: Department of the Army, 1960).

35. Memorandum on Alaska Highway, n.d., journal extracts, 26th P.J.B.D. Meeting, 25–26 February 1942, extracts from Cabinet War Committee minutes, 5 March 1942, *DCER 9*, pp. 1178–82, 1185–87.

36. Keenleyside memorandum: assistant under secretary of state for external affairs to under secretary of state for external affairs, 3 March 1942, ibid., pp. 1182–85.

37. Robertson note on Keenleyside memorandum, ibid., p. 1183n.

38. Extracts from Cabinet War Committee minutes, 5 March 1942, ibid., pp. 1185–87.

39. Adjutant General to Commanding General Field Forces, 10 February 1942, Ulio to CG WDC, 4 June 1942, WDC to AG, 25 August 1942, NARS, RG 407, AG 611.

40. R. M. Leighton and R. W. Coakley, *Global Logistics and Strategy, 1940–1943*, United States Army in World War II (Washington: Department of the Army, 1955), p. 583, appendix E; R. W. Coakley and R. M. Leighton, *Global Logistics and Strategy, 1943–1945*, United States Army in World War II (Washington: United States Army, 1968), appendix F-1.

41. Gerow to Cofs, 6 February 1942, NARS, RG 165; WPD 4327-27; extracts from minutes of 26th Meeting of P.J.B.D., 25–26 February 1942, *DCER 9*, pp. 1180–82.

42. B. D. Coll, et al., *The Corps of Engineers: Troops and Equipment*, United States Army in World War II (Washington: Department of the Army, 1958), p. 143; Ulysses Lee, *The Employment of Negro Troops*, United States Army in World War II (Washington: United States Army, 1966), p. 439. Ultimately, more than a third of the engineers working on the road were black, ibid., p. 609.

43. Leighton and Coakley, *Global Logistics and Strategy, 1940–1943*, pp. 294, 576, 582.

44. Dod, *Engineers, p.* 315; Stetson Conn, Rose C. Engelman, Byron Fairchild, *Guarding the United States and Its Outposts*, United States Army in World War II (Washington: Department of the Army, 1964), p. 225.

45. Western Defense Command, "History of the Western Defense Command," I: ch. 2, p. 17.

46. Lee, *The Employment of Negro Troops*, p. 609; Harold W. Richardson, "Alcan—America's Glory Road," Part I: "Strategy and Location," *Engineering Newsrecord* (17 December 1942): 859, copy in U.S. CMH, HRC 228.03, Geog., E., Alaska 611, "Alcan Highway."

Jim Crow in Alaska

The Passage of the Alaska Equal Rights Act of 1945

TERRENCE M. COLE

Terrence Cole, who teaches at the University of Alaska Fairbanks, is one of Alaska's leading historians. He has written on subjects as various as the Nome gold rush, the founding of Fairbanks, the environmentalist Robert Marshall, the history of the University of Alaska, and indoor baseball.

In the article reprinted here, Cole turns his attention to an important act passed by the Alaska territorial legislature in 1945 ending racial discrimination in public places. The act was passed nearly a decade before the landmark Brown v. Board of Education *decision ending public discrimination nationally. Three elements came together to generate the 1945 act. Governor Ernest Gruening was sensitive to the issue of Native equality, though as indicated in Stephen Haycox's article, he placed economic development for statehood ahead of all other issues. The second element involved the Alaska Native Brotherhood, which though politically active in the 1920s had withdrawn from politics in the mid-1930s. At Gruening's urging the ANB endorsed Native candidates in the 1945 election, and several won. But the catalyst for the legislature's action, Cole argues, was the sensitive letter of Alberta Schenck, whose honesty and courage captured the hearts of the territory's leaders.*

American society was racist in 1945, and Alaska was no different. While there were isolated voices which decried segregation and discrimination as well as prejudice, most Americans accepted minorities only when they were acculturated to mainstream values, behaviors, and attitudes; cultural differentiation still violated centrist perceptions of social validity and legitimacy. Alaska's act was remarkable in its overt, democratic rejection of discrimination, but the nature of what was acceptable in mainstream culture in 1945 must be kept in mind, as Cole notes in this valuable piece.

This article appeared originally in *Western Historical Quarterly* 23 (November 1992): 429–49; it is reprinted here by permission.

Americans have long believed that the western frontier offered more freedom, justice, and equality than the overcrowded, class-conscious cities of the East. This familiar theme of an egalitarian western society expressed by Frederick Jackson Turner and his followers has been sounded repeatedly in American history and literature. Though the Turner Thesis may no longer be fashionable among professional historians who advocate the "new western history," the significance of the frontier in the modern popular culture and politics of Alaska has never dimmed. No matter what political philosophers espouse, most residents of the "Last Frontier" share the conviction that Alaska's geographical isolation has made the northernmost state vastly different from the other forty-nine in the Union. Modern Alaskans prefer to think that their state offers greater freedom and opportunity than the more densely settled "Lower 48," and that Alaska is relatively free from the worst ills of the outside world, including poverty, pollution, racism, and crime. A popular bumper sticker often seen in Alaska claims, "We don't give a damn how they do it Outside."[1]

Modern Alaskans are therefore surprised and shocked to learn that before World War II racial segregation and Jim Crow policies toward Alaska Natives were standard practice throughout much of Alaska. So few blacks lived in the territory, especially before World War II, there was little organized discrimination against them. Natives, however, actually outnumbered the permanent white population of Alaska, and it was not until the late 1930s that whites became the permanent majority. In those pre-war years, pioneer Alaskans often refused Natives the right to vote, prayed every Sunday in segregated churches, and sent their children to segregated schools.[2]

Some Alaskans may have been blind to the inequities of their own society, but the unfair treatment of Natives was plainly evident to outsiders who could afford to be more truthful. During World War II, a visiting war correspondent noted in 1943 that the social position of Indians and Eskimos in Alaska "is equivalent to that of a Negro in Georgia or Mississippi."[3]

The Second World War laid the foundation for the great advances in racial equality that occurred in America during the 1950s and 1960s. As C. Vann Woodward once explained, U.S. pronouncements against the Nazis and Hitler's hated racist doctrines highlighted the "inconsistency" between "American practice at home and propaganda abroad."[4] In Alaska, as elsewhere in the American West, World War II thoroughly transformed virtually every aspect of life in the territory. Among the sweeping social, economic, and political changes that the war brought to the North, none was perhaps more painful than the successful battle in the 1940s to outlaw racial segregation in Alaska.

Eleven years before Rosa Parks refused to give up her seat on a bus in Montgomery, Alabama, a similar scene took place in Nome, Alaska. Alberta Schenck, a young half-Eskimo woman, was arrested in Nome in 1944 for daring to sit in the "white only" section of the local theater. Schenck's one-woman protest in Nome, and the fight against segregation across Alaska in the 1940s by crusaders such as Governor Ernest Gruening, the Native rights advocates Roy and Elizabeth Peratrovich, and the other Tlingit leaders of the Alaska Native Brotherhood and Sisterhood, illustrate that Jim Crow was a scourge to Alaska as well as to Alabama. The majority of white residents in pre-war Alaska took public discrimination against Natives for granted. Scars from such discrimination were largely invisible to those who did not have to suffer it. This hidden plague of prejudice was especially hard to cure in Alaska because so many whites chose to believe it never existed.

The early years of American control of Alaska in the late nineteenth century coincided with the peak of the Indian wars in the western states and the gradual legal entrenchment of segregation and white supremacy in the southern states. In 1896, the same year as the Klondike gold strike, the U.S. Supreme Court issued its landmark decision in *Plessy v. Ferguson* which formally approved segregation as the law of the land with the "separate but equal" rule.

The general American attitude toward Native Alaskans, as with blacks in the South, was reflected in a persistent pattern of discrimination. The Presbyterian missionary, trader, and territorial governor John G. Brady, according to his biographer Ted C. Hinckley, preferred to refer to Alaskan Indians as Natives or "Alaskans," because "for too many whites *Indian* was synonymous with *nigger*."[5] Hinckley explains that Brady ran a general store in Sitka in the 1880s but quit the business when his partner insisted on putting in two separate entrances with completely separate departments for Natives and whites "so that tourists would no longer be obliged to rub elbows with smelly, lamp black–smeared Tlingits."[6]

The situation at Brady's store in Sitka was not unique. Numerous bars, restaurants, and hotels in various Alaskan communities posted permanent signs stating "No Natives Allowed," while movie theaters habitually restricted Natives to seats in the balcony with signs such as "For Natives Only."[7] Native residents who migrated to white mining and fishing communities invariably settled in Indian ghettos on the outskirts of town. There were no legal prohibitions against Natives settling wherever they chose in Alaska, but economic, social, and cultural reality dictated that Natives live apart from whites. By both law and custom, however, Alaskan children attended segregated schools. As elsewhere, the deep feelings of parents for their children made the schools in Alaska a flash point for racial strife.

Originally, government officials and missionaries hoped to create a school system in Alaska "without reference to race."[8] In practice, however, whites in Alaska's major communities did not want their youngsters to be educated with Native children, and separate schoolrooms for whites and Natives were the rule. This informal "dual system" of education became law with the passage of the Nelson Act in 1905, which fractured Alaska's educational system into two separate and supposedly equal parts. The Nelson Act gave the responsibility to the territorial governor and local communities to fund fully the education of white children and children of "mixed blood who live a civilized life," while the costs of educating Indian and Eskimo children remained a federal burden.[9]

Some whites opposed the entrance of any "half breeds" into white territorial schools. Furthermore, the courts favored a narrow and highly arbitrary definition of what constituted a civilized person. In a test case brought in Sitka in 1908, the federal district court ruled a mixed-blood child ineligible to attend the Sitka public school because the child's stepfather "did not lead a civilized type of life." Apparently, only those who stopped speaking Native languages, eating Native foods, practicing Native religions, and associating with other Natives, and started speaking English, wearing blue jeans, eating canned food, living in a frame house, and working for wages, could be considered "civilized."[10] And only a Native who had come close to this interpretation of "civilized life" by abandoning his own culture could become an American citizen, since Native Americans throughout the United States were not granted universal citizenship until 1924.

The quest for Native citizenship and equality with whites inspired the establishment in 1912 of the Alaska Native Brotherhood (ANB), an association that evolved into the first significant Native political organization in Alaska. The mission-trained Native leaders of the ANB patterned their goals on the teachings of the missionary schoolteachers, from whom they had learned that Christianity and complete acculturation were the key to both heaven and the American dream. Anything less would doom

Native people to certain extinction. The ANB, whose official song was "Onward, Christian Soldiers," and whose official lapel pin was a prospector's gold pan, supported three major initiatives: citizenship for Natives, better education for Native children, and abolition of "uncivilized" Native customs.[11]

In the 1920s, under the leadership of William and Louis Paul, the ANB became a highly effective political machine. William Paul, a skilled Tlingit attorney, successfully battled in the courts for the Natives' right to vote, and he created a Native voting block that held the balance of power in southeastern Alaska. William Paul himself became the first Native to run for and win a seat in the territorial legislature in 1924, the year that all Native Americans were granted U.S. citizenship. Fear of Paul's political machine and his alleged manipulation of the many Natives who could not read (like a big-city ward boss, he distributed cardboard cutouts to his followers to enable illiterate voters to make their Xs in the right places on the ballot) helped spur passage of the 1925 Alaskan literacy law designed to limit Native voting.[12]

Some white residents responded with anger to the increasing signs of Native political power. A 1926 editorial in the *Fairbanks Daily News-Miner* under the headline "Alaska—A White Man's Country" expressed the fears of many when it charged that Indians were threatening to take control of Alaska. At the time, Alaska's economy was still reeling from the prolonged slump following World War I in its basic industries of mining and fishing, and the exodus of the white population as the economy declined actually had left the Natives in the majority. "NOTWITHSTANDING THE FACT THAT THE INDIANS OUTNUMBER US," the *News-Miner* claimed, "THIS IS A WHITE MAN'S COUNTRY, and it must remain such." The newspaper described the disaster that had overtaken Sitka when the Indians, whom the paper claimed were people of a "lower order of intelligence," of whom ninety percent could not read, write, or speak English, began to vote with stencils. "The result is that today Sitka has a city council controlled by the Indians," the editorial complained. "It has a half-breed Mayor, an Indian Chief of Police, who can and does put white people in jail—and no one can be so obnoxious as an Indian with a little authority."[13]

High on the ANB's list of political priorities was the reform of the Native educational system. The ANB targeted the dual system of education as a cruel hoax on those who had abandoned their own traditions, only to be rejected by the white culture they had tried to embrace. The Native schools stressed rudimentary education, primarily teaching English and vocational training, while the white schools, in contrast, generally had "a high percentage of high school graduates who continue education in institutions of higher learning."[14] In the larger communities of southeastern Alaska, such as Wrangell, Ketchikan, Juneau, and Sitka, Native children were generally barred from the local public schools and forced to attend the federal Indian schools. Paul nearly succeeded in 1921 in convincing the bureau of education to close the Indian school at Wrangell, in order to forcibly integrate education in the community.[15]

After two Native girls were expelled from the Ketchikan public school in 1929 and ordered to attend the Native school in nearby Saxman, William Paul served as the attorney in a suit against the school board. The case inflamed opinions on both sides of the issue. The tone of one Juneau newspaper editorial headlined "Color Line in Schools" gives an indication of the racial passions that had been stirred. The editorial complained that "breeds" were doomed to remain "social pariahs" because they were clearly inferior and made a "pathetic spectacle" when forced to associate with white children. In the federal schools, the editorial continued, half-breed and Indian children "can grow to manhood and womanhood without that inferiority complex which is bound to be theirs if they are permitted in the white schools."[16]

Despite the newspaper's professed concern for the feelings of Native children, the court reaffirmed the right of youngsters of mixed blood to attend the school of their choice. It was a landmark decision. From that time forward, one authority claims, Indian children began to attend schools regularly throughout Southeast Alaska.[17] But, restrictive policies nevertheless remained in force. In 1939, Charles Hawkesworth, a senior official in the Indian service, explained to a U.S. Senate subcommittee in Juneau that some years earlier the local school board had decided that only Indian boys and girls above the fifth grade "would be privileged to come to the city schools." Hawkesworth said he also knew of a case in Valdez where an eighth-grade Native girl "wanted to attend high school, but the school board didn't see fit to take her."[18]

School segregation remained one of the core problems of Alaska's racial dilemma. But race discrimination in other public places, such as restaurants, theaters, playgrounds, and swimming pools, also emerged as a battleground in the 1930s and 1940s. When a grand officer of the ANB was told to sit in the Native-only section in a Juneau movie theater in 1929, he walked out and vowed never again to suffer such an insult. At a meeting of the executive council, the ANB agreed to stage a boycott of the offending theater, not because its policies were any worse than other theaters' in town, but because it had a chain of theaters throughout southeastern Alaska and appeared to be more vulnerable to a boycott. In conjunction with the theater boycott, the ANB also recommended that its members refuse to patronize any establishment that discriminated against Natives. The action proved effective throughout much of southeastern Alaska. Within a month the "No Natives" signs at the theater and other businesses began to come down. As Philip Drucker's history of the ANB explains, "Apparently many white businessmen became aware for the first time of the strength and effectiveness of the Brotherhood."[19]

Though the ANB succeeded in forcing some white businessmen in southeastern Alaska to learn to value Native patronage, there were still glaring examples of blatant discrimination against Natives in the region and throughout Alaska in 1939, when Franklin D. Roosevelt appointed a crusading New Deal Democrat named Ernest Gruening governor of the territory. Gruening was shocked by the signs he saw excluding Natives from public facilities. The new governor met few white Alaskans who seemed to share his sense of outrage. "I found relatively little encouragement . . . from Alaskans with whom I discussed the matter," Gruening later wrote. "It was, they said, 'the custom of the country.' When I proposed to some that these discriminations be forbidden by legislation, I was told that it would stand little chance of enactment by the Territorial Legislature."[20]

On his first visit to Alaska, Gruening said he had been haunted by a sign that hung in Anchorage's leading restaurant, the Anchorage Grill on Fourth Avenue, which said, "We Do Not Cater to Native and Filipino Trade." In 1940, he returned to have a chat with the owner, George Grames, a naturalized American from Greece. In his memoirs, *Many Battles,* Gruening described how he rebuked Grames for the sign and asked him how he would like to see a sign that read "We Do Not Cater to Greeks." Gruening wrote, "I then gave George a pep talk about the meaning of America. He went over and removed the sign. 'It will never be up again,' he said."[21]

In Alaska, as in many other American communities, World War II demonstrated the contradictions between the nation's fight for freedom overseas and its denial of equal opportunities at home. On 30 December 1941, about three weeks after Pearl Harbor, Elizabeth Peratrovich, the grand vice-president of the Alaska Native Sisterhood, and her husband, Roy Peratrovich, the grand president of the Alaska Native Brotherhood, sent an angry letter to Governor Gruening complaining about the "No Natives Allowed" sign over the door of the Douglas Inn, across Gastineau Channel from Juneau. They complained that Natives in Alaska were being treated like Jews in Germany and challenged the hypocrisy of such prejudice. The Peratrovichs wrote that, especially because of "the present emergency, when unity is being stressed," wasn't such a sign "very UnAmerican?" "In the present emergency," their angry letter continued, "our native boys are being called upon to defend our beloved country, just as the White boys. There is no distinction being made there but yet when we try to patronize some business establishments we are told in most cases that natives are not allowed." The Peratrovichs said they appealed to Gruening because "we know you have the interest of the native people at heart and we are asking that you use your influence to eliminate this discrimination, not only in Juneau or Douglas, but in the whole Territory."[22]

In fact, Gruening had already taken action. He had previously asked both the mayor of Anchorage and the mayor of Douglas to use their influence to have any signs in their communities "indicating discrimination between natives and whites removed."[23] The governor had also personally asked the owner of the Douglas Inn, John Marin, an immigrant from Italy whose real name was Martini, to remove his offensive sign. Marin claimed he kept the sign up because "I can't have a lot of dirty, drunken natives in my place." After the war started and the Peratrovichs made their appeal, Gruening went back to talk to Marin again. The governor lectured the hotel owner about the U.S. fight against Nazis and fascists who believed they were a "master race." "The United States is opposed to that idea," Gruening said, "and all that goes with it. So I urge you to paint out that sign."[24]

When Marin still refused to remove the sign from the Douglas Inn, Gruening determined that legislation specifically outlawing such practices was the only answer. In July 1942, the governor informed Guy J. Swope, director of the Division of Territories and Island Possessions, about the situation and asked for the opinion of the solicitor's office on preparing "a suitable bill for introduction into the next Territorial Legislature." The war provided a strong rationale for legislative action. Signs forbidding Natives from entering a public establishment, the governor wrote, were not only offensive, but "are in my judgement distinctly destructive of morale and furnish . . . a psychological impediment to the war effort. They are in effect a replica of Hitlerist policies and cannot be justified." Despite his patriotic appeal, Gruening warned that a fight could be expected. "It should be stated that this prejudice reflects the views of a good many old time Alaskans but that does not alter the fact that such discrimination is inexcusable and disgraceful."[25]

Unfortunately, the most powerful person in Alaska during World War II, General Simon Bolivar Buckner, Jr., the commanding officer of the Alaska Defense Command, demonstrated an intense prejudice against Alaska Natives. Son of the famous Confederate general of the same name, who surrendered to U. S. Grant at Fort Donelson in 1862, General Buckner held racial views in the 1940s that were little different from those of any rabid Southerner during the Civil War.[26] Apparently on Buckner's orders (though he denied it), Alaskan military posts issued regulations prohibiting soldiers from fraternizing with Native women, ostensibly to protect Native virtue and to stop the spread of venereal disease among the troops. To ensure the separation of whites from Natives, the army encouraged soldiers to patronize restaurants, stores, and hotels that denied access to Natives. Military officials actually placed off limits to military personnel some establishments that welcomed all races, simply because they did not discriminate against Natives.

Roy Peratrovich of the ANB protested bitterly to the congressional delegate, Tony Dimond, and Governor Gruening against the army's discriminatory policies. "The matter of race discrimination is rather getting out of hand in Alaska," Peratrovich wrote in the spring of 1943. "Before the present war, it was the civilians that discriminated against the Indians. Now it is the civilians and the soldiers." He especially resented the rules that prohibited Indian girls, even those whose brothers were in the army, from becoming members of the USO. "Sometimes I wonder," Peratrovich wrote, "if we really are fighting for democracy."[27]

When Gruening argued against the army's policies of racial segregation in Alaska, Buckner angrily replied: "I can think of no better way to exterminate the native tribes than to encourage their women to associate with unmarried white men, far from home and from white women." If Indians wanted total equality with whites, he charged, then all government programs "giving to the native tribes special hunting, trapping and other privileges denied to white men" should be abolished.[28]

On another occasion, Buckner justified the separation of the races on both moral and practical grounds. He explained that, just as a white oak tree is different from a willow, "Similarly, the Lord in His infinite wisdom has, for reasons beyond our knowledge, created in the Indians a human being differing in many respects from a white man." According to Buckner, the only problem with race relations in Alaska was troublemakers who hoped to exploit the situation, as the general explained in a letter to the assistant secretary of war in July 1943. Buckner claimed that only "shyster lawyers," ambitious politicians, "fifth columnists," and misguided individuals "who see no appreciable differences between the Chinese, the Caucasians, the Japs, the Negroes, and Papuans, the Indians and the Australian Bushmen and who would be happy to intermarry with any of them" were inciting trouble among the Indians in Alaska.[29] When Buckner stubbornly failed to revoke his discriminatory policies, Governor Gruening and Delegate Dimond went over his head, taking their complaints about race discrimination all the way to Secretary of War Henry L. Stimson and to President Roosevelt himself, who ordered a stop to the exclusion of Natives from USOs.[30]

One of the most notorious incidents of racial discrimination in Alaska during World War II was the U.S. government's botched handling of the 1942 forced evacuation of nearly nine hundred Aleuts from their homes in the Aleutian Islands. Unlike the internment at about the same time of 120,000 Japanese Americans in concentration camps, an overtly racist measure born of wartime hysteria, the removal of the Aleuts from a combat zone for their own protection was theoretically a sounder public policy. In fact, the Aleut evacuation was administered so poorly that it caused a horrendous amount of death and hardship among the Native people. Many of the Aleuts died after their evacuation, while those who survived until the end of the war and returned to the Aleutians found entire villages burned to the ground and their personal belongings looted by American military personnel.[31]

The decision to evacuate the Aleuts came after the Japanese bombing of Dutch Harbor on 3 June 1942 and their subsequent occupation of Attu and Kiska islands; the Aleuts were given no notice before U.S. Navy ships arrived to take them away. Though virtually all Natives were required to leave the Aleutian Chain, some whites were permitted to stay. For instance Charlie Hope, a white man who lived at Unalaska, was allowed to remain in the village, while his Native wife was forced to leave.[32]

After the hasty government roundup of the Aleuts, most of the Natives were warehoused in abandoned canneries and camps in southeastern Alaska for the duration of the war. Sanitary conditions in the camps were deplorable. Small children and the elderly suffered most. About forty of three hundred people died at Funter Bay, where a physician who visited the camp in the fall of 1943 wrote, "As we entered the first bunkhouse the odor of human excreta and waste was so pungent that I could hardly make the grade."[33] Residents of Ketchikan feared that the two hundred Aleuts housed in an old CCC camp at Ward Cove eight miles from town would spread an epidemic of venereal disease and tuberculosis among the white population. The city of Ketchikan quarantined the camp, and businessmen urged the Aleuts be moved farther from the city. The proprietor of the Totem Inn said she wanted to keep Aleuts out of her establishment because "they were unsanitary and diseased and thus obnoxious to her regular customers besides requiring an unusual amount of trouble in sterilizing of their dishes."[34]

The cavalier attitude of the U.S. government toward the welfare of the Aleut people was due in part to the exigencies of war. But it was also part of a deeper problem: Alaska Natives were second-class citizens in their own land. In an effort to remedy that situation and to outlaw discrimination against Natives, Governor Gruening submitted an anti-discrimination bill to the territorial legislature in early 1943. Passing the bill proved to be difficult, especially because of the complete lack of Native representation among territorial lawmakers. At the time, there was not a single Native member of the Alaska legislature. Though Natives comprised about one-half the population of the territory, only one Alaska Native had ever been elected to the territorial legislature in its history—William Paul, who had served in the mid-1920s.[35]

The anti-discrimination bill failed to pass in the 1943 session by the narrowest margin possible, an 8-8 tie vote in the house. "While I am greatly disappointed in this result," Gruening told Secretary of Interior Harold Ickes in March 1943, "and consider it shocking that in this international crisis the Alaska Legislature should put itself on record before the whole world as in favor of discrimination—an incident which may well be utilized by enemy propagandists—the outcome was a good deal closer than I would have expected." The close vote, Gruening said, would "serve one very useful purpose"; it proved that if only a small number of Native Alaskans became involved in the next election they could make a major difference. "It will awaken the Indians from their political lethargy," Gruening explained to Ickes, "and induce them to take a more active part in politics. This is the first time . . . in which an issue involving an attitude for or against the Indians has been squarely posed and which could not be evaded."[36]

Gruening recognized the Native vote as a potentially powerful constituency in his fight against the Seattle fishing and mining interests that controlled the legislature and blocked his efforts to increase taxes on the huge profits of the canned salmon industry. In addition, the governor hoped that the grip of the "interests" on the territorial government would be loosened by the congressionally authorized 1944 reapportionment of the legislature, doubling the size of the senate to sixteen seats and increasing the house by fifty percent—from sixteen members to twenty-four. He actively campaigned across Alaska to ensure that some of the new lawmakers would be Alaska Natives.

In November 1943, Gruening sent a written message to the annual convention of the Alaska Native Brotherhood, urging the group to find Native leaders willing to serve in the legislature. The proof that Natives were needed in Juneau, he said, was the shameful rejection by the old guard of the anti-discrimination bill. The governor stated that "Native people have both a right and a duty to exert themselves, to assert themselves and, by taking an active part in our political life, to see that such an unfortunate exhibition of prejudice and bigotry is not repeated."[37] When the votes were counted in the 1944 fall elections, two Tlingit Indians had been swept into office with overwhelming support: Frank Peratrovich of Klawock, the older brother of the ANB Grand President Roy Peratrovich, and Andrew Hope of Sitka.[38]

In the spring of 1944, during Gruening's campaign to win support for the anti-discrimination bill in the next legislature, he received an emergency telegram from a seventeen-year-old Nome girl named Alberta Schenck, who had spent the previous night in jail for violating the segregated seating arrangements in the local theater. Her arrest was destined to inspire much debate in the battle for the equal rights bill in the coming legislative session.

Nome, like most other Alaskan towns, had its share of Jim Crow practices. Sadie Brower, daughter of a white father and an Eskimo mother, was a teenager in the early 1930s when she wanted to attend a Nome dance for a planeload of visiting soldiers. "There was a definite line between the natives and the whites," she remembered. "If it was a white man's dance, no one with native blood could go in there." Sadie and another half-Native friend were so eager to go to the dance that they bleached their hair with peroxide. They only began to worry afterwards when the time came for Sadie to return to her home in Barrow. "Well, we started looking for berets to cover our hair, because the roots were starting to come out black as you please, and there was no hair dye available in Nome then, no way to color your hair. So I was like that when I got off the boat in Barrow. Dad took one look at me and said, 'Foolishness. How foolish can you get!'" Sadie said it was a long time before her hair grew out and returned to its normal color, and she never forgot her embarrassment over what she had done for one night of dancing with the white soldiers.[39]

The threat of spreading tuberculosis was a common justification for keeping Eskimos separate from whites, as was the smell given off by Natives' skin boots, which were usually tanned in urine. According to one war correspondent, Eskimos and whites had "complete equality" in Nome in the early 1940s, except at the hotel and the music theater. "They can't live at the hotel," Howard Handleman wrote in 1943, "and they have to sit on their own side of the theater." The balcony, nicknamed "Nigger Heaven," was completely reserved for full-blooded Eskimos.[40]

In the spring of 1944, the forced seating arrangements at the theater particularly bothered Alberta Schenck, a young schoolgirl whose mother was an Eskimo and whose father was a white man. Two of her brothers were on duty with the U.S. Army, and her father was a veteran of World War I. Alberta worked as an usher at the Dream Theater after school and felt ashamed every time she had to tell Eskimos that if they found no seats on the right side of the theater or in the balcony they had to leave, even if there were empty seats on the left side.

She explained her frustrations to Major Marvin ("Muktuk") Marston, the head of the Alaska Territorial Guard and a staunch fighter for equal treatment of Alaska Natives. Marston, widely known by his Eskimo nickname Muktuk, had been hired by Governor Gruening to mobilize the Native population during World II, and he recognized the damage done by race discrimination in Alaska. At every available opportunity he bitterly protested white racism.

Alberta told Marston that she had been fired from her job at the theater for complaining about the management's segregated seating policies. She could not understand why such unfair treatment of those with a different color skin could be allowed in a land that professed such love for freedom and justice. When the major read an essay Alberta had written at school describing her feelings, he was astounded at the pain and suffering that came through her simple language. "There was no use in evading the issue nor in pretending to this intelligent adolescent that all was well," Marston wrote. "She knew and I knew that here was a festering core of racial prejudice and social injustice wholly incompatible with our loudly proclaimed 'equality and justice for all.'"[41]

Marston suggested that Alberta submit her essay to the editor of the

Nome Nugget and ask him to publish it. When the next issue of the paper came out he was surprised to find her hard-hitting letter to the editor on page three. "I believe we Americans and also our Allies are fighting for the purpose of freedom," Alberta wrote. "I myself am part Eskimo and Irish and so are many others. I only truthfully know that I am one of God's children regardless of race, color or creed. You or I or anyone else is not to blame [for] what we are." She then addressed the situation at the Dream Theater. "What has hurt us constantly is that we are not able to go to a public theater and sit where we wish, but yet we pay the SAME price as anyone else and our money is GLADLY received." Such actions, she said, were not in the spirit of Thomas Jefferson's Declaration of Independence or the U.S. Constitution that she was studying in school, but were instead "following the steps of Hitlerism."[42]

Alberta's letter caused a furor in Nome. The next issue of the paper carried an angry rebuttal from an anonymous reader. "The theater is a private institution, and has the right to make its own house rules and until the native people as a whole live up to public health standards, it would be hard for the management to change their present system even though some of the natives themselves do not like to sit next to 'odoriferous' persons. . . . I, therefore, suggest that those of the native group who are intelligent enough to complain and criticize, start working from within the native population, raise their own standards and earn the right for which they are asking."[43]

Marston said that Alberta wrote a second article in response, but the "newspaper was anxious to drop so hot an issue and the printed discussion came to a sudden close."[44] A few nights after Alberta's letter was published, she went out on a date to see a movie with a white army sergeant stationed at the Nome base. The sergeant escorted her down the aisle and they sat together on the white side of the theater. Suddenly, the manager came down the aisle and ordered her to move to the Native side of the auditorium with the other Eskimos and "half-breeds." When the sergeant told Alberta not to get up, the manager rushed out and returned with the Nome chief of police. When she still refused to get up, Marston said the chief "seized Alberta by the shoulders and literally pulled her into the aisle, pushed her down to the door, and out onto the street."[45]

Alberta Schenck spent that night in the Nome city jail. She was released the next day. Her arrest infuriated the local Native population who threatened legal action but felt helpless to fight the long-established policies of discrimination. As Muktuk Marston later wrote, "When the white man called the law in the Arctic, the native was always in the wrong and the white man was always in the right." According to Marston, on the Sunday night following the incident with Alberta, a group of Eskimos purchased tickets and stormed into the theater, sitting wherever they chose. Alberta's father, Albert Schenck, reportedly hired O. D. Cochran, a prominent local attorney and territorial senator, to represent Alberta in a suit against the theater manager and the Nome chief of police.[46]

Marston also helped Alberta compose a telegram to Governor Gruening describing what had happened. When the governor received the news, he immediately wired Nome's Mayor Edward Anderson demanding an explanation. The mayor, ashamed of what the local police had done, wired back a brief response: "A mistake has been made. It won't happen again."[47] In a personal letter to Alberta, Gruening praised her for refusing "very properly" to sit in the Native section. "The discrimination which crops out here and there in Alaska against people of Native blood . . . is very objectionable to me," Gruening wrote. "I consider it un-American. I feel that it violates the principles upon which our nation was founded. I deem it contrary to the spirit of our country and directly in conflict with the issues on which this great war is being fought. In this war, American boys of all races and creeds are enlisted. There is no discrimination when they are called upon to lay down their lives for their country and for liberty." Gruening promised Alberta that he would again push for passage of an anti-discrimination bill in the next legislature, and "if it becomes law, you may be certain that the unpleasant experience which has been yours will not happen again to anyone in Alaska. It should never have happened in America."[48]

A sign of how deeply Alberta's arrest angered some members of the Nome community came only a few weeks later in the annual election of the Queen of Nome. The yearly spring carnival was the highlight of the Nome social scene. In April 1944, only about a month after her experience in the city jail, Alberta Schenck, with massive support from the soldiers of the Nome garrison, was elected the Queen of Nome for 1944. She won the popularity contest by an overwhelming margin, thanks to soldiers who had been angered by the way she had been treated. Individuals could vote as often as they liked at various businesses around the community, and Alberta tallied 63,850 votes, three times the total of her nearest competitor. "The so-called 'Four Hundred' of Nome were dumbfounded," Major Marston wrote in his memoirs published twenty-five years later. "I suspect they have not yet fully recovered from the shock."[49]

Despite obvious resentment among some Nome residents at the way

Alberta Schenck had been treated, the Dream Theater continued its notorious segregation practices. On the night of 17 January 1945, Otto Geist observed an incident at the theater. Geist, a pioneer Alaskan archaeologist who served with the Alaska Territorial Guard during World War II, wrote immediately to Major Marston. "I happened to be witness this evening," Geist wrote, "to the unpleasant situation when, first one native woman (as I could see a full blood) was removed from the left side of the [aisle], then, a young white man married to what appeared to be a half caste. The full blood woman quietly moved over to the already crowded right side set aside for natives. The white man, however, remonstrated and did not move when the usher girl asked him to move." Eventually, the white man and his wife agreed to change their seats, but only after a woman from the theater office came out and ordered them to sit on the Native side. Geist said that if the man had not backed down, the "local police would have been called upon" to throw them out of the theater.[50]

Five days after Geist's visit to the Dream Theater, the 1945 Alaska legislature convened in Juneau. Near the top of its agenda was the equal rights bill that would abolish segregation as practiced at Nome's only theater. In his message to the legislature, Governor Gruening urged the lawmakers to meet the challenges of the post-war world. "First, let us live up, at home, to the principle for which American boys of every race, creed and color are giving all they have," Gruening said. "Let us get rid of soul-searing race discrimination in our midst to the extent that we can do it by legislative action."[51]

The bill to make segregation a crime was introduced in the house by Representative Edward Anderson of Nome, who as city mayor had apologized to Governor Gruening for Alberta Schenck's arrest. Alberta's lawyer, Senator O. D. Cochran, introduced a senate version. Crowded hearings were held in both bodies to debate the measure, which would guarantee "full and equal accommodations, facilities and privileges to all citizens" throughout Alaska. As one newspaper account of the house proceedings stated, "The ghost of Abraham Lincoln, the Great Emancipator, trod heavily through the halls of the House of Representatives yesterday as that body convened in a committee of the whole before a jammed gallery on the non-discrimination bill introduced by Anderson of Nome."[52] Speaking forcefully from the gallery in favor of the Anderson bill was Roy Peratrovich, the president of the Alaska Native Brotherhood. The ANB president blasted the "unscrupulous white men in our midst" whose actions were "a disgrace to the Democratic form of Government."

During his oration, Peratrovich tied the equal rights measure to the issue of aboriginal land claims for Alaska Natives. At the time, Secretary of Interior Harold Ickes was pushing for the establishment of large Indian reservations in Alaska, as Ickes and prominent Indian rights advocates, such as Felix Cohen, believed that Alaska Natives had a valid potential claim to millions of acres in the territory. White Alaskans were terrified at the prospect that the Interior Department was recommending to return "most of the territory to the Indians on the ground that they have owned it all along." Earlier in 1944, the *Ketchikan Chronicle* had warned that any attempt to give Alaska back to the Indians would only fan the flames of racial warfare.[53]

From the house gallery, Peratrovich told the legislators that the ANB, an organization with a strong assimilationist background, had so far rejected Ickes's "tempting" proposals for reservations. "We have opposed reservations," Peratrovich said. "We are opposed to accepting any form of special privilege. We want to take our chances with the white man." As the Juneau *Empire* reporter who covered the house hearing pointed out, however, "There was [an] implied threat in Peratrovich's speech when he declared ominously, 'I dare not prophesy what will happen if you folks do not pass this bill—we cannot stand beside you and aid you in your fight against Ickes unless you accept us as one of you.'"[54]

Opponents of the equal rights bill argued that it would not eliminate racial discrimination. An editorial in the conservative Juneau *Empire* admitted the next day that those who said there was no discrimination in Alaska were either "very much mistaken or else not very observant. Racial discrimination certainly does exist in Alaska as it exists not only in every State and Territory of the United States but throughout the world." According to the *Empire,* however, the bill would only make matters worse. "No law can force a business man, who is of one race, to deal pleasantly with a customer who happens to be of another race." The newspaper continued, "We honestly believe that a law which would attempt to force an elimination of racial discrimination, such as this measure now in question, would only serve to heighten racial discrimination." The *Empire* pointed with pride to the fact that it was no longer the custom in southeastern Alaska to have segregated seating in movie theaters. "Many more places of public accommodation are now opened to Indians than was the case 90 years ago. Not because laws were passed, but because this disease of the mind is being cured gradually."[55]

In both the house and senate debates, Senator O. D. Cochran used the Dream Theater as a "prime example" of the injustice of racial discrimination.[56] The notorious case of Alberta Schenck was a lurid reminder of how painful prejudice could be. Several of Cochran's Nome colleagues in the senate, including Tolbert Scott and Frank Whaley, bitterly opposed the equal rights measure. Scott claimed that "mixed breeds" who wished to associate with whites were causing all the problems and that the issue had only been raised to "create political capital for some legislators." Senator Allen Shattuck of Juneau argued that the races, rather than be brought closer together, should be kept farther apart for their own good. The Natives needed time, he said, to adjust to one thousand years of white civilization. "Eskimos are not an inferior race," said Senator Grenold Collins of Anchorage, another opponent of the measure, "but they are an individual race."[57]

After hearing all of the white senators expound on their racial views for nearly two hours, Elizabeth Peratrovich, wife of Roy Peratrovich, took the floor. In her moving testimony she told how it felt to be turned away from a place of business or denied the right to live in a certain neighborhood because of the color of one's skin. She said the opponents of the bill claimed the law would not stop racial discrimination, but that was hardly a reason to vote against it. "Do your laws against larceny and even murder prevent those crimes?" she asked the opponents of the bill. When Mrs. Peratrovich finished, one reporter wrote, the shrill opposition had been shamed into a "defensive whisper," and she drew "volleying applause from the galleries and Senate floor alike, with a biting condemnation of the 'super race' attitude."[58]

Though the anti-discrimination bill provoked hours of bitter debate in the legislature, in the end it proved to be one of the most popular pieces of legislation during the 1945 session. The legislature passed the equal rights measure by an overwhelming margin: 19-5 in the house and 11-5 in the senate. Governor Gruening signed the equal rights bill into law on 16 February 1945, officially abolishing Jim Crow practices in the Territory of Alaska. Standing behind Ernest Gruening as he put his signature on the bill were the key figures in its passage: Roy and Elizabeth Peratrovich, Senator N. R. Walker of Ketchikan, and the two Nome politicians who had come to Alberta Schenck's defense, Senator O. D. Cochran and Representative Edward Anderson.[59]

With the passage of the 1945 Alaska equal rights bill, the signs in Alaskan businesses prohibiting Natives came down. Discrimination did not end in Alaska, but the 1945 law was nevertheless a significant step forward, for it recognized that no one had the right to post his policies of race discrimination.

Even to this day, however, many Alaskans have blind spots when it comes to the subject of race discrimination toward Alaska Natives. Racism is virtually an invisible topic in Alaska's historical literature, and some old-timers would prefer that it stay that way. As one former white resident of Nome wrote me in 1989, regarding the Alberta Schenck incident: "I am sorry that I have no additional knowledge of the occurrence you are writing about probably because to me there was nothing unusual happening. Whenever two or more groups intermingle, be they of different races or just groups of the same race, there will be friction that will gradually be eradicated if no one keeps poking the embers."[60] With the massive social, political, and economic challenges that still face Alaska Natives today as they struggle for equality and cultural survival, it seems wishful thinking to believe that the problems of the past should be so easily forgotten, or worse yet, to pretend that they never happened at all.

NOTES

1. The best examinations of Alaska in relation to the Turner Thesis are Melody Webb, *The Last Frontier: A History of the Yukon Basin of Canada and Alaska* (Albuquerque, 1985), and Peter Coates, *The Trans-Alaska Pipeline Controversy: Technology, Conservation and the Frontier* (Bethlehem, 1991). See also Orlando Miller, *The Frontier in Alaska and the Matanuska* Colony (New Haven, 1975). For a recent sociological analysis of how Alaska's frontier philosophy shapes the culture and politics of the state, see Lee James Cuba, "A Moveable Frontier: Frontier Images in Contemporary Alaska" (Ph.D. dissertation, Yale University, 1981).

2. Ernest Gruening, *The State of Alaska* (New York, 1954), 306. For a discussion of various examples of segregation and discrimination in Alaska, see: Phillip Drucker, *The Native Brotherhoods on the Northwest Coast* (Washington, D.C., 1958), 45; *Fairbanks News-Miner*, 12 March 1990, p. 10; Stephen W. Haycox, "William Paul, Sr., and the Alaska Voters Literacy Act of 1925," *Alaska History* 2 (Winter 1986/1987): 17–37; Joseph E. Senungetuk, *Give or Take a Century: An Eskimo Chronicle* (San Francisco, 1971); John Tepton, "Between Two Worlds: Growing up Native in Alaska," *We Alaskans* (Sunday magazine of the *Anchorage Daily News*), 24 May 1987, p. 9.

3. Joseph Driscoll, *War Discovers Alaska* (New York, 1943), 302.

4. C. Vann Woodward, *The Strange Career of Jim Crow* (New York, 1974), 131.

5. Ted C. Hinckley, *Alaskan John G. Brady: Missionary, Businessman, Judge, and Governor, 1878–1918* (Columbus, 1982), 62, 136.

6. Ibid., 70.

7. Drucker, *The Native Brotherhoods*, 70.

8. David S. Case, *Alaska Natives and American Laws* (Fairbanks, 1984), 198–99.

9. Charles K. Ray, *A Program of Education for Alaska Natives* (Fairbanks, 1959), 30–57; see also Stephen W. Haycox, "Races of a Questionable Ethnical Type: Origins of the Jurisdiction of the U S. Bureau of Education in Alaska, 1867–1885," *Pacific Northwest Quarterly* 75 (October 1984): 155–63; Victor William Henningsen, "Reading, Writing and Reindeer: The Development of Federal Education in Alaska, 1877–1920" (Ph.D. dissertation, Harvard University, 1987); Case, *Alaska Natives and American Laws*, 197–207; Richard L Dauenhauer, *Conflicting Visions in Alaska Education* (Fairbanks, 1980).

10. Drucker, *The Native Brotherhoods*, 49.

11. Ibid., 18, 41; Andrew Hope, *Founders of the Alaska Native Brotherhood* (Sitka, 1975); Rosita Worl, "The Birth of the Civil Rights Movement," *Alaska Native News* 1 (November 1983): 10–37.

12. Haycox, "William Paul, Sr., and the Alaska Voter's Literacy Act," 17–37; Drucker, *The Native Brotherhoods*, 37–40.

13. *Fairbanks Daily News-Miner*, 29 October 1926.

14. William K. Keller, "A History of Higher Education in Alaska, 1741–1940," (Ph.D. diss., State College of Washington, 1940), 252.

15. Haycox, "William Paul and the Alaska voter's Literacy Act," 19.

16. *Stroller's Weekly* (Juneau), 14 September 1929.

17. Drucker, *The Native Brotherhoods*, 50; Case, *Alaska Natives and American Laws*, 200.

18. U.S. Congress, Senate, Committee on Indian Affairs, *Survey of Conditions of the Indians of the United States*, Part 36, 74th Cong., 2nd Sess. (Washington, D.C., 1939), 19833–19834. [These hearings were actually held in 1936, ed.]

19. Drucker, *The Native Brotherhoods*, 71.

20. Ernest Gruening, "Ernest Gruening and the Native People of Alaska: A Personal Account of the Record," Gruening Papers, General Correspondence, 1954–57, Box 8, Folder 72, Alaska and Polar Regions Collection, University of Alaska Fairbanks.

21. Ernest Gruening, *Many Battles: The Autobiography of Ernest Gruening* (New York, 1973), 318–19.

22. Roy and Elizabeth Peratrovich to Ernest Gruening, 30 December 1941, National Archives Microfilm Publication (MF Pub M939), General Correspondence of the Alaska Territorial Governor, 1909–1958 (Washington, D.C., 1973) [hereafter General Correspondence], Microfilm Reel 273, File 40-4b.

23. Gruening to Roy Peratrovich, 2 January 1942, General Correspondence, Reel 273, File 40-4b.

24. Gruening, *Many Battles*, 319.

25. Gruening to Guy J. Swope, 30 July 1942, General Correspondence, Reel 273, File 40-4b.

26. Morgan Sherwood, *Big Game in Alaska: A History of Wildlife and People* (New Haven, 1981), 3–4.

27. Peratrovich to Anthony Dimond, 26 April 1943, General Correspondence, Reel 273, File 40-4b.

28. General S. B. Buckner to Gruening, 7 June 1943, General Correspondence, Reel 273, file 40-4b.

29. Buckner to John J. McCloy, 29 July 1943, Papers of Harold L. Ickes, Secretary of the Interior file, AK-2, Container 93, Manuscript Division, Library of Congress, Washington, D.C.

30. Gruening, *Many Battles*, 321.

31. Committee on Wartime Relocation and Interment of Civilians, *Personal Justice Denied: Report of the Commission on Wartime Relocation and Internment of Civilians* (Washington, D.C., December 1982), 317–59. See also, *Fairbanks Daily News-Miner*, 10 March 1983; 23 April 1985; *Anchorage Daily News*, 1 October 1987.

32. Committee on Wartime Relocation, *Personal Justice Denied*, 334.

33. Ibid., 340.

34. Ibid., 349.

35. Alaska Legislative Affairs Agency, Alaska Legislature Roster of Members, 1913–1982 (Juneau, 1982).

36. Gruening to Harold L. Ickes, 17 March 1943, General Correspondence, Reel 273, file 40-4b.

37. Ernest Gruening, "Message to the 30th Annual Convention of the Alaska Native Brotherhood at Hoonah, November 8–13, 1943," Gruening Papers, General Correspondence, Box 8, Folder 72.

38. Evangeline Atwood and R. N. DeArmond, comps., *Who's Who in Alaska Politics: A Biographical Dictionary of Alaskan Political Personalities, 1884–1972* (Portland, 1977), 47, 77.

39. Margaret B. Blackman, *Sadie Brower Neakok: An Iñupiaq Woman* (Seattle, 1989), 96–97.

40. Howard Handleman, *Wartime Alaska, Alaska Life,* (December 1943), 46; Bud Richter, phone interview by Terrence M. Cole, 15 February 1989; Loretta Helle, phone interview by Terrence M. Cole, San Diego, California, February, 1989.

41. Marvin "Muktuk" Marston, *Men of the Tundra: Eskimos at War* (New York, 1969), 134.

42. *Nome Nugget*, 3 March 1944.

43. Ibid., 10 March 1944.

44. Marston, *Men of the Tundra*, 134.

45. Ibid., 135.

46. Ibid., 135–37; Bud Richter interview, 13 February 1989.

47. Marston, *Men of the Tundra*, 137.

48. Gruening to Alberta Schenck, 17 March 1944, Nome Correspondence, Box 6, Records of the Alaska Territorial Guard, Geist Collection, Alaska and Polar Regions Collection, University of Alaska Fairbanks.

49. *Nome Nugget*, 17 April 1944; Marston, *Men of the Tundra*, 138.

50. Otto Geist to Marston, 17 January 1945, Marston Correspondence, Box 15, file 11B, Records of the Alaska Territorial Guard, Geist Collection.

51. *Journal of the House of Representatives of the Territory of Alaska*, 17th session (Juneau, 1945), 71.

52. *Daily Alaska Empire* (Juneau), 31 January 1945.

53. Quoted in *Nome Nugget*, 1 November 1944; see also Stephen W. Haycox,

"Economic Development and Indian Land Rights in Modern Alaska: The 1947 Tongass Timber Act," *Western Historical Quarterly*, 21 (February 1990): 20–46, reprinted in this anthology; see also Kenneth Philp, "The New Deal and Alaskan Natives, 1936–1945," *Pacific Historical Review* 50 (1981): 309–27, also reprinted in this anthology.

54. *Daily Alaska Empire* (Juneau), 31 January 1945.

55. Ibid.

56. Ibid., 6 February 1945.

57. Ibid.

58. Ibid.

59. *Nome Nugget*, 11 April 1945; "The Birth of the Civil Rights Movement," 11. In memory of Elizabeth Peratrovich, who died of cancer in 1950, Alaska's Governor Steve Cowper signed a proclamation in 1988 declaring 16 February, the day Gruening signed the equal rights bill, as "Elizabeth Peratrovich Day." See *Anchorage Daily News*, 6 June 1988, p 1.

60. R. B. to Terrence M. Cole, 4 February 1989.

Economic Development and Indian Land Rights in Modern Alaska

The 1947 Tongass Timber Act

STEPHEN W. HAYCOX

As salmon packers moved into southeastern Alaska in the late 19th century, the Natives began to lose control of their traditional fishing sites. Although they complained, officials took no action. Alaska's first Organic Act (1884) required that Native land claims be settled by Congress, and Congress failed to act. Then, President Theodore Roosevelt created the Tongass National Forest, which encompassed almost all of southeastern Alaska. Not until 1935 did Congress pass the Tlingit-Haida Jurisdictional Act, authorizing southeastern Natives to seek compensation for lost land in the United States Court of Claims. That suit had not yet been filed when Congress passed the Tongass Timber Act of 1947, authorizing logging in the Tongass.

*Stephen Haycox, Professor of History at the University of Alaska Anchorage, has worked extensively on Alaska Native history and contemporary Native issues. His publications include "Sheldon Jackson in Historical Perspective: Alaska Native Schools and Mission Contracts, 1884–1894" (*Pacific Historian, *Spring 1984), "'Races of a Questionable Ethnical Type': Origins of the Jurisdiction of the U.S. Bureau of Education in Alaska, 1867–1885" (*Pacific Northwest Quarterly, *October 1984), and "William Paul and the Alaska Voter's Literacy Act of 1925" (*Alaska History, *Winter 1986). In 1988 he published* A Warm Past: Travels in Alaska History *(Anchorage: Press North, 1988), and he wrote a biography of Alaska's first Tlingit lawyer and politician, William Lewis Paul, for* Haa Kusteeyí, Our Culture: Tlingit Life Stories, *edited by Nora Marks Dauenhauer and Richard Dauenhauer (Seattle: University of Washington Press, 1994).*

In the following selection, Haycox describes the conflict between those, such as the Secretary of the Interior Harold Ickes, who wanted to protect Alaska Natives and their land and others who sought to open the Tongass to logging in hopes of creating a pulp industry but in disregard of the environmental impact.

This article appeared originally in *Western Historical Quarterly* 21 (February 1990): 20–46; it is reprinted here by permission.

He concludes that prodevelopment forces, including the U.S. Forest Service and Alaska's territorial officials, won this battle and that Native rights, Native claims, and environmental integrity lost.

Between 1933 and 1945 Secretary of the Interior Harold Ickes and Indian Commissioner John Collier attempted to extend the Indian Reorganization Act of 1934, the Indian New Deal, to Alaska. With other administration officials, Ickes was determined to protect Native land title and help Natives defend their fishing and hunting rights. He also hoped the act would provide Natives with desperately needed financial help. But although the IRA was amended to apply to Alaska in 1936 (the Alaska Reorganization Act), enabling Natives to establish village self-government and borrow money from a federal credit fund, implementation of other provisions of the act failed in the territory, due to poor administration by the Office of Indian Affairs, inadequate funding by Congress, and confusion and inconsistency in defining policy.[1] One historian has declared this attempted extension of the Indian New Deal a mistake, on the grounds that it increased tension between the territory's Native and white residents and delayed both the resolution of Native land title questions and the securing of social justice for Alaska's Native people.[2]

By 1945 the attempt to establish the Indian New Deal in Alaska had ended. In the next several years, as the direction of national Indian policy began to change, Congress debated several measures dealing with Alaska Indians. These included a bill to rescind the authority of the Secretary of the Interior to establish Indian reservations in the territory, a bill to guarantee in perpetuity a large number of fish traps owned by the absentee salmon industry, several versions of the Alaska statehood bill, and a bill to authorize the Secretary of Agriculture to sell timber leases in Alaska's vast Tongass National Forest.[3] While the first two did not ever become law, and Alaska statehood was delayed until 1959, the Tongass Timber Act did pass Congress and was signed by the President on August 8, 1947.[4]

The Tongass act authorized timber lease sales in Alaska, despite protests by the resident Tlingit and Haida Indians, by their Washington, D.C., attorneys, and by the last proponents of the Indian New Deal in the Interior Department. Debate turned principally on the question of Indian land rights and then on whether the economic development of Alaska should take precedence over protection of Indian rights and land title.[5]

Sharp debate divided departments within the government, and in part disagreement over the bill represented the clash between the last remaining supporters of the Indian New Deal and the new proponents of Indian assimilation and termination, to whom federal protection represented dictatorial guardianship contrary to the principles of individual freedom. Many conservatives in the 80th Congress were determined to reduce government involvement in the American economy. Some westerners chafed particularly under federal control which they thought impeded rather than encouraged development of the West's resources.[6] Opponents of New Deal policies undoubtedly saw in the Tongass Timber Act an opportunity to replace such control with private development of critically needed resources, development supported by the government rather than hindered by it.

Action on the Tongass bill also took place at the same time that Congress began to develop the policy of termination, and debate on the timber and other Alaska bills likely contributed to the growing opinion that Indians should be assimilated into the mainstream of American culture through the ending of special federal services for them.[7] A bloc of western Senators, including Hugh Butler of Nebraska and Arthur Watkins of Utah, led the effort to develop termination at that time.[8] Although in the Congress the House Committee on Agriculture did most of the work on the Tongass Timber Act, and debate on it in the Senate was desultory, Butler and Watkins were its two chief sponsors there.[9]

Though conceived by allies of Secretary Ickes and supporters of his policies as a way to protect Indian rights in Alaska, the Tongass bill became law in a form so different from its original version as to be angrily denounced by Ickes and New Deal advocates and by the Indians themselves as a betrayal. Some called it Alaska's Teapot Dome, claiming that the act was the result of collusion between the U.S. Forest Service and private investors, intended mainly to benefit developers who sought to establish a pulp industry in Alaska utilizing land and timber which belonged to the Indians by aboriginal title but to which the Forest Service was quite willing to provide access for the industry, over the Indians' objections and to their disadvantage.[10] At the same time, supporters of the final legislation, most particularly the U.S. Forest Service and Alaska territorial officials, hailed its passage as a victory for land and resource development and a reprieve from New Deal Indian policy.[11] In Congress, Senator Watkins proclaimed that the act actually did protect the rights of Alaska's Indians.[12] Such widely opposing interpretations suggest the significant degree of difference within the government over how to approach not only Alaska Indian matters, but national Indian policy as well.

The genesis of the Tongass Timber Act was a severe newsprint shortage which followed World War II.[13] Industry analysts searched the continent for untapped pulp timber, and spokesmen expressed considerable interest in Alaska's Tongass National Forest, where there were suitable stands of western hemlock, Sitka spruce, and red and yellow cedar.[14] Established in the first decade of the twentieth century, the forest comprised sixteen million of the eighteen million acres of Alaska's southeast panhandle.[15] Interest reached a high pitch in 1946 when the Senate established a special subcommittee to investigate the newsprint shortage and dispatched the chairman, Homer E. Capehart, to survey Alaska resources.[16]

Capehart reported favorably on the Tongass forest and encouraged investors to conclude negotiations already under way with the Forest Service. The regional forester of the Alaska National Forest Region (USFS), B. Frank Heintzleman, representing the government, had found three companies which were particularly anxious to establish pulp facilities in Alaska: Puget Sound Pulp and Timber, the D. & F. Co. of New York City, and American Viscose Corporation.[17] An enthusiastic advocate of Alaskan economic development, Heintzleman assured the potential investors that the Forest Service was just as prepared as the pulp industry to see the effort move ahead. With them he worked out a comprehensive pulp development program. The plan projected five mills to be built in the Tongass Forest, each with a fifty-year life-span. Each would produce daily five hundred tons of pulp or paper, an annual level of production which would supply a significant amount of the nation's demand for newsprint.[18]

The project would have a dramatic economic impact on Alaska. Heintzleman estimated that two and one-half persons would be employed in the forest and in the mills (combined) per ton of daily production, amounting to 1,250 persons per mill. There would also be a need for one and one-half service persons for each mill, an additional six hundred twenty-five. Adding wives, children, and other nonworking dependents of employees, Heintzleman said, the total would be 6,500 persons dependent on each mill, needing housing and services within commuting distance of the site.

This was a remarkable projection. The total population of Alaska in 1947 was approximately 120,000, but the population in the southeast approached only 30,000, of which about 6,500 were Tlingit, Haida, and Tsimshian Indians. The primary economic resource in the region was the salmon fishery, which dominated all other industry, but was seasonal and utilized a sizeable imported labor force.[19] By Heintzleman's calculations, establishment of the pulp industry in Alaska would provide significant economic livelihood for the entire population of the panhandle region, including the Natives, on a year-round basis.

But implementation of these ambitious plans was hampered by the question of Indian land title, for there were fourteen Tlingit and Haida Indian villages within the boundaries of the Tongass National Forest.[20] Moreover, much of the best timber was situated near the Native villages. One of Secretary Ickes's objectives in extending the IRA to Alaska was to protect forest lands in the vicinity of those villages.[21] He thought Forest Service policies threatened such lands, and in 1944 he had invited Indians in the Tlingit and Haida villages of southeast Alaska to prepare claims on lands they had traditionally used in the forest. He promised that the Interior Department would protect Indian lands once they were appropriately identified.[22]

Interior Department attorneys helped the Indians prepare their claims. In doing so they relied on a new interpretation of the theory of aboriginal title, in conjunction with unique circumstances involving Indian lands in Alaska. In American law, Indians are held to have "aboriginal title" to lands which they have demonstrably occupied at some time.[23] Such title does not include the ultimate fee, i.e., only the federal government or those authorized by it may purchase such lands. In some instances it has been held to include fishing sites in coastal waters and rivers. Only the United States can extinguish that title, either by purchase, the usual practice, or simply by taking it. The courts have found that takings of Indian lands by the U.S. are legal and not necessarily compensable, a controversial finding. Indians may sue for damages for lost value resulting from such takings.[24] Indians are regarded as having "possessory right" or title to lands in their actual use and occupation, even if such title has not been confirmed by an act of the government. Such title is made more secure by being formally recognized by the United States either by federal treaty or by statute. Though Indians were prohibited in 1863 from making claims for treaty violations or mishandling of tribal resources before the U.S. Court of Claims, Congress from time to time authorized an extension of the jurisdiction of that court in specific cases.[25] Before 1941, it had been assumed that lands once used by Indians but subsequently abandoned, the title to which had not been formally recognized by the federal government, came under the jurisdiction of the U.S. to dispose of as it might desire. However, in an important decision of the U.S. Supreme Court in 1941 involving the Santa Fe Railroad and the Walapai (Hualpai) Indians of Arizona, Indians were held still to retain aboriginal title over formerly used but abandoned lands.[26] This decision was highly significant, for it meant that, even if the U.S. had taken and disposed of lands formerly used by Indians, if the Indians could prove their former use of the land and its resources they could sue the U.S. for damages.

This new departure in Indian land law was seized upon by the brilliant Indian rights attorney Felix Cohen, who served in the Interior Department Solicitor's Office from 1933 to 1948.[27] Cohen saw the *Walapai* decision as providing the basis for protection of Indian lands in Alaska. The United States had never signed treaties with any of Alaska's Natives, as it had been done in other western territories, and had not established traditional reservations.[28] Nor, with the exception of a few townsites and some very small school reserves, had the government recognized Indian land titles in Alaska.[29] For the most part, the Tlingit and Haida Indians congregated in their fourteen southeast Alaska villages, although they also used some traditional salmon-fishing and berry-gathering sites. While some Tlingit and Haida were well assimilated, many others were not and pursued a subsistence life-style heavily dependent upon fishing and hunting.[30] Non-Native encroachment threatened the resources upon which they depended. Yet for all practical purposes, the Indians had abandoned most of the eighteen million acres of southeast Alaska. Thus, while they had a possessory right to the locations they actually occupied and used, it was assumed they had lost any rights to the rest of the land.

On the basis of the *Walapai* decision, Cohen and Ickes challenged that assumption, choosing to regard most of southeast Alaska as subject to aboriginal title. This was a highly controversial decision. But the Indian Reorganization Act of 1934, extended to Alaska in 1936, authorized the Secretary of the Interior to create new Indian reservations to protect Indian lands, and soon after the *Walapai* case, Secretary Ickes relied upon the IRA to establish seven new Indian reservations in Alaska, including a 1.4 million acre reserve for 202 Athabaskan Indians north of Fort Yukon deep in the interior north.[31] He relied upon it also in assuring the Tlingit and Haida Indians that he would protect their aboriginal lands in the Tongass National Forest. It was that assurance which later prompted Senator Butler to introduce legislation rescinding the authority of the Secretary of the Interior to establish Indian reservations in Alaska.

In making his promise, Ickes put the Interior Department, and Alaska's Indians, on a collision course with the Forest Service, for Indian or Interior Department control of forest lands might jeopardize the sale of timber leases on lands near the villages, and pulp mill development might be severely curtailed, if not rendered financially unfeasible. Predictably, the Forest Service reacted negatively. Heintzleman accused Ickes of "introducing a new, wholly impractical, unnecessary and harmful element" into the development of Alaska.[32] As it did in other national forests, the Forest Service treated all undeveloped land within the Tongass Forest boundaries as land under its jurisdiction, a practice affirmed by the courts.[33] Particularly, the agency claimed ownership of the trees and all forest resources, regardless of any land rights. The legislation establishing the Tongass Forest provided that "existing property rights" would be "respected and safeguarded."[34] But along with the General Land Office (reorganized as the Bureau of Land Management in 1947) and most non-Native Alaskans, the Forest Service had never regarded the shifting use of land by Indians on an infrequent basis for hunting and berry gathering as evidence of Indian possession. If there was visual evidence of active Native use, the land would be considered occupied. Otherwise, it was considered abandoned and available.[35]

Alaska's leading territorial officials, Governor Ernest Gruening and Congressional Delegate to Congress E. L. (Bob) Bartlett, also reacted negatively. Both were ardent supporters of Alaska's economic development and eventual statehood. A referendum held in the territory on the issue of statehood in October 1946 passed handily and was viewed widely as the beginning of the final statehood campaign. Bartlett and Gruening thought that economic development was critical to statehood.[36] New industry would attract additional population and would increase the tax base needed to finance state government. Gruening thought that the newsprint shortage would be short-lived and so believed that the readiness of the pulp industry to establish mills in Alaska must be seized upon quickly. Failure to implement Heintzleman's plan, he wrote at one point, would "shut off perhaps for all time, or at least for many years to come, the first important year-round industry that has ever been available to Alaska and which is ready to begin immediately."[37]

With Gruening's support, Heintzleman was prepared to move ahead despite Ickes's clear opposition and invitation to the Indians to submit land claims to the Interior Department. The Forest Service had sold some limited timber leases before the Indian New Deal was extended to Alaska, and Heintzleman assured the pulp investors that the agency was ready to auction sufficient stumpage to meet the long-term need projected by the industry, a fifty-year supply. But unlike Alaska's forester, the investors were unwilling to go ahead unless they could be assured there would be no litigation over Indian land rights. The capital investment to start the industry was too great to justify such a risk. Until the land issue was resolved, they thought there could be no pulp development.[38]

Before leaving the department in 1946, Secretary Ickes had arranged for hearings on Indian land claims to be held in three of the Tlingit and Haida villages, Kake, Klawock, and Hydaburg, to determine the extent of traditionally used land beyond the physical village sites, i.e., land to which the Natives might have aboriginal title. The hearing officer, Richard A. Hanna, a former chief justice of the New Mexico Supreme Court, found the evidence presented by the Indians to support most of their claims to prior use to be inadequate, and he confirmed Indian title only to very small areas in immediate proximity to the villages. He recommended that Congress investigate the evidence for title to greater acreage and provide compensation for any lands taken for which Indian title could be proven. Ickes thought Hanna's finding was too narrow and overruled it. Instead, he recommended the withdrawal of several hundred thousand acres (combined) in separate new reservations around the three communities. Under IRA provisions, village residents needed to vote on whether or not to accept the reservations. There was considerable ambivalence about reservations among the Indians in Alaska, however, and voting had not been completed when Ickes left office. The Tongass situation remained unresolved.[39]

Ickes's replacement, Julius A. Krug, was uncertain whether to proceed on the basis of the validity of aboriginal title, fearing government liability. He decided that the administration should gather more information on Indian land use before he could recommend any solution to the Alaska problem. In June he asked Theodore Haas, the chief counsel in the Office of Indian Affairs, to travel to Alaska in the company of Dr. Walter Goldschmidt, an anthropologist attached to the Department of Agriculture, the Forest Service's parent agency. In their joint report, Haas and Goldschmidt applied former Secretary Ickes's recommendation for reservations for Kake, Klawock, and Hydaburg to all fourteen Indian villages, proposing boundaries which would protect traditional lands adjacent to and beyond each village. But the total land area recommended for all villages combined was less than two million acres, or about ten percent of the Tongass National Forest, far less than the eighteen million acres to which Cohen thought the Indians had aboriginal title.[40]

Krug, who vacillated on Alaska policy throughout his tenure as Interior Secretary, was much less confident than Ickes that the courts would apply the doctrine of aboriginal title to Alaska in such a way as to protect extensive land for Indian claim or award damages to compensate Natives for land taken in the establishment of the Tongass National Forest. Therefore, much to the dismay of Cohen and other proponents of aboriginal title and much more extensive Indian reserves, Krug endorsed the Haas-Goldschmidt recommendation as a working proposal for solving the Alaska lands problem. He concluded that the acreage it projected as Indian land was the most land to which the Indians could expect to gain any title.[41] He directed a new assistant secretary in the Interior Department, Warner W. Gardner, to determine the acceptability of this proposal to the Forest Service and other interested agencies, including the Justice Department, the Office of Indian Affairs, and also attorneys for the Alaska Indians, and the absentee-owned Alaska canned salmon industry, whose right to certain fishing sites might be affected by confirmation of Indian land title.[42] Gardner, attracted to government service by New Deal reforms in 1935, had worked in the Attorney-General's Office and the Solicitor's Office at the Labor Department before serving in the Interior Department Solicitor's Office with Felix Cohen from 1942 to 1946.[43] The challenge of finding a solution to the Alaska problem would be one of his principal responsibilities over the next year.[44]

Gardner found that the Forest Service was adamantly opposed to the Haas-Goldschmidt recommendation. Protesting that the validity of aboriginal title would not stand the test of time, the Forest Service recommended that the government, by administrative or Congressional action, extinguish any Indian title which might exist beyond actual village sites and advise the Indians to sue for damages, if any.[45] Attorneys for the Agriculture Department also adopted this position. It was a method of appropriating Indian land which had been used often in the development of the West. Interior Department Solicitor Maston G. White acknowledged that technically the procedure was legal; Congress could extinguish any Indian title by simple legislation. But White and other Interior Department officials objected that for the government to solve the problem that way would violate the American sense of fair play. It was now "too late in the history of the country," White said, to act in such a cavalier manner toward its Indian citizens.[46] But the Agriculture Department and the Forest Service appeared unyielding. Agriculture Undersecretary W. E. Dodd pointedly warned Gardner that, if the Interior Department were to reserve ten percent of the land in southeast Alaska to protect Indian title, such action would create "competing jurisdictions" and make pulp development "very uncertain."[47] Seeking a way out of the impasse and skeptical that an administrative solution was likely, Secretary Krug recommended in January 1947 that Gardner draft legislation for Congress. But the positions of the departments were so far apart that Gardner told Krug, "No agreement is possible just now." There would need to be more cooperation before anything could be recommended to Congress.[48]

Delegate Bartlett already had proposed that the government mandate an administrative settlement. At the beginning of 1945 he introduced a bill modeled on Judge Hanna's recommendation, authorizing the Interior Department to negotiate with the Indians for relinquishment of any potential title to most of their claims in return for cash compensation and clear title to the remainder. The Indians debated this proposal at several annual conventions of their powerful political body, the Alaska Native Brotherhood.[49] A sophisticated organization, the ANB had acted as a focal point and forum for Native interests in Alaska since 1912.[50] It had helped to elect a Native lawyer, William Paul, Sr., to the territorial legislature in 1924. It also helped elect two Indians to the Alaska House in 1944, Frank Peratrovich and Andrew Hope, who fought successfully for an anti-discrimination law.[51] Peratrovich went on to the territorial Senate in 1946. Although ANB leaders were usually elected from among the well assimilated minority, the organization spoke for all Natives, including those in other parts of Alaska, and was well known to officers in the Bureau of Indian Affairs and the Interior Department.[52] In this regard the Tlingit and Haida differed somewhat from many western Indians who had less experience in articulating their concerns and interests with agencies and officers of federal and state governments.

The ANB had supported action on Alaska land claims for many years.[53] Its members had worked with the Indian Office toward passage in 1935 of the Tlingit-Haida Jurisdictional Act which authorized a case in the U.S. Court of Claims. As of 1947, however, no suit had been filed because of questions associated with the implementation of the Indian Reorganization Act in Alaska and because of difficulties securing Bureau of Indian Affairs approval of an appropriate attorney.[54] In 1947 the Indians selected a highly experienced lawyer to advise them on land claims and other matters relating to the federal government. He was James Curry, general counsel of the National Congress of American Indians. Curry had worked in the Office of Indian Affairs and in the Interior Department before going into private practice in 1945.[55] Like Gardner, he was a good friend of Felix Cohen, and like Cohen, he accepted the validity of aboriginal title. Curry began working with the Indians even before he received government approval of his contract.[56]

ANB leaders were divided on Bartlett's suggestion of a negotiated settlement. Some argued that the Indians should stake everything on Secretary Ickes's promise of protection of their ancestral lands. Others, however, argued for the expediency of negotiations, if extinguishment of title to some land would result in quick cash payment which could be used to secure title to the remainder. After prolonged debate, the ANB approved Bartlett's proposal, with that provision.[57]

In 1947, however, Curry advised the Indians not to relinquish any potential land title through administrative proceedings as proposed by Bartlett. They should wait, he counseled, for the courts to rule specifically on their claims, and he proposed to prepare the suit authorized by the 1935 act. In the meantime the Indians might consider a legislative settlement a more secure alternative, should they judge its terms to be advantageous. The ANB accepted Curry's advice, overturning its earlier endorsement of Bartlett's proposal. Bartlett and Gruening regarded Curry's involvment as obstructionist and detrimental.[58]

Bartlett agreed that a legislative solution was preferable, if an acceptable one could be drafted quickly. Legislation might settle the matter of land titles conclusively, he thought, but, he told Secretary Krug, to accommodate the pulp industry, Congress must act before recessing for the summer, that is, by the end of July.[59] Gardner also supported a legislative solution. So did Felix Cohen, who provided it in a proposal which he forwarded to Gardner and to the Agriculture Department in March 1947. Fearful that the Forest Service might go ahead on its own, Cohen suggested that Congress pass legislation neither confirming nor denying the Indian land claims but authorizing the Forest Service to sell timber leases free and clear of such claims. At the same time, however, the agency would give the Indians ten percent of the receipts from all leases sold. The Indians would then use the cash to finance their suit at the Court of Claims, testing the validity of aboriginal title in Alaska.[60]

Initially, most of the interested parties found the proposal attractive, as Cohen anticipated. He knew the Forest Service and Alaska territorial officials were increasingly anxious over the continuing delay and the possibility of protracted litigation which might discourage pulp industry investors. The solicitor in the Agriculture Department, Edward Mynatt, apparently persuaded the Forest Service to help facilitate the Cohen proposal by informally recognizing the Indians' right to an amount of land in the forest equal to one hundred sixty acres for each Native, just over one million acres, or six and one-half percent of the forest land.[61] This was the minimum which Mynatt thought the courts would award the Indians in a final disposition of the forest lands. During April, the other agencies involved also indicated their approval of the proposal, and Gardner agreed to have Mynatt draft a bill to take to the appropriate committees in Congress.[62]

Curry also accepted Cohen's proposal and the Forest Service's one-hundred-sixty-acre provision, though he cautioned Gardner that he was not sure of the Indians' support, and could not bind them. Gardner was concerned about Indian approval, for he doubted that any bill could be passed without it. Curry told Gardner he would send a representative to Alaska to explain the implications of the plan to the Indians.[63] Ten percent of Tongass timber receipts would adequately finance a comprehensive land suit, Curry thought. Recognition of six and one-half percent of the land area as clearly Indian-owned, though not the ten percent recommended in the Haas-Goldschmidt report, nonetheless offered protection of vital hunting areas in the vicinity of the villages. And confident that the claim of aboriginal title to the remainder of the forest would be upheld in the courts, Curry predicted a sizeable future damage or compensatory award for the Indians.[64] He assigned Ruth Muskrat Bronson, executive secretary of the National Council of American Indians and also an associate in his Washington, D.C., office, to go to Alaska to work with a local attorney there with whom Curry had entered into partnership, William Paul, Jr. Bronson and Paul would attempt to persuade the Indians to accept the proposal.[65]

Curry worried that this might be difficult. Non-Native Alaskans had protested strenuously, often in racial terms, the reservations which Secretary Ickes had created. They opposed unalterably any suggestion for additional withdrawals.[66] And in testimony at the Hanna hearings, both Forest Service administrators and Alaska officials of the Indian Office had disparaged the notion that aboriginal title to most of southeast Alaska had not been extinguished through abandonment.[67] In reaction, some Indian leaders argued that the Indians should make no agreements with government agencies or Congress but should stake everything on a court settlement of their aboriginal claims.[68]

It is significant that Felix Cohen did not consult the Alaska Native Brotherhood prior to suggesting his ten percent plan to Gardner. Cohen had traveled to Alaska in 1944 to attend the Hanna hearings and had been introduced to officers of the ANB.[69] In their discussions he had assured the Natives that they had substantial land rights in the Tongass National Forest and that he would do what he could to see that they were protected. Cohen's visit was important, for he and Secretary Ickes had acted without consulting the Alaska Indians in establishing the reservations in 1942 and in planning the Hanna hearings soon afterward.[70] Despite Cohen's solicitude for Alaska Natives and their rights, some ANB leaders found his and Ickes's presumption to act on their behalf offensive.[71] Cohen had spoken to Curry about the Alaskan Natives' need for representation, and he was pleased to have the experienced attorney involved in the Alaska problem. He looked to Curry to facilitate communication with the various Tlingit and Haida villages.[72]

In a long letter "To the Tlingit and Haida Indians of Alaska," an associate in Curry's Washington office, C. M. Wright, wrote that the proposed new legislation was the best they could hope for. Felix Cohen was "the best friend the Indians have in the government," Wright wrote. He had been responsible for Secretary Ickes's promise that Indian land rights would be fairly determined and fully protected. But the situation had changed from the Ickes period, and the Interior Department was no longer as friendly to the idea of broad aboriginal claims as it once had been. Cohen was "swimming against the tide." The pendulum had swung, and the New Deal was over. The suit over aboriginal claims could take years, he advised, and might be lost. The Indians should accept the proposal for ten percent of timber sales receipts. There was no immediate prejudice to their rights in doing so, and in any case, Wright wrote, "the Forest Service was prepared to sell timber to the proposed pulp mills in utter disregard of all your rights" if some agreement was not reached soon. The Forest Service's commitment to recognize a million acres as Indian land might be the best land disposition the Indians would ever achieve. Moreover, the new mills would provide jobs for large numbers Indians then unemployed.[73]

Even as Ruth Bronson was leaving Washington for Alaska at the first of May, however, agreement on the plan began to unravel. Attorneys for the canned salmon industry vigorously objected to it. Along with Forester Heintzleman and most non-Native Alaskans, the chief spokesman for the salmon industry, W. C. Arnold, thought that Indians had no right to land other than the actual sites on which their villages were situated. Payment of ten percent of timber sales receipts to the Indians might imply legal acknowledgement of their ownership of the timber sold to generate those receipts, he asserted, and thus open the door to recognition of Indian ownership of any and all timber in the Tongass Forest, and possibly any or all forest lands, and, more particularly, fishing sites within the forest where the industry operated salmon traps and cannery operations.[74]

The swiftness with which other critics of the proposal responded with their own objections manifested the power of the salmon industry where Alaska matters were concerned. Almost immediately, members of the Washington State Congressional delegation told Gardner they would oppose the legislation.[75] In addition to shipping a significant amount of the annual salmon pack through Seattle, industry investors had worked with Washington legislators for years to guarantee stability in the Alaska economy, a stability which benefited Seattle shippers and merchants as well. They would accept the legislation, the Washingtonians said, only if a provision were included to guarantee in perpetuity the number and location of the salmon industry's present trap sites. This was the subject of separate legislation also under consideration by Congress. Gardner knew that the Indians, who had objected to salmon trap sites since 1920, would never support such a provision.[76]

Delegate Bartlett also withdrew his support for the ten percent proposal. Upon learning of Arnold's opposition, he immediately telephoned Gardner to tell him that "the deal is off." No bill the salmon industry objected to, he said, would ever get through Congress.[77] At the same time, the Justice Department also notified Gardner that it could no longer support the legislation, echoing Arnold's argument that it might imply legal recognition of Indian claims.[78] Governor Gruening, unenthusiastic about the plan before, now notified Gardner that he, too, was opposed. Cohen, who was in close touch with Gardner, considered this the "death blow" for the plan, for Gruening made clear his intention never to allow any "crack in the door" which might doom both industrial development in Alaska and the statehood movement.[79]

With time running out on the legislative session, Gardner desperately tried to salvage something from the proposal which would allow pulp development while protecting the Indians' rights. Conceding the strength of the salmon industry, he arranged for Bartlett and Cohen to meet with him in Secretary Krug's office, where, in a tense session with Krug, a new bill was hammered out.[80] This was the bill Congress would pass as the

Tongass Timber Act of 1947. To quiet the major objection to the original version, the ten percent provision was dropped entirely. Instead, the Secretary of Agriculture was authorized to sell timber on any "vacant, unappropriated or unpatented land" within the forest, and all receipts from such sales would be put into escrow, "maintained in a special account in the Treasury" pending final determination of the extent of Indian claims. In the meantime, nothing in the act was to be construed "as recognizing or denying" the validity of such claims. This new version of the bill, in other words, simply ignored the question of aboriginal title and left the Indians to sue in court. In addition, the bill authorized the Secretary of the Interior to sell small tracts of lands, "notwithstanding any claim of possessory rights," for millsites and other processing needs.[81]

Although this legislation developed out of concern for Indian land rights, very little protection of those rights survived in the final version of the bill, for while the act did not expressly appropriate much Indian land, by effectively dismissing aboriginal claims, it left the Indians with a protracted, costly, and uncertain judicial appeal as their only recourse for determining the extent of their title and the amount of any damages they might recover from the taking and exploitation of that land by the U.S. And of immediate concern, it left them with no visible means to finance that appeal. In the meantime, the Forest Service (for the Secretary of Agriculture) could sell timber which might belong to the Indians, the cutting of which would irrevocably alter the character of the land on which the timber grew and the uses to which it might be put. And the Secretary of the Interior could sell lands which might later be found to be owned by Indians, but which would be used by non-Indians for non-traditional purposes. The Indians were removed from the process as active participants; they were made dependent upon the Secretary of the Interior to protect their villages, on the Secretary of Agriculture to get a fair price for the timber, and on the courts of the United States to determine what, if anything, they were entitled to as compensation.[82]

When Curry learned the provisions of the new bill he wondered why Cohen had approved it. Bartlett told Curry that Cohen had done so. But Cohen later told Curry that he had said in the meeting at Krug's office that he would not object to a bill which did not explicitly deprive the Indians of their rights but neither would he actively support it. Cohen thought Bartlett had misrepresented his position. In any case, Curry told Bartlett, Cohen, and Gardner that the Indians would never support the new proposal.[83]

In Alaska, Ruth Bronson learned this firsthand. At every village she and Paul visited, the Indians articulated their objections to the new measure. It did not answer their protest about land claims, they said, but instead left them facing endless litigation with no way to pay for it. Some argued that pulp was not the best use for much Tongass timber. But even if it was, if it was Indian timber, it should be sold by Indians, not by the Forest Service. And the Indians were "cynical," Bronson wrote, about work opportunities. The canners did not employ them if they could do otherwise, the Indians said, and the pulp industry would be the same. Moreover, the Indians feared destruction of their fishery. When the pulp mills come in, they said, "they will destroy the fish, shrimp and other seafood resources because of the poison that is generated." Not only would the Indians lose what little income they presently had from selling small amounts of fish to some canneries, but they would be forced to move great distances away from the millsites in order to continue their fishing. The new bill was a "blow" to the Indians, Paul wrote; there was nothing in it for them. The Indians made plans to send a delegation to Washington to protest the legislation.[84]

Determined to have the matter settled, however, Secretary Krug sent the new bill to the Congress on May 16.[85] In the Senate it was assigned to Butler's Committee on Public Lands which held brief, perfunctory hearings, which were not published. In the House, it went to the Committee on Agriculture, where Chairman Clifford Hope of Kansas scheduled immediate hearings. These were the primary hearings for the bill.[86] Most of the principals testified in the last week of May and the first week of June. Gruening repeated his assertion of the necessity to capitalize on the present willingness of the investors in the pulp industry. C. M. Granger, assistant chief of the Forest Service, seconded that assertion, and went on to say that the Service needed the lands which Interior had identified in the Haas-Goldschmidt recommendation because that was where the best timber was. Assistant Secretary of Agriculture Charles Brannon argued that the proposed bill carried out former Interior Secretary Ickes's desires by implicitly inviting the courts to make a final disposition of Alaska Indian claims, an assertion which Ickes would hotly deny in several news columns. Interior Solicitor Maston White assured the Congressmen that the Forest Service had the right to the timber, and could cut if it liked, but that the Indians would certainly seek an injunction if the government did so without their approval, perhaps tying up pulp development indefinitely. Whatever plan was worked out would need their approval. James Curry used extensive testimony to make a passionate case not only for the Indians' rights to timber and land, but also for the government's need to respect their right to a settlement prior to any lease sales, not after. He seemed to raise serious doubts with the Congressmen as to the constitutionality of the legislation.[87]

Members of the Indian delegation were able to make brief statements on the next to the last day of the hearings. They said that the bill violated both Secretary Ickes's promise to implement a just and definite determination of their land rights and the Haas-Goldschmidt recommendation for reservation boundaries. They also argued that the bill violated the U.S. Constitution by taking property without adequate judicial procedure. The resulting sale of timber leases by the Forest Service would pauperize the Natives, they said, and it violated the American sense of justice. Shrewdly, they suggested that the bill would not protect the investors, for the Indians were sure to sue the government and the pulp companies, and the litigation would probably hold up pulp development.[88]

Although he did not testify directly, Alaska Forester Frank Heintzleman was present at the sessions, and when questions about actual conditions in Alaska were raised, he supplied the answers. He also submitted a formal written statement. Although not a member, Delegate Bartlett was permitted to join the committee, to ask questions, and to make statements for the record.[89]

Regardless of testimony in opposition to it, the committee seemed determined to get the bill out for a full Congressional vote before the summer recess. The newsprint shortage loomed large in their questions and discussions, as did the need to develop Alaska.[90] There was considerable discussion of how much land was appropriate for the Indians and how a determination should be made. They were not in a position to make a judgment on that question, the Congressmen agreed, and they left the matter to be settled by the courts. Facilitating economic development was the critical factor, the committee summarized, and should not be jeopardized by the theory of aboriginal title. Judging that their colleagues would agree, they sent the bill forward with a recommendation for passage.[91]

There was little interest in the bill in the full House. In the last days of the session in late July, Chairman Hope called it up one morning immediately after the daily invocation, when the floor was nearly empty. It passed with no comment, though Hope did note the objections of the Indians.[92]

Interest in the Senate was nearly as desultory. Senator Butler, an outspoken advocate of Alaska development as well as a leader of the growing termination bloc in Congress, brought the bill up three days before the scheduled adjournment date and succeeded in having it placed on the unanimous consent calendar. Senator Warren G. Magnuson of Washington State spoke for the bill and quickly summarized its intent as he understood it. Speaking proprietarily, he said that what "we" seek to do "is to sell the timber, protect the Indians, and give Alaska a needed pulp and paper industry. That is all it amounts to." Taking aim at James Curry, he added that some "Indian lawyers downtown" wanted to justify their existence and continue to make their living "off the Indians" by telling their clients that they were protecting their rights in objecting to the bill. But everyone in the Pacific Northwest and Alaska, Magnuson asserted, "including the Indians themselves, wants to get this industry established." The senator seemed unaware of the Indian protest.[93]

While the bill was before the Senate, former Secretary Ickes criticized it vigorously in a regular newspaper column he wrote on government affairs, excoriating both Secretary of Agriculture Clinton Anderson and the Interior Department. Ickes called the bill a "timber grab." Indian ownership of "great stretches" of the Tongass Forest had been confirmed by the Interior Department, Ickes wrote, but the Agriculture Department "arrogantly" proposed to overrule Interior without even taking the matter to court. The urgent need for pulpwood, Ickes continued, did not justify the Forest Service conducting a "raid on privately owned property." Perhaps the "shadiest side" of the matter, he said, was that the Interior Department, the supposed "guardian" of the Indians, was equally guilty, refusing to fight any further for the Indians' rights. Ickes suggested that the Indians erect totem poles to Anderson and to the Interior Department. This old Indian custom was supposed to yield one of two results when someone took something which did not belong to him: either the property would be returned, or the person or persons to whom the pole was dedicated would have "an early demise."[94]

But Ickes's remarks had no effect, for the bill passed the Senate on a voice vote in the last fifteen minutes of the session, on July 26. Watkins, chairman of the Indian Affairs committee and a former judge, said that the question of land claims should be left to the courts. He confessed that he was not sure of the act's constitutionality. But he said he would vote for it and leave that question to the future. In the meantime, economic development in Alaska would benefit both Natives and whites.

Senator Butler in the meantime added to the record statements of support from mayors and chambers of commerce in several Alaska non-Native communities, some of them not in the southeast region. All the statements tied passage of the bill to pulp development in Alaska, and one repeated the argument that the Indians had no confirmed land rights outside their villages.[95]

President Truman did not sign the bill until August 8. In the interim, Curry and his associates launched a last-minute effort to persuade him to veto it. Curry published an article in which he argued that the measure was inconsistent with the defense of the rights of "little people" by the United States. That Indian ownership of resources was blocking "the road of progress" was, Curry wrote, "an old, old excuse." All the Indians were being offered, he said, was "the right to sue the Federal Government for the value of what is taken from them." But when the timber of the Chippewa Indians of Minnesota had been taken in 1908, he pointed out, adjudication had lasted thirty-one years, and then the court ruled that the timber had not been marketable in 1908, even though it had been sold for millions of dollars later. So the Chippewas were denied any compensation. California Indians had waited ninety-one years in a similar case, Curry wrote, and then had been awarded far less in compensation that the true value of the land and resources which had been taken from them.[96]

Bronson published an article on the day the President signed the bill; she charged that the act had been rushed through Congress in the last "hectic" days of the session to hide a "sickening" timber theft from the American public. She compared the government's action to the infamous Teapot Dome scandal of the 1920s, when Interior Secretary Albert Fall set aside Wyoming Indian lands as a petroleum reserve and then allowed Sinclair Oil Company to pump and market the oil on the commercial market, paying Fall a percentage of the profits. Bronson did not charge that any government officials were being paid by pulp developers for their support of the Tongass bill, and the comparison with the oil scandal was at best inflammatory. But Bronson apparently judged that it made "good press." Like Ickes, she also argued that the right to sue the government was of little use to the Indians. Law suits, she said, were of value "only to their grandchildren."[97]

Probably in response to the opponents' published articles and mailings by the NCAI, many concerned citizens wrote letters directly to the President protesting the bill and urging his veto of it. Most called the bill an "illegal land grab" and appealed for justice, "at long last," for the Indians.[98]

Unpersuaded, President Truman signed the bill on August 8. He made no public announcement upon doing so. But in a major statement on Alaska the preceding May, he had urged industrial and economic development in Alaska and had pledged his support.[99] Responses sent to the letter writers by the President's office staff were somewhat perfunctory but indicated that the President was certain that adequate protection of Indian land rights was contained in the bill, and that the measure would greatly aid development and population in Alaska. Indicating the degree to which the bill was seen as a victory in Alaska, soon after signing it the President received a telegram from the Ketchikan Chamber of Commerce requesting the pen which he had used. Unfortunately for the merchants of Ketchikan, it could not be located.[100] Governor Gruening too was much relieved by the bill's passage. Not long after it became law, he wrote to Secretary Krug that the territory had "had a narrow escape."[101]

Passage of the Tongass timber bill cleared the way for pulp development, as Gruening and others hoped it would, although the industry's ambitious plans for Alaska were not realized on the grand scale imagined. Eventually two pulp mills were constructed, but little of the pulp they produced was suitable for use as newsprint.[102] Assessing the contribution this development made to the Alaska statehood campaign is difficult, for the financing for the state government was projected to come mainly from oil and other mineral leases, and when the statehood bill passed, only one of the mills had been completed. However, its construction did somewhat validate the promise of industrial development.[103]

It is more difficult to determine the significance of the act for Alaska's Tlingit and Haida Indians. For a time, passage of the act fueled more protest by opponents. Secretary Ickes wrote more columns, adding Gruening and Heintzleman to his list of villains, and at least one newspaper editor called for the act's repeal.[104] The Alaska Native Brotherhood collected a number of such protests and, with the NCAI, published them in a pamphlet entitled "Alaska's Teapot Dome." A photograph of former Secretary Fall was printed opposite the title page.[105] The other bills in Congress which affected Alaska Indians were under active debate, and the protests were directed more toward these bills than toward repeal of the Tongass Timber Act.[106] Secretary Krug retired in November 1949. Still uncomfortable about unprotected Indian lands in Alaska, on his last day in office he executed an order creating three new Indian reservations there.[107] The continuing protests of the advocates of aboriginal title and the rights of the Tlingit and Haida people may have helped to convince

Krug that Alaska Indian lands needed administrative protection, considering Congress's action on the Tongass bill.[108]

Reaction to the Tongass act continued for many months after it became law. Early in 1948 Felix Cohen, recently retired from government service, published an article he called "Open Season on Alaska Natives" in which he charged that the actions of the Forest Service in assisting the pulp industry were an example of capitalist colonialism which denied the Indians their legitimate rights and, in addition to other consequences, condemned them "to die of diseases of malnutrition."[109] Employment opportunities for Alaska's Indians, only some of whom were well assimilated, were poor, health care was inadequate, and educational attainment was low. Governor Gruening estimated that ten percent of the receipts from timber sales for pulp development would have amounted to hundreds of thousands of dollars annually, which might have helped to alleviate Indian suffering. And while he could not approve an implied Congressional recognition of Indian land title by the provision that they be paid for the timber, nonetheless he was concerned about the Indians' plight. Not long after passage of the Tongass act, he recommended to Secretary Krug that it be amended to allow the government simply to use fifty percent of the sales receipts to aid the Indians "until some sum such as twenty-five or thirty million dollars has been expended."[110] Although Krug responded positively, the Forest Service objected to the proposal.[111]

As Curry's associate C. M. Wright had written to the Tlingit and Haida people before the Tongass bill passed, the New Deal in Alaska was over for the Indians.[112] Gruening's and Heintzleman's ideas for the economic development of Alaska and regarding the assimilation of the Tlingit and Haida Indians found support in Congress and among many officers in the federal bureaucracy. As they would for a time in national policy, those ideas were to take precedence in Alaska over protection of Indian land title and the question of justice for Alaska's Indians. Uncertain of the implications of reservations, and fearful and resentful of control by the federal government, Indians in the villages of Kake and Klawock rejected the reserves offered by Secretary Ickes; though the people of the village of Hydaburg approved their reservation, it subsequently was disallowed by the courts in 1952 as having been faultily established.[113] Following the Tongass act, the Tlingit and Haida Indians did not ask the courts to enjoin the Forest Service from auctioning Tongass timber. Instead, with Curry approved as their attorney by the Interior Department and working on contingency, they began earnestly to pursue their aboriginal claims suit to the whole Tongass National Forest.[114] They would win that suit in the U.S. Court of Claims in 1959 but would be awarded only $7.5 million in damages in 1965 for the taking of the forest and its resources.[115] The Indians considered the amount of the award inadequate. Six years later, in the comprehensive Alaska Native Claims Settlement Act, the Tlingit and Haida would obtain clear title to their villages and certain lands surrounding them. But the total acreage would be far less than either the ten percent of the Tongass forest proposed in the Haas-Goldschmidt recommendation in 1946 or the six and one-half percent the Forest Service had been persuaded to concede in early 1947.[116]

That outcome could not be anticipated in 1947, however, and the story of the Tongass Timber Act is one of a conflict of values and the policies which embodied them. For the Forest Service and advocates of Alaska statehood, the primacy of modern capitalist development in the Tongass National Forest was more important than the protection of potential Indian land rights and resources, which they interpreted as a threat to that development. Assimilation of Indians into the mainstream of white culture in Alaska seemed both necessary and appropriate to those who held this view, a position doubtless reinforced by the fact that the most articulate Indian spokesmen were themselves well assimilated. This fact likely obscured the negative effects of the curtailing of federal services. Congressional arguments in support of the Tongass Timber Act were similar to those which later would be made in support of the termination policy. On the other hand, supporters of the Indians argued for the primacy of aboriginal title and protection of Indian rights. To secure Indian lands, and Indian culture and identity, they placed the sanctity of Indian land title above the value of economic development. At the very beginning of the termination era, in the Tongass Timber Act of 1947, the advocates of Indian rights lost an important early contest over these values to the proponents of development and assimilation.

NOTES

1. Francis Paul Prucha, *The Great Father: The United States and the American Indians*, Vol. II (Lincoln: University of Nebraska Press, 1984), pp. 957–63; F. Cohen, *Handbook of Federal Indian Law*, 1982 ed. (Charlottesville, Va.: Michie Bobbs Merrill, 1982), pp. 750–52.

2. Kenneth Philp, "The New Deal and Alaskan Natives, 1936–1945," *Pacific Historical Review*, 50 (August 1981): pp. 309–27.

3. U.S. Congress, Senate, Committee on Interior and Insular Affairs, *Report, Rescinding Certain Orders of the Secretary of the Interior* (S.J. Res. 162), 80 Cong., 2 sess. (1948), *passim*; U.S. Congress, Senate, Committee on Interstate and Foreign Commerce, *Hearings on S. 1446, Leasing Salmon Traps in the Territory of Alaska,* 80 Cong., 1 sess. (1947), *passim;* U.S. Congress, House, Subcommittee on Territorial and Insular Possessions, Committee on Public Lands, *Hearings on H.R. 206 and H.R. 1808, Statehood for Alaska,* 80 Cong., 1 sess. (1947), *passim;* U.S. Congress, House, Committee on Agriculture, *Hearings on H.J. Resolution 205, Tongass National Forest,* 80 Cong., 1 sess. (1947), *passim.*

4. 61 *United States Statutes* 920–21; the bill was in the form of a joint resolution, 80 Cong., 1 sess., H.J. Res. 205, and S.J. Res. 118; U.S. Congress, House, Committee on Agriculture, *Authorizing the Secretary of Agriculture to Sell Timber within the Tongass National Forest,* H.R. 873, 80 Cong., 1 sess. (1947); U.S. Congress, Senate, Committee on Public Lands, *Authorizing the Secretary of Agriculture to Sell Timber within the Tongass National Forest,* S.R. 874, 80 Cong., 1 sess. (1947).

5. House Committee on Agriculture, *Hearings on H.J. Res. 205*, pp. 3–6, 7–10, 37–40.

6. Susan M. Hartmann, *Truman and the 80th Congress* (Columbia: University of Missouri Press, 1971), pp. 7–8, 37–38, 143–45; Hugh Butler to Arthur H. Vandenberg, file S.J. Res. 118, Box 262, Hugh Butler Papers, Nebraska Historical Society (hereafter Butler Papers, NHS).

7. Prucha, *The Great Father*, pp. 1013–40.

8. *Ibid.,* p. 1015; Donald L. Fixico, *Termination and Relocation: Federal Indian Policy, 1945–1960* (Albuquerque: University of New Mexico Press, 1986), p. 36.

9. *Congressional Record,* 80 Cong., 1 sess. (July 26, 1947), p. 10407; Harold L. Ickes, "Alaska Indians," *New York Post,* Aug. 21, 1947, p. 8.

10. Alaska Native Brotherhood, October 1947, Alaska Timber, Box 62, James Curry Papers, National Anthropological Archive (Smithsonian) (hereafter, James Curry Papers); Curry, the principal attorney for the Tlingit and Haida Indians in their dealings with the federal government, represented the Alaska Native Brotherhood (ANB) and several southeastern Alaska villages.

11. Gov. Ernest Gruening to Sec. of the Interior J. A. Krug, Sept. 18, 1947, file 40-04, reel 274, Record Group 348, Records of the Office of the Governor of Alaska, National Archives and Record Service Microcopy 939.

12. *Congressional Record,* 80 Cong., 1 sess. (July 26, 1947), p. 10407.

13. House Committee on Agriculture, *Hearings on H.J. Resolution 205,* pp. 2–3; David C. Smith, "Pulp, Paper, and Alaska," *Pacific Northwest Quarterly* 66 (April 1975), pp. 61–70.

14. *Ibid.*, 62; Ernest Gruening, *The State of Alaska* (New York: Random House, 1954), pp. 370–71.

15. U.S. Congress, House, Committee on Agriculture, *Disposition of Revenues from Tongass National Forest, Alaska*, H.R. 2568, 84 Cong., 2 sess. (1952), p. 2.

16. Smith, "Pulp, Paper, and Alaska," p. 67.

17. Heintzleman to Gruening, April 14, 1947, file 41-01, reel 280, RG 348, NARS Microcopy 939; House Committee on Agriculture, *Hearings on H.J. Res. 205*, p. 23; Lawrence W. Rakestraw, *A History of the United States Forest Service in Alaska* (Anchorage: Alaska Historical Comm. et al., 1981), pp. 125–26.

18. Heintzleman to Gruening, March 4, 1947, file R-10, Box 1500, Div. of Timber Management, Record Group 95, Records of the Forest Service, National Archives (NA).

19. House Committee on Agriculture, *Hearings on H.J. Res. 205*, pp. 7, 47.

20. These included Klukwan, Hoonah, Angoon, Kake, Klawock, Hydaburg, and Yakutat and parts of the white communities of Haines, Juneau, Douglas, Sitka, Petersburg, Ketchikan (Saxman), and Wrangell. The Tsimshian village of New Metlakatla on Annette Island, the only Tsimshian village in Alaska, was established under special circumstances and was not included in Tlingit and Haida land claims matters. Official counts of the villages ranged from eleven to sixteen.

21. Claude Wickard to Sec. of Interior Ickes, Feb. 5, 1945 file Alaska, Office Files of Oscar L. Chapman, 1933–53, RG 48, Records of the Office of the Secretary of the Interior, NA.

22. Felix S. Cohen, "Report to the Commissioner of Indian Affairs," July 10, 1944, and Interior Solicitor Maston G. White to Assist. Sec. of the Interior William E. Warne, Dec. 5, 1947, file Territories, Alaska: Indian claims, Box 68, Office of the Solicitor, RG 48, NA.

23. Cohen, *Handbook*, pp. 486–93; David S. Case, *Alaska Natives and American Law* (Fairbanks: University of Alaska Press, 1984), pp. 47–55; William C. Canby, Jr., *American Indian Law in a Nutshell* (St. Paul: West Publishing Co., 1981), pp. 221–24, 226–31.

24. Cohen, *Handbook*, p. 491; Case, *Alaska Natives*, pp. 55.

25. Cohen, *Handbook*, p. 160.

26. *United States, as Guardian of the Hualpai Indians of Arizona, v. Santa Fe Pacific Railroad*, 314 US 339; Cohen, *Handbook*, pp. 488, 490, 521–22; Lucy Kramer Cohen, ed., *The Legal Conscience: Selected Papers of Felix S. Cohen* (New Haven: Yale University Press, 1960), pp. 273–304.

27. House Committee on Agriculture, *Hearings on H.J. Res. 205*, pp. 5–6.

28. Cohen, *Handbook*, p. 743; Case, *Alaska Natives*, p. 86.

29. Cohen, *Handbook*, pp. 743–46.

30. Gruening to Krug, Sept. 18, 1947.

31. U.S. Congress, Senate, Subcommittee of the Committee of Interior and Insular Affairs, *Hearings on S. 2037, Repeal Act Authorizing the Secretary of Interior to Create Indian Reservations in Alaska*, 80 Cong., 2 sess. (1948), pp. 53–56; Case, *Alaska Natives*, pp. 101–104.

32. Heintzleman to Assist. Sec. of Interior Warner W. Gardner, March 15, 1947, file R-10, Box 1500, RG 95, NA.

33. Memorandum, Bureau of Indian Affairs to Sec. of Interior, through White and Warne, Sept. 26, 1947, file Alaska Salmon Trap & Timber Bill, Box 56, Office of the Solicitor.

34. White to Gardner, March 4, 1947, file Alaska Salmon Trap & Timber Bill, Box 58; Office of the Solicitor, House Committee on Agriculture, *Hearings on H.J. Res. 205*, p. 3; 36 *U.S. Statutes* 847.

35. White to Gardner, March 4, 1947.

36. Clause-M. Naske, *An Interpretive History of Alaskan Statehood* (Anchorage: Alaska Northwest Publishing Co., 1973), pp. 67, 73; Bartlett to Cohen, April 15, 1948, file 14.8, Box C1B, Curry-Weissbrodt Papers, Alaska Historical Library, Juneau. The Curry-Weissbrodt Papers consist of the office files of James Curry and Israel Weissbrodt, who followed Curry as principal attorney for the Tlingit and Haida Indians. Produced by the Sealaska Heritage Foundation (of the Tlingit and Haida Indians), they are available on microfilm.

37. Gruening to Frank Peratrovich, Andrew Hope, Frank Johnson, and Fred Grant (Tlingit Indians), July 1, 1947, printed in House Committee on Agriculture, *Hearings on H.J. Res. 205*, pp. 186–87; *Alaska Daily Empire*, March 25, 1948, p. 4.

38. Gardner to Krug, March 12, 1947, file Alaska, Box 73, Julius A. Krug Papers, Library of Congress (LC); Butler to Sec. of Agr. Clinton Anderson, March 12, 1947, file Alaska, Box 219, Butler Papers, NHS.

39. Editorial, *Journal of Forestry* 43 (June 1945): 391–92; Philp, "New Deal and Alaskan Indians," pp. 320–21.

40. Haas-Goldschmidt Report (Dec. 10, 1946), Acting Sec. William Zimmerman to Warne, Feb. 4, 1947, file Records Concerning Claims of Natives of Southeast Alaska, Box 56, Office of the Solicitor; House Committee on Agriculture, *Hearings on H.J. Res. 205*, pp. 8–9.

41. Department of the Interior Statement of Policy on Aboriginal Claims and Native Reservations in Alaska, Nov. 20, 1946, file Gen. Corresp., 1930–58, Box 60, Office of the Solicitor.

42. Gardner to W. C. Arnold, June 5, 1946, file Alaska-Fisheries, Box 3, Warner Gardner Papers, Harry S. Truman Library (hereafter HST Lib.); Philp, "New Deal and Alaskan Natives," pp. 321–22

43. Oral history tape OH-111, Gardner Papers, HST Lib.

44. House Committee on Agriculture, *Hearings on H.J. Res. 205,* p. 16.

45. Memorandum, Bureau of Indian Affairs to Sec. of Interior, through White and Warne, Sept. 26, 1947, file Alaska Salmon Trap & Timber Bill, Box 56, Office of the Solicitor.

46. White to Gardner, March 4, 1947, *ibid.*

47. Dodd to R. Welch, House Comm. on Public Lands, Feb. 24, 1947, file 17.2, Box C1B, Curry-Weissbrodt Papers.

48. Gardner to Krug, Jan. 27, 1947, file Alaska-Native Land Claims, Box 3, Gardner Papers, HST Lib.

49. Minutes, and Resolution No. 2, Angoon convention (1945), ANB, pp. 87–99, file 26.2, Box C3A, Curry-Weissbrodt Papers; Minutes, Wrangell convention (1946), ANB (no pag.), file 26.2, Box C3A, *ibid.*; Elizabeth Peratrovich to Curry, Jan. 27, 1950, file 11.4, Box C1, *ibid.*

50. Philip Drucker, *The Native Brotherhoods: Modern Intertribal Organizations on the Northwest Coast* (Washington, D.C.: Bureau of Ethnology, 1956), *passim.*

51. *Ibid.,* pp. 47–47, 70–73; Gruening, *State of Alaska,* pp. 376–77.

52. For example, Memorandum, Alaska Conferences, Feb. 5, 1937, file Alaska, 1933–44, Lands Division, Office File of John Collier, Records of the Bureau of Indian Affairs, RG 75, NA, and Memorandum, Jan. 25, 1941, file Alaska-S, Indian Organization, Office of the Commissioner, RG 75, NA.

53. *The Alaskan* (ANB newspaper, Petersburg, Alaska), Nov. 29, 1929; David Morgan to William Paul, Sr., June 1, 1940, file 23, Box C3A, Curry-Weissbrodt Papers.

54. Paul to Office of Indian Affairs, May 27, 1941, file Alaska-S, Office File of John Collier; Report of Land Suit Attorney, William Paul, Jr., Oct. 3, 1941, file 6, Box C3, Curry-Weissbrodt Papers.

55. Stanley James Underdall, "On the Road toward Termination: The Pyramid Lake Piautes and the Indian Attorney Controversy of the 1950s," unpub. doc. dissert., Columbia University, 1977, pp. 120–21; Joaqlin Estus and Glenda Choate, *Curry-Weissbrodt Papers of the Tlingit and Haida Indian Tribes of Alaska: An Inventory* (Juneau: Central Council of Tlingit and Haida Indian Tribes of Alaska, 1983), p. 10.

56. Acting Comm. of Indian Affairs William Zimmerman to Don Foster, Chief, OIA, Juneau, March 22, 1947, file 26.2, Box C3A, Curry-Weissbrodt Papers.

57. Paul to William Baker, editor, *Ketchikan Chronicle,* May 21, 1945, and Paul to Curry, March 18, 1947, file 19, Box C1B, *ibid.*

58. Curry to Paul, Jr., March 22, 1947, file 3.4, Box C3, *ibid.*; Gruening, *State of Alaska,* pp. 373–74; Gruening to Bartlett, April 15, 1947, file 40-04, reel 274, RG 348.

59. C. M. Wright (Curry associate) to file, March 21, 1947, file 19, Box C1B, Curry-Weissbrodt Papers.

60. Cohen to Edward F. Mynatt (Assoc. Solicitor, Agr. Dept.), March 17, 1947, file Alaska-Territories, Box 69, Office of the Solicitor.

61. Gardner to Curry, March 21, 1947, file 3.3, Box C3, Curry-Weissbrodt Papers; Gardner to White, March 21, 1947, file Alaska Salmon & Timber Bill, Box 56, Office of the Solicitor.

62. Wright to file, April 3, 1947, file 19, Box C1B, Curry-Weissbrodt Papers.

63. Curry to Gardner, April 7, 1947, *ibid.*

64. Ruth Bronson to file, May 8, 1947, file 19, Box C1B, Curry-Weissbrodt Papers.

65. *Ibid.*

66. *Ketchikan Chronicle,* Oct. 24, 1944, "Alaska-Wide Anti-Indian Reservation Issue" (Special Issue); Dec. 6, 1944, p. 4; Frank G. Johnson (mayor of the Tlingit village of Kake), circular letter to Alaska towns, Dec. 7, 1944, file 3.3, Box C3, Curry-Weissbrodt Papers.

67. *Hearings on Claims of Natives of the Towns of Hydaburg, Klawock, and Kake, Alaska,* file 40-04d, reel 274, RG 348.

68. Paul, Sr., to Frank G. Johnson, May 13, 1945, file Alaska Native Brotherhood, Box 2, William Paul Papers, Suzzallo Library, University of Washington (hereafter UW Lib.). Paul, Sr., was a principal Tlingit leader and officer of the Alaska Native Brotherhood from 1920 to 1960.

69. Johnson, circular letter, Dec. 7, 1944.

70. Minutes, Angoon convention, ANB (1945), pp. 37–39, file 26.2, Box C3A, Curry-Weissbrodt Papers.

71. *Ibid.,* pp. 40–42.

72. Cohen to Curry, Feb. 21, 1947, file Alaska Timber, Box 62, James Curry Papers.

73. Wright to the Tlingit and Haida Indians of Southeastern Alaska, April 11, 1947, file 19, Box C1B, Curry-Weissbrodt Papers.

74. Gardner to Cohen, April 23, 1947, file Alaska Lands, Box 143, RG 126, Records of the Office of Territories, NA.

75. Wright to file, Apr. 18, 1947, Bronson to file, May 8, 1947, file 19, Box C1B, Curry-Weissbrodt Papers; Gruening, *State of Alaska,* pp. 393–405.

76. Gardner to White, May 5, 1947, file Alaska Native Land Claims, Box 3, Gardner Papers, HST Lib.

77. Frances Lopinsky (Curry associate) to Curry, May 13, 1947, file 17.2, Box C1B, Curry-Weissbrodt Papers.

78. Gardner to White, May 5, 1947, file Alaska Native Land Claims, Box 3, Gardner Papers, HST Lib.

79. Lopinsky to Curry, May 13, 1947, file 17.2, Box C1B, Curry-Weissbrodt Papers; Gruening to Oscar Chapman, Feb. 15, 1949, file GRI-GRY, Box 46, Papers of Oscar L. Chapman, HST Lib.

80. Gardner to White, May 18, 1947, file Alaska Native Land Claims, Box 3, ardner Papers, HST Lib.; Lopinsky to Curry, May 19, 1947, file 17.2, Box C1B, Curry-Weissbrodt Papers.

81. 61 *U.S. Statutes* 920–21.

82. Curry's associates labeled it "Gov. Gruening and the Sec. of Agriculture's Bill"; Lopinsky to Curry, May 13, 1947, file 17.2, Box C1B, Curry-Weissbrodt Papers.

83. Curry to file, May 19, 1947, Lopinsky to Curry, May 19, 1947, *ibid.*

84. Bronson to Curry, May 19, 1947, *ibid.;* Paul, Jr., to Johnson, May 21, 1947, file 2, Box C3, *ibid.*

85. House Committee on Agriculture, *Hearings on H.J. Res. 205,* pp. 2–3.

86. Butler to Arthur Watkins, Aug. 12, 1947, file Alaska, Box 219, Butler Papers, NHS. Watkins was chairman of the Senate Indian Affairs Committee.

87. House Committee on Agriculture, *Hearings on H.J. Res. 205,* pp. 37–40 (Gruening), 25–26 (Granger), 175, 190–92 (Brannon) (Ickes, *Washington Evening Star,* July 23, 1947, p. 9), 185 (White), 51–150 (Curry).

88. *Ibid.,* pp. 151–67. The ANB did not take an official position on the bill until its 1947 annual convention, held in November, when it condemned the measure; clipping (unidentified), Nov. 15, 1947, file Alaska Native Brotherhood, Box 1, Paul Papers, UW Lib.; Nov. 17, 1947, file 6 (resolutions), Box C2, Curry-Weissbrodt Papers.

89. House Committee on Agriculture, *Hearings on H.J. Res. 205,* pp. 7, 27–28, 41, 129, 190 (Heintzleman), 151, 163, 167 (Bartlett).

90. *Ibid.,* pp. 9, 12, 38, 40–41.

91. *Ibid.,* pp. 43, 16–17, 32–33, 84–90.

92. *Congressional Record,* 80 Cong., 1 sess. (July 10, 1947), p. 5524; Ickes, *Washington Post,* Aug. 21, 1947, p. 8.

93. *Congressional Record,* 80 Cong., 1 sess. (July 23, 1947), p. 9809.

94. *Washington Evening Star,* July 23, 1947, p. 9.

95. *Congressional Record,* 80 Cong., 1 sess. (July 26, 1947), p. 10407.

96. *Commonweal,* Aug. 1, 1947, pp. 4–5.

97. *New York Herald Tribune,* Aug. 8, 1947, p. 2.

98. File 1-C, "Tongass National Forest," Official Office File, Harry S. Truman Papers, HST Lib.

99. Alaska Development Plan, May 22, 1947, Administrative Correspondence Files, Office of the Solicitor.

100. File 1-C, "Tongass National Forest," Truman Papers.

101. Gruening to Krug, Sept. 18, 1947, file 40-04d, reel 274, RG 348.

102. Smith, "Pulp, Paper, and Alaska," pp. 68–70; U.S. Congress, Senate, Special Committee to Study Problems of American Small Business, *Survey of Alaskan Newsprint Resources,* S.R. 852, 80 Cong., 2 sess. (1947), p. 3.

103. Claus-M. Naske and Herman E. Slotnick, *Alaska: A History of the 49th State* (Grand Rapids: William B. Eerdmans Publishing Co., 1979), pp. 173–74, 176–77; Smith, *op. cit.*

104. *New York Post,* Aug. 21, 1947, p. 8; *Richmond* (Virginia) *Times-Dispatch,* Sept. 1, 1947, p. 6.

105. Alaska Native Brotherhood, October 1947, Alaska Timber, Box 62, James Curry Papers.

106. Oliver La Farge to Philleo Nash, Aug. 17, 1949, file Alaska Native Land Claims, Box 76, Philleo Nash files, HST Lib.

107. Information Bulletin, Department of the Interior, Nov. 3, 1949, Central Office File, Box 90, RG 48, NA; Memorandum for the President, David Niles, Feb. 6, 1950, file Alaska Native Claims, Box 76, Philleo Nash files, HST Lib.

108. La Farge to Nash, Aug. 17, 1949.

109. *Newsletter,* Institute of Ethnic Affairs, February 1948, pp. 4–8, copy in file S.J. Res. 118, Box 262, Butler Papers, NHS.

110. Gruening to Krug, Sept. 18, 1947.

111. Warne to Krug, Feb. 2, 1948, file Alaska Field Staff, 1948–53, Box 77, Office of the Solicitor.

112. Wright to the Tlingit and Haida Indians of Southeastern Alaska, April 11, 1947, file 19, Box C1B, Curry-Weissbrodt Papers.

113. Case, *Alaska Natives,* pp. 102, 106–107.

114. Paul, Sr., to Curry, Nov. 2, 1947, file 6 (Hydaburg convention), Box C3, Curry-Weissbrodt Papers.

115. *Tlingit and Haida Indians of Alaska et al. v. U.S.,* 177 F. Supp. 452 (Ct. Cls., 1959); 79 *U.S. Statutes* 543; *Tlingit and Haida Indians of Alaska et al. v. U.S.,* 389 F. 2nd 778 (Ct. Cls., 1968).

116. Robert Arnold, *Alaska Native Land Claims* (Anchorage: Alaska Native Foundation, 1976), pp. 150–51.

The Governor Who Opposed Statehood

The Legacy of Jay Hammond

JOHN WHITEHEAD

John Simms Whitehead, Professor of History at the University of Alaska Fairbanks, earned his doctoral degree at Yale University in 1971. His works include Hydroelectric Power in Twentieth Century Alaska: Anchorage, Juneau, Ketchikan and Sitka *(Fairbanks: University of Alaska, Institute of Water Resources, 1983) and* Separation of College and State: Columbia, Dartmouth, Harvard and Yale, 1776–1876 *(New Haven: Yale University Press, 1973). He recently completed Arrell Morgan Gibson's unfinished* Yankees in Paradise: The Pacific Basin Frontier *(Albuquerque: University of New Mexico Press, 1993).*

Several of Professor Whitehead's articles concern the Alaskan and Hawaiian statehood movements, as will much of his forthcoming work. In researching opposition to statehood within Alaska, Whitehead found that Governor Jay Hammond had opposed statehood in the 1950s, in part because he opposed the rapid economic development that advocates of statehood believed statehood would bring. In this selection examining Hammond's political career, Whitehead suggests that Alaska's Permanent Fund, now one of the single largest investment accounts in the world, is a legacy of the same views which led Hammond to oppose statehood.

When Alaska became the forty-ninth state in 1959, one might have concluded that the political advocates of statehood, or the statehooders as they were known, had been the principal apostles of environmentalism and responsible management of the new state's natural resources. A major theme of the statehood movement, certainly in the words of the territorial governor Ernest Gruening, had been to free Alaska from the outside economic interests, particularly fishing

This article appeared originally in *Alaska History* 7 (Fall 1992): 15–30; it is reprinted here by permission.

and mining, that had plundered its natural wealth and perpetrated a boom-and-bust economy for most of the twentieth century. As a territory Alaska had been denied the legislative control over its natural resources, particularly over commercial fisheries, that the federal government had given other western territories. Instead, the government, through a maze of dozens of separate agencies, managed Alaska's renewable and nonrenewable resources. Statehooders perceived, accurately by most analyses, that Seattle-based fishing interests and other lobbies were effective in gaining the kind of federal regulation—or lack of regulation—they wanted.[1]

To emphasize the exploitation of the past, statehooders pointed with outrage to the depletion of the territory's salmon—a phenomenon they connected directly to overfishing by Seattle-based canning companies that utilized the fish trap. Fish traps were outlawed in all forty-eight states; only in Alaska, where the federal government controlled the fisheries, were such devices legal. Fish traps were so hated by Alaskans that popular support for their abolition was stronger than for any other single issue in the territory. In a 1948 referendum, Alaskans voted to abolish fish traps by an 8-1 margin of 19,712 to 2,624—a margin greater than statehood itself would achieve. Despite this overwhelming popular mandate, the federal government, under industry pressure, refused to comply with the wishes of the people. The fishing industry exerted pressure locally as well as in Washington, D.C. Bill Baker, editor of the prostatehood *Ketchican Chronicle*, said the salmon industry tried to put his paper out of business after he supported fish trap abolition.[2]

In the winter of 1955–56 statehooders met in Fairbanks to draft a proposed constitution for the new state. A prime feature of this "model" document was an elaborate article on natural resources. Making use of the newest theories in resource management, the constitution mandated that the new state would manage renewable resources on a sustained yield basis, and it gave the legislature the power to reserve lands from the public domain as areas of natural beauty or scientific interest. When the statehooders presented this proposed constitution to the voters for ratification in April 1956, they also submitted an ordinance which would prohibit the use of fish traps once the constitution became effective. Both the constitution and the fish trap ordinance were ratified—the latter gaining a 5-1 majority compared to a 2-1 majority for the constitution.[3]

While presenting themselves as the true lovers of the land, the statehooders consistently portrayed their opponents, the antistatehooders, as exploiters and degraders. Indeed, there was a basis for this attack. The most vocal, visible, and well-financed foes of statehood were representatives, including lobbyists and newspaper supporters, for the major economic interests operating inside the territory but generally owned outside Alaska. Though mining had been prominent in the territory's history, mineral production fell so drastically after World War II that mining ceased to be a potent force by the mid-1950s. By this time the specter of "outside economic interests" had largely devolved on the Alaska Salmon Industry, Inc., a trade group of Seattle-based canning companies. The canned salmon industry's chief lobbyist was the Seattle lawyer Winton C. (Bill) Arnold, sometimes referred to as Judge Arnold. Throughout the 1940s Arnold had pressured members of the territorial legislature to vote against taxes on the salmon industry, using tactics that shocked veterans of even the most influence-laden state legislatures. Statehooder Herb Hilscher of Anchorage, who devoted an entire chapter of his prostatehood volume *Alaska Now* to the chicaneries of Bill Arnold, said in a 1981 interview that he had even taken a picture of the Judge leaning over the balcony of the territorial legislature instructing members how to vote.[4]

Arnold did not face a setback until 1949, when Ernest Gruening persuaded the legislature to pass the territory's first comprehensive tax legislation. Stung but undaunted, Arnold quickly turned his attention to the United States Congress, where statehood legislation passed the House of Representatives in 1950. To block Senate approval Arnold appeared before the Senate Committee on Interior and Insular affairs with elaborate graphs and charts to defeat the statehood cause. The *Anchorage Daily Times* reported that the salmon industry had raised $150,000 for this effort.[5] Statehood legislation failed to reach a floor vote in the Senate that session. Arnold was not the sole cause of the defeat of statehood in 1950. But to listen to statehooders one could easily believe that every vote ever cast against statehood was bought or influenced by Arnold, and that every alternative suggestion to statehood was just a clever ruse by Arnold to divert the attention of the population. In the minds of many Alaskans, antistatehood meant Winton C. Arnold.

The rhetorical battle between statehooders and antistatehooders continued even after Congress passed the Alaska statehood bill in June 1958. In that decisive summer, newspapers such as the *Fairbanks News-Miner* continued to carry stories of plots and rumors to thwart admission. Finally in August 1958 Alaskans formally accepted statehood in a Congressionally mandated plebiscite by a vote of 40,452 to 8,010. Statehooders rejoiced at the 5-1 majority in the biggest voter turnout in Alaskan history.[6]

Most writers and speakers on statehood have paid little attention to the antistatehooders since 1959. Historians have ably recorded the thrust of the antistatehood position prior to admission but have assumed that it vanished on Admission Day, never to recur. Writing in 1969, Carroll Glines succinctly described the sudden death of the antistatehood press: "By Admission Day, all opposition to statehood had ceased. The Juneau Daily Alaska Empire, most vocal of the opposition newspapers, carried no editorials on the subject but headlined the issue . . . WE DOOD IT." Glines expressed amazement at the short memory of the editor. Alaska's most thorough student of statehood, the historian Claus Naske, also chronicles the opposition before statehood but finds little if any lasting significance in the antistatehood movement after 1959. Looking back at the time of Alaska's silver anniversary, he remarked, "In 1984, nobody questions the wisdom of Alaska statehood. In retrospect, the arguments used against Alaska statehood are of less significance today than during the struggle."[7]

During that same silver anniversary year, a group of statehood advocates assembled at the annual meeting of the Alaska Historical Society to reminisce. When asked if there was any lingering heritage of the antistatehood opposition, the group responded with a choral no and pinned antistatehood squarely on the back of the canned salmon industry and its chief lobbyist Winton C. Arnold. "Bill Arnold was the chief opponent," asserted Bob Atwood, publisher of the *Anchorage Daily Times*. "He was the only opponent of statehood that was backed by an organization that . . . raised money and spent it liberally to fight statehood. . . . We were bitter enemies. We called each other names publicly." What happened to such a bitter opponent after Alaska gained entry to the union? Atwood had a quick, disarming answer: "At the time statehood was achieved, the salmon industry collapsed and disappeared. He [Arnold] came to Anchorage, and practiced law here, and became a local citizen. We became friends."[8]

The antistatehooders, however, consisted of more than the allies of Seattle canning interests. One-sixth of Alaskans—over eight thousand voters—opposed statehood. They did not disappear, nor did they all cease to battle for the goals which caused them to oppose statehood. Even the statehooders would admit that there had been some individuals opposed to admission who were not necessarily tools of Judge Arnold. There were some Alaskans, particularly in the less developed northwest region of the territory, who believed that Alaska did not have the economic means to pay the costs of a state government. They feared ever-mounting personal taxes would result from statehood. In metropolitan Anchorage a few people, such as the one-time mayor John Manders, favored commonwealth status, like Puerto Rico's, under the assumption that Alaska would gain more self-government and be exempt from federal taxation. Some federal employees opposed statehood in reaction to widely circulated rumors that they would lose their jobs or at least their 25 percent cost-of-living pay bonus. Despite assurances from Bob Bartlett, Alaska's territorial delegate to Congress, that this was not the case, some of the "feds" remained suspicious.[9]

In addition to these recognizable groups, there was also a sizable but unorganized collection of individuals who often wrote singly against statehood but who alluded to the existence of a larger constituency that shared their views. The individuals in this assortment were a diverse lot. Some testified at Congressional hearings, while others confined their comments to the "Letters to the Editor" section of newspapers. The statehooders often tried to dismiss this group as kooks or "little old ladies" like Miss Alice Stuart of Fairbanks who testified to Congress in 1957 that one could not openly oppose statehood in "polite society."[10] However, one voice coming from this group did not die out with admission and ultimately promoted his vision of Alaska from the highest branches of government: Jay S. Hammond, a former bush pilot, wildlife guide, and commercial fisherman from the western Alaska village of Naknek who went on to serve as Alaska's fourth governor.

Hammond was a popular governor while in office, and in the decade since he left the governor's chair, he has become the virtual symbol and protector of all things Alaskan, particularly through the medium of his popular television series, Jay Hammond's Alaska. As governor, Hammond did not hide his antistatehood sentiments. In 1976 he told a reunion of the delegates to the constitutional convention, "At one time I was neither wildly enthusiastic over the constitution you produced nor the impending advent of statehood." Hammond had gone on record as early as 1953 as being in the opposition. He later stated in a letter to the editor of the *Anchorage Daily Times* in 1958: "Oddly, it is becoming increasingly apparent that many more Alaskans are opposed to immediate statehood than we once thought. To my astonishment, I have found upon questioning that the majority of my acquaintances fall in this category. Not a few of these, once ardent statehood supporters, have reversed their stand after living here a few years and becoming familiar with the situation. What goes on here? Could it be that they . . . simply have not been as thoroughly statehoodwinked?" A few weeks later he wrote to a prostatehood group that he did not believe Alaska could support a state government. He saw Alaska's economy in worse shape than it had been in thirty years, mining almost defunct and the salmon catch at its lowest point in decades. He questioned the statehooders' claim "that industry wants statehood for Alaska and is waiting to pour dollars into this country upon its advent." He even mused rhetorically, "If this is the case, why is the largest industry in Alaska, the salmon industry, fighting statehood tooth and nail."[11]

Hammond voted against statehood in the August 1958 plebiscite. But no sooner had he cast his ballot than he acquiesced to the request of a group of teachers in Naknek to run for the first session of the new state House of Representatives. He won, running as an Independent. After his first term he registered as a Republican and was reelected to the House in 1960 and 1962. After a stint back home as manager of the Bristol Bay Borough (1965–66), he was elected to the state Senate in 1966, where he stayed until 1972, serving as majority leader in 1970 and president in 1971–72. After a term as mayor of the Bristol Bay Borough (1973–74) he ran for governor in 1974, beating the ardent statehooder Walter Hickel in the Republican primary and narrowly edging out the Democrat William Egan in the general election. Egan had been the symbol of statehood, serving as president of the constitutional convention and as the state's first governor. Hammond beat both Hickel and the Democrats again in 1978 and held the governor's mansion for a total of eight years.

Hammond's background was a curious one for an antistatehooder. He was neither a sourdough nor an agent of the Seattle interests. The future governor was born in upstate New York in 1922 and later moved with his family to Vermont. World War II interrupted his college career, and he served as a Marine Corps pilot from 1942 to 1946. He had never shown any particular interest in Alaska but knew something about the territory from the drawings of Rockwell Kent, who lived near his family in New York. While in flight school at Corpus Christi, Texas, Hammond met a man he described as an "old time guide and bush pilot" who invited him to come to Alaska when the war ended. Hammond joined his friend in 1946 and worked with him off and on for three years at Rainy Pass. A war injury required some rest from the outdoor life during that time, and Hammond enrolled at the University of Alaska, completing a degree in biology in 1949. He joined the U.S. Fish and Wildlife Service that year, where he worked until 1956 when he started his own guide service and commercial fishing business. Young, educated, relatively recent arrivals to Alaska, particularly veterans who arrived after World War II, were often portrayed as statehooders. To Ernest Gruening, in particular, young veterans who had fought to preserve democracy were a source of energy to build the new state.[12] Why then was Hammond, a vigorous, well-educated man with a future ahead of him, opposed to statehood? And did he change his views after admission? A 1987 interview provided some fascinating answers.

Hammond seemed quite eager to talk about his early views on statehood. He noted that this was something people rarely asked him about but quickly observed, "I've had a penchant for being on the wrong side of the popular political issue of the moment." Hammond said he did not really think much about statehood when he first came to Alaska. He emphasized that he was "never opposed to the idealism inherent in statehood" but that he questioned at the time the ability of Alaska to finance and administer a new state government. The former governor admitted that he had obviously been wrong on the economic score, but he was quick to point out that in the first years after statehood Alaska was in dire financial straits. Said Hammond, "We would have been belly-up without oil. We would have been bankrupt. You know what bailed us out. We were almost over the edge and frantic—the earthquake. It was the 'best thing' that ever happened to the state financially at that stage in time." Indeed the infusion of federal reconstruction funds that came after the 1964 Anchorage earthquake was an important source of state funds. The euphoric view of the future that the statehooders had projected in 1959 had clearly become tarnished in the early 1960s when there were substantial fears that public revenues would not be adequate to meet the increased governmental functions Alaska inherited with statehood—particularly after the initial transition funds provided by the federal government ran out. These fears were so substantial that a number of Alaskans lost some of their previously held reticence to criticize statehood and the statehooders. Hammond remembered one conversation he had in the early 1960s with a group of eight legislators in which five claimed they voted against statehood. Whether or not their contentions were true, it was clear to Hammond that the vise grip that statehooders had once held on Alaskan political sentiment had weakened in the early 1960s.[13]

In addition to his worry about potential state finances, Hammond attributed some of his opposition to the fact that he had been a federal employee with the Fish and Wildlife Service. Many statehooders severely criticized all federal management of wildlife resources. Hammond admitted that he was probably "smarting under those sort of charges." He confirmed that many federal employees did fear the loss of their cost-of-living differential if statehood passed.

Despite his reservations about statehood, Hammond frankly stated that he did not really know all the facts in 1958. "If I knew everything I know today back then," he reasoned, "I would have been a proponent of statehood." So was it only ignorance that kept him from being a statehooder? When he learned the facts, did he fall in with the proponents? Not at all. As the interview went on, it became clear that Hammond had not been so much at odds with statehood as with the statehooders. The governor put it this way: "What troubled me mostly at the time of statehood was that it seemed to be advocated by those who had their sights on higher office. The would-be political plumpickers were the ones advocating statehood." Furthermore, Hammond saw the statehooders as the "advocates of aggressive, no holds barred growth." Their views, he said, were "at odds with what I thought was the best destiny for Alaska." Hammond explained that he came to Alaska because of the "environmental degradation" in the United States. He loved the openness, the exoticness of the remote territory. As he said with a smile, "When I came up, there were 72,000 people, and I thought it was a bit crowded." Statehood seemed to spell the end of Alaska's differentness. It would make Alaska just like the rest of the United States—particularly given the words of statehooders like Herb Hilscher who wrote as early as 1948 that those people who supported statehood did so "with an honest conviction that only through statehood can a new civilization be built in Alaska, with a million Americans guiding the destiny of a great new commonwealth."[14]

Though Hammond did not succeed in fending off statehood, as a political leader in the new state he continued to work toward his vision of Alaska as a place different from the too-developed Lower 48. He locked horns with such statehood supporters as Ernest Gruening, Bob Atwood, and the Anchorage Chamber of Commerce over plans for a giant dam on the Yukon River near Rampart and for the Trans-Alaska Pipeline. He opposed the aggressive developers' policy of state subsidies for economic growth. He thought this stimulated activities that brought people to Alaska who required substantial state services but who were in enterprises that could not yield tax revenues to pay for those services. This would increase the size of the state's annual operating budget beyond any level that could be sustained by a permanent tax base. Hammond took issue with the idea that the state needed to make the initial investment in an infrastructure to lure development. It's philosophy was "development must pay the price of admission." Only oil of all the major industries since statehood, Hammond noted, had paid its way and provided revenues to match the public services its employees required.

On the surface, Hammond's philosophy seems at odds with the record of his administration. During his two terms, particularly the second term, state revenues rose enormously from $599 million in fiscal year 1975 to a dizzy peak of $4.74 billion seven years later, thanks to a flood of Prudhoe Bay oil revenues. State subsidies for economic development and enlarged governmental operations increased as legislators found it irresistible to satisfy their constituents' requests. What did Hammond do in the face of this growth? In his 1987 interview, the governor noted that he vetoed $1.07 billion in legislation during his administration but admitted that this was a "drop in the bucket" in view of the size of the state's oil revenues. Instead, he pointed to the creation of the Alaska Permanent Fund as the principal achievement of his administration to stem runaway growth by diverting a portion of Alaska's oil revenues away from the annual political appropriation process—and hence away from overinflating both the operating and capital budgets.

The state legislature created the Permanent Fund through a constitutional amendment approved by the voters in November 1976. The amendment required that the state pay into the Fund "at least twenty-five percent of all mineral lease rentals, royalties, royalty sale proceeds, federal mineral revenue sharing payments and bonuses received by the State." Beginning with the first deposit of $4 million in fiscal year 1977, the Fund has grown to a $10.9 billion savings account as of June 30, 1991. The principal of the Fund is constitutionally inviolate, though the annual earnings may be appropriated by the legislature for governmental functions or any purpose provided by law. Since the fund's inception, however, the only major expenditures have been for annual per capita "dividends" to all Alaska residents beginning in 1982. Approximately 50 percent of the annual earnings, which amounted to $1.03 billion in fiscal 1991, go for the dividends, the remaining half being reinvested into the principal for inflation-proofing. In the first ten years of the program, the annual dividends ranged from $331 to $1,000 and totaled approximately $7,000 per

Alaskan. The Permanent Fund dividend program, which, in Hammond's words, countered the "selective greed" of the legislature with the "collective greed" of the people, has turned this state savings account into a virtually sacred institution in which all citizens feel a direct stake.[15]

Hammond sees the permanent investment account linked to a dividend as an enterprise he championed for years with little support. Hammond explained that he first proposed such a plan on a regional scale when he was manager of the Bristol Bay Borough in the 1960s. His proposal would have established a fund based on a 3 percent tax on commercial fishing. While serving in the state legislature, Hammond proposed a plan in 1970 called Alaska, Inc., which would have put the $900 million coming from the 1969 North Slope oil lease sales into an investment account with dividends to citizen shareholders. His fellow legislators rejected the plan and diverted the $900 million into annual state budgets, exhausting the nest egg by 1977. Hammond as governor revived the Alaska, Inc. proposal as a model for the Permanent Fund and the dividend program. Once again he encountered resistance in the legislature. Hammond recalled that initially "almost nobody was behind it" and that legislators thought the "idea of dividend was ridiculous."[16]

Even after the Permanent Fund was approved in 1976, the dividend program was not a foregone conclusion. The constitutional amendment merely stated that "all income from the Permanent Fund shall be deposited into the general fund unless otherwise provided by law." For the next four years a debate ensued over whether the fund's resources, both principal and income, should be used as a development bank to fuel the Alaskan economy or as a trust to produce maximum income for future distribution. The trust concept and Hammond's Alaska, Inc.–inspired dividend program prevailed. Legislation creating the program passed in 1980, and the first dividend was paid in 1982.[17]

The decision to manage the Fund as a maximum income-producing trust with a separate board of trustees independent of the state treasury has resulted in an exceedingly small investment of the Fund's capital in Alaska. Investments within the state can be made only if they are comparable in risk and return to outside investments. In 1991 only $85 million of the Fund's $11 billion in assets were invested in certificates of deposit in Alaskan banks, and a mere $26 million in Alaska home mortgages. Of the Fund's $962.8 million real estate portfolio, only $13.8 million was invested in Alaska. The outside Alaska investment philosophy has become almost an article of faith with the Fund's trustees.[18]

While the Fund's trustees divert capital from Alaska in the management of the principal, individual Alaskans have dispensed their dividends in a manner that inhibits both capital-intensive development and the growth of government bureaucracy. In general, the dividends that go into the disposable income of individuals are used on consumable items such as grocery bills or tickets for winter vacations. Like Humpty Dumpty after his fall, the dividend program breaks up half a billion dollars every year into half a million individual checks so that all the horses and all the men of governors and legislators can never put the Permanent Fund's earnings together again.[19]

By grabbing oil earnings from lawmakers, by channeling them to largely non-Alaskan investments, and by distributing much of the investment income to Alaskans' pockets, the Permanent Fund has diverted 20 percent of all state revenue from oil away from in-state capital development projects and from a further increase in the size of Alaska's state government. Is this phenomenon a legacy of the same ideas and philosophy that led Jay Hammond to oppose statehood in the 1950s? When asked in 1987 if he saw a direct connection between his prestatehood opposition to unquestioning supporters of economic development and his later support for the Permanent Fund, the former governor responded, "Absolutely, I felt [the Fund was] the only way you could sweep off the smorgasbord some of these monies to prevent [lawmakers] from just going absolutely ape and artificially stimulating the economy and trying to do everything for everybody." To Hammond the Permanent Fund was the way to smooth economic growth and ensure that the oil boom would provide permanent support for the state government in leaner times. To him it is the logical extension and development of the reservations and arguments he had with the statehooders before admission and throughout his years in state government as legislator and governor.

Having said this, Hammond was not unaware of the irony of the "growth" record of his administration and his economic philosophy. The governor quipped that if he had truly been an advocate of zero growth, as some statehooders accused him, he had failed miserably. Then speaking as if to respond to conservationists who might question his record, he added, "The only thing I can say in my defense is that had we not created the Permanent Fund and had I been an advocate of aggressive, gung-ho, all out growth, . . . where would we be now? . . . You know that entire $8 billion [the size of the Permanent Fund at the time of the 1987 interview] would have been spent on something. . . . When the flood tide of oil wealth receded, it would have left us that much worse off." With billions flowing into the state's coffers, Hammond could not completely restrain Alaska's development and keep the population at his ideal of a "crowded" 72,000, but he certainly could foil some of the dreams of statehooders who foresaw a million Alaskans.[20]

A full analysis of the economic thought of Jay Hammond and of the origins of the Permanent Fund awaits future historians. This brief treatment of both may well raise as many questions—and hackles—as it answers. Nonetheless, that should not divert us from the initial thrust of the article—the legacy of antistatehood thought. There is no question that Alaskans have thought extensively about the economic development of their state, in large part because of the peculiarities of its history. The statehooders reacted strongly to the exploitation and depletion of Alaska's natural resources by the absentee fishing and mining interests. They tried to correct what they saw as the sins of the past with their model constitution and its natural resources article. In doing so they went a step further and envisioned a more populated and economically developed state. But in the process of reacting to the "depleters," they spawned a counterreaction to themselves as "developers." Jay Hammond was one of the counterreaction's early voices. The statehooders paid only fleeting, if any, attention to this little-known game guide who wrote letters to the editor and posed no threat to their movement. But the antistatehooder from Naknek would leave as lasting a legacy to the state he once opposed as those who created it. In doing so he ensured that the debate over the best use and protection of Alaska's land and resources would remain open-ended.

NOTES

1. For Gruening's view of the exploitation of Alaska's resources, see Ernest Gruening, *The State of Alaska,* 2d ed. (New York: Random House, 1968) and *The Battle for Alaska Statehood* (Fairbanks: University of Alaska Press, 1967), particularly the reprint of his address to the 1955–56 Constitutional Convention "Let Us End Colonialism," 74–91.

2. For the fish trap controversy in Alaska politics and the political ramifications of the depletion of the salmon run, see George W. Rogers, *Alaska in Transition: The Southeast Region* (Baltimore: Johns Hopkins Press, 1960), 13, and Richard A. Cooley, *Politics and Conservation: The Decline of the Alaska Salmon* (New York: Harper and Row, 1963). Princeton University student David Felsenthal's

1992 undergraduate thesis, "The Alaskan Salmon Fishing Industry: A History of Exploitation and Depletion, 1912–45," details the level of packing industry influence on the federal regulation of the Alaskan salmon industry. The pressure on Bill Baker is related in William Baker's interview in Claus-M. Naske, John S. Whitehead, and William Schneider, *Alaska Statehood: The Memory of the Battle and the Evaluation of the Present by Those Who Lived It: An Oral History of the Remaining Actors in the Alaska Statehood Movement* (Fairbanks: Alaska Statehood Commission, 1981).

3. For the background to the natural resources article in the Alaska constitution, see Victor Fischer, *Alaska's Constitutional Convention* (Fairbanks: University of Alaska Press, 1975), 129–40. The April 1956 vote for ratification of the constitution was 17,477–8,180; for abolishing fish traps 21,285–4,004.

4. For background on W. C. Arnold, see Richard H. Bloedel, "The Alaska Statehood Movement January, 1945–June, 1950" (unpublished master's thesis, University of Washington, 1966), 21, 64–65, 72; and Gruening, *Battle for Alaska Statehood,* 52–54. For Hilscher's comments see Hilscher, *Alaska Now* (Boston: Little, Brown and Company, 1948), 273–80; 1981 interview with Hilscher in Naske, Whitehead, Schneider, *Alaska Statehood.*

5. U.S. Congress, Senate, Committee on Interior and Insular Affairs, Hearings on H.R. 331 and S. 2036, *Alaska Statehood,* 81st Cong., 2d Sess., 1950; *Anchorage Times,* June 26, 1950.

6. For rumors on the activities of the opposition prior to the August 1958 plebiscite, see *Fairbanks Daily News-Miner,* August 8, 9, 13, 14, 1958. Changes in Alaska's voting practices helped spur the large voter turnout. The new constitution allowed nineteen-year-olds to vote, and military personnel who claimed Alaska as a residence could also vote.

7. Carroll V. Glines, Jr., "Alaska's Press and the Battle for Statehood," (unpublished master's thesis, American University, 1969), 97; Claus-M. Naske, *A History of Alaska Statehood* (Lanham, Md.: University Press of America, 1985), 272.

8. Transcript of tape recording of 1984 Alaska Historical Society Annual Meeting, Anchorage, November 4, 1984, in author's possession. The panelists included Robert Atwood, Evangeline Atwood, John Hellenthal, Seaborn Buckalew, Vic Fischer, and Herb Hilscher.

9. For an excellent description of the commonwealth movement, see Naske, *A History of Alaska Statehood,* 193–203. For the concerns of the cost of state government in northwest Alaska, see G. R. Jackson and Ralph Lomen, "A Suggestion for the Reorganization of Alaska in Anticipation of Statehood," October 1953, pamphlet in author's possession. The opposition of federal employees to statehood was not organized, nor was there a pamphlet literature connected with it. It was widely rumored at the time. Hammond mentions it in his interview by the author, December 14, 1987, which was taped and is now stored in the Oral History Collection at the Rasmuson Library, University of Alaska Fairbanks. (Unless otherwise cited, all statements by Hammond quoted in this article and summaries of his views are based on this interview.) See *Fairbanks Daily News-Miner,* August 9, 1958 for rumors that federal employees would lose their cost-of-living differential with Alaska's admission to the union.

10. "Bob Bartlett's Washington News Letter," March 21, 1957, Bartlett Collection, Rasmuson Library; *Fairbanks Daily News-Miner,* August 9, 1958.

11. Jay S. Hammond, "Constitutional Convention Review," speech at Fairbanks, October 16, 1976; Gruening, *Battle for Alaska Statehood,* 69; *Anchorage Times,* April 4, 1958; Hammond to James Fischer membership chairman, Operation Statehood, April 20, 1958, Operation Statehood Papers, Rasmuson Library.

12. Gruening, *Battle for Alaska Statehood,* 16, 34; Ernest Gruening, *Many Battles: The Autobiography of Ernest Gruening* (New York: Liveright, 1973), 328–29, 341, 346. For efforts to encourage homesteading among veterans in Alaska, see Herb and Miriam Hilscher, *Alaska, U.S.A.* (Boston: Little, Brown and Company, 1959), 98–109.

13. For a description of the financial straits the new state experienced in the early 1960s, see Claus-M. Naske and Herman E. Slotnick, *Alaska: A History of the 49th State* (Grand Rapids: Wm. B. Eerdmans Publishing Co., 1979), 167–78.

14. Hilscher, *Alaska Now,* 289. Hammond's allusion to 72,000 people comes from the 1940 census population of 72,524. By 1950 the population stood at 128,643. Population figures cited in Naske and Slotnick, *Alaska,* 306.

15. For basic information and a description of the Permanent Fund, see Alaska Permanent Fund Corporation, *1991 Annual Report; Alaska Permanent Fund Corporation, An Alaskan's Guide to the Permanent Fund (*1991), 20.

16. Hammond's advocacy of Alaska, Inc. can be found in his "State of the State" addresses of January 13, 1976, and January 11, 1977. See also Jay Hammond, "Chance for Change," statewide radio and television address, May 3, 1977. I am grateful to Claus Naske, a member of Hammond's Alaska Growth Policy Council, for supplying me with an extensive pamphlet collection of Hammond's addresses while governor.

17. For background to the debate on how the Fund should be managed, see *An Alaskan's Guide to the Permanent Fund,* 2–7.

18. For the Fund's investments and investment philosophy, see Alaska Permanent Fund, *1990 Annual Report,* 8–19, 23 and *1991 Annual Report,* 6–23.

19. As of 1992, the only public program that reconcentrates the individual checks for a larger public purpose is the Alaska Education Trust Fund, which allows an individual to earmark 50 percent of his or her dividend to prepay tuition at the University of Alaska several years in advance. Legislation creating this program passed in 1990 effective with the dividends paid in 1991.

20. The figure of 20 percent of oil revenues being deposited into the Permanent Fund is based on revenues dedicated to the Fund by constitutional mandate and by other special legislative appropriations. For fiscal year 1977–91, total oil revenues were $36.686 billion; $6.966 billion was deposited in the Permanent Fund. See Alaska Permanent Fund, *1991 Annual Report,* 6.

Project Chariot

Alaskan Roots of Environmentalism

PETER COATES

The popular notion that Alaska is America's last frontier, a remote, unsettled wilderness, traditionally has been linked with the concept of economic development: the region's lack of development has been understood as an opportunity for investment and seems even to have beckoned investment, as a virgin snowfall tempts one to make the first footprint. But Alaska's remote regions are not uninhabited: 208 Native villages are scattered throughout this northern wilderness. Planners far from Alaska have not always been well informed about the region. And on a number of occasions various government agencies have sought to test exotic and potentially harmful devices where they assumed there would be little human impact or notice. In the late 1960s, for example, the U.S. Atomic Energy Commission undertook a series of underground nuclear tests on Amchitka Island. The government halted the program after three tests because of protests over potential contamination of area fisheries. Earlier plans by the U.S. Army Corps of Engineers to dam the Yukon River in Rampart Canyon deep in the Interior went awry when protests over the extermination of millions of acres of migratory waterfowl habitat could no longer be ignored. In the 1970s the U.S. Army kept secret the placement of a nuclear reactor to generate electric power at Fort Greely near Delta, again in the Interior.

In the late 1950s the nuclear physicist Edward Teller, Father of the Hydrogen Bomb, proposed blasting an artificial harbor on the Alaskan Arctic coast as part of the AEC's Atoms for Peace program to show the domestic uses of nuclear power. Teller and AEC scientists argued there would be no human or environmental impact. Most Alaskans accepted their representation and whole-heartedly supported the project. Several scientists at the University of Alaska, however, pointed out that there would in fact be high detrimental impacts, particularly on remote Eskimo villages. Rather than gratitude for their warning, these scientists received criticism,

This article appeared originally in *Alaska History* 4 (Fall 1989): 1–31; it is reprinted here by permission.

and most eventually were fired, a story told well in Dan O'Neill's 1994 book Firecracker Boys *(New York: St. Martin's Press, 1994).*

Peter Coates has published one of the few important studies of the history of the relationship between technology and environment in Alaska, The Trans-Alaska Pipeline Controversy: Technology, Conservation, and the Frontier *(Toronto: Associated University Presses, 1991), in which he argues that the embrace of technology and economic development has inhibited substantive debate on the nature and role of the Alaska environment. In the article reprinted here, Coates (no relation to Ken Coates) traces the origins of much of the modern environmental movement to Project Chariot, Teller's Alaska project. Protesters organized as the Alaska Wilderness Society to call the attention of national environmental groups to the dangers posed by the radioactive fallout from the proposed blast, to the government's obfuscations, and to society's vulnerability to false government assurances about the safety of this and other technological advances tied to economic development. Other historians have also addressed the need for environmental histories of Alaska, among them William Cronon and Donald Worster, major scholars of the American West.*

Ever since the wartime Manhattan Project, the potential for virtuous and constructive applications of the most destructive force in history has enthralled the emerging American nuclear establishment. Most scientists and officials thought about "taming the atom" in terms of generating vast quantities of cheap electricity by atomic reactor. Others believed that atomic power could be harnessed to propel airplanes, ships, trains, and even automobiles. In the late 1950s, however, some researchers also began to investigate the use of atomic explosives for civil engineering. The biblical image of the sword beaten into a plowshare provided the civilian Atomic Energy Commission with a persuasive symbol for this benevolent vision. In 1957 the AEC established Project Plowshare to develop and promote peaceful uses of nuclear explosives and assigned technical direction to the University of California's Lawrence Radiation Laboratory (LRL). The AEC conceived a spectacular multitude of what it called "geographical engineering" schemes as part of Plowshare, including the use of atom and hydrogen explosives to dam and redirect rivers, create underground water reservoirs, cut tunnels through mountains, and release mineral wealth from the ground. None of these was considered technologically or economically feasible with conventional methods.[1]

Under contract to the LRL, the United States Geological Survey, the E. J. Longyear Company (an oil-drilling concern), and the U.S. Army Corps of Engineers carried out the search for the most suitable site for what the AEC called an "excavation application." The AEC established three criteria to govern the selection: the need to protect humans and wildlife (1957 was marked by increasing public unease about nuclear testing in Nevada), certain geological and engineering features necessary to provide essential data, and the demonstration of "possible long-term utilitarian value."[2] On these grounds, the consultants ruled out the traditional Nevada Test Site seventy miles north of Las Vegas and all other locations in the States. Instead, they identified eleven sites between Point Barrow and Nome which met the AEC's definition of remote—at least twenty miles from human settlement—and chose Cape Thompson on the Chukchi Sea as the most promising.[3] Here, at the mouth of Ogotoruk Creek, one hundred and ten miles north of the Arctic Circle, the AEC proposed to excavate a deepwater harbor by detonating two 1-megaton and two 200-kiloton "devices" just below ground level.[4] Each of the smaller explosives was ten times larger than the bomb dropped on Hiroshima. The AEC named the plan Project Chariot.

Though it attracted some local support, Project Chariot, which eventually underwent substantial modification, engendered considerably more opposition—locally and nationally—for a mixture of social, economic, environmental, and political reasons. Like many of the grandiose schemes devised as a part of Plowshare, such as a second Panama Canal, Chariot never materialized. A quarter of a century after it was canceled in 1962, the full story of this bold proposal and the bitter controversy it precipitated remains to be told.[5]

Project Chariot has not been neglected because it was just a curious parochial incident. Chariot played a pivotal role in awakening Native awareness and political power in Alaska. The controversy is an attractive springboard for discussion of profound matters such as the ethics of research, the political control of scientific endeavor, and the relationship between scientific advance and moral development. Chariot also had a role in the nascent antinuclear movement in the United States. A thorough discussion of these facets, however, lies beyond the scope of this paper. Addressed here instead are the evolution of attitudes toward the Arctic and the emergence of an environmental consciousness locally and elsewhere in the nation. Arguments in favor of environmental protection and values, which attained widespread acceptance among conservationists and environmentalists during more recent, better-publicized Alaskan natural resource controversies—over the authorization of the Trans-Alaska Pipeline, the "national interest" lands proposals that culminated in the Alaska National Interest Lands Conservation Act, and, currently, oil leasing in the Arctic National Wildlife Refuge—can be observed in their infancy during the dispute over Project Chariot.

The AEC's initial proposal came as Alaskans faced a precarious economic future. In 1957 the government provided 60 percent of all employment in Alaska; more than two-thirds of that was in the military sector. From 1957 onwards, however, defense spending fell sharply as Alaska's military population shrank.[6] At the same time the long-term decline of the traditional economy based on fur, salmon, and gold continued. Thus a prominent feature of Alaskan politics and economics upon the attainment of statehood in 1959 was the search by local politicians and businessmen for a broader and more secure economic base. The AEC promoted Chariot as a public works–style internal improvement. The first announcement of the proposal in June 1958, a week after the House of Representatives voted approval for statehood, claimed that "the absence of harbors on the northwest coast of Alaska close to important mineral deposits has in the past hampered development of such deposits. Fishing in this area has also been impeded by lack of a safe haven." The AEC explained that field studies would be carried out that summer to verify that the explosions would not harm humans, fish, or wildlife. The blast was scheduled to the summer of 1959.[7]

The initial advertising of Plowshare in Alaska encompassed other earth-moving possibilities in addition to Chariot. Edward Teller, the director of the LRL, undertook the primary responsibility for marketing nuclear engineering in Alaska. A week after President Eisenhower signed the Alaska Statehood Act, Teller, popularly known as the Father of the Hydrogen Bomb, and Gerald W. Johnson, the associate director of the LRL, came to Juneau to introduce the peaceful atom to a hastily convened assembly of officials and businessmen. According to Teller, the AEC had slated $5 million for such a project in Alaska, two-thirds of which would pay Alaskan workers or buy supplies in the state. He reassured his audience that an excavation application would not be performed unless it could be economically justified. Johnson explained, "We don't just want a hole in the ground." Teller then traveled to Fairbanks, where he addressed a group at the university consisting of science faculty, university administrators, and local businessmen. His speech was replete with references to

Alaska's physical size and frontier ebullience. In Juneau he had professed that "we looked at the whole world, almost the whole world." Now he explained that the AEC had chosen Alaska to host a daring nuclear innovation because of its remoteness, sparse population ("You have the fewest people"), and its inhabitants' receptivity to innovation ("You have the most reasonable people"). He stressed that here, at last, was a venture commensurate with the spirit and proportions of the land itself and its residents' pioneering aspirations.[8]

Alaskans' response to the proposal and Teller's hyperbole was mixed from the beginning. Politicians in Juneau were not impressed by Chariot's economic value, though some expressed interest in the possibilities for nuclear engineering elsewhere in the state. Most newspapers were delighted with Chariot. The editor of the *Fairbanks Daily News-Miner*, George Sundborg, enthused that a nuclear engineering project, possibly resulting in a commercial harbor, would "center world scientific and economic attention on Alaska just at the time when we are moving into statehood and inviting development."[9]

Yet, in other circles, Chariot mustered scant support. George W. Rogers, a prominent economist employed by the state whom Teller attempted to woo during his trip to Alaska, expressed early private reservations over Chariot's feasibility. Rogers indicated to Teller that the ocean at Cape Thompson was navigable for a maximum of two months each year and explained that coal that the AEC projected might be mined in northwest Alaska was a considerable distance from Ogotoruk Creek and on the other side of the Brooks Range. Undaunted, Teller retorted that the AEC would build a railroad and overcome the short shipping season by providing tank farms and warehouses to store oil, coal, and other minerals.[10] Group protest in Alaska originated in the fall of 1958, when a handful of biologists at the University of Alaska recommended studies to ascertain the project's social and environmental effects.[11]

In January 1959 two other officials from the LRL, Harry B. Keller and A. V. Shelton, seeking a firmer commitment to the project, visited Alaska. Concentrating on the business community, they warned that Chariot would not materialize unless it received widespread Alaskan backing. The *Fairbanks Daily News-Miner* explained that "Alaskans are being given an opportunity to 'vote' on the matter through their Chambers of Commerce." The new state's chamber promptly announced its approval. Soon afterwards the chamber at Fairbanks, the closest major city to the blast and a likely supply center, gave the project a unanimous vote of support.[12]

Following Keller and Shelton's visit, a series of critical letters appeared in the *Fairbanks Daily News-Miner*, whose publisher, C. W. Snedden, was a staunch supporter of Chariot. Irving Reed, a member of the Fairbanks city council, was convinced there were far better ways to spend $5 million in federal funds for the worthy cause of Alaskan development. Other critics believed that the project was hazardous as well as economic folly. Virginia (Ginny) Wood, who, along with Celia Hunter, ran the Camp Denali wilderness camp, alleged that the AEC had dumped Chariot on Alaska because of protest from inhabitants of the desert states and southern California against further testing in Nevada. Albert W. Johnson, a botanist at the University of Alaska, wrote to deplore the absence of a full discussion of the harmful effects of radiation.[13]

In January, a group led by Carl Hamlin, the assistant manager of the Matanuska Valley Farmers' Cooperating Association Creamery, met in Fairbanks and formed the Committee for the Study of Atomic Testing in Alaska. It was affiliated with the Greater St. Louis Citizens' Committee for Nuclear Information (CNI), founded in 1958. CNI aimed to provide scientific information comprehensible to laymen as an antidote to AEC-distributed information.[14]

In 1959, though, other factors were also leading the AEC to modify Chariot. Nuclear test ban talks were under way in Geneva, and the United States, the Soviet Union, and the United Kingdom had observed a voluntary nuclear testing moratorium since November 1958.[15] The Soviet Union, whose territory lay only 180 miles from the site of a blast expected to hurl debris 30,000 feet into the air, opposed Chariot, while America's western allies were skeptical about the Plowshare program in general.[16] These pressures undermined the project, and during the fall and winter of 1958–59 the AEC made statements suggesting that Chariot might be canceled or delayed.

In these statements the AEC referred only to its difficulties selling the harbor as an economic project. One AEC commissioner, Willard F. Libby, noted at a United Nations conference on peaceful uses of atomic energy: "The only trouble with the plan is that we haven't been able to find anyone who really wants a harbor there."[17] On February 17 the AEC's chairman, John A. McCone, reported to Congress's Joint Committee on Atomic Energy that the agency had set aside the harbor-blasting proposal. McCone, a California industrialist, gave the same reason, explaining that "we couldn't find a customer for the harbor." He informed the committee that, until the AEC found one, it would look for an alternative to

Chariot "which would demonstrate exactly the same thing, and might be more useful."[18] The AEC did not try to explain why there had been no commercial interest. The U.S. Geological Survey, however, offered a clue in a report it released in October 1959; minerals in the vicinity of Cape Thompson were of doubtful commercial value.[19]

But the AEC did not give up on Chariot because of the moratorium on testing, the project's unmarketability, and Alaskan criticism. The agency tried to revive the proposal by reducing its size from blasts of 2.4 megatons to 460 kilotons and reclassifying it as an "experiment" instead of a "harbor." The AEC's new stated purpose was observation of cratering effects of simultaneous detonations between 63 and 210 feet underground involving two 200-kiloton and three 20-kiloton explosives. Building on theories and prediction models suggested by recent underground tests in Nevada, the AEC also wanted to obtain basic data on radioactive distribution and to measure its effects and those of the air blast and seismic shock on the local biota.[20]

In late February officials from the LRL visited Juneau to introduce and promote the scaled-down project, which, they hoped, would be more acceptable internationally and would not arouse as much Alaskan opposition. The Alaska House of Representatives passed a supportive resolution on March 9. Yet the state's political leaders were still less than enamored. Governor William Egan and U.S. Senator Ernest Gruening were concerned about potential federal abuses. Throughout the summer of 1959 they pressed the AEC to fund a state representative with the agency to ensure some degree of state oversight, something the AEC refused to do, citing its lack of authority to hire nonfedreal employees.[21] Alaska's other U.S. senator, E. L. Bartlett, endorsed the original Chariot proposal on February 9. Less than two weeks later, however, he disavowed the modified scheme and urged the AEC, which he felt had no clear purpose, to conduct its experiments elsewhere. While welcoming federal spending in Alaska, Bartlett was wary of any potential violation of states' rights. This sensitivity was particularly acute immediately after statehood, and it applied especially to land withdrawals. In April Bartlett called for hearings on the AEC's land withdrawal at Cape Thompson. His disquiet focused on its size, originally publicized as forty square miles, but actually sixteen hundred square miles.[22]

In addition to economic and political objections, Chariot faced criticism on social and environmental grounds. The AEC and its Alaskan supporters had always claimed that "the project is located in the wilderness, far away from any human habitation." While this claim was possibly valid with respect to whites, it overlooked the Native villages of Point Hope and Kivalina, both within forty miles of the blast site. Their combined population was almost five hundred. These Eskimos subsisted to a large extent on caribou meat. The major component of the caribou's diet is lichens, which are rootless and, unlike most forms of vegetation, receive nutrition directly from the air in the form of precipitation, dust, and other airborne material. After the first atomic blasts in 1945, these nutrients were contaminated with fallout, and lichens became saturated with radionuclides such as Strontium-90 and Cesium-137. Further, because of their slow growth and longevity, lichens concentrated radioactivity. These radionuclides attained higher levels of concentration as they passed up the short and relatively simple arctic food chain.[23]

Concern over the project's impact on local Natives featured prominently in a detailed list of questions the Committee for the Study of Atomic Testing in Alaska sent to the AEC in mid-February 1959. The committee wanted to know why Alaska had been chosen for the experiment and why there was no provision for comprehensive social and environmental studies. A. R. Luedecke, the AEC's general manager, explained that the agency had chosen Alaska instead of Texas or California, where the committee had suggested it might prove more useful, primarily "for technical suitability and sufficient isolation." He noted that Chariot was designed to "test theories and obtain data which are needed before nuclear explosives can be utilized in excavation work near population centers." To allay public fears, Luedecke declared in late March: "We believe that the experiment could be conducted without hazard to the public and without serious disturbance to the marine and onshore life or food chains. . . . We are now proceeding to verify this opinion."[24]

The AEC had commissioned a one-year bioenvironmental research program in late February. The program, which the AEC claimed had always been an integral part of the proposal for Project Chariot but which critics believed was a response to public pressure, was to determine the conditions for the blast which would cause the least damage. A related purpose was to measure the biological effects of a nuclear explosion by contrasting the pre- and post-shot ecology of the region. To carry out this program, the AEC's San Francisco Operations Office established the Committee on Environmental Studies for Project Chariot (CESPC) under the direction of John N. Wolfe, head of the Environmental Sciences Branch of the AEC's Division of Biology and Medicine, to lead the effort.

The agency negotiated contracts with the University of Alaska for some of the studies.[25]

A group of University of Alaska biologists who had been in the forefront of criticism became part of the research team. Albert W. Johnson was appointed Senior Scientist, Botanical Investigations, with Leslie A. Viereck as his assistant. L. Gerard Swartz was placed in charge of sea bird cliff investigations, and William O. Pruitt was assigned to lead the terrestrial mammal investigations. The AEC hired Don C. Foote, a twenty-eight-year-old graduate student at McGill University in Montreal, to lead investigations of the human geography. The AEC allocated $100,000 for this program, which consisted of some forty individual studies.[26]

Afraid that Alaskan support for Chariot would dwindle further, one AEC commissioner assured Senator Gruening that the experiment, costing $2 million, "would still provide an excavation suitable for a harbor." Some boosters of Alaskan economic development remained captivated by this prospect, and the project continued to enjoy the support of the state's leading newspapers—the *Anchorage Daily Times* and the *Fairbanks Daily News-Miner*. Six months after reclassification, Albro Gregory, the editor of the *Nome Nugget,* in a contribution to the *News-Miner,* still insisted that this harbor would be able to handle the largest ocean-going vessels.[27] In the spring of 1959, Harry B. Keller had visited Kotzebue, 125 miles southeast of Ogotoruk Creek, the settlement with a significant white population which was closest to the blast site. In response to this first trip of an AEC official to the region, the Reverend William T. McIntyre, the president of the Arctic Circle Chamber of Commerce representing Nome and Kotzebue, wrote to AEC Chairman McCone:

> Alaskans, who are all pioneers, if not in fact then in heart, should feel proud that our state has been singled out to play yet another leading role in the Drama of the Century. We who live in this part of the state . . . feel this project will be the means of paving the way for the future development of this area . . . possessing vast potentialities in the mineral, coal, oil and hydroelectric fields, indeed, want the original harbor plan rather than [the] scaled down experiment.[28]

At the heart of McIntyre's exhortation lay the storehouse image of Alaska. For generations this image typified the reaction of those who believed that Alaska's natural resources were of great material value and who advocated their rapid and thorough development; negative appraisals of the economic value of Seward's Folly were epitomized by the time-honored icebox image.

In contrast, and for a quite different purpose, some conservationists also rejected the image of Alaska, and the Arctic in particular, as a wasteland of ice and snow. On February 12, 1959, the *News-Miner* printed a letter from Olaus J. Murie, a nationally renowned wildlife biologist with extensive research experience in the Alaskan Arctic. In a prophetic statement, Murie progressed from specific criticisms of the planned detonation at Cape Thompson to a general assault on what might be called the myth of the barren Arctic. Murie objected to the Arctic being thought of as a "dump-ground" for projects unwanted elsewhere. Instead, he emphasized the rich and subtle beauty which he saw behind the Arctic's hostile and harsh facade. The Wilderness Society, based in Washington, D.C., of which Murie had been director since 1946, passed an anti-Chariot resolution later in February—the first conservation organization to do so. The San Francisco–based Sierra Club did likewise in March.[29]

Teller's efforts to promote the new version of Chariot resembled his first lobbying campaign in many respects. Delivering the commencement day address at the University of Alaska, he flattered Alaskans: "Anything new . . . is repulsive and frightening. . . . Anything new that is big needs big people in order to get going. . . . And big people are found in big states." Teller told the audience that the AEC had the power to "reshape the land to your pleasure." It could, he boasted, "dig a harbor in the shape of a polar bear if required." Here, indeed, was a tantalizing technology to extend human mastery over nature beyond the wildest imaginings of the nineteenth-century pioneers who pushed the American frontier westward.

Seeking to demonstrate the wide benefits of Project Chariot, Teller introduced a fresh element. The AEC was finding it increasingly difficult to ignore the Native people of Cape Thompson, whom the agency had never directly informed of its plan. Teller's strategy, returning to the original economic justification for Chariot, was to include them as beneficiaries. He argued that these indigenes, strait-jacketed in poverty for centuries, stood to gain the most because Chariot would transform them into coal miners by making it possible for them to mine and ship coal.[30] Later that summer, when Teller addressed a meeting of the Arctic Circle Chamber of Commerce in Nome, he added Japan to the list of beneficiaries. He maintained that the coal the former hunter-gatherers mined would help supply Japan's energy needs. He saw a measure of justice and atonement in this: "The Japanese were the first to suffer by atomic blast; how wonderful it would be if they might be the first to benefit.[31]

Even before the AEC had announced its bioenvironmental studies, some Alaskans were convinced that Chariot was safe as well as economically sound. Robert Atwood, the editor-proprietor of the *Anchorage Daily Times,* drew the following analogy:

> Asking Alaskans for a decision on this proposed atom experiment is like a doctor asking his patient whether he wants an operation. The easiest answer is "no." The doctor usually tells the patient he must have one for his own good, and the patient does what the doctor says. The atom scientists are the doctor in this case. If they say that adequate safeguards for life and property have been provided, how can laymen say otherwise?[32]

William R. Wood, who had recently come from the University of Nevada to become the president of the University of Alaska, was another loyal local ally. Three months into the studies, Wood echoed Atwood's faith in the AEC and his deference to its experts: "If the U.S. government decides that the project is a safe one, there is no reason for concern." Albro Gregory indicated that the bioenvironmental studies were superfluous because "most scientists . . . already believe [it] to be feasible" and concluded that the danger to humans was minimal since "only a few Natives pass by."[33]

At the beginning of 1960, after only two months' work, the CESPC submitted its first report to the AEC. Confirming the AEC's prestudy determination, the committee recommended that the blast take place in March or April. At that time, it explained, few birds were in the area, little hunting took place, plants and many animals were under a protective blanket of snow, and the subsequent spring melting would flush radioactive particles out to sea where they would be diluted and decay harmlessly on the ice.[34]

At a meeting of the CESPC in Anchorage in March, however, Foote, Pruitt, Swartz, Viereck, and Johnson disagreed with these conclusions. Their research indicted that high winds and low precipitation meant that much of the area around Ogotoruk Creek was bare in the spring, when hunting by Natives on land and sea reached its annual peak. They also expressed skepticism that venting of radioactive particles from the blasts could be kept to less than 5 percent as the AEC predicted.[35]

AEC releases and the Alaskan press did not address these arguments. Albro Gregory did mention that there had been some criticism from "misinformed" sources but ridiculed them as people who worried that "a caribou might be hit in the head with a rock." In August 1960, the AEC invited reporters to the site for the first time. Though the agency stressed that the bioenvironmental studies had been an integral part of the project since 1958, Wolfe's comments to the press ("We are sort of riding the coat-tails of an engineering project of great magnitude") reinforced the impression of some critics that these studies were scrambled together later in response to public complaints.[36] Subsequent press reports did not mention any dissent from the official position.[37]

Chariot also faced mounting opposition from Alaska Natives. In November 1959 the Point Hope Village Council sent the AEC a petition condemning the project. In December the council voted unanimously against Chariot. Many villagers had received information from CNI through tape recordings. "We . . . know about strontium 90," explained one Native, "how it might harm people if too much of it get in our body." Urged by Egan, Bartlett, and other top Alaskan officials, three AEC officials paid a hasty visit to Point Hope. There Russell Ball, the assistant manager of the AEC's San Francisco office in charge of general planning for Chariot, told an audience of one hundred Natives: "We no longer have any expectation that there will be any commercial value to the hole that will be produced." Daniel Lisbourne of the village council suggested that, on the basis of remoteness, the coast between Barrow and Barter Island was more suitable. Ball, without explaining the problem, retorted that the climate there was too severe.

The officials showed an eleven-minute film accompanied by a technical script which was incomprehensible to most educated whites, to say nothing of its Point Hope audience, many of whom were not highly proficient in English. In response, a villager told the officials: "We really don't want to see the Cape Thompson blasted because it [is] our home, homeland. I'm pretty sure you don't like to see your home blasted by some other people who don't live in your place like we live in Point Hope." Rod Southwick, an AEC publicity chief, tried to reassure the villagers by promising that, "if we cannot find a time to do it safely, we won't do it." He added that cattle grazing in the vicinity of the Nevada Test Site had been unaffected by blasts there and pledged that in the event of any property damage—such as broken windows and cracked plaster—the AEC would provide financial compensation. Southwick said that villagers would be invited to watch the blasts, as Nevadans had been. In early summer, replying to the petition the villagers had sent the previous November, the AEC emphasized that no decision had been made to conduct the experiment and that Chariot ultimately would require presidential approval.[38]

In August the Wilderness Society registered the major conservationist protest of 1960. At its annual meeting, the organization's governing council passed a resolution opposing the project. It referred to the threat to Alaska Natives and expressed anxiety over the blast's impact on the wilderness qualities of the DeLong Mountains, which form the westerly extension of the Brooks Range. The society considered this region, of which it saw Cape Thompson as an integral part, "our last great wilderness area in the world not in the tropical region."[39]

The CESPC issued its first summary report in December 1960. It conceded the existence of "certain bioenvironmental problems," notably the importance of springtime hunting by Natives on the land and sea ice in the blast area, and admitted that "in some areas the data were incomplete." Nevertheless, it repeated the assurance that radiation effects would be "negligible, undetectable, or possibly nonexistent in the environment beyond the throw-out boundary." Even before the report appeared, the *Fairbanks Daily News-Miner* hailed it as the best scientific analysis of any area ever undertaken. The paper printed an Associated Press story which claimed that every conceivable aspect of the region and the behavior of its inhabitants had been painstakingly researched and faithfully recorded: "If an Eskimo takes a notion to go hunting, the investigators note and record where he went, what he bagged and when he returned."[40]

Others were not so approving. The CESPC report infuriated the project's critics, not least of whom were certain members of its contracted university personnel. These scientists had taken the contracts, as Leslie Viereck explained to a leading member of the Wilderness Society, "with the idea that we could do more to oppose the project in this way than we could if we sat on the sidelines." But it became apparent to them that the AEC "is using us to their own advantage. . . . The time has now arrived when we . . . must do something very drastic in nature." Nine days after the CESPC issued its report, Viereck announced that he intended to resign after the current contract. In his resignation letter to the University of Alaska's President Wood, he claimed that the AEC's manipulation of science for political ends was intolerable. He felt he could no longer maintain his "personal and scientific integrity and work for the AEC project." He cited the agency's conclusion that spring was the best time for the blast before the studies had begun, its suppression of contrary evidence, and its public denial of the existence of any dissent among its researchers.[41]

By then Don Foote had assumed a solid critical stance. Foote concluded that he had been naive and had had "absolutely no idea what Chariot was" when he joined the bioenvironmental studies team. In November he told a member of the CESPC that he had launched a personal crusade to "lift the lid off Chariot" and expose a project he considered "rotten to its very bottom." Four months later he explained to Wolfe that his dissent emerged gradually as his "politically immature mind awakened to the modern interplay of politics and science."[42]

State and national conservation organizations stepped up their opposition to Chariot in 1961. The recently founded Fairbanks-based Alaska Conservation Society, of which Viereck, Pruitt, Swartz, and Johnson were charter members,[43] devoted its spring newsletter entirely to the controversy and printed far more than its regular mailing. Slowly the Alaskan opposition's case was spreading. *National Wildlands News, Defenders of Wildlife News,* and the *Sierra Club Bulletin* published critical articles or news items on the AEC's proposed experiment. *Outdoor Life,* the organ of the Izaak Walton League of America, noted criticism by Alaskan sportsmen, the efforts of the scientists, and indicated that the project required watching.[44] In June the Committee for Nuclear Information released a major report based in part on studies by dissenting Alaskan members of the AEC's bioenvironmental research team. It emphasized the dangers of radioactive contamination in the arctic food chain. Barry Commoner, professor of plant physiology at Washington University in St. Louis and one of the founders of CNI, wrote in depth on the nature of the dust-lichen-caribou-man link. He cited evidence that as a result of this flow of energy in the Arctic, levels of Strontium-90 (Sr-90) in the bones of Native Alaskans were much higher than in other Americans, despite far lower ground levels of the element in northern Alaska than elsewhere in the country. In another contribution, Michael W. Friedlander, a physicist, argued that food chain contamination by Sr-90 as a result of Chariot could be ten times higher than AEC estimates.[45] Commoner and Friedlander subscribed to the view that Sr-90 causes leukemia, bone cancer, and, eventually, mutation of the gene structure. The spirit of inquiry also extended to the *News-Miner,* which featured a series by Tom Snapp in August which was more skeptical than anything that had previously appeared on Chariot in its pages.[46]

Opposition spread in late 1961 and during 1962. In March 1961, Point

Hope villagers had sent a protest to President Kennedy, denouncing Chariot as being "too close to our homes at Point Hope and to our hunting and fishing areas." That November, Native Alaskan arctic peoples met at Barrow, in large part as a direct response to the threat of Chariot. This *Inupiat Paitot* was the first such political conference for these groups. The delegates denounced the permit the BLM had issued to the AEC for the Cape Thompson area as a violation of legally recognized aboriginal land rights and demanded its revocation.[47] Opponents of Project Chariot achieved a major break-through in April 1962 when *Harper's* published a comprehensive summary of their case. Its authors were Paul Brooks, a Sierra Club director, and Joseph Foote, the brother of Don Foote.[48]

In August 1962, after spending $3 million on Chariot, the AEC announced its decision to defer making a recommendation to the President that the project proceed. Though it gave no reasons, the AEC stressed that this was not because the bioenvironmental studies, resumed for a third and final year, had suggested a likelihood of any danger to Natives or the flora and fauna upon which they depended for food, shelter, and clothing.[49] The AEC explained that the anticipated data on crater formation, radioactive distribution, and seismic shock were already available or soon would be from other sources.[50] (The United States had resumed underground nuclear testing in May 1960.) Nevertheless, the *Anchorage Daily Times* felt that the AEC had capitulated to pressure and interpreted cancellation as "a victory over atomic science by Alaskan Eskimos," an opinion echoed in the *Washington Post.* According to Sharon Francis, an aide to the Secretary of the Interior, the department's disapproval had been a factor in Chariot's defeat. Francis explained that Interior had an influential role in assessing the AEC's bioenvironmental studies. On August 29 she wrote to Don Foote: "Those involved with the project at the AEC and at Livermore knew that Interior was prepared to exercise severe judgment in the matter of Project Chariot. Rather than have us issue a counter-report to the President which we would have publicized, and which would have been most embarrassing to the AEC, they withdrew early in the fray, and in the most face-saving manner."[51]

There was no euphoria that fall, however, among the project's Alaskan critics, who remained suspicious of the AEC's plans as long as the land withdrawal remained in force. The Assistant Secretary of the Interior John A. Carver, who had a particular interest in Native Americans, also wanted the status of the withdrawal amended to specify that its sole purpose was biological research.[52] In January 1963, the AEC informed the department that its land needs at Cape Thompson could be reduced from the approximately sixteen hundred square miles then withdrawn to an area less than a tenth the size. This placed the site on "caretaker status," deemed suitable for continuing scientific studies.[53] In April, control over the AEC research station at Ogotoruk Creek transferred to the Navy's Arctic Research Laboratory at Point Barrow.[54] On May 29, 1963, under pressure from an increasingly impatient Department of the Interior, the AEC recalled in entirety its application for the remaining 96,000 acres. The land was restored to the public domain on September 2, 1963.

The Project Chariot story is a landmark in the history of conservation in the United States in three major respects: in connection with the origins of environmentalism, in the context of the emergence of the now ubiquitous environmental impact statement, and as part of the development of a more appreciative American attitude toward the Arctic as a natural environment.

The late 1950s and the early 1960s were a critical transitional period in American conservation history, and the Chariot controversy highlights the relationship between elements of continuity and change. The controversy over Chariot should be contrasted with the debate some ten years later over the Trans-Alaska Pipeline proposal, when a project with powerful momentum and solid private, state, and federal backing was confronted by a wide-ranging coalition of conservationists and environmentalists. There were two major differences between the debates. First, no amount of promotion could disguise the original Chariot's inherent lack of economic appeal to Alaskans. Moreover, the LRL and the AEC had achieved no greater success convincing other federal agencies of the project's value in its modified form. Senator Bartlett's comment in 1959 on the demise of the harbor project was just as valid for cancellation of the experimental plan. Chariot, he declared in his senatorial newsletter, had "failed for want of horses to pull it."[55]

Second, it would be inaccurate to characterize the protest against Chariot as part of a "movement" in the sense that opposition to the pipeline was an integral part of the environmental movement—arguably its cause célèbre. A leading historian of conservation in the early twentieth-century Progressive Era has defined a movement as a popular force deriving from a broad social base.[56] This was not the case with the opposition to Chariot. The anti-Chariot campaign was of modest size, fought principally by a cadre of committed Alaskans united by professional and personal ties within the Alaska Conservation Society and supported by the Committee on Nuclear Information and a scattered assortment of aroused individuals.

Many members of national conservation organizations were slow to respond to the call-to-arms from their Alaskan compatriots. Members of the Alaska Conservation Society on publicity missions to the Lower 48 often despaired at the dismal state of awareness they found. "Chariot is an unknown," lamented Celia Hunter, one of the organization's founders. Sportsmen tended to leave the issue alone, and for those conservationists who did become involved, Chariot was an atypical cause. Some individuals felt strongly because they were directly acquainted with Cape Thompson or other parts of the Far North. In the case of James and George Marshall, brothers of Bob Marshall, the Brooks Range adventurer of the 1930s, identification with the Alaskan Arctic and concern for its fate was vicarious. These officials of the Wilderness Society, which their brother had founded, had never been to Alaska. These alarmed conservationists encountered considerable apathy and resistance in their efforts to recruit their colleagues.[57] CNI and the Association on American Indian Affairs (AAIA) gave these conservationist critics the most support. Neither organization became involved in the struggle against Chariot for traditional conservation reasons, namely, protection of scenic beauty, wilderness, and wildlife.

This relative lack of conservationist support is not entirely surprising. Even to its first Alaskan critics, the blast did not immediately commend itself as a conservation issue.[58] Nuclear matters, whether military or energy related, were not a major item on the agenda of conservation during the early Cold War. If anything, some conservationists in the early 1960s were impressed by the potential of nuclear power as a "clean," cheap, and renewable energy source which offered an attractive alternative to damming wild rivers and flooding wilderness to provide hydropower.[59]

The Chariot controversy was not another familiar debate about pristine wilderness and splendid scenery. In 1960 Leslie Viereck observed that wilderness in the vicinity of Ogotoruk Creek had already been ruined by the construction of over forty buildings, including power and radio stations and two 2,200-foot airstrips, not to mention the extensive damage to the tundra by tracked personnel carriers. There was little discussion of the nuclear experiment as a threat to a prized scenic and recreational resource; spectacular landscape features and dramatic topography were conspicuously absent at Cape Thompson, which conservationists had never proposed for protected status of any sort. Many conservationists questioned Project Chariot's merits and legitimacy as a conservation issue. Allied to this question of suitability was the matter of competence. "We must be careful not to get into genetic and other fields we are not expert in," warned Richard Leonard, the secretary of the Sierra Club.[60] Leonard evidently was more comfortable with the customary pursuit of wilderness and scenic protection policies, for which he believed the club was better equipped.

Those conservationists who did become critics of Chariot were as concerned with how the proposal jeopardized the Native way of life as they were with the implications for the land and its fauna. Rarely did critics refer to one threat without discussing the other. This concern with the quality of the human environment in addition to the ecological health of the natural environment, and the emphasis on the inseparability of humankind from the rest of nature, gives the Chariot controversy much of its significance. The Chariot debate provides one of the earliest examples of the combination of the conventional nature-protection concerns of conservation and preservationism with the larger and more complex issues engendered by mid-twentieth-century science, technology, and industrial culture. As the 1960s advanced, these latter concerns, especially the impact of pollution from pesticides, crude oil, and radioactivity on people and the rest of nature, became identifiable collectively as environmentalism.[61]

By illustrating how traditional ways of thinking and established organizations first came to cope with some of these new issues, the Chariot debate sheds light on the roots of environmentalism and was a harbinger of what the media dubbed the "age of ecology" in late 1969 and early 1970. Barry Commoner of CNI became, for many, the prophet and leader of the environmental movement. Commoner remembers Project Chariot as his personal introduction to ecology and the beginning of his career as an environmentalist. Referring to his new-found concern with ecological matters, he recalled recently, "It is absolutely certain that it began when I went to the library to look up the behavior of lichen in connection with the Chariot program."[62] Lichens, with their unique biological properties and striking connection with human life through the distinctive arctic food chain, provided tangible evidence of the interrelatedness of all forms of planetary life within a single community.

The bioenvironmental studies for Chariot were a further indication of the controversy's seminal role. At the end of 1960, despite his criticisms and decision to resign, Viereck had already conceded the character and intrinsic value of the study as a whole, which he praised as "one of the best ever conducted in an Arctic region."[63] This was the first time the AEC had conducted ecological investigations of any significance prior to a detonation, and it had carried out over 150 tests between 1948 and 1958. Part of the explanation lies in Chariot's status as the first unclassified American nuclear experiment. The CESPC bioenvironmental studies chief, John Wolfe, described Chariot as "the first opportunity to do a good biological study prior to a nuclear explosion and it may be our last." CESPC's research became a de facto, integrated environmental, biological, and social study of the region. *Outdoor Life* praised the studies as "the best overall fact-finding job that any of our government agencies has ever done before starting work on a large-scale project involving our natural resources."[64] John C. Reed, a scientist with the Arctic Institute of North America, felt that the Chariot studies could become a model for "coordinated investigations of the environments of other areas."[65] It certainly was the first environmental study to precede a proposed engineering project in Alaskan history. The final report issued in 1966 was essentially a catalogue of life forms designed to serve as baseline data for measuring the biological costs of a nuclear explosion.[66] In some ways, however, it might be seen as a forerunner of the formal environmental impact statement which became mandatory with the passage of the National Environmental Policy Act of 1969 for any project involving the federal government and the use of public lands.

In its official comments, the CESPC criticized the image, exploited by the AEC and its local allies, of the Arctic as an environment which no human activity or technology could destroy, an environment where there simply was nothing to destroy. In contrast, the CESPC noted, "Not infrequently it is described as remote, desolate, barren, and climatically rigorous. Probably none of these adjectives is accurate, and very possibly they are misleading. . . . It is not remote to the Eskimo, the arctic fox, or the ptarmigan; the flowering plants . . . belie its barrenness and desolation." The CESPC described Cape Thompson as part of a thriving ecosystem where "the caribou range at will, as did once the buffalo on the great plains."[67] These were early expressions of the belief that the Arctic is a complex, fragile, and still comparatively intact ecological whole, reminiscent in this respect of much of the West before the coming of the railroads.

Don Foote, Chariot's most persistent critic, was particularly sensitive to the global significance of what he saw as an increasingly embattled Far North and the region's meaning for future generations. Cape Thompson, he wrote to his brother on the East Coast at the end of 1961, "as the entire Arctic, is on the verge of a tremendous transition. The Arctic is important not only to the people who now live in it but to the people who are your next door neighbors." He did not assign value to the Arctic as a storehouse of mineral resources or as an outdoor laboratory for nuclear physicists. Foote wanted the Arctic left alone because it exemplified "a sane and peaceful world where people love and respect beauty, [and] cherish life and the natural world." Moreover, he saw a further threat to the Arctic in petroleum development. "The new explorers up there are after oil," he wrote, and "we must prevent the destruction of the Arctic as wilderness."[68]

James Marshall once mused wryly that Edward Teller was "gambling on creating even more" wilderness in Alaska than already existed, in the sense that wilderness was synonymous with wasteland. In Marshall's view, Cape Thompson was not aesthetically or ecologically a wasteland, but the nuclear experiment would turn it into one.[69]

The AEC continued to present what some conservationists perceived as fresh threats. Reflecting on Chariot's demise, Senator Gruening had remarked, "If they wanted to blow a hole in the ground they should have picked an uninhabited island where there would be no possible danger to anyone."[70] Though the AEC did not proceed with any further Plowshare projects in Alaska, the agency did not lose interest in the state as fertile ground for nuclear experimentation. As if taking Gruening's advice, the commission shifted its attention to Amchitka, which, it noted, was "far from people, as far as any place that can be found in the fifty states."[71] Amchitka, in the western Aleutians 1,340 miles southwest of Anchorage, was part of a national wildlife refuge. The closest peopled place was the Adak Naval Station, 190 miles away; the nearest Native settlement was 270 miles distant at Atka.

The executive order creating the Aleutian Islands National Wildlife Refuge in 1913 contained the proviso that this designation would not interfere with the use of the islands for military purposes. So, despite rising Alaskan, national, and international indignation, the AEC's Division of Military Application and the Department of Defense conducted underground tests on Amchitka in 1965 (Long Shot), 1969 (Milrow), and 1971 (Cannikin).[72] At 5.2 megatons, Cannikin (under the technical direction of the Lawrence Livermore National Laboratory, formerly the LRL) was the largest underground blast in American history and illustrates how nuclear testing in Alaska continued to play a catalytic role in the history of conservation. Concern that Cannikin would trigger a huge tidal wave and seismic activity and result in large-scale radioactive contamination of the marine ecology led to the formation of Greenpeace, the direct-action international environmental organization, in Vancouver, British Columbia. In an attempt to prevent the blast, a crew of Canadian and U.S. activists attempted to take a converted fishing boat into the test zone.

After detonating Cannikin, the AEC announced that it had no plans for further tests in the Aleutians. In 1973, the agency "evacuated" Amchitka. The Battelle Memorial Institute's laboratory in Columbus, Ohio, organized bioenvironmental studies in 1967 modeled on those for Chariot. The studies, published in 1977, concluded that the ecological impact of testing on Amchitka had been slight and that any adverse effects had already been reversed.[73]

In the late 1960s and early 1970s, Project Plowshare was increasingly on the defensive, facing stiff opposition from environmentalists. Two underground Plowshare tests which did take place—Gasbuggy in New Mexico in 1967 and Rulison in Colorado two years later—were designed to "stimulate" natural gas to the surface by disintegrating the rock containing the gas. The gas these blasts released, however, was highly radioactive. Glenwood Springs and Aspen declined to use the gas Rulison produced. After the 1973 Rio Blanco shot, Coloradans voted 3 to 2 and much to Teller's chagrin to ban further gas stimulation shots in their state. This effectively killed Plowshare, which the AEC terminated soon afterwards.[74]

Recently, the attention of an influential member of the American nuclear establishment has been drawn back to the Alaskan Arctic as an attractive setting for the adventurous propositions of nuclear physicists. In June 1987, Edward Teller revisited Alaska to promote the Reagan administration's Strategic Defense Initiative, of which he is a chief architect and leading proponent. Addressing Commonwealth North, an Alaskan economic development lobby in Anchorage, Teller argued that Alaska would provide the best site for launching laser defenses against incoming Soviet missiles. He gave three reasons: its location near the likeliest route of any missile attack; its abundant energy resources which could fuel laser technology; and the low temperatures of the Arctic which would aid superconductivity.[75] Alaskans, he argued in tones reminiscent of the late 1950s, are "reasonable" people open to new ideas and sympathetic to the scientific duty and national security imperative "to find out what kinds of weapons are possible." Illustrating the persistence of entrenched views, Teller still characterized the Alaskan Arctic as a previously uninhabited and largely worthless land, now redeemed by substantial oil development and the prospect of further exploitation in the Arctic National Wildlife Refuge. Before the discovery of oil at Prudhoe Bay, he remarked, "Nobody was there."

A question posed by someone who had heard Teller speak at the University of Alaska in 1959 about digging a harbor "in the shape of a polar bear" led Teller to reflect on his previous involvement with Alaska. He restated his faith in the potential for the peaceful uses of nuclear explosives and recalled Chariot as a fine engineering project, which "should have been done." He also offered an explanation for the project's demise which was entirely at odds with the reasons the AEC had given in 1962 and in its final report four years later. In a concession to the influence of Chariot's conservationist critics, Teller explained that "the environmentalists" stopped the project "with no good reason."[76] How important "environmentalists" were to the cancellation of Chariot is open to debate, but Chariot clearly outlined the concerns and ideology of the nascent environmental movement.

NOTES

1. Plowshare was born at a meeting of nuclear scientists in LRL in February 1957 and formally established that June. The AEC's Division of Military Applications controlled the project until 1961, when the commission placed it under the newly created Division of Peaceful Nuclear Explosives. Useful studies of Plowshare are Harlan Zodtner, ed., *Plowshare Series: Industrial Uses of Nuclear Explosives,* University of California Radiation Laboratory (Department of Commerce, 1958); Frederick Reines, "The Peaceful Nuclear Explosion," *Bulletin of the Atomic Scientists* 15 (March 1959): 118–22; Ralph Sanders, "Nuclear Dynamite: A New Dimension in Foreign Policy," *Orbis* 4 (Fall 1960): 307–22; Ralph Sanders, *Plowshare Series: Industrial Uses of Nuclear Explosions* (Washington, D.C.: Public Affairs Press, 1962); Richard T. Syles, "U.S. Nuclear Exotica: Peaceful Use of Nuclear Explosives" (paper delivered at the Midwest Political Science Association's annual conference, April 1985).

The Soviets may have been working on a comparable program. Gerald W. Johnson, "The Soviet Program for Industrial Applications of Explosions," *Bulletin of the Atomic Scientists* 16 (November 1960): 366–69.

The author expresses appreciation to Dan O'Neill for his considerable assistance in preparing this article.

2. Atomic Energy Commission, Division of Peaceful Nuclear Explosives, "Plowshare Program, Fact Sheet, Project Chariot," revised, April 1962, 1–2, Box 13, Don C. Foote Papers, University of Alaska Archives, Fairbanks.

3. T. L. Péwé, D. M. Hopkins, and A. H. Lachenbruch, *Engineering Geology Bearing on Harbor Site Selection Along the Northwest Coast of Alaska from Nome to Point Barrow*, USGS Open File report, October 14, 1959; R. Kachadoorian, "Engineering Geology of the Chariot Site," in Norman J. Wilimovsky and John N. Wolfe, eds., *The Environment of the Cape Thompson Region, Alaska* (Springfield, Va.: AEC, 1966): 86–95; E. J. Longyear, "Report of the University of California Radiation Laboratory on the Mineral Potential and Proposed Harbor Locations in Northwest Alaska," April 18, 1958, Box 11, Foote Papers.

4. AEC, "Plowshare Program, Fact Sheet, Project Chariot," 3.

5. Two general texts—Claus-M. Naske and Herman E. Slotnick, *Alaska: A History of the 49th State* (Grand Rapids: William B. Eerdmans Publ. Co., 1979) and William R. Hunt, *Alaska: A Bicentennial History* (New York: W. W. Norton, 1977)—devote a few pages to the controversy. The source for both of these is Paul Brooks, *The Pursuit of Wilderness* (Boston: Houghton Mifflin, 1971). The account in all its essentials was first rendered in Paul Brooks and Joseph Foote, "The Disturbing Story of Project Chariot," *Harper's* 224 (April 1962): 60–67.

6. Alaska's military population decreased from 48,000 in 1957 to 34,000 two years later. George W. Rogers, *The Future of Alaska: Economic Consequences of Statehood* (Baltimore: Johns Hopkins Press, 1962): 94.

7. AEC Press Release No. 131, June 9, 1958, San Francisco Operations Office, Oakland (hereafter AEC-SAN), Box 11, Foote Papers.

8. *Juneau Daily Empire,* July 15, 1958; *Fairbanks Daily News-Miner* (hereafter *FDNM*), July 15, 16, and 24, 1958; Joe Foote, Background Materials, brief, March 1, 1961, p. 12, Box 10, Foote Papers.

9. *FDNM,* July 24, 1958. In Juneau Teller asked for further suggestions about how the AEC could assist the young state's economic development. On July 15 the *Juneau Daily Empire* reported that Teller had heard people who urged various projects, including a seven-mile canal across the Alaska Peninsula between Herendeen Bay and Balboa Bay, a deepwater port on Norton Sound to serve Nome, the excavation of a shipping basin near Katalla on the southcentral coast, and a dam on the Yukon River at Rampart Canyon. Though Teller gave the impression that the AEC was open to ideas, there is little indication that it seriously considered any earth-moving scheme in Alaska apart from Chariot. A possible exception was the Katalla plan. Reuben Kachadoorian, *Engineering Geology Bearing on Harbor Site Selection Along the Gulf of Alaska form Point Whitshed to Cape Yakataga, Alaska,* Trace Element Investigations Report 642, USGS, December 1959.

10. George W. Rogers, interview by Ronald K. Inouye, April 1986, transcript, p. 44, Alaska and Polar Regions, Oral History Program, UAF. In February 1961, Rogers sent Don Foote a critique of Longyear's economic feasibility study of Chariot. Rogers believed it contained "a strong element of predetermination" and was naive because it failed to examine the demand for minerals from Cape Thompson and did not calculate the disadvantages of trying to compete with more favorably located regions of the world. Box 11, Foote Papers.

11. Ernest Patty, president of the university, conveyed these concerns to the AEC on October 7, 1958. Box 21, Foote Papers.

12. *FDNM,* Jan. 10 and 12, 1959.

13. *FDNM,* Feb. 3, Jan. 19 and 23, 1959.

14. *FDNM,* Jan. 29 and 31, 1959; Donald Worster, *Nature's Economy: A History of Ecological Ideas* (1977, entitled *Nature's Economy: The Roots of Ecology;* reprint, Cambridge: Cambridge University Press, 1985), 340.

15. One reason Teller was so adamantly opposed to any test ban treaty was that, he told President Eisenhower in June 1957, a ban would interfere with the use of completely "clean" nuclear devises which he believed could be perfected in six to seven years for peaceful purposes, such as creating harbors. Robert A. Divine, *Blowing on the Wind: The Nuclear Test Ban Debate, 1954–1960* (New York: Oxford University Press, 1978), 149, 193. For similar expressions by Teller a year later, see Robert C. Williams and Phillip L. Cantelon, eds., *The American Atom: A Documentary History of Nuclear Policies from the Discovery of Fission to the Present, 1939–1984* (Philadelphia: University of Pennsylvania Press, 1984), 193.

16. At the Second United Nations International Conference on Peaceful Uses of Atomic Energy in Geneva in September 1958, American delegates, including Teller, argued that Plowshare should not be included in the test ban debate. Soviet representatives, however, claimed that Plowshare, especially Chariot, was a facade for military testing and could be a way for the United States to continue weapons testing despite a ban. *New York Times,* Sept. 12, 1958. On this general topic, see Reines, "Peaceful Nuclear Explosion."

17. *Bulletin of the Atomic Scientists* 15 (January 1959): 47.

18. U.S. Congress, Joint Committee on Atomic Energy, *Hearings: Development, Growth, and State of the Atomic Energy Industry,* 86th Cong., 1st sess., Feb. 17, 1959, 13, 28. McCone denied that a specific site had already been selected at Cape Thompson.

19. Reuben Kachadoorian, R. H. Campbell, C. L. Sainsbury, and D. W. Scholl, "Geology of the Ogotoruk Creek Area, Northwestern Alaska," Trace Element Memorandum Report 976, USGS, Nov. 1, 1958. These geologists also examined the potential for subsequent problems posed by disturbing frozen ground and by natural forces which might act to fill or seal the harbor. While some silting and filling by ocean currents would occur, they concluded these problems were not severe and that a harbor would require "little maintenance." The AEC conceded that the mineral potential of Cape Thompson was doubtful. AEC, "Plowshare Program, Fact Sheet, Project Chariot," 3.

20. AEC, "Plowshare Program, Fact Sheet, Project Chariot," 3. Simultaneous detonations at depths greater than 63 feet in permanently frozen ground were unprecedented features of the Chariot experiment. The AEC expected the deeper detonations at far greater depth. There would be one 200-kiloton device and four others of 20 kilotons. The small ones would be set off 400 feet underground and create a channel 900 feet wide, 200 feet deep, and 1,600 feet long. The large one placed 800 feet underground would produce a turning basin 400 feet deep and 1,800 feet in diameter. This last modification, according to the AEC, was necessary for technical and financial reasons. AEC, "Plowshare Program, Fact Sheet, Project Chariot," 3–4; AEC to Sen. Bartlett, Jan. 13, 1961, Box 11, Foote Papers.

21. D. L. Anderson to John N. Wolfe, June 15, 1959, Cape Thompson file, Ralph J. Rivers Papers, University of Alaska Archives. In a press release, Governor Egan requested that state officials receive "full information necessary for them to

perform their primary responsibilities to the citizens of Alaska." The AEC responded that it had already gone beyond any previous efforts to inform state officials. Press Releases, Aug. 20 and 27, 1959, Box 10, Foote Papers.

22. E. L. Bartlett, *Newsletter,* Feb. 20, 1959, Box 10, Foote Papers. The BLM announced its intention to withdraw forty square miles in September 1958 and asked for public comment. It only received two comments—one asked for further information, and another expressed concern about the withdrawal's threat to the Native community and asked about provisions for restoring the land to the public domain after the project. The BLM announced the full size of the withdrawal in April 1959. *Federal Register,* Sept. 5, 1958, April 30, 1959. Bartlett remained ambivalent toward Chariot. Though unpersuaded by the economic benefits that were supposed to accrue from the harbor, he remained enthusiastic about the opportunities for further "adventures" which might prove more beneficial, such as a waterway through the Alaska Peninsula, should Chariot be a successful experiment. Bartlett to Richard Cooley (Dir., Alaska Natural Resources Research Center, Juneau), July 28, 1959, Cape Thompson file, Rivers Papers.

23. *FDNM,* Jan. 10, 1959; *Nuclear Information* 3 (June 1961): 8–12.

24. Committee for the Study of Atomic Testing in Alaska to AEC, Feb. 19, 1959, and A. R. Luedecke to Ralph J. Rivers, March 27, 1959, Cape Thompson file, Rivers Papers. The AEC promised studies when Project Chariot was first announced in the summer of 1958, but it had not yet reported on the nature or extent of these studies or the conclusion it had drawn from them.

25. AEC-SAN, *Chariot Environmental Program,* July 1959 (copy courtesy of LLNL Archives, Livermore, California).

26. AEC, "Plowshare Program, Fact Sheet, Project Chariot," 3.

27. Willard F. Libby to Gruening, March 13, 1959, Box 20, Foote Papers. Libby was the only AEC commissioner who was a scientist. *FDNM,* Aug. 24, 1959.

28. William T. McIntyre to John McCone, April 11, 1959, Box 25, Foote Papers.

29. *FDNM,* Feb. 12, 1959. Due to ill health, Murie, then resident in Wyoming, did not play a very active role in the struggle against Chariot.

30. Edward Teller, Commencement Day Address, University of Alaska, May 18, 1959, transcription, Box 10, Foote Papers. One of Teller's favorite quips that summer was, "If your mountain is not in the right place, just drop us a card." *Anchorage Daily Times* (hereafter *ADT*), June 26, 1959. According to George Rogers, Teller talked about turning Eskimos into coal miners during their meeting in July 1958, but Teller apparently had not used this argument in public before. Rogers interview, 44.

31. *Nome Nugget,* June 29, 1959. Teller saw few disadvantages to the blasts. In Anchorage, while refusing to respond to the Soviet charge that Chariot was a weapons test in disguise, Teller did indicate that the AEC was considering allaying Russian concerns on the impact of the blasts on their people by carrying out the experiment when the winds would blow radiation to America rather than Asia. *ADT,* June 26, 1959.

32. *ADT,* Feb. 10, 1959.

33. *FDNM,* Aug. 18, 20, 22–24, 1959.

34. CESPC, AEC-SAN, "Statement," 2, Box 25, Foote Papers.

35. Foote, "History Notes (C)," 37; *FDNM,* April 27, 1960.

36. *Jessen's Weekly,* Aug. 18, 1960; *New York Times,* Aug. 17, 1960.

37. See for example, *New York Times,* Aug. 17 and 18, 1960.

38. Paul Brooks and Joseph Foote, "The Disturbing Story of Project Chariot," 61; AEC representatives' meeting with residents of Point Hope, March 14, 1960, transcript of a tape recording by the Reverend Keith Lawton, pp. 9, 21–25, 35, Box 12, Foote Papers; E. C. Shute (Manager, AEC at San Francisco) to David Frankson (President, Point Hope Village Council), June 11, 1960, Box 25, Foote Papers.

39. *Living Wilderness* 22 (Autumn-Winter 1960–61): 43.

40. *Bioenvironmental Features of the Ogotoruk Creek Area, Cape Thompson, Alaska, A First Summary by the Committee on Environmental Studies for Project Chariot,* TID-12439 (Department of Commerce, 1960), 52–57; *FDNM,* Dec. 5, 1960.

41. Leslie Viereck to Lois Crisler, Aug. 27, 1960, Alaska Wilderness file, George Marshall Papers, Bancroft Library, Berkeley; Viereck to William R. Wood, Dec. 29, 1960, Box 22, Foote Papers. The university did not review Viereck's contract after May 1961. According to *Time* (Sept. 13, 1963, p. 63), Pruitt was fired from the University of Alaska following his protest that the blast might harm local Natives. In a letter to the AEC, Pruitt charged that Brina Kessel, the head of the university's zoology department and in charge of the university's contract with the AEC, modified the final report of his findings as a member of the bioenvironmental research team prior to its submission to the AEC. Pruitt charged that in this way his three years' work was "diluted and aborted." (Pruitt to AEC, April 25, 1962, Foote Papers, Box 25). Furthermore, the ACLU, investigating a possible breach of academic freedom, questioned President Wood about allegations that his intervention eventually led to the denial of a one-year appointment of Pruitt to the faculty of Montana State University. (*Polar Star,* Oct. 18, 1963). However, the ACLU was unable to obtain sufficient evidence to proceed with legal action. Albert Johnson eventually left the university due to dissatisfaction with Kessel and Wood. (Albert Johnson, interview by Dan O'Neill, San Diego, April 11, 1988, transcript, pp. 41–42).

42. Foote, "History Notes (C)," 37; Foote to Arthur H. Lachenbruch, Nov. 25, 1960, Box 21; and Foote to John N. Wolfe, March 11, 1961, Box 25, Foote Papers. According to Foote, his affiliation with the AEC ended on March 31, 1961. He, however, remained at Point Hope until the end of August 1962. Wolfe and Wilimovsky, *Environment of the Cape Thompson Region,* 1042.

43. The Alaska Conservation Society emerged in 1960 out of the campaign to establish a wildlife range in northeast Alaska. See the recollections of Celia Hunter, a charter member, in Maxine E. McCloskey, ed., *Wilderness: The Edge of Knowledge* (San Francisco: Sierra Club Books, 1970), 186–87.

44. *Outdoor Life* 127 (January 1961): 10–11, 137; *National Wildlands News* 2 (February 1961): 2; *Defenders of Wildlife News* 36 (Spring 1961): 2; "Project Chariot—The Long Look," *Sierra Club Bulletin* 46 (May 1961): 5–9, 12–13. In December 1961 the *Bulletin of the Atomic Scientists* carried a short critical article on Chariot which extensively quoted Foote and Viereck.

45. *Nuclear Information* 3 (June 1961): 8–12. *Nuclear Information* was the publication of CNI. This issue was entitled "Project Chariot: A Complete Report on the

Probable Gains and Risks of the AEC's Plowshare Project in Alaska." Reports in the issue by Foote, Viereck, and Pruitt had appeared in the Alaska Conservation Society's spring 1961 bulletin. The report also included contributions from John S. Kelly and Gerald W. Johnson of the AEC.

46. *FDNM,* August 19, 21, 22, and 23, 1961. Snapp's probing series did not indicate an editorial shift. Snedden continued to support atomic harbor-creating schemes on the coast of northern Alaska to encourage resource development and provide jobs for local people.

47. *FDNM,* Nov. 18, 1961. The AAIA sponsored this conference, which Assistant Secretary of the Interior John Carver attended. The U.S. Fish and Wildlife Service's enforcement of a seasonal ban on Native hunting of migratory waterfowl was the other issue which precipitated the conference. One of the conference's lasting legacies was the establishment within a year of the *Tundra Times* by Howard Rock, with the financial backing of Henry S. Forbes, who was the chairman of the AAIA Policy Committee. Two of the first three issues of the paper discussed Chariot. Patrick Daley and Beverly James, "An Authentic Voice in the Technocratic Wilderness: Alaskan Natives and the *Tundra Times,*" *Journal of Communication* 36 (Summer 1986): 23–27; Lael Morgan, *Art and Eskimo Power: The Life and Times of Alaskan Howard Rock* (Fairbanks: Epicenter Press, 1988), 182–200.

48. Brooks and Foote, "The Disturbing Story of Project Chariot," 60–67.

49. AEC-SAN Press Release, Aug. 24, 1962, Box 25, Foote Papers. The CESPC's second summary report repeated that the chance of damage to plants, animals, and people "appears exceedingly remote." Bette Weichold, ed., *Bioenvironmental Features of the Ogotoruk Creek Area, Cape Thompson, Alaska (Including Predictions and Assessments of the Effects of Nuclear Detonations Proposed for an Excavation Experiment): A Second Summary Report,* compiled by CESPC, TID-17226 (Oak Ridge, Tenn: AEC, 1962): v.

50. A. R. Luedecke to Ralph Rivers, Aug. 22, 1962, Cape Thompson file, Rivers Papers.

51. *ADT,* Aug. 24, 1962; *Washington Post,* Aug. 25, 1962; Sharon Francis to Foote, Feb. 1 and May 8, 1962, Box 22, Foote Papers.

52. Foote to Howard Rock, March 5, 1963, Box 22, Foote Papers.

53. John S. Kelly (Dir., AEC Div. of Peaceful Nuclear Explosives) to Rivers, May 2, 1963, Cape Thompson file, Rivers Papers.

54. *FDNM,* April 18, 1963.

55. E. L. Bartlett, *Newsletter,* Feb. 20, 1959, Box 10, Foote Papers.

56. Samuel P. Hays, *Conservation and the Gospel of Efficiency: The Progressive Conservation Movement, 1890–1920* (Cambridge: Harvard University Press, 1959), 1.

57. Hunter to Foote, Nov. 27, 1961, Box 21, Foote Papers; George Marshall to Richard Leonard (Secr., Sierra Club), April 29, 1960, Alaska Wilderness file, George Marshall Papers. In 1956 James Marshall's wife, Lenore Marshall, cofounded the National Committee for a Sane Nuclear Policy.

58. Vierick to Crisler, Aug. 27, 1960, Alaska Wilderness file, George Marshall Papers.

59. Peter A. Coates, "The Trans-Alaska Pipeline Controversy in Historical Perspective: Attitudes toward the Transformation of the Last American Frontier"

(Ph.D. diss., University of Cambridge, 1987), 153; Dan Swift, "The Economics of Rampart Dam," *Alaska Conservation Society News Bulletin* 5 (December 1964): 5.

60. Viereck to Crisler, Aug. 27, 1960, and Richard Leonard to David Brower, April 17, 1961, Alaska Wilderness file, George Marshall Papers. For details of damage to the terrain and subsequent melting of the permafrost at Ogotoruk Creek, see Reuben Kachadoorian, "Engineering Geology of the Chariot Site," in Wolfe and Wilimovsky, eds., *Environment of the Cape Thompson Region,* 95.

61. Only a few historians have recognized the importance of public concern over radioactive fallout as a factor in the onset of environmentalism. Thomas R. Dunlap and Ralph H. Lutts argue that the debate in the 1950s over fallout prepared Americans for Rachel Carson's *Silent Spring* in 1962, from which many historians date the beginning of environmentalism, and helps to explain the book's enthusiastic reception. Worster, *Nature's Economy,* 340; Thomas R. Dunlap, *DDT: Scientists, Citizens, and Public Policy* (Princeton: Princeton University Press, 1981), 102–4; Ralph H. Lutts, "Chemical Fallout: Rachel Carson's 'Silent Spring,' Radioactive Fallout, and the Environmental Movement," *Environmental Review* 9 (Fall 1985): 211–25.

62. Barry Commoner, interview by Dan O'Neill, New York, April 27, 1988.

63. Viereck to Wood, Dec. 29, 1960, Box 22, Foote Papers.

64. *Daily Alaska Empire,* March 17, 1960; *Outdoor Life* 127 (January 1961): 137. Limited studies of the impact on fisheries had been carried out prior to the Navy's Bikini Atoll tests in 1946.

65. *Science* 154 (October 1966): 372.

66. Wolfe and Wilmovsky, eds. *The Environment of the Cape Thompson Region.*

67. Weichold, ed., *Bioenvironmental Features of the Ogotoruk Creek Area,* 3, 165; Brooks and Foote, "The Disturbing Story of Project Chariot," 67.

68. Don Foote to Joseph Foote, Dec. 20, 1961, Box 20, Foote Papers.

69. James Marshall to Harvey Broome, March 17, 1960, Alaska Wilderness file, George Marshall Papers.

70. Undated, unidentified newspaper clipping, Rivers Papers.

71. Melvin L. Merritt and R. Glen Fuller, eds., *The Environment of Amchitka Island, Alaska* (Energy Research and Development Administration, 1977), vi. Though the AEC and the Department of Defense eventually chose Nevada for the first nuclear rests on American soil, they had recommended Amchitka Island in 1950. Richard G. Hewlett and Francis Duncan, *Atomic Shield, 1947–1952,* vol. 2 of *A History of the United States Atomic Energy Commission* (University Park, Pa.: Pennsylvania State University Press, 1969), 535.

72. According to the AEC, Long Shot (eighty kilotons) was designed to provide data on the differences between a nuclear blast and an earthquake or other natural shock. Improving the American capability to detect Soviet and Chinese underground tests, the AEC claimed, would help enforce the test ban treaty of 1963. The AEC described Milrow (one megaton) as a "calibration" test designed to see if larger tests were possible. Critics claimed its purpose was to test Spartan missile warheads. Cannikin was partially classified; it involved testing Spartan antiballistic missiles, warheads, or both.

73. Merritt and Fuller, *The Environment of Amchitka Island,* 647–48; Robert

Hunter (one of the crew members on the converted fishing boat), *The Greenpeace Chronicle* (London: Picador, 1980), 12–13, 16, 53, 113–15.

74. Gerald M. Clarfield and William M. Wiecek, *Nuclear America: Military and Civilian Nuclear Power in the United States, 1940–1980* (New York: Harper and Row, 1984), 366. No above-ground test ever took place as part of Plowshare.

75. *ADT,* June 9, 1987.

76. Edward Teller, Commonwealth North address, June 1987, videotape, KUAC-TV, University of Alaska Fairbanks.

Corruption

Alaska Size

JOHN STROHMEYER

John Strohmeyer is Writer-in-Residence at the University of Alaska Anchorage. After retirement from a Pulitzer Prize-winning career as editor of the Bethlehem, Pennsylvania, Globe Times, *he accepted an appointment as the Atwood Journalism Professor at the university for two years, and then retired permanently.*

In his insightful book on the role of oil, and oil money, in modern Alaska, Strohmeyer assesses the ways in which the state's leaders and people dealt with their newfound wealth. The massive Prudhoe Bay oil field, at an estimated 15 billion barrels the largest field in North America, was discovered in 1968. Though planned to begin in 1970, construction of the Trans-Alaska Pipeline was delayed by environmetnal suits until 1974. Production began in 1977. By 1987 the oil industry had taken an estimated $44 billion in profit, and by 1995, an estimated $110 billion (after costs of exploration, development, production, transportation, adminstration, and marketing, etc.). Through an aggressive taxing regime, 85 percent of general fund revenue in Alaska is generated from petroleum production.

In 1976 the people of Alaska, by constitutional amendment, created a permanent investment fund from about 10 percent of state oil revenue. By 1995 the fund held about $15 billion. By legislation adopted in 1980, about half of the earnings from the Permanent Fund are distributed annually and equally to every Alaska citizen; most of the remainder is used to "inflation-proof" the fund. Although the legislature can determine how the principal of the fund is used, the dividend distribution creates significant pressure not to use the principal. Alaskans repealed the state income tax at the same time they created the Permanent Fund.

Oil revenue has paid for numerous important capital projects in Alaska and has kept alive a variety of grant and bonus programs. The extent of population in the state and the quality of life of many Alaskans could not be sustained except by

This article appeared originally as a chapter in *Extreme Conditions: Big Oil and the Transformation of Alaska* (New York: Simon and Schuster, 1993): 123–50; it is reprinted here by permission.

oil taxes. But oil has had significant negative effects as well, including the first major white-collar crime in the history of the young state. In the chapter of his book reprinted here, Strohmeyer reconstructs the details of the North Slope Borough corruption case which resulted in the conviction of several highly placed individuals. Money is, of course, neutral; it is what is done with it that matters. But analysts have argued that capitalism plays to the "selfish gene" in the human constitution. Among other things, students of history study likelihoods as well as possibilities. Strohmeyer's account raises familiar questions about what might be expected when people suddenly become the beneficiaries of unaccustomed wealth and opportunity.

A bright glow from the Prudhoe Bay oil-pumping stations lights up much of Alaska's North Slope during the winter darkness, but it runs out well before you get to Barrow.[1] That's when ice fog generally takes over, as it does on this day late in November 1990, while our MarkAir pilot hunts for the Barrow airport. We land through the gloom just after noontime, and it is no lighter on the ground. I can see only a blur of a town. Its buildings are dim outlines in clouds of swirling snow and frozen steam from the exhaust of trucks and cars that are kept running even when people stop for lunch, for fear it will be impossible to restart them.

It is cold in Barrow in November. The temperature is twenty-nine below with a windchill factor of sixty below. As the northernmost city in Alaska, Barrow sits on the edge of the Arctic Ocean, hemmed in by ice much of the year. The sun disappears in mid-November and doesn't appear again until mid-January. Polar bears sometimes come into town across the packed ice floes in search of defenseless dogs tied in their pens.

It costs $915 round-trip to fly to Anchorage from here, bootleggers charge $50 for a fifth of whiskey, and gasoline is $2.80 a gallon. You can't drive to Barrow. And nobody drives very far around Barrow—the longest road goes only twelve miles. "Why would anyone want to live here?" I wonder. Yet thirty-three hundred people do.

"It's peaceful here," replies Marie Adams, an amiable, college-educated Inupiat whose father was a reindeer herder. One of twelve children, Marie got through Evangel College in Missouri with financial help from the Assembly of God church, but she chose to return to her subsistence family in Barrow instead of staying with a good job in the lower forty-eight. She is a dedicated whale researcher and recently opened Barrow's first public information agency, which publishes a newsletter on community activities.

Marie is proud that her people have survived for thousands of years in what some say is the world's most hostile inhabited environment. Each generation handed down the skills to capture migrating caribou, net returning salmon, and identify edible plants on the tundra, among other necessities for survival. The pride of the Inupiat to this day is the harpooning of the giant bowhead whale. In 1977, the International Whaling Commission tried to put a moratorium on the taking of bowhead whales, but so intense was the Eskimo protest that U.S. authorities helped the North Slope Borough[2] obtain special quotas for subsistence harvest. Each catch of these monsters (they weigh as much as fifty tons) is shared among the villagers and is an occasion for festivals and prayers.

The Eskimos in Barrow escaped contact with the Russian trappers who came in the eighteenth century. Other Alaska Natives were not so lucky. The invaders decimated the sea otter population and often enslaved the aboriginals who lived in the Aleutians. But the Inupiats had to overcome the hardships inflicted on their food chain by flotillas of American whaling ships that all but eliminated the whales that migrate in the Arctic. Yet they continue to hang on to their harsh world, to the perplexity of anthropologists and historians.

A visitor to Barrow quickly senses that Marie and much of the Native community are fighting harder than ever to save their culture. Over the past fifteen years, the threat to their traditional way of life has been greater than any they endured through centuries of famine, disease, and natural disaster. The discovery of oil on the North Slope has transformed these once primitive people into privileged people. Their land has created billions of dollars of wealth, and they have had serious problems dealing with it.

As the seat of the North Slope Borough, which taxes all of the Prudhoe Bay oil fields, Barrow is the richest city, per capita, in the United States, and possibly in the world. In recent years it has also probably attracted the greatest number of unscrupulous people, per capita. That they have managed to extort many millions of dollars of Eskimo wealth is a scandal little known beyond Alaska.

Oil companies did their utmost to prevent the incorporation of the North Slope Borough. Early in the 1970s, they sought injunctions in court, arguing that it did not make sense to create a municipality of 56.6 million acres (about the size of the state of Minnesota) just so a small band of once nomadic people could tax the Prudhoe Bay oil complex, plus every future oil well, the pipeline, and service centers across the entire top of Alaska. "Who Will Control the Dazzling North Slope Wealth?" one Anchorage newspaper headlined the battle.

With the several thousand oil company workers who had recently arrived in Alaska barred from voting, an essentially Eskimo electorate voted 402–27 in June 1979 to create the North Slope Borough. Citing the terms of the state constitution, the Alaska courts validated the election, thereby certifying the largest local government in the world. The borough starts where Alaska meets the Chukchi Sea on the west and encompasses the entire oil-rich tundra north of the Brooks Range to the Canadian border on the east.

The fifty-seven hundred predominantly Inupiat Eskimos who occupied the eight isolated villages in this desolate land probably had no idea of the wealth that would be theirs. Newspapers estimated that the oil company facilities at Prudhoe Bay alone would swell the assessed value of taxable property to $10 billion. It reached $13.6 billion by 1987. Meanwhile, "Outsiders"[3] scrambled even before the vote was in to advise the Eskimos on how such a solid tax base could be used to create instant millions for themselves and, of course, their advisers. Investment houses were begging to sell municipal bonds backed with such guarantees of oil revenues.

The borough elected Eben Hopson, an Inupiat whaling captain and respected patriarch, as its first mayor. He had a clear vision of how to apply the money. "The caribou and the whale have formed the base of our existence, but cash has become a way of life," he stated. "We have been introduced to dwellings heated by oil, with running water and even indoor toilets." He pledged that the people of the North Slope henceforth would have all the amenities of Anchorage or Fairbanks. No longer would they have to carry their wastes to village tank trucks or hunt for blocks of blue ice to melt for drinking water. And never again would they have to worry about the caribou not returning or the salmon disappearing. There would be well-paying cash jobs for everyone.

As the center of his improvement program, Hopson authorized the Barrow Utilidor, an extraordinary sewer and water system that would be installed in heated tunnels burrowed beneath the permafrost.[4] He promised to connect it to every home in the city. To give his people the finest education, Hopson started building the largest and most up-to-date high school in Alaska. It would occupy 119,532 square feet and include an

Olympic-size swimming pool, a college-size basketball auditorium, plus separate rooms for wrestling, gymnastics, and karate—an impressive facility for a district that averages about 150 high school students.

Hopson died in 1980. He did not live long enough to see either project completed. Nor did he live to learn of the massive corruption his well-intentioned building program would spawn. That sad distinction belongs to the administration of Mayor Eugene Brower, a boyish Inupiat who took office in 1981 at the age of thirty-three. Brower, also a whaling captain, had been the public works director but had grown impatient with the slow pace of the capital improvements started by Hopson and the interim mayor, Jake Adams, another whaling captain. (Barrow has 144 whaling captains.) When the baton passed to Brower, he set out to take Barrow from the Stone Age to the space age as fast as he could get vessels and planes to ship the lumber and hardware from Seattle.

Coached by outsiders, Brower borrowed hundreds of millions of dollars—the debt swelled from $453 million to $1.2 billion during the three years he served—by floating bonds backed by the borough's oil property-tax base. This was quite a spectacular feat for a municipality of fewer than six thousand people. Moody's Investors Service rated the bond issues A or better. Wall Street bond brokers and their Alaskan agents feasted.

As the debt began to approach that of Philadelphia and other large cities, several alarmed lawmakers started to call for legislation to put a cap on Barrow's runaway borrowing. They feared the state could be left paying off the debt in the long term when oil revenues started declining and Barrow could no longer meet its payments. In response to these threats from Juneau, Brower signed multimillion-dollar construction contracts the way some mayors sign proclamations. And with about the same amount of scrutiny. Brower, whose education was limited to Bureau of Indian Affairs schools, could not have masterminded so massive a capital program by himself. Experts of all stripes from the Outside streamed in to help, and Natives often stopped to admire their shiny Lear Jets and Cessnas parked at the airport. But there were two figures who emerged from the shadows of Alaska's political life to grab the inside track from the day that Brower took office.

Lew Dischner, then sixty-five, was a portly, glad-handing political veteran who had been part of the power structure in Juneau for as long as Alaska had been a state. He had been appointed first commissioner of labor in 1959 by Governor William Egan, a Democrat. Dischner left the post after a year and resurfaced in Juneau as a lobbyist for several large clients, including the Teamsters, the most powerful labor group in the state. Along the way, he demonstrated an adeptness at getting government loans and state contracts to build a private business empire. He developed a waterfront mall in Juneau, won the contract to operate a laundromat in a state-owned residential high rise, and acquired a hotel that leased rooms to the state.

Dischner also built a network of influence. With the help of the Teamsters, he became a leading fund-raiser for the Democratic party and certain helpful Republican candidates. His ability to deliver hefty campaign contributions earned him a reservoir of return favors at all levels of local and state government, to be tapped when needed.

With the birth of the North Slope Borough in 1972, Dischner headed north to the future. He arrived bearing a campaign chest for Eben Hopson, who rewarded Dischner by hiring him as a borough lobbyist. When Hopson died, the borough assembly president Adams served out Hopson's term and was expected to win the next election, in October 1981. But Dischner decided the next mayor should be Brower, the young Eskimo rising in the public works department.

Dischner masterminded Brower's campaign, raising $100,000 to fund it. Much of the money was laundered, given in the names of a variety of people but actually coming from Dischner and an assortment of slope contractors who expected to be rewarded once their man was safely in office.

It was a daring gamble. Brower won by only twenty-four votes, but he lost no time in rewarding Dischner. He made the lobbyist consultant to the mayor on capital improvement projects, a lucrative combination that would set Dischner up to make $250,000 a year for lobbying services alone, two and a half times Brower's own salary.

The mayor's other confidant was Carl Mathisen, then forty-nine, a small-time political wheeler-dealer who dripped gold. As glum as Dischner was cheerful, Mathisen made his statement with what must have been a record-size wristwatch studded with gold nuggets, featuring two twenty-karat bears growling at each other across the timepiece. Mathisen had worked in the 1970s for the borough's bond counsel, Bob Dupre of Juneau. While helping Dupre reap a bounty of commissions by floating $1.2 billion in bond issues, Mathisen had been laying the foundation of his own future. Though short on formal education, Mathisen had enough contracting experience in Anchorage to understand the ways of government and bureaucrats. He convinced Mayor Hopson to hire him as borough training program coordinator. That was how he got to know Brower in the public works department.

Mathisen became Brower's mentor, teaching the young Inupiat ways of government not found in textbooks. Mathisen also ingratiated himself with the Brower family, showering its members with gifts and even became godfather to a Brower son. Brower reciprocated by persuading his father, yet another whaling captain, to appoint Mathisen a member of his renowned crew. The only white man ever to be so honored, Mathisen bowed out after he had a terrifying nightmare about a polar bear in camp on his first outing and injured his leg on the second.

But when Brower ran for mayor in 1981, Mathisen and his wife were in the forefront of his supporters, with a $5,000 check. One of Brower's first acts in office was to install Mathisen as a consultant to the mayor and to the public works director handling capital projects, a post that would pay him an average of $300,000 a year. His initial consulting contract paid him $156,500.

The two consultants were well paired. Dischner was skilled in siphoning money, and Mathisen had the nuts-and-bolts savvy to provide respectable projects. Together they recruited a compatible cast of engineers, architects, technicians, and construction and service companies to do their business. Many were struggling specialty firms, and some did not exist until the borough started letting contracts. But all were expected to abide by the house rules, which required them to systematically kick back 10 percent of every borough contract to Dischner and Mathisen.

Awed by the way his two advisers got things moving, Brower didn't question them when they picked a Seattle firm, the H. W. Blackstock Company, to purchase all materials, all shipping, and anything else that had to do with servicing the borough's capital construction projects. As an influence peddler, Dischner had had a long relationship with Blackstock. He took good care of his client.

Dischner engineered a contract that permitted Blackstock to tack 30 percent on top of the cost of anything it provided, an arrangement unheard of in municipal government or private industry. The president of the lucky company was Kenneth Rogstad, the former Republican chairman of King County, which includes Seattle. Dischner knew that Rogstad could be counted on to contribute to campaigns of well-positioned Democrats in Alaska as well.

"The consultants became the government," Chris Mello, then contract reviewer for the borough, says. A California native, barely thirty years old and fresh out of California Western School of Law in San Diego, Mello was working at his first real job. He admits he was puzzled at first by what he saw, and then was simply dismayed. "In my first meeting with Lew Dischner, he told me he was a blood brother to the mayor, and what he said went," Mello says. "Suddenly the borough was starting hundreds of projects and running them was wrested away from the borough employees and turned over to the consultants. We were reduced to clerks."

Brower signed contracts for more schools, firehouses, health clinics, roads, worker camps, incinerators, engineering studies, and architectural renderings, plus expensive change orders for the Utilidor and other projects in progress. At one point, the sparsely populated borough's capital budget soared to $300 million a year, which rivaled what the city of Chicago then spent for the capital needs of its millions of residents. "Consultants identified the projects," Mello says. "We were spending as much as a million a day. Projects were coming so fast that those that should have been bid were not bid. I was supposed to review the contracts before they went to the mayor. But sometimes those documents would arrive in the legal department already signed by the mayor. What was the point of reviewing them then?

"We hear rumors of kickbacks. Then we find out later that Lew and Carl formed their own companies to work on projects. The next thing you know they are negotiating contracts on behalf of the borough with their own companies, and the costs of the projects go way out of line."

Harold Curran, another young law school graduate, was also among those who felt uneasy. He had come to Alaska as a VISTA volunteer and followed his girlfriend, an environmental planner with the Trustees for Alaska, a nonprofit public interest law firm specializing in Alaska environmental issues, to a project in Barrow. Hopson welcomed the talent and hired him as borough attorney. "When I found out that a sole-source contract was awarded for six health clinics, I advised Brower that it should have been a bid contract," Curran says. "At one point I wrote him a memo noting that some of the contracts that had not been bid seemed to be in the high dollars. Soon after, I got a letter from Brower's litigation counsel telling me that the price of a contract was not a legal issue."

Frustrated, Curran tried to interest John Larson, news director for Channel 2 in Anchorage, Alaska's largest television station, in looking at the way the borough handed out contracts. Larson said the station didn't have the staff to investigate a situation so far away. But the Eskimos in Barrow did not need media exposure to see that things were getting out of hand at borough hall, or that Outsiders were helping themselves to millions of dollars of their money.

The Utilidor was initially estimated to cost $80 million, but Brower's change orders helped send the total up to $250 million by 1984, when only 10 percent of the buildings were hooked up. (The cost had reached $330 million by 1991, when still only slightly more than half of the homes were being serviced. It is by far the most expensive public works project ever attempted in Alaska.) The bill for the high school, initially projected at $25 million, soared to $80 million, which amounts to $320,000 per student. In his book *Alaska,* James Michener gives the impression that it is an ugly building. To me, the appearance did not register as forcefully as did the distortion of educational priorities. An expensive, life-size bronze statue of Hopson greets a visitor at the entrance, and a $75,000 mural decorates an inside wall. Yet the library is no larger than the gym's smallest exercise room, its book supply is glaringly meager, and its current periodical shelf does not contain any out-of-state newspapers or even one from the state capital.

What attracted even more public attention than the skyrocketing cost of these projects, however, was the change in the mayor's life-style. Brower now traveled by private jet to Anchorage, Seattle, Palm Springs, and, it was rumored, the casinos in Las Vegas. After one trip, he returned sporting a huge diamond ring and expensive new suits. The mayor's new boat, worth at least $35,000 according to local mariners, was the envy of all who boated upriver to the caribou grounds. Brower also started showing off a new Browning semiautomatic shotgun.

The prevailing wisdom is that an incumbent mayor who provides full employment and more than the usual amenities for his constituents is bound to be reelected. Brower did all that and had a reelection war chest of $950,000 to boot, raised with Dischner's expertise. But the people of the North Slope could feel their fortune being drained by Outsiders, and quiet resentment was mounting. In the fall of 1984, they voted Brower out of office. The victory of George Ahmaogak, a borough worker who is only part Inupiat (but a whaling captain, of course), was the political shocker of the year.

During Brower's last five days in office, his administration pushed through more than $15 million in checks and signed $7.6 million in contracts. The frenzy was described in a story filed from Barrow by Bill White, business editor of the *Anchorage Daily News*: "'There are planes leaving in a half-hour. Get the checks out,' outgoing mayor Brower barked at an accounting officer. While the planes waited, the men they had brought hovered over the mayor and the accounting clerks. They wanted checks for millions of dollars and they wanted them cashed before Brower left office." Among the principal beneficiaries were Dischner, Mathisen, and Kenneth Rogstad, the head of the H. W. Blackstock Company.

The incoming mayor, George Ahmaogak, immediately noticed that many borough files were missing. He assumed they were shredded, whereupon he went to the assembly and asked for an audit of borough finances. The audit, performed by the Fairbanks accounting firm of Main Hurdman, surprised even those who had expected the worst. Besides finding many contracts that had not been legally bid, the report showed that millions of dollars had been spent on services for which no invoices existed. It also identified an array of contracts with "an improper scope and fee relationship," meaning that the amount paid appeared to be excessive for the service. The auditors particularly questioned the propriety of nearly $20 million that went to H. W. Blackstock. Not only were many of the payments in cash, contrary to purchasing procedures, but sometimes goods were never delivered. Among the many discrepancies cited was a $363,134 payment for borough housing development furniture. Neither invoice nor furniture appeared to have been received.

The most eye-opening finding was that Dischner and Mathisen, while on the borough payroll as consultants, had set up firms of their own to get borough business. The largest, North Slope Constructors, had been favored with many millions of dollars in contracts. It was incorporated, with Dischner, Mathisen, and Rogstad as equal owners, one year after Brower took office. North Slope Constructors was able to shut out other firms by bidding low and then negotiating change orders. "That substantially increased the size of the contract without substantially increasing work to be done," the auditors reported.

The whiff of wholesale fraud inspired newspapers in Fairbanks and Anchorage to dig deeper. They soon exposed layers of lesser players—lawyers, architects, engineers, consultants, public-works employees, and even a state senator—who had benefited from the questionable payments, kickbacks, and tainted gifts that flowed like water during the Barrow building boom. Public attention inevitably shifted to Governor William Sheffield. What was he going to do about the North Slope corruption?

The governor's first response was that he was not aware that any state money had been involved. The *Anchorage Daily News* quickly challenged him, showing that the state had budgeted more than $4 million for a half dozen projects questioned by the audit.

Then the Anchorage representative Fritz Pettyjohn charged that the state attorney general Norman Gorsuch was dragging his feet in investigating the matter because several of those who landed lucrative contracts in Barrow were heavy political contributors to the governor's campaign. Dischner himself was one of Sheffield's largest contributors. A secretary in the governor's office says Dischner walked into the office one day and tried to drop off a $60,000 check for the governor's campaign committee. The secretary, recognizing the illegality of the gift, refused to accept it. But the surprise was that Rogstad, a Republican power in the Seattle area, figured so prominently in raising money for Sheffield, a Democrat. According to newspaper reports, which were not denied, employees of Blackstock sent $7,000 in checks to Sheffield, and the company helped organize a fund-raiser in Seattle to reduce the sizable campaign debt Sheffield carried into office.

Suddenly, the question of whether Sheffield would act became academic. By the spring of 1985, the governor himself was in deep trouble. Someone had tipped off the *Fairbanks News-Miner* that there was something shady about a ten-year, $9.1 million lease the state had signed for office space in a Fairbanks building. The specifications had been written so narrowly that only the one building had qualified.

Stan Jones, a reporter on the *News-Miner,* dropped the Barrow story and plunged into a round-the-clock investigation of the Fairbanks lease. He reported that a labor leader named Lennie Arsenault, who had helped raise $92,000 for Sheffield's campaign, had a financial interest in the favored building. Further, he found that Arsenault had had discussions with the governor regarding the lease and that employees within the state leasing office had protested the circumvention of leasing procedures.

The stories troubled the state prosecutor Dan Hickey, a Georgetown Law School graduate who, like Curran and Mello in Barrow, was among the young lawyers who had answered ads for jobs in the emerging state of Alaska. He became chief prosecutor in 1975. In spite of Sheffield's public declarations of propriety, Hickey quietly started to investigate the Barrow mess without the governor's knowledge. But other disturbing events soon demanded his full attention. Two employees from the administration's procurement office visited Hickey and bared their concerns about the Fairbanks lease. They also told him Stan Jones had filed a request under Alaska's Freedom of Information Act to see the file, which, they said, was damaging to the governor.

Crusades against corruption in government have a poor record in Alaska. In fact, the system seemed to find ways to abort aggressive law enforcement, a fact no one knew better than Hickey. In 1982, he had led a grand jury investigation into the dealings of the state senator Ed Dankworth, former head of the Alaska state troopers. While co-chairman of the senate finance committee, Dankworth and a business partner had bought the former Isabel Pass pipeline camp for $1 million and tried to sell it to the state for use as a correctional facility—at an asking price of $3 million.[5] The grand jury indicted Dankworth for conflict of interest, but the courts gutted the case, ruling that the senator was protected by legislative immunity. None of his conversations or actions to persuade the legislators to appropriate money for the camp purchase could be used against him; they were considered part of the legislative process. Hickey had no choice but to dismiss the case.

Hickey was also well aware of what happened to another whistle-blower, Representative Russ Meekins, Jr., the upstart who had captured the speaker's chair in the famed 1981 legislative coup.[6] In the spending frenzy of 1982, Meekins publicly accused the state senator George Hohman (D-Bethel) of trying to bribe him with promises of a bag of money in exchange for support of a water-throwing plane.[7] Hohman was convicted and expelled from the senate. However, ten years later he still had not paid his $10,000 fine and was gainfully employed as acting city manager of Bethel. Meanwhile, Meekins's brilliant political career suddenly came to a screeching halt. He did not run for reelection and left the state.

These were parables Hickey could not ignore as he began to probe the affairs of the highest officer in the government of Alaska. Nevertheless, he impounded all the leasing records in the procurement office and launched a grand jury investigation.

Governor Sheffield made two appearances before the grand jury. Soon after the first, Hickey went to his boss, Attorney General Gorsuch, with an unappealing prognosis. The ramifications of the case required outside expertise. A pained Gorsuch agreed. They looked to Washington, D.C., and brought in George Frampton, who had worked as a special prosecutor with the Watergate grand jury that led to the downfall of President Nixon in 1974. Tensions in the state escalated as politicians and the public soon suspected that the inquiry into Sheffield's administration involved more than the lease of a building. The grand jury worked for ten weeks, calling in more than forty-four witnesses and preparing 161 exhibits as it built a case against Sheffield.

Meanwhile, two key state housing administrators died under circumstances that many continue to find troubling. In February 1985, Bruce Moore, a Department of Administration Services employee who complained that superiors were pressuring him to process the Fairbanks building contract, was found dead on a sidewalk beneath the balcony of his condominium in Hawaii. He was an apparent suicide, though he left no note, and friends noticed no indication of depression or ill health. Three months later, Lisa Rudd, a Sheffield cabinet officer who also had expressed skepticism at the building contract, died within hours of contracting a virulent bacterial infection. No evidence of foul play was found in either of the deaths, but the newsman Stan Jones and state housing employees of that era still shake their heads over the deaths and call them "an incredible coincidence."

On July 2, 1985, the grand jury returned a devastating report. It charged "a serious abuse of office" by Governor Sheffield and his chief of staff, John Shively, in their alleged intervention into the lease process and in their attempt to frustrate official investigations into the matter. Inspired, according to some, by the climate of the Watergate hearings, the jurors called Sheffield unfit to hold office and recommended the senate be called into special session to consider impeaching the governor.

Shaken by the finding, Sheffield stuck by his testimony that he did not remember meeting with Arsenault and that consolidating state offices in the Fairbanks building would have saved the state money. Nevertheless, about six hours after the grand jury's report, Gorsuch issued a legal opinion stating that the administration should cancel the lease because it was tainted by favoritism. The attorney general, who had already said he wanted to resign, left office the next week. Sheffield quickly appointed Hal Brown, a lawyer from Ketchikan, to succeed him. One of Brown's first acts was to call in the state prosecutor. "I was told to get out quietly," Hickey says. He left, but not quietly. He issued a blistering parting message citing the work to be done, including the state's responsibility to investigate the situation at Barrow.

The senate impeachment debate even more strongly took on aspects of Watergate. The Republicans, who had 11-9 control of the senate, hired the former Watergate committee counsel Sam Dash to oversee the proceedings. Meanwhile, Sheffield also reached down to Washington for another Watergate pro, Philip Lacovara, counsel to the Watergate prosecutor Leon Jaworski, to defend him.

Dash advised the senate that Sheffield's tampering with state leasing procedures might not amount to an impeachable offense, but perjury would. (The broad pattern of lying to cover up the crime rather than actual complicity in the Watergate break-in was the biggest factor in Nixon's ouster from the presidency.) Dash pointed out that Sheffield had testified four times that he could not recall ever meeting with Arsenault, while not only Arsenault but John Shively, the governor's own chief of staff, told the grand jury in detail about a meeting in which the governor and Arsenault discussed lease specifications.

Many thought Dash had made a case for impeachment, but at the moment of truth, the majority crumpled. Observers speculated that some didn't understand what was wrong with helping a campaign contributor, and others were bound to the unwritten political code that you don't stone anyone in your own circle today lest you be stoned tomorrow. Still others clearly saw official misconduct but simply did not have the courage to make a stand.

In the end, the senators not only rejected Dash's recommendation but gutted a subsequent rules committee resolution denouncing Sheffield for questionable veracity and "significant irregularities." Instead, they called for a study into state procurement procedures and then added a rebuke to the investigators in the form of a resolution asking that the Alaska Judicial Council "study the use of the power of the grand jury to investigate and make recommendations . . . to prevent abuse and assure basic fairness." Five years later, as memories faded, the legislature even reimbursed the governor for his legal expenses. A catchall bill, ostensibly passed to fund the state's longevity bonuses and legal expenses to recover disputed royalty payments from oil companies, included a payment of $302,653 for Sheffield. And when the Democrats regained the U.S. presidency in 1992, Sheffield emerged as President Clinton's dispenser of patronage in Alaska.

The trauma of the Sheffield controversy plus the departure of Hickey doomed any state action against government corruption in Barrow. The new state attorney general had no appetite for searching out corruption in remote villages, much less for the turmoil of another grand jury investigation. By now just about every element in the protection system was prepared to do nothing about Barrow. The reason seemed clear to Roger McAniff, a University of Alaska engineering professor who, as a business consultant, had analyzed the inflated contracts let during the Brower years: "Alaska simply had no experience in dealing with white-collar crime."

But while the desire for money induces corruption, it can also counter it. The millions lost to favored contractors on the North Slope had infuriated many contractors who sought and were denied the chance to compete. Several refused to accept the affront without a fight. Reports of kickbacks for contracts and of the millions Eugene Brower had dished out during his final days in office came to the attention of the FBI. The bureau dispatched an agent, G. Bruce Talbert, to Barrow to investigate. He came back with a harrowing story. The payouts appeared to be the desperate final stages of a sophisticated system in which a tight circle of white manipulators had been making personal fortunes by milking the newly rich Eskimo municipality. Only someone knowing how to match political greed with free-enterprise chicanery could have masterminded such a scheme, Talbert reported, and Brower's consultants, Lew Dischner and Carl Mathisen, had just those skills.

Meanwhile, North Slope's escalating bond indebtedness was receiving attention around the state. Representative Fritz Pettyjohn of Anchorage had been urging fellow legislators in Juneau to support a bill to cap the borough's extraordinary borrowing spree, lest the state eventually get stuck with the debt. Some Natives assailed Pettyjohn as a racist for denying Eskimos the right to use their own money to upgrade their living conditions, but their complaint was unlikely to pacify an uneasy legislature for long.

By the spring of 1985, the FBI, now joined by Internal Revenue Service investigators, was able to piece together a picture of the dimension of corruption. The bureau handed the Justice Department a bribery, extortion, and fraud case the likes of which the nation had rarely seen.

Alaska's U.S. attorney was a tall, trim, low-key lawyer in his late thirties named Mike Spaan. His training was solid—Boalt Hall law school at the University of California, Berkeley; two years as a legal assistant for Alaska's senior U.S. senator, Republican Ted Stevens, and six years with a private law firm. But he also was very conscious of whose turf he was treading on. While many of his peers would have jumped at the chance to establish a political reputation as a foe of crime and corruption, Spaan was reluctant to preempt the state. Further, he felt state laws could be applied more directly and effectively than the Racketeer Influenced and Corrupt Organizations (RICO) Act, the federal antiracketeering law that covers local corruption.

But the FBI gave Spaan little choice. It was possible, the bureau reported, that Alaska was sitting on the biggest bribery, extortion, and tax-evasion case in municipal history. The FBI identified more than a dozen people—public officials, contractors, engineers, architects, and assorted lesser players—as members of Barrow's inner circle who had enjoyed grossly inflated contracts in return for which they'd kicked back a steady stream of millions to the masterminds in the mayor's office. The bureau wanted the authority to start subpoenaing records.

Whatever the difficulties of using federal law to crack a state corruption case, Spaan was persuaded. Appalled at the amounts of money and instances of public betrayal involved, he was further dismayed to find that he did not have the staff to move against everyone at once. He could prosecute only in stages and hope that he could finish the job before the five-year statutes of limitations ran out. While much of the state's attention was still occupied by the Sheffield impeachment battle, Spaan moved quietly to start a federal grand jury investigation into the North Slope mess.

Early in 1985, Spaan and the FBI's Talbert began mapping out the first full-scale white-collar corruption case ever prosecuted by the U.S. attorney's office in Alaska. Spaan decided to move first against the lesser figures, hoping he could get them to plea bargain for lighter sentences in exchange for a promise to testify for the government in the bigger cases.

On May 30, 1986, the federal grand jury finally handed down its first indictment. After more than a year of news reports of intense witness traffic in the federal building, it was an anticlimax. A lone Inupiat named Irving Igtanloc, Brower's public works director, was indicted on six counts of extortion, wire fraud, and income tax evasion. Nor was the substance of the charges particularly earthshattering. Igtanloc was accused of extorting gifts from a Washington State firm doing business with the borough, to wit: a remodeling job on his home, a .44-caliber revolver, and the mounting of an 18-inch lake trout his wife had caught while they were guests of the contractor at a fishing lodge.

Quite incidentally, Spaan announced, the man charged with providing the gifts to Igtanloc had been indicted for bribery but had pleaded guilty to a reduced charge in exchange for an agreement to cooperate with investigators. The lesser charge—illegal shipment of gifts of liquor—was laughable, especially in Alaska, but Spaan felt he had at least made a crack in the inner circle.

The name of the plea bargainer was Joseph P. Brock, and he had been a $250,000-a-year executive for a consulting group called MMCW. Based in Anchorage, the firm was a partnership of McCool McDonald Architects of Seattle and Anchorage and the Bellevue, Washington, engineering firm of Coffman and White. Dubbed "the engineers" in the FBI investigation, MMCW was a major player in the borough's capital improvement program. It had been handed an annual $7.8 million, no-bid contract to administer the technical side of the project development. MMCW determined the scope of the work and the estimated cost, then placed the contracts. Many of the contracts, the FBI found, were steered to architects and engineers within the MMCW family, at suspiciously lucrative terms. Brock was an important point man for the MMCW operation. But his feeble penalty—two years' probation and a $4,000 fine—made some wonder whether the state was in for another round of typical Alaska white-collar justice.

By the end of 1986, the indictments had picked up speed, and a picture of looting in the North Slope had finally begun to emerge. Martin Farrell, Brower's top lawyer, was charged with fraud for getting Brower to sign a $720,000 contract, with a $150,000 nonrefundable advance, two days before leaving office in 1984. Thomas Gittins, a contractor, was charged with kicking back 10 percent on all borough contracts to Lew Dischner and with doing a $601,000 home-remodeling job—at Dischner's expense—on the home of Myron Igtanloc, Irving's brother. Myron maintained an 8,500-square-foot Anchorage residence with gold-plated plumbing fixtures while serving as the North Slope's capital improvement projects coordinator. Myron Igtanloc himself was charged with three felony counts of tax evasion for failing to report $600,000 in income over a three-year period.

It was also disclosed at this point that Gittins claimed he had been paying an additional 3 percent on all contracts to a North Slope Native legislator, Al Adams, who soon after had been elected to the state senate. He at first insisted he had received "a little more than his legislative pay"—$45,000—for helping Gittins get contracts, most of which were funded by public money. Subsequent testimony would charge that Adams received at least $700,000 for services described as "public relations, ensuring compliance with local hire, and such other duties as Gittins might assign him." Those allegations did not figure in the indictment, nor did the Alaska state legislature find any breach of ethics after it made a cursory investigation.

The North Slope grand jury investigation went on for two years before it touched principal figures. On February 2, 1987, the ex-mayor Eugene Brower was indicted on fourteen counts of receiving bribes, gifts, and loans from contractors and lobbyists in return for preferential treatment. Several big names—Dischner, Mathisen, and Rogstad among them—were identified as having provided the favors, but they were not indicted, to the consternation of the public and the press. Spaan dodged the questions. As it turned out, he was buying time to negotiate with Brower in the hope that the ex-mayor would agree to reduced charges in exchange for testifying against those who extracted the heavy money.

For several months Brower held out, vowing to prove his innocence in court. Finally the FBI agent Brent Rasmussen, who had worked with Talbert on the investigation, set up a meeting with Brower and showed him the government's evidence of the "10 percent clause," the secret deal Dischner and Mathisen had with the engineers, architects, and contractors under which the latter kicked back 10 percent of their payments from the borough. "I don't know if words can describe it," Rasmussen said. "Brower went into a state of shock. He broke down entirely; he was sobbing, and the interview had to stop. He was unable to continue."

Soon after, Brower pleaded guilty to a single charge of tax evasion and agreed to help the government. This time there was not only the uneasy feeling that a truly major player in the corruption case was getting off with a sweetheart deal but also a lingering question in the public's mind whether Brower might have feigned his remorse.

Nevertheless, Spaan was convinced he now had what the case needed—an Eskimo leader to testify against the white exploiters. On November 10, 1987, Dischner and Mathisen were indicted. The government alleged that their illegal take from the borough amounted to $21 million. Each was charged with thirty-six racketeering counts of fraud, bribery, kickbacks, and extortion in the North Slope Borough.

The inquiry had so drained the short-staffed U.S. attorney's office that the state attorney general agreed to lend Spaan two lawyers from his staff to help out. An attorney named Peter Gamache had been assigned there earlier, and now a second was urgently needed.

Karen Loeffler got the call. A petite, dark-haired, cheerful young woman only four years out of Harvard Law School, she had come to Alaska when she became bored with her job at a private law firm in Minneapolis. She landed a job with the oil and gas section of the state attorney general's office in 1985, when the gubernatorial impeachment controversy dominated the news. She had heard only a little about the North Slope, and since the state had at that point decided not to pursue the case, she had never dreamed she would become part of it.

As soon as she reported for duty, Spaan handed her a pile of grand jury transcripts, exhibits, and financial records with instructions to read them thoroughly. The tone in his voice said, "From now on, Karen, the North Slope corruption case is your life."

Loeffler had limited experience as a prosecutor and very little exposure to criminal law. But she did not have to read very deeply into the North Slope file to discover that she had been handed an incredible mission. For the next year, she devoted long days, nights, and weekends trying to put together blocks of the evidence in a way that a jury of ordinary citizens could understand. She evaluated the grand jury testimony of hundreds of witnesses. She pored over reports of FBI agents, often meeting with them and Peter Gamache to analyze prospective witnesses. She buried herself in a small mountain of documents to unravel the workings of complicated interlocking corporations.

On October 14, 1988, the racketeering trial of Lewis Dischner and Carl Mathisen finally began. In a crowded courtroom on the second floor of the federal building in Anchorage, the U.S. attorney Mike Spaan stationed his erect six-foot-four-inch frame before the jury. "This is a case about fraud, bribery, kickbacks, extortion, and corruption," he said. "The sticky fingers of Dischner and Mathisen managed to grab twenty-one million dollars in public funds from the borough in just three years. We are going to prove that twenty-one million dollars dollar by dollar."

Mathisen smiled weakly. Dischner leaned over to confer with his attorney, Douglas Pope, giving the impression he was puzzled by what Spaan was saying.

"This entire case," Pope countered, "is here because the prosecution misunderstands the situation on the North Slope." The government was confused about the law, he said, and about the duties of Lew Dischner, "a man with a strong sense of values being unfairly prosecuted for his strong commitment to the people of the North Slope borough." Taking his turn, Laurence Finegold, Mathisen's attorney, declared, "This isn't a case about money. It is far more complex than the government wishes to have you believe. . . . It was not illegal payments that created expensive projects, but the [arctic] conditions. . . . In less than fifteen months Mathisen helped bring dramatic, if expensive, changes to the North Slope." The lawyers took about four hours to outline their cases, and then the court recessed for the weekend.

Brower was the government's first witness. In a hesitant, almost sheepish manner, he testified that while in office he had been showered with gifts by Dischner, Mathisen, and their contractor friends. Dischner provided him with the use of a home in a fashionable section of Anchorage. Brower also admitted to accepting a $45,000 diamond ring from him. Mathisen had paid for a customized 27-foot dory valued at $35,000. Brower's benefactors flew him to Las Vegas several times and on two occasions handed him $1,000 in gambling money. Contractors flew him to Palm Springs, where he was provided the use of a Cadillac, and he never asked who paid his hotel bills and airfare to Hawaii.

Brower admitted that many of the borough contracts he had approved were issued to companies totally or partly owned by Dischner and Mathisen. He conceded that he had pretended not to know of their involvement when he testified before the grand jury and had lied under oath to protect them. Yes, he said, he had known about Mathisen's ownership of Alaska Management Services, about Dischner's part-ownership of North Coast Mechanical, and about both defendants' ownership shares in Igloo Leasing and North Slope Constructors, all big beneficiaries of Brower's public works spending. Under questioning by Spaan, Brower even said he was aware that Dischner and Mathisen had started jet service, called Tri-Leasing, with Dana Pruhs, a lobbyist for the nationally known Ensearch contracting firm, which was based in Texas but also had sizable operations in Alaska. He conceded he had heard that North Slope contractors had to use the service or lose future contracts. (According to the indictment, Tri-Leasing extorted $570,979 from borough contractors in 1984.)

In cross-examination, however, the defense attorneys went to work. Incredibly, they got Brower not only to deny that the gifts were bribes or were used to gain his approval of contracts but to agree that the borough had benefited from them. By providing Brower with a house in Anchorage, where he had the free use of a telephone and a Cadillac, hadn't the defendants saved the borough money when the mayor was away on business? "Yes," Brower answered.

Dischner's lawyer, Douglas Pope, even sought to portray the gifts as part of an Eskimo *pamaq,* a Native gift-giving ritual that signifies a partner for life and involves no expectation of something in return. Longtime Alaskans in the courtroom had to suppress chuckles. They knew that *pamaq* is based on helping those in need when food runs out or when disability restricts subsistence activity. A $45,000 diamond ring, a $35,000 dory, and $1,000 handouts to gamble in Las Vegas hardly sounded like aid to a Native in distress. In short order, the defense attorneys reduced

Brower to total confusion. Suddenly, what had seemed an open-and-shut case of bribery had been recast as big government coming down on well-meaning people who had tried to befriend the Eskimos on the North Slope.

The case became a trial of legal finesse. Spaan concentrated on building a paper trail showing calculated bribery. He placed in evidence an array of official records, painstakingly assembled by Karen Loeffler and an IRS agent, Ronald G. Chan, to show how money flowed to the borough, then to the contractors, and then in 10 percent increments to the bank account Dischner shared with Mathisen.

Spaan got some unexpected help from witnesses who suddenly began talking to save their own skins. Charles Hinson, a construction project engineer with Coffman and White of Seattle, which was part of MMCW, reluctantly testified that the engineering firm paid Dischner $1.3 million between 1981 and 1984—an amount equal to 10 percent of its engineering fees to the borough. Geoffrey Fowler, another member of the inner circle of consulting engineers, gave an even more vivid account of what it was like to do business on the North Slope. Testifying with immunity after having pleaded guilty the year before to a single charge of bribery, Fowler said his original firm, Frank Moolin and Associates, was down to a single employee in 1980 when he got a call from his brother to come to the North Slope Borough, which was having design troubles with the underground Utilidor. It turned out to be a timely call. Fowler's struggling firm eventually redesigned the entire $330 million project and emerged as a flourishing business, but he had to play by the rules. Fowler testified that, besides paying bribes to Dischner, he bought guns, portable dishwashers, and tape players for borough officials, raised campaign funds, and laundered campaign money at Dischner's behest, fully aware he was breaking laws.

Thomas Gittins, a self-made contractor who started as a janitor, already had his own indictment for bribery to worry about, but he testified without immunity to assist the government. He said he met Dischner and Mathisen in Palm Springs and asked them about lining up work on the North Slope. During the discussion, he said, Dischner agreed to represent him—for 10 percent. Gittins already was allegedly paying the legislator Al Adams 3 percent on all contracts, but according to Spaan, he needed Dischner for additional protection. Gittins was rewarded with a $6,155,000 service-area project that included building a well-appointed barracks for oil field workers. It didn't matter that oil companies already maintained their own living quarters—public money to build was there. (In a 1991 visit, I found the building vacant and apparently never used.)

But while the paper trail and witnesses had clearly established a 10 percent kickback pattern, for conviction under RICO the government had to prove that the municipality had been harmed. Spaan took no chances with the jury. He had hired Roger McAniff, an associate professor of engineering at the University of Alaska Anchorage, to do a project cost summary of contracts awarded to the inner circle principals on the North Slope. Working from a large chart that Spaan posted in front of the jury, McAniff analyzed twenty-three contracts involving nine projects, testifying that each was grossly overpriced. Blackstock had been paid $8,785,000 for its services in building health clinics, when a more realistic cost would have been $3,523,000. MMCW had been paid $24,435,000 for consulting, but McAniff's analysis showed that it had done work worth about $13,200,000. A firm named Olympic faithfully kicked back 10 percent of the $25,639,000 it was paid to build fire stations that could have been built for less than half that amount.

The defense attorneys pounced on McAniff. They grilled him for two months, attempting to show that he had greatly underestimated the cost of building on arctic permafrost. They cited the extraordinary costs of the high school and Utilidor, which had been started by Brower's predecessor. But while the defense attorneys parried with the witness, jurors were studying the project cost summary chart in front of them. Several could be observed doing their own math.

Finally, the government opened the subject of the defendants' personal wealth. Now jurors saw figures they didn't need a math course to understand. The FBI's Talbert, an accountant by training, calculated Dischner's net worth at $150,000 at the start of 1981. By 1984, he said, Dischner's net worth rose to between $11 million and $12 million and included properties in Anchorage and Palm Springs. The government introduced Dischner's income tax records, over strong objections by the defense attorneys. The returns showed that Dischner had listed the numerous companies associated with the North Slope construction as "clients." The largest was H. W. Blackstock. In one year alone, Blackstock paid $1.6 million in fees to Trust Consultants, a business solely owned by Dischner. The government maintained that Dischner not only had failed to pay proper income taxes in 1981 and 1982, but filed no tax returns at all in 1983 and 1984: his estimated income for those two years was $19 million.

In May 1989, eight months after it started, the longest and most expensive criminal trial in Alaska's history came to an end. More than one hundred witnesses, including nearly everyone who had any connection with the government in Barrow, had been called by the prosecutors. Thousands of documents and other items introduced as evidence filled the courtroom. Neither Dischner nor Mathisen took the stand, and the court had seemed relieved when Mathisen's defense attorney called only one witness. By the end, the attorneys, the jurors, and even the judge appeared on the edge of nervous exhaustion.

The jury deliberated for sixteen days. On May 23, it found Dischner, now seventy-three, and Mathisen, fifty-seven, guilty of more than twenty counts each of racketeering, fraud, bribery, and accepting kickbacks from contractors. The U.S. district judge James M. Fitzgerald sentenced each man to seven years in federal prison and ordered them to forfeit more than $5 million in property.

But the euphoria in the U.S. attorney's office was short-lived. Exhausted, Spaan resigned, saying he needed a year off to refresh body and spirit with a trip around the world. An assistant, Mark Davis, was named acting U.S. attorney. It was up to him to direct the prosecution of the two major bribery cases that remained—against the MMCW engineers and the Seattle businessmen who ran the H. W. Blackstock Company, who together had profited more than anyone from the North Slope contracts.

The MMCW gang, the architect Allen McDonald and the engineers Peter White and David Coffman, had been indicted on thirty-nine counts of racketeering, bribery, and tax fraud. If convicted, they faced more than twenty years in prison. Their trial was initially scheduled for Fairbanks, but no judge was available because federal courts were too busy and recent retirements had drained the judicial ranks The search for a federal judge elsewhere took on comic proportions.

First, the trial was moved to Los Angeles. The prosecutors in Alaska protested. Then it was moved back to Fairbanks, but the Los Angeles judge, a one-time amateur ski champion, balked because, among other reasons, he considered the skiing inferior in Alaska. The case was finally assigned to federal court in Portland, Oregon, where it simply evaporated in March 1990. Despite protests from his young assistant, Neil Evans, the assistant U.S. attorney Stephen Cooper from the Fairbanks office negotiated and signed an appalling plea bargain.[8]

Cooper agreed to reduce the thirty-nine-count indictment against the MMCW defendants to a single felony with no jail time, no fine, no community service, and, worst of all, no commitment to testify in the Rogstad corruption trial yet to come. In comparison, back in 1987, Geoffrey Fowler, a fourth member of the MMCW group who had agreed to testify for the government, was sentenced to six months in prison, a $10,000 fine, and one thousand hours of community service.

The acting U.S. attorney Mark Davis claimed he had no idea such a plea bargain was being signed and said it was done without his approval. He sped to Portland in an attempt to get the presiding judge, James Burns, to rescind it. Judge Burns was incensed. He castigated Davis for "this thoroughly unedifying display" and threatened to reconsider the constitutionality of all the charges. The plea bargain stood, and a chastened Davis returned to Anchorage. Mike Spaan, back from his vacation and now in private practice, called the whole matter "unconscionable." Neil Evans, the assistant, resigned in protest. Cooper did not respond to media queries.

The third and last of the three major racketeering cases was placed in the hands of Peter Gamache, who was on loan from the state attorney general's office. In February 1990, Gamache had successfully indicted the two Seattle men who ran the H. W. Blackstock Company. Kenneth Rogstad, the president, and Wayne Larkin, the director of administration, were charged with paying more than $2.5 million in bribes and kickbacks to obtain slope business worth $140 million during the Brower administration. If convicted, each faced twenty years in prison and the forfeiture of millions of dollars.

The case had more than usual media interest because Rogstad was a politically prominent former chairman of the Republican party in King County, which encompasses Seattle. Newspapers reported that he had connections to the White House through a Blackstock director, the Seattle lawyer James Munn, who had run Ronald Reagan's 1980 presidential campaign in Washington State.

The case began to unravel before it began. Right off, the Seattle pair succeeded in moving the trial to federal court in Tacoma, Washington, roughly three thousand miles from Barrow. Next, Peter Gamache unexpectedly resigned to take a state job in Kodiak. His departure further crippled the U.S. attorney's office. Almost by default, the case fell into the lap of Karen Loffler. With barely a month to prepare, she would have to take on two nationally prominent defense lawyers—the noted San Francisco attorney Marc Topel, representing Rogstad, and the Chicago attorney Thomas Decker, retained by Larkin. Both had had plenty of time to do their homework.

In September 1990, Karen Loffler packed up three thousand pounds of documents and headed for the U.S. district court in Tacoma. A senior judge, Jack Tanner, had been assigned to the case. Karen soon discovered that Tanner, a retired jurist, was also an impatient judge. "The government's case depended upon building a forest of evidence as it did in the Dischner and Mathisen cases," remarked Hal Spencer, the Associated Press court reporter who covered the trial. "But every time Karen tried to produce a tree, the judge or the defense knocked it down."

Meanwhile, the government's Eskimo witnesses, Brower and Irving Igtanloc, were torn apart by the defense. Yes, they had received items of value ranging from $37,000 boats to groceries and free housing from Blackstock. No, they conceded, these were not bribes, only gifts. Yes, they had been billed for these items by Blackstock—after the government started its investigation in 1984. No, they had never paid. Several of the more experienced witnesses who might have helped, such as the borough lawyer Chris Mello or Roger McAniff, were never called to the stand at all.

"There is no question that the mayor and the public works commissioner were bribed," Judge Tanner commented after the prosecution rested its case. But, he said, whether Rogstad and Larkin had been involved remained at issue. Topel and Decker quickly built a wall of doubt for the jury. First, they argued that Blackstock had been paying fees to Dischner for years in return for consulting services. What Dischner did with the fees was of no concern to them. As for the items the company had given to Mayor Brower, those were not favors, they stressed, but items he was expected to pay for. It happened that Brower was something of a deadbeat, Topel declared, but Blackstock, however belatedly, had billed him for the boats and housing.

The trial of Dischner and Mathisen, which involved similar allegations, had lasted eight months. This one lasted two weeks. The jury acquitted both defendants. Afterward, a juror remarked, "We felt something was fishy, but the government never proved it."

It was a sad ending to a long and courageous investigation. The FBI agent Bruce Talbert had devoted six years of intense work to the case and paid for it with a broken marriage. Karen Loeffler is now saddled with responding to eternal appeals as Dischner and Mathisen, among others, fight going to jail. She still manages to be cheerful, although she feels she was betrayed by a lower forty-eight jury with an ingrained perception that such doings were just normal for Alaska.

More than a dozen North Slope officials, contractors, and consultants were convicted. The Eskimo community still hopes to recover some of the splurged funds through a maze of civil suits that were still slowly moving through the Anchorage courts in 1992. But the only sure winners will be the lawyers.

Aside from Rogstad and Larkin, only one other defendant, Brower's lawyer, Marty Farrell, was acquitted. Dischner and Mathisen were ordered to begin serving their jail terms on March 2, 1993. Until then, the only ones to serve time were three Eskimos. Ex-mayor Brower, sobbing before the court, was sentenced to thirty days and three year's probation for tax evasion. Irving Igtanloc did six months in a halfway house for bribery. His brother, Myron, spent six months in a minimum-security prison in Washington State for tax evasion.

At best it was a cloudy victory that left Alaskans wondering why neither the U.S. Justice Department nor the state congressional delegation had helped arm the U.S. attorney's office to see the battle through.

NOTES

1. This account is based on extensive newspaper research and interviews with virtually all of the principals noted.

2. The borough is a unit of regional government provided in the Alaska constitution. It has less self-governing authority than an incorporated city and may be "organized," its administration being carried out by an elected council, or "unorganized," in which case the state provides minimum services. See Gerald A. McBeath and Thomas A. Morehouse, *Alaska Politics and Government* (Lincoln: University of Nebraska Press, 1994), 123–24.

3. *Outsider* is an informal term used in Alaska (and the Canadian North) to indicate non-residents.

4. Permafrost is permanently frozen soil. It underlies most of Alaska north of about 60 degrees latitude. The city of Anchorage is not underlain by permafrost, but areas just a few miles north of the city are. The top few inches of permafrost usually melt in summer, refreezing with the return of winter.

5. Isabell Pass was one of nine major construction camps along the route of the trans-Alaska oil pipeline, 1974–77; the camps were abandoned once construction was completed, and the materials dismantled and sold.

6. Russ Meekins of Anchorage, a dissident member of the majority party in the legislature, staged a coup in which he successfully took over the leadership with the support of the minority. Strohmeyer discusses Meekins in other chapters of his book. See also McBeath and Morehouse, 135–36, 160–61.

7. The bribe was for Meekins's support for purchase by the state of fire-fighting aircraft from a company owned by Hohman's associates.

8. Assistant U.S. Attorney Stephen Cooper should not be confused with former Alaska Governor Steve Cowper, 1986–90.

The End of Wilderness

MORGAN SHERWOOD

Morgan Sherwood, Professor Emeritus at the University of California, Davis, is one of Alaska's more important historians. His many carefully researched books and articles and his encouragement of new students in the field have advanced the understanding of the subject as has the work of few other scholars.

Sherwood grew up in Anchorage and completed his undergraduate and advanced studies at the University of California, Berkeley. He has taught at the University of California, Davis, since receiving his doctoral degree for a study published in 1965, Exploration of Alaska, 1865–1900 *(New Haven, Conn.: Yale University Press), a pioneering work which is perhaps the single most important book in Alaska studies. He has published numerous journal articles, including "Ardent Spirits: Hooch and the Osprey Affair at Sitka" (*Journal of the West, *July 1965), and "Science in Russian America" (*Pacific Northwest Quarterly, *January 1967). His* Big Game in Alaska: A History of Wildlife and People *(New Haven: Yale University Press, 1981) traces the history of game regulation in Alaska from 1925 to 1945 and argues that Alaskans were slow to recognize the necessity for regulation of the resource. In 1967 Sherwood published the first anthology of scholarly articles on Alaska history,* Alaska and Its History *(Seattle: University of Washington Press).*

The article reprinted here offers the challenging thesis that the Alaska wilderness may be a thing of the past. Access to the wilderness having become easy and commonplace, man has become a part of the landscape everywhere. Hikers and pilots lost in the wilds now have their positions located by reconnaissance satellites. It may be that, if wilderness means "wild," the taming reach of man may have gone so far as to render the term wilderness *meaningful no longer.*

This article appeared originally in *Environmental Review* 9 (Fall 1985): 197–209; it is reprinted here by permission.

Environmental historians should face the problem of wilderness, which is a problem of definition, or the failure to frame our analysis of wilderness precisely. If historians continue to treat wilderness only as an idea, the meaning of which has changed over time, they will have little to contribute to the preservation of natural environments and, *reductio ad absurdum*, "wilderness" will become a city park or perhaps a suburban lawn.[1] Historiographically, wilderness will cease to be a place or even an idea and become only a word. Maybe it already has.

My thesis may be stated simply: We are in the wilderness about wilderness. The central reason for the confusion is our inability or reluctance to treat technology as a crucial factor. To argue the case, I will assay a number of definitions of wilderness and indicate the failure of these definitions to define what is called wilderness in Alaska (not always officially designated wilderness units), given the availability of certain technologies. In the conclusion, I will deal briefly with policy for existing natural environments.

But first, if you do not think that the meaning of wilderness has become too vague, your attention is called to the title of a recent television documentary about Alaska, narrated by Lorne Green and entitled "New Wilderness," as though our lawmakers can declare an area "wilderness" and make it so, as though wilderness can be "new." The Kachemak Bay Wilderness Lodge, a few miles across the bay from the town of Homer, has been listed as America's best wilderness lodge in Sterling Publications' "America's Best 100"[2]; apparently, the trail to wilderness lodges is brightly blazed by their own version of the Michelin guidebook. Still another example of confusion over the meaning of wilderness comes from a summer issue of the *Homer News*.[3]

An Alaska Wilderness Marathon was planned for the Kenai Peninsula last summer. It would cross fifty miles of the Kenai National Moose Range, through which motorized access was requested to set up a check point. Runners could carry portable rafts, tents, and other modern accoutrements needed to "rough it" outdoors. Michael Hedrick, manager of the refuge, denied a permit, saying, "There have to be places where some species of wildlife have top billing." The organizer of the race was a biologist with the Alaska State Fish and Game Department; he responded: "I deal with environmental issues every day and this just isn't an environmental issue." He said that a dogsled race was held in the Gates of the Arctic National Wildlife Refuge last year and argued: Why not a marathon through the Kenai Moose Range? Ted Stevens, one of Alaska's U.S. senators, persuaded the federal agency to reverse Hedrick's decision. Stevens told a newspaper reporter: "The agency implied that the traffic, 50 to 75 pairs of feet, running over the Resurrection Trail is too much. I couldn't buy that. If people can't walk or run in the Alaska wilderness, what can be in it?"

Evidence from the wilderness marathon controversy supports the notion that citizens who wish to protect the natural environment may sometimes have reason to fear public employees charged with its protection as much as exploitative entrepreneurs. Another example of this problem, and also of the strange ways in which the word "wilderness" is used, appears in a questionnaire distributed by the Alaska Division of Parks. Respondents were asked whether they favored development of recreational facilities in Kachemak Bay State Wilderness Park. The developments included boat-launch facilities, lodges, shelter cabins, and landing strips for airplanes.[4] (The response for both the Wilderness Park and neighboring State Park was overwhelmingly for low or no development.)

If you still do not think that "wilderness" is a vague concept, so vague that it may not really be a place anymore, read the third part of John McPhee's *Coming into the Country*, in which the Yukon River people are forever proclaiming themselves to be genuine frontiersmen and -women while they criticize their neighbors for the lack of ennobling frontier virtues. One of them characterizes another as more frontiersman-like because he hand-loads his ammunition.[5] The hand-loader thinks that *how much* technology is the issue. He is correct, but the insight dissolves when he says: "People who have tried to get away from technology completely have always failed. Meanwhile, what this place has to offer is wilderness that is nowhere else." One may read that part of McPhee's book as an attempt to determine how much technology is permissible in a wilderness and to measure it by the amount of technology available where civilization ends, which supports my thesis that technology is the crucial variable.

Sadly, however, McPhee concludes that he must carry a gun out of fear of the bears, which brings us to solitude, one quality invoked to identify wilderness. According to this definition, wilderness provides solitude that inspires a kind of subtle unease and quiet wonder. The definition is one of a large category that dwells on the literary and psychological effects of wilderness on the individual. Wilderness (or a natural environment where one is alone) inspires poetry, impresses one philosophically with, for example, man's insignificance, tempering his destructive impulses, or inspires a kind of delicious fear. McPhee's fear of bears brings home to him a deep philosophical contradiction. He writes: "If bears were no longer in the country, I would not have come. I am here . . . because they survive. So I am sorry—truly rueful and perplexed—that without a means of killing them I cannot feel at ease."[6] McPhee thought he needed a gun to travel alone in a natural environment relatively unpopulated by other humans. He might have carried a toy cap pistol to frighten the animal or, more mundanely, a couple of saucepans to rattle the bears. Better still, using no technology whatever, he might have done what a Swedish-American pioneer in Alaska once recommended: "Sing loudly on the trail." (I know of no case of an experienced outdoorsman being attacked without provocation by a bear, although I admit the point hangs on the definition of provocation.)[7]

In his firearm, McPhee had the power of industrial technology to help him appreciate the wilderness. There was more than a gun in his wilderness. He was carried there in airplanes and in boats propelled by outboard motors. There is a road to Eagle; it is gravel, narrow, tortuous, and not maintained from October to April, but for half of the year it will take you 160 miles to the Alaska Highway, which will in turn get you by auto to Chicago (if the urban wilderness happens to be your cup of tea). All-terrain vehicles and snowmobiles penetrate McPhee's country, along with airplanes equipped with "tundra tires" and skis to reduce the need for cleared landing strips. Bulldozers tear up the country looking for gold, chainsaws reduce the spare forests for fuel, just as axes and saws—even power saws at an early date—did to feed steamboats from the late nineteenth century to quite recent times. Voices fill the radio waves to reduce still further the isolation from urban environments. Probably, like many rural Alaskans, some of McPhee's people have erected satellite antennae for television reception of the same adolescent inanities that are inflicted on the remainder of American society.

There is no solitude (read "wilderness") if an aircraft may thunder overhead at any time and land, if a skiff with a noisy outboard motor may splash by your "wilderness" beach at any time, if jet boats ignore low water to crunch over sandbars on their way up a remote stream, if a snowmobile marathon can scatter wildlife, if a bear's misunderstood ferocity can be silenced by a bullet before the animal's intentions are determined. So much for solitude as a sign of wilderness, given the widespread use of modern technology in Alaska.

In one sense, solitude is only a variation of Frederick Jackson Turner's famous criterion. According to him, the frontier disappears, and by implication wilderness too, when a certain man-land ratio changes. Turner and the Superintendent of the Census of 1890 "regarded as unsettled" any area with less than two inhabitants in a square mile[8] (table). The number of square miles per person in Alaska dropped, between 1880 and 1980, from a high of 18.3 square miles in 1890 to 1.45 in 1980. By this measure, Alaska, as a whole, is still a frontier region. But that conclusion is unsatisfactory for a couple of reasons. First, the method is arbitrary and fails to account for the distribution of population. As recently as 1950, the population of Alaska was only 27 percent urban; now the population is about 50-50, urban-rural. Most of the urbanites and suburbanites live in an area embracing Anchorage, part of the Kenai Peninsula, and the lower Matanuska and Susitna river valleys near the big city. The concentration of population means that large areas of Alaska are sparsely settled; with a low man-land ratio, they may qualify as wilderness. However, such areas are *accessible* with modern transportation technologies, and *vulnerable* if other technologies employed in the war against nature are introduced. One person (it does not require two) could make a mess of his one square mile even in 1890. Imagine what a bulldozer operator can quickly do to a square mile, nowadays. Instead of counting people in rural areas, machines should be counted in the entire area which they may affect.

Date	*Population*	*Square Miles Per Person*
1880	33,400	17.5
1890	32,000	18.3
1900	63,600	9.2
1910	64,400	9.1
Jan. 1, 1920	55,000	10.65
Oct. 1, 1929	59,300	9.9
Oct. 1, 1939	72,500	8.1
Apr. 1, 1950	128,600	4.6
Apr. 1, 1960	226,200	2.6
1970	300,400	1.95
1980	401,800	1.45

The figures are rounded, and 586,000 square miles is divided by the population. Source: A. M. Rollins, comp. *Census of Alaska: Numbers of Inhabitants, 1791–1970* (Anchorage: University of Alaska Anchorage Library, 1978). U.S. Bureau of the Census, *General Social and Economic Characteristics: United States Summary, 1980.*

Scrappy data on airplanes will illustrate the importance of counting machines that permit access to what people call wilderness. As early as 1944, sixty-two airplanes were used by hunting parties flying out of Anchorage, then a city of perhaps six thousand or seven thousand people.[9] In one month of the following year, Merrill Field, the town's airstrip, had 10,000 landings and takeoffs, more than LaGuardia Field in New York City.[10] There were twenty-nine "air carriers" operating out of Anchorage in 1947, or about one air service for every 325 people in town.[11] These were mainly bush pilots, taking people to and from natural environments. In 1956, 77 percent of the hunters who traveled by air were successful at killing caribou from the Nelchina herd; only 20 percent of the hunters traveling on foot were successful, although they came a long part of the way by auto. Later regulations prohibited aircraft from driving animals to exhaust them and make them easier to kill, and also prohibited herding animals to landing places, shooting from the air, and spotting (locating) animals from the air.[12] Spotting is still common. In 1960 there was one aircraft for every 194 Alaskans, including children, and in 1967 there was one for every 100 persons. That year, one in fifty residents had a pilot's license, and Lake Hood in Anchorage was the largest seaplane base in the United States. A Federal Aviation Administration pamphlet describing all of this is entitled *The Alaskan Region: A Family Affair*.[13]

Counting machines is not the most dramatic way to argue that accessibility made possible by modern technology is the important determinant of wilderness status. Instead, consider a place which would, at first thought, be chosen by many people as the least accessible spot in Alaska: the slopes of Mount McKinley, the tallest mountain in North America. Surely, Denali (as romantics prefer to call the mountain) can be "regarded as unsettled" and offers the psychological rewards of solitude. Not necessarily true, during the summer months. In 1970, 124 people were on the mountain, in 1976 nearly 600, a number topped in each of the next four years.[14] During early May of 1983, perhaps 200 people were already on the mountain or waiting for an air taxi to fly them from Talkeetna to Kahiltna Glacier, elevation 7,000–8,000 feet. This year one pilot told a reporter: "Packing the plane is like loading a sports car for a two-week vacation."[15] Size and distance are difficult to estimate from Kahiltna Glacier except during climbing season, when perspective is provided by other mountaineers; in the words of the pilot, "you can see people coming into view . . . and you can see them all day long." From Kahiltna Glacier, climbing parties may be guided as high as 14,000 feet.[16] The mountain is 20,300 feet in elevation.

One guide climbed it twenty-five times.[17] If you do not have the physical stamina, the sense of adventure, or the suicidal drive it takes to ascend Mount McKinley, you can sightsee around the mountain by airplane or fly to a camp on Ruth Glacier that offers dogsled tours.

A third definition of wilderness refers to the biological integrity of an area and the absence of man and his works. In the Wilderness Act of 1964, that means an area "where the earth and its community of life are untrammeled by man . . . ," an area which "generally appears to have been affected primarily by the forces of nature, with the imprint of man's work substantially unnoticeable."[18] How noticeable are the works of man, his technology, in remote areas of Alaska? In answer to that question, this paper should, but will not, discuss the greenhouse effect on the earth's climate, or "Arctic haze," or the sight and the sound of airliners flying the Great Circle Route between Europe and Asia. Instead, a single example will suffice here to demonstrate that man's work is ubiquitous.

The example is Anaktuvuk Pass, in the Brooks Range, and its residents in 1963, including a five-year-old Eskimo girl named Dorothy Ahgook. In that year the *Tundra Times* reported unhappily that Dorothy had "the highest, or one of the highest radiation counts of any person in the United States."[19] Her sister Vera, one year older, had a high count too. The village council was told by a representative of the Atomic Energy Commission that "whole body counts" of radiation—strontium 90 and cesium 137—had increased substantially in Anaktuvuk. A reporter for the *Tundra Times* claimed that residents had "about forty times the amount of radiation absorbed by the average U.S. citizen," another record for Anaktuvuk.

The problem was ecological. Radioactive debris from the atmospheric testing of nuclear bombs had been carried by air currents over the Arctic. Common plants of the tundra, lichens and sedges, got their nutrients from dust in the air as it fell with rain and snow, not from the soil, and stored what they absorbed. Migrating caribou had several times as much strontium 90 as the flesh of cattle elsewhere in the U.S. The Eskimos of Anaktuvuk relied heavily on caribou for food. Among some Alaskan Natives, the marrow of caribou bone is especially favored.

What the long-range effects are of overdosing radiation by the people of Anaktuvuk is not clear. Events there did help to cancel the Atomic Energy Commission's Project Chariot, which was intended to blow a hole on the Arctic coast west of Anaktuvuk. Opposition to Project Chariot united northern Alaskan Eskimos politically for the first time and led to publication of the *Tundra Times*, which became an influential voice for Eskimo causes. (The physicist Edward Teller, in promoting Chariot, told an Anchorage audience jokingly: "If your mountain is not in the right place, just drop us a card.")[20] Anaktuvuk Pass is now the principal village in Gates of the Arctic National Park and Preserve, though not in an area designated wilderness. The village is just north of Mount Doonerak, made famous by Robert Marshall, founder of the Wilderness Society.[21] Residents still hunt, fish, and gather in the region. The *Alaska Geographic* reported in 1981: "A desire to maintain cultural integrity for Native communities and rural life style within the newly created national parks generated provisions [in the Alaska National Interest Lands Conservation Act of 1980] to continue subsistence activities including hunting, fishing and trapping using motorized vehicles such as snow machines and motorboats *where traditionally practiced.*"[22] And so much for the natural biological integrity of wilderness areas, where man's technology is unnoticeable.

The fourth and final characteristic of wilderness considered here is the oldest, in many ways the most attractive, and, at first glance, the easiest way to identify wilderness. In this scheme, wilderness is measured by the presence of wildlife, especially the large animals, living more or less as they did before the appearance of mechanized man. The abundance and variety of wild creatures in a natural environment define the wilderness condition.

Most of the wild species that were in Alaska when the Russians came in 1741 are still there, though certain species have been threatened over time, for example, the whales, fur seals, and otters at sea and large mammals on land during the gold rushes. One may still see the giant Kenai moose going its own way, and the formidable Kodiak brown bear still ranges the island after which it was named. But "things are not what they seem." The presence of wildlife in Alaska is due to the rise of conservation as a potent political movement, and a social institution—wildlife management—created to achieve the goals of conservationists has itself become heavily dependent on technology. Not even the brown bear, once called by DeWitt Clinton "the ferocious tyrant of the American Woods,"[23] can count on roaming freely in his territory without being shot with a tranquilizer, tagged, and equipped with a radio transmitter.

Management of Alaska's wild animals began long before such high technology was available and predates wildlife management as a profession. In the 1830s, the Russians introduced conservation practices to the Pribilof Island fur seal rookeries.[24] The United States, after 1870, also regulated the killing of fur seals on land. The decisions of both governments followed periods of indiscriminate slaughter. Alaska's first game laws were a response to wholesale destruction of edible wildlife during the gold rushes northward in the late nineteenth century and early in the twentieth. A decision made late in the nineteenth century to import reindeer from Siberia for the relief of Eskimos suffering from the commercial depletion of marine mammals contributed to a little-publicized ecological disaster. The reindeer competed with the native caribou for browse, overgrazing the range. Both populations crashed dramatically in the 1930s and 1940s. Meantime, the federal Alaska Game Commission policed the health of other wildlife, a job made easier by the low human population.[25]

Major demographic, economic, political, and technological changes occurred during and after World War II. "Traditional" uses of aircraft, snowmobiles, and motorboats became common *after* the war. The population tripled, federal spending for defense boomed the economy, and the new state of Alaska assumed management of its resources in 1959, when public support of science was more generous than it had been before the war. High-tech wildlife biology came to Alaska with these changes. The Eskimos were not uniformly delighted.

The *Tundra Times*, in 1966, reported that two investigators from eastern universities had killed several polar bears while conducting a scientific experiment. The *Times* did not have all of its facts straight, but using other sources as well, a rough picture of what happened can be sketched. The two biologists came to Alaska to develop methods of immobilizing the bears in order to tag them and, eventually, attach radio transmitters which would be monitored by satellite and thus track the animal around its frigid habitat. Two airplanes were used, one to spot the bear; when spotted, another airplane would deposit the scientists someplace ahead and return to help the first aircraft herd the bear toward the waiting savants, who were armed with a rifle and tranquilizing dart or syringe. The syringe was loaded with succinylcholine chloride; the size of the dose was determined by an estimate of the bear's size, made by the pilot of the spotter airplane. When the bear was chased, perhaps exhausted, within range, it was shot with the dart, then marked with a long-lasting red dye. *Splattered* would be a better word than *marked*; the dye could not be sprayed on because of low temperatures, so it was dumped on the animal's backside.

The first polar bear to be anesthetized stirred during the handling and was given another dose of succinylcholine chloride; it died. The second bear was "marked recovered," the scientists reported; it may be the bear that was shot soon thereafter by a hunter who easily could have spotted its red posterior on the white landscape. (The hunter was distressed because the fur was spoiled.) A third bear was not immobilized. The fourth bear that was hit died in five minutes; the fifth in ten minutes; the sixth in twenty-five minutes. Succinylcholine chloride had no effect on the next two bears coming within range, according to the two investigators. They also anesthetized two other polar bears, but their data about these animals are incomplete. The score: four bears killed and three immobilized and marked, one of which was shot by a hunter shortly thereafter. The experiment was reported at a national conference and in *Scientific American*. Newspaper reports emphasized the derring-do. Whether any science needed to protect the polar bear emerged from the carnage (as both biologists firmly believe) is moot because the effect of the drug on large animals apparently was known before the episode.[26]

More than 3,000 polar bears have been immobilized, marked, and studied worldwide since then, 12–15 percent of a total population estimated at 20,000–25,000. Alaska's polar bears number either 6,000–9,000 animals, or 3,000–5,000, depending upon the expert you consult. The discrepancies suggest that all of the capturing and tracking can only have been partially successful. The presence of scientists in the polar bears' Alaskan wilderness has not even resulted in a wildlife management program for the animal. The Marine Mammal Protection Act of 1972 gave supervision of polar bears to the federal government. Sport hunting was prohibited, but Congress allowed Natives the right to hunt the animal using "traditional" methods at any time, without bag limits and with no protection for females and cubs. Products made from the bear's skin may be sold, reviving the specter of market hunting which wildlife protectionists thought they had banished decades ago. Clearly, the polar bear is not "master of the northern ice," as a federal biologist titled his article about Nanook.[27] Man and his technology are.

Biologists continue to drug and tag Alaska's wild animals and to equip them with radios. An article in *Alaska* magazine by a state biologist entitled "Wildlife That Goes Beep-beep" describes how transmitters have been attached to brown bears, black bears, polar bears, caribou, moose, wolves, walruses, and geese.[28] Another article in the same magazine reports how the Forest Service and the State Department of Fish and Game moved mountain goats by helicopter to a place where they could be seen by tourists from a highway. The reclusive animals were tranquilized with a dart shot from a helicopter, examined, tagged, and then carried in a net by helicopter to a place where motorists could better appreciate the Kenai "wilderness."

"Darting wildlife from the air is tricky," said one biologist. "A goat can travel some distance in the seven to eight minutes it takes the drug to work. . . . If a goat reaches a steep slope before going down, chances of retrieving it are slim."[29]

The state undertook a large investigation during the 1970s to explain the disappearance of moose from an area in the interior that is not officially a wilderness unit. Moose is a favorite game meat of Alaskans. The wolves were blamed by the hunters, and when the state decided to shoot some wolves, the national news media triggered a popular uproar. In the experiment, more than 100 adult moose were tranquilized and fitted with radio collars or other identification devices. One hundred twenty calves were also equipped with radios; this was accomplished by chasing the cow away with a helicopter. One hundred wolves were killed, sixty wolves were removed from the area, and another 150 wolves were given radio collars. Twenty-three adult brown bears were also equipped with radios, and forty-seven were drugged and taken miles away by helicopter, airplane, and truck; 70 percent returned in sixty days. The main culprit was the brown bear, which feasted on baby moose and cut the calf survival rate, which eventually reduced the moose population.[30]

Did this massive intrusion of technology into a natural environment end the wolf control controversy? No. It and other studies have led to specific population goals for moose, caribou, and wolves in several areas. Statistics on the effects of these management practices on the individual animals are not readily available. One hopes that mortality rates are lower than they were in the polar bear experiment or in the record of management in Yellowstone Park, where eighty-six grizzlies have been killed by wildlife professionals since 1970, most by drug overdoses.[31]

The public is apparently not alarmed by the adventures of its wildlife managers. Perhaps people have become accustomed to such activities by watching Marlin Perkins, Jacques Cousteau, and William Conrad tinker with wild animals weekly on television. In outdoor magazines, thrilling stories by biologists confronting dangerous wild beasts often replace the bear stories of hunters. Frequently the articles feature cute pictures of, for example, a tranquilized brown bear embracing a biologist, or a giant sedated polar bear resting on the lap of a scientist, or a wildlife expert with his arm around the neck of a cow moose. Such photographs are becoming as common in outdoor magazines as pictures of big game hunters posing with rifle and kill were in former times.

So, if you spot a mountain goat while visiting Alaska, remember that it may have been placed there for you to see, in order to provide you with "photo opportunities" (a term that wildlife managers have borrowed from the public relations industry). If you agree with Aldo Leopold that knowledge alone of the presence of wildlife certifies an area's classification as wilderness, remember that the biggest game animal out there may have tatooed gums, a tag on its ear, and go beep-beep. Even the fish in your Alaskan wilderness may have been put there by humans. In Kachemak Bay, state biologists have planted thousands of young salmon where they cannot reproduce. The fish return at the end of their cycle to mill around, vainly searching for a freshwater stream with gravel in which to spawn, turning red and black and decaying. Fishermen are invited to catch them by net or snag in an orgy of unsportsmanlike "taking" that would chill the spirit of Izaak Walton. The other rotting salmon are left for the eagles, ravens, and bears.

Is all of this wildlife management—or is it farming or ranching or zookeeping? Sam White was a veteran warden who pioneered the use of airplanes when he worked for the Alaska Game Commission. In the late 1970s I asked him what he considered the gravest threat to Alaskan big game. He answered in one word: "Biology." His judgment was too severe. Some reductionist science and high-tech game management may be necessary to the animals' survival. But modern technology has made "wildlife" management a contradiction in terms, and these days, the presence of indigenous animals does not necessarily identify wilderness.

In 1967 Robert Heilbronner published his controversial article which asked: "Do Machines Make History?" The answer sounded too much like technological determinism.[32] But if machines do not always make history, machines do unmake wilderness. The lesson for policy makers is fairly clear. Just as early conservationists leaned heavily on technological obsolescence and outright prohibition of certain technologies to protect wildlife, fisheries, and national parklands, society should now move with deliberate speed to restrict the use of destructive technologies in relatively untouched natural environments. Congress should legislate off-road vehicles, all-terrain vehicles, airplanes, helicopters, snowmobiles, and motor boats out of such areas, except when the machines are on rescue missions. Purchase anywhere of an off-road vehicle for recreational purposes should be considered *prima facie* evidence of intention to engage in destructive trespass, and the sale of these vehicles should be prohibited except for occupational purposes. This action would be a major step forward to environmental sanity, in town as well as in the woods (and, incidentally, improve America's balance of payments with Japan).

What about policy for high-tech wildlife management? The wolf-moose-bear study concluded with the statement: "Unfortunately, the answers we have found, although they provide valuable clues and good basic information for other parts of Alaska, apply only to the Nelchina Basin and our study area, and for the years 1975 through 1981."[33] In other words, the study was inconclusive for Alaska as a whole and will have to be repeated again and again in the Nelchina basin and all other places where the moose population declines. The scientific caution is admirable in principle, consistent with ecological theory, and promotes full employment of wildlife technicians. It also raises an economic question: Has the cost of management been translated into dollars-per-pound of moose meat? Political and ethical questions arise too. The Alaska State Department of Fish and Game defers to wildlife advisory boards for policy based on such experiments, and these advisers encourage the management of animals for use by people, whether as sport and food or for "photo opportunities," or to protect people from those animals. In addition to these concerns, which will not disappear from Alaska in the foreseeable future, the beasts should be managed and studied with the welfare of the animals themselves a consideration. The ethical issues associated with animal science are almost never addressed in print by the biologists involved. Meanwhile, in response to pressure from animal rights organizations, the federal government and universities in the contiguous United States have created institutions to oversee the ethical use of animals in research. University committees, consisting of scientists mainly but also public representatives and representatives from the humanities, now appraise an experiment with the animal's welfare in mind. Does it suffer unalleviated pain or distress, and if so, is the distress justified, given the significance of the experiment? Perhaps similar institutions are needed to evaluate wildlife studies.

To conclude: existing definitions of wilderness as a place where there is solitude, a low man-land ratio, biological integrity, and wildlife do not work because disruptive modern technologies are not taken into account. Technologies that provide easy access have threatened Alaskan natural environments increasingly since the end of World War II. Between then and the 1960s, Alaska lost its frontier innocence, and wilderness became only a word, not a place. Ironically, wilderness in America may have ended at the same time that society, by passage of the Wilderness Act of 1964, decided that it was worth saving. There are still ways, however, to reverse or at least to ameliorate the damage.

NOTES

1. The tendency to view the history of wilderness as the history of an idea comes, of course, from Roderick Nash's deservedly successful *Wilderness and the American Mind* (New Haven: Yale University Press, 1967).

2. Reported in a brochure for the Lodge, 1984.

3. July 12, 1984.

4. Alaska Division of Parks, 1982.

5. *Coming into the Country* (New York: Bantam Books, 1981; originally published 1977), p. 195.

6. Page 339.

7. The issue is discussed in M. Sherwood, *Big Game in Alaska: A History of Wildlife and People* (New Haven: Yale University Press, 1981), pp. 36–38.

8. Frederick Jackson Turner, "The Significance of the Frontier in American History," in Turner, *The Frontier in American History* (New York: Henry Holt, 1950; originally published 1920; the paper was read in 1893), p. 3. U.S. Census Office, *Compendium of the Eleventh Census, 1890, Part I* (Washington: GPO, 1892) p. xlv.

9. Annual Report, Alaska Game Commission, 1944, A.G.C. Records, Alaska State Library, Juneau.

10. Jean Potter, *The Flying North* (New York: Macmillan, 1965; originally published 1945), p. 7.

11. Tewkesbury's *Who's Who in Alaska and Alaska Business Index* (Juneau: Tewkesbury Publishers, 1947).

12. *Annual Report*, Alaska Game Commission, 1956, A.G.C. Records.

13. (Washington: GPO, 1967). U.S. Federal Aviation Agency, *General Aviation in Alaska* (Washington: GPO, 1960).

14. *Alaska* 49 (May 1983): 27.

15. C. Swaney, "Air Taxi Owner Picks High Life in Talkeetna," *Anchorage Times*, July 1, 1983, business section, p. 1.

16. National Public Radio, "Alaska," cassette ME-82-08-23.

17. *The Milepost, 1983* (Anchorage: Alaska Northwest, 1983), p. 231.

18. The law is reprinted in C. W. Allin, *The Politics of Wilderness Preservation* (Westport, Conn: Greenwood Press, 1982), Appendix A.

19. Sept. 3, 1963. Information about Anaktuvuk, and background, is drawn from this issue and from: *Tundra Times*, Dec. 23, 1966; P. Brooks and J. Foote, "The Disturbing Story of Project Chariot," *Harper's* 224 (Apr. 1962): 60–67; R. D. Arnold

et al., *Alaska Native Land Claims* (Anchorage: Alaska Native Foundation, 1976), pp. 94, 95.

20. Quoted in Brooks and Foote, "Disturbing Story," p. 67.

21. Marshall, *Alaska Wilderness* (Berkeley: University of California Press, 1970; originally published 1956).

22. *Alaska National Interest Lands* (Anchorage: Alaska Geographic Society, 1981), p. 12. Italics added. See U.S. Statutes at Large, 94 Stat. 2371 et passim, especially 2423, 2428, 2430.

23. Quoted in J. M. Holzworth, *The Wild Grizzlies of Alaska* (New York: G. P. Putnam's Sons, 1930), p. 232.

24. C. L. Andrews, *The Story of Alaska* (Caldwell, Idaho: Caxton Printers, 1947), p. 147.

25. Sherwood, *Big Game in Alaska*, pp. 27, 84, 85, passim.

26. The incident can be documented from periodicals, a paper by the biologists, and correspondence with one of them and with Alaska officials, but names are not important. The episode is included here to demonstrate further that high-tech science can be dangerous to wildlife. Specific documentation will be provided upon request, if needed for scholarly purposes.

27. F. Bruemmer, "Nanook Bears Watching," *National Wildlife* 21 (December-January 1983): 38–42. S. C. Amstrup, "Masters of the Northern Ice," and J. Rearden, "Alaska's Unmanaged Polar Bears," *Alaska* 50 (November 1984): 35, 36.

28. By Sterling Miller, *Alaska* 50 (June 1984).

29. D. Allen, "Movin' Goats," *Alaska* 50 (October 1983): 71.

30. W. G. Ballard, "The Case of the Disappearing Moose," *Alaska* 49 (January 1983): 22–25, (February 1983): 36–39, (March 1983): 38–41.

31. Bill Gilbert, "Can We Live in Peace with the Grizzly?" *Sports Illustrated* 61 (July 1983): 72.

32. *Technology and Culture* 8 (July 1967): 335–45.

33. Warren G. Ballard, "The Case of the Disappearing Moose," *Alaska* 49 (January-March 1983): 42.